SOCIAL PROBLEMS

SOCIAL PROBLEMS
Fourth Edition

JAMES WILLIAM COLEMAN
California Polytechnic State University,
San Luis Obispo

DONALD R. CRESSEY
Late, University of California,
Santa Barbara

HarperCollinsPublishers

Sponsoring Editor: Alan McClare
Art Direction: Kathie Vaccaro
Text and Cover Design: Kay Wanous
Cover Art: Jack Tworkov
Text Art: Accurate Art, Inc.
Photo Research: Mira Schachne
Production Manager: Jeanie Berke
Production Assistant: Beth Maglione
Compositor: Waldman Graphics
Printer and Binder: R. R. Donnelley & Sons Co.
Cover Printer: The Lehigh Press, Inc.
Cover Art: Tworkov, Jack. *West 23rd.* 1963. Oil on canvas, 60 ⅛″ × 6′8″ (152.6 × 203.3 cm).
Collection, The Museum of Modern Art, New York. Purchase.
Photograph © 1989 The Museum of Modern Art, New York.

Library of Congress Cataloging in Publication Data

Coleman, James William, 1947–
    Social problems.—4th ed./James William Coleman.
      p.   cm.
    Bibliography: p.
    Includes indexes.
  ISBN 0-06-041334-4 (Student Edition)
  ISBN 0-06-041336-0 (Teacher Edition)
  1. Sociology.   2. Social problems.   3. Social institutions.   4. United States—Social conditions—1980.   5. United States—Social policy—1980.   I. Cressey, Donald Ray, 1919–1987.   II. Title.
  HM51.C593   1990
  361.1—dc20   89-34883
                                                                                    CIP

        91 92 9 8 7 6 5 4

CONTENTS

7 · The Ethnic Minorities 188

8 · The Sick and the Health Care System 221

12 · Mental Disorders 331

13 · Drug Use 359

14 · Crime and Delinquency 393

15 · Personal Violence 431

PART FOUR
PROBLEMS OF A CHANGING WORLD   457

16 · Urbanization 459

17 · Population 486

18 · The Environment 512

19 · Warfare and International Conflict 543

PREFACE

From the rough draft for the first edition through this fourth edition, our goals in writing *Social Problems* have remained the same. We write for students. Our objectives have been to familiarize them with the crucial problems of their times and to stimulate them to think in a critical, scientific way. We try to challenge the half-truths and pat answers that are so often repeated about our social problems and to get students to participate in the dialogue about these issues rather than merely stand back and observe.

Professors familiar with the third edition will notice that I have continued the special features that helped make this book so successful—the broad coverage of social problems, the strongly worded debates, the clear and informative graphics, and the consistent theoretical organization, which includes a theoretical perspective section in each chapter.

This fourth edition is, however, different from the other revisions in two important ways. Since it has been almost 10 years since the first edition of *Social Problems*, we decided that a major rewrite, not just an update, was necessary. I worked to maintain the overall structure of the book, but the individual chapters have been extensively rewritten with the goal of making each chapter fresh, contemporary, and relevant.

The new material added during this process includes the following:

Chapter 1—new coverage of the analysis of public records and statistics as a method of sociological research

Chapter 2—the impact of growing debt and government deregulation, and new material on the current economic crisis

Chapter 3—new coverage of government spending and taxation, and corruption in defense spending

Chapter 4—new research on the quality of education and the reform proposals

Chapter 5—new studies of the changes in family structure and household inequality

Chapter 6—new information on the widening gap between rich and poor and the problems of the working poor, the homeless, and the underclass

Chapter 7—new material on the role of race and class in perpetuating ethnic injustice

Chapter 8—new information on the AIDS crisis and the shortage of health care for the poor

Chapter 9—new coverage of the problems of the young as well as the elderly

Chapter 10—new information on women's roles, feminist theory, and gender issues

Chapter 11—new coverage of sexually transmitted diseases and child molestation

Chapter 12—new research on sexism in the mental health care system, and the new APA classification system

Chapter 13—new research on the physical and social effects of drug use

Chapter 14—new material on white collar and corporate crime

Chapter 15—new coverage of suicide and the controversial new evolutionary theories of violence

Chapter 16—new coverage of the farm crisis, and new studies of suburbanization and the effects of the cutbacks in public housing

Chapter 17—new research on China's population control program and the current trends in world population

Chapter 18—new studies of the "green house effect," the destruction of the ozone layer, and the problems of desertification and deforestation

Chapter 19—new theories of revolution and new information on nuclear proliferation

These changes were, of course, planned long in advance, but another change came on quite unexpectedly—the death of Donald R. Cressey. Don was one of the great contemporary sociologists, and he is deeply missed. Although Don wasn't able to review all the changes in this edition, his influence pervades the new material as much as the old. I have tried hard to live up to the demanding standards he set and to listen to his often repeated advice to "cut the B.S. and get to the heart of the matter."

Space permits the mention of only a few of the many people who contributed to this edition. First and foremost are the hundreds of students who have given invaluable suggestions over the years. I would also like to thank the following professors who served as academic reviewers for this edition: Michael F. Morris, Pensacola Junior College; Merry Shernock, Norwich University; D. A. Rozas, Milwaukee Area Technical College; John Pease, University of Maryland; Robert Bolin, New Mexico State University; Louis Kriesberg, Syracuse University; Michael Pastor, University of Pennsylvania; Carol Handy, University of Calgary; John O'Brien, Kent State University; Sam Josephs, Luzerne County Community College; Bernard Green, Texas A&I University; and Ellen Horgan, Northeastern University.

Professors Richard Shaffer, Barbara Mori, and William Preston of the California Polytechnic State University also made extensive comments on several individual chapters. The insightful suggestions of all these reviewers were of great assistance, as were those made by the professors who used earlier editions of *Social Problems* and kindly volunteered their comments. The work of Alan McClare, Nora Helfgott, and the other members of the Harper & Row team who have labored on this project is greatly appreciated. Finally, my special thanks and gratitude go to Maureen Jung, who was the researcher for this edition. Her diligent work and her brilliant comments made this a far better book than it would otherwise have been.

James William Coleman

Chapter 1
SOCIOLOGY AND SOCIAL PROBLEMS

Poverty, discrimination, war, violence, overpopulation, pollution—the list of our social problems is depressingly long, so long that many people throw their hands up in despair. Though a picture of a starving Asian baby or the sight of a lonely old woman may stir our concern, most of us quietly decide that there is nothing we can do to help. But is this true? Can we do nothing? The sociological study of social problems is founded on the belief that something can indeed be done if we first make the effort to study our problems systematically and then act on our understanding.

Understanding our problems does not mean that they can be easily changed. Medical scientists have been able to conquer dread diseases by applying the knowledge they have built up over the years. But social problems are woven into the fabric of social relationships in ways that diseases are not; effective action to deal with them is almost always painful and difficult. However, history has repeatedly shown that failure to act is likely to lead to far more devastating consequences.

Politicians and community officials spend much of their careers trying to solve social problems that include everything from double parking to nuclear war. Voters select the candidates who claim to have the best solutions, but the average citizen's ideas about many social problems can be distorted or confused. While serious study of social problems will clear up much confusion and misunderstanding, beginning students often have the uncomfortable feeling that the more they read, the less they understand. There are so many conflicting viewpoints. One group sees a social problem one way and another group with conflicting interests sees it another way. Even the results of objective, scientific research may appear to be contradictory.

Sociology is a framework for sorting out all these facts, ideas, and beliefs. It provides the perspective and the tools needed to make sense of our social problems. Use of the sociological perspective helps reduce confusion in the minds of those who wish to participate intelligently in public discussions of these important issues. With this perspective we can develop programs to deal with our problems and evaluate their results once they have been put into effect. This is not to say, of course, that sociologists agree on just what a social problem is or how it can be explained. But fortunately such disagreements often result in a richer understanding for the student who is willing to examine all sides of the issues involved.

WHAT IS A SOCIAL PROBLEM?

Most people define a **social problem** as a condition that is harmful to society. But the matter is not so simple, for the meanings of such everyday terms as *harm* and *society* are far from clear. Conditions that some people see as social problems harm some segments of society but are beneficial to others. Consider air pollution. On the one hand, an automobile manufacturer might argue that government regulation of free enterprise is a social problem because laws requiring antipollution devices on cars raise costs, decrease gasoline mileage, and stimulate inflation. On the other hand, residents of a city with heavy air pollution might argue that the government's failure to outlaw noxious automobile emissions is a social problem because the smog created by automobiles harms their health and well-being. One person's social problem is another person's solution. Clearly, most people define social problems as conditions that harm or seem to harm their own interests.

A more precise sociological definition holds that *a social problem exists when there is a sizable difference between the ideals of a society and its actual achievements.*[1] Social problems are created by the failure to close the gap between the way people want things to be and the way things really are. According to this definition, racial discrimination is a social problem because although we believe that everyone should receive fair and equal treatment, some groups are still denied equal access to education, employment, and housing. Before this definition can be applied, someone must first examine the ideals and values of society and then decide whether these goals are being achieved. Sociologists and other experts thus decide what is or is not a problem, because they are the ones with the skills necessary for measuring the desires and achievements of society.

Critics of this approach note that no contemporary society has a single, unified set of values and ideals. Instead, there are many conflicting and contradictory beliefs. Thus, sociologists must decide which ideals and values will serve as standards for judging whether a certain condition is a social problem. Critics charge that sociologists select those ideals and values on the basis of their personal opinions and prejudices, not objective analysis.

The most widely accepted sociological definition holds that *a social problem exists when a significant number of people believe that a certain condition is in fact a problem.*[2] Here "the public"—not a sociologist—decides what is or is not a social problem. The sociologist's job is to determine which problems concern a substantial number of people. Thus, in this view pollution did not become a social problem until environmental activists and news reports attracted the public's attention to conditions that had actually existed for some time.

The advantage of this definition is that it does not require a value judgment by sociologists who try to decide what conditions are social problems. Such decisions are made by "the public." However, a serious shortcoming of this approach is that the public often is uninformed or misguided and does not clearly understand its problems. If thousands of people were being poisoned by radiation leaking from a nuclear power plant but didn't know it, wouldn't radiation pollution still be a social problem?

All the topics discussed in the chapters that follow qualify as social problems according to both sociological definitions. Each problem involves conditions that conflict with strongly held ideals and values, and all are considered social problems by significant groups of people. We have tried to discuss every problem fairly and objectively. However, it is important to understand that even selecting the problems requires a value judgment, whether by social scientists or by concerned citizens, and honest disagreements about the nature and importance of the various issues competing for public attention cannot be avoided.

SOCIAL PROBLEMS AND SOCIAL MOVEMENTS

The social issues that concern the public change from time to time, and examination of the Gallup poll's surveys reveals some interesting trends. War and peace and various economic issues have consistently ranked high on the public's list of social concerns. Interest in other problems seems to move in cycles. Thus, concern over taxes, foreign policy, drugs, and lack of religion and morality is high in some years and low in others. Still other social problems are like fads, attracting a great deal of interest for a few years before dropping from public attention.[3]

These changes have many different causes: shifts in ideals and values, the solution of an old problem, the creation of new ones. But the most important forces affecting changes in public opinion are **social movements** that focus attention on a certain social problem. For example, none of the Gallup polls in the 1930s and 1940s showed civil rights or race relations to be significant problems, even though racial discrimination was widespread and openly practiced. It was not until the civil rights movement began in the late 1950s that the polls began to reflect an interest in this problem. The civil rights issue would probably have remained buried if a powerful social movement had not developed.

Such movements begin when a large number of people start complaining about something they feel is a social problem. This group may be composed of people who believe they have been victimized, such as black victims of racial discrimination or female victims of sexual discrimination. Or it may be made up of concerned outsiders, such as opponents of alcohol use or those favoring the death penalty. As people with a common interest in an issue begin to talk with one another and express their feelings about the problem leaders step forward to lead the developing movement.[4] Martin Luther King, Jr., was such a leader for the civil rights movement, as Ralph Nader has been for the consumer movement. Jerry Falwell, leader of the Moral Majority, is another example.

The leader's first job is to mold separate groups of dissatisfied people into an organized political movement. The success of the movement depends on publicity, for it is only through publicity that the general public can be made aware of the problem and encouraged to do something about it. In other words, it is through publicity that the problem of a particular group becomes a social problem.

Three factors help a social movement gain public support and favorable action by government. The most important is the political power of the movement and its supporters. If the movement's supporters are numerous, highly organized, wealthy, or in key positions of power, it is more likely to be successful.

Social movements create public awareness about social problems and push the government to take action to resolve them.

A second factor is the strength of the movement's appeal to the people's values and prejudices. A movement to protect children from sexual abuse by adults is much more likely to gain widespread support than an effort to protect the civil liberties of child molesters.

The strength of the opposition to a movement is a third element determining its success or failure. Money is always limited, and the advocates of various social programs must compete with one another for funds. For example, few people object to the proposition that our elderly citizens deserve a higher standard of living. However, a variety of opponents quickly emerge when someone suggests raising taxes to pay for improving the living conditions of the elderly. Opposition to social movements also comes from people whose special interests are threatened by the goals of the movement. Thus, a proposal to raise the minimum wage for farm workers is bound to be opposed by farm owners.

A principal goal of many social movements is to create awareness of a social problem and then mobilize government action to resolve it. But even when a movement achieves these objectives, government action may be ineffective. A new government agency is often the means chosen to deal with a problem. Governments all over the world have created huge bureaucracies to deal with poverty (departments of welfare), health care (medicare and medicaid), pollution (the Environmental Protection Agency), and crime (police, courts, and prisons). Like all bureaucracies, these agencies are clumsy and slow moving, and are often more concerned with their own survival than with the problems they are designed to solve. After all, if narcotics enforcement agencies stopped all drug abuse, if police departments prevented all crime, or if mental hospitals quickly cured all disturbed people, the employees of these agencies would soon be out of work. Occasionally, it appears that the agencies set up to deal with a particular social problem are not actually expected to solve it. Politicians have been known to approve funds for a social program just to silence troublesome protesters, creating new agencies with impressive titles but no real power.

THE SOCIOLOGICAL APPROACH: BASIC IDEAS

In their attempt to study society scientifically, sociologists have often borrowed standards and methods developed in the physical and biological sciences. But they have found that human behavior is more complex and more difficult to understand than the topics studied by physicists, chemists, and biologists. Despite these handicaps, sociologists have developed a body of knowledge, theories, and methods that guides their research and forms the heart of sociology. Like other sciences, sociology has its own terms to describe what it studies, often words taken from everyday language. But because precision is necessary, sociologists give special meanings to common terms such as *role, group,* and *culture.*

Roles   In the theater or the movies, a role is the part a particular person plays in the show. Sociologists use the term in much the same way except that the role is played in real-life social situations. A **role** is usually defined as the set of behaviors and expectations associated with a particular social position (often known as a status). All roles—daughter, son, student, automobile driver, and countless others—offer certain rights and duties to the player. A student, for example, has the right to attend classes, to use the school's facilities, and to be graded fairly; the student also has the duty to read the texts, complete assigned work, and behave in an orderly manner. However, the way actual people carry out their roles often differs enormously from such idealized expectations.

Everyone plays many roles. A woman may be a wife, mother, sister, worker, consumer, student, and criminal—all at the same time. Some people experience **role conflict** because what is expected of them in one role clashes with what is expected in another. For instance, the roles of student and employee may each require large amounts of time and energy; the individual who attempts to fulfill both is likely to experience considerable role conflict.

Roles are one of the basic building blocks of our social world, and every society has countless positions with roles attached. Roles are interwoven in complex ways, so that it is often impossible to understand a particular role apart from the social network in which it is embedded. For example, it is not possible to define the role of wife without reference to the roles of husband, daughter, son, mother, and father. This interdependence stems from the fact that the rights of one position—wife, for example—are interlaced with the duties of other positions—husband, daughter, son. Each of us is judged by our performance as we carry out our roles, and the negligent mother, the abusive father, the incompetent professor, and the disruptive student who fail to meet role expectations are judged harshly.

Norms   A **norm** is a social rule that tells us what behavior is acceptable in a certain situation and what is not. Every human group, be it a small circle of friends or an entire society, generates norms that govern its members' conduct. Individuals who violate norms are often labeled **deviants** and given some kind of formal or informal punishment. A person who violates the norm against taking the lives of others may be tried and formally punished with a prison term, whereas a person who violates the trust of his or her friends is informally punished by ridicule or exclusion from the group. But like roles, the norms of various groups may conflict. Thus, some people are placed in the uncomfortable position of being forced to violate the norms of one group to which they belong in order to meet the norms of another.

It should be obvious that not all social norms are of equal importance. Norms that are merely customary procedures and are not strongly held by the group involved are called **folkways**. The Western custom of eating with a knife and fork, not fingers, is a good example. Those who eat with their fingers at a formal dinner are not sent to jail. They might not even be shunned by their friends, yet they are certainly considered odd, crude, or unsophisticated. Norms that a group considers very important are called **mores**. People who violate our mores, such as the prohibition of murder and rape, are punished severely. Many ancient mores have been absorbed into criminal law.

Groups   In the sociological sense a **group** is not just a gathering of people in the same place at the same time. Instead, it consists of a number of individuals who have organized and recurrent relationships with one another. Within the group, members quickly identify the roles and norms that govern their behavior and relationships. Groups have boundaries, and most group members share some common purpose or goal, even if it is only to enjoy one another's company.

To take a simple example, there is a great difference between students who sit quietly in a college library reading their sociology books and a similar number of students who have formed a study group. The group has norms. All members are expected to come prepared to discuss and criticize what they have read and to be helpful rather than competitive. No member is to waste time discussing the weather or last week's football game. In time the group develops specialized roles such as "the brain," "the joker," and "the plodder." A few students may even make their contribution to the group by looking intelligent and dignified while saying little or nothing. The group thus has a division of labor whereby various individuals help achieve the group's goal, each in his or her own particular way.

Socialization   **Socialization** is the process by which individuals learn the appropriate ways of behaving in their culture. Put another way, it is the process of be-

In the process of socialization, children learn to play the roles expected of them from their inter-actions with other people.

coming human. Roles, norms, customs, values, how to speak, even how to think—all these are learned in the process of socialization. Almost everything humans think or do is influenced by what they have learned from those around them.

Our basic socialization occurs in the early years of life. The rare child who has been hidden away from contact with the world in a closet or attic has limited speech and appears to be mentally defective. But socialization is not confined to the childhood years; it continues throughout our lives. As we enter new social groups, we begin a new process of socialization and begin acquiring new attitudes, perspectives, and behavior patterns.

Institutions   Social **institutions** are relatively stable patterns of thought and action centered on the performance of important social tasks. All societies have institutions for producing children and giving them guidance and support (family), relating to the supernatural (religion), producing and distributing food and other goods and services (economics), training its people (education), and making and enforcing rules (politics). Social institutions thus are organized around one or more of the necessities of social life. But sometimes the norms of one institution conflict with those of another, as when the norms of an economic institution that stresses free competition and accumulation of individual wealth clash with the norms of a family institution that stresses cooperation, mutual care, and sharing.

Social Classes   A **social class** is a category of people with similar shares of the things that are valued in a society. They have common life chances—a similar chance to get an education, to get health care, to obtain material possessions, to gain a position in life, and so on. This concept of social class is one of the most important and most useful in all sociology. Virtually all the problems examined in the next eighteen chapters of this book—from crime to the population explosion—are profoundly influenced by the class structure in which they are embedded. Karl Marx and many other nineteenth-century writers defined social class solely in economic terms. Today most sociologists use a broader definition taken from the work of the German sociologist Max Weber. According to Weber, the valuables a society distributes include social status and power as well as money. **Status** rests on a claim to social prestige, inherited from one's family or derived from occupation and life style. **Power** is the ability to make others do something whether they want to or not. Power is often associated with politics, though it may have other sources as well. In order to assess the class positions of individuals and groups, we must know their social and political standing as well as their income.

Sociologists use several different schemes to describe the class system in Western societies, but the most common divides these societies into four different classes (see Figure 1.1). The **upper class** is composed of individuals with great wealth, who often hold key positions of corporate power as well. Next comes the **middle class**, made up of an upper segment of highly paid

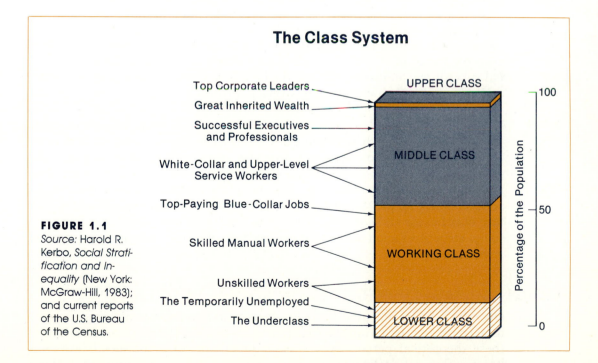

The Class System

Top Corporate Leaders

Great Inherited Wealth

Successful Executives and Professionals

White-Collar and Upper-Level Service Workers

Top-Paying Blue-Collar Jobs

Skilled Manual Workers

Unskilled Workers

The Temporarily Unemployed

The Underclass

UPPER CLASS

MIDDLE CLASS

WORKING CLASS

LOWER CLASS

Percentage of the Population

100

50

0

FIGURE 1.1
Source: Harold R. Kerbo, *Social Stratification and Inequality* (New York: McGraw-Hill, 1983); and current reports of the U.S. Bureau of the Census.

professionals and successful executives and entrepreneurs, and a much larger group of middle-level managers and white-collar (nonmanual) workers. The **working class** is about the same size as the middle class, but its members are mainly blue-collar (manual) workers and lower-level service workers. Although the best paid blue-collar workers earn more money than many middle-class employees, members of the working class make, on the average, far less than their middle-class counterparts. At the bottom of the social hierarchy is the **lower class**, whose members live in conditions of poverty or very close to them. This class can be further divided between an upper segment composed of the working poor and the short-term unemployed, and an **underclass** who have few prospects for a permanent job and are heavily dependent on the welfare system (see Chapter 6).

There is a popular belief that most Americans are middle class, perhaps because the majority of the people we see on television and in the movies are from that class. But the truth of the matter is much different. Of every 100 people in the United States, only one is from the upper class, 15 to 20 are from the lower class, and the remainder are more or less evenly divided between the working class and the middle class.

Culture   In everyday speech *culture* refers to the refinements of civilization, such as art, music, and literature. But to sociologists **culture** is the way of life of the people in a certain geographic area, and particularly the ideas, beliefs, values, patterns of thought, and **symbols** that make it possible. A culture provides individuals a way of understanding the world and making it meaningful. A **subculture** has its own ideas and beliefs yet is influenced by the larger culture. It is thus a culture within a culture. In industrialized nations it is accurate to speak of a working-class subculture, a youth subculture, a criminal subculture, and so on, despite the fact that working-class people, youths, and criminals all share the same overall culture.

Society   Although culture and society cannot be separated in real life, sociologists sometimes distinguish between the two so that each can be studied more easily. In such studies, **society** refers to a group of people in a particular geographic area who share common institutions and traditions, while the physical and mental products of those people are known as their culture. All societies have an overall **social structure**, which is simply an organized pattern of behavior and social relationships. They also have many more focused social structures such as a particular pattern of family life, social class, and government.

SOCIOLOGICAL PERSPECTIVES ON SOCIAL PROBLEMS

Over the years sociologists have developed and refined several broad theories to account for the nature of society and its problems. An understanding of these theoretical perspectives is essential to the study of social problems because they are designed to make sense of the conflicting claims made about social issues. But all theories do not serve the same purpose. **Macro theories** try to make sense of the behavior of large groups of people and the workings of entire societies; **micro theories** are concerned primarily with the behavior of individuals and small groups.

The **functionalist perspective** and the **conflict perspective** are the two most widely used types of macro theories. The micro theories are **social psychological theories** because they focus on the psychological effects of social groups and the social effects of individual behavior. We will consider only four of most important of these: the **biosocial, personality, behavioral, and interactionist theories.** (See Tables 1.1 and 1.2.) The supporters of these various theories often disagree with one another, but none of the theories can be said to be "right" or "wrong." Some theories, however, are more effective than others in analyzing a particular social problem, and more than one theory can be applied to the same problem. In fact, the greatest understanding comes when the insights gained from different theoretical perspectives are combined.

The Functionalist Perspective   Functionalism has been one of the most influential schools of social thought of recent times. Starting with the work of the French sociologist Émile Durkheim, functionalist theory was refined by Talcott Parsons, Robert K. Merton, and many others. Functionalists see society as a well-organized system in which most members agree on common norms and values. Roles, groups, and institutions fit together into a unified whole. Peo-

TABLE 1.1   Theories of Society (Macro Level)

Basic issues	The functionalist perspective	The conflict perspective
What holds society together?	Agreement on basic norms and values	Power, authority, and coercion
What is the basic nature of modern society?	A balance among various institutions, each performing different functions necessary to the survival of society	A competitive struggle for dominance among various social groups
Is society normally static or dynamic?	Static—when significant changes occur, a healthy society quickly readjusts and returns to a stable equilibrium	Dynamic—society is in a continual state of flux as it adjusts to the shifting balance of power among its competing groups
What is the major cause of social problems?	Social disorganization caused by rapid social change	The exploitation and oppression of some groups by others

TABLE 1.2 Social Psychological Theories (Micro Level)				
Basic issues	**Biosocial theories**	**Personality theories**	**Behaviorist theories**	**Interactionist theories**
What is the most fruitful area for research?	The physical human organism and its hereditary makeup	Individual personality	Behavior	Social interaction
What is the principal source of human behavior?	Human biology	Individual personality	Reinforcements from the environment (human and physical)	Interaction with people and groups through symbols and shared meaning
What is the major cause of social problems?	Innate human characteristics; biological defects in certain individuals	Personality disorders, maladaptive personality traits	The reinforcement of inappropriate behavior	Social support for deviant or dysfunctional behavior

ple do what is necessary to maintain a stable society because they accept its rules and regulations.

According to functionalist theory, the various parts of society are in delicate balance, and a change in one part affects the others. Each part has a **function** in maintaining the balanced order. For instance, the function of the economic institution is to provide the food, shelter, and clothing that people need in order to survive, while the function of the educational institution is to train individuals in the skills needed to keep society operating.

But societies, like machines and biological organisms, do not always work the way they are supposed to work. Things get out of whack. Changes introduced to correct a particular imbalance may produce other imbalances, even when things are going well. When an action interferes with the effort to carry out essential social tasks, it is said to be **dysfunctional**. For example, educators may train too many people for certain jobs. Those who cannot find jobs in their special line of work may become resentful, rebelling against the system which they feel has treated them unfairly. Thus, "overeducation" may be said to be a dysfunction of modern education.

Some of the functions and dysfunctions of an organization are *manifest*, that is, obvious to everyone. A manifest function of police departments, for example, is to keep crime rates low. Other functions and dysfunctions are *latent*—hidden and unintended. A latent function of police departments is to assist people in distress. Sociologists who study social problems have placed particular emphasis on exposing **latent dysfunctions** that are unknown to the general public. For instance, sociologists who have studied police departments note that these agencies burden the people they arrest with stigmatizing labels ("criminal," "delinquent," "outlaw," "hoodlum," and so on), and those who have been labeled may actually commit more crimes than if they had been left alone. Thus, in trying to stop crime, criminal-justice agencies may unintentionally contribute to its increase (see Chapter 14).

According to functionalists, social problems arise when society or some part of it becomes disorganized. This **social disorganization** involves a breakdown of social structure, so that its various parts no longer work together and norms lose their influence on particular groups or individuals. Functionalists see many causes of social disorganization. Norms may be violated because of inadequate socialization, or society may fail to control the aggression produced in its members. A society's relationship to its environment may be disrupted, so that it no longer has sufficient food, oil, building materials, or other resources. However, in modern industrial societies, one cause of social disorganization underlies all the others—namely, rapid social change. According to most functionalists, society responds well to change only if it occurs slowly.

Social disorganization is particularly severe in the modern era because more change has occurred in less time than in any other period of human history. Basic institutions have undergone drastic changes, with technology advancing so rapidly that other parts of the culture have failed to keep pace. This **cultural lag** between technological changes and our adaptation to them is one of the major sources of social disorganization. For instance, when knowledge about nutrition, public health, and modern medical technology began spreading through the world in the nineteenth century, many lives, especially those of the newly born, were saved. Yet traditional attitudes toward the family have not changed fast enough to adjust to the fact that more children survive to adulthood. The result has been a worldwide population explosion.

Although functionalism has been a standard theoretical approach to social problems for many years, it has a growing number of critics. Despite its claims of objectivity, many sociologists see functionalism as a politically conservative philosophy that automatically assumes that society is good as it is and should be preserved without major changes. Functionalism blames social problems on individual deviance or temporary social disorganization while seeming to ignore the basic injustices of society. The critics of functionalism claim that it is impossible to separate the functions of the various segments of society from each other. They also argue that one person's disorganization is another person's organization, and that what functionalists really mean when they say something is functional is that it works for the benefit of the privileged social classes.

The Conflict Perspective   The conflict perspective is the major alternative to the functionalist approach to the study of social problems. This perspective is based on a different set of assumptions about the nature of society and comes to different conclusions about the causes of social problems. As the name implies, conflict theory sees society as a struggle for power among various social groups. Conflict is believed to be inevitable and in many cases actually beneficial to society. For instance, many needed social changes arose from such conflicts as the French Revolution and the American War between the States.

The conflict perspective can most easily be understood by contrasting it with functionalist theory. Functionalists assume that society is held together by the agreement of its members on a common set of values, attitudes, and norms. For example, they say that most people obey the law because they believe it is fair and just. In contrast, conflict theorists insist that social order is maintained by authority backed by the use of force. One or more groups hold legal power, and use it to make others obey their will. To this way of thinking, most people obey the law because they are afraid of being arrested, jailed, or even killed if they do not obey. Another important difference between functionalism and the conflict perspective may be seen in their assumptions about social change. Functionalists tend to view society in relatively static terms, asserting that too much change is disruptive and that society has a natural tendency to regain its balance whenever it is disturbed. But conflict theorists see society in more dynamic terms. Because people are constantly struggling with one another to gain power, change is inevitable. One individual or group is bound to gain the upper hand, only to be defeated in a later struggle.

Neither the conflict perspective nor the functionalist perspective can be said to be a single unified theory. Rather, each consists of a number of related theories that share many common elements. The conflict perspective not only contains a large number of sociological theories but also encompasses a wide range of political views.

At least in part because of these political differences, different conflict theorists tend to focus on different kinds of conflict. Some are primarily concerned with **value conflict**, which arises from the differences in attitudes and beliefs among different social groups; others focus on **class conflict**, rooted in differences in power, wealth, and prestige; and still others emphasize conflicts based on gender or ethnic differences. There is, however, no reason why a conflict theorist must focus on only one of these and ignore the others. Different social problems involve different conflicts, and it is important to be sensitive to them all.

Sociologists who emphasize value conflict strongly disagree with the common functionalist assumption that most people in a society share the same set of norms and values. They point out that modern societies are composed of many different groups with different attitudes, values, and norms, and that conflicts are bound to arise. For instance, consider the abortion issue. Many conservative Christians believe that the human fetus, at any stage of its development, is a complete, living human being and that aborting a pregnancy is a form of murder. Feminists and others who support the right to a legal abortion hold that an unborn child is not yet a human being because it is unable to survive outside the womb. They assert that if the state forbids a woman to obtain an operation that she desires, it is violating her right to control her own life. Conflict theorists say that the clash between these two groups is a result of conflicting values and does not reflect social disorganization.

The great size and diversity of North American societies make such value conflicts inevitable. The continent is the home of hundreds of ethnic groups: white Anglo-Saxon Protestants, French Canadians, Germans, Ukrainians, Italians, Irish, Navahos, Mexicans, Chinese, and Africans, to name only a few. Each of these has its own set of cultural values and norms. In addition, all the world's major religions are represented, not to mention thousands of cults and splinter groups. There is also a rich diversity of subcultures within the dominant cultures, including punks, physicians, organized criminals, and hundreds of other groups who have developed their own perspectives on the world.

Value conflicts arise from other sources as well. Values shared by the members of the same group or society may be inconsistent or even directly opposed to one another. For example, the values of freedom and equality that are so fundamental to democratic societies often come into conflict. The individual who values equality may believe that only an unjust system could allow the children of a Rockefeller or a Du Pont to inherit tremendous wealth while many others receive nothing. However, another person may feel that any attempt to change this system violates the freedom of those who possess inherited wealth. Even freedom itself can be interpreted in conflicting ways. To some, affirmative action laws requiring factory owners to hire members of a minority group violate the owners' freedom to run their businesses as they see fit. To others, repeal of such laws would violate the freedom of minority workers to make a decent living.

But not all conflicts stem from disagreement over values and their interpretation. Some conflicts arise in part *because* people share the same values. If two groups of people place a high value on wealth and power and only one group has access to them, conflict is likely to result. Many sociologists believe that conflict over wealth, power, and status is the basic cause of most social problems. Although these competing groups may be based on various characteristics such as ethnicity, race, or gender, conflict sociologists have traditionally focused most heavily on class differences.

One of the first theorists to focus on class conflict as the underlying cause of social problems was Karl Marx, who wrote in the 1800s. For Marx, the position a person holds in the system of production determined his or her class position. In a capitalist society a person may be in one of two different positions. Some people own capital and capital-producing property (for example, factory owners, landlords, and merchants) and are therefore members of the **bourgeoisie**. Other people work for wages as producers of capital (for example, factory workers, miners, and laborers of all kinds). Marx called this class the **proletariat**. Marx asserted that these two classes have directly opposing economic interests because the wealth of the bourgeoisie is based on exploitation of the proletariat.

Class conflict, according to Marx, is a result of an inevitable historical process. He thought that the workers (proletariat) would develop an increasing awareness of their exploitation by the bourgeoisie and that that awareness, combined with growing political organization, would eventually lead to violent class conflict. A revolution won by workers over their masters would, Marx contended, lead to a classless society. Private property and inheritance would be abolished; steeply graduated income taxes would be introduced; education and training would be free; and production would be organized for use, not profit.

Marxist theory is an activist approach to social problems and social change. It guides the actions of millions of people throughout the world. However, not everyone who sees class conflict as a cause of social problems is a Marxist. All sociologists recognize that modern industrial society has a class system and that the classes have competing interests that generate conflict. But most sociologists, at least in Western nations, do not believe that a classless society is possible under present conditions, or that a violent social revolution is inevitable. Many social scientists who use the class conflict approach believe that society can best be changed through gradual reforms rather than violent revolution.

Just as functionalism has been criticized for being too conservative, the conflict perspective has been criticized for being too radical. Critics say that

The conflict perspective holds that the unequal distribution of wealth, power, and prestige is one of the most basic causes of social problems in contemporary society.

conflict theorists overemphasize the role of conflict, arguing that if there were as much of it as these theorists claim, society would have collapsed long ago. Functionalists do not agree that the maintenance of a capitalist society benefits only the bourgeoisie. Finally, many conflict theorists, particularly Marxists, are criticized for judging capitalist society too harshly. Critics argue that the classless utopia that Marx envisioned is impossible to achieve and that capitalist societies generally do a good job of dealing with their social problems.

Functionalism and conflict theory are the two principal macro-level approaches to social problems. While some sociologists claim that one or the other is the only valid approach, most use whatever theory seems to work best for the problem at hand. The use of both functional and conflict approaches often sheds more light on a problem than either approach used alone. For instance, crime can usefully be studied as a product of social disorganization, of class conflict between the poor and the other classes, and of value conflict between those who accept the law and those who don't. Obviously, all of these perspectives are useful if we are to understand social problems.

The Social Psychological Perspective Social psychological theories operate on a level different from that of the functionalist and conflict theories. Social psychology is concerned with the behavior of single individuals and small groups, and their relationships with one another and with the larger society. Socialization and the part that group interactions play in the individual's psychological development are a central concern of social psychology. A second major concern is to explain why some individuals conform to the norms and expectations of their groups while others become deviant. Most contemporary explanations of crime, mental illness, and sex role behavior are based on the findings of social psychologists.

Even social problems that seem to stem from social disorganization or class conflict have a social psychological side to them. Therefore, micro social psychological theories supplement the macro theories. However, the supporters of various social psychological theories are often at odds with one another. Of the many micro theories, the ones most commonly applied to the study of social problems include biosocial theories, personality theories, behavioral theories, and interactionist theories.

Biosocial Theories Scholars have long tried to explain social behavior by pointing to the biological traits of the human species. At one time such explanations were extremely influential in economics, political science, psychology, and sociology. A host of different behaviors were said to be instinctual. Warfare was seen as stemming from an "aggressive instinct," cooperation from a "social instinct," capitalism from an "acquisitive instinct," and so on. As the list of such "instincts" grew, critics began to charge that these theories had little factual support and added nothing to understanding human behavior. They argued that even if there were, for instance, an instinct of aggression, this biological fact would help very little in the understanding of the complex economic, political, religious, and social conflicts that lead to wars. Most scientists eventually lost confidence in instinct theory and turned instead to explaining human behavior in terms of social and cultural conditions. "To explain a social fact," Émile Durkheim said, "seek other social facts." However, many social scientists believe that the pendulum has now swung too far in the other direction, and biosocial theories of human behavior have begun to receive new attention.

Some of the new biosocial theories seem to imply that virtually all human behavior is inherited. It is argued that even such values as altruism (unselfishness), which appear to be entirely cultural, have actually been built into our genetic structure in the process of evolution.[5] After studying the incredible diversity of behavior in human societies, few anthropologists or sociologists can accept the idea that most human behavior is directly determined by genetics. Most contemporary biosocial theorists therefore emphasize the importance of the interaction between biological predispositions and the social environment. For example, many criminologists who argue that there is a hereditary predisposition toward crime see the problem as being as much with society as with genetics. They argue that people with low intelligence, which they hold to be a biological characteristic, are rejected by teachers and more competent students because they do poorly in school. As a result, they are more likely to become rebellious and antisocial (see Chapter 14). Whether we accept this argument or not, there is little doubt that the structure of the human body and its biological needs have enormous influences on both individual and social behavior. After all, the most basic task of any society is to provide for the biological needs of its members. Imagine how different human society would be if we reproduced without sexual intercourse, as some plants do, or if human beings matured into adults in a few weeks, as some animals do.

Although no single, broad biological theory is accepted by all social scientists, dozens of different theories are relevant to discussions of specific social problems. Although some are very convincing, others are based on little more than myth and prejudice. Sociologists have traditionally avoided biological explanations of social problems, in part because the social policy implications of these theories are often very pessimistic. If a social problem is believed to be biologically caused, policy makers have little incentive to try to solve it because they obviously have little chance of changing human biology. For example, if people live in poverty only because they are biologically inferior (a proposition that virtually no contemporary social scientist would support), there is little chance that policy makers could do much to eliminate poverty. Even more disturbing is the blatant racism of some biosocial theories. In the past many reputable scientists believed that blacks and members of other minorities were poor because they were racially inferior. But the obvious errors in this theory should not be taken as evidence that all biosocial theories are in error. On the contrary, many sociologists believe that the biosocial perspective will make an increasingly important contribution to the understanding of human behavior in the years ahead.

Personality Theories Personality is one of the most widely used words in psychology. It refers to the stable characteristics and traits that distinguish one person from another and that account for differences in individual social behavior. For example, criminals are said to break the law because they have "sociopathic personalities" (impulsive, unstable, and immature). Racial prejudice is said to stem from an "authoritarian personality" (rigid, insecure, with repressed feelings of guilt and hostility).

Although there are many different personality theories, the one developed by Sigmund Freud has been the most influential. Freud asserted that an individual's personality is formed during the early years of childhood and that the family is therefore the major force in personality development. If children experience a serious emotional trauma, their psychological development may be impaired, leading to difficulties later in life. For example, traumas caused by the parents' negative reaction to infantile sexual behavior may create an unconscious conflict between the desire for sexual gratification and the desire for approval from parents and society. This conflict may emerge later in the form of impotence, frigidity, or other psychological problems.

Freud divided the personality into three parts. The most basic is the **id**—the instinctual drives, particularly sex, which are said to motivate all human behavior. The second part of the personality to develop is the **ego**—the individual's conscious, reality-oriented experience. The **superego**—the individual's conscience or sense of morality—is the last to develop. Freudians assume that these three parts of the personality are balanced in normal people and that personality disorders arise either from disturbances in one part or from an imbalance among the different parts. Freudians also place much importance on the unconscious mental life that is presumed to go on without the individual's awareness.

Freud's theory has been attacked because of its overemphasis on the sex drive, its neglect and misunderstanding of females, and its departure from standard scientific procedure. As a result, few sociologists or psychologists today apply Freud's theory in its original form. However, many psychologists have used Freud's ideas as a basis for new theories that try to avoid these faults. Still other psychologists have developed entirely different perspectives on the nature and origins of personality. But because most theories of personality rely upon subjective reports in which people try to describe how they think and feel, they are often subject to criticism for an alleged vagueness and lack of supporting factual evidence.

A different approach focuses on *personality traits* rather than on the structure and dynamics of personality. Trait theories classify people according to basic personality characteristics, such as dominance–submissiveness, impulsiveness–self-control, and introversion–extraversion. Many tests have been developed to determine the presence of such traits in particular individuals, and attempts have been made to link specific traits with specific types of deviant behavior. But, so far, this line of research has produced few satisfactory results. Critics of this approach note the great differences among the traits that various psychologists claim to have found with their tests, arguing that personality is not composed of the simple, distinct traits that the tests are said to measure. Instead, the critics assert, personality can be understood only as a unified whole.

Behavioral Theories Some social psychologists are convinced that it is a waste of time to try to figure out what is going on inside people's heads. They argue that because the psychological traits that are said to determine behavior cannot be observed, such efforts ultimately reflect the subjective judgments of the theorist. Because these social psychologists confine their studies exclusively to observable behavior, this theoretical perspective, founded by J. B. Watson and developed by B. F. Skinner, is known as **behaviorism**.

Behavior, from this perspective, depends on the **reinforcements** the actor receives from its performance. If an individual is rewarded (one type of reinforcement) for a certain behavior in a certain situation, he or she is likely to repeat the behavior when the situation recurs. If punishment is given, the behavior is less likely to be repeated. For instance, if parents respond to their daughter's temper tantrum with concern and attention, she is likely to repeat that behavior the next time she wants attention. But if the girl's tantrum is ignored, she will use a different means to attract attention. Thus, behavioral theory explains human action primarily in terms of the individual's environment. Of course, the process of learning is not nearly as simple as our illustration implies; behaviorists have developed an elaborate set of principles about the many kinds of reinforcements that encourage or discourage the learning of specific behaviors.

Critics of behavioral theory object to its exclusion of mental processes and the subjective outlooks of individuals, arguing that it is impossible to understand human behavior without understanding the way people think and feel and the structure of their personalities. They agree that it is difficult to study personality directly but assert that this is hardly enough reason to conclude that personality has no influence on human behavior. A newer school of thought known as **social behaviorism** attempts to take account of such criticism by explicitly recognizing the importance of such things as ideas, culture, and social groups in the learning process, thus bringing them much closer to our next group of theorists—the interactionists.

Interactionist Theories Interactionist theories see behavior as a product of an individual's social relationships. Because the socialization process forms the foundation for human interaction, interactionists study it in detail. Their theories hold that individuals are products of the social relationships and the culture in which they participate. People develop their outlook on life from participation in the symbolic universe that is their culture. They develop their conceptions of themselves, learn to talk, and even learn how to think, as they interact early in life with family and friends. Unlike the Freudians, interactionists believe that an individual's personality and self-concept continue to change throughout life in response to changing social environments.

The work of the American philosopher George Herbert Mead has been the driving force behind the interactionist theories of social psychology. Mead argued that the ability to communicate in symbols (principally words and combinations of words) is the key feature that distinguishes humans from other animals. Individuals develop the ability to think and to use symbols in the process of socialization. Young children blindly imitate the behavior of their parents, but eventually they learn to "take the role of the other," pretending to be "Mommy" or "Daddy." From such role taking children learn to understand the interrelationships among different roles and to see themselves as they imagine others see them. Out of this process children eventually formulate a **self-concept;** that is, they create a mental image of who and what they are. The concept of self is one of the most important in social psychology, for our self influences almost every aspect of individual behavior. Eventually, according to Mead, children also begin to take the role of a **generalized other.** In doing so, they adopt a system of values and standards that reflect the expectations of people in general, not just those who are present at any particular time. In this way **reference groups** as well as actual **membership groups** come to determine how the individual behaves.

After Mead's death in 1931, his ideas continued to gain stature among sociologists and social psychologists. Those who adhered most closely to Mead's original ideas became known as symbolic interactionists.[6] They have been very active in the study of social problems and have contributed a great deal to our understanding of critical social issues. For example, differential-association theory, an important explanation of delinquency and crime, is a direct offshoot of Mead's theories, as is the labeling theory of mental illness and the cultural-learning theory of drug use (see Chapters 12, 13, and 14). Despite his enormous influence, Mead has many critics. As with Freudian theory the most common criticism of interactionist theory is that it is vague and difficult to substantiate.

DOING SOCIOLOGICAL RESEARCH

The theoretical perspectives we have discussed serve as a guide and a point of reference for the student of social problems. However, theories are of little value unless they deal with facts. Unfortunately, showing how a theoretical process actually works to produce its effects is much more difficult for a sociologist than it is for most other scientists. In the study of social problems, people rarely agree on what "the facts" are. Many sociologists long for the simplicity of sciences like physics because it is much easier to study the movement of inanimate objects than to predict or explain human behavior.

Because their task is so difficult, sociologists give a great deal of attention to determining the best ways of doing social research. Volumes have been written on the subject, yet there is no widespread agreement about the most effective methods. The selection of research techniques must be based on the particular problem under study. Among the many available sources of data, public records and statistics, the case study, the survey, and the experiment are most commonly used by sociologists.

Public Records and Statistics Governments and organizations like the United Nations and the World Bank publish a wealth of statistics and information. A look through the footnotes of this book will reveal numerous references to data from the Bureau of the Census, the Bureau of Justice Statistics, the Department of Labor, and similar organizations, for such information is vital to the efforts of sociologists to understand today's social problems. One of the oldest and most reliable sources of statistics is the U.S. census, which is taken every ten years. The goal of the census is to count every person in the United States and determine such characteristics as their age, gender, and employment status. This is obviously a massive undertaking, and so many organizations also take surveys that question only a sample of the total population. There are periodic government surveys of selected groups such as the elderly or the unemployed, as well as general surveys designed to measure, for example, the number of people who have been the victims of crime. Another important source of data is the bureaucracies that register births, marriages, divorces, and deaths; and the official records of government agencies, such as the federal budget and the Congressional Record.

Despite their importance to the sociologist, such statistics still have serious shortcomings. Almost every researcher has had the experience of spending long hours looking through official publications searching for a particular figure that is nowhere to be found. You might, for example, be interested in comparing the income and educational levels of Chinese Americans and Filipino Americans, only to find that the Department of the Census lists only whites, blacks, Hispanics, and "others." More serious is the problem of bias and distortion. It has, for example, long been known that many black males from the underclass vanish from census reports in their early years of adulthood only to reappear in middle age. Government statistics may also be biased by political considerations. Such things as the rates of poverty, unemployment, and crime are often hot social issues, and many sociologists have charged that the standards and procedures for calculating those figures are sometimes slanted for political reasons.

The Case Study A detailed examination of specific individuals, groups, and situations is known as a **case study**. There are many different sources of information for such investigations, including the official records just discussed, biographies, and newspaper reports. But **personal interviews** and **participant observation** are the most common.

Suppose you were interested in studying juvenile delinquency. You might locate a gang of delinquent boys and interview them, asking each boy why he became involved in the gang, what he does with the other gang members, what his plans for the future are, and so on. You would then study the replies, put them together in some meaningful way, and draw your conclusions. On the other hand, in a participant observation study you would actually take part in gang activities. You might disguise yourself and work your way into the gang as a regular member, or you might tell the boys your purpose and ask their permission to watch their activities. One problem with the interview technique is that we can never be sure the subjects are telling the truth, even if they think they are. Although the participant observation technique avoids this problem, it is difficult and sometimes even dangerous to study people in this way, for they often resent the intrusion of nosy outsiders. Another problem is that the presence of a sociologist may make the people being studied change their behavior.

When compared with other research methods, the case study has the advantage of allowing researchers to come into close contact with the object of their study. Interviews and direct observation can provide rich insights that cannot be obtained from statistics. But the case study method has its limitations, especially when the cases selected for study are not typical. For instance, a researcher might unknowingly select a group of delinquents who are strongly opposed to drug use, while all the other gang members in the same area are heavy drug users. Another common criticism of the case study method is that it relies too heavily on the ability and insights of the person doing the study. Although this problem is common to all research methods, it is especially troublesome in case studies because all the "facts" that are disclosed for examination are filtered by the researcher.

The Survey   Rather than concentrating on an in-depth study of a few cases, the **survey** asks more limited questions of a much larger number of people. Because it is seldom possible to question everyone concerned with a certain social problem, a **sample** is used. For instance, suppose you were interested in the relationship between age and attitudes toward the abortion issue. You might select an appropriate city for your study and randomly select a sample of 100 names from the city directory. If the sample is properly drawn, it will be representative of all the people in the city. Each person in the sample would then be interviewed to determine his or her age and attitude toward abortion. You would then analyze the responses statistically to determine the relationship between these two variables.

The survey is an invaluable tool for measuring the attitudes and behaviors of large numbers of people. The famous Gallup poll is a good example of how the survey method can be used effectively. However, because this method reports answers to a limited number of fixed questions, it is not as effective as the case study approach in developing new ideas and insights. Another problem is that people do not always answer the questions honestly, particularly if they deal with sensitive issues such as sexual behavior or crime. A third difficulty is that surveys are expensive and time consuming to conduct. But when conducted properly, a survey ensures that the people studied are not misleading exceptions, and case studies seldom provide this assurance.

The Experiment   In social science, as in the physical and biological sciences, the **experiment** provides an opportunity for the most carefully controlled type of research. Although there are many types of experimental designs, experimenters usually divide their subjects into an experimental group and a control group. Then, the experimental group is manipulated in some way the other group is not. By comparing the two groups at the end of the experiment, researchers try to discover the effects of what was done to the experimental group. To illustrate, suppose you were interested in the effects of violent programs on television viewers. You might select two groups of people and show one, the experimental group, a number of violent television programs and the other, the control group, nonviolent programs. You would then test the two groups to see whether the violent programs caused any increase in violent behavior or attitudes.

A major problem arises because most experimental studies of human behavior must be conducted in laboratory settings. Watching violent television programs in a laboratory is likely to have different effects from watching the same programs at home because the conditions in the two settings differ so greatly. True "social experiments," in which a social change is introduced into real-life settings to determine its effect on a social problem, are very rare because control is difficult in such conditions and few social scientists have the authority or the money to carry out such research. Another problem with experimental research is that the subjects may be inadvertently harmed by the experimental manipulations, and many potentially valuable experiments cannot be done for ethical reasons.

INTERPRETING CLAIMS ABOUT SOCIAL PROBLEMS

Even those of us who never do research on social problems sooner or later will have to interpret claims about them. Politicians, journalists, and sociologists, as well as an assortment of cranks and oddballs, constantly bombard the public with opinions and "facts" about these problems. Each citizen must decide whether to believe or disregard these assertions. Many of the claims are patently false, but some are presented with impressive-sounding arguments. Reasonable skepticism is an important scientific tool. It should be practiced by anyone who is interested in knowing how social problems arise, persist, and change.

Some people find it easy to believe almost anything they see in print, and even accept the exaggerated claims of television commercials and newspaper advertisements. The ability to speak well may be taken as a sign that the speaker is trustworthy and honest. The belief that those who lie in public are usually sued or even put in jail adds to the credibility of public speakers.

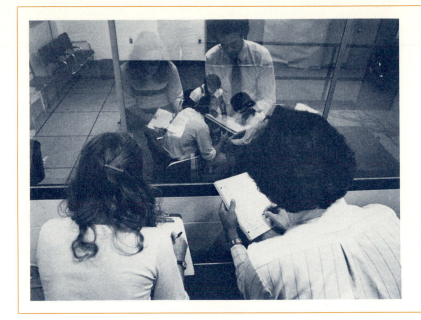

The experiment permits more carefully controlled research than any other technique. It is extremely difficult, however, to re-create everyday social conditions in the labora-tory when working with human subjects.

But there are many ways of telling lies without risking trouble with the law. One technique is to lie about groups rather than individuals. While a speaker could not say that John Jones is a narcotics addict without some proof, the speaker could say that college students or musicians are addicts. Another technique is to imply guilt by association. A speaker might charge that Judge Mary Jones is "frequently seen in the company of thugs, degenerates, and narcotics addicts." Consider the difference between these two statements:

> Mary Jones, the Communist Party, and student revolutionaries agree that there are great injustices in the American economic system.

> Mary Jones, the National Council of Churches, and Supreme Court judges agree that there are great injustices in the American economic system.

Another way of conveying a misleading impression is to quote out of context. This sort of misrepresentation has been brought to the level of a fine art by the merchandisers of paperback books. For example, a reviewer in *The New York Times* might say something like this: "This book is somewhat interesting, but certainly not one of the greatest books of the decade." And it might end up being quoted like this: "Interesting . . . one of the greatest books of the decade.—*The New York Times.*"

It is essential to read claims about social problems and their solutions carefully. Wild propaganda and intentional distortions usually are self-revealing. However, most people who are concerned about social issues do not intentionally lie or distort the truth. They may merely be vague, using phrases such as "many people believe" and "it is widely thought" because their knowledge is incomplete. But people also tend to unconsciously distort their perceptions to fit their own biases, and misleading statements are hardest to detect when the speaker is sincere. There are a number of standards that can be used to measure the validity of a statement, but none of them is foolproof.

The Author   One of the best places to begin evaluating an article or speech is with the author. What are his or her qualifications? Why should the speaker or writer know anything more about the problem than the audience? Titles and academic degrees in themselves do not mean very much unless they have some clear relation to the problem under consideration. For instance, a professor of physics might be qualified to talk about nuclear power, but her opinion about the influence of international politics on our oil supplies could well be of little value. A professor of sociology might be well qualified to comment on the causes of crime but know little or nothing about how police departments should be organized. An impressive title does not always guarantee authority or expertise.

It is also helpful, when possible, to know an author's biases. They will often become clear if one looks at the author's other work. For example, suppose that an economist who has always supported the social security system publishes a study concluding that the system has been a failure. These findings should be given more weight than the same conclusions published by a long-time opponent of social security. The same is true of articles published by people with special interests. An article concluding that criminals have been mistreated by the police is more persuasive if it is written by a police officer than if it is written by a burglar.

The Support   Scientific research projects are expensive. If authors say their assertions are based on research, it is important to know who paid for the research and what, if anything, its supporters stand to gain from its conclusions. Few organizations, including federal agencies, will fund a study that is likely to arrive at conclusions harmful to their interests. It is not very surprising to find a study funded by an oil company that asserts that oil drilling will produce little environmental damage, or to find a study funded by a tobacco company that says that smoking cigarettes is as safe as playing badminton. However, a study funded by an oil company that concludes that oil drilling will cause serious damage to the environment merits attention.

The Distribution   Where an article is published or a speech is given can be another important guide to the reliability of the statements made. One can usually assume that articles published in recognized professional journals such as *The American Journal of Sociology* or *Social Problems* meet some minimal professional standards. But an article on race relations published in a newspaper affiliated with the Ku Klux Klan, an article on minimum wages published in a trade union weekly, or a speech on gun control before the National Rifle Association is likely to contain few surprises.

The Content   There are no firm rules for judging which conclusions are reasonable and which are not. Some research papers are so technical that only an expert can judge their value. But most books, magazine articles, and speeches about social problems are not directed at expert audiences; so readers and listeners need no special qualifications when they make a judgment about the accuracy of what is said. Asking the following questions is a good way to begin when judging the value of an article or speech.

Does the Article or Speech Make Sense? It is important to get involved with what is being said rather than just passively accepting it. Are the author's arguments logical? If a person says that drug addiction is widespread because enemy agents are trying to weaken the country by enslaving its youth, ask yourself whether it is reasonable to claim that such methods could be used in secret. It is also logical to ask why those who are being enslaved by drugs are the least powerful people in the population. Do the author's conclusions seem to follow from the evidence presented? There is good reason to reject an argument that, for example, asserts that college students who smoke marijuana do so because of poverty. Subtler gaps in logic can also be detected by the attentive listener.

Why Does the Writer or Speaker Use a Particular Style? A book or speech need not be boring to be accurate. Nevertheless, there is a difference between a calm, thoughtful analysis and demagoguery. Skillful speakers who give emotion-packed examples of human suffering may only be trying to get an audience's attention, or they may use such examples to cloud the issue. Most articles, speeches, and books necessarily contain some vague claims or assertions. One should always ask whether the vagueness is necessary because some facts are unknown or because the author is trying to obscure the subject or conceal information. Conversely, a collection of numbers and statistics does not guarantee that conclusions are valid. An old saying holds that figures don't lie but liars figure.

Do an Author's Claims Fit in with What Others Say About the Subject? The truth of a proposition is not decided by democratic vote. Majorities can be wrong and minorities right. Even an individual who strays far from what most people—including experts—accept as true is not necessarily wrong. In scientific work especially, a successful experiment by a lone researcher can change truths that have long been accepted. But if an author's claims differ greatly from those of others who know something about the subject, there is reason to be skeptical. The question to be asked is whether the author presents enough evidence to justify rejection of the old ideas and the accepted beliefs.

SUMMARY

There are two major sociological definitions of the term *social problem.* One says that social problems are created by gaps between a society's ideals and actual conditions in that society. The other defines a social problem as a condition that a significant number of people consider to be a problem.

The public's perceptions of social problems change from time to time. The major forces influencing these changes are social movements that try to bring about social change. These movements usually begin when people who share a common problem start to communicate with each other and commit themselves to finding a solution. If the supporters of a social movement are powerful, or if they can appeal to popular values and prejudices, the movement has a good chance of success. If the opponents of the social movement have more influence, the desired action is less likely to be taken. But even if the government takes official action, the agencies that are supposed to deal with the problem may do little or nothing to change it.

Over the years sociologists have developed a body of knowledge, theories, and methods that aid in the study of social problems. Eight basic sociologic terms essential to the understanding of the sociological approach are *roles, norms, groups, socialization, institutions, classes, culture,* and *society.*

Sociologists approach the study of social problems from different theoretical perspectives. The two major approaches dealing with large groups and entire societies are the functionalist perspective and the conflict perspective. Functionalists see a society as a delicate balance among its basic components. Every society has a set of needs that must be fulfilled if it is to survive and all the components of a society have functions that they perform to meet these needs. But they may also have dysfunctions or harmful consequences for society. Social problems occur when a society becomes so disorganized that its basic functions cannot be performed as well as they should be. Conflict theorists see social order as a set of power relationships. Coercion, not shared values and beliefs, is the cement that holds a society together. Some conflict theorists emphasize conflicts between people whose values are incompatible; others emphasize conflicts between people from different classes, ethnic groups, or genders. But they agree that the oppression of one group by another is a basic cause of our social problems.

Social psychological theories focus on individuals and small groups rather than on entire societies. Biosocial theories emphasize the role of heredity in human behavior. Personality theories focus on the traits that an individual develops in early socialization. Behavioral theories discount internal mental processes and are concerned only with observable behavior and the ways in which it is learned. Interactionist theories note the important effects of social interaction on behavior.

Theory is an important guide, but it becomes effective only when applied to facts. Social scientists use four principal methods to gather data to test theories and uncover the facts. Public records and statistics provide social scientists with a rich source of data without having to collect it themselves.

The case study is a detailed examination of specific individuals, groups, or situations. Surveys put questions to cross sections of the population. Experiments usually try to duplicate the social world in a laboratory so that the various factors being studied can be carefully controlled.

Even those who never do research on social problems should be able to interpret and judge the claims of others. There are at least four commonsense methods for evaluating speeches, books, and articles about social problems: (1) Check the qualifications and biases of the author. (2) Check the biases of the people who pay the bills of the speaker or author. (3) Check the publishers of magazine articles and the special interests of the audience listening to a speech. (4) Check the content of the speech or article and the logic of the arguments the author uses to support a point.

KEY TERMS

behavioral theory

biosocial theory

case study

conflict perspective

culture

experiment

functionalist perspective

group

institution

interactionist theory

norm

personality theory

role

social class

social problem

social psychological theory

socialization

society

sociology

survey

FURTHER READINGS

Introducing Sociology

C. Wright Mills, *The Sociological Imagination,* New York: Oxford University Press, 1959.

Randall Collins, *Sociological Insight: An Introduction to Non-Obvious Sociology,* New York: Oxford University Press, 1982.

Anthony Giddens, *Sociology: A Brief but Critical Introduction,* San Diego: Harcourt Brace Jovanovich, 1982.

Robert E. Kennedy, Jr., *Life Choices: Introducing Sociology,* New York: Holt, Rinehart & Winston, 1985.

The Sociological Approach to Social Problems

Malcolm Spector and John I. Kitsuse, *Constructing Social Problems,* Menlo Park, N.Y.: Cummings, 1977.

Earl Rubington and Martin Weinberg, *The Study of Social Problems,* 2d ed., New York: Oxford University Press, 1977.

Jonathan H. Turner, *The Structure of Sociological Theory,* Chicago: Dorset Press, 1986.

Conducting Sociological Research

Earl Babbie, *The Practice of Social Research,* 4th ed., Belmont, Calif.: Wadsworth, 1986.

PART ONE
Troubled Institutions

- What is the "world economy"?
- Who controls corporations?
- Is the "work ethic" dead?
- Why has the economy stagnated?
- What can the government do to solve our economic problems?

Chapter 2
PROBLEMS OF THE ECONOMY

What has happened to the American dream? People seem to be losing their faith in the promise of unbounded opportunity and success for anyone who is willing to work hard enough to achieve it. Stores are flooded with foreign products that are not only cheaper but often of better quality than domestic goods. Inflated real estate prices and high interest rates have put the price of owning a home beyond the grasp of millions of young Americans. And most troubling of all, there seems to be a new spirit of selfishness as people in comfortable economic circumstances strain to protect their position at the expense of those below them, and those at the top get an ever larger share of the economic pie.

Of course, the American dream has always been just that—a dream, In the past, women and minorities were always excluded from the dream; and countless others tried and failed to win the promised success. Moreover, despite some recent setbacks, the standard of living is still much higher today than could have been imagined 100 years ago, and the Great Depression certainly brought greater economic hardship than any we know today. Still, such facts are little consolation to people who have grown used to the seemingly endless prosperity that followed World War II. American society has grown to depend on its growing affluence to provide the wherewithal to deal with its other social problems. Now the economy is undergoing fundamental changes that are calling that assumption of ever-greater prosperity into question, and American society is facing one of the most difficult adjustments in its history.

MYTHS AND REALITIES

Most people are surprisingly uninformed about the way our economy operates, and many widely accepted economic beliefs are just plain wrong. The first step toward understanding our economy and the changes that are transforming it is to examine those myths and find the underlying realities.

The World Economy   The world is a vast and confusing place, and most people are familiar with only a small part of it. When economic problems crop up, people seek explanations by looking at familiar events close to home. Although some problems can be understood in terms of a single nation or even a single city, today's economic problems are world problems. No one can understand the causes of inflation, unemployment, or economic stagnation by looking only at a single nation in isolation from the **world economy**.

Day by day, year by year, the world is becoming smaller and more interdependent. Because of its large size and relative geographic isolation, the United States traditionally enjoyed a large measure of economic independence. But such independence is fast becoming a thing of the past for all the nations of the world. The size of the grain harvest in the Soviet Union, the import tariffs in France, and the average wage paid to Japanese industrial workers all have a profound effect on our economic destiny.

But although all nations are part of the world economy, all nations do not play the same part in it. The principal dividing line in the modern world is between the wealthy industrialized nations and the poor agricultural nations of the **Third World**. Although most of the world's products are manufactured in the industrialized nations, more than three-fourths of the world's people live in the Third World.[1] Another important division in the world economy is between the socialist nations, which have centrally planned economies, and the capitalist nations with which we are more familiar.

Contemporary Capitalism   Almost everyone will agree that the United States, Canada, and many European countries have capitalist economies. But exactly what does this mean? Although it is difficult to define **capitalism** precisely, capitalist economic systems display three essential characteristics. First, there is private property. Second, there is a market that controls the production and distribution of valuable commodities. Third, privately owned businesses compete with one another in this free market, each aiming to make the greatest possible profit. The classic statement of the principles of free-market capitalism was set forth in Adam Smith's book *The Wealth of Nations,* first published in 1776.[2] Smith argued that individuals will work harder and produce more if allowed to work for personal profit. Private greed will be transformed into public good through the workings of a free market regulated only by supply and demand. The profit motive will drive manufacturers to supply goods that the public demands, and competition will ensure that the goods are reasonably priced. The market will regulate itself in the most efficient possible way—as though guided by an "invisible hand"—if the government does not interfere with the free play of economic forces.

Adam Smith's revolutionary ideas won great international acceptance. And because of their popularity, many people continue to believe that our economy operates the way Smith said it should. However, there have been drastic economic changes since the early nineteenth century, when North America came closest to the ideals of Adam Smith's capitalism.

Business people have long realized the great advantages that can be gained with the help of the government. Political pressure by entrepreneurs won franchises, patents, tax breaks, tariffs, and other special privileges that restricted the competition that Smith envisioned. Producers also worked together to reduce competition on their own. They banded together to limit the supply of goods so that prices would rise. Trade associations, chambers of commerce, and similar organizations were formed to foster this collusion. Even Adam Smith recognized the problem: "People of the same trade seldom meet together, even for merriment and diversion, but the conversation ends in a conspiracy against the public, or in some contrivance to raise prices."[3]

But Smith did not foresee another development that would reduce competition even more: the rise of the giant corporation. Huge banks, multinational corporations, newspaper chains, and broadcasting companies all represent the merging of competing interests. In some industries a single corporation was able to take over complete control of the market and create a **monopoly**. Great companies like Standard Oil and United States Steel drove their competition out of business and then could charge virtually any price they wanted for their products. In response, the government tried to restore competition by breaking up the monopolies and regulating the giant companies. However, such regulation was not very successful. There are few outright monopolies today, but they have been replaced by **oligopolies:** industries dominated by a few large companies.

In addition, government intervention in the economy transferred competition from the marketplace to the offices of regulatory agencies, where businesses compete for favorable rules and regulations. The government is deeply involved in the modern economy, sometimes intervening in the interest of the public, sometimes in the interests of manufacturers or other special-interest groups, but always involved.

THE CORPORATIONS

Although huge corporations are relatively recent arrivals on the economic scene in the capitalist countries, they have quickly come to dominate it. Unlike businesses owned by single individuals or partners, corporations are owned by their stockholders. Most large corporations have thousands of owners, although some are controlled by a few major stockholders. One of the most important trends of recent years is that an increasing percentage of corporate stock is now owned or controlled by institutional investors such as banks and insurance companies instead of private individuals. Because it would be impractical for all stockholders to be involved in important corporate decisions, they elect a board of directors to set general policies and oversee the running of the corporation. Executives and managers who are full-time employees make the day-to-day decisions and carry on the work of the corporation.

Business Giants   If all the world's largest enterprises, including governments, were listed in order of size, half would be corporations. Such American giants as General Motors and Exxon have assets worth billions of dollars. Antitrust laws prohibit a single corporate giant from monopolizing an entire industry. But corporations can get around these laws by expanding into related fields, buying out suppliers and distributors. Others have become **conglomerates:** large firms that own businesses in many areas of production and distribution.

Another distinctive characteristic of today's major corporations is their **market control.** The markets for many important products, ranging from automobiles and gasoline to aspirin and broadcasting, are dominated by just three or four giant firms. About 60 percent of all the goods and services produced in the United States (not counting those produced by the government) are made in industries dominated by such oligopolies. And even in these restricted markets there is usually one giant that is larger and stronger than any other. For instance, General Motors produces more cars than all other American car manufacturers combined. (See Figure 2.1.)

Because there are so few major corporations in some industries, it is

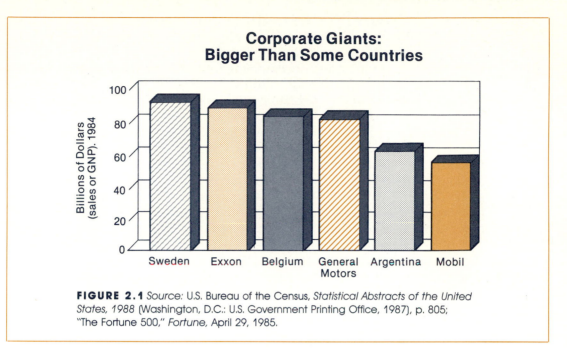

Corporate Giants:
Bigger Than Some Countries

FIGURE 2.1 *Source:* U.S. Bureau of the Census, *Statistical Abstracts of the United States, 1988* (Washington, D.C.: U.S. Government Printing Office, 1987), p. 805; "The Fortune 500," *Fortune,* April 29, 1985.

easy for them to restrict the "free competitive market." The largest corporation in an industry often becomes the **price leader.** It sets the prices for the merchandise it sells, and other corporations set theirs at the same level, ignoring the principles of supply and demand envisioned by Adam Smith

Because the same individuals serve on the board of directors of many different firms, most large corporations are said to have interlocking directorates. *These interlocking directorates create channels of communication among major corporations and encourage them to cooperate to promote their common interests.*

and his followers. The business giants also communicate and cooperate through **interlocking directorates.** Although it is illegal for a member of the board of directors of one large firm to sit on the board of a competing firm, it is not illegal for directors of competing firms to be on the board of a third firm in a different industry. Accordingly, powerful individuals sit on the boards of directors of several giant corporations, exchanging views and ideas and plans with other corporate leaders.

Some business giants are linked together as **corporate interest groups** based on common family holdings or controlled by the same giant banks. For instance, when Richard K. Mellon died, his obituary indicated that the Mellon family still held dominating interests in six companies with total assets of over $15 billion (Gulf Oil, Aluminum Corporation of America, Mellon National Bank, Koppers, Carborundum, and General Reinsurance).[4] The enormous power of the major banks comes not only from the control of loans and other essential financial services but also from the control of pension funds and trust accounts that own huge blocks of corporate stock.[5] Obviously, corporations that are controlled by the same financial interests are more likely to cooperate than to compete.

Although competition among domestic firms has declined, recent years have seen the arrival of strong new foreign competitors. In the automobile industry, for example, mergers and bankruptcies have left only three significant American automobile manufacturers. Because they tend to make similar products that sell for similar prices, their strongest competition often comes from Japanese firms like Toyota or Honda or from cars produced in low-wage countries, such as the Korean Hyundai.

Who Runs the Corporations?   The modern corporation is a vast financial network. The relationships between a given corporation and its competitors, banks, subcontractors and suppliers, stockholders, directors and managers, workers, unions, and various local and national governments are extremely complex and may change without warning. Researchers who try to determine who, or what, controls this network rarely have the cooperation of corporations. Because they must rely on secondhand data on this politically charged issue, their conclusions are often contradictory.

Supporters of the corporate system claim that corporations are democratic institutions owned by many different people, and they point to the fact that almost 50 million citizens own stock in American corporations.[6] However, critics note that although many people own some stock, most stock is owned by a small group of wealthy individuals.[7] In 1985, over 93 percent of the people who owned stock had incomes over $25,000, and, of course, those with the highest incomes also had the biggest stock holdings.[7] Institutional stockholders such as banks, insurance companies, and investment companies also hold major blocks of stock. Most of the public trading on the New York Stock Exchange is conducted for institutional stockholders, not private individuals.[8] Although the stock in these financial institutions is held by individual investors, the directors nevertheless have considerable influence on the affairs of the corporations whose stock their company owns. Moreover, banks and other financial institutions exercise great influence over corporate decision making through their power to grant or reject loans to finance corporate projects.[8]

Most economists agree that there is a significant separation between ownership and control in most modern corporations. Because there are so many stockholders, most of them simply vote for or against the current management and have little influence on individual corporate decisions. The technical complexity of modern business is so great that many stockholders do not even understand the key issues facing management. Economist John Kenneth Galbraith calls the group of managers who make the important decisions the **corporate technostructure**. He points out that most national and international corporations are no longer run by a single powerful person like Andrew Carnegie or John D. Rockefeller. Decisions are made by anonymous executives and managers who spend their entire careers gaining the technical skills and knowledge needed to manage a modern corporation. However, corporate managers must still serve the primary interest of their stockholders—making profits—or risk losing their jobs. James and Soref, for example, found that declining profits were the single major reason that corporate presidents lost their jobs, regardless of whether the firm was owned by a large number of stockholders or a single individual.[9]

Considering the huge size of the modern corporation and the interlocking of corporate directorships, the top business leaders in the United States are a relatively small group—perhaps 5,000 to 10,000 people.[10] C. Wright Mills argued that these managers are part of a unified **power elite** that includes other very wealthy people and pursues its own interests at the expense of the average person (see Chapter 3).[11] Proving or disproving Mills's thesis is very difficult and rests largely on conflicting interpretations of inconclusive data about how cohesive a group those in a position of power actually are. Still, Mills's thesis has been gaining increasing acceptance. When he published *The Power Elite* in the 1950s, Mills was branded as a dangerous radical; today his ideas are widely accepted in the social sciences. Perhaps Mills's most telling argument is that corporate managers, regardless of their backgrounds, must accept the ideology of the corporate elites and behave like them if they are to be successful. As Mills put it, "In personal manner and political view, in social ways and business style, he [the new manager] must be like those who are already in, and upon whose judgments his own success rests."

The Multinationals In recent years most large corporations have expanded across national boundaries, setting up a complex web of sales, manufacturing, distribution, and financial operations. About 60 percent of the world's largest corporations are American, but other nations have also produced giant multinationals, such as the Swiss Nestlé Company and the Royal Dutch Shell Petroleum Company.

These powerful multinational corporations have generated tremendous controversy. Some people see their growth as the first step toward world unity. They are convinced that by linking together the economies of the world's nations, the multinationals are laying the foundations for a world government that will usher in a new era of peace and prosperity. But the critics of the multinationals see them as lawless international bandits who exploit small countries and play large ones against one another.

The expansion of multinational corporations among the industrialized capitalist countries has created problems of international control and regulation that have yet to be solved. Concern has been mounting in Canada, for instance, over the transmission of U.S. laws and policies to the Canadian branches and affiliates of American companies. The economic power of American multinationals, which hold 80 percent of all foreign investments in Canada, has grown steadily.[12] Even though the government has made repeated efforts to promote economic independence, more of Canada's economy is in foreign hands than in any other industrialized nation. Despite the creation of Petro-Canada, a popular government-owned petroleum company, foreigners still control about 60 percent of the Canadian gas and oil industry as well as 52 percent of the textile industry, 11 percent of printing and publishing, and the entire tobacco industry.[13] Many Canadians have come to see this foreign economic domination as a grave threat to their national independence.

The decline in the value of the American dollar in the late 1980s has even created such fears in Canada's giant neighbor. Foreigners have direct investments of over $230 billion in the United States, and some estimate that they control as much as 40 percent of the pharmaceutical industry, 25 percent of the kitchen appliance industry, and 20 percent of the tobacco industry.[14]

But the worst abuses of the multinational corporations have resulted from their expansion into the poor Third World countries of Africa, Asia, and Latin America. Although the multinationals bring in advanced technology and encourage some types of economic development, the "host" nations must pay a heavy price. Even in wealthy countries like Canada, reliance on foreign technology decreases economic and political independence. In less developed nations foreign corporations with heavy investments wield tremendous power. Too often the critical economic decisions in poor nations are made by foreign corporate executives with concern for the welfare of the local people.

One of the most famous examples of political interference was International Telephone and Telegraph's involvement in Chile. ITT, one of the largest and richest corporations in the world, used its international financial influence in an effort to stop Salvador Allende, a Marxist, from coming to power. After he had been democratically elected, ITT and the U.S. Central Intelligence Agency tried to create economic havoc and overturn Allende's government. Their aim was finally achieved when Allende and many of his supporters were killed in a military coup. Allende's government was replaced by a military dictatorship that soon became notorious for its brutality and intolerance.[15]

Multinational corporations ship products all over the world. The expansion of such powerful corporations in weak and impoverished nations brings a threat of foreign economic domination.

In addition to the problem of foreign political domination, there are increasing grounds for questioning how much poor nations actually benefit from multinational investments. A careful statistical comparison of nations that depend on their own resources for economic development with those that encourage foreign investment indicates that such investments do produce immediate economic benefits. However, once the initial investment is made and the multinationals begin taking home their profits, the economies of the nations with large foreign investments begin to falter.[16] Thus, more self-reliant nations have greater economic growth in the long run.

Corporate Crimes   The business world is sometimes described as a lawless jungle where profits rule and where those who let honesty and ethics stand in their way are considered fools. Although this is a gross exaggeration, there is ample evidence that the crime rate is high in the business world.

Everyone has had the experience of buying an article of clothing or an appliance that seemed to fall apart after the slightest use. Although the manufacture and sale of such merchandise is not a violation of the law, selling an inferior product while making false claims for it is **fraud**. There are countless examples in industries ranging from cosmetics to automobiles. A particularly trouble-prone group are the defense contractors who have repeatedly been caught selling food and equipment to the military that falls far short of the standards they certify their products to have met. Some fraudulent claims endanger the health or even the life of the consumer. The major pharmaceutical companies have, for example, frequently been caught making fraudulent claims about their products or concealing information to cover up their hazards. Two well-known examples are the painkiller known as Oraflex, which is believed to have killed 49 people and injured almost a thousand more, and the Dalkon Shield contraceptive, which is believed to have killed at least 17 women and caused about 200,000 injuries.[17]

Price fixing (collusion by several companies to cut competition and set uniformly high prices) is another common corporate crime. A survey of the heads of the 1000 largest manufacturing corporations asked whether "many" corporations engaged in price fixing. Among those heading the 500 largest corporations, a surprising 47 percent agreed that price fixing is a common practice. An overwhelming 70 percent of the heads of the remaining 500 corporations also agreed.[18] It is quite possible that violations of the laws against price fixing cost consumers more than any other crime.

The most famous price-fixing case was a conspiracy in the heavy electrical equipment industry. Highly placed executives of such companies as General Electric, Westinghouse, and McGraw-Edison admitted that they had been meeting secretly for years to set their prices. The executives did not associate in public, used only public telephones, and even had a secret code. This conspiracy alone is estimated to have cost the public over $1 billion.[19] But the single biggest price-fixing case, and perhaps the single most costly crime of all time, was known as the oil cartel case. The oil cartel was first created in 1928, when the major oil companies signed written agreements to divide up the world market and set an artificially high price for petroleum. There is some disagreement about when the cartel was dissolved, but there is evidence of its continued existence as late as 1974. Yet despite the enormous magnitude of the crime, the government's original effort to prosecute the criminals dragged on for over 15 years and ended with nothing more than an agreement with the petroleum multinationals to stop their illegal activities.[20]

Consumers are not the only victims of corporate crimes. Companies steal from each other as well. **Industrial espionage** is a thriving industry in which investigators are hired to "bug" the offices and telephones of competing companies. Valuable data stored in the computers owned by one company are stolen by the use of computers belonging to another. Employees are bribed to cheat their own companies or governments by paying more for a product than is necessary. A few years ago Lockheed Aircraft Corporation admitted bribing dozens of foreign officials to buy Lockheed planes. Lockheed officials claimed that this was a common practice among international businesses, and their claim was soon supported by a rash of bribery scandals in other companies. When the government later made an offer of amnesty, 95 major corporations admitted involvement in commercial bribery.[21]

Many companies also use illegal practices to drive their competitors out of business. One technique is for a big company to sell certain products at a loss in order to bankrupt a small competitor. The loss is recovered and profits increased by selling products at much higher prices after the competition has been eliminated. Another technique is for a giant corporation to buy out producers of key raw materials and cut off supplies to its small competitors.[22] Like many corporate crimes, the damage extends far beyond the immediate victims to the general public, who in one way or another foot the bill.

THE GOVERNMENT

Although many conservatives argue that the government should avoid all interference in the economy and allow the free market to regulate itself, the governments of all industrialized nations are deeply involved in directing their economies. Actually, governments play two key economic roles in contemporary capitalist societies. First, government is a major employer, providing jobs and paychecks for millions of people who do everything from sweeping streets to flying jet bombers. Second, government regulates the economic activities of the private sector. Some regulation is done directly through the legal system—for example, when the courts decide civil suits involving private business or when the government brings legal action for the violation of antitrust laws. But government also has many other means to direct a country's economic activities.

Government officials can influence the economy by manipulating the amount of money in circulation and the interest rates on loans. By increasing the money supply and lowering interest rates, the government can give a boost to the economy—but at the risk of increasing inflation. Restricting the money supply and raising interest rates help reduce inflation but are likely to reduce economic growth and increase unemployment. Tax policies also have a tremendous impact on the economy. Taxation influences the general rate of economic growth as well as providing special benefits or problems to specific industries. Whatever techniques it uses, the average citizen now expects the government to do everything possible to ensure economic prosperity. When the economy is in decline, the government is blamed and politicians have a difficult time getting reelected. Conversely, a prosperous economy is a great asset to officeholders.

One of the most common economic myths is the idea that big business and big government are bitter rivals competing for economic power. In fact, government and business cooperate more often than they compete. As Galbraith put it, "The industrial system, in fact, is inextricably associated with the state. In notable respects the mature corporation is an arm of the state. And the state, in important matters, is an instrument of the industrial system.''[23] Of course, this does not mean that corporation executives wouldn't like lower taxes and less government control, or that government officials wouldn't like the corporations to show more concern for the welfare of citizens. Businesspeople are sometimes antagonistic toward government, but they nevertheless look to the government when they are in economic trouble. In most capitalist countries, the government's economic strategy has been to encourage general prosperity by ensuring the prosperity of the big corporations. Many of today's corporations are so large and important that the government cannot afford to let them fail. In 1971, when the Lockheed Corporation found itself on the brink of bankruptcy, the American government stepped in to guarantee a $250 million loan to the "private company," just as the government was later to do for the Chrysler Corporation.

Government regulatory agencies such as the Federal Trade Commission and the Food and Drug Administration have come under strong attack in recent years. Consumer groups charge that although these agencies were set up to protect the public interest, they often end up helping the industries they regulate rather than the public: "The regulatory agencies have become the natural allies of the industries they are supposed to regulate. They conceive their primary task to be to protect insiders from new competition—in many cases, from any competition."[24] One problem is that the directors of these agencies often come from the industries they are supposed to regulate and return to those same industries when they leave the government. In such circumstances the regulators are unlikely to sacrifice their future by offending powerful corporation executives. But even when the officials try to do their job, the power of the corporation is so great that these small, underfunded government agencies are too weak to get the job done.

Business groups often make the opposite criticism, charging that government regulation damages the economy by requiring a mountain of costly and time-consuming paperwork and placing unnecessary restrictions on their activities. As a result of these criticisms, the 1980s have seen a trend toward the deregulation of some important industries. Unfortunately, the results of deregulation have often been disappointing. Deregulation of the airline industry, for example, produced not only a drop in ticket prices but also a decline in the safety and quality of service. Moreover, it touched off a wave of mergers and buy-outs that have reduced competition and have once again led to higher prices. Deregulation of the savings and loan industry had even worse results. Many managers pursued speculative high-risk investments, often as a part of fraudulent schemes to enrich themselves. Hundreds of savings and loans went bankrupt, and the government insurance agency has been left with billions of dollars in debts.

SMALL BUSINESS

Although overshadowed by the huge bureaucracies of the corporations and the government, small business still plays a key role in the economy. Numerically, small business has always been in the majority. About 60 percent of the 2.5 million firms filing tax returns report assets of less than $100,000.[25] And with the current limitations in the growth of government employment and the decline in many traditional manufacturing industries, small business has played a larger and larger role in creating new jobs for the growing work force. Employment in big business, in contrast, has shown little growth in recent years. As *Forbes* magazine put it, large corporations "do not appear to be efficient engines of job creation."[26]

But those who do find work in small businesses quickly discover that working conditions are very different from those in the government or corporations. The main attraction of small business is the independence it offers to its many owner-operators. But most new businesses go bankrupt in their first year or two, and many of the entrepreneurs who succeed work long hours for a modest return. The employees of many small businesses share their boss's economic insecurity, but without the compensation of greater independence. In comparison with corporate workers, the employees of small businesses are less unionized and receive lower pay and fewer fringe benefits.

Although small business and corporations are often lumped together as part of the "private sector," there are fundamental differences between the two. The large corporations are able to restrict competition among themselves and thus safeguard their profitability. Small businesses generally face a host of competitors in a very real struggle for survival. Another important difference is political. The corporations wield enormous political power and as a result can obtain many benefits and special favors from the government. Small business is much less influential, which means that small businesses pay higher taxes, receive fewer government benefits, and cannot expect a government bailout when they run into financial trouble. For that reason, some economists refer to the corporations as the monopoly sector of the economy and small business as the competitive sector.

Perched between the corporate giants and the legions of "mom and pop" businesses are the medium-sized firms that are at the center of much economic innovation and technological development. Unlike small companies, medium-sized firms have the size and economic resources necessary to get the job done. But unlike the giant corporations, medium-sized firms have less cumbersome bureaucracies and are more subject to the competitive pressures of the marketplace. Because medium-sized firms are not large enough to dominate their principal markets, they are faced with the same choice as small businesses: be efficient and competitive, or go under.

THE WORKERS

The difference between thinking of oneself as an unemployed street sweeper or as an outstanding surgeon is enormous. People's self-concepts—their ideas of who and what they are—are profoundly affected by their occupations and their place in the occupational hierarchy. Not only are workers the heart of the economic system, but their work is often a central focus of their lives. Workers' occupations bring them into contact with specific social worlds and specific groups of people. If we consider, for example, the differences between the social world of a police officer and that of a ballet dancer, it becomes obvious how deeply people are influenced by their work.

Attitudes Toward Work To the citizen-philosophers of ancient Greece, work was a curse on humanity, fit only for slaves and barbarians. In their view, work took the mind away from higher pursuits—art and philosophy—and made it impossible for workers to attain true virtue. The ancient Hebrews had a more favorable attitude toward work, regarding it as sheer drudgery, but drudgery that might help them atone for Adam's original sin. The early Christians generally accepted the Hebrew idea of work as a punishment for original sin with little value in itself. It was the Protestant reformers, particularly the Puritans, who transformed the meaning of work in the Western world. To John Calvin and his followers, work was the sacred duty of every person, and economic success was a sign of divine favor. However, Calvinists were forbidden to enjoy the fruits of their labor and admonished to value work for its own sake.

This "work ethic" remains a potent force found among people of all religious backgrounds. Studies have shown that many people would continue working even if they had enough money to live comfortably without doing so. Workers gave a variety of reasons for wanting to continue to work, ranging from the positive idea that work is fun to the negative notion that not working would make them feel lost or nervous. Despite such views, many people seem convinced that the work ethic is dying out. Some feel that the affluence of contemporary society and the use of so many labor-saving devices encourages people to ignore the value of honest work. Others argue that we are drifting toward a "consumer culture" oriented toward leisure and personal pleasure rather than production. However, the desire for more personal wealth continues to be a powerful motivation for hard work. For instance, when productivity increases, workers may receive higher wages or more leisure time. Research shows that workers generally prefer more pay to more free time.[27] In fact, recent surveys indicate that there has been a sharp decline in leisure time in the last decade as more and more wives have gone to work outside the home.[28]

The Work Force Both the types of jobs and the kinds of people who work at them have changed radically in this century. Two significant trends are apparent in the job market. First, farm workers, owners, and managers—once the largest job category—have steadily declined. They now make up only 3.1 percent of the work force in the United States.[29] Mechanization and modern technology have enabled a handful of workers to feed millions, so fewer people are needed on the farm. Second, because of the increasing competition from foreign products and labor-saving automation, there has been a shift of workers away from manufacturing and other **blue-collar** occupations and into **white-collar** and service occupations (see Figure 2.2). Employment in **smokestack industries** such as steel and automobiles has shown an especially

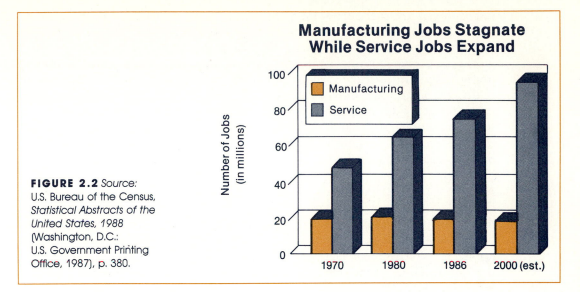

Manufacturing Jobs Stagnate While Service Jobs Expand

FIGURE 2.2 *Source:* U.S. Bureau of the Census, *Statistical Abstracts of the United States, 1988* (Washington, D.C.: U.S. Government Printing Office, 1987), p. 380.

sharp decline. Millions of blue-collar jobs in basic industries have been permanently lost as the proportion of the work force employed in manufacturing dropped from 34 percent in 1950 to 19 percent in the late 1980s. During that same period, however, service jobs increased from 59 to 76 percent of the total work force.[30]

These changes have brought great hardship to many people in the working class. Most former industrial workers lack the skills necessary for well-paying positions in **high-tech industries** such as computers and communications. Some find factory jobs as assemblers, but such jobs pay much less in high-tech fields than they do in unionized heavy industry. Further, the high-tech industries have not created nearly as many new jobs as have been lost in basic industries. The only alternative for many workers is the service industries. Although working in a service job may sound more attractive than working in a factory, the reality is often quite different. Most service work is just as dull, menial, and repetitive as most factory work, but on the average the pay is only 70 percent as high. The result has been a growing income gap between the working class and more highly trained managers and professionals, and the deterioration of entire towns that depend on failing manufacturing concerns.

There have also been significant changes in the participation of women in the work force. Particularly important changes are occurring in the role of married women who are entering the work force in unprecedented numbers. In 1900 only 1 out of 20 married women participated in the work force; today more than half of all married women hold jobs (see Chapters 5 and 10).[31] The resulting increase in the number of people looking for work has been an important contributor to the unemployment problem.

Although they are often overlooked, it should be remembered that these

unemployed are still part of the work force. During the 1980s, they averaged about 7.7 percent of all workers—a very substantial number of people. Although unemployment insurance may help for a time, many unemployed workers receive nothing from the government; and those who do collect unemployment insurance receive less than half of their previous salaries. In addition to the unemployed, another 20 million Americans hold part-time jobs. About a quarter of these people are **underemployed;** that is, they want full-time work but are unable to find it. On the average, part-time workers earn less than 60 percent as much per hour as full-time workers, and most of them receive no medical or retirement benefits.[32]

Worker Alienation   The mechanization of the workplace during the industrial revolution led to a progressive dehumanization of workers. Although the hours may not be as long as they were in the past, many of today's factory workers still find their jobs dull and trivial and see themselves as little more than cogs in a machine. These feelings are so common that they have been given a name: the "blue-collar blues." It is hardly surprising that some workers who perform the same repetitive tasks hundreds of times a day, year in and year out, become dissatisfied. David Charrington's survey of worker attitudes found that "feeling pride and craftmanship in your work" was one of the most highly desired characteristics in a job.[33] Yet modern technology is rapidly eliminating the skilled craftsperson and replacing him or her with complex computer-controlled machinery. The people displaced from such jobs often drift into low-skilled service industries. But even those who are retrained to repair and maintain such equipment often lose the old sense of pride that came from being directly responsible for producing a high-quality product.

By these standards, professionals, upper-level managers, and the self-employed are most likely to be satisfied with their work. Programs to help blue-collar workers gain greater satisfaction have generally attempted to broaden the task that a single worker performs, making the work less repetitive and enabling the worker to see the finished product. Some corporations, for example, give a group of workers responsibility for assembling a finished

The repetitive work so common in industrial labor often creates feelings of alienation and boredom, which have been called the "blue-collar blues."

product rather than give each individual responsibility for only one small part of it. Other companies encourage workers to rotate from one job to another in order to vary their tasks. Some managers allow employees to set up their own working procedures and schedule their own hours. Allowing workers to participate in management decisions that affect their jobs has also proven to reduce alienation.

Of course, these new approaches have not always been successful. Some workers seem happier in simple repetitive jobs than in jobs requiring decision making, and a few observers have charged that such programs are just a fad that will soon blow over. However, many others attribute much of the enormous success of the Japanese economy in recent years to their ability to get workers involved in the decision-making process and to commit themselves to the goals of their organization. Conflict theorists, on the other hand, argue that worker alienation will not be reduced significantly until workers receive a greater share of the profits of the companies using their labor.

Death on the Job   Boredom and alienation are not the only problems workers have to face on the job. Working for the wrong company or in the wrong industry can have fatal consequences. The National Safety Council estimates that 14,000 people are killed in industrial accidents every year, and most of those deaths are preventable. Data from Wisconsin indicate that 45 percent of the industrial deaths in that state result from violations of the state safety code, and the safety codes themselves often fail to provide adequate protection for workers.[34] In addition to the thousands of workers who die as a direct result of accidents, a much larger number die more slowly from the effects of occupationally caused diseases. The U.S. government estimates that there are 100,000 such deaths a year, but that figure is only an educated guess.[35] Many workers who die from occupational diseases never know the source of their problem. And in addition to this huge death toll, at least 2.2 million workers a year are injured in occupational accidents, and many more are probably made ill by the work they do.[36]

It is clear that some employers simply do not care about the deaths and injuries they cause to their workers. New processes and procedures are constantly being developed by industry, but few employers take time to test them adequately before putting them into use. There are now over half a million chemicals used in modern industry, but only a few thousand have been thoroughly tested to see if they are dangerous. And even when tests do show a chemical to be hazardous, some firms try to keep the results secret. For example, when an Italian scientist discovered that vinyl chloride (a popular plastic) causes a rare form of cancer that had been found among vinyl chloride workers, the Manufacturing Chemists Association joined with the European firm that sponsored the research in a coordinated effort to keep the findings secret. Confidential memos indicate that the manufacturers of asbestos followed the same policy, and intentionally concealed the dangers of asbestos exposure from their workers. The ultimate death toll among these men and women is expected to be well over two hundred thousand.[37]

The Labor Unions   The early period of industrialization created misery among workers. Entire families labored in mines and factories. Industrialists paid the barest subsistence wages, claiming that workers were lazy and would stop working if they were better paid. Working conditions were terrible, and deaths from occupational accidents were rampant. Work days were long, often 14 hours or more, and holidays were few and far between. Conditions were so bad that Karl Marx proclaimed that the workers would soon destroy capitalism in a violent revolution. But the workers did not respond with revolution. They responded with unionization.

The early labor unions faced bitter struggles with employers and the government, which supported the employers' interests. In many places unions were outlawed and organizers jailed; even when unionization became legal, organizers found themselves harassed at every turn. But the unions gradually gained official recognition and acceptance, and as they won power the conditions of the average worker improved.

Today unions are a major economic and political force. Union endorsements are sometimes critical to the success of political candidates, and corporation executives no longer denounce union leadership. But there are signs of serious trouble on the horizon. Union membership in the United States peaked in 1945 at about 35 percent of the civilian work force, but by 1987 it had declined to only 17 percent. In contrast, about 38 percent of Canadian workers are union members, as are 40 percent of West German workers and half of British workers. Unions used to win over 90 percent of collective

The threat of a strike has been the unions' most effective weapon in their struggle for better pay and working conditions. In today's anti-union climate, however, the number of successful strikes is far lower than it was in the past.

bargaining elections, but that figure is less than 50 percent today. Sensing the weakening of labor's political and economic power, union members are much more timid than they were in the past. There were only 63 major strikes in 1984, the lowest figure since 1947, when the first statistics were compiled.[38] There is, however, evidence that although union power has declined, the strikes that do occur have become longer and more bitter.[39]

Unions tend to be concentrated in the corporate sector of the economy, particularly in manufacturing and blue-collar jobs. A significant part of the decline in union membership in the United States was caused by a decline in the importance of these occupations to the economy. Unions are now directing more efforts toward organizing government workers and white-collar employees, but resistance remains strong. Today's unions face other serious problems as well. On one side are the increasingly sophisticated industrial robots that threaten more and more union jobs; on the other are the masses of the world's poor who will eagerly work for a fraction of union wages. Ironically, increasing worker output through automation is one of the few ways workers in high-wage countries like the United States can continue to compete with low-wage workers in the Third World. Thus, the unions are increasingly faced with the choice of losing jobs to automation or to foreign labor. To make matters worse for the unions, the conservative political trend of the 1980s has led to increasing government hostility toward the labor movement.

Like giant corporations, labor unions have become larger and more bureaucratic. About 42 percent of all union members in the United States are in eight unions, and most of the smaller ones are affiliated with the gigantic American Federation of Labor–Congress of Industrial Organizations (AFL–CIO). The very size of modern unions creates problems for their members, who often feel lost and unimportant in such huge organizations.

As the power and importance of union leaders has grown, some have become less responsive to the needs of the members. Gangsterism and violence have also plagued a few American unions. Especially notorious is the Teamsters Union, whose former president, Jimmy Hoffa, was murdered in 1975 amid allegations that organized criminals had taken control of the union's pension funds. Moreover, Hoffa, Dave Beck (his predecessor as president), and Roy Williams (his successor) were all convicted of criminal offenses for their actions as union officials and sent to prison at one time or another in their careers.[40]

Like similar ideas about corporations and the government, the assumption that unions and corporations are always bitter enemies is not true. Unions and corporations perform many services for each other. Obviously, unions rely on corporations to employ their members. If the corporation goes out of business, the workers are unemployed. Good relationships with management permit union leaders to deliver better contracts without strikes, thus winning favor with the membership. On the other side of the coin, unions perform some valuable services for corporations. If wage differences among the various companies in an industry are eliminated by uniform labor contracts, the most powerful firms can control prices more easily. The big unions also help eliminate unauthorized ("wildcat") strikes and work stoppages. Union contracts give stability to an industry and ensure that if a strike comes, it will occur only at a predictable time. Yet there are still many bitter union-management conflicts, and the relations between unions and corporations range widely from intense competition to close cooperation, sometimes swinging back and forth unpredictably between those two extremes.

THE ECONOMIC CRISIS

The American dream that we all can improve our standard of living through hard work and diligence, and that each generation will be better off than the preceding one, has been a major element of American culture for centuries. But after generations of growing prosperity, the 1970s saw a sharp reversal in economic prospects, and the 1990s hold serious questions about the validity of the old assumptions and ideals.

The traditional measures of economic hardship have been the rates of unemployment and inflation. However, a comparison between single years is misleading because all capitalist economies go through a **business cycle:** alternating periods of "boom" and "bust" in which the economy swings from growth and prosperity to stagnation and recession. During downturns in the cycle, **inflation** is supposed to decline while **unemployment** goes up; and during upswings, the opposite is supposed to happen, with inflation increasing and unemployment declining. To see the long-term trends behind these swings in the business cycle, we must compare the changes in inflation and unemployment during a fairly long period of time. An examination of statistics from the last four decades shows that both of these economic problems have been on the increase. Inflation was almost three times higher in the 1970s and 1980s than it was in the 1950s and 1960s, and unemployment was about 50 percent greater.[41]

As important as these statistics are, they still tell only part of the story. There were several periods in the 1980s when both unemployment and inflation were declining, yet the real income of workers was also going down. When we control for inflation, we find that real wages grew about 4 percent a year from the end of World War II to the mid-1960s. But since 1973, the average hourly wage has dropped 10 percent, and the average weekly wage 15 percent.[42]

The worst period for the economy followed the oil crisis that began in 1973. Oil prices soared, and there was a massive transfer of wealth from the industrialized nations to the oil-exporting nations. In the 1980s, petroleum prices returned to more normal levels, and the performance of the American economy improved. Inflation showed a sharp decline from the years of runaway oil prices, and the second half of the 1980s even saw some improvement in unemployment.

But the current economic picture is far from bright. Real wages are still shrinking, although more slowly than they were a decade ago, and most worrisome of all are the huge federal deficits that were necessary to fuel this

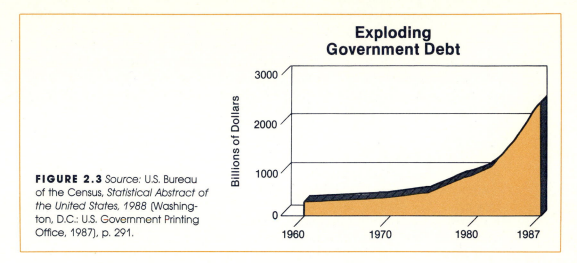

Exploding Government Debt

FIGURE 2.3 *Source:* U.S. Bureau of the Census, *Statistical Abstract of the United States, 1988* (Washington, D.C.: U.S. Government Printing Office, 1987), p. 291.

modest economic recovery. In its first three years alone, the Reagan administration ran up more government debt than all its predecessors combined, and the mountain of red ink has continued to grow since then (see Figure 2.3). Today, about one in every five dollars the federal government takes in must be used to pay the interest on the national debt.[43] To finance this debt, the United States has had to borrow huge amounts of money abroad. Traditionally a creditor nation, the United States became a net debtor in 1985, and today it has larger debts than any other nation in the world. We cannot go on borrowing from the future forever. Sooner or later these debts must be paid off, and when that happens there will be a real danger of another sharp decline in the standard of living.

The Causes   To solve these economic problems, we must understand their causes, and the first place to look is the changing world economy. At the end of World War II, all the major industrialized nations, except for the United States and Canada, lay in ruins. Because the factories of North America emerged from the war undamaged, their products were sometimes the only ones available. And as Europe and Japan began to recover from the war, they became hungry consumers of North American goods. The United States became the world's dominant economic power, and the American dollar was virtually an international currency. But that era is over. Europe and Japan now have vigorous industries of their own that compete with American firms in the world market.

But all the new competition does not come from foreign companies. As we have seen, the big American corporations have become truly international organizations with little allegiance to the interests of their home country. Because the United States was the most prosperous country in the world during the postwar period, its workers received the highest wages. But the availability of cheap labor in the poor nations led large American corporations to shift many of their manufacturing operations to other countries, thus increasing unemployment in the United States.

The increase in world competition was an inevitable result of the recovery from the devastation of World War II. But many American industries have failed to keep up with that foreign competition. For example, the American markets for radios, record players, video tape recorders and cameras are now dominated by Japanese firms. Many other domestic industries, such as shoe manufacturing, survive only because they are protected from foreign competition by tariffs (taxes on imports) or by import quotas.

Why aren't American products more competitive? The high wages paid to workers and managers is certainly one factor. But Americans have enjoyed a higher standard of living than most of the rest of the world for generations; moreover, the cost of labor in some European countries is now actually higher than in the United States. (U.S. managers, however, continue to earn much more than their European counterparts.) The key to maintaining a high standard of living and competitiveness in the world market lies in high productivity. If workers make more products per hour, they can be paid high wages without increasing the price of the products they make. But the productivity of American workers has been increasing more and more slowly. Between 1948 and 1955, productivity increased an average of 3.4 percent a year; for the next 10 years the increase averaged 3.1 percent. From 1965 to 1973, the average increase was 2.3 percent, and from 1973 to 1982 the increase averaged only 1 percent. The rate of increase in productivity has improved substantially since 1983, but it remains below the level typical of other postwar periods of economic recovery (the upswing of the business cycle).[44] And although the productivity of the American work force remains the highest in the world, it has been increasing more than three times faster in Japan and about twice as fast in countries such as France and Italy.[45]

The most obvious cause of this faltering productivity is the fact that the United States continued to use some aging and inefficient factories built well before World War II. In contrast, such nations as West Germany and Japan were forced to rebuild their factories virtually from scratch after the war. The war alone is not, however, a sufficient explanation. After all, American businesses could have built new factories, since the United States was the world's strongest financial power during most of the postwar period. As compared with its principal competitors, the United States has reinvested a significantly lower percentage of its national income in new plants and equipment. On the average, Japan invests twice the proportion of its national economy in new plants and equipment as the United States does, and nations like West Germany and Australia invest about 50 percent more.[46]

There are many reasons why the United States has failed to reinvest enough money to keep its industries leaders in the world market. Part of the problem is psychological. Americans became complacent about their technological edge and decided to enjoy the fruits of their labor instead of investing for the future. The oligopolistic control of key manufacturing industries is another crucial factor. When the major corporations in an industry work together to control the market for their products, they have less incentive to make big new investments in plants or equipment because their profits are already assured. The huge overseas investments made by American companies in the last 30 years are also important because this flow of money out of the country has reduced the pool of capital available for domestic investment.

The economic domination of the large corporations has hurt reinvestment in another way: when large firms decide to use some of their profits to move into a new industry, they generally buy out an existing firm rather than build a new factory of their own. Thus, money that would otherwise have been used for basic investments ends up being paid out to the stockholders of the firms that are being bought out. The desire to expand into a new business is not the only, or even the most harmful, motivation for corporate acquisitions. In the 1980s, an increasing number of "corporate raiders" were buying up corporations with borrowed money, and paying it back by selling off the corporations' most valuable assets.

One of the biggest drains of investment comes from the heavy military burden carried by the United States (see Figure 2.4). The enormous cost of the American defense establishment siphons off billions of dollars that might otherwise be used for more economically productive ventures. Of every dollar the United States invests in fixed plants and equipment, 33 cents goes to the military; in contrast West Germany spends only 13 cents, Japan a scant 2 cents. The effects of the military burden are even more obvious if we look at research and development. Between the end of World War II and the early 1970s, the United States spent a total of $200 billion on research and devel-

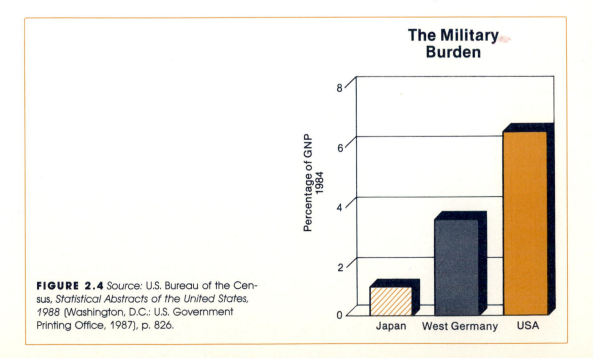

FIGURE 2.4 *Source:* U.S. Bureau of the Census, *Statistical Abstracts of the United States, 1988* (Washington, D.C.: U.S. Government Printing Office, 1987), p. 826.

The Military Burden

Percentage of GNP 1984

opment; but a full 80 percent of that money went for defense, the space program, and atomic energy.[47]

There are, nonetheless, some nations that devote a far greater percentage of their national economy to the military than the United States. The percentage in the Soviet Union is about twice as high, and in Israel it is four times higher,[48] but it is no coincidence that America's strongest economic competitors are carrying a lighter military burden.

One final factor in our current economic problems must be mentioned: the environment. Much of the reason North Americans traditionally enjoyed a higher standard of living than the rest of the world was because of the vast stores of natural resources that were easily put into use—productive farmlands, timber, coal, iron, and petroleum, to name just a few. But North Americans were foolish and shortsighted in their use of these natural treasures. Seeing the environment as an endless horn of plenty, whole forests were razed, farmlands overworked, and petroleum reserves pumped dry. Moreover, the dizzying growth in population has meant that the resources that remain must serve the needs of more and more people every year (see Chapter 18).

The Consequences All these facts and figures may seem distant and abstract, but they reflect fundamental economic changes that are transforming the way we live. Despite these economic difficulties, Americans have managed to keep their standard of living growing. From 1973 to 1988 the average household income increased about 1.9 percent a year,[49] but this was achieved only because more and more married women have gone to work outside the home (see Chapter 5). In other words, declining real wages have meant that more people have to work to earn the same or a slightly higher standard of living. One obvious consequence of this trend is a sharp drop in leisure time and a high level of personal stress. According to the Harris poll, the amount of leisure time enjoyed by the average American has decreased 32 percent since 1973.[50] Almost 60 percent of Americans report that they experience "high stress" at least once or twice a week, and 30 percent say they live with high stress every day.[51] This growing burden has probably been an important contributor to the declining birth rate, as couples have less time for children and the demands they inevitably make.

Another major consequence of these economic changes is an increasing gap between the "haves" and the "have-nots." The old saying about the rich getting richer and the poor getting poorer was not true for most of the postwar years until the 1970s. But according to a study by the Congressional Office of the Budget, the portion of the national income earned by the bottom half of the population dropped 9 percent from 1977 to 1988. While during that same period, the top 1 percent's portion of the national income increased by a huge 46 percent.[52] These changes hit particularly hard at young people at the beginning of their careers. In the years from 1973 to 1983, home ownership declined 54 percent among those under 25, and 22 percent among those between 25 and 34 (see Chapter 6 for an explanation of the causes of this trend).[53]

RESPONDING TO THE ECONOMIC CRISIS

A staggering number of proposals for dealing with the economic crisis have been put forward. Most of them can be grouped into two broad categories. The first category contains ideas about ways to improve the economy and reverse the economic stagnation just described. The second category includes proposals for adjusting to our new economic environment and improving the quality of life regardless of the ups and downs of the economy. Advocates of the first kind of proposals often claim that their theories can restore the vigorous economic growth of the past, whereas advocates of the other approach are more likely to feel that those days are gone forever. Despite such disagreements, both kinds of responses will be needed if this critical problem is to be brought under control.

Rebuilding the Economy   Those who are concerned with revitalizing the economy generally agree that more money must be invested in plants, equipment, and basic research if gains in productivity and quality are to be achieved. The controversy is about how that increase in investment is to be accomplished. One popular approach among conservatives is known as *supply-side economics,* because it focuses on increasing the supply of goods rather than increasing demand, as most economic programs have tried to do since the Great Depression. Supply-siders and conservatives in general are strongly opposed to what they see as excessive government regulation of business in such areas as environmental pollution and consumer product safety. They feel that a sharp reduction in the government's role in regulating the economy would free business to be more productive. The other major component of the conservative program is a sharp across-the-board reduction in taxes. Supply-siders feel that such tax cuts will stimulate the economy, which will in turn increase government revenues enough to make up for the money lost in the original tax cuts. Other conservatives call for deep cuts in government spending to bring the budget back into balance. Both argue that the reductions in income taxes will give the wealthy more money than they are likely to spend, and the surplus will be invested in productive business ventures. Critics point out that such policies are likely to widen the gap between the rich and the poor. They also note that tax benefits received by the wealthy are often invested in things like gold, antiques, and overseas businesses, and thus are likely to produce no significant benefits for the domestic economy.

The principal alternative to the supply-side program takes the opposite approach and calls for much greater *economic planning* on the part of the federal government. Advocates of economic planning point out that the governments of America's successful economic competitors such as West Germany, Sweden, and Japan are much more deeply involved in planning and directing the economies of their nations than is the American government. Many more businesses in those nations are owned directly by the government. In addition, government, private industry, and labor unions work much more closely together. Proponents of this approach argue that the government must develop a comprehensive economic plan that identifies areas of economic strength and weakness and outlines a coherent series of programs to improve the economic environment.

Although advocates of economic planning have not agreed on a set of specific programs, many suggestions have been made. There is increasing support for the proposal to create a federal bank or finance corporation to provide special low-interest loans to high-growth industries and to assist older industries to become more competitive. Another common proposal is to reduce American military spending to the same level as our economic competitors, so that more scientists can be put to work in productive high-tech industries. Along the same lines, American schools—faced with declining budgets, shrinking salaries, and shortages of science and math teachers—must be revitalized so that they can teach their students the skills needed in a high-tech economy.

In addition to the call for greater economic planning, many progressives advocate new programs to encourage *economic democracy*. Past experience has shown that workers have a more cooperative attitude, accept necessary cuts in wages, and work harder when they are working for themselves. It therefore seems logical that the government assist workers to take over the ownership of financially troubled firms, help workers start new cooperative enterprises, and pass new legislation to force financially healthy employers to give workers more power to control their economic destiny. Many supporters of economic democracy feel that forceful action must also be taken to loosen the big corporations' domination of the economy. They therefore advocate much tougher enforcement of antitrust laws, new legislation to require major corporations to place publicly elected representatives on their boards of directors, and the nationalization of corporations that restrict free competition or repeatedly act against the public interest.

Critics of the government's role in the economy point to the damage done by some government programs in the past. They argue that the more deeply the government becomes involved in running the economy, the more inefficient and wasteful it will become. Supporters of greater economic planning say that the problems with other government programs have been caused by powerful special-interest groups that have corrupted the programs or used them to serve their own narrow interests. To solve that problem, they recommend the kinds of political reforms discussed in Chapter 3.

There are also many ways private firms can improve their own operations. American management has recently come under strong criticism from such unexpected sources as the *Harvard Business Review* and *Business Week*. These new critics are charging that American managers are too concerned with short-term profits and paying big dividends to their stockholders and that such attitudes are very harmful to the long-term interests of their companies. The critics also charge that far too many American managers are accountants and lawyers who don't understand their firm's products and how they are made. To deal with this problem, it is often proposed that American managers adopt some of the techniques of their successful foreign competitors. More specifically, it is suggested that managers be rewarded

DEBATE

Should We Increase Tariff Barriers to Protect Our Industry from Foreign Competition?

YES Our basic industries are in the midst of an unprecedented economic crisis. The stores are flooded with cheap imports, the rates of industrial unemployment and bankruptcies are soaring out of control, and large parts of the industrial Midwest are turning into a "rust bowl" reminiscent of the "dust bowl" of the Great Depression. Something must be done or we will soon be facing an economic collapse.

The cause of all these problems is not difficult to find. It is unfair competition from corporations that pay virtual starvation wages in poor countries around the world. How can North American workers ever compete with workers who are eager to accept jobs that pay only a few dollars a week? Some claim we can do it by increasing our productivity. Such an increase may help, but it can never solve the fundamental problem. For one thing, increased productivity means using fewer workers to produce more goods, and that obviously will do nothing to help unemployment. More important, we must realize that the world is now a single integrated community, and technological advances that used to give our workers a big advantage in productivity now spread quickly to factories in other parts of the world.

The only solution to this growing crisis is to put up stronger barriers to foreign imports. Critics claim such a program would spur other countries to raise their trade barriers and touch off a devastating trade war. Such fears are not groundless, but a carefully thought out program that only retaliated against countries that consistently sell far more products to us

NO It is always tempting to pursue easy solutions to complex problems. Our economic difficulties have many causes, but they cannot be cured by the quick fix of protectionism. It seems simple enough to say that the best way to help firms losing sales and jobs to foreign competition is to keep foreign products out of the country. But the matter is much more complex than that. History has shown that when one country raises its trade barriers, other nations respond by raising theirs, which in turn spurs more retaliation. If the spiral is not checked, the ultimate result is a trade war like the one that contributed so much to the Great Depression. We dare not be fooled into thinking that a depression as severe as the one in the 1930s can never happen again. It can, and a new wave of protectionism is likely to set it off.

But even if protectionist policies do not start another depression, they are likely to have other harmful consequences. The absence of cheap foreign goods will lead to an increase in prices that will make us long for the double-digit inflation of the 1970s, and some goods we do not produce at home will not be available at any price. Without foreign competition the pace of technological innovation will slacken, our industries will become less and less efficient, and the quality of our products will decline. But the most devastating consequences will be to the poorest people of the world. Without the North American market, many foreign companies would fail, and the already staggering levels of unemployment in the Third World would grow unmanageable.

than they buy could avoid this problem. For example, if we reduced our trade deficit with Japan from $40 or $50 billion a year to $10 billion, how could the Japanese retaliate without hurting themselves still further? Another objection to raising trade barriers is that it will hurt American consumers by increasing the cost of the goods that are available. But what is the use of low-priced goods, if we have no jobs to earn money to pay for them? The ultimate choice is simple: either our workers must learn to live on wages comparable to those paid in India and Hong Kong, or we must protect them from foreign competition. Surely we must choose the second alternative.

The ultimate result would be starvation and massive political unrest.

The proposals to raise our trade barriers are not really intended to help the economy as a whole. Rather, they are designed to benefit a small group of workers in old heavy industries who are so overpaid that they have simply priced themselves out of the world market. The majority of our people would be better off without trade protectionism. The best way to solve our economic problems is to make our industry slimmer and more efficient so that it can compete on the world market, not to let it rot behind artificial trade barriers.

---

for actions that contribute to the long-term, not the short-term, interests of their company and that more engineers and scientists be promoted to top management positions.

Many experts recommend that American managers learn from the Japanese approach to labor, which has worked so successfully in the last three decades. One component of this success has been greater worker involvement in the decision-making process, which not only fosters a greater commitment to the organization but also takes advantage of the workers' intimate knowledge of the day-to-day problems that arise on the job. One successful technique, known as the *quality circle*, was originally conceived by American social scientists and then refined and put into practice by the Japanese. The quality circle is a group of workers and managers who meet together to discuss ways they can improve the quality and efficiency of their operation. The wider use of quality circles or some other technique to bring workers into the decision-making process holds great promise for American business. But greater commitment by workers to their company requires the company to show greater commitment to its workers by avoiding layoffs and making a genuine effort to improve their welfare.

Adjusting to Economic Change   The economies of the North American nations are now operating in a new environment. Because of increasing international competition and dwindling natural resources, even a massive surge in investment is unlikely to stimulate economic growth comparable to that of the 1950s and 1960s. Many social scientists are therefore convinced that we must take new measures to adjust to slower growth and longer periods of recession.

Because most nations depend on rapid economic growth to create enough new jobs for their growing work force, the economic stagnation of the 1980s threatens millions of people with permanent joblessness or under-employment. While middle-class people with managerial or technical skills will probably avoid serious harm, the outlook for the working class is grim. Moreover, the programs to improve productivity discussed above will only make unemployment worse. When an employer buys more efficient ma-chines to increase the worker's productivity, fewer people are needed on the assembly line and surplus workers are laid off.

Western European nations have responded to this problem with large-scale programs of job retraining. The idea is to train unskilled workers for new occupations, as well as to retrain skilled workers who have lost jobs in declining industries. Such a program is clearly needed in the United States. However, even if all unemployed workers were retrained, there would still not be enough jobs to go around. Either workers must put in fewer hours to spread the work around, or new jobs must be created. The most commonly heard response to this problem is the call for government to create jobs for those who are unable to find any other work. Critics charge that such "make-work" programs are wasteful and inefficient, but it is difficult to see how they could be more wasteful than unemployment itself. Nonetheless, it is highly important that new job programs be effectively managed and targeted to meet pressing social needs, such as rebuilding decaying highways and railroads, constructing systems of mass transit, and building new hydro-electric and solar plants. If these goals are met, such a program could provide a major boost for the economy.

In this uncertain economic climate, more and more people are com-ing to believe that the economy should be made as diversified and as self-sufficient as possible. For example, it is more than a decade since the first "energy crisis," yet the United States is still so dependent on foreign oil that a new crisis in the Middle East could have the same or even worse conse-quences. Communities therefore could be given more help to develop local hydroelectric and solar resources and to conserve energy with better insu-lation and effective systems of mass transit. By the same token, no one can predict how well any product will sell in the ever-changing world market. But a domestic program to stimulate the construction of new housing (for example, a program that provided special low-interest loans to first-time buyers) would not only improve the quality of life for buyers of the new housing, but would also stimulate an industry that is largely immune to foreign competition.

Finally, it is important to note that the quality of life is not measured solely by the economist's computations of average income or the standard of living. The quality of life can be improved regardless of the economic climate. Numerous suggestions for such improvements are discussed in the chapters of this book, including proposals to clean up the environment, make the workplace safer, reduce crime, improve the lives of the elderly and poor, and improve the educational system so that people can better understand the complexities of the world around them.

SOCIOLOGICAL PERSPECTIVES ON PROBLEMS OF THE ECONOMY

The rising cost of living, the control of prices by corporations, the hardships of unemployment, and similar difficulties seem to be matters for technically trained economists. Indeed, some economists devote their lives to the study and solution of these problems. But sociologists feel that a "dollars and cents" approach cannot, by itself, yield genuine understanding of our economic problems. To the sociologist, economic problems can be understood only in their social context. It makes no more sense to study economic problems apart from their social background than it does to try to solve social problems without understanding their economic basis. Sociologists use the three perspectives discussed in Chapter 1 to analyze economic problems and their relationship to society as a whole.

The Functionalist Perspective Functionalists see the economic system as a machine that produces and distributes the commodities a society needs. If the system functions efficiently to give the society what it wants, there are few economic problems. But sometimes the machine balks or strains. One part may run faster or slower than others, throwing the whole system out of balance. For example, distribution may not keep up with production, or we may produce too many goods of one kind and not enough of another. Such maladjustments may correct themselves (free enterprise) or may be corrected by officials (government intervention). Economic crises occur when the whole machine becomes disorganized and coordination throughout the system falters.

Functionalists blame contemporary economic problems on rapid changes that have thrown the traditional system out of balance. It took hundreds of years for Western society to develop and perfect an economic system based on open competition among private individuals in a free market. But as the system became larger and more complex, its problems multiplied. As we have seen, huge corporations sprang up and gained control of many vital markets; the government stepped in to regulate the economy; and powerful unions began to control the labor market. Thus, three new cogs—corporations, government, and unions—threw the old machinery out of balance. Under these conditions, old economic ideas were no longer effective, and dysfunctional economic decisions followed. In addition, the economy has continued to change so rapidly that it has been unable to achieve a new and stable balance, with serious economic problems remaining unresolved while new ones continue to arise.

Most functionalists shy away from radical, far-reaching proposals for solving economic problems, principally because they know that change brings problems as well as solutions. Disruptive change in an unbalanced system makes a new balance even more difficult to achieve. Functionalists favor specific, limited cures for specific, limited problems. Education and training for the unemployed and better law enforcement to deter corporate crime are functionalist solutions to economic problems. The basic goal of the functionalist is to reduce the disorganization in economic institutions and improve the coordination between them and other social institutions. Only when this goal has been reached will the economic system function smoothly and efficiently.

The Conflict Perspective   Conflict theorists take a very different view of the economic system. Unlike functionalists, they do not consider society a unified whole based on a consensus about norms and values. Consequently, they do not say that the economic system performs either well or badly for the entire society; rather, they believe that it benefits certain groups at the expense of others, and that who benefits, and to what degree, changes from time to time.

From the conflict perspective, society is composed of many different groups, each trying to advance its economic interests at the expense of the others. Most economic problems arise because one group—or a coalition of groups—seizes economic power and acts in ways that advance its own interests at the expense of the rest of society. Thus, conflict theorists say that recent changes in the economic system reflect competition among different groups. Each works for its own selfish interests as Adam Smith said they should. But conflict theorists do not, like Smith, assert that this competition brings advantages to everyone. They say it benefits only the most powerful competitive groups. Conflict theorists charge that ever since businesspeople and industrialists seized power from the landed nobility, they have busily enlarged their power and their affluence.

According to the conflict perspective, the underlying cause of most economic problems is the exploitation of workers by their employers and other members of powerful elites. If these problems are to be solved, the workers must somehow gain enough power to make the elites give up their advantages and create a more just economic order. The first step, according to Marxists, is for oppressed workers to develop "class consciousness," a sense of unity based on the realization that they are being exploited. Then the workers must organize themselves for political action and achieve change either through peaceful conflicts—elections, protests, and strikes—or, if need be, through violent conflicts.

Social Psychological Perspectives   Because social psychologists are concerned mainly with individuals, they rarely address large-scale economic problems. Instead, they are more interested in the impact of the economic system on an individual's psychological makeup, attitudes, and behavior patterns. They also examine the impact of these ways of behaving on the larger economic system. Social psychologists have found, for example, that unemployment has devastating psychological consequences for many workers. Feelings of boredom, uselessness, and despair are common, and some frustrated workers suffer much more serious difficulties. Studies show that the rates of such stress-related problems as suicide, alcoholism, mental disorder, and high blood pressure are significantly higher among the unemployed. Unemployed workers are also more likely to lash out at those around them. An increase in the unemployment rate increases the rate of child abuse and other family violence.[54]

But the psychological damage caused by the economic system is not limited to the unemployed. According to social psychologists, our open, competitive economic system encourages a strong achievement orientation that often leads to dissatisfaction and anxiety. When a large percentage of a population is oriented toward individual competition, the culture they share is likely to show many forms of innovation and creativity. But this system also creates a considerable amount of insecurity, anxiety, and hostility. Social psychologists have observed, however, that the economic system's norms are not equally shared by everyone in a society. Those who are upwardly mobile or are dropping in occupational standing are likely to be more oriented toward competitiveness and conflict than those in secure economic positions. The unskilled and the downwardly mobile have more social and psychological problems than other people. They also are more likely to be hostile, aggressive, and anxious.

Effective solutions to the psychological problems created by our economic system are not easy to find. One possible solution would be to deemphasize the values of competition and achievement and to emphasize instead cooperation and mutual support. But despite the fact that a noncompetitive orientation has long been stressed in family and religious institutions, its application to society at large meets with strong resistance. This opposition seems to be based on fear that reducing competitiveness will destroy initiative and creativity. Perhaps this is why emphasis is placed on clinical treatment of psychological disorders rather than on changing the economic and social conditions that seem to produce them. But many social psychologists continue to argue that reducing economic insecurity, even in a competitive society, would improve the mental health of our entire population.

SUMMARY

Change has come so rapidly to our economic system that many people have difficulty seeing things as they really are. One common mistake is to look at the American economy as though it were an independent, self-contained system and to overlook its dependence on the web of international relationships that make up the world economy. A second is the belief that the American economy is an open, free-market system much like the one described by Adam Smith; in reality, the growth of giant corporations, labor unions, and big government has wrought fundamental changes in the way the economy operates.

The corporation is a major force in the modern economic system. Some corporations have grown so large that they control dozens of different companies in many countries. Although the government no longer permits most markets to be controlled by a monopoly (one corporation), many industries are controlled by an oligopoly (a few large corporations). Corporations work together in a variety of legal and illegal ways to exercise market control.

Accordingly, prices are often determined by the corporations and not by changes in supply and demand.

There is considerable debate over who runs the corporations. Some people see small stockholders as the owners and controllers, while others claim that a few large stockholders dominate most corporations. Others argue that control rests with corporate managers, who have the special technical skills needed to make decisions that will increase profits. Most sociologists hold that high-level corporate decision makers represent the interests of a "power elite" that dominates the economic and political systems. Others suggest that the decision makers represent a wide variety of conflicting interests.

Most large corporations are multinationals; that is, they have offices and facilities in many different nations around the world. Although most of the big multinationals are American, many other countries are represented as well. Some think the multinationals are laying the foundation for a new era of world peace and cooperation, but others see them as exploiters of poor and powerless people.

In the United States, government, like corporations, has come to play a key role in the economic system. The government is not only a major employer but also is deeply involved in managing the economy.

Workers are at the heart of any industrial economy. Recent years have seen a sharp decline in the number of workers in the old "smokestack" industries, but white-collar and service jobs have been on the increase. Women, especially married women, have been entering the work force in increasing numbers, and unemployment and underemployment remain a significant problem.

The United States is faced with a crisis posed by the stagnation of its economy. Numerous explanations for this stagnation have been offered, including increased competition in the world economy, faltering American productivity, and less abundant natural resources. In a growing number of families, these changes have forced both husbands and wives to take jobs outside the home, and there is a significant widening of the income gap between the rich and the poor. Many proposals have been made for dealing with this crisis, most of which focus on either rebuilding and improving the economy or adapting to the changing economic realities of our times.

The three main sociological perspectives see our economic problems in very different terms. Functionalists see economic problems as products of poor organization. Conflict theorists see them as a result of struggles between competing groups. Social psychologists note that personality problems are closely linked with economic problems.

KEY TERMS

blue-collar worker   oligopoly
business cycle   power elite
capitalism   underemployment
economic planning   unemployment
inflation   white-collar worker
monopoly   world economy

FURTHER READINGS

Origins and Solutions of the Economic Crisis

Paul Blumberg, *Inequality in an Age of Decline,* New York: Oxford University Press, 1980.

Barry Bluestone and Bennett Harrison, *The Deindustrialization of America,* New York: Basic Books, 1982.

Jerome H. Skolnick and Elliott Currie (eds.), *Crisis in American Institutions,* Boston: Little, Brown, 1985.

Specific Economic Problems

James William Coleman, *The Criminal Elite: The Sociology of White-Collar Crime,* 2d ed., New York: St. Martin's Press, 1989.

Michael Goldfield, *The Decline of Organized Labor in the United States,* Chicago: University of Chicago Press, 1987.

Diane Werneke, *Productivity: Problems, Prospects and Policies,* Baltimore: Johns Hopkins University Press, 1984.

Laurence White, *Human Debris: The Injured Worker in America,* New York: Putnam, 1983.

- Why do we have so much bureaucracy?
- Do special-interest groups serve a useful purpose?
- Is there a power elite?
- How can government be made more responsive to social problems?
- Does the growing use of computer technology threaten civil liberties?

CLAIM INFORMATION

The essence of politics is **power**—the power to determine what is a criminal act and what is not, the power to start or avoid wars, the power to collect vast sums of money and spend them on everything from ballpoint pens to nuclear bombs. Those who wield political power regulate thousands of aspects of our daily lives, from issuing birth certificates to demanding burial licenses. Clearly, the political institutions are of crucial importance to modern society; when the government stumbles, it's everybody's problem.

A government may fail its citizens in countless ways, but the central problem of any democratic government is democracy itself: the need to reflect fairly the will of the people. Despite centuries of developmental changes and reforms, true democracy is still a long way off. Democratic governments are subjected to fierce pressures from powerful groups seeking special privileges at the public's expense, and the people themselves sometimes give up their democratic rights and responsibilities. In times of war or severe economic depression, for example, people seem willing to give almost unlimited power to leaders who promise to set things right.

Government is also crucial in providing solutions to social problems. Even such personal problems as divorce, mental disorder, and drug addiction have their political side. In modern societies such problems are given to the government to solve, usually by passing new laws or spending tax dollars in ways that are expected to help. As government has grown in size and influence, it has become the principal institution for dealing with social problems. It is hard to imagine effective solutions to such diverse problems as crime, poverty, environmental pollution, or urban decay without political action. Yet the government's efforts to deal with such pressing problems are often disorganized, underfunded, and ineffective.

THE GROWTH OF GOVERNMENT BUREAUCRACY

Governments throughout the world have been growing rapidly since the beginning of this century. For example, in 1940 government spending equaled about 10 percent of the goods and services produced in the United States; by 1986 it equaled about 23 percent.[1] In 1929, the year of the great stock market crash, there were a little more than three million government employees in the United States; today there are almost 17 million. Of course, the country's population was also increasing, but the percentage of all workers who were employed by the government still rose from 6.5 to 14.5 percent. The charge that there has been runaway growth in the size of the government in recent years is false, however. There has actually been a significant decline in the percentage of the labor force employed by the government since 1970, when it totaled 15.7 percent; and the share of our national income that goes to taxes has also gone down since then.[2]

The influence of government on the daily lives of its citizens has grown along with its size. In past centuries most centralized governments were distant and ineffective. Important decisions were made locally and were based on custom and tradition. Today governments are much stronger and less tightly bound by traditional restraints. But most of this growth in size and influence has been a response to changes in other social institutions. As the family became smaller and less stable, the government had to assume some of the functions that the family once performed, such as educating children and caring for the elderly. Similarly, industrialization has produced economic instability that has proven too great for private firms to manage. Even in the United States, with its deep suspicion of centralized authority, conditions became so bad during the Great Depression that the government was forced to get more involved in the economy.

The Nature of Bureaucracy   When they hear complaints about the problems of bureaucracy, most people think of government waste and corruption, but most large private corporations are just as bureaucratic as the government and face many of the same difficulties. Max Weber, one of the founders of modern sociology, was among the first to study public and private bureaucracies. He concluded that the typical **bureaucracy** has the following five characteristics:

1. A clear-cut *division of labor*. Each office has its own task to perform, and workers are specialists.
2. A *hierarchy of authority*. Each worker is part of a ranked order in which superiors supervise and direct their subordinates.
3. A set of *formal rules* that guide the workers and supervisors and the operations of the organization as a whole.
4. *Impersonal enforcement of rules*. Officials treat all people impersonally, applying the rules to specific cases without feelings for or against the person involved.

Both public and private bureaucracies have grown rapidly in the twentieth century, and complaints about their dehumanizing effects are voiced by many people.

5. *Job security.* Employment in a bureaucracy is based on technical qualifications; the employee who does his or her duty is protected against arbitrary dismissal. Promotion is decided on according to objective standards and rules.[3]

Everyone complains about bureaucratic waste, yet Weber saw bureaucracies as the most effective form of social organization. Although some bureaucracies are inefficient, the alternatives are even worse. Organizations based on personal loyalty and allegiance without formal rules may function efficiently for a time, but sooner or later their complete dependence on the person at the top leads to trouble. As Weber pointed out, bureaucratic organization "is, from a purely technical point of view, capable of attaining the highest degree of efficiency. . . . It is superior to any other form in precision, in stability, in the stringency of its discipline, and in its reliability."[4]

More recent studies reveal that bureaucratic employees do much more than follow formal rules. Bureaucracy has another face: the everyday activities and informal procedures that develop among individual employees. It is common, for example, for the duties of an incompetent official to be performed on an informal basis by a lower-status employee. Sometimes rules are so awkward that employees must develop ways of circumventing them if they are going to get the job done. Some job actions that fall short of outright strikes take the form of "working to the rules": all employees do exactly as the rules direct, and productivity inevitably decreases. Obviously, no matter what the rules say, bureaucratic employees are human beings, not impersonal machines, and they are bound to act like it.

The Problems of Bureaucracy   The strength of a bureaucracy can also be its weakness. The formal rules that permit a government agency to function smoothly can also drown it in a sea of red tape. No system of rules is perfect, and when unusual cases occur, it may be necessary to break the rules to meet the organization's goals. But meeting these goals is not the only concern of most bureaucrats. Holding onto their jobs is often a more important goal, and because they can be fired for breaking rules, the tendency is to play it safe. Employees try to give at least the appearance of following rules to the letter, regardless of the consequences for the organization. For example, a welfare worker may know that a family is needy and deserves government assistance but is ineligible because of some technicality. An employee who is afraid to violate the rules "passes the buck" by sending the applicant to another office. At the next office the applicant may be referred to someone else, and so on through the bureaucratic maze while the family goes hungry. Such **displacement of goals** is extremely common in bureaucracies both in the government and in private industry.[5] Even Max Weber had doubts about the depersonalizing effects of bureaucratization. He came to fear that the unending drive for bureaucratic efficiency would imprison people in an "iron cage" of reason, with little room for human emotions.

The problems of depersonalization and goal displacement are produced by the structural demands of bureaucratic operation, but other common problems come from the activities of individual employees or the way the organization as a whole is run. Foremost among these is the favoritism and corruption that plagues so many government agencies around the world. A second common problem is the inefficiency and waste that often results from the failure of the legislature or executive to provide clear goals and to closely supervise the operation of public bureaucracies. Finally, bureaucracies often become a powerful political force in themselves, lobbying for programs and policies that may not be in the public interest.[6]

THE AMERICAN SYSTEM OF GOVERNMENT

There are many different forms of government in the world today, ranging from the vast Communist party bureaucracy in the Soviet Union to feudal Saudi Arabia. Governments that try to carry out the will of their citizens through elections are in the minority. The American system is one of these, as are the parliamentary systems of Canada, Australia, Japan and the Western European nations.

The problems of any government, democratic or dictatorial, are closely associated with its structure and organization. In the United States and Canada, national affairs are handled by a central government and local affairs are left to semiindependent local governments, each with its own geographic boundaries. The goal of this **federal system** is to provide overall unity and cohesion while allowing for local autonomy and self-direction. It permits smaller local governments to operate on a more human scale and provides for the expression of regional differences. But the federal system has its drawbacks. The overlapping of the responsibilities of federal, state, county, and city governments is inefficient, and officials at these different levels of government often work at cross-purposes, wasting valuable resources on useless squabbling. Duplication of services is another characteristic of the federal system. For example, in the United States it is possible for a single criminal case to be investigated by a city police officer, a county sheriff, a state police official, and a federal investigator, with each asking the same questions of the same witnesses and suspects. The delicate balance among the various governments in a federal system may also promote inaction. Officials at one level of government who try to deal with a pressing social problem may come into conflict with officials at another level who have different ideas about what should be done.

Geographically, government in the United States is highly decentralized, with authority and power spread among 50 independent states and thousands of local communities. Politically, there has been a trend toward increasing concentration of power in the federal government, particularly the executive branch. This growing dominance can be seen in the pattern of federal spending. At the turn of the century, about two-thirds of all government spending was done by the state and local governments; but the relationship has now been reversed. The federal government accounts for about 60 percent of all government spending.[7] One cause of this centralization was American participation in one war after another and the consequent need for centralized control and coordination. The growing involvement of the federal government in economic and social problems has been another factor, since state and local governments cannot manage the national economy or respond effectively to nationwide problems.

Political Parties American **political parties** are loosely organized. National officials have little control over state and local party activities. This decentralization is so great that it might be said that there are really 50 separate Democratic parties and 50 separate Republican parties. Indeed, there may be even more, since local party officials are quite independent of state officials. American political parties seldom meet until election time draws near. Then they assemble to nominate candidates and plan strategy for the coming contest. Membership in a political party requires no more than claiming a preference when registering to vote. Few party members actively involve themselves in party activities, and the parties have little control over candidates after they are elected.

The two major parties in the United States do not have distinct political ideologies. Republicans tend to be conservative and Democrats incline to liberalism, but both parties are broadly based, and each has a conservative wing and a liberal wing. Indeed, both parties tend to move toward the middle of the ideological road, where most of the voters are presumed to be. The parties seem to be held together mainly by the members' desire to elect their candidates, but there is little unity even in elections. Many Republicans vote for Democrats, and many members of the Democratic party vote Republican.

Despite their lack of concern for ideology, American political parties do reflect class differences. The Republicans have closer ties with business, the Democrats with blue-collar workers and minorities. The two parties consistently take different positions on important political issues. Studies show that Democrats favor government regulation of business, social-welfare spending, and higher taxes for the wealthy, whereas Republicans favor minimal government controls on business, low expenditures for social welfare, and a smaller government.[8] Democrats receive larger contributions from organized labor, whereas Republicans receive more money from business.

Unlike many other democratic nations, the United States has only two political parties of national significance. Consequently, the attitudes and values of political minorities often cannot find expression in the political process. The main reason for this is the winner-take-all system used in American elections. For example, if a minority party received 15 percent of the vote in every congressional election in the nation, they still would not win a single seat in Congress (and, indeed, at the present time almost all the elected officials in the federal government come from just two parties). In a system of **proportional representation,** parties win legislative seats in proportion to the percentage of the votes they receive. Thus, under this system, our hypothetical minority party would win 15 percent of the vacant seats.

Separation of Powers In addition to dividing power geographically, the nation's founders partitioned the federal government into separate branches in the hope that each branch would check and balance the powers of the others. The **legislative branch** was designed to enact laws, the **executive branch** to carry out the laws, and the **judicial branch** to interpret the laws and decide on their constitutionality. The theory was that a balance of power would develop among these three branches of the federal government and prevent any one of them from gaining dictatorial power.

The Legislative Branch The U.S. Constitution gave Congress broad legislative powers, and for about 150 years it dominated the other two branches. However, in the twentieth century Congress became more of a reactive than an active force in American government. It still exercises great power, but this power tends to take the form of approving, modifying, or rejecting presidential proposals. Rather than trying to tell the executive branch what it should do, Congress more often tries to tell it what it should not do.

Congress does most of its work in committees. The Senate currently has 17 standing committees and the House 21. In addition, there are almost 250 subcommittees specializing in issues ranging from agriculture to foreign affairs. Congress could not function efficiently without specialized committees to consider specialized matters. However, the committee members, who must approve proposed legislation before it goes to the entire body, usually get their jobs on the basis of seniority. In most cases, the chairperson of a committee is the member who has been in Congress the longest. This means that legislators from "safe" districts, who are reelected year after year, end up with the lion's share of power. These older members are usually firmly opposed to any innovation, no matter how valuable, that might threaten the traditions that are the foundation of their power.

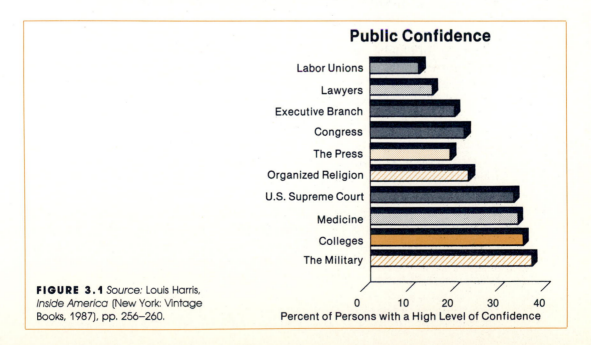

FIGURE 3.1 *Source:* Louis Harris, *Inside America* (New York: Vintage Books, 1987), pp. 256–260.

Another reason Congress is ineffective is that many legislators are afraid to make any move that might arouse controversy. Even trying to restrain the executive branch through budgetary controls is likely to be politically dangerous, especially if the president proposes to spend money in ways that the taxpayers think are in their immediate interests. As former Republican Representative Paul McCloskey put it, "The penalties in the profession of politics are applied to those who attempt to lead, take controversial positions and, most of all, allow those controversial positions to become known to constituents."[9] McCloskey noted that Congress has three informal rules that function to restrict its power: (1) Never take a position on a controversial issue unless you have to. (2) When you do take a position, try to be as vague as possible. (3) Try to keep your votes secret or unrecorded. To put it bluntly, members of Congress do not exercise strong national leadership on social issues because they do not care to take the political risk of doing so. (See Figure 3.1, p. 73.)

The Executive Branch In recent years the executive branch has gained power at the expense of the legislature. The president is the only federal official elected by all the people, and as the symbol of the American nation has tremendous moral authority that can be translated into political power in many ways. The president is now a major initiator of congressional legislation. In addition, the president has the power to veto legislation and is the commander-in-chief of the armed forces. Even though the Constitution requires a declaration of war by Congress before the nation can enter into deadly international combat, the Korean and Vietnam wars were initiated entirely by the president. War was never declared by Congress in either case.

Another source of presidential power is control of the federal bureaucracy. The president can reward supporters with federal jobs or muster the massive resources of the federal bureaucracy in conflicts with the other two branches of the government. The president has generally proven more effective than Congress in making and carrying out important decisions. While congressional decisions require extensive debate and slow progress through various committees, the president is much freer to act quickly.

The growth of executive power raises some troubling questions. The fact that the president can arrive at important decisions more quickly than the legislature does not mean that presidential policies are better than those created in Congress. Continuing erosion of the system of checks and balances may create an executive branch so powerful that Congress will not be able to restrain it.

The Judicial Branch The federal judicial system consists of 89 district courts, 10 circuit courts of appeal, and the Supreme Court. Because the Supreme Court is at the top of this hierarchy, it has the greatest political impact. Whether the Court is liberal, conservative, or somewhere in between, it does much more than interpret laws. In its decisions it makes social policy as well. In the earlier years of this century, the Court was a strong supporter of the privileges of the elite. For example, the Court held that corporations have all the rights guaranteed to individual citizens by the Fourteenth Amendment, and it prohibited all sorts of federal regulation, even restrictions on child labor. But under the leadership of Chief Justice Earl Warren during the 1950s and 1960s, the Court was extremely active in protecting the rights of the poor and the powerless. It attacked racial segregation, demanded that state legislators be elected in ways that give more equal representation to all voters, restrained zealous police officers, and held that criminals are entitled to free legal representation if they cannot afford to pay an attorney. Today, the Court has swung back to a conservative stance and is far more hesitant to step in to right a social wrong.

Throughout its history the Supreme Court has been the focus of numerous political storms. Debate has raged about whether an appointive body should have such great power in a democracy. On one side of the debate are those who argue that "nine old men and women" should not have the power to block the will of the entire nation. On the other side are those who assert that the Court's insulation allows it to protect the rights of minorities who are being abused by majority rule. For better or worse, the Court is not as immune from the political currents of its time as many people suppose. The justices are well-informed people who understand their political environment and respond to it. If there is sufficient opposition to a decision, it is often modified in later rulings.[10]

THE PARLIAMENTARY SYSTEM OF GOVERNMENT

The British **parliamentary system** is used in one form or another by most of the democratic governments in the world. It differs from the American system in that the American executive has more independent power than the executive in a parliamentary system. In Great Britain, Canada, and other nations with parliamentary governments, the prime minister is not directly elected by the people. A political party's objective is to elect a majority to the House of Commons; the House, in turn, elects a prime minister. The parties also have a strong voice in the selection of the members of the prime minister's cabinet. If the party or coalition of parties in power (called "the government") loses an election and no longer has a majority, the prime minister resigns. In many parliamentary systems there is also an upper house, called the House of Lords in Britain and the Senate in Canada. In Britain, most lords inherit their title and the right to sit in the House of Lords. In Canada, members of the Senate are not called lords or ladies but are appointed for life.

Canada, like the United States, is a federal system. Its ten provinces would be called states in America. The national parliament, like the federal government in the United States, has jurisdiction over foreign relations, national defense, the postal system, transportation and communication between provinces, trade with other countries, and other national affairs. The remaining areas of legislation—education, administration of justice, administration of public lands, and so on—are in the hands of the provincial governments. Unlike the United States, however, Canada has only one set of criminal laws, those made by the federal government. In America, each state has its own criminal laws in addition to the federal laws.

The principal advantage of a parliamentary government over the American system is its flexibility. In the United States, the chief executive officer (president) is elected for four years and remains in office for the entire term, no matter how unpopular the policies of the administration may prove to be. In Canada or England, a chief executive officer (prime minister) who antagonizes the voters can be replaced much more quickly. The Watergate scandal, for example, would not have caused as great a furor in Great Britain or Canada as it did in the United States. Shortly after the first crimes were discovered, new elections would have been called, and a new government would probably have been elected.

The main advantage of the American system is its stability. In times of political crisis parliamentary systems can become extremely unstable. Prime ministers are elected with weak parliamentary support and are sometimes thrown out of office before they have a chance to take effective action. If the parliament is divided among many small parties, it is often difficult for any candidate to get the votes needed to be elected prime minister. American presidents are in a much more secure position, for they know they will be in office for at least four years. Thus, it is easier for a president to take unpopular actions that are nonetheless in the public interest.

WHO RUNS THE GOVERNMENT?

Many governments claim to be democratic, but few actually are. Even the claims of such countries as England, the United States, and Canada that "the people" hold the political power are open to question. Does power really reside in the people, or is it in the hands of special-interest groups or an exclusive "power elite"? There is no simple answer. An enormous number of factors influence important government decisions—including court rulings and administrative decisions as well as actual lawmaking. Exactly how these decisions are made, or by whom, has been the subject of much research, but the results are open to many conflicting interpretations.

The Citizens In an ideal democracy, political power is shared by all citizens. But today's nation-states are too large for direct participation by everyone, making elected representatives a special power group in and of themselves. This is not to say that elected representatives never express the interests of the majority of their constituents. Majority rule is certainly possible, but there are sizable obstacles in its way.

One of the major problems of any democracy is the apathy and indifference of its citizens. Only about 60 percent of the registered voters actually cast a ballot in presidential elections, less than 50 percent vote when only the Congress is up for election, and the turnout for local offices is often far smaller.[11] And because many eligible voters never even register, these figures actually overestimate public interest. Other forms of political participation, such as working in a political campaign or participating in a political rally, are even less common than voting.

It is not necessary for all the citizens in a democracy to participate if those who do are representative of those who do not. But this is not the case. Studies of citizen participation reveal a strange paradox. Those who most need the government's help are least likely to participate in the political process. People with higher incomes and better educations are much more likely to participate, while minorities and the poor are less likely to get involved.[12] Thus, it seems that wealth and education create the interest and the resources necessary for political participation (see Figure 3.2).

There are, however, some signs of hope. Years of effort by black leaders to register voters and get them to the polls seemed to have paid off in the 1986 congressional elections, when for the first time ever young blacks were more likely to vote than young whites. Although older whites were still more likely to go to the polls than their black counterparts, the increasing political participation of young blacks is a very positive sign for the future.[13]

But even citizens who are interested in politics often find it difficult to decide where a particular politician really stands on the issues. As pointed out earlier, politicians often try to conceal their opinions about controversial issues. In addition, the voters seldom get a chance to talk directly with candidates, relying instead on the mass media for their information. Effective campaigners try to project a positive image in their advertising and television speeches, which often have little to do with the issues. Advertising agencies sell candidates like soaps and deodorants. In a 30-second television commercial there is little time for serious consideration of political issues. Moreover, candidates of minor political parties and those without strong financial backing have little access to the media and are thus frozen out of the arena of serious political debate.

Another source of voter apathy is distrust of the government and a feeling of powerlessness. Many people do not think their votes or opinions count for much against the powerful special-interest groups and the huge number of

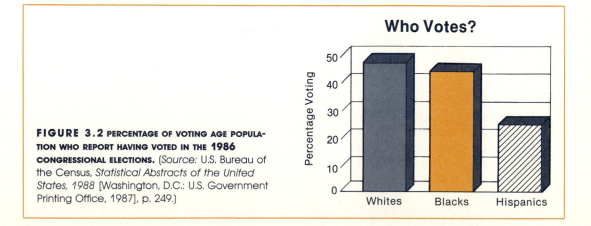

FIGURE 3.2 PERCENTAGE OF VOTING AGE POPULA-TION WHO REPORT HAVING VOTED IN THE 1986 CONGRESSIONAL ELECTIONS. (Source: U.S. Bureau of the Census, Statistical Abstracts of the United States, 1988 [Washington, D.C.: U.S. Government Printing Office, 1987], p. 249.)

other voters. A single vote, the argument goes, is almost never decisive, in even the closest elections.

Special-Interest Groups   Legislators and other government officials are strongly influenced by **special-interest groups** with a particular stake in specific legislation. Physicians, realtors, women, small businesses, big businesses, labor unions, ethnic minorities, and numerous others are special-interest groups. Many such groups are concerned about the laws and policies that affect their economic well-being. Other groups come together because of their feelings about a certain issue. Examples include antiabortion groups, civil liberties groups, and patriotic groups. The influence of these groups depends to a large extent on their size, their degree of organization, and the money at their disposal. Big business is the most powerful of all interest groups because it has command of more of these resources.

Lobbying various legislative bodies is the principal activity of most special-interest groups. The lobbyists' principal aim is to convince lawmakers to pass the kind of legislation they desire. One of their most effective tools is information. Because individual legislators are seldom well informed on all the bills they must consider, and because legislative bodies lack the funds to make independent investigations of all the issues before them, the facts and figures supplied by lobbyists are often quite influential. Lobbyists also try to influence legislation by cultivating the friendship of individual legislators. Many well-heeled Washington lobbyists are notorious for their lavish parties and their ingratiating manner. Moreover, a lobbyist's promise of political support from a powerful special interest often determines an elected official's decision. Threats by a special interest can be effective too. Opposition by a powerful labor union or an important corporation has resulted in the defeat of many politicians.

Money is one of the special-interest groups' main tools. Political campaigns are becoming more and more expensive, and the special interests are supplying the money. In 1986 the winning candidates for the House of Representatives spent an average of $340,000 each, and winning candidates for the Senate spent about $3 million—five times more than a decade before (see Figure 3.3). Political action committees (PACs) representing various special interests gave over $130 million in 1986, and, of course, many of the direct contributions also came from individuals with some special interest in a particular policy or program.[14] Politicians inevitably claim that such contributions are merely a sign of support from those who favor their policies and have no influence on their votes, but few outside observers find such statements very convincing. It is too simplistic to say that most politicians overtly sell favors and influence for campaign contributions (although periodic corruption scandals show that it certainly does occur), but all those millions of dollars often do exert a dominating influence on the outcome of the political process.

In theory, the ability of special interests to hire lobbyists and give campaign contributions that help elect sympathetic politicians wouldn't make much difference as long as both sides of important issues had roughly the

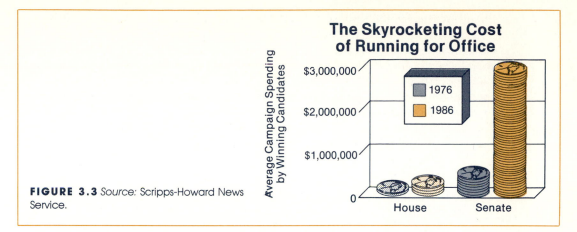

The Skyrocketing Cost of Running for Office

Average Campaign Spending by Winning Candidates

$3,000,000

$2,000,000

$1,000,000

0

1976

1986

House   Senate

FIGURE 3.3 *Source:* Scripps-Howard News Service.

same amount of money to spend. But that is clearly not the case. In the year and a half from the start of 1985 to June of 1986, PACs representing corporate interests gave over three and a half times more money to politicians than the PAC representing labor.[15] Even more unequal was the battle between corporate polluters and the environmentalists. In 1983 and 1984, environmental groups gave $275,000 to members of the House, while the chemical industry alone gave $4.5 million in an effort to head off tougher environmental restrictions.[16] This same disparity is reflected in the contributions to political parties. In 1985–86 the Republican party's three main campaign committees raised $252 million, while the Democrats raised only $61 million.[17] Obviously, the poor and the underprivileged will never be able to spend as much money to advance their political interests as the wealthy do, just as broadly based "general interest" groups such as the environmentalists and the consumer advocates are unable to match the financial power of the big corporations whose policies they oppose.

Some political scientists argue that, despite their abuses, lobbyists and special-interest groups are important to a political democracy. Like political parties, they provide a channel of communication between citizens and their government. Moreover, reasonable political compromises can come out of the conflict between competing interest groups. But the poor, the uneducated, and the deprived lack the resources to create an effective interest group and are therefore denied the right to participate in this key political arena.

Is There a Power Elite?   As was noted in Chapter 2, one of the most heated debates in the social sciences concerns the existence of what C. Wright Mills called a power elite—a small unified ruling class. Supporters of the idea that the United States and other capitalist nations are ruled by a small upper class are called **elitists.** Those who believe that political decisions are made by changing coalitions of many political forces are called **pluralists.**

The Elitists Although radicals have long argued that America is dominated by a small group of powerful men, it was Mills's book *The Power Elite*, published in the 1950s, that started the current debate. According to Mills, the power elite is a coalition of people in the highest ranks of the economy, the government, and the military who together form a unified and self-conscious social class:

> There is no longer, on the one hand, an economy and, on the other hand, a political world, containing a military establishment unimportant to politics and to money-making. There is a political economy numerously linked with military order and decision. This triangle of power is now a structural fact, and it is the key to any understanding of the higher circles in America today. For as each of these domains has coincided with the others, as decisions in each have become broader, the leading men of each—the high military, the corporation executive, the political directorate—have tended to come together to form the power elite of America.[18]

According to Mills, one of the major sources of the unity of the power elite is its members' common social background. They come from upper-class and upper-middle-class white families living in urban areas. They attend the same Ivy League colleges and, by and large, share the same attitudes toward the world and their position in it. In addition, the social networks that they represent are closely interconnected, with many common interests. Finally, although the power elite does not represent some great conspiracy, its members do meet both socially and professionally and often coordinate their activities.

Below the power elite Mills saw two other levels of power in American society. At the bottom of the heap are the great masses of people—unorganized, ill informed, and virtually powerless. Between these masses and the elite are the "middle levels" of power, where some true competition between interest groups still exists. Mills saw the U.S. Congress as a reflection of these middle levels of power. Although Congress decides some minor issues, the power elite ensures that no serious challenge to its control is tolerated in the political arena.

More recent writings of the elitist school accept Mills's conclusion that power is concentrated in the hands of the few, but question his inclusion of the military leadership in the power elite. Although they recognize the importance of the military, they are convinced that the most critical decisions, even in the field of international relations, are made by an economic-political elite. This elite is not, however, an equal partnership between top corporate and top government officials. The lion's share of the power is held by those in key positions of corporate power, for they not only greatly outnumber powerful government officials but hold far more wealth, and their careers are not dependent upon the uncertainties of the electoral process.[19]

The Pluralists Pluralists believe that democratic societies are indeed democratic. Although they recognize that there is a large apolitical mass with little power, they argue that critical political decisions are not made by a single group but are decided in a contest among many competing groups. David Riesman, a pluralist writing at about the same time as Mills, arrived at some very different conclusions. He called interest groups "veto groups" because he thought their main objective was merely to block policies that might threaten their interests.[20] Where Mills saw common interests among powerful groups, Riesman saw divergence; where Mills saw growing concentration of power, Riesman saw growing dispersion of power.

Current pluralist thought runs along the lines taken by Riesman. However, his idea that interest groups are concerned mainly with stopping unacceptable proposals is no longer widely accepted. Arnold M. Rose, a sociologist who was also a state legislator, pointed out the obvious fact that interest groups take action on their own behalf. From Rose's perspective, the pluralist:

> conceives of society as consisting of many elites, each relatively small numerically, and operating in different spheres of life, ... While it is true that there are inert masses of undifferentiated individuals without access to each other (except in the most trivial respects) and therefore without influence, the bulk of the population consists not of the mass but of integrated groups and publics, stratified with varying degrees of power.[21]

The debate between the elitists and the pluralists is not likely to be resolved quickly. As G. William Domhoff has pointed out, "These disagreements often reflect differences in style, temperament and degree of satisfaction with the status quo as well as more intellectual differences concerning the structure and distribution of political power."[22] Indeed, both sides seem to agree on more than they are willing to admit. Most elitists will grant that conflicting interest groups play a political role at some level of power and most pluralists will grant that a disproportionate share of the power is held by elites. The real question is a factual one: How unified or competitive are the elites?

An Iron Law of Oligarchy? The influence of powerful interest groups on the democratic process has made some experts doubt the very possibility of a truly democratic government. One of the most famous doubters was Robert Michels, a political sociologist who did his major work between World Wars I and II.[23] Michels was a socialist who became disillusioned when he discovered that European socialist parties that claimed to stand for freedom, equality, and democracy were actually controlled by elites just like other political parties. He concluded that all large organizations, including governments, are inevitably ruled by a few powerful people at the top. Michels called this conclusion the **iron law of oligarchy**.

Michels' studies convinced him that the administration of any political party or government requires delegation of power to an individual or a small group. The entire membership simply cannot make all the day-to-day decisions. The leaders, who are talented and capable, gain access to information and facilities that are not available to the average member, enabling them to improve and refine their skills. The leaders then use their growing power to protect their position. Michels said the masses have a natural respect, even reverence, for people in positions of power, and many follow their leaders almost automatically. Moreover, the masses lack the knowledge and skills to understand the technicalities of modern organizations and their administration. Even if the leaders are committed to democracy, the structural and psychological demands of the organization still create an oligarchy. "Thus the majority of human beings, in a condition of eternal tutelage, are predestined by tragic necessity to submit to the domination of a small minority, and must be content to constitute the pedestal of an oligarchy."[24]

Most social scientists are not as pessimistic as Michels. They note that even the strongest elites do not have unlimited power but are restricted by the political structure and expectations of their society. Pluralists argue that because there are many competing elites in democratic societies, the masses can wield great influence by shifting their support from one elite to another. Elitists deny that such a system exists in modern-day democracies, but they do not deny its possibility. Indeed, elitists call attention to a "power elite" at least in part because they believe that doing so will stimulate action to build a more democratic system.

THE MILITARY

The military poses a dilemma for democratic societies. It is essential but at the same time extremely dangerous. With its traditions of command, authority, and unquestioning obedience, the military often responds when disorganization and confusion paralyze a democratic government. The list of struggling democracies that have been taken over by their military is a long one, particularly in the less developed nations of Asia, Africa, and Latin America. In fact, there are more military governments than democratic governments in the world today. However, developed countries with long democratic traditions—such as Great Britain, Canada, the United States, and Switzerland—appear in little danger of a direct military takeover because civilian control of the military is so well established. But even these nations face the danger of growing too dependent on the military, both politically and economically.

Because a military force is necessary for defense, the critical question is not whether or not to have one, but how much of the national budget should be spent for this purpose. Different nations answer this question in different ways. The United States spends a higher percentage of its income on its military, while Japan and West Germany, with similar economic and political systems, spend comparatively little, in part because American military forces help protect those nations.[25]

One point is clear, however. Although military spending can give a temporary boost to a lagging economy, serious long-range damage results. Most military products have no practical use unless there is a war: you can't eat them, wear them, or live in them. Moreover, military research and development takes scientific talent away from more productive civilian research. As was noted in Chapter 2, the military burden borne by the American economy is an important part of the reason the United States is growing less and less competitive with such nations as West Germany and Japan.

The prolonged warfare of World War II, closely followed by the cold war with the Soviet Union and by the Korean and Vietnam conflicts, left the United States with an enormous military establishment. At the peak of the Vietnam war, the United States had over 3.5 million men and women in the armed forces. The current *peacetime* figure remains over 2 million. Workers in defense industries and civilian employees of the Air Force, Army, and Navy swell the number of defense personnel to over 5 million, not counting those who depend indirectly on military spending.[26] The military budget was about $282 billion in 1987. And when the costs of veterans benefits and of military expenditures in other budgets are added in, about one-third of all federal funds go to the military, making it the single largest customer of American business.[27]

There are, moreover, persistent reports that the business operations of the Department of Defense are riddled with waste and corruption. Most of the charges surround the Department of Defense's huge yearly purchases of equipment and supplies for the U. S. military, and the cost overruns and the failures of major weapons systems. In 1982, the General Accounting Office concluded that there was a 91 percent chance of a major cost overrun (53 percent or more) on the average military contract, and that fraud and waste cost the Department of Defense at least $15 billion a year.[28] Publicity about some of the outrageous amounts the Department of Defense paid for supplies,

The spectacular failure of the test flight of this Trident II missile underlines the growing concern about corruption and inefficiency among defense contractors.

such as a $1,118.26 plastic cap for the leg of a stool, and public pressure to clean up the corruption in the Defense Department led to numerous prosecutions of contractors and government officials during the last decade on charges that included fraud, bribery, and price fixing.

Given the enormous size and economic strength of the American military, it is not surprising that many observers have expressed concern about its influence in a democratic society. One of the most unexpected warnings came from President Dwight D. Eisenhower, a career Army officer. In his farewell address President Eisenhower warned against the influence of the "military-industrial complex" and the growing interdependence between the military and giant corporations. Such companies as General Dynamics, Lockheed, and Rockwell International are not owned by the military, but their profits come largely from military contracts. Hundreds of other companies also sell a substantial percentage of their product to the military, with the result that corporations and the armed forces have many interests in common. President Eisenhower feared that this "complex" could come to dominate the nation.

The military has its own lobbyists, who wield tremendous influence in Washington. They are assisted by lobbyists for organized labor, which sees military spending as an important source of jobs, and by lobbyists for corporations, which see military spending as good business. Even if there were no military lobbyists, senators and representatives from states with high concentrations of military bases or defense industries would still be vigorous supporters of military appropriations. Although all this does not add up to military control of the American government, the military-industrial complex obviously has enormous influence and power.

FREEDOM OR OPPRESSION?

Of all the problems and dilemmas confronting democratic government, none strikes closer to home than the issue of how to maximize personal freedom and protect civil rights while still maintaining social order. The fear that the government wants to control every aspect of our lives and strip us of our basic human rights is shared by people in many walks of life. The nightmare that could come from a fusion of technology and totalitarianism, depicted in such books as George Orwell's *1984* and Aldous Huxley's *Brave New World*, has haunted the Western world for decades.

Lists of human rights usually include freedom of speech, assembly, and movement and the right to privacy, autonomy, and political expression. But the ideas embodied in these noble generalizations are difficult to apply in practice. The expression of one person's rights may interfere with those of another, and there is always someone to claim that "the common good" or "the general welfare" requires the suppression of individual freedom.

The list of systematic violations of individual liberties is tragically long, even in democratic countries. One famous example was the anticommunist "witch hunts" that took place in the United States in the 1950s. The hysterical search for communist subversives led to the blacklisting and professional

The growing sophistication of computer technology has made it possible to store and retrieve detailed records of citizens' private lives. The creation of a centralized data bank for all personal records poses an obvious threat to individual liberties.

ruin of many people whose only offense was belonging to the wrong political organization or holding an unpopular opinion. A more recent example comes from Canada, a country with a long democratic tradition. When two prominent Canadians were kidnapped in 1970 by members of a group seeking independence for the province of Quebec, the national government invoked the War Measures Act, thereby suspending civil liberties. Membership in or support for the group responsible for the kidnapping was forbidden and about 490 "separatist sympathizers" were rounded up and jailed. Of these, 435 were eventually released without ever being charged with a crime. Polls indicated that the Canadian people clearly approved the use of the War Measures Act, just as the American people approved of the anticommunist crusades.[29]

Watergate, the biggest political scandal in American history, involved a different sort of violation of civil liberties. President Nixon's White House was not riding a wave of popular fear and resentment but rather was working behind a cloak of official secrecy to harass and silence its political opponents. Among other crimes, the Watergate scandal involved burglaries of the offices of political groups including the Democratic party and the use of illegal wiretaps, listening devices, tax audits, and false rumors against those on the "enemies list" put together by the White House. Once the scandal began to come to public light, administration officials perjured themselves, paid bribes, and destroyed evidence in order to obstruct the investigation.[30]

Very similar tactics were used by several presidential administrations to try to crush the opposition to the Vietnam War. Evidence gathered after the end of the war shows that the FBI and other government agencies used a variety of illegal surveillance techniques including wiretaps and burglaries to gather information. More serious, they engaged in a direct campaign of political harassment and repression. Phony letters were sent to the friends and families of political activists accusing them of everything from embezzlement to cheating on their spouses, false stories were planted in the media, police were urged to arrest activists for minor charges, utilities were encouraged to shut off their services, and some activists were attacked and even killed by those acting under government sponsorship.[31]

It should not be assumed that such threats to civil liberties will disappear if the wrong sort of people are kept out of public office. The momentum of cultural and technological change is a much more powerful force than the ambitions of a few unscrupulous politicians. Modern technology has provided the means for establishing a more powerful totalitarian state than has ever existed before. Even democratic nations are now using sophisticated electronic eavesdropping and wiretapping techniques and assembling computerized files on large numbers of their citizens.

Many private corporations are following the same path. Until recently about 20 percent of America's largest companies used polygraph machines (lie detectors) to test job applicants or to uncover employee theft. A 1988 law banned most of these tests,[32] but while the use of the polygraph has been sharply curtailed, drug testing has grown alarmingly. Today, about half of America's largest corporations have some kind of program to test their employees' urine for traces of illegal drugs. Moreover, many experts feel that poorly trained operators and shoddy lab work make the results of most of these tests highly unreliable.[33]

People of all political persuasions are becoming concerned about the threat that the use of these new technologies may pose to civil liberties. The federal government maintains a staggering number of files of information about its citizens. At latest count, there were over 3½ billion of these files, an average of 15 files on each American.[34] They range from files on "subversives" and criminals kept by investigative agencies such as the FBI, the CIA, and military intelligence agencies to the massive record-keeping systems of the Internal Revenue Service and the Social Security Administration. The Department of Justice alone maintains at least 10 major files, including lists of persons involved in civil disturbances, organized criminals, narcotics addicts, criminal defendants, individuals wanted by the police, passers of forged checks, and aliens. Clearly, government agencies need many of these files if they are to do their work efficiently. But is such efficiency dangerous?

The prospect that all these files might be centralized frightens civil libertarians. It is now technologically possible to establish a system that could, at the punching of a single identification number, reveal all the significant events in an individual's entire life history. The power available to the controller of such a system would be immense.

The Privacy Act of 1974 was supposed to prevent the indiscriminate sharing of files between government agencies, but it has failed to do the job. A loophole that exempts routine sharing "compatible" with the purpose for which the information was collected has been used to justify virtually any kind of exchange of information. An additional concern is the fact that some of the information in these data files is false or misleading. People have lost their jobs, or been unable to find new ones, because false information was included in one of their files. But even if all the information were accurate, the prospect of hapless individuals being followed forever by a single mistake is not a pleasant one. Clearly, the totalitarian nightmares of such authors as Orwell and Huxley are now technologically possible. The problem facing all free people is to prevent them from coming true.

BURDENS AND BENEFITS

Taxes are one of the most difficult issues our political leaders must face. The voters constantly demand more and more government services, yet they don't want more taxes to pay for them. There is, of course, nothing new about this dilemma. But it has grown worse in recent years as the economic decline that started in the 1970s has made it increasingly difficult for many people to maintain their standard of living. In 1978, California's famous Proposition 13 slashed property taxes, which were being pushed up by skyrocketing real estate values, and touched off a nationwide "tax revolt." Yet while taxpayers were demanding lower taxes, neither the cost of running the government nor the demand for its services was going down.

The federal government took the easy way out. In 1981 federal income taxes were substantially reduced, but instead of cutting away at the programs the voters wanted, the government simply borrowed the extra money and ran an ever larger budget deficit. Although the long-term economic consequences are likely to be grave, in the short run this approach has allowed us to have our cake and eat it too. The problem at the state and local level has been much more severe. The federal government's shift from social to military spending forced state and local governments to pick up the tab for an increasing number of services. But because it is much more difficult for them to run big deficits year after year, many state and local governments have been faced with a severe financial crisis.

Along with the issue of how high taxes should be, there is the critical question of who is to bear the tax burden and who is to get the benefits of government spending. In the last decade there has been a significant shift in taxes from the rich to the poor and middle class, and a shift in spending from social programs to the military. A report from the Congressional Budget

Office concluded that between 1977 and 1984 the taxes on the poor went up 2.5 percent, while the taxes of the most wealthy Americans dropped 7.8 percent.[35] The tax reforms of 1986 resulted in some improvement in the situation of the poor, but they were still paying higher taxes in 1988 than they were in 1977. During those years, the real income of the wealthiest 1 percent of the American people increased a full 46 percent, while their share of the taxes paid increased by less than half that much. In contrast, the real income of the poor declined by 9 percent, while their share of taxes declined by only 8 percent.[36] At the same time taxes on the rich were being cut, federal spending was shifted away from social programs that help the poor, such as Aid to Families with Dependent Children, food stamps, and housing assistance. Between 1980 and 1987, the proportion of the federal budget spent on the military increased by 25 percent, while the share for education and social services declined 28 percent.[37]

RESPONDING TO PROBLEMS OF GOVERNMENT

Practically all social problems are in part governmental problems. But "the" problem of government is the problem of democracy itself: creating and maintaining political systems that are truly a government "of the people, by the people, and for the people." In recent years there have been three principal responses to the challenge of getting people involved in the affairs of their own government.

Being More Democratic   Democracy is not just a system of government, it is a process of constant struggle to protect and expand the power of the people. There are several simple structural reforms that could be made to make our system of government significantly more democratic. Of these, campaign finance reform is clearly the most pressing need. In their present form, the campaign finance laws do virtually nothing to limit the power of wealth to frustrate the will of the majority. The law limits direct contributions to a candidate's election committee, but the wealthy can still spend all the money they want to help a candidate as long as they do so as individuals, or give the money to PACs that support their views. Presidential candidates are eligible for federal funds if they agree to a fixed spending limit, but there are no spending limits or federal financial assistance for other candidates. And even in presidential elections, individuals and PACs are once again allowed to spend an unlimited amount to support a candidate so long as they do so independently of the candidate's election committee.

The plain fact is that the current system forces politicians to sell the powers of their office to the highest bidders and creates grossly unequal contests between candidates running for the same office. The best solution to this problem is to provide federal financing in all campaigns for national office, not just in presidential elections. This new law would have to be written so that third-party candidates would be eligible for government financing along with Republicans and Democrats. But if properly drawn, such a law would eliminate the problems of campaign financing that make our current system so undemocratic. Another proposal, intended to discourage the slick professional television commercials that tell so little about the real political issues, is to provide free media time for all candidates to discuss their views in depth. Finally, some people advocate the use of a system of proportional representation rather than the winner-take-all system now used in the United States, so that political minorities would have a more significant role in the governmental process.

Limiting Government Secrecy   There are good reasons for government secrets. National governments must keep military and sometimes economic information from potential enemies. Local governments must not let speculators know that a certain piece of land is about to be purchased for public use. But the "secret" stamp used for these purposes can also be used to cover up official mistakes and incompetence and, worse yet, crimes and violations of civil liberties. The cold light of publicity can do a great deal to restrain overzealous government officials, and that is the reason the Constitution prohibited Congress from making any law that abridges the freedom of the press. In effect, the press was given the duty of uncovering government secrets.

Making sure government bureaucrats inform the public about their behavior is not easy. In 1966 the Freedom of Information Act became law. This act requires U.S. government agencies to hand over any information they have about an individual citizen if that person requests it. However, many government bureaucracies responded to requests with months of stalling, and some charged fees for the information they furnished. Other agencies protect information they do not want the public to see by classifying it as secret. In response Congress added tough new amendments to the bill, providing a deadline for responding to requests for information, limiting the fees that could be charged, and providing for judicial review of classified material. This new legislation gave the public much greater access to government records, but the bureaucracies continue to put up a determined resistance.

Unfortunately, as the Watergate scandal fades from memory, the attitudes of our elected officials seem to be changing as well. In 1982, the Intelligence Identities Act was enacted, providing jail sentences for Americans who reveal the names of undercover agents working for the government, even if those agents are involved in criminal violations of civil liberties. President Reagan also sharply reduced restrictions on CIA operations, for the first time allowing that agency to conduct covert operations within the United States and to infiltrate domestic political organizations. And the FBI later admitted that it was investigating such organizations as the National Council of Churches, the United Automobile Workers, and the National Education Association because they opposed administration policy in Central America.[38] Such developments show that stronger laws are still needed to limit government secrecy and protect the right of free political expression.

DEBATE

Do We Need New Laws to Restrict Government Secrecy?

YES Information is the lifeblood of democracy. If the people are to control the activities of their government, they must know what it is doing. The totalitarian government cloaks its activities behind a screen of secrecy; the democratic government acts in full public view with the knowledge and consent of its people. The totalitarian government restricts what its people are allowed to know, spreading lies and half-truths and releasing accurate information only when it reflects favorably on the government. Democracy requires that the voters know the failures as well as the successes of their leaders.

Time and again the opponents of real democracy wrap themselves in the flag and tell us that we must keep secrets from our people so that our military leaders can protect us from our foreign enemies. But in this age of electronic surveillance, spy satellites, and high-tech snooping, foreign agents already know most of the information our government tries so hard to conceal. The real reason for most of the government's secrecy is to hide its mistakes and its unpopular policies from the public.

If we are to protect our individual liberties, the public and the press must be given the right to inspect government records and find out the secret policies, the clandestine operations, and the hidden blunders. Of course, there are some things, such as the technological details of new weapons, that the public doesn't need to know. But with a few such exceptions, the wraps of government secrecy must come off if the people, and not the privileged few, are to control the government.

NO This is a dangerous world. Our nation is confronted by a host of foreign enemies and domestic subversives, and we must protect our military plans, operations, and technology from their prying eyes. Our adversaries do not give away their secrets to anyone who asks, and if we did, we would be at a hopeless disadvantage in the struggle for national survival.

The voters in a democratic society must be politically informed, but the greatest obstacle to full public participation is apathy, not government secrecy. We already have strong legal safeguards protecting the public's right to know about its government, and an aggressive press skilled at uncovering government blunders and cover-ups. It is virtually impossible to conceal political secrets for any length of time, and new laws wouldn't bring much additional information to the public.

Further restrictions on government secrecy would actually hurt, not help, democracy because they would weaken our military and make us vulnerable to foreign domination or even outright military conquest. The secret operations that our government undertakes in foreign countries have been critical to our efforts to stem the spread of communism throughout the world. But when such operations become public knowledge, they become far less effective. Oftentimes they become such a political liability that they must be abandoned altogether. Our survival in this dangerous world requires that we be able to use the tools of secrecy and deception, as all nations have throughout human history.

Getting Politically Involved   Despite the range of complex and difficult political problems facing modern democracies, there is one response that can help resolve them all: increased involvement of ordinary citizens in the process of government. But while that sounds simple enough, there are enormous obstacles to be overcome. Some sociologists argue that in politics, as in sports, the media have transformed the average citizen into a passive spectator rather than an active participant. Although there is some truth in such assertions, political apathy has many other causes as well. The sheer increase in total population has meant that each elected official represents more and more people and as a result is less responsive to any single individual. The growing anonymity of the modern metropolis has broken down the sense of social responsibility and shared community so essential to the political life of traditional small-town America. And, as we have seen, the political deck is stacked against the average citizen, who has little influence compared with the powerful and the privileged.

There is, however, reason for optimism. It is easy to idealize the political life of small-town America, but in many important respects we are far more democratic than they were. In the early days of the republic only white males who owned property could vote. But step by step the poor, minorities, and finally women were let into the political process, even if they still do not enjoy equal representation. Today's mass society presents daunting obstacles to individual citizens who want to influence the government, but history has shown us that those individuals can have an important impact when they ban together in political organizations to press their demands for change.

SOCIOLOGICAL PERSPECTIVES ON PROBLEMS OF GOVERNMENT

Practically everyone agrees that the government has serious shortcomings. Indeed, pointing out these weaknesses has become a career for some public figures. Yet there is considerable disagreement over exactly what the problems are. Conservatives are usually concerned about government inefficiency and waste, maintenance of military preparedness, and what they consider excessive interference with the economy. Liberals and progressives are more concerned about violations of civil liberties, protection of minority rights, and the democratic process, and the government's effectiveness in dealing with society's other problems.

The Functionalist Perspective   The government performs at least five basic functions that are essential to modern society. First, government is a system for using force to ensure conformity to society's norms and values when other means of control have failed. Police departments and other criminal-justice agencies enforce the norms that have been made into law. Second, government maintains order by acting as the final arbiter of disputes arising between individuals and groups in the thousands of lawsuits settled by the courts every year. Third, government is responsible for the overall planning and direction of society and the coordination of other social institutions. Fourth, government must deal with the social needs that are left unmet by other social institutions, for example, maintaining roads and caring for homeless children. Finally, government is responsible for handling international relations and, if necessary, warfare.

According to functionalists, the rapid social changes of the past century have made it very difficult for many governments to perform these functions effectively. Government has accepted more and more responsibilities but has been ill prepared for its new tasks. Many governments are saddled with old-fashioned systems of organization that were adequate in the eighteenth and nineteenth centuries but are ineffectual today. Government officials often fail to understand their duties, or they pursue their own interests rather than the public's. High offices are given out to reward the supporters of victorious candidates, and bribery and corruption are everyday occurrences. Another problem is created by technological changes that take place so rapidly that government officials are unable to control their applications. As a result of all this, government fails to function effectively.

Functionalists suggest that steps be taken to reduce this disorganization by reshaping the government. The tasks of government bureaucracies should be spelled out in detail, and each bureau should be rationally organized to achieve them. The decision-making machinery should be revamped to remove the awkward traditional structures that impede efficiency. For example, the U.S. Congress should reform its committee system so that more effective laws can be enacted. Tougher laws that reduce unnecessary secrecy and protect civil liberties should also be passed. Finally, functionalists recommend that a more vigorous law enforcement campaign be launched to root out bribery and corruption.

The Conflict Perspective   Conflict theorists see the government as a source of tremendous political power that is used to advance the interests of those who control it. Government works to repress conflict rather than to resolve it. That is, the groups in control of the government (the upper class) use its power to smother their opposition. Vagrancy laws, for example, have been used to force the poor to work in dangerous, low-paying jobs. Tax laws with loopholes that benefit the rich are another example of the expression of class interests through legislation. When value conflicts produce tension, opposing groups often go to the government asking for favorable legislation. For instance, those who believe homosexuality, drug use, or abortion to be immoral often seek to outlaw such behavior. When successful, such efforts result in the use of the power of the state to oppress those who think or act in unpopular ways.

According to the conflict perspective, control of government is a prize that is won through political conflict. Once a group gains such control, it uses the power of the government to maintain its position, and thus the group becomes difficult to dislodge. The law and its administration become tools of the power elite and are used to exploit the masses. The solution to this problem is to give a stronger voice to the "common" man and woman. Such measures as providing government financing for political campaigns, restricting lobbying, and requiring full disclosure of all government deliberations and proceedings are steps in this direction. But conflict theorists believe that greater economic equality is also necessary to achieve a true democracy. The key to a more equal distribution of both wealth and power is greater political activism and organization by those who are not being represented in government. The government will change only when those groups gain enough power to force it to change.

Social Psychological Perspectives   Social psychologists focus on relationships between political systems and individual personality. Some suggest that the character of a nation's people affects its political system; others assert that political systems affect personality just as economic systems do. The citizens of some nations seem to accept their leaders with almost unquestioning obedience, while other cultures breed rebellious individualists who are suspicious of all higher authority. One of the most famous psychological studies of fascism concluded that many of the followers of totalitarian leaders have "authoritarian personalities."[39] Such persons are said to be rigid, extremely conformist, and uncomfortable with ambiguity and uncertainty. As a result, this type of individual favors strong leadership that provides order and conformity at the expense of individual liberty. It could well be, however, that fascism generates authoritarian personalities rather than the reverse.

Another concern of social psychologists is **political socialization**: the ways in which people learn their political values and perspectives, whether authoritarian or democratic. Children learn most of their political attitudes from their parents and early in life develop attachments to such symbols as the flag, patriotic slogans, and well-known public figures. As they grow older, their views are affected by their peer groups, teachers, and others. A democratic society can do little to change the home environment of its children because to do so would threaten basic civil liberties. However, schools can teach children to respect the rights of others, to understand how governments actually operate, and to work for the equality of all people.

SUMMARY

Governments and their bureaucracies have expanded rapidly in the last century. Although both public and private bureaucracies are often criticized, they are still more efficient than other forms of organization. However, today's huge government bureaucracies are not without problems. Employees sometimes become more concerned with protecting and enhancing their jobs than with the efficiency of the organization. And for the same reason, they resist attempts to reduce the size of their organization, even if some of its functions could be performed more efficiently elsewhere.

The American government is a federal system with three distinct levels: local, state, and federal. The federal government is divided into three branches—executive, legislative, and judicial—so that each branch counterbalances the others. The legislative branch, consisting of the Senate and the House of Representatives, has been declining in power and influence. The executive branch, headed by the president, contains most of the huge federal bureaucracy. With the growth of the federal bureaucracy has come an increase in presidential power. Although a powerful president has the means to provide effective leadership and take quick, decisive action, some people fear that excessive presidential power may pose a threat to democratic government. The judicial branch is the federal court system. It is headed by the Supreme Court, which also has tremendous political power. Some authorities are convinced that the Court has more power than any nonelected body in a democratic government should have, but others see it as our best protection for civil liberties.

American political parties tend to be broadly based and nonideological. The Republican and Democratic parties both have liberal and conservative wings; nevertheless, there are significant differences between them. The Democrats receive greater support from poor people, minority groups, and organized labor, whereas the Republicans receive more support from business interests and the wealthy.

The American system of government has its roots in the parliamentary system found in most of the world's democratic governments, including Canada and Britain. In the parliamentary system the executive branch is not distinctly separated from the legislative branch. Members of the parliament are elected by the people, and the majority of the members of that body select one of their members as the prime minister. If the party in power cannot get enough votes to carry out its policies, the parliament is dissolved and a new election is called.

Social scientists have spent much effort trying to determine who really controls democratic governments. Theoretically, the power of the vote should give control to the people. But citizens are often apathetic, and they can be misled as well. The richest and most highly educated citizens are most active in expressing their opinions to government officials.

Special-interest groups wield tremendous power through their lobbying activities, by giving large sums of money to candidates they like, and by using their influence to defeat those who oppose them. Some social scientists, known as elitists, believe that the government is controlled by a small, unified power elite. Others, the pluralists, see many different groups competing for power and are not convinced that a single ruling class exists. According to Robert Michels' iron law of oligarchy, every large organization is ruled by a small group of individuals, no matter how great its efforts to be democratic.

The military poses a basic dilemma in a democratic society. Its traditions of unquestioning obedience and authoritarianism can be a real threat to democratic institutions, yet its power seems essential to national survival.

Protection of civil liberties is a critical task in every democracy. There are many recent examples of governments violating individual rights and interfering with democratic processes. The use of modern technology to collect, store, and retrieve information about individual citizens is a growing threat to civil liberties.

Local, state, and national governments have been caught in a financial dilemma caused by a revolt of taxpayers demanding lower taxes, combined with a continued insistence on a high level of government services. In the last decade there has also been a shift in federal priorities from social services to military spending.

Many responses to these problems have been proposed, including federal financing of election campaigns, limiting government secrecy, and maximizing political participation by citizens.

Functionalists see the problems of government as signs of failure; the political institution has failed to work correctly and must be adjusted so that it runs smoothly again. Conflict theorists are more likely to note that the political system itself, not just parts of it, produces the conditions that we call social problems. Value conflicts and class conflicts are part of the political system, but the balance of power now favors the elite and special interests rather than the poor and the deprived. If political problems are to be resolved, this dominance must be ended. Social psychologists note that there is a relationship between political systems and personality; they have found that people's political behavior is learned, just as other behavior is learned.

KEY TERMS

bureaucracy
elitist
executive branch
federal system
iron law of oligarchy
judicial branch
legislative branch

lobbying
parliamentary system
pluralist
political socialization
power
special-interest group

FURTHER READINGS

The Operation of Government

Thomas R. Dye, *The Irony of Democracy: An Uncommon Introduction to American Democracy,* 7th ed., Monterey, Calif.: Brooks/Cole, 1987.

Francis E. Rourke, *Bureaucracy, Politics and Public Policy,* 3d ed., Boston: Little, Brown, 1984.

The Power Elite Debate

Thomas R. Dye, *Who's Running America: The Conservative Years,* Englewood Cliffs, N.J.: Prentice-Hall, 1986.

C. Wright Mills, *The Power Elite,* New York: Oxford University Press, 1956.

G. William Domhoff, *The Powers That Be: The Process of Ruling Class Domination,* New York: Random House, 1978.

Arnold Rose, *The Power Structure,* New York: Oxford University Press, 1967.

- Why is an educated population so important to modern societies?

- Does our educational system favor middle-class children?

- How does school integration affect students?

- What is the cause of declining scores on student achievement tests?

- How can we improve our educational system?

We place tremendous faith in education. We expect it to provide a "guiding light" for the young and to pass on the democratic traditions of our society. Education is seen as a path out of the slums for new immigrants and out of poverty for the sons and daughters of the disadvantaged. But it is also essential for the "good life" and professional careers so highly valued by the middle class. As technology becomes more complex and sophisticated, even our hopes for the future of the economy are coming to rest on the quality of our educational system and the graduates it produces.

But while our goals and aspirations continue to grow, our educational institutions seem to be mired in one crisis after another. On the one hand, the poor and minorities are charging that the educational system has shut them out, and they are demanding their share of the educational dream. At the same time, the middle class, which has long been the backbone of the educational system, is beginning to have some very real doubts about how well it is serving their needs. Several national reports have issued stinging attacks on the quality of American education, and the glut of young men and women seeking a career in education has turned into a serious shortage of high-quality teachers.

The picture is not really so bleak, however, for North Americans are still among the most educated and best-informed people in the world. The educational system is a "failure" only because the goals we set for it are so high. Yet if we are to keep up with the technological race necessary to maintain our competitiveness in the world economy and meet our pressing social needs, those goals will have to be set still higher.

EDUCATION IN CONTEMPORARY SOCIETY

In small traditional societies education takes place in the home and in children's informal day-to-day association with adults. Training for the few specialized occupations that exist is the responsibility of those who hold the jobs, usually members of the same family. Customs and traditions are passed along from one generation to the next without the assistance of schools or professional teachers.

In more complex societies specialized organizations for the transmission of knowledge by highly educated teachers have developed. In the beginning, these schools were mostly for the training of priests and other religious officials, but secular education soon followed. Until the second half of the nineteenth century, education was reserved for aristocrats and a few of their important servants. The masses had little need to read or write, and some aristocrats saw any attempt to develop these skills in the lower classes as a threat to their power. Only 200 years ago the governor of the colony of Virginia viewed ignorance as bliss, at least for the common man or woman: "Thank God there are no free schools or printing; . . . for learning has brought disobedience and heresy into the world, and printing has divulged them. . . . God keep us from both."[1]

It was not until the end of the eighteenth century, when democratic revolutions took place in America and France, that the idea of education for the common people began to catch on. Education for the lower classes became more important as the masses began to share in important governmental decisions and religious groups emphasized the need for everyone to be able to read the Bible. Yet progress toward equality has been slow, and children of the wealthy continue to receive more and better education than children of the poor.

A high school education is now the rule, not the exception. In 1890 only 7 percent of children of high school age in the United States were in school; today more than 10 times that percentage actually graduate.[2] Because of this growth, education has become a big business. Virtually every American receives some formal education, and most people spend a good portion of their lives in schools and classrooms. There are now about 1.5 million primary school teachers and 1 million secondary school teachers in the United States. Another 320,000 people teach at the college and university level, making the total number of teachers around 3 million.[3]

Despite the growing number of teachers, there is still much confusion about what they are supposed to do. The most obvious job of the school system is to teach young people the skills they will need when they become adults. The "three Rs"—reading, writing, and arithmetic—are basic, but schools also teach many other skills, ranging from sewing and automobile mechanics to elementary engineering. Another of its functions is that of grading students on how well they have mastered their studies. The educational system thus performs a kind of "sorting service" for the rest of society by directing the most talented and motivated students toward the most important and highest-paying jobs. Education then becomes a channel for the upward mobility of capable people from the lower classes, as well as a downward conduit for people from other classes with little talent or motivation.

It would be a mistake to assume that the schools teach only knowledge and skills, however. A third important function of the schools is to transmit culture: values, attitudes, roles, and patterns of behavior. Most socialization still takes place in the family, but schools also try to inspire children to behave according to accepted customs. Students are instructed to respect property, avoid violence, and obey the law. However, not all of the socialization that occurs in the schools is beneficial. Many feminists argue, for instance, that the schools help teach and perpetuate **sexism**. Until recently most primary and secondary school textbooks showed boys and girls in stereotyped sex roles even at a very early age. Boys were usually shown as active doers and makers, whereas girls were shown as passive observers admiring the boys' skills. When occupations were shown, the males were doctors, lawyers, and engineers, while most of the females were full-time homemakers or had low-status jobs. Although things have begun to improve, these old stereotypes are still very much a part of our educational system.[4] (See Chapter 10 for further discussion of sexism in education.)

The educational system has at least four **latent** (that is, hidden) **functions** that rarely come to the attention of the general public. One such function is

The schools do much more than teach reading, writing, and arithmetic. One of their most important functions is to provide for students' social and recreational needs.

to preserve the class system. Schools help some lower-class youngsters advance, but also help to keep most of them right where they are. In other words, the schools perpetuate social inequality. For example, much of the "sorting" mentioned earlier is based on class and ethnic background rather than on talent and motivation. Because schools are staffed largely by middle-class whites, they tend to stress middle-class values and attitudes. Students from different subcultures are thus at a disadvantage, and although a few especially talented individuals do succeed, most do not. Those who are not successful in school are likely to remain disadvantaged when they move into the job market.

A second latent function of education is to reduce unemployment. By keeping millions of students off the labor market until they are young adults, the school system absorbs those who are not needed in the economy. The unemployment rate would skyrocket if all the people in school suddenly started looking for full-time jobs. Indeed, education for the masses did not expand until the industrial revolution had produced a vast army of surplus laborers.

A third latent function of the schools is to serve as an agent of social control, attempting to regulate and control the behavior of students. Many teachers and students report that their schools are obsessively concerned with obedience and respect for authority. While this may not be characteristic of all schools, it is true that teachers and administrators spend an enormous amount of effort enforcing rules that have little to do with learning. More generally, schools are expected to prevent juvenile delinquency by keeping young people off the streets, counseling them about personal problems, and reporting "predelinquent" youths to juvenile authorities.

A fourth latent function of the schools is to provide for students' social and recreational needs. By providing a meeting place and a host of common activities, schools foster friendships among students and even offer a setting in which future husbands or wives may be chosen. Also, the school environment allows young people to develop and share norms and values that differ from those of their parents. It is in schools that the "youth culture" flourishes. Ideally, school life is a sheltered one where social errors are not too costly and where new ideas can be tried safely.

EQUAL EDUCATIONAL OPPORTUNITY FOR ALL?

In the past the keys to economic success usually involved such things as the ownership of good farmland or the canny skills of the small businessman. As formal education and professional training have gained more and more importance, so has the issue of educational equity. Many have charged that our educational system fails to provide equal opportunity for all, and as a result the poor, immigrants, and minorities have far less chance of "making it" than they did in the days of the frontier. To understand this important issue we will first examine the role social class plays in a student's academic success, and then look at how good a job the educational system does of meeting the needs of minority students.

Social Class and Achievement   Grade-school teachers and university professors alike can easily see that the daughters and sons of middle- and upper-class parents do better in school than the children of the poor. In fact, numerous studies have found social class to be the single most effective predictor of achievement in school. As Parelius and Parelius put it:

> Whether we look at scores on standardized ability or achievement tests, classroom grades, participation in academic rather than vocational high school programs, involvement in extracurricular activities, number of years of schooling completed or enrollment in or completion of college and professional school, children from more socioeconomically advantaged homes outperform their less affluent peers.[5]

There are two principal explanations for this difference. One focuses on the advantages higher-status children have because they come from home environments in which books, a large vocabulary, and an emphasis on achievement are common. The other notes that the schools themselves are organized and operated in ways that fail to meet the educational needs of the poor.

Family Background Lower-class children live in a very different world than do middle-class children. The homes of the poor tend to have fewer books, newspapers, and magazines, and the parents have less education. People with low incomes are less likely to read for entertainment; thus, children in low-income homes are less likely to be encouraged to learn that vital skill. Lower-class families are also larger and are more often headed by only one adult. Children in such families are likely to receive less parental contact, guidance, and educational encouragement. Another factor is health: poor children are more likely to be undernourished than their middle-class counterparts and they are sick more days a year.[6] And unhealthy children simply do not learn as well as healthy ones.

More positively, the academic success of children from affluent homes stems from the value their parents place on education. A number of surveys have shown that children from wealthy families want more education than children from poorer backgrounds.[7] Some of this difference results from the fact that middle-class homes place a higher value on education and long-range planning. But some of it also reflects a realistic adjustment to the fact that poor children have less chance of getting a good education.

Children who speak only Spanish or some other language foreign to the schools are obviously handicapped. But language also makes an important difference to the educational achievements of the various social classes in the *same* ethnic group. Standard English is more commonly spoken by middle-class blacks, while lower-class blacks are more likely to speak "black English" dialects. Because schoolwork is done in standard English, lower-class blacks are handicapped. Similar language differences are found among

The current system of school finance is often grossly unequal. The poor frequently pay a higher proportion of their income in school taxes and receive an inferior education in return.

DEBATE

Is the Quality of Public Education Deteriorating?

YES The decay of public education is obvious to anyone who cares to look. The cheap, run-down buildings that house so many public schools are the most visible signs of trouble, but those walls contain much greater problems. Year after year, our schools have been given more responsibility to solve social problems. We now expect our schools to combat racism, stop drug abuse, prevent unwed pregnancies, help the handicapped, and reduce delinquency. But at the same time, we are cutting away at already inadequate school budgets instead of providing the additional money necessary to deal with the demands of our technological age. Teachers are paid less than cocktail waitresses, and positions in math, science, and engineering go begging. Our schools often lack basic supplies, much less the expensive computer systems that are necessary if students are to learn the skills contemporary society demands.

Not only have our schools failed to meet the challenge of the 1980s, considerable evidence shows that they are not even teaching the basics of reading, writing, and arithmetic very well. Many of our classrooms exhibit a kind of educational paralysis. Students are unruly, attendance is sporadic, the use of drugs and alcohol is common, and an atmosphere of violence prevails. Too many teachers have given up on discipline, and too many administrators allow students to dodge academic classes and take trivial electives instead. The private schools aggravate these already serious problems by skimming off the wealthiest and most motivated students. Not only does this tend to lower classroom standards even further, but it deprives the

NO Determining the quality of public education is not like weighing a cabbage. There are enormous disagreements about the ends that a good education ought to achieve and few effective ways to measure how well those ends are met. It is easy to point to the decline in standardized test scores as proof that our educators are not doing a good job. But the realities are much more complex than that. The fact is that the explosive growth of electronic communications and the ever-increasing number of children living in single-parent homes have changed students in a very fundamental way. If our students are given less family support and less exposure to the written word, how can we expect them to earn higher marks than their predecessors? Moreover, there is reason to doubt the validity of standardized tests as a measure of educational achievement. At best, these tests, which ask students to fill in hundreds of little bubbles, measure only the narrowest of educational skills. What about the appreciation of good literature and music, the knowledge of world affairs, the ability to communicate verbally, and the countless other skills that sound education should impart?

The growing emphasis on equipping our students to deal with the social problems they will meet in the real world makes today's education more relevant and more valuable for the average student than it ever was in the past. Aren't students better off gaining the knowledge that helps them prevent an unwanted pregnancy and an early marriage than learning calculus? Our schools are reaching out to meet the emotional and social needs of a generation that lacks the public schools of the support of the parents who would be most effective in pushing demands for reform. The tragic fact is that a growing number of students are emerging from high schools illiterate and uneducated.

family support that was assumed by traditional education. All in all, our educational system is doing a better job of meeting the needs of students; those needs have simply changed.

raise a more fundamental issue, arguing that such tests focus on only a single type of educational skill and should not be used to make an overall evaluation of educational achievement. The other side generally agrees that these tests do not measure all aspects of educational achievement, but they argue that the tests are a valid indicator of some very important educational skills. And they point out that in addition to doing more poorly than past generations, American students also do very poorly on international comparisons. The National Commission on Excellence in Education reports that on 19 academic tests, the United States never scored first or second among industrialized nations and was last on seven of them.[33]

Those who blame the schools for the decline in test scores attribute much of it to a decline in academic standards. In response to the protests of the 1960s, many schools reduced the number of required courses and gave students more freedom in course selection. As a result, enrollments in basic academic courses declined. A report to the National Commission on Excellence in Education found that since 1969, the amount of time spent on academic courses has declined from 70 to 62 percent of all class time, while the time spent on such courses as driver education has increased from 8 to 13 percent. It seems reasonable to expect that achievement scores will decline if students do not enroll in courses designed to teach basic skills. It can also

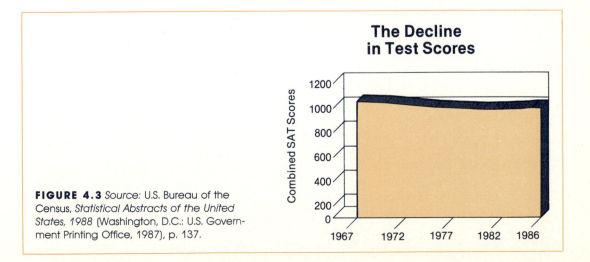

FIGURE 4.3 *Source:* U.S. Bureau of the Census, *Statistical Abstracts of the United States, 1988* (Washington, D.C.: U.S. Government Printing Office, 1987), p. 137.

The Decline in Test Scores

Combined SAT Scores

1200
1000
800
600
400
200
0

1967   1972   1977   1982   1986

be expected that scores will go down even more if the content of basic courses is watered down. The commission found, for example, that homework has decreased to the point that only a third of high school seniors spend more than an hour a day on it.[34] Such softening of standards has often been covered up by the practice of **grade inflation**: assigning grades of A or B to students who have barely learned to read and write.

But whatever the shortcomings of the schools, experts agree that students' home environment has an enormous influence on how well they master their studies. And there are good reasons to believe that the environment of today's students is less conducive to educational achievement than it was in the past. For example, the average student now spends more time watching television than in any other activity except sleep. Obviously, children who sit in front of television sets instead of playing basketball will not become good basketball players. Just as obviously, children who watch television instead of reading books will not become good readers and, consequently, will not learn to write very well either. Some also blame dependence on electronic calculators for the decline in math scores, although there is at present little evidence to support such a conclusion.

Teachers commonly complain that their students have been growing more rebellious and less interested in their studies. Such changes are often blamed on growing permissiveness in child-rearing practices or the sharp increase in the percentage of children living in single-parent homes. It is, however, very difficult to determine whether students really are less interested in their studies than they used to be or whether teachers are just idealizing the past. But the increase in single-parent and two-income families may influence educational achievement in a different way: by reducing the amount of time parents have to help their children with their studies and to get involved in the educational programs of their schools.

Financial Problems   During the 1960s and early 1970s American education expanded rapidly. The nation built new schools and universities, hired more teachers, and devoted an increasing percentage of its total income to education. But in the second half of the 1970s this trend came to an abrupt halt, then reversed itself. The percentage of national income the United States devotes to education peaked in 1975 and has declined substantially since then.[35] The first cutbacks came at the local level, but they were soon followed by sharp reductions in federal aid to education and in student loans.

There appear to be several reasons for these problems: the stagnation of the economy; the increasing strength of conservative ideology, which opposes all kinds of government spending; and the aging of the population and the decline in birth rates, which have reduced the base of political support for education. The "tax revolt," which began with the passage of California's famous Proposition 13 and later spread to many other states, sharply reduced revenues that have traditionally gone to the schools. At the same time, the federal government under President Reagan sharply reduced its support to education—between 1980 and 1985 federal spending on education declined by 30 percent.[36] The result has been the elimination of many libraries, health services, and field trips, reductions in school maintenance, the inability to purchase the modern equipment needed to keep students abreast of the latest developments in science and technology, and the imposition of fees that keep many poor students from participating in extracurricular activities such as after-school sports and music.

Defenders of these cutbacks point out that researchers have not found a direct one-to-one relationship between the amount of money spent per student and academic achievement. But there is little doubt that in education, as in other parts of our society, you get what you pay for. In the long run, these cutbacks are bound to have a devastating effect on the equality of education if they are not reversed.

The Teacher Shortage   One of the most important tasks facing our educational system is hiring and retaining capable and highly motivated teachers. We will need to hire hundreds of thousands of new teachers in the next decade as the children of the "baby-boom" generation (1947–1957) work their way through the schools, and as many of our current teachers reach retirement age. But the evidence indicates that the schools will have a very difficult, if not impossible, time meeting that goal. A 1985 survey found that only 2 percent of all first-year college students were considering jobs in elementary education (which currently has the most urgent need for teachers), and less than 6 percent of these students said they were interested in any kind of career in education. Yet it is estimated that a huge 23 percent of our college graduates would have to go into teaching to meet the demand in the next decade.[37] Moreover, education majors are not attracting top-quality or even middle-quality students. The average SAT scores of education students ranks among the lowest of all college majors. Moreover, too few of these students are specializing in the areas that are in the most demand. Less than half of the newly hired teachers in English and mathematics are currently certified in the field they teach.[38]

There are many reasons for the shortage of qualified teachers. The most obvious is low pay. The average pay for all teachers is lower than many less skilled occupations such as plumbers and electricians, and far below the comparable professions. As the authors of a 1981 National Institute of Education study put it, the United States "gets approximately what it pays for: the bottom one-third of the college-going population seeking positions paying salaries in the bottom one-third of the economy." But there are other reasons for the shortage as well. School teachers used to have great prestige in their community, but as the educational level of the entire population has risen, people no longer hold the college-educated teacher in such awe. Also, our educational institutions used to be major beneficiaries of sex discrimination because teaching in elementary schools was one of the only challenging occupations open to bright young women. But now that more opportunities are opening up, many of the most talented women seek careers in other areas.

RESPONDING TO PROBLEMS OF EDUCATION

The problems of education are economic and political problems as well. Some proposals for change call for modification of the entire structure of our society, including the institution of education. But educational problems are also bureaucratic problems, and other proposals for change call for improved efficiency in the existing school system and its teaching methods. Some of these suggestions have already been implemented in private schools with varying degrees of success. The proposals to improve the educational system fall into two broad categories: proposals for providing more equal educational opportunities for all citizens and proposals for improving the quality of education.

Toward Equal Educational Opportunity   Almost everyone agrees with the idea that there should be equal educational opportunity for all. But as we have already noted, there is widespread disagreement about what this means and how it can be achieved. Integration of students from different ethnic backgrounds into the same schools is often proposed as a solution to educational inequality. A second approach is to set up special **compensatory education** programs to help disadvantaged students. A third widely accepted idea is to remedy educational inequality by spending an equal amount of money on each student's education.

Effective Integration For years the American government, particularly the judicial branch, has been trying to achieve racial and ethnic integration in the schools. Despite many advances, this goal has still not been achieved. Following court-ordered integration, unofficial resegregation often occurred as whites moved to the suburbs or enrolled their children in private schools. It has been suggested that resegregation should be reduced by merging suburban school districts with inner-city school districts and then busing children within each district. One difficulty with this proposal is distance. Some suburban communities are so far from the city centers that students would have to spend a large part of their school day on a bus. Another difficulty is prejudice. The proposal does nothing to discourage white parents from putting their children in private schools, and in fact would encourage them to do so.

As an alternative, some have proposed voluntary desegregation plans that give students the right to attend any school they wish, provided that it does not have a higher percentage of students of their ethnic group than their neighborhood school. The goal of this plan and the related proposals to create **magnet schools** to attract students from all ethnic groups is to reduce "white flight" while still allowing minority and lower-class students to attend integrated middle-class schools if they wish. Critics of such plans argue that they are not likely to significantly reduce segregation because most students choose to attend their neighborhood school.

Another possibility would be to encourage the integration of residential areas so that neighborhood schools would automatically be integrated. In many ways this is the most appealing solution, for it would provide the broadest possible opportunity for development of interracial friendships and cooperation. However, daunting obstacles stand in the way of any effort to create truly integrated communities. For one thing, a long history of prejudice and suspicion makes many Americans prefer to live in neighborhoods in which everyone shares their own economic and ethnic background. Moreover, the poor and minorities simply cannot afford to live in affluent neighborhoods with the best schools. One possible solution is to create more subsidized housing for low-income families in wealthy neighborhoods, and tax incentives for affluent families to refurbish older homes and move back into lower-income neighborhoods. But specific proposals usually run into intense opposition from wealthy home owners who fear that low-cost housing will decrease their property values, or from the residents of low-income neighborhoods who fear they will be displaced by more prosperous newcomers.

Compensatory Education Another way to boost the educational achievement of the poor and minorities is to provide them with special programs and extra assistance. The most popular and widely known compensatory program of this kind is Project Head Start, which gives preschool instruction to disadvantaged children. At first the results of the project seemed quite promising, but follow-up studies found that most of the early gains made by those in the program faded away by the time the children reached the second or third grade.[39]

However, results from the Perry Preschool Project indicate that such programs can have long-range benefits if they are properly run. The Perry Project selected a group of poor black children from Ypsilanti, Michigan, gave half of them an intensive preschool program for two years, and then carefully followed their educational and social progress. They found that the students who went to preschool had higher scholastic achievement throughout their school years, were twice as likely to graduate from high school, and were even less involved in delinquent behavior.[40]

A related program under Title I of the Elementary and Secondary Education Act provides federal money to give extra help to disadvantaged students who are already in school. Over five million elementary school students are given help under this program, and its supporters credit it with much of the reduction in the gap between the achievement scores of black and white students that has occurred in recent years. But critics point to studies showing that the benefits of elementary school programs do not carry over into high school.[41]

Two conclusions seem warranted from the studies of the preschool and Title I programs. First, although these programs are no cure-all for the educational problems of the disadvantaged, they have had some very positive effects. Second, long-term benefits can best be achieved by continuing supplemental help throughout high school instead of cutting it off after a few years.

A variety of educational-opportunity programs have also been established on the college level. Generally, these programs make special provisions for the admission of disadvantaged and minority students who do not meet standard admissions requirements. They also provide tutoring and special assistance to help these students stay in school. Although these programs have their critics, they have become an accepted part of most colleges and universities. The greatest conflicts have arisen over special admissions programs for graduate and professional schools. Competition for places in these schools is intense, and white students complain that they are the victims of reverse discrimination because some whites are being rejected in favor of less qualified minority students. Supporters of special admissions programs argue that minorities have already been subjected to a great deal of discrimination and that **affirmative action** programs merely attempt to compensate for some small part of it (see Chapter 7).

Reforming School Finance As was pointed out earlier, schools in rich districts often receive more money per student than do schools in poor districts. Such inequality could be erased if the federal government paid for all primary and secondary education, giving equal financial support to each school. However, there is a strong tradition of local control of the schools in the United States. Many people believe that federal financing would mean federal control and that federal bureaucracies would not be responsive to the needs of local communities. They point to the maze of costly federal regulations that accompany federal support of colleges and universities.

There are, nonetheless, few alternatives to more federal aid to education, even if it stops far short of complete financial support. Economic problems have caused more and more troubled cities and towns to cut back on education. And in the long run that will produce even greater economic decay because of the lack of the trained workers necessary in today's high-tech economy. Federal money is needed to break this vicious circle. But such a program must also aim to maintain as much local autonomy as is consistent with high educational standards.

Improving the Schools The original Coleman report created a furor when it was first published in 1966, because it found that none of the measures of school quality it used—funding, teacher qualifications or physical facilities—had much effect on the educational achievement of the students. These results were widely interpreted to mean that "schools don't make any difference." Subsequent research has shown that those results were largely a product of the extremely narrow questions the researchers asked and were highly misleading. Michael Rutter's 1979 study of London high schools found that they had a critical impact on student achievement. Not surprisingly, the best schools were those that maintained high standards, required more homework, and had clear and well-enforced standards of discipline yet still created a comfortable, supportive atmosphere for students.[42] Coleman himself later acknowledged that schools do make a substantial difference. In a comparison of private and public schools published in 1982, Coleman and his colleagues wrote that "the indication is that more extensive academic demands are made in the private schools, leading to more advanced courses, and thus to higher achievement."[43] Thus, it seems clear that the first place to start to improve student achievement is to raise academic standards and require more homework.

Changing the Curriculum One of the most common reactions to new educational problems is to change the school curriculum. In response to the protests of the 1960s, a variety of new courses were introduced in an attempt to make schoolwork more relevant to the lives of minority students. In addition, history and social-studies classes began to include discussions of the significant contributions made by blacks and Hispanics to the United States. Criticisms of rigidity and authoritarianism in schools brought increases in the number of electives in high schools and a reduction in the number of required "academic" classes. Now that concern is growing over the decline in academic achievement, the curriculum is being changed again, this time toward stiffer academic programs. Many of the requirements for basic academic courses that were dropped during the 1960s and early 1970s were reinstated in the 1980s.

Better Educational Techniques In recent years much concern has been shown for refining and improving teaching methods and the learning environment. Many reformers, unhappy with public schools, have opened their own private schools. Some of these are called **free schools** because the relationships between students and teachers are relaxed and friendly. The combination of inexperience and underfinancing is too much for most of these schools, and the majority close within a few months.

Probably the most notable exception is A. S. Neill's highly successful Summerhill school.[44] Founded on faith in "the goodness of the child," Summerhill was conceived as a place where children were to be granted freedom without repression. Pupils are not ordered to be "nice" or "decent," and they are allowed to use profanity. Because Neill wanted to establish self-confidence and self-discipline in the children, Summerhill is run on a democratic basis. The children vote in weekly "parliamentary" meetings and are not required to attend classes. Learning is based on the child's interests, allowing each pupil to proceed at his or her own speed.

The graduates of Summerhill have generally done quite well in college and in their careers. Their success is not surprising, however, for the cost of attending the school has generally restricted enrollment to the upper and middle classes. Whatever the shortcomings of Summerhill and similar institutions, these schools have demonstrated that there is a workable alternative to the traditional school setting.

In a different attempt to improve teaching methods, there has been a trend toward organizing schools to give what is called **fundamental education**. Schools using this approach stress the teaching of basic skills and play

Great improvements in computer-assisted education have been made in recent years, but to take full advantage of these advances, schools must have better-trained teachers and more equipment.

down as "frills" such subjects as art, music, home economics, and traffic safety. They also try to teach children to be patriotic, respect authority, and lead moral lives. Many of these schools have strict dress codes and frown on unconventional behavior.

It is difficult to evaluate these attempts to find better educational techniques because they are not trying to accomplish the same things. The free schools try to develop spontaneity, creativity, and psychologically well-adjusted children. The fundamental schools try to develop academic competence and respect for authority and tradition. The public schools, caught between interest groups with profound differences in basic values and perspectives, try to strike the best balance they can, often satisfying neither side.

In the last few years public schools have been moving closer to the "back to basics" philosophy. This trend has been particularly pronounced at the elementary level, where fundamental skills are receiving a renewed emphasis. At least partially as a result of these changes, scores on achievement tests among elementary students have increased. Yet some educators believe that the rigid educational goals being set for elementary students may actually be harming their later performance in higher grades. The tests by the National Assessment of Educational Progress found that high school students now do better on tests of grammar and spelling but cannot write good essays; they do better on comprehension of words and sentences but cannot understand more complex passages; they do better on basic math computations but worse on word problems that require thought and analysis.[45] There is a growing feeling that schools ought to focus more effort on teaching students to read, write, and understand mathematics. But it must be remembered that those are not simple skills and that programs aimed primarily at improving scores on standardized tests are likely to produce narrower and less well-educated students.

Better Teachers In the long run, the quality and dedication of teachers is far more important than the particular techniques they use. There is no more important task facing our schools than keeping the best possible faculty on the job. The most obvious way to achieve that goal is to recognize the fact that there is less prestige in being an elementary or secondary teacher than there was in the past, and then to offer a substantial increase in pay to attract and retain high-quality professionals. One proposal already implemented in many school districts provides additional *merit pay* for superior teachers. A related approach is to create *master-teacher* programs in which a school's best teachers are given extra pay to provide counseling and assistance to other teachers.

Money, however, is not the only problem. Teachers also complain about the frustrations of working within a bureaucracy that is often more concerned about the smooth functioning of its schools than about education. They also complain about excessive paperwork, and the conflicts between the demand that they be classroom police officers and the need to be educators. Given all these problems, it is no surprise that teachers suffer such a high "burnout" rate. Fewer than one in five new teachers are still in the profession after ten years.[46]

But streamlining the bureaucracy and increasing pay will not guarantee that enough top-quality teachers will be recruited. Success will depend largely upon society's attitude toward education. As Tom Hayden, chairman of the California Assembly's Subcommittee on Higher Education, put it:

> The desire to teach is fostered in a social climate that supports the personal mission of helping others grow, of creating and sharing knowledge and pursuing a higher quality of life. Such values are not promoted in a climate of self-serving shortsightedness that lures people toward the quick fix, the fast buck, and the easy answer. Until a new emphasis on public service and social responsibility arises to balance narrow self-interest, the teaching crisis will remain difficult to resolve.[47]

SOCIOLOGICAL PERSPECTIVES ON PROBLEMS OF EDUCATION

In recent years our educational institutions have come to be seen as a means of dealing with other social problems. The schools are expected to improve the mental health of the nation, prevent delinquency and drug abuse, fight the spread of sexually transmitted diseases and teenage pregnancy, as well as reduce economic, political, and social inequality. At the same time, a new wave of concern about foreign competition in an age of high technology has led to demands that our schools improve their academic performance. These conflicting expectations have placed a great burden on our educational system and have made political footballs of some school programs.

The Functionalist Perspective As was noted earlier, functionalists see education as a basic institution that must fulfill many essential social needs. In modern times, the schools have grown increasingly important in the education of children from all social classes. The school is expected to teach youngsters the skills essential to members of modern society and to transmit important cultural values. But functionalists note that the educational system is often so disorganized that it does not perform its functions very well, in part because of the increasing demands placed upon it. Schools are confronted with so many different tasks that they are not doing any of them very well, and efforts to achieve one goal often conflict with efforts to achieve others. For example, the turmoil caused by some integration programs can interfere with the educational process. Efforts to modify the curriculum and make classes easier so that disadvantaged students will not get discouraged also reduces the achievement levels of more gifted students. Thus, many functionalists feel that the schools have gone too far in trying to meet the demands of special-interest groups and have neglected the needs of society as a whole.

Not all functionalists agree on how to make the schools more effective. Many advocate the elimination of the new goals and programs that have been introduced in recent years. Although such changes might well improve fundamental education, they are also likely to disrupt the efforts to deal with other pressing social problems. Proposals for employing more effective teaching methods are also compatible with the functionalist perspective. But most functionalists argue that such changes can be effective only if they are accompanied by a reorganization of the schools. For example, teachers must be rewarded for good teaching, rather than for being efficient bureaucrats or for the length of time they have spent on the job. Finally, many functionalists advocate better planning and coordination with other social institutions in order to reduce the problem of unemployment and underemployment among the educated. But such a program must be combined with an effort to reduce the instability of our economic institutions, since it is impossible to train students to meet the needs of an economy that is in a state of rapid and unpredictable flux.

The Conflict Perspective   Conflict theorists are not convinced that providing equal educational opportunity and upward mobility for the poor have ever been goals of our educational system. Rather, they argue that the schools are organized to do the opposite: to keep members of subordinate groups in their place and prevent them from competing with members of the ruling class. They point to the fact that free public education for all children is a relatively new idea and that even today many poor children must drop out of school to help support their families. Moreover, expensive private schools provide a superior education for children from the upper classes, whereas the public schools that serve the poor are underfunded, understaffed, and growing worse. Conflict theorists also argue that the old system of officially segregated education and the current system of de facto segregation serve to keep blacks and other oppressed minorities at the bottom of the social heap. The general principle is that the social and cultural biases in the educational system are not accidents but rather are reflections of a social system that favors the powerful.

Conflict theorists also see the schools as powerful agents of socialization that can be used as a tool for one group to exercise its cultural dominance over another. The most striking examples come from the educational system's treatment of minorities. Until relatively recently, young American Indians were likely to be taught that their ancestors were bloodthirsty savages, and blacks often read in history textbooks that their forebears were happy-go-lucky "darkies" who actually enjoyed being slaves. But this **cultural imperialism** is not limited to ethnic conflicts. The recent attempts of some religious groups to require that their beliefs about the origins of the human race be taught in the public schools is another example of the same process.

From the conflict perspective, the best and perhaps the only way to change these conditions is for the poor and cultural and ethnic minorities to organize themselves and reshape the educational system so that it provides everyone with equal opportunity but does not indoctrinate students in the cultural values and beliefs of any particular group. All children must be given the same quality of education that is now available only in private schools; cash subsidies must be provided for poor students who would otherwise be forced to drop out of school; and special educational programs must be set up to provide extra help for children whose parents have a weak educational background. Nevertheless, most conflict theorists probably agree with Christopher Jencks, who concluded that the educational system can do little to reduce inequality without changes in the broader society. Even if there were complete educational equality and everyone were given a college education, social and economic inequalities would remain. Such changes would not produce more interesting, highly paid professional jobs, nor would they reduce the number of menial, low-paying jobs. Thus, educational and social change must be carried out together.

Social Psychological Perspectives   Social psychologists are concerned with how schoolchildren learn. They also study the impact of the educational system on students' psychological development. Many have commented on the possibility that the authoritarianism so common in our schools impedes learning and encourages undemocratic behavior in later life. Moreover, schools create serious psychological problems for students who for one reason or another do not fit into the educational system. The heavy emphasis on competition and the consequent fear of failure are disturbing to those students who are already anxious and insecure. Students who do not do well in school are often troubled by feelings of depression and inadequacy, and the failure to live up to the academic expectations of parents and teachers is a major contributor to teenage suicide. Summerhill and other free-school experiments are attempts to improve the socialization process and, thus, to deal with these problems.

Other social psychologists, however, are not convinced that the social relationships in most traditional schools are harmful. They note that rational discipline may benefit children by exposing them to the rules and regulations that they will be expected to follow after they leave school. Moreover, some behaviorists have charged that children in free schools are reinforced for behavior that is unacceptable outside the school. This does not mean that these social psychologists necessarily favor the programs of fundamental schools. Some children need a great deal of discipline and an emphasis on obedience to authority, but social relationships of this kind impede the ability of other children to learn and to function effectively. Thus, it seems logical to provide the greatest possible range of educational alternatives so that the needs of each student can be met.

SUMMARY

Schools, colleges, and universities were originally reserved for the elite. Today, however, education has become a big business, employing around 3 million teachers in the United States alone.

Schools perform a number of important tasks. They teach essential skills such as reading, writing, and arithmetic. They transmit the society's values and attitudes. They perform a "sorting service," channeling students toward jobs for which they can qualify. The educational system also protects the advantages of dominant social groups by keeping most lower-class people in their "place." Schools serve as agents of social control but also provide a great number of social opportunities for students.

Children from the lower classes do not do as well in school as children from the middle and upper classes. Poor children usually come to school with a variety of economic and cultural handicaps, and the school system discriminates against these children in a number of ways. Teachers expect lower-class children to do poorly, and their expectations often become self-fulfilling prophecies. The schools attended by poor and working-class children often have lower budgets than other schools.

Racial and ethnic discrimination in the American educational system goes back to the days of slavery. Since the Supreme Court's decision outlawing school desegregation (1954), most legal (de jure) discrimination has been abolished. However, de facto (actual) segregation arising from segregated housing patterns is still widespread.

Schools are always struggling to deal with the twin problems of authority and rebellion. If schools lack discipline, students run wild and education suffers. But if discipline is too strict and authoritarian, students learn anti-democratic values and attitudes, and the likelihood of rebellion and delinquency is increased.

There has been a growing concern about the quality of our educational system because of the decline in high school students' scores on standardized achievement tests. Some argue that those tests are not a good measure of educational quality, others claim that the problem lies in the changing family environment of today's students, while still others hold the schools themselves responsible. Much concern has also been expressed about the financial problems of our schools and the increasing shortage of qualified teachers.

There are many proposals for creating more equal education. These include programs to achieve more effective integration, programs to give special assistance to poor and minority students, and reforms in school finance. Proposals for improving the educational process itself include increasing academic standards and requiring more homework, the use of better educational techniques such as those used in free schools or fundamental schools, changing the curriculum so the schools can do a better job of meeting students' needs, and making education a more attractive career so that the schools can hire better teachers.

Functionalists argue that the educational system is not running smoothly and that solving the problems of education is mostly a matter of reorganizing schools so that they will operate more efficiently. Conflict theorists are prone to look behind the stated goals of the educational system and argue that economic and political elites have an interest in achieving other, unstated goals that favor those in positions of power. Social psychologists are concerned about the harmful effects our educational system may have on individual students and about the best ways to correct these problems.

KEY TERMS

affirmative action
compensatory education
de facto segregation
de jure segregation
free school

fundamental education
grade inflation
hidden curriculum
latent function
magnet school

FURTHER READINGS

The Quality of Education

Michael Rutter, *15,000 Hours: Secondary Schools and Their Effects on Children*, Cambridge, Mass.: Harvard University Press, 1979.

Christopher Jencks et al., *Inequality: A Reassessment of the Effect of Family and Schooling in America*, New York: Harper & Row, 1972.

James S. Coleman, Thomas Hoffen, and Sally Kilgone, *High School Achievement: Public, Catholic and Private Schools*, New York: Basic Books, 1982.

Problems of Education

Keith Baker and Robert Rubel, *Violence and Crime in the Schools*, Lexington, Mass.: Lexington Books, 1980.

National Commission on Excellence in Education, *A Nation at Risk: The Imperative for Educational Reforms*, Washington, D.C.: Government Printing Office, 1983.

Meyer Weinberg, *The Search for Quality Integrated Education*, Westport, Conn.: Greenwood Press, 1983.

Ann Bastian et al., *Choosing Equality: The Case for Democratic Schooling*, Philadelphia: Temple University Press, 1986.

- How is the modern family changing?

- Is divorce a social problem?

- What are the causes of family violence?

- Are children victims of their parents' problems?

- How can the family be strengthened?

Chapter 5
PROBLEMS OF THE FAMILY

The family is found in one form or another in every known society. Yet observers dating back as far as ancient Greece have bemoaned its "decay," complaining of everything from youthful rebelliousness to a breakdown of traditional moral values. But these age old complaints have taken on new meaning in the industrial era. Traditional beliefs about the family, from the assumption of male dominance to the restriction of sexual relations to the married couple, are being challenged. The divorce rate has soared, and an increasing number of women are having children without ever having been married at all.

Some take all this as a sign of the impending collapse of our family system, but such arguments ignore the many strengths of today's families. The family is certainly changing, but it shows no signs of disappearing. Almost everyone eventually marries, and most people who divorce marry again. And it is not at all clear that people who lived in different family systems were any happier than people are today. In fact, the opposite may very well be true. In traditional family systems marriage partners were pressured to maintain even bitterly unhappy marriages that would be quickly dissolved today. The fact that the divorce rate was lower a hundred years ago than it is today hardly means that families then were healthier or happier. Although the erosion of traditional family structure has caused problems for many people, it has also given many others the opportunity to create a new family network that is better suited to the needs and desires of our times.

THE NATURE OF THE FAMILY

A **family** is usually defined as a group of people related by marriage, ancestry, or adoption who live together in a common household. Although the family is universal to all human societies, its structure and traditions vary enormously from one place to another. In some societies a wide variety of relatives are considered members of the family, while in others the family consists of only parents and children. Some societies permit only one husband and wife, while others allow many more. Anthropologist George Murdock's classic study of 565 societies found that about one-fourth followed our pattern of **monogamy** (only one husband and one wife at a time), whereas over 70 percent allowed **polygyny** (more than one wife). Murdock also found 4 societies in which a woman is allowed more than one husband.[1]

In some societies each parent plays an important role in child rearing, but in others the father has little to do with his children. For instance, among the Nayar of southern India the mother and her relatives (both male and female) carry the entire responsibility for the children. Some societies allow sexual relations only between the married couple, while others encourage a broad range of sexual contacts. Marriage is considered permanent and unbreakable in some societies, but others allow for easy divorce and remarriage. There are many other variations as well, for the family is as diverse and varied as culture itself.

Nuclear and Extended Families   Different types of families are usually classified according to their structure. One of the most useful classifications divides families into two categories: nuclear and extended. The **nuclear family** consists of a married couple and their children. Although there are often close ties between the members of the nuclear family and the other relatives of the husband and wife, nuclear families are independent, self-controlled units. When two people marry, the couple and their children become a separate family unit, usually living apart from the families in which the wife and husband were reared. The nuclear family is the dominant family pattern in modern industrialized nations in North America, Europe, and Asia.

Although the nuclear family is the norm in our culture, anthropologists have found that the **extended family** is the ideal in most agricultural societies around the world. The extended family consists of two or more related nuclear families living together in the same place. At the time of marriage the wife usually becomes a member of the husband's family, which consists of his grandparents, their sons and their wives, and their grandchildren. There are also a substantial number of societies in which the husband joins his wife's family. In a few societies, the grandparents are excluded and the extended family is based on the tie between brothers and sisters of the same generation.

Many people in industrialized societies romanticize the extended family, seeing it as somehow more natural than their nuclear families. But the first human societies, which relied on hunting and gathering to obtain their food, had nuclear families. Hunters and gatherers moved from place to place; consequently it was difficult for them to maintain large family groups. The extended family came into its own only with the development of settled agriculture. As people began to stay in one place and farm single plots of ground, the extended family helped fill the need for a steady supply of labor to work the fields. Also, ownership of land by an extended family often meant that the land would not be cut into smaller and smaller pieces to be divided among their heirs whenever the parents died. Even today most agricultural societies have extended family systems that provide for the essential needs of their members.

Life in an extended family is very different from the life we know in the nuclear family. For one spouse at least, marriage does not represent a sharp break with the past, as it does in our culture. He or she continues to live with his or her parents as before. Although the adjustment is more difficult for the spouse who must move into a new family, husband and wife both remain under the authority of the older generation. They have little chance of controlling their own lives unless they outlive their siblings and take over the responsibility for the entire family. Each child is reared and socialized by many adults, not just by the parents.

Family life in China before the changes of the twentieth century was a classic example of an extended family system. Except in a few coastal cities, control by the older generation affected every aspect of life. Marriages of children were arranged with an eye to public expectations and the family's best interests. Love between the newly married couple was of little concern, since newlyweds were virtual strangers. Individuals were surrounded by relatives, and this larger family determined each person's career and ambitions. Each person was secure within the group, which cared for its members in case of sickness, accident, old age, or an emergency. Such charity involved no stigma or disgrace, and indeed was accepted as a social duty. The surrounding community, sharing similar values, supported the extended family. In societies where the nuclear family pattern dominates, most people can look forward only to increasing isolation and loneliness as they grow older, but the Chinese could expect their status and authority to increase year by year.[2]

Young people were given more say in the selection of a mate in the traditional American family, and parents held less absolute control over their married children. But the ideals of traditional America were far different than the ones most of us hold today. Everyone was expected to be married and have children, and women who were not married by their middle twenties were derided as "spinsters" and "old maids." The needs of the family were considered more important than those of its individual members, and no one was expected to leave a marriage no matter how bad it became. The father was the absolute head of the family, and he exercised great authority over his wife and children. The woman's place was in the home, and she was denied the right to control her own property, to vote, or to participate in society as an independent person.[3]

The Impact of Industrialization   The industrial revolution transformed family life as the large extended family deteriorated under the impact of changing economic conditions. Because most production took place outside the home, the economic base of the family weakened, causing younger members to leave home to find employment. Like the hunting and gathering economy, industrialization requires a high degree of mobility, forcing workers to move from one place to another as some jobs close and others open. The extended family is far too rigid to adapt to such rapidly changing economic conditions. The industrial revolution also had a tremendous impact on traditional culture. As ideals of individualism and competition spread, many of the attitudes and values that had supported the extended family system were abandoned.

Because the emerging nuclear family was smaller and less stable than the extended family, the development of the industrial economy spurred other institutions to take over part of the tasks that used to be the exclusive responsibility of the family. In the past, the family was the primary unit of economic production, but in industrialized nations corporate farms and factories have taken over most of that responsibility. The schools are playing an increasing role in the socialization of the young, just as government welfare programs are helping the family in the economic support of the young and the old. The extended family also was once the primary agency of social control. In many agricultural societies the victims of a crime first looked to the family of the offender to make restitution before they attempted to com-

The contemporary nuclear family typically consists of only the married couple and their children.

plain to outside agencies (if such agencies even existed). Today, police, courts, and schools have a very significant role in controlling the young, while the criminal-justice system has almost completely taken over responsibility for the control of adult behavior.[4]

Because many of the family's functions have been taken over by other social institutions, it is much easier to live without family support. Marriage has become a matter of individual choice. Couples now marry out of the desire for companionship and personal happiness, not out of duty to their families or economic necessity. Romantic love has taken on tremendous importance as the process of mate selection has focused on finding a compatible person and "falling in love." Love is considered a kind of magic potion that can overcome almost any problem. In sharp contrast, traditional societies see romantic love as a frivolous basis for marriage and a threat to the smooth operation of the family system.

And in one sense it is, for our emphasis on love and personal happiness leads to the belief that unhappy marriages should be dissolved. When we say that two people have "fallen" in love, we imply that the matter is beyond their control, a bit like fate. It follows that they can also fall out of love.

THE MODERN FAMILY

Although modern industrial societies have already gone through the wrenching change from the extended to the nuclear family system, that does not mean that we have reached a new plateau of stability. The pattern of family life continues to show the same restless change that seems to characterize all facets of industrial society. The most important trends are the continuing decline in the size of the family, the changing relationships between husbands and wives, and the continued importance of the family in the daily lives of most people.

Growing Smaller   Year by year, generation by generation, the American family has been getting smaller. In 1790 the average American household had almost six persons, and today it contains less than three.[5] One important reason for this trend is that people are staying single longer than they did in the past. (See Figure 5.1.) Between 1955 and 1985 the average age at marriage increased by about two years, and the statistics also indicate that people are waiting longer after a divorce before they remarry. Industrial society's ever-increasing demand for education and training is certainly one reason more marriages are delayed, but there are other important factors as well. Greater acceptance of premarital sex makes the single life more attractive, and the public's attitude toward singles has undergone a remarkable change. The nineteenth-century stereotypes of the lonely bachelor and the neglected spinster have been replaced by the new stereotype of the "swinging singles," who often elicit envy instead of pity among their married friends. Singles' high disposable income has made them the focus of a new consumer industry that includes everything from singles-only apartment buildings to packaged singles vacations. These changes, along with a significant increase in the population of young adults, led to a 70 percent rise in the number of single people during the 1970s and another 16 percent increase between 1980 and 1986.[6] But these figures should not be misinterpreted. The vast majority of all Americans do eventually get married (over 90 percent); they are simply choosing to remain single for a somewhat longer part of their lives.

Another reason our families are shrinking is that we are having fewer children. We will examine the reasons for this more thoroughly in Chapter 17, but there is little doubt that they all are closely linked to the process of industrialization. Modern technology has helped to bring down the death

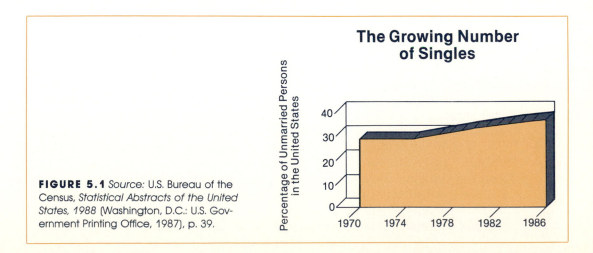

FIGURE 5.1 *Source:* U.S. Bureau of the Census, *Statistical Abstracts of the United States, 1988* (Washington, D.C.: U.S. Government Printing Office, 1987), p. 39.

The Growing Number of Singles

Percentage of Unmarried Persons in the United States

40 30 20 10 0

1970   1974   1978   1982   1986

rate, so that it is no longer necessary to have many children to ensure that a few survive. And although children were an asset in a traditional agricultural society, they have become an economic burden in the industrial world.

Finally, there has been a significant growth in the number of single-parent families. As recently as 1970, single-parent families made up less than 13 percent of all American families, but today that figure is over 22 percent; and those families contain about a quarter of all American children.[7] The causes of this increase are easy to find. As we shall see in the next section, the percentage of single-parent families headed by widows has declined, but there has been a sharp increase in the number of families headed by women who have been divorced or have never married.

Changing Roles   Our ideas about what role the wife and the husband should play in the family are undergoing a profound change. The traditional ideal of the breadwinning husband who makes the decisions and rules the family and his stay-at-home wife who raises the children and does the housework is being challenged by a new vision of marital equality. In the egalitarian marriage, husband and wife are considered equal partners. They make important decisions together, and they share the work necessary to keep the family going. Both husband and wife often work outside the home, but the key is that the tasks of child care, housework, and breadwinning are fairly distributed so that each partner shoulders an equal share of the burden. As recently as 1974 a majority of both men and woman surveyed by the Harris poll considered "a traditional marriage" best, "with the husband assuming responsibility for providing for the family and the wife running the home and taking care of the children." But little more than a decade later in 1985, a majority of women (57% to 37%) and men (50% to 43%) were convinced that a better marriage is one "where the husband and wife share responsibilities more—both work, share the housekeeping and the child responsibilities."[8]

But although more and more people claim to believe in marital equality, we are still a long way from realizing those ideals. Most wives still assume the primary responsibility for the "women's work" of child care and housekeeping, and most men continue to see their role as the primary breadwinner. The great importance that our society attaches to financial success, the relatively low status given to child rearing, and the cultural traditions of male dominance often mean that the husband has a disporportionate share in the decision-making power.

One area where there has been the most obvious change is in the economic role of the wife. In 1938 a national survey found that three-fourths of all Americans disapproved of a woman working if her husband could support her. But 40 years later, another survey found a complete reversal of public opinion: three-fourths of those surveyed approved of wives holding a job.[9] And the statistics show that behavior has changed along with the attitudes. In 1986, 54.6 percent of all married women were employed outside the home, as were 64.3 percent of married women with children.[10] Since less than one-third of all families have only a single male breadwinner, the typical American family is now a **dual-earner family.** It should be noted, however, that males still continue their primacy in the breadwinning role, both because they usually earn higher wages than their wives (see Chapter 10) and because a much greater proportion of working wives are employed in part-time jobs.

Continued Importance   Critics of contemporary society often see a rising tide of narcissism that is washing away the sense of commitment and self-sacrifice necessary to maintain a healthy family. In this view, we have become so obsessed with our personal satisfactions that we have no time left over for anyone else. Public opinion polls offer no support for this dismal view of modern life, however. The American public consistently rates a good family life as their single most important goal—more important than good health, self-respect, or personal happiness. Moreover, the public sees no contradiction between personal happiness and the demands of family living. When the Harris poll asked Americans who is happiest, 65 percent said married people and only 18 percent said single people.[11]

Thus, there is no reason to believe that we see the family as any less important than we did in the past. If anything, we demand more of it. The expectation of love and emotional gratification from one's spouse is probably higher than it has ever been, and the increasing impersonality of modern society has made the family into the only island of warm personal relationships that many people have. There is, moreover, evidence that most people are happy with their married life. A 1976 survey found that 80 percent of

Most nuclear families still maintain close ties to grandparents even though they do not usually live in the same home.

DEBATE

Are Dual-Earner Families Harmful to Children?

YES The wrenching changes of industrialization gravely weakened the family. Just two parents are now expected to perform all the duties that had been carried out by a whole team of relatives working together. Moreover, most of these new responsibilities were placed on the mother. It is ridiculous to argue that the children do not suffer if the mother works outside the home in addition to all her other duties. There are only so many hours in the day, and the working mother simply cannot do as much for her children. The father may be able to assume a few of her responsibilities, but he is likely to be just as busy and overworked as she.

Children in families with two wage earners return from school to an empty home, or worse, simply run wild on the streets until their parents get home from work. Even those who are in day care are little better off. Most day care facilities are private businesses, and the children's emotional needs take a backseat to the demand for profit. Even the best day care facilities cannot provide the love and attention we expect from a child's parents.

Children in dual-earner families also suffer from an increase in conflict between the parents. The demands of trying to manage two careers and perform the many duties of child rearing at the same time place continual pressure on both partners. The result is more fights and more hostility. Tired, overworked parents lose their tempers more quickly with their children and each other. Some even come to resent the burdens their children place on them. But whatever the parents' attitude toward their children, their sons and daughters are bound to be affected

NO There is no scientific evidence to show that children are harmed when both their parents work. On the contrary, there is good reason to believe that they actually benefit. The most obvious advantage is the extra income that enables children to have things they otherwise would be denied. A higher standard of living does not simply mean more toys, hamburgers, and sweaters. It means music lessons, travel, special tutoring, a computer, or perhaps even a private school with superior academic standards.

Contrary to the charges of traditionalists, working mothers are often more satisfied with their lives than are those who stay at home. As a result, they do a better job of parenting. Certainly the working mother provides a much more positive role model for her children. And daughters and sons both benefit from the fact that fathers generally assume more responsibilities of parenting in dual-earner families. Finally, an independent income gives the mother more power in the dual-earner family; the children are therefore more likely to believe in the value of equality because their families are in fact more egalitarian.

Critics charge that professional day care harms children, but the evidence indicates that children benefit enormously, if the parents carefully select good quality care. Children in day care centers are exposed to new ideas and playmates, and as a result, they have a broader background and do better in school.

Although critics of dual-earner families make a lot of charges, they haven't proven any of them. The real reason for their objections is that these families violate their prejudiced notion that a woman's place is in the home. In modern by the increase in tension in the home.

There are some families in which both parents must work just to keep everyone fed. In most cases, however, it is sheer greed that sends both parents off to work, for our people are already among the richest in the world. Children are more important than money, and their needs must come first.

industrial society, the woman's place is anywhere she chooses to be. Dual-earner families promote greater human freedom and more equality and therefore benefit both children and adults.

---

married Americans described their marriages as "very happy" or "above average,"[12] and a more recent Harris poll found that 85 percent of married people said that they would remarry the same person if they had it to do all over again.[13]

Most of the early studies of the modern nuclear family pictured it as an independent unit relatively isolated from other kin.[14] But other researchers argue that our kinship networks are much stronger than was first believed.[15] Most nuclear families are certainly enmeshed in a very significant web of relationships with other relatives. Substantial amounts of financial aid flow from one generation to another, usually from parents to young married couples and later from middle-aged couples to aging parents. Members of kinship networks also provide one another with important services, ranging from babysitting to emotional and financial support in times of personal distress. There are extensive social and recreational contacts between the members of many kinship networks. However, kinship ties are much narrower in modern society than they were in the past. The primary bonds are with parents, siblings, and children, and other kinship ties are usually much less important.[16]

FAMILY PROBLEMS

The modern family is in much better shape than is commonly believed, but our times nonetheless present us with a host of difficult problems we are still struggling to solve. In this section we will examine five of today's most important family issues: divorce, births outside of marriage, violence, child rearing, and the inequalities of family life.

Divorce This century has seen a dramatic increase in divorce rates. In 1920 there was one divorce for every seven marriages in the United States; 50 years later the rate had climbed to one divorce for every three marriages. There is now about one divorce for every two marriages, making the divorce rate in the United States one of the highest in the world.[17] Even though most people who get divorced ultimately remarry, the ratio of divorced people to married people living with their spouses more than doubled from 47 per 1000 in 1970 to

19th-Century Social Problems

John and Leo Koelbel, well-to-do farmers residing in the town of Newton, had a hearing in Manitowoc in the county court before Judge Anderson, having been cited there on the charge of contempt for failing to comply with an order of the court commanding them to pay 60 cents a week each for the support of their aged parents. . . . The 2 sons have positively refused to give a single cent toward the support of their father and mother. The court ordered them both to be committed to the county jail until they saw fit to comply with the order. . . .

June 11, 1900

These selections, which appear throughout the text, are from the *Badger State Banner*, a newspaper published in Black River Falls, Wisconsin.

131 per 1000 in 1986.[18] In the last few years, however, the divorce rate has leveled off. But at this time it is unclear whether this is a temporary pause or if the years of steady increase are over.

Who Gets Divorced? In the nineteenth century, divorce was mainly for the wealthy. Great Britain and many American states required a special act of the legislature for each divorce, and the poor lacked the influence and money necessary for such decrees. Now divorce is most common among the poor, and the divorce rate declines as education and income increase.

One cause of the higher divorce rate among the poor is the special economic problems they experience. As an old saying puts it, "When poverty comes in the door, love goes out the window." It is possible, too, that divorce is less frequent among the wealthy because dissolution of marriage requires complex arrangements for distributing wealth and income among family members. Also, the availability of travel, entertainment, and servants helps the wealthy adjust more easily to married life.

Age is an important factor in marital instability. A teenage marriage is almost three time more likely to end in divorce than a marriage of partners over 30.[19] The divorce rate also varies significantly among different ethnic groups. Black males are about 12 percent more likely to be divorced than white males, and the differences for females are larger: about 34 percent.[20]

Most divorces occur fairly soon after marriage. About 5 percent of all divorces occur within the first year of marriage, and the divorce rate peaks at 9 percent for the second and third years and then slowly declines.[21] Considering the length of time it takes to get divorced in many states, this means that many couples begin divorce proceedings shortly after their wedding.

Why the Upward Trend? The increase in the divorce rate has caused considerable alarm among those who consider it a sign of moral decay. Sociologically, this increase is most clearly related to the decline of the extended family. The partners in today's marriages receive considerably less support and assistance from relatives than their great-grandparents did. Thus, when trouble arises, they have fewer resources on which to draw. At the same time, unhappy couples are now under much less pressure from their families to stay together and avoid divorce. Even if parents want a married couple to stay together, they no longer have the economic power to enforce their wishes.

The shift from the extended family system to the nuclear family has made it easier to see marriages as unions that are not permanent. The romanticism on which courtship is now based leads many young people to expect marriage to be a state of perpetual happiness and conflict-free bliss. When they start quarreling about money matters, about how much time they should spend with each other, about recreational or intellectual interests, or about who is supposed to sweep the floor and carry out the garbage, they imagine that love has flown out the window and that they can no longer continue their relationship.

Changes in the economic role women play in our society have made divorce a more practical alternative than it was in past years. More and more women are working outside the home, making them less dependent on their husbands and, thus, less likely to stay married to men whom they dislike. Attitudes toward divorce have changed too. Only 50 years ago divorce was seen as an immoral act, an affront to "decent" people. The divorced woman was stigmatized as a "grass widow" and her virtue exposed to public question. Public sentiment was so strongly against divorce that it was forbidden in some countries, and many others made it extremely difficult. Today divorce carries less stigma, and the consensus seems to be that it is better to separate than to continue in an unhappy marriage. And as attitudes have changed, so have the laws. In 1969 California became the first state to pass a "no-fault" divorce law, and its example has been followed by other states. Instead of having to go through the painful process of proving that one partner did not fulfill the conditions of the marriage contract, the "no-fault" law allows for divorce by mutual agreement, substantially reducing the legal costs of a divorce.

Is Divorce a Social Problem? There is no doubt that a divorce is often the only satisfactory solution to an impossible family situation. Nevertheless, divorce continues to be seen as a sign of failure—an admission by the marriage partners that they lack the ability, trust, or stamina to continue an intimate relationship. Many of the problems confronting divorced people stem from such attitudes, and because the parties to a divorce often share such convictions, they feel guilty and ashamed about the breakup of their marriage. Those who dissolve their marriages are still made to feel that they have failed in their duty to God, country, parents, and children. Despite the high frequency of divorce, we have not developed effective means for helping newly divorced people make the transition to a different life style. When a spouse dies, relatives rally around the widow or widower to provide emotional and financial support. There are also a variety of rituals, such as the funeral service, to help ease the pain of transition. Yet the divorced person, who shares many of the same problems, seldom receives the same kind of support.

But whatever social support a couple may receive, divorce is bound to cause personal suffering. The termination of an intimate relationship and the accompanying feelings of guilt and failure make divorce a painful experience, even if there are no serious clashes. From a social viewpoint, the major cost of divorce is the division of families with children into smaller and therefore weaker units. Because of the occupational discrimination against women, a family consisting of a mother and children is likely to have a lower income than a two-parent family. And single parents, regardless of their sex, have great difficulty handling both the role of breadwinner and the role of parent.

The greatest concern about divorce centers on the children. The parents chose to have their divorce, and hopefully have the maturity and experience to deal with it. The children are clearly another matter. Studies of the children of divorce show high levels of fear, grief, sadness, and anger at what has happened to them.[22] Although most children eventually learn to adjust to their new situation, a divorce can have lasting effects. Children whose parents are divorced have higher rates of school absenteeism and delinquency and are themselves more likely to become divorced when they grow up.[23] But all this does not mean that children are better off if an unhappy marriage is preserved, for little research shows this to be beneficial. For example, a study of 1,400 children ages 12 to 16 found that the effects of persistent conflict in the home were just as harmful as the breakup of a marriage.[24]

Births Outside of Marriage   Like divorce, the number of childbirths by single women has shown a remarkable increase in recent years. The percentage of babies born to single women more than tripled between 1960 and 1984, and is now about 21 percent of all births. But such general statistics obscure some very important differences between ethnic groups. Almost 60 percent of black babies are born to single women, whereas that figure is about 28 percent for Hispanics and 13 percent for whites.[25]

The reasons for the high birthrate among single black women are a matter of heated debate. When a widely publicized report by Daniel Moynihan first called attention to this issue in 1965, it was denounced as a racist attack on black Americans. But there is now a growing concern with this problem in the black community itself. Although the causes are not entirely clear, several factors stand out. First and foremost, blacks are much more likely to be poor than whites, and the illegitimacy rate is much higher among poor people from all ethnic groups. Second, the prejudice and discrimination

19th-Century Social Problems

Lena Watson of Black River Falls gave birth to an illegitimate child and choked it to death.

October 9, 1890

that have been aimed at blacks for so many years have hit particularly hard at black males from poor homes. The extremely high rate of unemployment among this group makes it much harder to live up to the expectations of fatherhood, and fathers who feel inadequate to meet the needs of their families are far more likely to withdraw and leave their support to the welfare department. Third, the pattern of early pregnancy and single-parent homes has been passed down from one generation to the next in the black underclass.

It is, however, easy to exaggerate the differences between blacks and whites. The birthrates of unmarried women are growing rapidly among all ethnic groups; blacks were merely the first ones to feel the effects of this trend. In fact, since 1960 the birthrate has increased almost twice as fast among single white women as among single black women.[26]

The overall increase in the birthrate of single women is ultimately a result of the same process of industrialization that broke down the extended family. Among the more immediate causes, however, the increase in sexual activity among teenagers, combined with the failure to use appropriate contraceptive techniques, also stands out as the major contributor (see Chapter 11). Although American teenagers have about the same level of sexual activity as European teenagers, they are less likely to use birth control, and consequently their illegitimacy rate is far higher. Another important factor is the growing unwillingness of young couples to marry simply because the woman is pregnant. Studies of births in past centuries, when illegitimacy rates were low, show that about 20 to 25 percent of all weddings occurred after the conception of a child.[27] Today the "shotgun wedding" (in which a pregnant woman's father threatens the young man if he does not marry the virgin he has "spoiled") has gone out of style. The children of unwed mothers are still often condemned, but the stigma has decreased over the years.

The social position of an unmarried woman with a child in today's society is not very different from her divorced counterpart. However, she is likely to face some special problems, such as feelings of embarrassment and guilt, the belief that she has been deserted by the father of the child, and the lack of emotional support she needs during the difficult months of pregnancy. But the greatest problem of unmarried mothers comes from the fact that most of them are not ready for the responsibilities of parenthood. Most single mothers are under 25, and over a third of all births outside of marriage are to teenagers.[28]

These births are seldom planned, usually resulting from carelessness or lack of knowledge about contraception. The arrival of the unexpected and often unwanted child may have wrenching consequences for the young mother. Teenagers who become pregnant are more likely to drop out of school, work at lower-paying jobs, and are more often unemployed than their peers. Their children have a higher rate of infant mortality and more serious health problems than those of others. Three of every four children born to unmarried women live in poverty.[29]

Violence Beatings, slashings, stabbings, burnings, and chokings are common events in many families. Pagelow estimates that about 12 million wives are beaten by their husbands every year in the United States, and that somewhere between 1 and 2 million children are abused each year.[30] Family violence ranges in severity from the spanking of a troublesome child (which, though usually socially acceptable, is still a form of violence) to cold-blooded murder. Until quite recently, much family violence remained hidden behind closed doors. Even now, law enforcement agencies seldom get the cooperation they need to prosecute wife beaters and child abusers.

Violence Between Husband and Wife The relationship between husbands and wives is one of the strongest bonds in our society. It is deep, passionate, and often violent. The exact amount of husband-wife violence is difficult to determine, but it is one of the most common of all forms of violence. More calls to the police involve family disturbances than all other forms of violent behavior combined. In one of the most comprehensive studies of family violence to date, Straus, Gelles, and Steinmetz found that about a quarter of the husbands and wives they interviewed admitted that there had been violence between them at some time in their marriage. But the researchers suspect that their study may have underestimated the rate of husband-wife violence. They estimate that it actually occurs in some form in about one of every two marriages.[31]

In many societies, such as those in the Middle East, husbands have traditionally had the legal right to physically punish wives who refuse to accept male authority. Although this practice is no longer approved of in Western culture, it still occurs. Thus, the threat of violence is often used by husbands to control their wives. However, as women gain financial and social equality, they also gain greater power in the home, making it easier for them to demand an end to the violence or to leave abusive husbands. Straus, Gelles, and Steinmetz found that families that make their decisions democratically have lower rates of both child abuse and husband-wife violence than families in which one member dominates the other.[32]

The effort of husbands to dominate their wives is, however, only one of many causes of family violence. The Straus, Gelles, and Steinmetz survey also found that a surprising number of violent incidents are actually begun by the wife, not the husband. There is a great deal of evidence that there is a "cycle of violence" that is passed down from one generation to the next. Children raised in violent homes learn that violence is a way to deal with frustration and anger and are therefore much more likely to be violent themselves.[33] (See Chapter 15 for a more complete discussion of the causes of violence.)

Child Abuse No one knows how many children are abused by their parents each year. For one thing, there is no clear line between "acceptable" punishment and child abuse. The vast majority of parents spank their children at some time or other. All these parents are certainly not child abusers. Yet severe and repeated spankings can be just as cruel as other forms of violence. According to one estimate, 14 percent of all children are severely beaten by their parents each year.[34] Straus, Gelles, and Steinmetz found that 8 percent of the married couples with children they questioned admitted having kicked, bitten, or punched their children, and 4 percent admitted having "beaten up" their children.[35]

Although such figures are shocking, we probably do not abuse our children as much as our ancestors did. Traditionally, severe physical punishment was considered essential to the learning process. Many parents believed that "if you spare the rod, you spoil the child." In colonial America a statute even provided for the execution of sons who were "stubborn and rebellious" and failed to follow parental authority. However, there is no record of such an execution actually taking place.[36] A comparison of the rates of child abuse in a survey first done in 1975 and repeated again in 1985 found a 47 percent decrease in that ten-year period.[37] Although some of that difference may reflect a greater reluctance to admit having abused a child, it seem that all the recent attention given to this problem is paying off.

Gil's study of officially reported child-abuse cases provides some interesting insights into the type of child who is most likely to be mistreated.[38] Contrary to popular opinion, children of all ages, up to their senior year in high school, are abused. Abused children are much more likely to come from broken homes, and less than half of the abused children in Gil's sample were living with their natural father. Children from large families are also more likely to be abused. Gil found that the usual indicators of social class—income, occupational prestige, and education—are all negatively related to child abuse. In other words, the lower the parents' social and economic status, the more likely they were to hurt their children. The children in Gil's sample were more likely to be abused by their mothers than by their fathers, in part because the fathers were not present in many homes. Many of Gil's findings, such as those concerning the sex and class differences in child abuse, were confirmed by the Straus, Gelles, and Steinmetz survey.[39]

There are many explanations of child abuse. Psychologists tend to picture child abusers as people who are mentally ill or at least have severe emotional problems. The typical child abuser is described as impulsive, immature, and depressed, with little control over his or her emotions. Social workers are inclined to see environmental stress as the most important cause of child abuse. They note that an unwanted pregnancy, desertion by the husband, or unemployment and poverty put special pressures on a parent that may result in child abuse. Social psychologists have found evidence that most child abusers learned to be abusive when they were children. That is, they themselves were beaten when they were young, and they in turn beat their own children.

Many sociologists argue that child abuse occurs so frequently in America because the physical punishment of children is condoned and even encouraged. They call for laws that would make it a crime to inflict physical punishment on children, as has already been done in Sweden. But it is important to remember that child abuse can be psychological as well as physical. Countless parents cause severe emotional damage to their children without ever being physically violent.

Child Rearing   Raising children to replace those who grow old and die is the most critical function of the family. The vitality and even the survival of a society depends on how effectively the family does this job. Thus, every society is only about 20 years from extinction, for if a society fails to socialize its children for that length of time, it will cease to exist. Of course, this is very unlikely to happen. But it is clear that there are many "pathological" families

Child rearing has always been one of the most important and most difficult tasks of the family.

in which the relationship between parents and children is warped, and even "healthy" families often fail to socialize their children effectively.

Child rearing has never been an easy task, but it is particularly difficult today. Our nuclear family system gives parents almost exclusive responsibility for the support and upbringing of children, and they receive far less assistance from other relatives than parents did in the past. If one of the parents is unable to perform his or her duties, the family is almost automatically plunged into crisis, since there are no other relatives in the household to help out. There is, moreover, a growing feeling among parents that our society has turned its back on their problems. In 1986, pollster Louis Harris found that 74 percent of all adults believed that the problems our children face are getting worse, and that 63 percent believed that too little effort had been made to solve them. In Harris's words: "For nearly a generation now, there has been a gradual but steady decline in the attention that society has paid to children."[40]

The growing number of **single-parent families** has made these problems worse (see Figure 5.2). The percentage of children living with only one parent has more than doubled since 1970, and about one-quarter of all American children now live in single-parent homes.[41] Financially, most single-parent families are always on thin ice, for the majority of them are headed by women, and women on the average earn far less money than men. To make matters worse, they usually have to pay for child care service out of their meager earnings. Child support payments from the father sometimes help, but in 1985 only about 61 percent of women with children were awarded support payments in their divorce or separation;[42] and the typical father fails to pay about one-quarter of the amount due.[43] As a result of these factors, the *majority* of the children in single-parent families now live in poverty. To make matters worse, the federal government has, in the words of one researcher, "abandoned children." Since 1981, 3 million children have been cut from free school lunch programs, 1 million children have lost eligibility

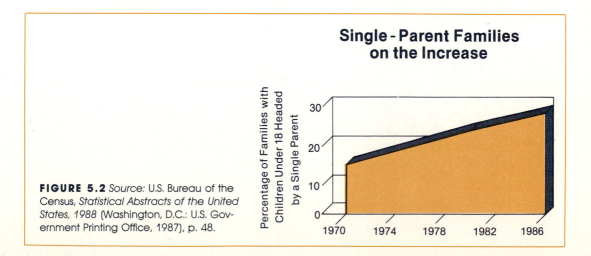

FIGURE 5.2 *Source:* U.S. Bureau of the Census, *Statistical Abstracts of the United States, 1988* (Washington, D.C.: U.S. Government Printing Office, 1987), p. 48.

Single-Parent Families on the Increase

Percentage of Families with Children Under 18 Headed by a Single Parent for aid to families with dependent children, and health care for poor families has been sharply reduced.[44]

Another child-rearing problem in single-parent families is the lack of parental supervision and guidance. Often single parents do not have time to perform both their breadwinning and their child-rearing roles. Some studies of delinquency, for example, indicate that children from "broken homes" are more likely to engage in rebellious behavior than other children.[45] There is also clear evidence that children from single-parent families are more likely to get into trouble with the police, although many criminologists feel that the difference results from police bias or the fact that single-parent families tend to have lower incomes.[46] The relationship between discipline and delinquency is not, however, a simple one. Studies show that parental discipline promotes delinquency when it is too strict as well as when it is too lax.[47]

A great deal of concern has also been expressed about the children of dual-earner families. But although working mothers often bear extra burdens, the fear that maternal employment somehow harms children apparently is unfounded. Having reviewed all the available research on this subject, Thomas Taveggia and Ellen Thomas concluded that "there are no substantial differences between the children of working and nonworking mothers" in terms of the characteristics tested, such as intelligence, personal development, school achievement, and social adjustment.[48]

Dual-earner families do have some special difficulties in rearing their children, however. The biggest problem reported by working mothers, whether single or married, is the lack of accessible high-quality child care.[49] A recent Harris poll found that 42 percent of nonworking mothers said that they would look for work if there were more day-care centers where they live.[50] Because of this shortage, only about 10 percent of dual-earner families with children are currently sending them to day-care centers. Twenty-five percent of those families leave their children with relatives, and 29 percent arrange their work so that one or the other parent is home with the children. But at least 13 percent provide no adult supervision for a substantial part of the day.[51]

A different sort of problem arises from the growth of the mass media and the expansion of formal education, which have greatly reduced the control parents used to have over what their children learn. Some of the greatest concerns are about the effects of profit-oriented television programming. It is estimated that by the time the average American child graduates from high school, he or she will have spent 15,000 hours watching television, compared with only 11,000 hours spent in the classroom. During that time he or she will have seen about 18,000 fictional murders and watched over 650,000 commercials. Research shows that children who watch a lot of television see the world as a more dangerous and frightening place than children who watch little television.[52]

Contributing to all these problems is the so-called generation gap. The pace of social change has been so rapid that the world in which children grow up is very different from the one their parents knew, making mutual understanding and communication more difficult than in traditional societies. Parent-child conflicts are typically most acute during adolescence, when children are trying to establish their independence and are straining to deal with growing sexual drives. Children who feel they should be independent and "modern" rebel against parents who try to keep them under tight control; but parents who allow their children more freedom may also have more difficulty protecting them from the many hazards of modern life.

One of the clearest indicators of the difficulties modern families are having with child rearing comes from the increasing number of **runaways.** The General Accounting Office of the United States estimates that about one million young people run away from home every year. Although four out of five return within a few days, the rest are likely to suffer serious hardships. Both males and females turn to crimes such as prostitution and shoplifting to support themselves. Because they are often on the streets and vulnerable, they are also victims of sexual abuse, and their rates of alcoholism and drug addiction are extremely high. The label of "runaway" that is applied to these young people is, however, quite misleading in some cases. A substantial number are actually **pushouts** who are forced to fend for themselves because their families no longer want them.[53]

Work and Family Inequality Our ideas about the proper role of wives and husbands have, as we have seen, been undergoing some remarkable changes, and this redefinition of traditional roles has placed considerable stress on the modern family. In the past each partner in a marriage generally had a clear-cut idea of what to expect from the other. But today a bride and groom can no longer assume that their conceptions of their respective roles coincide, and considerable compromise is required to resolve such differences. More women are working outside the home and demanding an equal share of the decision-making power within the family. Some husbands, socialized to see women as inferiors, consider these demands a threat to their masculinity, particularly if the wives are more successful in their careers than are their husbands. But even when both partners accept the ideal of sexual equality, career conflict can still arise. For example, one partner may be offered an important promotion that requires a move that would be disastrous to the career of the other, or a sick child may require one parent to miss a critical assignment at work.

The dramatic increase in the number of wage-earning women often leads us to forget about the other essential type of family labor: housework. Although many people assume that fewer children and modern home appliances have greatly reduced the total amount of housework, that has not proven to be true. New expectations for "sparkling" dishes and dust-free tabletops have raised the standards that homemakers strive to meet. Some technological "advances" have in fact created more rather than less work. The classic example is the automobile, which created a new category of household work (driving) that slowly demanded more and more time. As the automobile became increasingly common, door-to-door peddlers, home delivery by retail stores, and house calls by physicians were sharply curtailed, and automobile-based surburbanization placed schools and jobs farther away from home. These changes transformed the car from a convenience to a costly necessity.[54] Many of the other "labor-saving" devices women went to work to buy actually saved less time than was required to earn the money to pay for them. As a result there has been a sharp drop in leisure time. Despite the dreams of science-fiction writers that modern technology would create a society in which most of us would not have to work at all, the Harris poll found that the amount of leisure time available to the average American has actually declined 32 percent since 1973.[55]

The growing shortage of leisure time makes the division of labor in the family a particularly important issue. In general, men tend to work more hours outside the home and perform automobile and home repairs and other heavy household tasks. Women tend to work fewer hours outside the home but generally do most of the work that needs to be done around the house, including child care, cooking, cleaning, and laundry. How fairly are the family burdens divided? Research shows that when the husband is the only wage earner, the wife works about the same number of hours in the house as he does on the job. But since he also does some work at home, the husband puts in more total hours of work than does his wife. In dual-earner families, however, a sharp increase in the wife's duties reverses this relationship. Although the husbands of working wives generally do a little more around the house and more services are purchased from outsiders, the total number of hours the wife must work is greatly increased.[56] Perhaps that is why employed mothers report being less satisfied with their lives than are other women.[57]

RESPONDING TO PROBLEMS OF THE FAMILY

In one sense there are as many responses to family problems as there are families. Because each family is unique, its members respond to their problems in unique ways. In another sense, however, family problems are institutional, and therefore affect us all. Despite its weaknesses, the nuclear-family system is very much in tune with the economic and social institutions of modern industrial society. For this reason, most reformers have chosen to direct their efforts toward strengthening the nuclear family rather than trying to reestablish the larger and possibly more durable family units typical of the extended-family system.

Better Preparation   One way of strengthening the nuclear family is to see that people are better prepared for marriage. Perhaps the easiest way to achieve this goal is simply to discourage early marriage, so that partners are older and more mature when they do marry. Census Bureau figures show that the average age of couples at the time of their first marriage has gradually increased during the last three decades. From 1970 to 1984 the average age at marriage jumped from 20.6 years to 22.8 years for women, and from 22.5

years to 24.6 years for men.[58] Publicizing the problems of early marriage might encourage this trend and stop some young couples from marrying, but it is far from certain that such a campaign would be effective.

Another approach is to prepare the young for marriage through educational programs in high schools and colleges. Although such programs encourage realistic expectations about married life and teach techniques for dealing with marital problems, most of them have not been notably successful. Regrettably, a few hours of classroom instruction are not likely to change long-held attitudes and expectations about marriage.

All educational efforts fortunately do not have to change deep-seated attitudes in order to be successful. One of the most serious family problems is unwanted pregnancy among teenage girls. More effective sex education programs in the schools could go a long way toward reducing this major problem. But to be effective, such educational programs must be combined with a well-publicized effort to provide unrestricted access to birth control devices for teenagers who need them. Studies show that the single most effective way to prevent pregnancies among teenage girls is to establish birth control clinics in high schools (see Chapter 11). However, many people are now pushing to restrict rather than expand the availability of birth control information and devices. For example, an unsuccessful effort was recently made to require family-planning clinics that receive federal aid to notify the parents of teenagers who ask for birth control devices. Experience shows that the effect of such a policy would be to scare teenagers away from birth control clinics and thus increase the number of teenage pregnancies.

Efforts are also being made to restrict the availability of abortions to teenagers and mature women alike. Many states and the federal government have cut back on financial assistance to poor women who desire abortions, and the result is not only more social inequality (wealthy women can afford to pay for their own abortions) but an increase in the number of unwanted babies. Since about 45 percent of all teenage pregnancies end in abortion, the complete elimination of abortion in the United States could be expected to nearly double the birthrate among teenagers. (See the debate in Chapter 8 for arguments for and against the prohibition of abortion.)

An increasing number of young couples are living together before deciding on marriage. There are those who feel that this promotes stronger marriages, as well as others who feel that it promotes weaker ones, but the effects of this trend are still unclear. A four-year study by Newcomb and Bentler found no differences in marital satisfaction or divorce rates between couples who "cohabited" before marriage and those who did not,[59] and Jacques and Chason found no differences in the way married couples described their marriages when they compared couples who had cohabited with those who had not.[60] But such studies are far from conclusive, because there are probably many differences in attitudes and values between cohabitors and noncohabitors that would also influence such things as marital adjustment and divorce rates.

Reducing Family Conflicts Ideally, the family is a cooperative, trouble-free unit that shelters its members from the stresses of the outside world. But real families seldom, if ever, achieve this ideal. Periodic episodes of tension and conflict are the rule, not the exception, in family life. Indeed, open disagreements and even arguments are an excellent way of resolving the differences that inevitably develop between family members. Families that avoid conflict by avoiding unpleasant subjects or conflict-laden situations are weaker, not stronger, for it. As feelings of resentment build up, such families are likely to break up or deteriorate into an "empty shell," where family members carry out the obligations of their roles but without mutual love, affection, or understanding. Thus, an open and honest airing of disagreements is an excellent way to manage family conflict and keep it within acceptable bounds.

Often, however, differences become so great that they cannot be resolved within the family unit. Friends and relatives can sometimes be helpful, but there has been a significant increase in the number of people seeking professional counseling for marital problems. When there are fundamental conflicts between personalities, attitudes, or life-styles, even the best professional counseling may prove futile. Such counseling is most helpful for couples with specific, limited problems. For example, the sex therapy pioneered by the famous Masters and Johnson research team has been helpful to many couples because it deals with specific problems, such as impotence or frigidity, that respond to straightforward treatment.[61] A growing number of counseling programs are also being established to deal with family violence. A number of these programs have apparently achieved significant reductions in family violence among their clients, but sufficient scientific evidence has not yet been collected to make a final judgment on their effectiveness.

Many conflicts are rooted in the way family roles are defined by our society. Traditional family patterns—in the extended family as well as in the nuclear family—have subordinated women and deprived them of the power to control their own destinies. As a result, some women feel frustrated and angry about their position in the family, while the traditional role expectations of their husbands blind them to the problem. Moreover, the traditional division of labor in the family may require both men and women to do work for which they are poorly suited. Some families clearly would be much better off if the husband stayed home to care for the children while the wife worked. It therefore seems likely that the nuclear family system will be strengthened by the continuing growth of the new pattern of marriage based on sexual equality. In such families the division of labor is based on the skills and abilities of each partner rather than on their gender, and decision-making power is equally shared. Although many families already function in this manner, our traditional standards lead some people to brand any deviation from the customary patterns as wrong and unnatural, and the entire family system is weakened by this attitude. Public opinion polls show that the ideal of sexual equality is gaining increasing acceptance, but that those who condemn any violation of traditional standards remain a significant group. In 1970, 63 percent of Americans said they would have less respect for a man who stayed home with his children, but by 1985 that figure had dropped to 25 percent.[62]

Today, more couples are sharing child-rearing responsibilities by allowing each member to perform
the tasks he or she does best regardless of sexual
stereotypes.

Helping Single Parents   The evidence shows that a strong program of family planning
that makes birth control directly available to teenagers could significantly
reduce the number of unmarried teenage mothers (see Chapter 11). But whatever measures we take, the number of single-parent families is likely to keep
increasing for the immediate future, and much more needs to be done to
deal with their special problems. Women head most single-parent families,
and an effective program to eliminate sexual discrimination in the work
place would go a long way toward reducing the acute financial problems
experienced by many of these families. But to reach all needy families, the
government must also increase its direct welfare benefits to poor families
whether headed by one or two parents (see Chapter 6).

Another important step would be the creation of government-supported
day care centers, as has already been done in many European countries.
Federal financing would reduce the economic problems faced by both single-
and two-parent families, and increased government supervision would help
to ensure the highest possible standards were met. Nonetheless, opposition
to this plan has been strong. Critics argue that government agencies are poor
substitutes for parents and point to the bureaucratic indifference and cold-
ness that are typical of many orphanages, institutions for delinquents, and
schools. They fear that day care centers will harm children by depriving
them of motherly love. Advocates of day care centers respond that children
in day care still have ample contact with their parents and that properly run
day care centers enrich children's lives rather than deprive them. Alison
Clarke-Stewart's study of children in average or above-average day care centers found no evidence of harm done to the children. In fact, the day care
children were more advanced in cognitive and social skills than children
who stayed home.[63]

Expanding the Kinship Network   The nuclear family system is clearly well suited to
life in modern industrialized societies. But the fact remains that the nuclear
family, no matter how strong, is not as effective as the traditional extended

family in performing many social functions. For this reason some people long for a return to the extended family system. But this dream is unrealistic. No attempt to turn back the clock and reestablish the family system of the past is likely to withstand the economic and political forces that broke up the extended family in the first place.

Nevertheless, members of modern nuclear families have more significant contacts with their relatives than is commonly believed. And establishing even closer ties among relatives can provide one of the most practical and effective solutions to the problems of the family. Of course, this solution will not work for everyone. Many people simply have no compatible relatives living nearby who are willing to help. A more radical step in the same direction are the attempts to establish what might be called "substitute kinship networks" through communal family living.

A **commune** is a close-knit group of people living together in a supportive family environment that offers many of the advantages of the extended family. Ideally, the group provides love, financial assistance, and emotional support for children and adults alike. But most do not survive. Administrative authority often becomes a critical problem. Democratic communes in which members' independence is paramount may find it difficult to get even the simplest household tasks done. Communes with powerful leaders and a common ideology are more efficient. Things get done. But in such authoritarian settings conflicts are inevitable. Some members eventually come to believe that they are being exploited and either rebel or leave. Another source of problems is the fact that most of the people living in modern communes come from nuclear families that have not prepared them for life in a commune. Finally, many communes disband because of harassment from neighbors who neither understand nor accept the communal life style. Although some rural communes succeed in isolating themselves from outsiders, most communes must expend precious economic, psychological, and social resources to protect themselves from the hostility of outsiders.

SOCIOLOGICAL PERSPECTIVES ON PROBLEMS OF THE FAMILY

Concern for the "decaying" family is nothing new. Because the family is such a basic social institution, it has always been the center of great social concern. But the rapid change that the family has undergone since the industrial revolution has created new and difficult problems for sociologists to study and has led to considerable debate among the proponents of the different sociological theories.

The Functionalist Perspective Functional analyses of human society have led many sociologists to conclude that the family is *the* most basic social institution. Not only is it found in one form or another in all societies, but no other social institution is responsible for performing as many important tasks. Most of us begin and end our lives in the family context, and we are seldom far from its influence during the years in between.

Most social scientists agree that the family's most important function is to provide replacements for those members who have died or are disabled.[64] Such replacement has four aspects. First, the family *provides for reproduction* by creating a stable mating relationship that supports the mother during the pregnancy and the children during the critical early months of life. Second, the family *socializes the young*. It is in the family that the child learns how to think, talk, and follow the customs, behavior, and values of his or her society. The family, therefore, is an important agency of social control. Third, the family *provides support and protection* for its children. The family must satisfy a wide range of emotional needs as well as physical needs for food and shelter. Fourth, the family is a primary *mechanism of status ascription*. Each child is given a social status on the basis of the family into which he or she is born. Thus, children of the wealthy are automatically upper class, while children of low-income families are assigned to the bottom rungs of the social ladder. The family also performs important functions for adults. It provides emotional support and reinforcement and is a primary group of great importance. It provides physical care and support in times of illness and old age. The family also transfers wealth from parents to young children and, later, from older children to aging parents.

Functionalists see family problems as stemming from the disorganization caused by industrialization. The extended family is compatible with the traditional cultures in which it is found but ill suited to the modern industrial world. Industrialization broke up the extended family and forced changes in the nuclear family system. The resultant disorganization and the structural weaknesses of the nuclear family have made it increasingly difficult for the family to perform its functions efficiently. Nor did change cease with the industrial revolution. The increase in the number of women in the work force and the ideal of sexual equality are bringing about another realignment of family structure. From the functionalist perspective, the present family system is in trouble because it has not had enough time to adapt to these ceaseless social and economic changes.

Functionalists agree that the prosperity and even the survival of contemporary society depend on the strength of its family system. However, functional analysis does not lead to any single proposal for improvement. One possibility would be for other agencies—such as day care centers and schools—to assume more of the family's functions, permitting the family to handle its remaining functions more effectively. Another approach is to promote trial marriages as a test of compatibility and easier divorce for marriages that fail. However, many functionalists fear that such proposals would contribute to the erosion of the traditional family and the vital functions it performs. These functionalists therefore recommend a return to the values associated with the traditional nuclear family, such as a stronger prohibition of divorce and greater restrictions on sexual behavior.

The Conflict Perspective Many conflicts of values and attitudes affect the modern family. Traditionalists place great importance on the value of a stable family environment for child rearing and thus reject the idea of divorce; modernists see personal happiness as the most important goal of family life and believe that a child will suffer more from an unhappy home than from a broken one. Traditionalists are convinced that sexual relations should be restricted to one's spouse; modernists advocate greater sexual freedom. Modernists condemn traditional attitudes toward women as exploitive and unjust, and they support full sexual equality. Traditionalists, in contrast, are likely to believe that male dominance is based on innate differences between the sexes and that any other sort of family relationship is unnatural. Traditionalists condemn the increase in dual-earner families and working women as a threat to the welfare of children. Modernists see the increasing financial power of women as a positive development that may help create a more egalitarian family and a more just society.

When conflict theorists look beneath these conflicts in values they see a fundamental struggle between male dominance and female liberation. Freidrich Engels felt that the oppression of women in the family was the original form of human exploitation. Present-day conflict theorists argue that the traditional family is organized for the benefit of the husband at the expense of his wife. The husband has more authority, prestige, and independence, while the wife must carry out the subordinate role. It would be wrong to assume that these statements apply to all families. There are certainly egalitarian families, and families in which the wife plays the dominant role, but conflict theorists hold that these are the exceptions, not the rule.

Conflict theorists are also concerned about the effects class conflict has on the family. The poor have significantly higher rates of divorce, illegitimacy, and overall family instability than do other classes, and conflict theorists attribute these conditions to exploitation of the poor by the upper classes. For instance, many men cannot get decent jobs because the financial pressures of a life of poverty and the low quality of local public schools prevented them from learning basic reading, writing, and mathematical skills. Because these men cannot provide their families with the standard of living our society has led everyone to expect, they come to see themselves as failures. This sense of failure may in turn lead to a host of other problems, including the breakup of the family, alcoholism, and violence against other family members.

In the eyes of most conflict theorists, the solution to family problems will come only from greater equality, both within the family and in society as a whole. They recommend that the government undertake a vigorous program to eliminate occupational discrimination against women and minorities, and make a serious effort to reduce unemployment and the overall levels of economic inequality in our society (see Chapters 2, 6, 7, and 10 for more details). They also support proposals for a nationwide system of federally funded day care centers and shelter houses for the victims of wife abuse. Finally, they advocate a concerted effort to combat sexism in all sectors of our society, including education, business, and the media, to free women from exploitation by men

Social Psychological Perspectives   Most social psychologists have focused on the family's role in the socialization of children. Social psychological research has linked faulty socialization to problems ranging from mental disorder to juvenile delinquency. Clearly, some families socialize their children to play conformist roles, whereas other families encourage children to behave in ways that others consider indecent and even illegal. But most problems with the process of socialization in the family come from neglect and indifference or, in more extreme cases, from the hostility and even violence parents direct at their children. For adults, the nuclear family's most critical social psychological role is to provide emotional support and comfort. For some, the family is the only shelter from the relentless demands of modern civilization—the one place where the individual can develop a sense of stability and belonging—and for that reason dissension and conflict within the family can have devastating psychological consequences for all its members.

Social psychologists point to several possible ways to create the kind of stable, emotionally supportive families that do an effective job of socializing their children and providing security and comfort for all their members. The ideal of romantic love is so heavily emphasized in our culture that young people approach marriage expecting more of each other than either can possibly give. Too often they end up bitter and disappointed when their romantic fantasies fail to come true. More realistic expectations, encouraged by schools and the mass media, may be one way of solving the problem. Another approach to creating more supportive families would be to promote the development of the kinds of alternative family forms discussed earlier, thereby generating a wider network of kin and friends to share the emotional burdens of family life. Such family structures might also do a better job of socializing children. Because more adults would be involved in the socialization of each child, the harmful effects of an incompetent or abusive parent could be neutralized more easily.

SUMMARY

The institution of the family is found in all societies, but in many different forms. The two main types of family are the *extended family* and the *nuclear family*. The nuclear family consists of a married couple and their children. The extended family usually includes several generations of parents, grandparents, and children and is typical of agricultural societies. The demands of the modern industrial system place tremendous pressure on these large, cumbersome family units. As industrialization has transformed one country after another, the nuclear family has largely replaced the extended family. The traditional extended family had the sole responsibility for many different tasks, but in modern society the family's role is supplemented by specialized government agencies such as schools and juvenile courts.

The modern family has continued to change even after the breakup of the extended family, and three trends are particularly important. First, declining birthrates, the increase in single-parent families, and the tendency to stay unmarried longer have led to a steady decline in the size of the average household. Second, the sharp increase in the number of women working outside the home and the growing popularity of the ideals of sexual equality have led to major changes in the roles that husbands and wives play in many contemporary families. Third, despite generations of rapid change most of us continue to see the family as one of the most important and satisfying facets of our daily lives.

Of all family problems, the rising divorce rate has generated the most public concern. This trend has many causes. As the extended family has deteriorated, married couples have become freer to divorce. At the same time, the stigma against divorce has decreased. Because love and personal happiness are receiving increasing emphasis, there is greater willingness to end marriages that fail to achieve these goals. Both women and men are more economically independent than in the past, and it is usually easier for them to live apart after a divorce. Many problems are associated with divorce, including personal stress, family instability, and increased difficulty in child rearing. But it is not at all clear that divorce is worse than the alternative of continuing an unhappy marriage.

Like divorce, the number of births to single mothers has increased in recent years. There seems to be a growing reluctance on the part of young couples to marry just because of pregnancy. The unmarried mother who keeps her child has many of the problems experienced by other single-parent families, but because so many of these mothers are teenagers, they are generally less prepared for the changes a baby brings into their lives.

Although there are no dependable statistics, it appears that violence between husband and wife is a common way of settling disputes and leads to a substantial number of injuries and homicides every year. Another form of family violence, child abuse, is even more dangerous because the victims are unable to defend themselves. Studies indicate that child abuse is most likely to occur in large families with low incomes in which the natural father is not present. Many explanations of child abuse have been advanced, including emotional disturbances in the parents and the transmission of child abuse from one generation to the next through learning.

Because the modern nuclear family often has little support from its kinship network, child rearing can be difficult. The single-parent family in particular is likely to have economic and behavioral problems because a single adult must play all the roles that are customarily divided between two people.

Another source of strain in the modern family is the changing expectations about the behavior of husbands and wives. Because increasing numbers of women have gone to work outside the home, and because there are now a variety of alternatives to traditional sex roles, the expectations of husband and wife may conflict. One particularly common problem is that the burdens of housework are not fairly reallocated to take into account the time working women must put in on the job.

Many proposals have been made for resolving problems in the family. One approach would strengthen the existing nuclear family system through education, marriage counseling, and a reduction of unwanted births among teenage girls. Sexual equality and greater fairness within the marriage are also frequent suggestions. Many people recommend expansion of the kinship network and a return to something similar to the extended family.

Sociologists of the functionalist school are convinced that problems of the family are symptoms of the social disorganization caused by rapid social change. Industrialization broke up the extended family but has not produced a strong nuclear family system to replace it. Conflict theorists note the many conflicting values and beliefs about modern family life and point to them as a major source of problems. They also stress the notion that many problems, from divorce to family violence, arise because modern society allows the powerful to make profits at the expense of the weak and encourages the exploitation of women by their husbands. Social psychologists are concerned about the ineffectiveness of the nuclear family as a socializing agency. They hope to encourage the development of stable families that will provide continuity in children's lives and, at the same time, provide more security and emotional support for all family members.

KEY TERMS

dual-earner family
extended family
family
monogamy

nuclear family
pushout
runaway
single-parent family

FURTHER READINGS

The Contemporary Family
Randall Collins, *Sociology of Marriage and the Family: Gender, Love, and Property*, 2d ed., Chicago: Nelson-Hall, 1988.
James M. Henslin (ed.), *Marriage and Family in a Changing Society*, New York: The Free Press, 1985.

Problems of Child Rearing
Sheila Kamerman, *Parenting in an Unresponsive Society*, New York: Wiley & Sons, 1981.
Alison Clarke-Stewart, *Daycare*, Cambridge, Mass.: Harvard University Press, 1982.

Family Violence
Mildred Daley Pagelow, *Family Violence*, New York: Praeger, 1984.
Murray Straus et al., *Behind Closed Doors: A Survey of Family Violence in America*, Garden City, N.Y.: Anchor Books, 1980.

Divorce and Financial Problems
Andrew V. Cherlin, *Marriage, Divorce and Remarriage*, Cambridge, Mass: Harvard University Press, 1981.
Marian Wright Edelman, *Families in Peril*, Cambridge, Mass.: Harvard University Press, 1987.

PART TWO
The Problems
of Inequality

Chapter 6
THE POOR

The modern industrial economy has produced fantastic wealth. Middle-class Americans have luxuries that were undreamed of in past centuries, and an image of mass luxury and comfort is reflected daily in television dramas, movies, and books. But there is an underside to our industrial affluence— the millions of faceless people who do not share in the abundance. Poverty is a basic characteristic of our industrial society; it is the other side of affluence.

The poor in North America do not look like the starving millions in famine zones of the Third World, but their misery is just as real. Poverty can be more difficult in a rich country than in a poor one. There is no shame in poverty in India because most people are poor; but the North American poor are constantly confronted by the affluence that they are denied.

Although the poor are a minority in every sense of the word, they are a sizable one. According to official government estimates there were over 32 million poor people in the United States in 1986, which means that 13.6 percent of all Americans were poor.[1] Such figures should, however, be viewed with a skeptical eye, for as we will see, there is considerable debate about how to determine if someone is poor or not. But whatever measure is used, the problem is an enormous one.

Despite the appearance of widespread affluence, some of the worst slums in the industrial world are found in North America. Poor nutrition, nagging hunger, shabby clothing, and a crowded room or two in a deteriorating old building are all that many families can hope for. Moreover, North Americans' attitudes toward the poor appear remarkably callous when compared with those of people in many European countries.

THE RICH AND THE POOR

Poverty and wealth are closely related. In North America and in most of the rest of the world, the good things of life are not distributed evenly, and wealth is concentrated in the hands of a few individuals and families. The deprivation of some people creates abundance for others. We must therefore look at the problem of poverty as part of the larger issue of social and economic inequality.

Economic Inequality: The Widening Gap There are two ways of determining the extent of economic inequality: by measuring differences in income and by measuring differences in wealth. Although these two yardsticks are related, there are some important differences between them. **Income** refers to the amount of money a person makes in a given year; **wealth** is a person's total assets: real estate and personal property, stocks, bonds, cash, and so forth.

The distribution of income in the United States is extremely unequal. In 1985 the richest 20 percent of American families received 43.7 percent of all income, while the poorest 20 percent received only 4.6 percent. The top 5 percent received 17.0 percent of the total income—more than three times as much as the poorest 20 percent of American families.[2]

Examining the distribution of wealth is more difficult because the Census Bureau does not publish yearly reports as it does for the distribution of income. However, all the available research indicates that wealth is far more unequally distributed than income. A study made for the Joint Economic Committee of Congress concluded that in 1983 a small group of "super rich" families (about one half of one percent of the population) owned 35 percent of all assets. The top 10 percent owned about 72 percent of all assets, while the other 90 percent of the people shared only a little more than a quarter of the wealth. But as bad as these figures are, the reality may be even worse. The single major asset of most American families is their home, and if that is dropped from the figures the top 1 percent own over half of all wealth.[3] A study by Daphne Greenwood indicates that the bottom 30 percent of the population have virtually no measurable wealth because their debts equal or exceed their assets[4].

Why is wealth so much more unequally distributed than income? There appear to be two principal reasons. First, lower-income people usually have to spend everything they make just to get by and are therefore unable to build up savings accounts or investments. Second, wealth tends to be passed on from one generation to another. Poor people usually have poor parents and receive no inheritance. Wealthy people, on the other hand, usually have wealthy parents and are much more likely to come into a substantial estate. (See Figure 6.1.)

Although many Americans see their country as the land of opportunity and equality, international comparisons do not bear out this view. There is far more economic inequality in the poor nations of the Third World than in any of the developed countries. But most research shows the United States and France to have the highest economic inequality of any industrialized nations, while Japan and the Scandinavian countries have the lowest.[5] The

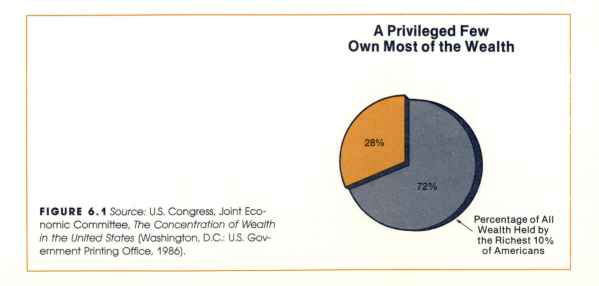

A Privileged Few Own Most of the Wealth

28%

72%

Percentage of All Wealth Held by the Richest 10% of Americans

FIGURE 6.1 *Source:* U.S. Congress, Joint Economic Committee, *The Concentration of Wealth in the United States* (Washington, D.C.: U.S. Government Printing Office, 1986).

In our materialistic society, people are judged as much by what they have as by who they are. Thus along with their material abundance, the children of the wealthy receive the assurance that they are valuable and important individuals. Because the children of the poor lack so many of the things everyone is "supposed" to have, they often feel that there is something wrong with them or their families.

But the poor are deprived of more than just material possessions. In comparison with the sophistication and elegance of the rich, those brought up in poverty appear to speak crudely, with heavy accents and a limited vocabulary. They have less education, are less informed about the world, and are less likely to vote. Significant numbers of poor people cannot even read or write. In such an environment, the poor can hardly avoid feelings of insecurity, inadequacy, and frustration. Some bottle up those feelings, contributing to the high rates of schizophrenia and psychosomatic illnesses among the poor. In others, the hostility and anger is expressed in violent crime. The rates of murder, assault, and rape are all much higher among poor people than the rest of the population (see Chapter 15).

Economic uncertainty is also a part of being poor. Even the poor people who are lucky enough to have a permanent job work in the low-paying dead-end positions that are the first to be cut in bad economic times. Others work as temporary laborers or are simply unemployed. To make this insecurity even worse, the poor have far higher rates of family instability than the rest of society. The poor marry younger and have the highest rates of divorce, separation, family violence, and childbirth by single women.

This pattern of inequality even carries over into matters of life and death. We hear a great deal about medical miracles like artificial hearts and organ transplants, but these miracles are reserved for people with health insurance. As a rule, the poor receive second-rate health care, a deficient diet, and inadequate shelter. Consequently, they have twice the rate of infant mortality, triple the rate of premature births, and double the rate of maternal deaths from childbirth than the rest of the population.[11] The poor are also more likely to contract contagious diseases, and their average life span is considerably shorter than that of wealthy people.

MEASURING POVERTY

Even though everyone has a general idea of what poverty is, it is a difficult term to define precisely. Certainly, poor people lack some of the goods and services that others enjoy. This may mean insufficient food, shelter, clothing, or entertainment, but how much is "insufficient"? Are people poor if they have no means of private transportation at all, no bicycle, no car, only one car? Everyone agrees that some people are poor, but it is difficult to draw a precise line between those who are poor and those who are not.

The Absolute and the Relative Approach   Poverty may be defined in two ways: absolute and relative. The **absolute approach** divides the poor from the nonpoor by using some objective standard, such as the lack of money to purchase adequate food, shelter, and clothing. The **relative approach** holds that people are poor if they have significantly less income and wealth than the average person in their society.

Supporters of the relative approach argue that what is really important is not the fact that the poor have a low standard of living but that they are psychologically and sociologically excluded from the mainstream of society. In this view, people come to need what their society tells them they should have. To the average American, who needs a great deal, the migrant farm workers on the bottom rung of the social ladder lack the essentials for comfortable living. Yet these beliefs obviously are not shared by the hundreds of thousands who enter the United States to become migrant workers. In the social world of the Mexican villager, these jobs represent affluence, not poverty.

But despite the appeal of such arguments, the absolute approach is far more widely used both by government agencies and social scientists—perhaps because what most concerns the public is not the **relative deprivation** of the poor but the fact that they lack sufficient food, shelter, and clothing.

Every year the U.S. government publishes a "poverty line" for several different types of families. If a family's income falls below the line, they are officially considered to be poor. The poverty line was originally based on studies showing that the average low-income family spent about a third of its budget on food. The Department of Agriculture's Economy Food Budget was then multiplied by three to calculate the poverty line. Beginning at $3000 in 1964, the poverty line for a family of four had reached $11,203 by 1986.[12]

Although such precise numbers make the poverty line sound fair and objective, it is actually a rather arbitrary figure. A different approach to these computations could easily lead to a very different figure, and there is considerable debate about whether the poverty line is too high or too low. Some conservatives feel that it is too high (thus overestimating the amount of poverty), because welfare benefits that are not given in cash, such as food stamps and medicaid, are not counted as income. Advocates for the poor counter that the original calculation that a poor family spends a third of its income on food didn't count such benefits either (although it is true that benefits are higher now than they were in 1964). Furthermore, they point out that the Department of Agriculture itself admits that the Economy Food Budget was intended only as a temporary or emergency budget and is not adequate to meet long-term nutritional needs. Moreover, in 1969 the government stopped adjusting the poverty line on the basis of the rising cost of food and used a measure of overall inflation instead. But the cost of food and other necessities has gone up much faster than the consumer price index as a whole, thus leading to a lower estimate of the amount of poverty.[13] When it was first created, the poverty line was about 50 percent of the average income of an American family, but now it is only about 40 percent.[14] Significantly, when the Department of Labor defined a "high," a "moderate," and a "low" budget for a family of four, their low budget was about three-fourths higher than the official poverty line.[15]

Is Poverty Increasing or Decreasing? Once a standard for measuring poverty is established, social scientists can use it to explore many important issues. But it is important to remember that the results often depend on the assumptions made at the beginning. Some relative definitions of poverty, for example, hold that a person is poor if his or her income is in the bottom 10, 15, or 20 percent of the population. Using such a definition, the rate of poverty never changes unless we change our definition of poverty. With other relative definitions, the amount of poverty varies with changes in economic inequality, which as we have seen, has increased significantly in recent years.

A look at the official government statistics based on an absolute definition also reveals some interesting trends. According to these figures poverty declined sharply in the 1960s: from over 22 percent of the total population at the start of the decade, to around 11 percent in the early 1970s. The two main reasons for this improvement were the economic prosperity of the times and a strong government commitment to what was known as the War on Poverty. In the middle 1970s the oil crisis sent the economy into a tailspin, and the poverty rate leveled off. Continuing economic problems and a sharp reduction of government assistance to the poor sent the poverty rate back up in the early 1980s, peaking at over 15 percent in 1984. Economic recovery sent the poverty rate back down in the late 1980s, but without a reversal in government priorities, it seems likely to increase substantially with the next recession.[16]

WHO ARE THE POOR?

One of the major reasons for trying to determine who is poor and who is not to discover which segments of our society have the greatest poverty and what the differences are between different groups of poor people. Studies show that the chances of being poor are influenced by many general characteristics, including age, gender, family structure, and ethnic background. But the poor are as diverse as the middle class or the wealthy, and there are at least three important groups of poor people who deserve special attention: the homeless, the working poor, and the underclass.

General Characteristics

Family Structure, Gender, and Age The rapid growth in the number of single-parent families (see Chapter 5) has had a major impact on the problem of poverty. From 1970 to 1986 the percentage of all families headed by a single woman (the vast majority of all single-parent families) almost doubled from 10.8 to 21.0 percent.[17] And because such families have an extremely high poverty rate, single mothers and their children are the fastest-growing segment of the poverty population. In fact, about two-thirds of all families below the poverty line are now headed by single women, and the poverty rate in such families is almost two and one-half times the rate for the total population. Largely as a result of this trend and the higher birthrates among the poor, children under 18 are now almost 50 percent more likely to be poor

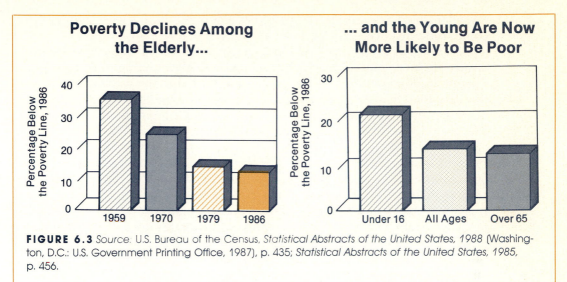

FIGURE 6.3 *Source:* U.S. Bureau of the Census, *Statistical Abstracts of the United States, 1988* (Washington, D.C.: U.S. Government Printing Office, 1987), p. 435; *Statistical Abstracts of the United States, 1985,* p. 456.

than the average American. In 1986, 19.8 percent of all American children lived below the poverty line.[18] (See Figure 6.3.)

Although there are many reasons why so many families headed by a single woman are poor, the fact that women with dependent children find it difficult to hold full-time jobs is a major factor. But even if these women find and hold jobs, sex discrimination often confines them to low-paying service, clerical, or sales positions. Welfare is often the only means of survival for these families, yet that too has been sharply reduced in recent years.

At the same time that the poverty rate has been rising among the young, it has been dropping for the old. Although the elderly used to have the highest poverty rate of any age group, it is now substantially below average. In 1986 the poverty rate for persons over 65 was 12.4 percent, which was 1.2 percent points below the national average.[19] Although the health problems and impaired mobility experienced by many elderly people mean that they may actually need a higher income to live at the same standard of living as younger people, there has nonetheless been a dramatic improvement in their overall financial status. And the reason for that much needed improvement is a single government program: social security. Since 1970, increases in social security checks have been tied to the cost of living, and because of the way the formula was written, the real spending power of those checks (after correcting for inflation) has actually increased 25 percent since then.[20]

Ethnic Background Contrary to popular stereotypes, most poor people in the United States are white, not black. Census figures indicate that about two-thirds of all poor people are white. However, the *percentage* of whites below the poverty line is considerably lower than the percentage of minorities below that line. For example, about 11 percent of all whites were poor in 1986, compared with over 31 percent of all blacks.[21]

In 1986, the average white family earned $29,152, and the average black family 16,786.[22] Moreover, unemployment is higher among most minorities. The unemployment rate for blacks is usually double the rate for whites, and the rate for Hispanics is only slightly lower. To make matters worse, discrimination in housing and various other services often means that minorities must spend more than whites for the same goods and services.

Place of Residence   When we think of the poor, most of us see crowded urban ghettos. But the percentage of rural people below the poverty line is actually greater than the percentage of urban people below that line, despite the fact that most poor people live in the large metropolitan centers.[23] Unemployment is generally higher in rural areas, while wages are lower. The mechanization of agriculture has left many unskilled rural people with no means of support. What work they can find tends to be seasonal, and those who follow the harvest fare little better than those who try to hire out at home. Migratory workers have a very high poverty rate, as do native Americans who live on barren reservations where it is impossible for them to make a living.

The urban poor in run-down city slums remain the largest group in terms of numbers, and they share many of the problems of the rural poor. Although there are more economic opportunities in the cities, urban slum dwellers are often denied an equal chance to succeed. Lacking adequate transportation, job skills, and a decent education, and often facing ethnic or racial discrimination, the urban poor are unable to take advantage of opportunities available to the affluent.

The Underclass   Most people who fall below the poverty line do not stay there their entire life. Greg Duncan and his colleagues found that about half of the people who were below the poverty line between 1969 and 1978 were poor for less than two years.[24] Typically, the loss of a job, a divorce, a serious health problem, or some other personal crisis pushes these people below the poverty line. Eventually, when their problem is resolved, their income goes up again. But there is another group of poor people, the so-called **underclass,** who are isolated from the mainstream of American society and who suffer repeated long-term bouts of poverty.

Although this underclass has been the focus of a great deal of recent sociological attention, there are several different ways of defining it, different estimates of its size, and even disagreements about the usefulness of the term itself. Robert Hill of the National Urban League estimated that 30 percent of those below the poverty line are "acutely poor," another estimate put the figure at 45 percent,[25] while Bane and Ellwood concluded that 60 percent of those who are poor "remain poor for a very long time."[26]

Whatever its exact size, the underclass is, in the words of sociologist William Julius Wilson, "the heart of the problem of poverty."[27] Members of the underclass are far more likely to have been raised in poverty than the population of poor people as a whole. They tend to come from single-parent families with a poor educational background and a history of welfare dependency. A substantial proportion of the people in the underclass can't read or write and lack other basic job skills. As a result, they are trapped in a self-perpetuating cycle of poverty that is extremely hard to break. Studies of social mobility show that it is less likely that members of the underclass will improve their economic position than it is for those above them in the social hierarchy.[28] The frustration and hopelessness of life in the underclass exacts a heavy toll. Compared with other Americans, members of the underclass have significantly higher rates of mental disorder, alcoholism, drug abuse, and suicide, and they more often fall victim to murder and other violent crimes.

The Homeless We have all seen them—the bag ladies who push around everything they own in a rusty shopping cart, the disheveled men sleeping on park benches or over heating grates to keep warm, an entire family living in an abandoned car. Of all the many forms of poverty, there is little doubt that the homeless are the most deprived. Protection from the elements is the most obvious problem they face: in the summer they swelter, and in the winter some literally freeze to death. But even getting enough food to eat is a continual problem for many of the homeless. Because they are almost always on the streets, they are easy targets for criminals and thugs. And aside from a few overworked charity and social-work agencies, the homeless confront a society that seems indifferent to their plight. The police to whom most of us turn for protection see the homeless as a nuisance who must be moved out or arrested when their numbers become too great.

There is, once again, considerable disagreement about exactly how many Americans are actually homeless. The U.S. Department of Housing and Urban Development estimated that there are only 250,000–350,000 homeless in the United States.[29] But a subcommittee of the House of Representatives later charged that HUD had pressured its consultants to keep their estimate low. The Department of Health and Human Services put the number of homeless Americans at about 2 million, and a 1987 estimate from the Coalition for the Homeless put the figure at 3–4 million.[30] One thing about which virtually everyone agrees is that the number of homeless men and women has grown substantially in recent years.

There are several reasons why homelessness appears to have increased even in years when poverty has not. The most popular explanation is that the deinstitutionalization movement, which sharply reduced the population of our mental hospitals, has left many severely disturbed patients to wander the streets (see Chapter 12). Although there is little doubt that this has contributed to the ranks of the homeless, it is not the only factor. Articles in national magazines such as *Time, Newsweek,* and *People* have claimed that the majority of the homeless are mentally disturbed, but several scientific studies have put the figure much lower than 50 percent. Most research sug-

The number of homeless women and men has increased sharply in recent years. This photo shows a homeless man, who spends his nights walking the streets or riding buses, being interviewed by a researcher.

gests that somewhere around a third of the homeless have mental problems.[31] A recent study of homeless adults in Texas found that only about 10 percent had psychiatric problems and concluded that, "The most common face on the street is not that of the psychiatrically-impaired individual, but one caught in a cycle of low-paying, dead-end jobs that fail to provide the means to get off and stay off the streets."[32] Another cause of the increase in the numbers of the homeless is that the federal government seems to have turned its back on their problems. Since 1985 the amount of money spent on federal housing subsidies, for example, has been cut by over 75 percent. Moreover, high inflation in the cost of rental housing has simply priced many poor people out of the market. One study found that the poverty population of 12 large U.S. cities increased 36 percent between the late 1970s and the early 1980s, while the supply of low-income housing decreased by 30 percent.[33]

The Working Poor   Many people assume that the solution to the problem of poverty is simply to find jobs for the poor. But statistics from the U.S. Bureau of the Census show that in 1984 almost one in ten poor adults worked full-time the entire year, and of course, many more poor people worked part-time or for part of the year.[34] One estimate holds that almost 7 million poor people worked over 30 hours a week in 1987. Furthermore, the working poor have been one of the fastest-growing segments of the poverty population—increasing by 50 percent from 1975 to 1986.[35] How can so many people hold full-time or nearly full-time jobs and still be poor? The answer is simple. A person working full-time at minimum wage for an entire year will earn less than $7000. That is barely enough to keep a single person above the poverty line, and far below the $11,203 a year necessary to keep a family of four out of poverty.[36]

Despite working long hours for little pay, the working poor do have some important advantages over other poor people. Psychologically, they have the self-respect that comes from knowing that they are working and contributing to society. They also have far better prospects of eventually moving out of poverty. But unfortunately, a great many poor people do not really have the option of working, even if they could find a job. About a third are below the age of 15, and another substantial group are elderly or in bad health. Even the welfare mothers who bear the brunt of so much criticism cannot realistically be expected to take a minimum wage job without continued public assistance, since the cost of child care alone would eat up most of their take-home pay.

UNDERSTANDING THE WELFARE SYSTEM

Before we can go on to examine the general causes of poverty, we must first take a look at the welfare system, which has become so much a part of the phenomenon of poverty in the twentieth century. And the first step toward understanding the welfare system is to understand the public's attitude toward the poor.

Attitudes Toward the Poor   The rejection of the old European class system and the availability of a vast new land to conquer helped create a tremendous faith in the value of hard work and competition among North Americans. To this way of thinking, each individual is responsible for his or her own economic destiny. Many people believe that even in a period of economic depression and high unemployment, anyone who works hard enough can be successful. It is also generally held that "there is always room at the top" for capable and hardworking people, no matter how humble their origins.

Despite its attractiveness, this belief in individual responsibility has a negative side. If the rich are personally responsible for their success, it follows that the poor are to blame for their failure. "Poor folks have poor ways," the old saying goes. Joe Feagin has summarized the principal points in this "ideology of individualism" as follows:

1. Each individual should work hard and strive to succeed in competition with others.
2. Those who work hard should be rewarded with success (seen as wealth, property, prestige, and power).
3. Because of widespread and equal opportunity, those who work hard will in fact be rewarded with success.
4. Economic failure is an individual's own fault and reveals lack of effort and other character defects.[37]

19th-Century Social Problems

Within 5 miles of Milton Junction and in a thickly settled part of Rock County, Mrs. Ira Ames starved and froze to death. The case was reported to the authorities at Janesville and it was found that the father had spent most of his time fishing while his wife and 7 children were in a rickety shanty without fuel or food. The youngest child died a week ago and was buried under the snow by the father in a soap box.

March 16, 1893

These selections, which appear throughout the text, are from the *Badger State Banner*, a newspaper published in Black River Falls, Wisconsin.

A recent nationwide survey showed that this ideology is still a potent force in American life. When asked about the causes of poverty, most of the people surveyed responded with individualistic explanations that blame the poor themselves, rather than with structural explanations that hold society responsible or with fatalistic explanations that blame such things as bad luck or illness. For example, 58 percent of the respondents said that lack of thrift and proper money management are significant causes of poverty, and 55 percent said that lack of effort by the poor is a very important cause of poverty.[38]

The ideology of individualism has had an enormous impact on the response to poverty in both the United States and Canada. Those receiving government assistance are stigmatized even when they are recognized as "legitimately poor" or "truly needy." Welfare programs tend to be designed in such a way that obtaining benefits is difficult and degrading. Piven and Cloward argued that the growth of the modern welfare system resulted more from an attempt to silence the political discontent of the poor than from a desire to improve their living conditions, and their findings have been supported by several more recent studies.[39]

The History of the Welfare System In traditional societies many people lived close to the subsistence level, but poverty did not carry a strong stigma. The extended family had the primary responsibility for the welfare of its members. However, the industrial revolution fostered the growth of small nuclear families, which are often too weak and isolated to care for their members in times of distress. At the same time, industrialization took more and more people from the land, where most could at least scratch out enough food to avoid starvation. As a result, the government was slowly required to assume an increasing share of the responsibility for the poor.

Modern welfare systems can be traced to England, where the effects of the industrial revolution first appeared. Thousands of peasant farmers were thrown off the land and migrated to the towns in search of work and freedom, and political power slowly shifted from the landed aristocracy to manufacturers and businesspeople. These elites responded to the mass migration in two contradictory ways. First, they enacted vagrancy laws that punished "sturdy beggars" (people who were able but seemingly unwilling to work). Second, they began giving government assistance to the "deserving poor." England's sixteenth-century Poor Laws placed the responsibility for the care of the poor with local officials, requiring them to establish poorhouses for the sick, disabled, and aged and work programs for the able-bodied poor and their children.[40]

The North American colonies copied the English Poor Laws, and as in England, public welfare was made a local responsibility. Outsiders were not eligible for aid and were forced to leave town if they showed signs of becoming destitute. Mayors opened fairs and other public meetings by asking "all idle and evilly disposed persons" to depart. The destitute were publicly stigmatized. In Pennsylvania, for instance, poor people had to wear the letter P on one of their sleeves. Those who were considered idlers or vagrants were punished. Massachusetts, Rhode Island, and Connecticut all had laws calling for the whipping or imprisonment of the able-bodied unemployed.[41]

Urbanization, industrialization, and the steady flow of immigrants produced a growing poverty problem in North America during the eighteenth and nineteenth centuries. But attitudes toward the poor seemed to grow even more hostile. As in England, workhouses were established for the poor. In these institutions employment was furnished for those who were able to work, and industrial training was provided for the young. The theory was that workhouses would cure the character defects that the poor were presumed to have, converting them to a life of Christian hard work and sober living. Poorhouses continued to shelter the aged and disabled, and houses of correction were established to compel vagrants and other sturdy beggars to work. Private welfare organizations also grew rapidly.

Few changes were made in this welfare system until the Great Depression of the 1930s, when unemployment rose dramatically and armies of the newly impoverished demanded assistance: "Groups of men out of work congregated at local relief agencies, cornered and harassed administrators, and took over offices until their demands were met."[42] Despite such determined protests, reforms were made grudgingly. Poor relief was still largely a local matter, but cities and counties proved unable to shoulder the financial burden. The federal government began to give small direct cash payments to the unemployed, but it soon shifted to work relief programs, which were more in tune with the ideology of individualism. With the coming of President Franklin D. Roosevelt's New Deal, a host of new government agencies were created to make work for unemployed Americans. But public opposition to these and other welfare programs remained strong through the Depression, and one of the few New Deal programs that still survives is Old Age and Survivors' Insurance (social security), which requires workers and their employers to set aside money for the workers' old age and for surviving dependents at the time of the insured person's death.

The 1950s brought only modest increases in welfare support for the poor, but a "welfare explosion" occurred in the 1960s. From December 1960 to February 1969, Aid to Families with Dependent Children (AFDC) increased by 107 percent.[43] Daniel Patrick Moynihan laid the blame for this increase on the deteriorating black family and on the general increase in female-headed families.[44] Piven and Cloward disagreed, maintaining that family deterioration made only a minor contribution to the growing welfare rolls and that the real cause was increased activism among the poor, who began to demand greater social support.

The 1960s also saw the launching of President Johnson's War on Poverty. Most of its programs were based on the assumption that people are poor because they lack education and job skills, and not on the more realistic assumption that poverty is a defect in the system for producing and distributing wealth. Such programs as the Job Corps, the Neighborhood Youth Corps, VISTA, Head Start, and family planning clinics were launched to help the poor improve their lot. Many of these programs missed their mark because they were poorly organized or because they were aimed primarily at young urban males, and neglected females, the rural poor, and the elderly. Yet despite all its faults, most researchers agree that the War on Poverty did help bring about a significant reduction in poverty in the United States.

The 1970s did not bring any new initiatives against poverty comparable to those introduced in the 1960s, but progress continued to be made for most of that decade. There was, however, a sharp reaction against welfare programs for the poor in the 1980s. Between 1981 and 1985, a period of unprecedented growth in the number of single-parent families, federal welfare spending dropped by 19 percent, about 400,000 families were cut from AFDC rolls, food stamps recipients were reduced by about 1 million people, and 3 million children were cut from school lunch programs.[45]

The Structure of the Welfare System   America's current welfare system is a confusing hodgepodge of overlapping programs and agencies. Funding comes from various mixtures of federal, state, and local governments, depending on the program. Benefits also vary widely from one state to another and even from one city to the next. The two major programs making direct cash payments to the poor are AFDC and Supplemental Security Income (SSI). SSI was launched in 1974 to replace Aid to the Blind, Aid to the Permanently and Totally Disabled, and Old Age Assistance. The federal government also finances and runs a variety of noncash programs that provide goods or services. For instance, food is supplied through food stamps and surplus commodities, health care through medicaid, and housing through rent subsidies and public housing projects. States, counties, and cities supplement these federal programs, most often with short-term emergency payments for people who are waiting for their applications to be processed by federal programs.

Generally speaking, welfare payments cease as soon as recipients become self-supporting. For this reason it has been charged that these programs discourage the poor from working. The rules of AFDC—the major form of direct welfare—were revised in the 1960s, so that only about two-thirds of the money recipients earned (after allowing for working expenses) was deducted from their welfare checks. Thus, they were rewarded for getting a job. But the Reagan administration's welfare reforms and reductions eliminated this two-thirds rule. The total amount of earned income must now be deducted from the welfare check, once again eliminating the financial incentive to work.

Canada has taken a somewhat different approach to public assistance. All Canadians receive government-financed health care, a small family allowance for each child, and an old-age pension at 65. This approach to welfare eliminates the costly bureaucratic red tape necessary to determine who is eligible for welfare payments. And because people are not excluded from these programs on the grounds that they earn too much money, work is encouraged rather than discouraged. The Canadian Pension Plan is an important supplement to the Old Age Security Pension, operating like the American social security system. Citizens are required to contribute a certain percentage of their income and are paid retirement benefits based on their previous earnings. The Canadian Assistance Plan provides 50 percent federal funding for payments to the needy, blind, and disabled, among others. However, Canadian welfare programs often suffer from the same lack of coordination among federal, provincial, and municipal governments that plagues American programs.

The Myths and Realities of Welfare   Many Americans have a distorted picture of the welfare system. They believe that the welfare rolls are full of able-bodied loafers and mothers who have children just to get a government handout, that people stay on welfare for their entire lives without ever working, and that the benefits provide a comfortable standard of living for those who qualify.

In reality, welfare benefits are meager and getting worse. Among the eight major industrialized nations, the United States ranks last in all types of family support.[46] As of 1986, there wasn't a single state in which the combined total of ADFC benefits and food stamps was sufficient to keep a family above the poverty line.[47] Moreover, after adjusting for inflation, average welfare benefits in the United States have decreased by about a third since 1970.[48]

In 1986, about 15.3 million people received some kind of welfare payments from the government in an average month; about two-thirds of these received AFDC. A comparison of these figures with the total number of people who live below the official poverty line shows that only about half of the poor receive welfare. (These figures do not, however, include people receiving food stamps or other non-cash aid.)[49]

Contrary to popular belief, less than 1 percent of welfare recipients are able-bodies males; most are over 65 or under 18, and many are blind or disabled. The only substantial group of able-bodied adults on welfare are mothers, usually without husbands, who cannot support their children. Also contrary to what many seem to believe, the payment for an additional child is actually less than the cost of raising that child, so there is no incentive for welfare mothers to have more children so that they will get more benefits. The average welfare family has only about 2.2 children.[50]

AFDC is probably the most controversial welfare program in the United States. Perhaps this is because it was created with the intention of assisting children whose fathers had died or been disabled, but only a small percentage of AFDC recipients now fit this description. Others have charged that AFDC inadvertently serves to perpetuate the cycle of poverty. For one thing, AFDC children may grow up without a working parent as a role model and therefore fail to learn the basic work habits and attitudes required for most jobs. Another problem is that families are sometimes broken up when support is denied because an unemployed man is present in the home. But there is a different reason that AFDC is so unpopular, and that is simple racism. When many white Americans think about AFDC, they think of a black welfare mother in the ghetto. And if they are also racially prejudiced, there is little doubt about what they will think of the value of the AFDC program.

EXPLANATIONS OF POVERTY

The economic base of some societies is so fragile that hunger is a daily reality for most people. Such extreme scarcity of food, clothing, and shelter clearly does not characterize modern industrial societies or even most traditional ones. The poverty problem in these societies is one of distributing wealth rather than one of producing it. From a global viewpoint the fact that some modern nations are poor while others are rich can also be seen as a problem in the distribution of wealth. There are many explanations of economic inequality, but most fall into three overlapping categories: those explanations based on an analysis of economic structures, those based on an analysis of the culture of the poor, and those based on an analysis of political relationships among power groups.

Economic Explanations   Much poverty can be traced directly to simple economic causes: low wages and too few jobs for those at the bottom of the social hierarchy. In technological societies like Canada and the United States, people without education and skills find it hard to get any kind of employment, and those who find work are likely to be employed in low-paying jobs. We have already seen that even a full-time job at the minimum wage isn't enough to keep a family out of poverty, and there are a growing number of people who are forced to take part-time or temporary jobs because they cannot find full-time work.

Although the unemployment rate goes up and down with the changes in the business cycle (see Chapter 2), the underlying trend in the last three decades has been toward increased unemployment. In the 1950s the unemployment rate averaged 4.5 percent; in the 1960s, 4.8 percent; in the 1970s,

6.2 percent; and in the 1980s it has averaged 7.7 percent.[51] A downswing in the unemployment cycle brought the rate down to 5.7 percent for the first quarter of 1988. But the problem is much worse than it looks, because these unemployment figures all understate the real size of the problem. In addition to the 6.8 million people who were counted in the 1988 figures, about a million unemployed workers were not included because they had become so discouraged that they had given up looking for a job,[52] and another 4.8 million workers had only part-time jobs when they wanted full-time work.[53]

In addition to the overall national problem, there are many areas with particularly high local unemployment rates—for example, the Appalachian coal region of Kentucky and West Virginia. Early in this century thousands of workers left their homes and farms to take jobs in the Appalachian coal mines. Soon the coal industry dominated the area, and it became almost impossible to find a job that was not dependent on coal mining. The mines, however, were owned and controlled by outside corporations. After World War II the mines were automated, the work force dropped from a high of 700,000 to about 140,000, and there were no new jobs for the workers who became unemployed. A similar problem can be found in areas that depended on old heavy industries that are no longer competitive in the world economy, and in the slums of the central cities, where high crime rates and a lack of local services discourage outside investment.

Unskilled labor and poverty go together. Unskilled laborers have been particularly hard hit by automation because they are unable to operate the machines that have taken over their jobs. While it is true that automation has not eliminated most lower-level service jobs, such as those of janitors, waitresses, and domestics, these jobs pay poorly and offer few fringe benefits or chances for advancement.

To add to the other problems, the poor often get less for their hard-earned dollars than other consumers do. Slum dwellers, for example, may pay more rent for a run-down apartment than people living in a small town pay for a house with a garden. More generally, because the poor are not mobile, it is difficult for them to shop around for sales and special values. They are obliged to patronize local merchants, who usually charge higher prices than those in affluent areas. When unexpected expenses occur, the poor must borrow money; but because they are not considered good credit risks, bank loans at standard interest rates may be impossible for them to get. Instead, they must go to loan companies, which charge much higher interest rates, or to loan sharks, who charge exorbitant illegal rates. Many stores in slum areas actively solicit sales on credit because the interest charges are more profitable than the sale itself. If the customer cannot meet the installment payments, the merchandise is repossessed and sold to another poor customer.[54]

Cultural Explanations   There are clear cultural differences between the social classes in all modern societies, and some social scientists see these differences as a major cause of poverty. The foremost advocate of this position has been Oscar Lewis, who argued that some poor people share a distinct "culture of poverty.''[55] Lewis did not ignore the economic basis of poverty; his thesis was simply that a separate subculture has developed among the poor as a reaction to economic deprivation and exclusion from the mainstream of society. Once a culture of poverty has taken hold, it is passed down from generation to generation. Children who grow up in poverty acquire values and attitudes that make it very difficult for them to escape their condition.

In the culture of poverty the nuclear family is female centered, with the mother performing the basic tasks that keep the family going. The father, if he is present, makes only a slight contribution. Children have sexual relations and marry at an early age. The family unit is weak and unstable, and there is little community organization beyond the family. Psychologically, those who live in the culture of poverty have weak ego structures and little self-control. Although Lewis did not use the term, most people living in the culture of poverty would clearly be part of what is now called the underclass.

Lewis studied a number of societies and concluded that the culture of poverty is international. It develops in societies with capitalist economies, persistently high unemployment rates, low wages, and an emphasis on accumulation of wealth and property. However, Lewis found a number of societies that have a considerable amount of poverty but no *culture* of poverty. India and Cuba, for example, have no culture of poverty because the poor are not degraded or isolated. But even in the United States, most poor people do not live in the culture of poverty. Because of the influence of the mass

Supporters of the culture of poverty theory believe that the children of the poor learn attitudes and values that trap them in a life of poverty.

media and the low level of illiteracy, Lewis estimated that only 20 percent of the poor live in a culture of poverty.[56]

Most social scientists agree that poor people are more likely to have some of the characteristics described by Lewis, but there is much skepticism about claims that they have any special personality type or that they value work less than other groups. Some of Lewis's critics are not even so sure that a distinct life-style is passed from one generation to the next. Rather, it is argued by "situationalists" that each generation of the poor exhibits the same life-style because each generation experiences the same conditions: poor housing, crowding, deprivation, and isolation. Charles A. Valentine, for example, argued that the conditions Lewis described are imposed on the poor from the outside rather than being generated by a "culture of poverty."[57] But most sociologists accept the notion that some poor people are members of a self-perpetuating underclass, and it follows that those individuals will need special government assistance if they are ever to escape from a life of poverty.

Political Explanations   Poverty is as much a political problem as a problem of economics and culture. This is evident from the fact that industrialized nations that are less wealthy than the United States have been more successful in reducing the gap between the haves and the have-nots. A high degree of inequality persists in the United States because most Americans have little concern about the problems of the poor, and those who do care are not politically organized. Politicians win votes by promising to eliminate inflation and high taxes, but few votes are won by promising to eliminate poverty. The ideology of individualism has convinced most Americans that the world is full of opportunities and that the poor deserve to be poor because they are too lazy or incompetent to seize those opportunities. As long as the poor are held responsible for their poverty, political action to change the conditions that cause poverty is unlikely.

Poverty, as Herbert Gans has pointed out, is valuable to the wealthy, and many powerful groups do not want it eliminated.[58] First, it ensures that society's dirty work gets done, for without poverty few people would be willing to do the low-paying, dirty, and dangerous jobs. Second, the low wages the poor receive for their work subsidize the wealthy by keeping the prices of goods and services low, and profits high. Third, poverty creates jobs for the many people who service the poor (such as welfare workers) or try to control them (such as police officers and prison guards). Fourth, the poor provide merchants with last-ditch profits by buying goods that otherwise would be thrown away: stale bread, tainted meat, out-of-style clothing, used furniture, and unsafe appliances. Fifth, the poor guarantee the status of the people above them in the social hierarchy. The poor provide a group that "respectable" people can brand as deviants—examples of what happens to those who break social rules. Thus, the contribution of poverty to the comfort of the middle and upper classes creates powerful opposition to any program that is likely to reduce it significantly.

RESPONDING TO PROBLEMS OF POVERTY

No one knows whether it is possible to create a classless industrial society in which all people are economically equal. Certainly, no such society exists today. It does, however, seem possible to eliminate poverty in an absolute sense, even if some people remain richer than others. Many societies have certainly made much greater progress toward alleviating the hardships of those at the bottom than the United States has.

Tax Reform   The simplest and most effective way of bringing about a more equal distribution of wealth is through the tax system. To be fair, a tax system should be progressive; that is, the higher someone's income, the greater the proportion of that income that should be paid in taxes. In theory, that is exactly how the income tax system works. In practice, however, loopholes, exemptions, and other special breaks for the rich mean that the income tax is only mildly progressive. And many other taxes, such as social security and sales taxes, are actually regressive; that is, the poor must pay a higher percentage of their income than the rich. One recent study found, for example, that the poor pay five times as much of their earnings in state sales and excise taxes as do those making over $600,000 a year.[59] And although there has been a great deal of talk about tax reform and closing the loopholes, the last two major overhauls of the tax system have not done anything to help the poorest Americans. The 1981 "reforms" increased the poorest tenth of the population's share of the tax burden by about 2.5 percent, and the 1986 reforms brought things back to about where they were before the changes in 1981.[60] But despite the failures of previous reforms, there is no doubt that the creation of a genuinely progressive tax system that was fairly enforced would be a giant step toward greater economic equality.

Reducing Unemployment   Reducing unemployment is a continuing concern of governments around the world. Despite repeated efforts, most programs have not met with long-term success. Providing employment for all who are willing and able to work is not as simple as it may seem. For example, it appears reasonable to assume that if the government takes action to stimulate the economy, businesses will boom and more jobs will open up. However, as was noted in Chapter 2, such indirect programs may have harmful effects on the poor because they create inflation.

Job retraining is widely used in European countries. The idea is a simple one: teach unemployed workers skills that are in demand so that they can find new jobs. While this approach is reasonable in this age of rapidly changing technology, it has basic limitations. For one thing, many of the hard-core unemployed can barely read and write and thus are unable to learn the high-tech skills that are in demand. These people need financial support for remedial education, not job training. But there is an even more fundamental problem: if all the millions of unemployed workers were taught the latest skills, there would still not be enough jobs to go around.

For that reason, many governments have attacked unemployment by creating new government jobs. It is often suggested that government work programs should be greatly expanded to permit the government to give a job to anyone who is unable to find one in the private sector. Making government an "employer of last resort" could virtually end unemployment.

Critics have repeatedly charged that such programs are wasteful and inefficient, and the funding for job programs of all types has been greatly reduced in the last few years. The largest federal job program, CETA (Comprehensive Employment and Training Act), was entirely eliminated by the Reagan Administration and was replaced with a much smaller substitute. After accounting for inflation, funding for work and training programs was cut by 50 percent between 1981 and 1986,[61] and only 2 million of the 17 million Americans who cannot find steady work are able to participate.[62] But despite such criticisms and cutbacks, there is little doubt that in the long run a well-run government job program would be much less costly to society than the lives and productive energy wasted by unemployment.

Workfare or Welfare?   One of the most popular proposals for changing our welfare system is the notion of making employment or job training mandatory for mothers who receive AFDC. The goal of these so-called **workfare** programs is to get mothers off the welfare rolls by training them and placing them in jobs, thus improving the lives of the poor and saving tax dollars at the same time. With this goal in mind, the current federal program known as WIN (Work Incentive Program) is being expanded, but it is still likely to run into serious problems. The first one is cost, since at least at the beginning an effective program will cost considerably more money to set up and run than it saves. The second difficulty is finding and paying for enough good day care to handle the participants' children while they are in training or at work. The third problem is that most current proposals are based on unrealistic expectations for success. In the past, even the most successful of these programs still failed to place about a third of the participants in a job, and typically those who do find work still do not make enough money to get off welfare.[63] Despite these difficulties, a well-designed employment program for welfare mothers could be a very positive step, but only if it avoids the kind of punitive approach based on unfair stereotypes of welfare mothers as loafers living high at the taxpayers' expense.

Extending Public Assistance   America's welfare system has many bureaucratic problems. Programs are administered by a patchwork of federal, state, and local agencies. A tremendous amount of time and money that might be used to help poor people is spent on determining who is eligible for assistance. Such administrative waste would be drastically reduced if certain welfare services were provided to all citizens, not just to those who can demonstrate special needs. As mentioned earlier, Canada has taken this approach, providing all citizens with medical care, a small retirement pension, and a family allowance for each dependent child. Most European countries have similar pro-

DEBATE

Should the Government Provide Free Housing for the Homeless?

YES A new wave of homeless men, women, and children are flooding across the nation, and we must do something more than just pick up their bodies when they freeze to death. Some people say that we should rely on churches and other private charities to handle the problem. But although that may have worked in a nation of small tightly knit farming communities, it is hopelessly inadequate in a complex urban society. The charities themselves openly admit that they do not have the money or the resources to solve this problem.

The government is the one organization that can provide adequate housing for our most needy citizens. The only question is whether or not these people deserve to be helped, and the answer is a resounding yes. More fortunate people often look down their noses at the homeless and blame them for their own misery. But no one chooses to be born in the underclass, to have a mental disorder, or to fall victim to the disease of alcoholism. And even the most zealous ideologue would have a difficult time finding a reason to blame homeless children for their plight. The real reason so many wealthy people oppose aid to the homeless is simple greed. They would rather see these unfortunates die on the streets than pay another $25 a year in taxes. But surely we are a more generous and public-spirited people than that. Our values and our traditions demand that we take forceful action to solve this tragic problem, and it is time we stopped talking and got the job done.

NO As soon as we hear about a new social problem, the first thing some people want to do is rush in and start throwing money at it. But a gigantic new government program to house the homeless would inevitably prove as wasteful and ineffective as other welfare programs have been. For one thing, the government is so inefficient and hamstrung by political pressures that most of the money is likely to be wasted before it ever gets to the homeless. And even if enough free housing were created to put a roof over their heads, that would do nothing to solve the underlying problems that made them homeless in the first place. The alcoholics and the mentally disturbed would simply be suffering from the same problems indoors rather than on the streets.

A free housing program for the homeless would be a financial monster. It would grow bigger year by year and eventually we would be forced to abandon it. We might begin by providing housing only to those who are now homeless, but what about the poor people who are working at low-paying jobs and still paying rent? They would soon walk away from their old apartments so that they too could become "homeless" and claim a free place to live.

The solution to the problem of the homeless is for individual citizens to give more to the private charities that have already proven that they can do an efficient job in dealing with the problem. Setting up another huge government bureaucracy would only make things worse, not better.

grams. The poor are not discouraged from working by the threat of a reduction in their welfare benefits when they start to earn some money. Welfare fraud and the time and money spent on detecting and apprehending chiselers are also greatly reduced.

Another approach to simplifying the complex maze of welfare programs is called the guaranteed annual income. A central feature of these proposals is a negative income tax. The basic idea is simple: Families earning less than a certain amount (the poverty line) would receive a government grant, called a negative tax, from the Internal Revenue Service. Families with incomes above the poverty line would pay "positive" taxes, just as they do now. Most proposals provide some incentive to ensure that poor families with working members make more money than the nonworking poor. The main advantage of such a program is that it eliminates a lot of unnecessary bureaucracy and therefore reduces the cost of delivering welfare services.

Organizing the Poor   Reducing unemployment, extending public assistance, and guaranteeing a certain minimum income all have very high price tags. Americans

In the 1960s, poor people won significant political and economic gains by organizing and working together for social change. But that spirit of political activism declined, and many of those gains have slipped away.

give much lip service to the ideal of equality, but they appear unwilling to put the ideal into practice with financial support. As we have seen, sociological research shows that programs to help the poor are created only when the poor organize and demand a bigger piece of the economic pie. Amid the activism of the 1960s, a number of poor people's organizations sprang up to press such demands and were able to win support from more broadly based groups. As a result, the welfare system was improved and poverty decreased. If the government is once again to become concerned with the plight of the poor, new organizations and new coalitions will have to be formed to push for change.

SOCIOLOGICAL PERSPECTIVES ON PROBLEMS OF THE POOR

Poverty has not always been a social problem. Although concern for poor people has a long history, until quite recently poverty was considered an inevitable part of social life or the fault of the poor themselves—a lowly status deserved by the lazy and incompetent. But in the past 50 years poverty has increasingly come to be seen as an institutional matter rather than a personal one. The Great Depression of the 1930s, tragic though it was, made a significant contribution to social science. It helped people see that the conditions of poverty are determined by economic, political, and social processes that are beyond the control of individual citizens. Most social scientists now view poverty as a social problem rather than as a collection of personal problems, but they disagree about the causes and solutions to this problem.

The Functionalist Perspective Functionalists consider the extremes of poverty and wealth, common in many nations, to be a result of malfunctions in the economy. In many parts of the world, rapid industrialization has disrupted the economic system, leaving it disorganized and unable to perform many of its functions. At first, people who lack job skills are forced into menial work at low wages and then, with the coming of automation, find that they are not needed at all. Industrial products become outdated (horse carriages, steam engines, milk bottles), and unless rapid adjustments are made, workers lose their jobs. Training centers and apprenticeship programs may continue to produce graduates whose skills are no longer in demand. Discrimination, whether it is based on sex, age, race, or ethnic status, also wastes the talents of many capable people, and society is the loser.

Functionalists point out that the welfare system intended to solve the problem of poverty is just as disorganized as the economy. Administrators often show more concern for their own well-being than for that of their clients. Too often the poor go hungry because bureaucrats are afraid to help a deserving family that is technically ineligible for assistance. Legislative bodies establish programs without enough funds for efficient operations. Inadequate communication systems fail to inform the poor about benefits to which they are entitled. Job training and educational programs are not coordinated with the needs of agriculture, commerce, and industry.

The best way to deal with poverty, according to the functionalist perspective, is to reorganize the economic system so that it operates more efficiently. The poor who have been cast out and neglected must be reintegrated into the mainstream of economic life. Members of the underclass must be provided with training and jobs so that they can resume their roles as productive citizens. But they must also be given a new sense of hope based on the knowledge that the rest of society cares about them and is willing to help them overcome their poverty. Functionalists also recommend reforms to help stabilize the economic system so that it will not produce new poor people to replace those who have escaped from poverty.

In general, functionalists are much more concerned about absolute poverty than about relative poverty. They doubt that relative poverty (economic inequality) can or should be eliminated. Davis and Moore, for example, argued strongly that economic inequality is functional (that is, good for society).[64] Their main point is that the desire for more money motivates people to work hard to meet the standards of excellence that are required in many important jobs. Without inequality of reward, the most capable people would not be motivated to train for or perform the demanding jobs that are essential to the economic system. It should not be concluded, however, that functionalists are convinced that the social system should remain unchanged or that the amount of economic inequality should not be reduced. The functionalist conclusion is simply that *some* inequality is necessary for the maintenance of society as we know it.

The Conflict Perspective   Conflict theorists start with the assumption that because there is such enormous wealth in industrialized nations, no one in such societies need be poor. Poverty exists because the middle and upper classes want it to exist. Conflict theorists argue that the working poor are exploited: they are paid low wages so that their employers can make fatter profits and live more affluent lives. The unemployed are victims of the same system. Wealthy employers oppose programs to reduce unemployment because they do not want to pay the taxes to support them. They also oppose such programs because the fear of unemployment helps keep wages down and workers docile. Thus, conflict theorists argue that the economic system of capitalist countries operates to create and perpetuate a high degree of economic inequality.

Conflict theorists also note that wealthy and middle-class people are more likely than the poor to say that unemployment and poverty stem from a lack of effort rather than from social injustice or other circumstances beyond the control of the individual. This application of the ideology of individualism enables the wealthy to be charitable to the poor, giving some assistance freely while ignoring the economic and political foundations of poverty. Charity, including the government dole, blunts political protests and social unrest that might threaten the status quo. Moreover, some poor people come to accept the judgments passed on them by the rest of society and adjust their aspirations and their self-esteem downward.

Conflict theorists view these adjustments to poverty as a set of chains that must be broken. They believe that the poor should become politically aware and active, organizing themselves to reduce inequality by demanding strong government action. In other words, political action is seen as the most effective response to inequality and, thus, to the problem of poverty. Most conflict theorists doubt that economic inequality can be significantly reduced without a concerted effort by poor people that gains at least some support from concerned members of the upper classes.

Social Psychological Perspectives   Social psychologists study the effects of attitudes and beliefs on behavior, pointing out that poor people learn to behave like poor people. The values of those who live in the culture of poverty are passed on to their children, thus directing them into lives of poverty. Stated differently, socialization practices among the poor promote attitudes and behavior patterns that make upward social mobility difficult. For example, the children of the poor learn to seek immediate gratification. Unlike middle-class achievers, they are not inclined to defer small immediate rewards so that long-run goals, such as a college education, can be reached.

Interactionists emphasize the fact that the main reference group for poor people is their poor neighbors. In many parts of the world, including some places in North America, a successful person is one who knows where the next meal is coming from, and a "big success" may be the assistant manager of a shoe store. People with such attitudes become trapped in their own poverty. More generally, interactionists point to cultural differences in the ways poor people and wealthy people define their worlds, and they note that even if new economic opportunities arise, these differences in definitions persist and function to keep the poor at the bottom of the social ladder.

Social psychologists also study the psychological effects of being poor in a wealthy society. The easy availability of television and other media of mass communication encourages the poor to compare themselves with more fortunate people. And when they do so, many come to believe that they are failures. Some attribute their failure to personal shortcomings rather than to social forces that are beyond their control. The outcome is likely to be a low sense of self-esteem, which may be combined with a variety of personal problems, ranging from drug addiction and mental disorders to delinquency and crime.

The social psychological perspective implies that poverty traps poor people psychologically as well as economically and socially. The trap can be sprung by eliminating absolute poverty (the lack of adequate food, shelter, and clothing) and by opening up more opportunities for the children of the poor, thus reducing overall inequality. Social psychologists also agree that the poor must be encouraged to redefine their social environment. Even if avenues for upward mobility are created, little change will occur as long as the poor are convinced that they can expect no better than a life of poverty. Many poor people will also have to be helped to change a self-image shaped by defeat and rejection before they will be able to take advantage of any new opportunities that are created.

SUMMARY

Whether economic inequality is measured by income distribution or by distribution of wealth, there are large gaps between the rich, the middle class, and the poor that have grown much wider in recent years. Significant differences also exist in the cultural perspectives and life-styles of these different groups. In cities the poor are trapped in run-down, crime-ridden neighborhoods, while the affluent have a multitude of opportunities from which to choose. Psychologically, the poor have to cope with feelings of inadequacy and inferiority because they lack the money and goods that everyone is expected to have. The families of the poor are more unstable, and they have more health problems and a shorter life span.

There are two common ways to measure poverty. The relative approach holds that people are poor if they are significantly less well off than the average person in their society. The absolute approach, which is used by most government agencies, defines poverty as the lack of the essentials of life, such as sufficient food, shelter, and clothing. Using the official figures, poverty decreased during the 1960s and early 1970s, leveled off for a while, and then began increasing sharply in the first half of the 1980s. More recently, the poverty rate has dropped again, but most experts do not believe that this will be a long-range trend unless substantial changes are made in the federal government's approach to the problem.

A look at the distribution of poverty shows that the young are more likely to be poor than the middle aged or the elderly. Children from single-parent families and the members of ethnic minority groups are also more likely to be poor. The poverty rate is highest in rural areas and lowest in the suburbs. But even if they have the same general characteristics, all poor people are not the same. The working poor are those who hold down a job but still make too little to be above the poverty line. The underclass is composed of the long-term poor who are shut out of the mainstream of society. And at the very bottom of the social heap are the homeless who seem to lack almost all the essentials of the life-style expected in our society.

The ideology of individualism, which stresses personal responsibility and self-reliance, has fostered the belief that the poor are to blame for their own condition. From the beginning, the welfare system was established on the assumption that being poor was one's own fault.

Today the welfare system in the United States includes a variety of overlapping programs and jurisdictions. Included are programs that make cash payments to families with dependent children (AFDC) as well as to the blind, the aged, and the disabled (SSI). Other programs distribute food stamps and assist with housing and medical costs. In Canada, the federal government has emphasized programs that provide welfare services to all citizens. Among these are government-financed health care, old-age pensions, and a small family allowance for each child.

There are many explanations of poverty. In some societies the economic base is so weak that many people must go hungry. In modern industrial societies poverty results from unemployment, low wages, and unequal distribution of wealth. The poor do not receive a proportionate share of the wealth, and they often pay more than wealthy people for the same goods and services. Another explanation for poverty is based on Oscar Lewis's idea that some nations develop a "culture of poverty" with its own distinctive characteristics. In addition, there are political reasons for the continued existence of poverty in North America. Poverty is valuable to the rich and the powerful. It ensures that dirty work gets done, that prices remain low, and that welfare workers have jobs.

There are many proposals for reducing poverty. First, the tax system might be reformed to require the rich to pay higher taxes than the poor. Second, unemployment could be reduced by stimulating the economy, providing job training, and increasing government employment. Third, welfare rolls might be reduced by helping AFDC mothers to get a job. Fourth, administrative waste could be cut if the welfare system were reformed by eliminating some categorical assistance programs and replacing them with welfare assistance for everyone. Fifth, the poor might organize themselves to influence legislation and government policies.

Functionalists see extremes of poverty and wealth as resulting from breakdowns in social organization. Conflict theorists are convinced that poverty thrives because the wealthy and powerful benefit from it. Social psychologists note that the socialization of the poor develops attitudes and behavior patterns that make upward social mobility difficult.

KEY TERMS

absolute approach	relative deprivation
income	wealth
poverty	workfare
relative approach	

FURTHER READINGS

The Rich and the Poor

Harold R. Kerbo, *Social Stratification and Inequality: Class Conflict in the United States,* New York: McGraw-Hill, 1983.

Leonard Silk and Mark Silk, *The American Establishment,* New York: Basic Books, 1980.

Ken Auletta, *The Underclass,* New York: Vintage, 1983.

Social Welfare

Michael B. Katz, *In the Shadow of the Poorhouse: A Social History of Welfare in America,* New York: Basic Books, 1986.

Frances Piven and Richard Cloward, *The New Class War: Reagan's Attack on the Welfare State and Its Consequences,* New York: Pantheon Books, 1982.

William Julius Wilson, *The Truly Disadvantaged: The Inner City, the Underclass and Public Policy,* Chicago: University of Chicago Press, 1987.

Being Poor in Hard Times

Paul Blumberg, *Social Inequality in an Age of Decline,* New York: Oxford University Press, 1980.

Michael Harrington, *The New American Poverty,* New York: Viking Penguin, 1984.

- What are the sources of prejudice and discrimination?

- How do today's immigrants differ from those of the past?

- Does education reduce discrimination?

- How do prejudice and discrimination harm society?

- Can political action bring ethnic equality?

Chapter 7
THE ETHNIC MINORITIES

The violent face of ethnic relations—riots, beatings, and murders—is familiar to anyone who watches the evening news. From Northern Ireland to South Africa, ethnic conflict is a burning issue. Virtually every nation with more than one ethnic group has had to deal with ethnic clashes. Some have managed to achieve long-term stability and harmony; others have been torn apart by violence and hatred. But most have just muddled through with alternating periods of conflict and cooperation.

The exploitation and oppression of one group by another are particularly ironic in democratic nations, for these societies claim to cherish justice and equality. But attempts to create real ethnic equality always meet stubborn resistance. The dominant group that controls the economic and political institutions seldom agrees to share its power. Because the members of minority groups tend to be less skilled and less educated, they are unable to unseat those at the top. Moreover, the fear of change causes people from all ethnic groups to hold fast to the way things are.

ETHNIC GROUPS

The members of an **ethnic group** share a common set of cultural characteristics or at least a common national origin.[1] What sets an ethnic group apart from others is its sense of common identity and the belief that its members share a unique social and historical experience.

Although a racial group is often an ethnic group as well, the two are not the same. A **race** is supposed to be based on some common set of physical characteristics, but the members of a race may or may not share the sense of unity and identity that holds an ethnic group together. Americans and Russians hardly have a sense of togetherness, even though they believe that they are members of the same race. However, when there are marked physical differences between different groups within a single society, race is likely to become an important factor in ethnic relations. Physical characteristics such as skin color are more visible than cultural characteristics, and are much harder to change or disguise.

Race is more a social idea than a biological fact. Among the 5 billion people in the world, there is an incredible range of skin colors, body builds, hair types, and other physical features. And there is little agreement about how people with these characteristics should be classified. For instance, in the United States people are considered "white" if all their ancestors came from Europe, and "black" if they have any significant amount of African ancestry. In contrast, Brazilians recognize about forty different racial groups with varying combinations of skin color, facial features, and hair texture.[2] Even scientists who study racial types do not agree on a single classification system. Thus, physical characteristics are biological in origin, but the way they are classified and the meanings they are given are socially determined.

People from all ethnic groups tend to see their own culture as the best and most enlightened. This is known as **ethnocentrism**.[3] Because values and behavior patterns differ from one culture to another, one's own culture naturally appears superior when judged by its own standards. Ethnocentrism, therefore, seems to be universal. All cultures show prejudice against foreigners, who are commonly viewed as heathens, barbarians, or savages. Such ethnocentric beliefs have often served as the justification for bloody foreign conquests. Similar ethnocentric attitudes are found in the various ethnic groups that make up a single society. Feelings of ethnic superiority are usually accompanied by the belief that economic and political domination by one's own group is both reasonable and natural.

Unlike ethnocentrism, racism is more closely related to physical than to cultural differences. **Racism** can be defined as the belief that human beings are divided into superior and inferior racial groups that ought to be treated differently by society.[4] Racism is common throughout the world. It can be seen in relations between African tribes with great differences in body build, in relations between the Spanish-speaking majority and the native Indians of South America, and of course in relations between whites and blacks in North America and in Western European nations.

Because racism involves active discrimination, it is usually more vicious and divisive than ethnocentrism. In most racist ideologies members of the subordinate group are seen as inferior, yet at the same time as a threat to the dominant group. Extreme racism may result in an attempt to exterminate the "inferior" group. Two chilling examples are Hitler's mass executions of European Jews and Gypsies, and the colonists' nearly successful attempt to wipe out the native population of North America.

PATTERNS OF ETHNIC RELATIONS

The relationships between ethnic groups take a bewildering variety of forms. Even the relationships among ethnic groups in North America can be difficult to grasp. Sociologists have helped by describing three general patterns of ethnic relations based on the distribution of economic and political power. In some cases, termed **domination,** one group holds power and others are subordinate to it. In other cases groups are roughly equal economically, politically, and socially. One form of equality is termed **pluralism** and a second **integration.**

It is important to note that these are only general patterns and that conditions of domination, integration, and pluralism may exist together. Further, the exact form these characteristics take in any society is bound to differ from the one described by general models.

Domination   When two ethnic groups come into close contact for the first time, ethnocentrism stimulates competition and conflict, and one group usually emerges as the winner. That group becomes dominant, holding most of the political and economic power and discriminating against the subordinate group.

Ethnic dominance was present in ancient civilizations and it continues to exist today. The domination of black slaves by white Americans is a typical

19th-Century Social Problems

The right of colored people to attend public places of amusement under the laws of Wisconsin is to be tested. Rachel and Clara Black are the nearly white and attractive daughters of a colored barber, Alfred Black. The young women visited the Century Roller Skating Rink at Oshkosh as spectators. The next day they received a note requesting them to discontinue their visits. They went again and were invited to leave, which they did. The reason assigned by the management of the rink is that it had established a rule not to let colored people frequent the place.

February 9, 1899

These selections, which appear throughout the text, are from the *Badger State Banner,* a newspaper published in Black River Falls, Wisconsin.

example. Politically, the displaced Africans were powerless, sharing none of the rights of other Americans. They had no weapons or organizations with which to fight their oppressors. Their work produced riches for plantation owners, but their lowly condition was far beneath mere poverty. They were isolated, rejected, and considered more animal than human. Although American slavery is an extreme case of ethnic domination, the pattern in other cases is the same.

Segregation is a part of most systems of ethnic domination. In segregated societies, contacts between the haves and the have-nots are held to an absolute minimum. After slavery was abolished in the United States, a rigid system of segregation was created that was much like the one found in South Africa today, where it is a crime for blacks or whites to cross the racial barriers established by the government. Legally defined residential areas, separate public toilets, and strict limits on the political rights of nonwhites are all part of the South African system of apartheid (segregation). By keeping the subordinate group separate and isolated, the dominant group tries to keep the myth of its own superiority alive and to prevent political action to change the existing order of things.

Pluralism   In pluralistic systems ethnic groups maintain a high degree of independence. The ethnic groups in a pluralist society identify with the larger society but control some of their own social and political affairs. Each group tries to keep its own identity and cultural traditions rather than blending together in a "melting pot." Although different groups in a pluralist system are roughly equal, in practice some inequality exists, so that deciding whether a relationship is one of domination or pluralism is a matter of judgment. For instance, French Canadians are usually considered part of a pluralistic system. Although they maintain a distinct identity and have a strong cultural tradition, there are some ways in which they are dominated by English-speaking Canadians. Anglo-Canadians (and Americans) control the Canadian economy, and the English and American cultural influence is very strong throughout Canada.

When ethnic groups occupy the same geographic area, competition is usually more intense and maintaining independence more difficult.[5] In many of the most successful pluralist nations, different ethnic groups are concentrated in different parts of the country. One of the best examples is Switzerland, which has ethnic divisions between Protestants and Catholics and among French-, German-, and Italian-speaking people. Each group lives in districts populated largely by people of the same ethnic background. The government recognizes no national language and proclaims its respect for all cultures and ethnic groups. But even in Switzerland the history of ethnic relations has not always been harmonious.

Cultural pluralism, even when it is regionally based, may result in ethnic conflicts, as in Belgium, or in warfare, as in Northern Ireland. In the extreme, separatist movements may divide the pluralist nation into two or more independent countries. This was the case in the division of India and Pakistan and of Pakistan and Bangladesh. A similar process is even possible in Canada, where some French Canadians want to divide the country into separate French- and English-speaking nations.

Integration   An integrated society, like a pluralistic one, strives for ethnic equality; but the interests of one ethnic group are not balanced against those of another. Ethnic backgrounds are ignored and, ideally, all individuals are treated alike.

In a truly integrated society all people attend the same local schools, go to the same churches, and vote for political candidates on the basis of merit alone. Politicians do not feel the need to try to win votes by publicly dining on spaghetti on Monday, blintzes on Tuesday, and sukiyaki on Wednesday.

Many Americans with northern European backgrounds have given up their ethnic identities. Many people with names like Seele, Soppeland, and Sutherland are unaware that their ancestors came from Germany, Norway, and Scotland. There are also instances in which several ethnic groups have fused into one, as in the case of Jewish immigrants who came from widely different backgrounds—Spanish, German, Russian, Polish—and now are likely to identify themselves as a single, unified ethnic group. A similar fusion now seems to be taking place among some immigrants from Latin America.

In the long run, integration replaces domination and pluralism. Peoples who live in close contact, marry each other, watch the same television shows, and eat at the same McDonald's hamburger stands are bound to integrate as time passes. Even racial differences may begin to fade, as they have in Mexico. However, integration is often resisted by members of ethnic groups who believe that their culture is superior to others and by those who want to maintain their distinctive ethnic traditions. It is also opposed by minority citizens who are convinced that they will be at a disadvantage if they are forced to compete in a society that reflects the cultural assumptions of other ethnic groups. Although they would prefer to be treated as equals, they fear that integration would really mean domination.

PREJUDICE AND DISCRIMINATION

Prejudice and discrimination are closely associated, but they are not the same. **Prejudice** refers to attitudes, **discrimination** to actions. Prejudiced people prejudge others, but not everyone who prejudges others is prejudiced. Prejudgment becomes prejudice when the attitude is so rigidly held that it cannot be changed by new information. For example, some Americans erroneously believe that "all Mexicans are lazy." Such a belief is unreasonable, but it is not prejudiced unless the believer refuses to change his or her mind after being shown proof that Mexicans work just as hard as anyone else. Gordon Allport used the following definition in his classic study, *The Nature of Prejudice:* "Ethnic prejudice is an antipathy based upon a faulty and inflexible generalization. It may be felt or expressed. It may be directed toward a group as a whole, or toward an individual because he is a member of that group."[5] Prejudice may be expressed in terms that seem favorable to members of an ethnic group. Thus, the belief that all blacks are good athletes may be just as prejudiced as the belief that all blacks have low IQs.

Discrimination is the practice of treating some people as second-class citizens because of their ethnic status. Usually, it surfaces when members of a dominant group deny equality to the members of a subordinate group. For instance, social clubs may discriminate against Jews by denying them admission, or the registrar of voters may discriminate against blacks by denying them the right to vote. Robert K. Merton has pointed out that some of us discriminate even if we feel no prejudice toward the person we discriminate against.[6] The reverse is also true. Sometimes we are prejudiced toward a person but reject discrimination because of moral convictions or other social influences.

The Sources of Prejudice and Discrimination Like other types of human behavior, prejudice and discrimination are not easily accounted for. Many influences come together to create them, and their origins cannot be found entirely in individual psychology or oppressive social institutions. Psychological and social processes blend together, like prejudice and discrimination themselves.

Authoritarianism One of the most influential works on prejudice, *The Authoritarian Personality,* was based on studies done at the University of California at Berkeley shortly after World War II.[7] The researchers sought the psychological causes of the development of European fascism, and their study described a distinct type of personality believed to be associated with intolerance and prejudice. The **authoritarian personality** is rigid and inflexible and has a very low tolerance for uncertainty. People with this type of personality have great respect for authority figures and quickly submit to their will. They place a high value on conventional behavior and feel threatened when others don't follow their own standards. Indeed, their prejudices help reduce the threat they feel when confronted by unconventional behavior. By labeling unconventional people ''inferior,'' ''immature,'' or ''degenerate,'' the authoritarians avoid any need to question their own beliefs and attitudes.

The notion that authoritarian personalities are responsible for prejudice and discrimination has, however, come under severe attack. Some critics have pointed out serious weaknesses in the methodology used in the original research. Others charge that the characteristics that are said to make up an authoritarian personality are not a unified whole but are merely a number of undesirable traits gathered under a single label. Still others say that the concept of authoritarianism is just a political attack on conservatism. Despite these and other criticisms, the idea that some individuals show authoritarian personality traits, and that authoritarianism is expressed in prejudice and discrimination, has become extremely popular both in the scientific community and among the general public.

Scapegoating Unpopular minority groups are often used as **scapegoats** for other people's problems. They are blamed for a wide variety of things that they could not possibly have caused. The term originates with a Hebrew tradition. On Yom Kippur a goat was set loose in the wilderness after the high priest had symbolically laid all the sins of the people on its head (Leviticus 16:20–22). Ironically, the Jews themselves often became scapegoats in Western history. When hundreds of thousands of people died in the plagues that swept through medieval Europe, rioters stormed into Jewish ghettos and burned them down, believing that Jews were somehow responsible for the epidemic. Six centuries later, when Hitler and the Nazis set up their extermination camps, Jews were still being blamed for the troubles of Europe.

One explanation of scapegoating is the **frustration-aggression theory**.[8] Its three basic principles are that (1) frustration produces aggression; (2) this aggression cannot safely be directed against powerful people; and (3) the aggression is therefore transferred to weaker individuals who cannot fight back, such as members of an unpopular minority group. Although the theory seems to make sense of scapegoating, it has some serious weaknesses. For example, frustration does not always produce aggression, and even when it does, the aggression is not necessarily directed at an ethnic scapegoat.

Learning Although prejudice and discrimination are sometimes associated with certain personality traits or with frustration, both are learned. South Africans do not need authoritarian personalities to have strong racial prejudice, because they learn such attitudes from their culture. Most prejudice is acquired early in the socialization process. Children adopt their parents'

19th-Century Social Problems

Some of the boys in this city have been indulging in a kind of sport of late which may soon prove to be something besides sport. They have been harassing the Chinese laundryman by tapping on his windows, throwing stones and sticks of wood against the side of the house, against the doors, and even through the windows. They have even gone so far as to open the door and throw in a dead cat. . . . We advise the boys to desist or some of them may soon be called to answer for their folly before the magistrate.

1894

prejudices as naturally as they adopt their parents' language, and discrimination follows prejudice as regularly as night follows day.

Some of the most common prejudices are taken from ethnic **stereotypes**—ideas that portray all the members of a group as having similar fixed, usually unfavorable, characteristics. The "happy-go-lucky Mexican," the "lazy Negro," and the "cunning Jew" reflect ethnic stereotypes that most of us learn at one time or another.[9] In situations of ethnic conflict, "contrast conceptions" often develop. That is, people from two ethnic groups develop strong negative stereotypes about each other. For instance, while white racists in the United States perpetuate vicious antiblack stereotypes, black racists have developed their own stereotypes that depict all whites as greedy, selfish, and bent on subjugating the black race.

Although the prejudice expressed in ethnic stereotypes is usually obvious, it can also be quite subtle. For example, a white schoolboy living in an integrated neighborhood learns prejudice when he hears his mother explain that it is all right for him to sleep overnight at the home of a black friend because "that house is so clean you could eat right off the floor." An unspoken but potent prejudice is at the base of the mother's praise: blacks are crude and dirty, but this family is an exception. Social psychologists have shown, too, that as some children are taught to be "tolerant" of ethnic minorities, they are quietly being taught to be bigots. If a father says to his daughter, "Some of my best friends are Jews," he is telling her that Jews are somehow bad but he is generous enough to make some exceptions. There may even be prejudice in the attitudes of a white employer who tries to document his lack of prejudice by bragging that in his factory "half the workers are black, and they do the job as well as anyone else."

Economics Conflict between ethnic groups fosters prejudice and discrimination. Some social scientists, particularly Marxists, are convinced that all conflict stems from economic causes. Whether one accepts this idea or not, there is ample evidence that the realities of economic competition lie beneath much prejudice and discrimination. If Jews, blacks, or members of other minority groups cannot get into elite colleges and professional schools, they obviously will not be able to compete with members of the dominant group in occupations requiring a high degree of training. In times of high unemployment, members of the dominant group can protect their jobs by making sure that minorities are the first to be fired and the last to be hired. It has long been noted that antiblack prejudice is highest among white working-class men who compete with blacks for low-paying unskilled jobs.

In other cases as in South Africa the practice of discrimination is so firmly entrenched that subordinate groups have practically no chance to compete. Members of the dominant group are not necessarily aware of the exploitation, however, because their stereotypes of ethnic and racial inferiority justify their behavior. Those in subordinate groups, however, realize that they are being exploited, and their anger and resentment find expression in their own prejudices, and may ultimately lead to revolutionary violence.

Racism and prejudice can also play an important part in class conflict. Marxists point out that racial animosities between black and white workers in the United States have been used to divide and weaken the working class. Employers often intentionally encourage racial conflicts to keep workers from forming a united front in their demands for higher wages and better working conditions. In the early part of this century, when most unions excluded black workers, it was common for employers to bring in black strikebreakers to end union disputes. The unions eventually realized that all workers were being hurt by these racial divisions and began recruiting black members, although a good deal of more subtle racism still remains in some unions.[10]

Politics The quest for power promotes prejudice and discrimination, just as the quest for money does. Dominant groups use discrimination as a technique for maintaining their power, appealing to popular prejudice to justify their discrimination. In some societies political discrimination is an obvious and accepted fact of life. For example, South Africa does not allow native Africans to vote, and until quite recently many American communities denied the same right to their black citizens. But most political discrimination is more subtle. Minorities who speak a language different from that of the dominant group can be excluded by a literacy test or discouraged by ballots and election information printed only in the language of the dominant group. The political participation of ethnic minorities can also be discouraged by charging a poll tax (a fee for voting) that they cannot afford, or by drawing the boundary lines of electoral districts in such a way as to dilute their influence.

Culture Much prejudice is just another form of ethnocentrism, as when those who are reared in one moral tradition think those who are reared in a different way are their natural enemies. When members of two or more ethnic groups live side by side, such cultural conflict seems to operate independently of economic and political competition. As the people of one ethnic group go about their everyday routines, they may violate the most sacred rules of their neighbors. For instance, Indian Hinduism absolutely forbids eating beef—the meat of a sacred animal—but Indian Muslims have no such objections. However, Muslims are forbidden to eat pork. To an orthodox Hindu, knowing a man who eats beef is akin to knowing a man who eats babies. To an orthodox Muslim, a man who eats pork is almost as bad. Such differences are not merely differences in food preferences. They reflect different moralities.

But cultural competition is not limited to competition between alternative sets of moral standards. In some multiethnic societies each ethnic group expects its behavior patterns to be given equal, or even special, recognition by the institutions of that society. Language is a good example. The language of the dominant group automatically becomes the language of business and government. This is obviously seen to be unfair by linguistic minorities, even if they speak the national language as well as that of their ethnic group. When aroused, they demand that their language be given equal status with the language of the dominant group. If these demands are successful, government and some economic activity must be carried on in two or more languages. Canada, Belgium, and southern India have all experienced such linguistic conflicts in recent years. Even in Norway all school-children must pass examinations in two different forms of Norwegian. Cultural competition also appears with reference to dress, the time of day at which lunch is eaten, national and religious holidays, and hundreds of other cultural traditions.

ETHNIC MINORITIES IN NORTH AMERICA

In North America we see all three of the patterns of ethnic relations discussed earlier. Most non-European ethnic minorities, such as blacks, Hispanics, and native Americans, live under a system of domination. Pluralism—the pattern in which each minority group maintains its cultural distinctness and controls its own economic and political affairs—is not as common in North America. The closest approach to it may be seen in Canada, where French Canadians are concentrated in Quebec and are in political control of that province. On a smaller scale, there are some relatively independent towns in the southwestern United States that are predominantly Chicano (Mexican American) in culture and population. In neither of these cases, however, is it accurate to say that these groups are independent and equal.

Members of some European ethnic groups have assimilated the dominant cultures of Canada and the United States and are now completely integrated. Irish, Italian, Polish, Hungarian, and other European Catholics seem headed in that direction, but they are not as fully integrated as earlier Protestant immigrants. Thus, the pattern of ethnic relations in North America is a mixture of domination and integration, with some elements of pluralism.

Historical Background   The Indians were the first Americans and for that reason they are often referred to as native Americans. Contrary to popular stereotypes, not all Indians were nomadic warriors. Indeed, there were many different Indian cultures. Some Indians were wandering hunters, but many others lived in stable villages and grew their own food. In some areas, principally Mexico and South America, the Indians had very advanced civilizations. American Indians spoke about three hundred different languages in just the area that is now north of the Mexican border.[11]

Three major groups of European colonists settled in North America: French, British, and Spanish. In the beginning, European–Indian relations were generally peaceful, and a lively trade developed. But the influx of colonists disrupted this early system of pluralism. Colonists came to dominate the eastern tribes and then slowly moved westward, first driving Indians from their lands at gunpoint, then restricting them to isolated reserves, and finally requiring even reservation Indians to obey their law.

Conflict was not restricted to whites and Indians, for the European powers also were bitter enemies, fighting among themselves for power, money, and Indian lands. The British emerged as victors in North America, and the lands north of what is now the Mexican-American border have been dominated by English-speaking peoples ever since. The boundaries of the newly independent United States changed slowly, moving westward as Americans took over vast sections of land formerly held by Spain, France, and Mexico. This westward conquest meant, of course, that sizable European and non-European minorities were brought under the domination of the English-speaking majority.

The two new North American nations took very different approaches to the problems of their Indian minorities. Canadian treaties with Indians were usually honored, and the government attempted to minimize stealing, looting, and pillaging by the white settlers. In tragic contrast, the United States government repeatedly signed treaties with the Indians and then broke them as white settlers demanded more and more Indian lands.[12] The loss of their land, the disruption of their economy, and the spread of European diseases almost led to the annihilation of the Indian people in North America. In 1500, there were between 12 and 15 million Indians in North America (excluding Mexico), but by 1850 only about a quarter of a million still survived.[13] After the Indians' resistance was broken, they were subjected to cruel domination:

> Most Indian people were denied the vote, had to obtain passes to leave the reservation and were prohibited from practicing their own religions, sometimes by force. Children were dragooned off to boarding schools where they were severely punished if they were caught speaking their own language.[14]

The French minority in Canada and the Spanish minority in the United States took divergent paths after they fell under Anglo domination. French Canada had a substantial population at the time of the English conquest, and it has maintained itself as a self-perpetuating community with little new immigration. Quebec has become an island of French in an English-speaking sea. In contrast, the Spanish-speaking population in most of the areas taken from Spain and Mexico was quite small. With the advent of the transcontinental railroad and the California gold strikes, these people were soon overwhelmed by waves of English-speaking immigrants. However, substantial immigration from Mexico and other Latin American countries eventually led to significant increases in the Hispanic population in the United States.

In the first century following the American Declaration of Independence, most immigrants to the United States came from the Protestant countries of northern Europe. But from 1870 to 1920 new immigrants came increasingly from the Catholic areas of Europe: Italy, Poland, Ireland, and eastern Europe. At first it was assumed that these immigrants would quickly assimilate into British Protestant culture; when they failed to do so, ethnic tensions and hostilities grew. In addition, nonwhite immigrants, principally from China and Japan, arrived on the West Coast to be greeted with even more prejudice and discrimination. A federal law passed in 1924 severely restricted immigration from southern Europe and stopped all immigration from Asia.

The history of the Africans in North America is unique because all the early African immigrants arrived in chains. American slavery was concentrated in the southern plantation regions, and slaveholders intentionally tried to extinguish African culture. The African family system was broken up, and fathers were routinely separated from their children. Slaves who shared common cultural roots were systematically separated and forbidden to speak their own language. They were even forced to abandon their own religion and to become Christians.

Unlike other immigrants, blacks were forced to come to North America against their will. Most were put to work as slaves on Southern plantations.

After slavery had been abolished, blacks continued to be plagued by racism. Black political power blossomed briefly after the Civil War, but this fragile flower was soon plucked. Blacks were systematically murdered, terrorized, and subjugated. Terrorist organizations such as the Ku Klux Klan and the Knights of the White Camellia drove blacks back into their subordinate status. Slavery was replaced by a system of segregation that denied blacks full rights of citizenship and isolated them from the mainstream of American society.

The rigid segregation system in the southern states and the more informal segregation practiced in the rest of the country thrived for a hundred years. It was not until the 1950s and 1960s that the civil rights movement finally broke the back of legal segregation. With a new sense of political awareness, thousands of blacks and their white supporters, backed by Supreme Court decisions, organized, demonstrated, and demanded equal rights. However, despite major improvements, racial domination continues to be fueled by prejudice and discrimination.

The new sense of black pride and political awareness that developed out of this struggle had an impact on other ethnic groups as well. Militant Hispanics, Asians, and native Americans organized and demanded better treatment, echoing demands for "black power" with calls for "brown power," "yellow power," and "red power." In Canada, the *Quebeçois* (French Canadians) also began to assert their cultural identity, and some demanded a new nation separate from Canada. "White ethnics"—especially descendants of immigrants from Italy, Poland, the Ukraine, and Ireland—also intensified efforts to maintain their ethnic identities.

The ethnic conflicts that were simmering in the 1960s quieted in the following years, but new problems arose. The Immigration Act of 1965 modified the quota system that favored European immigrants and opened the door to more people from the Third World. In the last 25 years, about 39 percent of the legal immigrants to the United States have been from Latin America and the Carribean, 32 percent from Asia, and only 22 percent from Europe.[15] About half a million legal immigrants are now admitted to the United States each year. No one knows how many people immigrate illegally each year, but in 1986 over 1.6 million illegals were deported from the United States.[16]

This new wave of immigration differs from its predecessors in some important ways. For one thing, the vast majority of the immigrants are from the poor countries of Latin America and Asia, not from the European countries that fed past waves of immigration. This shift in immigration from Europe to the Third World has created the same kind of groundless fears about the destruction of American culture caused by the previous shift from northern to southern Europe. The fears created by the new immigrants are intensified by the fact that they are not evenly dispersed through the country but are heavily concentrated in a few areas. Over 60 percent of the Asian population of the United States lives in California; Mexican immigrants are most heavily concentrated in the southwestern states, Cubans in Florida, Puerto Ricans in New York City. In fact, New York City has proven so attractive to immigrants that about 30 percent of its current population were born outside the United States.[17]

The heavy preponderance of Spanish speakers among the legal, and especially the illegal, immigrants has created another fear as well: that these immigrants will not follow the traditional pattern of assimilation but will become permanently isolated in Spanish-speaking communities. There is, however, no evidence that Spanish-speaking immigrants are any less interested in learning English than their counterparts from other parts of the world or any more likely to isolate themselves from the rest of society.

Institutional Discrimination   Most people think of discrimination as an action by one person against another. Although such personal discrimination is widespread, its consequences are not as serious as the discrimination that is built into economic, educational, and political institutions. Although the term *institutional racism* is sometimes used to define this problem, it is too narrow. **Institutional discrimination** is a more accurate term because bias can be based on ethnic status as well as race.

Education Our culture puts tremendous faith in education. Numerous studies have shown that people with more education are likely to have higher-paying and higher-status jobs (see Chapter 4). But blacks, Hispanics, and native Americans receive significantly less education than others. In 1986, 76 percent of whites had finished high school, whereas only 62 percent of blacks and 48 percent of Hispanics had finished.[18] Some Asian groups (Japanese, Chinese, Koreans, and Filipinos) are exceptions to this pattern and actually have a higher level of educational achievement than white Americans, but others such as Laotians and Cambodians are far below the American average.[19]

The sources of this educational inequality are rooted in domination. During the period of slavery most black Americans received little schooling, and after emancipation they were put into separate schools of decidedly inferior quality. The civil rights movement and the Supreme Court eventually ended legal segregation. But as was noted in Chapter 4, school segregation has continued, largely as a result of segregated housing patterns in cities. In response to this new problem, courts have ordered that schoolchildren be bused from one school to another to achieve racial balance. But a storm of protest and conflict has made the courts back away from this approach.

The history of native American education is in many ways even more dismal than that of black education. Many of the early Indian schools were run by missionaries who were determined to civilize and Christianize the "heathen savages." The government-run boarding schools that eventually replaced the missionary schools were no better:

> The young Indian, torn from his family, was shipped to the school where his hair was immediately cut and where he was given a military uniform and taught close order drill. One of the prime objectives of the system was to teach him the English language as rapidly as possible. He was given demerits for

speaking in his native language. Since the incoming student could speak no other language, great personal tragedies resulted, leading to high suicide rates.[20]

Many young Indians returning from boarding school were adrift: they did not fit into the white world, yet they no longer fit into the traditional world of their parents either.

The cultural assumptions of the white middle class are built into today's schools, and ethnic minorities have behavioral as well as learning problems as a result. For example, success in school depends largely on the student's ability to meet middle-class standards of discipline and self-control. Students from homes that allow free emotional expression and provide few controls on behavior are therefore at a disadvantage. In addition, textbooks and other course materials are often culturally biased. Imagine native American children's reaction on reading that traitors in their ancestors' struggle to keep their land are to be called "friendly" Indians. Only recently have American textbooks acknowledged the contributions of ethnic minorities to American society.

Cultural biases are also institutionalized through language. Immigrant children have always been required to do their schoolwork in English whether or not they are fluent in that language. Even though this system of instruction gave a distinct advantage to descendants of British immigrants, it seemed reasonable enough at a time when immigrants spoke dozens of different languages. But now that the United States has only two principal languages—English and Spanish—this policy is open to question. Some Spanish-speaking Americans are asking for bilingual education.

It should not be concluded that the differences in educational achievement among ethnic minorities stem entirely from the cultural biases built into the school system. For one thing, the children of the poor are under strong economic pressure to drop out of school, and ethnic minorities are likely to be poor. Further, there are significant differences in the value placed on education and in the family structure of various ethnic groups, and these differences affect achievement. For instance, Japanese Americans and several other Asian groups who are noted for their strong family have been very successful in school despite the barriers of language and racial prejudice.

Employment   Most minority-group members have low-status and low-paying jobs, and are more likely than whites to be unemployed. Whites are more than twice as likely as blacks or Hispanics to work as managers or professionals.[21] Similar patterns are found in the distribution of income. In 1986 the average black family earned only about 58 percent as much as the average white family, down from a high of 61 percent in 1970. Hispanic families earned about 70 percent as much as white families, putting them ahead of blacks but substantially behind the average American.[22]

These figures are misleading, however, because Hispanics have larger families than blacks. When we look at income per person instead of per family, Hispanics are actually slightly behind.[23] A similar thing happens

DEBATE

Should We Try to Stop the New Wave of Immigration?

YES The flood of new immigrants pouring into this country is out of control and must be stopped as soon as possible. Factory owners and investors reap huge profits from cheap immigrant labor, while the poor suffer. Because immigrants are willing to work for wages far below the minimum standards accepted in our society, they take jobs away from our own workers and drive down the pay for all unskilled work. Because several immigrant families are often willing to share the same cramped apartment, they outbid our own poor people for the limited supply of affordable rental housing. This human flood places a heavy burden on taxpayers, who must finance new schools, hospitals, prisons, and other facilities to meet the needs of all these new residents. It also creates serious new health problems by bringing contagious Third World diseases into this country.

Although some claim that the current wave of immigration is no different from those of the past, such statements are clearly false. The most obvious difference is that so many of today's immigrants come into this country illegally, thus showing disrespect for the laws and standards of the country they claim to admire. By allowing so many illegals to stay here, we reward their criminal behavior and in effect punish their law-abiding countrymen who stay at home. Another important difference is not in the immigrants but in the economic realities of present-day America. When previous waves of immigration reached these shores, there was a vast untamed continent to be explored and developed. Now the frontier is gone, and with it has gone our ability to assimilate large numbers of new immigrants.

NO The greatness of this nation was founded on the determination, sacrifice, and skill of the millions of immigrants who came to these shores over the years. Everyone now recognizes the great contribution immigrants have made to our nation, but the same objections raised about the immigrants of a hundred years ago are being voiced about the new immigrants of today. The real reason for these complaints also remains the same: prejudice and fear. Italians, Jews, Poles, and Irish helped strengthen, not weaken, America, and so will Latin Americans and Asians. The fact that the color of the new immigrants' skin is a little different does not mean that their contribution will be any less.

Some claim that new immigrants harm our economy by taking jobs away from our citizens and placing an extra burden on local and state governments. The exact opposite is true. Immigrants have always held the dirty, dangerous, unpleasant, and low-paying jobs that nobody else wanted, and the same is true today. Without the plentiful supply of low-cost labor immigrants provide, many of our hard-pressed domestic industries would be driven into bankruptcy by foreign competition. Nor are the immigrants a burden to government. They pay the same taxes as everyone else, and many of them actually receive fewer services for their money because they are afraid of being deported if they step forward to claim their due.

Perhaps more important, it would be morally unconscionable to shut the door to the world's poor and oppressed. How can we, the sons, daughters, and grandchildren of immigrants, tell those coura-

Effective action to stem this tide of immigration is needed now before these problems threaten the very survival of our society.

geous few that they may not gamble their future on a new land?

Economically, socially, and ethically, the United States will be far better off by encouraging new immigration than by trying to shut it off.

when we compare Asians and whites. According to data from the 1980 census, family income for Asians and Pacific Islanders was about 10 percent higher than for whites.[24] But the average Asian family also had more people working, and each Asian worker actually made only about 80 percent as much as his or her white counterpart.[25] A look at the unemployment figures shows much the same story. In 1986, only 6 percent of white workers were unemployed, while that figure was 10.6 percent for Hispanics and a huge 14.5 percent for blacks.[26]

Much of this inequality can be explained by the educational differences already discussed. Because minorities have less education, they have fewer members who qualify for high-paying jobs. But education is not the whole story, for minority members receive less pay than whites with the same level of education. On the average, a black family headed by someone who has completed four years of high school has about the same income as a white family headed by someone with only eight years of education.[27] Because blacks are physically the most distinct ethnic group, they are most often the victims of job discrimination. Such racism is common in labor unions as well as in businesses and results in the exclusion of blacks from union apprenticeship programs that pave the way to high-paying jobs (see Figure 7.1).

A related problem arises from cultural discrimination. Despite the talk about equal opportunities for those with equal ability, many people are hired and promoted because of their personal relationship with an employer or manager. And generally speaking, it is mutual understanding and a common background that promote such friendships. If the personnel manager and boss are white (which is likely to be the case), members of a minority group may be at a distinct disadvantage even if company policy prohibits job discrimination. A recent survey of 24 of America's largest corporations found that eight out of ten blacks and about half of the members of other ethnic minorities felt that women and minorities were excluded from informal networks and work groups in their company.[28]

Law and Justice   Discrimination in the legal system has a long history. The U.S. Constitution did not explicitly mention race or slavery, but it nonetheless provided for the return of escaped slaves and held that a slave should be counted as two-thirds of a person for congressional apportionment and

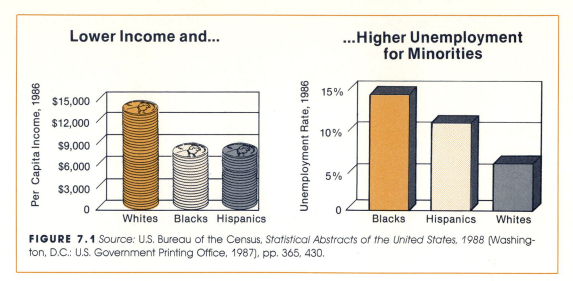

Lower Income and...   **...Higher Unemployment for Minorities**

FIGURE 7.1 *Source:* U.S. Bureau of the Census, *Statistical Abstracts of the United States, 1988* (Washington, D.C.: U.S. Government Printing Office, 1987), pp. 365, 430.

tax purposes. In 1857 the Supreme Court ruled that constitutional rights and privileges did not extend to blacks:

> We think . . . that they [blacks] are not included, and were not intended to be included, under the word "citizen" in the Constitution, and can therefore claim none of the rights and privileges which that instrument provides for and secures to the citizens of the United States. On the contrary, they were at that time considered as a subordinate and inferior class of beings, who had been subjugated by the dominant race, and whether emancipated or not . . . had no rights or privileges but such as those who held power and the government might choose to grant them.[29]

Even though such racist ideas are no longer part of the law, criminal-justice procedures continue to discriminate against ethnic minorities. Our legal system was built by whites, and it incorporates their cultural orientation both in its structure and in the attitudes of those who control the system. Numerous studies have shown that blacks are more likely than whites to be arrested, indicted, convicted, and committed to an institution. Similar studies have shown that blacks have a poorer chance than whites to receive probation, a suspended sentence, parole, or a pardon.[30]

Some sociologists say that these differences appear because blacks are more often involved in serious and repeated offenses than whites, and several studies support this conclusion. Others say that the differences appear because of personal and institutional biases: Police officers, prosecutors, and others tend to stereotype blacks and members of some other ethnic minorities as having a "natural tendency" to commit crimes. The idea that members of a minority group are "criminal types" becomes a self-fulfilling prophecy. Because blacks are expected to commit more crimes, they are watched more closely and therefore are arrested more often than other people. The same stereotypes make it seem reasonable to punish blacks and other minority group members more severely than whites. In sum, prejudice and discrimination still have a powerful influence on our criminal-justice system.

Housing The quality of housing is another index of ethnic discrimination. Blacks, Hispanics, and native Americans tend to be isolated in districts where the quality of housing is poor. Five times as many black families as white families live in housing with inadequate plumbing. Black families also have less space per person,[31] and are less likely to own their own home.[32] The same is true of Mexican Americans, who are about four times more likely

Many members of minority groups must live in cheap, rundown housing because they cannot afford anything else. Even members of minority groups who can afford better housing, however, may be barred by ethnic prejudice from obtaining it. Unscrupulous landlords take advantage of this situation by charging exorbitant rents for decaying apartments in minority neighborhoods.

than whites to live in overcrowded housing. Yet of all minority groups, some of the worst housing conditions are found among native Americans, who often live in decaying old homes in isolated reservations.

Most blacks and Hispanics, and some native Americans, live in segregated ghettos and *barrios* in run-down sections of large cities. Joan Moore's description of Mexican American barrios applies to other ethnic slums as well:

> . . . . when a visitor enters Mexican American *barrios* . . . ordinary urban facilities tend to disappear. Streets are unpaved; curbs and sidewalks and street lights disappear, . . . and the general air of decay and neglect is unmistakable. Abandoned automobiles, uncollected refuse, and the hulks of burned out buildings are monuments to the inadequacy of public services.[33]

When members of minority groups try to escape to other neighborhoods, they often run into a wall of prejudice. Many whites fear that the presence of minority group members in their neighborhood will depress property values. Unscrupulous realtors play on such fears through a practice known as **blockbusting.** Once a minority family has moved into a neighborhood, these realtors try to convince residents that property values will fall. If they are successful, the residents sell out cheaply to the realtors, who in turn sell the houses to incoming minority members at much higher prices. But all of the blame cannot be placed on realtors. Most people prefer to live with neighbors from their own ethnic group. Families from one ethnic group living in a neighborhood being invaded by another are sometimes harassed and intimidated until they pack up and move.

Class or Race? It is clear that minorities occupy the bottom rungs of the social ladder of North American society. But are their problems the result of past or present discrimination? In the late 1970s sociologist William Julius Wilson published an influential book arguing that there has been a significant decline in the importance of race as a source of discrimination.[34] The principal source of today's problems is, according to Wilson, the fact that blacks are trapped in a self-perpetuating cycle of poverty. Minority children are more likely to live lives of poverty because they are more likely to be born into poverty. Thus, the historical effects of the racism and discrimination that originally forced minorities into a subordinate position in the class system are seen to be more important than the discrimination they currently encounter.

The supporters of this theory can cite considerable evidence for their conclusions. Surveys show that racial and ethnic prejudice have been declining in recent years, and explicit laws have been passed against occupational discrimination. There is, moreover, a vigorous and expanding black middle class that seems to have been able to overcome the barriers of racism. And on the other hand, there are a substantial number of whites in the underclass who seem every bit as disadvantaged as the minorities (see Chapter 6). But it is important to recognize that although progress has been made

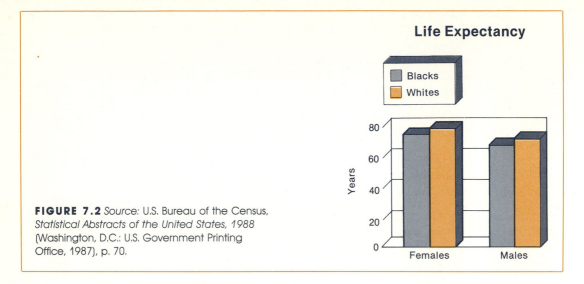

FIGURE 7.2 *Source:* U.S. Bureau of the Census, *Statistical Abstracts of the United States, 1988* (Washington, D.C.: U.S. Government Printing Office, 1987), p. 70.

in the fight against prejudice and discrimination, it is still a powerful force in American life. The members of most minority groups must still deal with major obstacles that whites do not have to face.

The Social Impact of Prejudice and Discrimination   Prejudice and discrimination, both past and present, have many far-reaching effects on our society—some of them obvious, others hidden. The harm that prejudice and discrimination do to a minority group member who can't find a job is clear for all to see. The harm that is done to society as a whole is not so obvious, but it is no less real. Arbitrary exclusion of certain individuals from important occupations wastes badly needed talent. Minority members feel only weak allegiance to a government that permits discrimination against them, and this may become a source of political unrest and violence. Prejudice and discrimination can also have a devastating psychological impact on their victims.

Discrimination is also a matter of life and death. In 1986 the average black American died about four years sooner than the average white.[35] Much of this difference is due to the higher infant mortality rates among poor minorities. A black baby is more than twice as likely to die in its first year of life than a white baby.[36] But even as adults, members of most minority groups still have a lower life expectancy than whites (see Figure 7.2). The plain fact is that these people die earlier than others because they receive inferior food, shelter, and health care.

RESPONDING TO PROBLEMS OF ETHNIC MINORITIES

Until recently most people saw North America as a "melting pot"—a crucible in which people from around the world were blended to form a new and distinct culture. The process of ethnic merging (integration) was believed to be the ultimate solution to the ethnic-relations problem. If everyone was blended into one group, ethnic prejudice and discrimination would be impossible.

But supporters of the **melting-pot theory** have come under increasing attack. First, it is now clear that ethnic merging has not really occurred. Native Americans, blacks, Hispanics, French Canadians—even Irish and Italians—maintain strong cultural and ethnic identities. Second, a rise of ethnic consciousness has led to a new determination to maintain traditional ethnic identities. More and more people are saying that they do not want to blend into the majority.

Nevertheless, all the ethnic groups in North America have undergone significant cultural changes resulting from mutual contacts. Although some elements of a common culture are shared by every ethnic group, the current emphasis on strong ethnic traditions and identity appears to work against further merging in the near future. Most recent proposals for change recommend a more pluralistic system. In the long run, however, it seems likely that domination will be reduced most effectively by programs promoting integration rather than pluralism. With the exception of native Americans and French Canadians, the various ethnic groups in North America are mixed together in the same towns and cities. They will therefore have to continue to share economic, educational, and political institutions, and for this reason greater equality is likely to be achieved only through further integration.

The problem of balancing the ideals of pluralism and integration while moving as rapidly as possible toward full ethnic equality is one of the greatest challenges facing North America today. The responses to this problem have taken two principal forms: political activism and institutional reforms.

Political Activism   Prejudice and discrimination have been hot political issues in the United States at least since the time of the Civil War. The political issues in the bloody conflict between the North and the South went far beyond the question of freeing the slaves. Constitutionally, however, the significant outcome of the war was a political push toward integration. The Thirteenth Amendment to the Constitution (1865) prohibited slavery; the Fourteenth Amendment (1869) gave citizenship to the former slaves and granted them the "equal protection of the law"; and the Fifteenth Amendment (1870) established their right to vote on an equal basis with other citizens.

But despite these amendments, the system of segregation that followed the end of slavery still denied blacks the basic rights enjoyed by other citizens. It was not until the 1950s that the Supreme Court finally ruled the key elements of the segregation system unconstitutional. Yet even then, a tremendous political effort was necessary to force their implementation. The civil rights movement—a coalition of liberal whites and indignant blacks—awakened poor southern blacks to the fact that they were being denied the right to vote. Civil rights activists used demonstrations, marches, and sit-ins to call attention to many forms of unconstitutional discrimination against blacks, and they used the federal courts to do something about it.

The civil rights movement was eventually supplemented, if not replaced, by what came to be called the black power movement. With the growth of ethnic awareness, many white liberals who had been working for the enforcement of antidiscrimination laws were eased out by black activists who demanded equality in a pluralist society rather than the blending of ethnic groups in a "melting pot." Believing integration to be just another form of domination, they pressed for separation of the races, but on an equal basis. Violence became common as black activists were increasingly frustrated in their attempts to realize their goals. Finally the black power movement was repressed by force and its most militant leaders killed or jailed.

But the spirit of the black power movement lives on. It serves as a guide for other minorities, who have formed their own activist groups. Political action against the system of ethnic domination also continues. But the activists, many of whom now hold government offices, are increasingly working within "the system." Native American activists have been particularly successful in using legal actions to win back the rights granted in treaties with the U.S. government. They won the right to fish in Puget Sound and Lake Michigan and legal title to lands in North Dakota, Maine, and Rhode Island.

Political activism has proven to be the most effective tool for winning social justice for minority groups. Here, the late Dr. Martin Luther King, Jr., is shown leading a protest march in Boston, Massachusetts. Such protests were part of the civil rights movement that brought an end to official racial segregation in the United States.

Even the Black Panthers, famous as the most militant of the black power groups, ended up running their own candidates for political office.

The success of black political activism can be seen in the fact that there are now about three hundred cities in the United States with black mayors.[37] Yet despite these advances, much of the efforts of minority leaders in the conservative 1980s have been devoted to merely protecting the victories won in the past.

Institutional Reforms   Political activism is only a means to an end. To advance the goal of ethnic equality, activists must decide on which changes they want in the social structure. Some of the most commonly voiced proposals call for the expansion of bilingualism, changes in the image of minorities presented in the mass media, effective school integration, and equal employment opportunities.

Bilingualism The most obvious way to eliminate institutional discrimination against those who do not speak English as a native language is through **bilingualism**—that is, giving minority languages equal status with the dominant language. This approach, which promotes equality through pluralism, has been quite successful in Switzerland but not in Canada. For most of the past century, Canadian bilingualism has meant protection of the rights of English speakers in Quebec but not protection of the rights of French speakers in the rest of Canada. The Official Languages Act sponsored by Prime Minister Pierre Trudeau forced the federal government to become truly bilingual, but to many French Canadians this was too little, too late. In August 1977 the legislature of Quebec rejected bilingualism and passed the Charter of the French Language, making French the only official language of the province and requiring its use in business and government.

It is not clear whether the recent proposals for bilingualism in the United States are a call for pluralism or for integration. Although a desire for pluralism is apparent among some advocates of bilingualism, educators have tended to use the Spanish-speaking students' language as a tool for teaching them in English. When this is done, the bilingual program can have the effect of heating up the melting pot, thereby promoting integration but defeating the aims of pluralism.

It would be extremely difficult to achieve linguistic pluralism in the United States, for true bilingualism would require that everyone learn to speak both English and Spanish even if their native language is Italian, Chinese, or Greek. Instead of linguistic equality, this would produce domination by two language groups instead of one. And although Spanish is the second most commonly spoken language in the United States, dozens of other languages are spoken. Full equality for so many languages is clearly impossible. It therefore seems reasonable to continue the American policy of using English as the main language, but supplementing it with more effective efforts to teach children in their own language so that they can keep up with their studies until they learn English.

The Mass Media Before the arrival of television, the mass media promoted ethnic stereotypes rather than trying to eliminate them. When black men committed crimes, newspapers were likely to run a story beginning in this way: "John Doe, a Negro, was arrested for the murder of his wife last night." Similar identifications were not made for crimes committed by whites, creating the impression that the crime rate among blacks was much higher than it was. In films and radio dramas, blacks played the roles of the inferiors that they were assumed to be in real life: janitors, maids, clowns, dancers. In the early days of television, too, there were few black roles, and the blacks who were seen on the screen were almost always depicted as inferior to whites.

It was probably the drive for profits, rather than concern for equality, that led to better treatment of minority groups in the mass media. Producers discovered that movies with black actors in leading roles attract blacks to the box office, and television soon began using more minority actors too. Then it became standard practice to use minority group members in television commercials and as announcers and newscasters.

At first these changes in the mass media seemed to be directed toward achieving integration, employing people on the basis of merit rather than ethnicity. But a trend toward greater pluralism developed as it was discovered that there is a market for national magazines, movies, and television shows produced especially for blacks or Hispanics. This new pluralism differs from the old approach in one highly significant respect, however: it is based on the assumption that whites, blacks, and other ethnic minorities are equal.

Schools The basic issue in the school integration controversy is not inequality per se. Of course, some people continue to believe that blacks are inferior and therefore are not entitled to an education equal to that given whites. But the vast majority of Americans now favor educational equality. The real controversy is over whether equal education is to be achieved through integration (as supporters of mandatory busing believe) or through pluralism (as supporters of "neighborhood schools" believe). (See Chapter 4.)

A side issue, but an important one, is whether the schools, like television, should be used to reduce racial and ethnic prejudice. Integrationists point to research showing that under the right conditions—cooperation among groups sharing common goals—integration does reduce prejudice. Pluralists say that the same conditions can be achieved without fully integrating the schools. They favor equality, but they want to retain separate ethnic identities, especially their own. Some school districts with large minority populations are attempting to recruit black and Hispanic teachers who are familiar with the culture of their students and can present positive role models. Thus, they have joined the pluralists.

Responses to proposals and programs for eliminating bigotry and cultural bias from school textbooks have been positive. As in the case of television and movies, integrationists and pluralists alike have accepted the idea that ethnic domination was promoted by elementary-school books picturing only middle-class whites and by history books portraying blacks as happy-go-lucky "darkies" and Indians as savages who murdered innocent settlers. Contemporary schoolbooks do a much better job of showing the great contribution of ethnic minorities to American life.

Employment The idea that everyone deserves an equal opportunity to make a living has a long history and a great deal of popular support. But implementing this idea has been difficult. Originally, most proposals called for an end to discriminatory practices in hiring and firing. For example, the Fair Employment Practices Commission, established by President Roosevelt's executive order during World War II, tried to end discrimination in war industries. The American Federation of Labor and the Congress of Industrial Organizations (which have since merged) both tried to organize blacks in the late 1940s and early 1950s. With the civil rights movement came the Civil Rights Act of 1964, which forbids discrimination by unions, employment agencies, and businesses employing more than 25 workers. But the problems in enforcing such a law have been immense, for it is extremely difficult to prove why someone was not hired or promoted.

The laws forbidding discrimination have now been supplemented by affirmative-action programs that require a positive effort to recruit and promote qualified minority-group members. Employers can no longer defend themselves by claiming that a decision not to hire a minority-group member was based on some criterion other than ethnic-group membership. They must prove that they are not discriminating. If the percentage of minority-group members in their employ is significantly lower than the percentage in the work force, companies must accept a goal for minority employment and set up timetables stating when these goals are likely to be met.

These procedures have created a powerful "white backlash." Critics charge that the ratios are not goals but quotas and that affirmative-action programs really call for reverse discrimination (discrimination against white males). Resolution of this conflict will be extremely difficult. It is true that some minority-group members are given preferential treatment and that therefore some whites are discriminated against. But it is also true that minority-group members still face far more discrimination than whites do.

The Supreme Court has yet to resolve these difficult legal issues. In the 1978 *Bakke* decision the Court upheld the general principle of affirmative action but ruled that Alan Bakke (a white) had suffered illegal discrimination when he was denied admission to a medical school that reserved a fixed quota of its admissions for minority students. In 1984 the Court struck down layoff procedures that protected the jobs of blacks by requiring layoffs of whites with greater seniority.

But in a series of rulings in 1986 and 1987, the Court upheld affirmative action in the workplace as a remedy for past discrimination by the same organization. Programs to promote blacks ahead of whites with higher test scores, requiring a union to meet a fixed quota of minority membership, and a fixed ratio of white to minority promotions were all approved on these grounds.[39] Thus, it is still not clear which kinds of affirmative-action programs are constitutional and which kinds are not. Because laws that merely prohibit employment discrimination against minority-group members do not seem to be enforceable, some form of affirmative-action procedures must be continued if equality of opportunity is to be achieved. Nevertheless, the dangers of allowing, indeed requiring, employers to consider ethnic group membership as a criterion for employment are great.

Directions for the Future   Although the history of the past several decades shows significant progress toward racial and ethnic equality, improvement has been slow. Complete equality remains a distant goal. Elimination of the school segregation system was a major step forward, as was the U.S. government's official stance against ethnic discrimination in housing and employment. Illiteracy rates among minorities have dropped, and their level of education has increased. Although racism and ethnic stereotypes remain, these prejudices are not publicly expressed by business and political leaders as often as they once were. Moreover, public-opinion surveys show that prejudice against minorities has diminished. In 1963, for example, 66 percent of the whites questioned by the Harris poll agreed that "blacks have less ambition than most other people," but by 1985 only 23 percent of whites agreed.[40]

Yet the picture is not without blemishes. The surveys showing a reduction in prejudice among whites also show that racism is still widespread on both sides of the color line. Despite years of struggle, little progress has been made in reducing the economic inequality among ethnic groups. In fact, the gap between the average white family's income and the average black or Hispanic family's income has actually widened in the last decade.[41] Perhaps most disturbing of all is the growing feeling that many Americans, hard-pressed by economic troubles, are turning their backs on the problem of ethnic injustice.

Spanish-speaking Americans are now facing special problems as a result of the flood of new immigrants from Mexico and other Latin American countries. Uneducated, unable to speak English, and in the country illegally, these young immigrants are willing to work for lower wages than American-born Hispanics. These "undocumented workers" often labor under deplorable conditions for less than the legal minimum wage, while fear of deportation keeps them from reporting their employers to the authorities. These immigrants seldom show up in census reports or unemployment figures, though they are estimated to number between 1 and 8 million persons.

A sweeping new program was enacted in 1986 to deal with the problem of illegal immigration. Illegals who could prove that they had lived in the United States since January 1982 were granted amnesty and allowed to apply for citizenship, and for the first time penalties were placed on employers who knowingly hired illegal workers.[42] The final results of this program are yet to be known. But it is doubtful that any long-term solution to this problem can be found as long as economic conditions are so desperate in Latin America and Asia.

Today's black community is clearly a house divided. On the one hand, there is the growing black middle class. Typically composed of families with two working parents, membership in the black middle class has more than doubled since 1960. While still facing considerable prejudice and discrimination, these families have slowly managed to improve their economic position. On the other hand, the economic position of lower-class black families, most of which are headed by single women, has continued to decline. Some observers predict that this economic and cultural gap will continue to widen, with the black middle class ultimately winning full acceptance into white society while the black underclass is completely shut out of the mainstream and its enormous problems ignored. More optimistic are predictions that the unique bond among American blacks forged by their long history of oppression will remain strong, and that the middle class will be able to help the children of poverty improve their social position.

In the 1970s many native American tribes were for the first time able to use their unique position in American society to make some significant economic gains. Tribal leaders began to demand that the resources of their reservations be utilized for their people's benefit and that the rights granted to them in numerous treaties with white America finally be honored. Many tribes took over direct control of the mineral and petroleum rights to reservation land and forced would-be developers to grant them much better terms. But it is easy to be misled by such generalizations, for this transformation has been an uneven one. Although some tribes have seen a very substantial increase in their fortunes, other tribes without valuable natural resources have not benefited at all, and the decline in petroleum prices in the 1980s has created serious problems even for the more fortunate tribes. About half of all American Indians live on reservations, and despite the roughly $2.5 billion the Bureau of Indian Affairs spends every year, many reservations are places of poverty and hopelessness. There is, for example, more than 80 percent unemployment among the Navahos who live in America's largest reservation;[43] and the poverty rate for native Americans is more than twice the national average.[44]

Finally, something must be said about the European ethnics—immigrants from countries like Ireland, Poland, and Italy—who maintain strong ties to their native culture. Because these "white ethnics" came with nothing and worked their way up in the face of considerable prejudice and discrimination, they generally have little sympathy for the demands of other ethnic groups. No one helped them gain equality, and they see no reason why non-Europeans—blacks, Hispanics, native Americans—should get special treatment. Indeed, some of these white ethnics both fear and hate their black- or brown-skinned neighbors. Long-term progress toward ethnic equality will come only when white ethnic groups are given more attention and understanding than they have so far received and when they, in turn, support demands for equality by the ethnic groups that have replaced them at the bottom of the heap.

SOCIOLOGICAL PERSPECTIVES ON PROBLEMS OF ETHNIC MINORITIES

Public concern about ethnic inequality waxes and wanes with the political climate. Interest in equality is particularly intense in times of change, when old patterns of ethnic relations are breaking up and there is conflict over future directions. In the United States, ethnic relations raised the most public concern during the Reconstruction period after the Civil War and during the era of the civil rights and black power movements that marked the end of the segregation system 100 years later. At both times ethnic inequality became a pressing social problem because an old system of ethnic relations was deteriorating and a new pattern was taking shape. But even in most stable periods, the problem of fairly managing ethnic relations in so diverse a society is never far below the surface.

The Functionalist Perspective   Functionalists believe that shared values and attitudes are the cement that holds a society together. The more disagreement there is over basic values, the more unstable and disorganized a society is likely to be. Although the various ethnic groups in North America have come to share many values over the years, significant differences remain, and these differences are an important source of conflict. North America lacks the unity, consensus, and organization that are essential to a harmonious society. Although the efforts of the largest ethnic groups to dominate others have become less and less successful, neither pluralism nor integration has replaced domination. Society is disorganized, unable to muster its people to work together for the common good.

From the functionalist perspective, ethnic discrimination is both a cause and an effect of contemporary social disorganization. The failure to give minorities full equality wastes valuable human resources and generates ethnic hostilities that reduce economic production and undermine political authority. These hostilities, in turn, contribute to prejudice and discrimination as different ethnic groups come to see one another as enemies.

To functionalists, the best response is to reduce discrimination by reorganizing social institutions. Unity is the objective, whether it is achieved through domination, pluralism, or integration. But integration is the ideal because an integrated society is likely to have the fewest conflicts. Functionalists ask for an attack on discrimination in housing, education, criminal justice, and elsewhere, arguing that an effective reform movement must increase support for "the system" among ethnic minorities while at the same time maintaining the allegiance of the majority.

The Conflict Perspective   Conflict theorists see the history of ethnic relations in North America as one of conflict and oppression. European colonists fought with each other and with the Indians. Eventually English-speaking whites conquered most of the continent, but conflict did not end there. As new groups settled in the "promised land," some were assimilated. Those who refused to give up their ethnic identity were shunted into inferior positions: employees rather than employers, police officers rather than judges, farmhands rather than landowners, blue-collar workers rather than white-collar workers, and so on.

From the conflict perspective, the history of all ethnic relations is the history of a struggle for power. When one group is more powerful than others, a system of domination develops in which weaker groups are exploited for the political, social, and economic advantage of the dominant group. When power is more equally distributed, pluralism develops. But whether ethnic groups are in a relationship of domination or equality, there is no guarantee that the system will remain stable. Social change is primarily a process by which one group grows stronger at the expense of others. Those who have power want peace and stability; those who are out of power want conflict and change. Institutionalized discrimination is, thus, a technique for keeping the dominant group in power and protecting it from competition.

Conflict theorists assert that ethnic equality can be achieved only through struggle. A group that has improved its status is by definition a group that has seized some political and economic power. Conflict theorists argue that political change is often necessary to bring about economic change in such things as employment, education, housing, and health care. The key to increased power is organization for political action. Even a small ethnic group that is unified can wield much greater power than its numbers would suggest. In a democratic society, political change can be achieved by outvoting and outmaneuvering one's opponents according to the established rules of the game. Political change can also be achieved by attacking the established rules in demonstrations and protests that may threaten—or provoke—violence. Both techniques are being used in ethnic struggles in North America and around the world, and conflict theorists counsel those who would change the system to study the historical record of the successes and failures of such efforts.

Social Psychological Perspectives   Social psychologists have put much effort into investigating the causes of prejudice and discrimination and their effects on individual victims. Interactionist theory, for instance, holds that individuals develop their concepts of personal identity from their interaction with the people around them. When members of a minority group are constantly treated as though they were inferior, they are bound to be affected. Some become convinced that they really are inferior, resulting in low self-esteem and feelings of inadequacy. They are also more likely to develop other personal problems, such as alcoholism and drug addiction. The rate of heroin addiction among blacks and Hispanics is much higher than the national average, and alcoholism is an especially severe problem among native Americans. Other minority-group members reject these ethnic stereotypes, forcefully asserting their own value and importance—behavior that occasionally results in trouble with the law. Still others try to avoid the effects of prejudice and discrimination by isolating themselves in segregated ethnic communities.

Proposals by social psychologists for reducing ethnic discrimination and prejudice fall into two broad categories. Those in the first category are based on the fact that whatever is learned can be unlearned. Included here are recommendations for more ethnic contact and communication and for direct attacks on ethnic stereotypes in the media and in schools. By showing people from different ethnic groups as they actually are, and not as stereotypes depict them, barriers to communication and understanding can be removed.

Proposals in the second category go to the root of the problem, recommending long-term changes that will reduce ethnic competition. More contacts and communication among ethnic groups will enable people to overcome their prejudices. But research shows that these contacts must be among ethnic groups of equal social status who are working together for a common goal rather than competing with one another for survival. In other words, social psychologists say that prejudice and discrimination will decrease as fear of economic competition decreases.

Unlike other social psychologists, biosocial theorists have concerned themselves with the effects of biological rather than social differences between ethnic groups. The visible physical differences between people from different ethnic backgrounds, for instance, make it easier to identify members of ethnic minorities, in turn making it easier to discriminate against them. A few biosocial theorists have even claimed that heredity is the cause of important differences in the behavior of different racial groups. For instance, some argue that blacks have lower intelligence than whites. Such claims have stirred up a storm of controversy, but the overwhelming majority of social psychologists hold that the hereditary differences between people from different racial backgrounds are very slight. Indeed, social psychologists point out that the practice of grouping people into common categories on the basis of such characteristics as skin color and type of hair is simply a cultural tradition, and one that has caused enormous social problems. The best solution to the "racial problem" is to abandon those traditional attitudes and adopt the more scientifically supportable view that all people are members of a single human race.

SUMMARY

Throughout history, tension and conflict have existed between ethnic groups living in close contact with one another. People who share a sense of identity and togetherness tend to be ethnocentric, believing that their ways of doing things are better than those of other groups. Ethnocentrism becomes racism when it is based on the idea that people with certain physical traits are superior to others and deserve special privileges.

The relationship between ethnic groups usually follows one of three general patterns. Domination exists when one ethnic group holds the power and exploits another group or groups. When two or more ethnic groups have roughly equal power so that each controls its own affairs, a system of pluralism exists. Finally, when two or more ethnic groups blend together and share power, customs, and social institutions, the relationship is known as integration.

Prejudice and discrimination are related, but they are not the same. The former refers to attitudes, the latter to actions. A prejudiced person has a strong dislike for members of a certain ethnic or racial group. Discrimination is the practice of penalizing some people because of their ethnic status.

Social scientists have found several causes of prejudice and discrimination. Some find their roots in rigid and inflexible authoritarian personalities; others say that frustration produces aggression, which is directed against safe scapegoats. Prejudice is learned in the process of socialization. Prejudice is used to justify discrimination, which is a device for preserving the economic and political dominance of a particular group. Finally, social scientists have noted that prejudice and discrimination are associated with moral and cultural conflicts as well as with economic competition.

Historically, North America has seen the conquest and domination of the Indians, French, Spanish, and Mexicans by English-speaking peoples. They also dominated black Africans and immigrants from other parts of the world. But that domination has not gone unchallenged. Some ethnic groups have retained a separate identity and added a pattern of pluralism to the pattern of dominance. There is no doubt, either, that the United States and Canada were "melting pots" in which some European cultures blended together in a pattern of integration.

Discrimination is built into our economic, educational, and political institutions. Some of this institutional discrimination is intentional, designed to protect the interests of whites, but some of it seems to have begun accidentally. Because our basic institutions were designed and are run primarily by whites they reflect the cultural values and assumptions of that group. Some sociologists argue that economic and social changes have reduced the impact of discrimination in today's society and that the long-term effects of past discrimination are now a more important cause of the problems of most minority groups.

Prejudice and discrimination have many negative consequences, including the exclusion of talented people from important jobs, the weakening of overall social unity, the creation of psychological problems, and the production of unnecessary pain and suffering. There have been many responses to the problems of ethnic relations. For 100 years the goal of political activism was to secure a pattern of integration by eliminating discrimination on the part of the dominant majority. More recently, some minority activists, believing that integration is just another form of domination, pressed for pluralism. Affirmative-action programs now attempt to make employers treat members of ethnic minorities fairly. A variety of institutional reforms have been suggested to reduce prejudice and discrimination, including bilingualism, reduction of cultural biases in the mass media and in schoolbooks, school integration, and equality of employment opportunity.

According to functionalists, North American society is disorganized and unable to muster its many ethnic groups to work in harmony for the common good. But conflict theorists see institutionalized discrimination as an intentional way of protecting the economic and political power of the dominant groups. The key to increasing the power of minority groups, in their view, is to organize for political action. Social psychologists point out that prejudice and discrimination are learned and that both are associated with fear of competition. They recommend more ethnic contacts and a reduction of economic competition among ethnic groups.

KEY TERMS

bilingualism
discrimination
domination
ethnic group
ethnocentrism
institutional discrimination

integration
pluralism
prejudice
race
racism
stereotype

FURTHER READINGS

Sociology of Ethnic Relations

Richard T. Schaefer, *Racial and Ethnic Groups*, Glenview, Ill.: Scott, Foresman, 1988.

William Wilson, *The Declining Significance of Race*, 2d ed., Chicago: University of Chicago Press, 1980.

Ethnic Groups in North America

Alvin M. Josephy, Jr., *Now That the Buffalo's Gone: A Study of Today's American Indians*, New York: Alfred A. Knopf, 1982.

Joan Moore and Harry Pachon, *Hispanics in the United States*, Englewood Cliffs, N.J.: Prentice-Hall, 1985.

Alphonso Pinkney, *Black Americans*, 3d ed., Englewood Cliffs, N.J.: Prentice-Hall, 1987.

- How do modern life-styles affect health?

- Why is health care so costly?

- Why do the poor receive inferior medical care?

- What are the benefits of national health insurance?

- What are the ethical dilemmas posed by modern medicine?

- How can our health care be improved?

Chapter 8

THE SICK AND THE HEALTH CARE SYSTEM

Good health, like good food and water, is easy to take for granted. It is not until our health is threatened that we realize how important it is. The physical suffering accompanying most serious illness is obvious, but the psychological cost is often much greater. The nagging fear of death or permanent disability torments many sick people. Their inability to carry out their normal social roles places burdens on their friends and relatives. Long-term illness requires a family to change its role structure: wives must go to work and husbands must care for the children. Some families even shut themselves off from outsiders and make the sick person the focus of their daily life. Too often the result is a growing sense of guilt and resentment that ends in the disintegration of the family.

Illness and death are, of course, an unavoidable part of human life. But society still has a profound influence on our health problems. For one thing, social factors such as public sanitation and safety, diet, stress, environmental pollution, and occupational hazards all help determine how healthy we are. And when we do get sick, the availability, quality, and organization of health care plays a major role in determining how quickly we recover, or whether we recover at all.

HEALTH AND ILLNESS

To many people, good health means simply that they have no obvious illnesses or physical problems. But some people who are depressed, lack vitality, and say they are "not feeling well" cannot be shown to have any specific illness. For this reason, the World Health Organization defines **health** as "a state of complete physical, mental and social well-being and not merely the absence of disease and infirmity."[1] It is clear that health involves social and psychological conditions as well as biological ones. The definition of good health varies between nations and even between different classes within the same nation. The tired, listless feeling associated with poor nutrition is considered normal by poor people in most parts of the world but is seen as a sign of illness by the wealthy.

People who are alive today are healthier and will live longer than any other generation in history. In the eighteenth century the average life span in even the most prosperous nations was no more than 35 years. Today, the life span in the industrialized world averages 70 years or more, largely because of a dramatic decline in infant mortality and deaths from contagious diseases.[2] As the average life span increased, the degenerative diseases of later life became the number one killers. In 1900 the leading causes of death were pneumonia, influenza, tuberculosis, and diarrhea. Today the leading causes of death are heart diseases, cancer, and strokes; influenza and pneumonia rank fifth (see Figure 8.1).[3]

The great improvement in living conditions in the twentieth century is the principal reason we are living longer. A rising standard of living and increased agricultural production mean better food, shelter, and clothing for

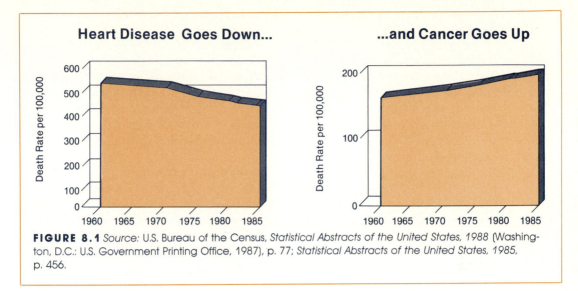

FIGURE 8.1 *Source*: U.S. Bureau of the Census, *Statistical Abstracts of the United States, 1988* (Washington, D.C.: U.S. Government Printing Office, 1987), p. 77; *Statistical Abstracts of the United States, 1985*, p. 456.

the average person. The installation of sewer pipes and the construction of water purification plants sharply reduced epidemics of waterborne diseases.

Physicians and medical researchers have contributed to the decline in death rates in three principal ways. First, they discovered the causes of contagious diseases and pressed for preventive measures based on this knowledge. Without the discovery of germs, our modern sewage disposal and water treatment facilities would never have been built. Second, immunization techniques were invented to prevent such killers as diphtheria and smallpox. Third, new techniques for treating dangerous diseases were developed, the most important being antibiotic drugs. Contrary to popular opinion, sophisticated and expensive medical procedures such as open-heart surgery have added little to the average life span.

THE HAZARDS OF MODERN LIVING

Not all the changes that have transformed the twentieth-century world have been beneficial to health. Stress, pollution, and overindulgence can kill and cripple as effectively as typhoid or tuberculosis. The widespread belief that medicine can perform miracles has created many unrealistic expectations. Many people eat, drink, and smoke too much, expecting that their physician will repair the damage to their bodies. But modern medicine is no substitute for a healthful life-style and common sense.

Exercise, Diet, and Smoking   Most North Americans are far less active than their ancestors were. Labor-saving devices ranging from the automobile to the electric toothbrush have reduced the amount of physical effort required for daily living, and automation has created an increasing number of "thinking jobs" that demand no harder work than picking up a pencil or making a phone call.

Current medical research shows regular exercise to be essential to good health. Not only do people who exercise regularly report that they feel better, but exercise has been shown to reduce the risk of heart disease—the leading cause of death in North America. A San Francisco study found that longshoremen who did hard physical labor had fewer heart attacks than longshoremen who did only light work. In their study of Boston men, Charles Rose and his associates found the amount of exercise to be one of the best predictors of longevity.[4]

Modern technology has enabled industrialized nations to conquer the most acute dietary problem: starvation. But though most of us now get enough to eat, we often eat the wrong kind of food. Although there is some disagreement over what type of diet is most conducive to good health, virtually no nutritionists feel that the high levels of fats and sugar in our diet are beneficial, and there is substantial evidence that such foods cause serious health problems.[5] A population of Canadian Eskimos who quadrupled their sugar consumption in just eight years experienced alarming increases in diabetes, arteriosclerosis (hardening of the arteries), obesity, and gallbladder disease.[6] A study of Japanese Americans whose diets were high in fat found that they had significantly more arteriosclerosis than Japanese living in Japan, where the diet is much lower in fat.[7]

A comprehensive report by the National Academy of Sciences in the late 1970s advised Americans to eat fewer fatty foods such as red meat, to eat little or no salt-cured foods such as ham, bacon, and hot dogs, and to eat more fresh fruits and vegetables.[8] And there is evidence that North Americans are finally paying heed to such warnings and are starting to change their dietary habits. The consumption of red meats such as beef and lamb has declined about 7 percent since its peak in 1970, while the consumption of fish, chicken, and fresh fruits and vegetables has increased.[9] But in 1988, the Surgeon General's Report on Nutrition and Health concluded that Americans were still eating too much fat and not enough fruits, vegetables, and whole-grain products.[10]

North Americans still love high-calorie foods, and our tendency to overeat has caused obesity to become a serious problem. Current research shows that heart disease, high blood pressure, and diabetes are associated with being overweight.[11] Many nutritionists are also concerned about the growing use of food additives. Some additives have been found to cause cancer or other serious ailments only after years of extensive use, and no one knows how many of today's additives will later be proven dangerous.

Despite heated denials from the tobacco industry, there is no longer any doubt that smoking is a serious health hazard. It has been linked to a long list of diseases, including lung cancer, emphysema, ulcers, and heart disorders. The Surgeon General's yearly reports on smoking state that, among other things, the death rate of smokers is 70 percent higher than that for nonsmokers of the same age, and the death rate for heavy smokers (two or more packs a day) is double that for nonsmokers. They also concluded that tobacco is a highly addictive drug comparable to cocaine or heroin.[12] Ironically, at the same time that the U.S. government was issuing these warnings, it was paying millions of dollars in subsidies to help tobacco farmers grow their deadly crop.

Stress Contemporary industrial societies put their citizens under great stress. Workers labor harder and longer than in agricultural societies and are under constant pressure to meet deadlines and quality standards. The initial symptoms of stress, such as irritability, insomnia, and a queasy stomach, are usually minor, and a certain amount of stress may even be necessary to good mental health (see Chapter 12). But high levels of stress over long periods of time can lead to serious health problems.

Evidence for this conclusion can be found in the fact that people in stressful occupations are more likely to suffer from a variety of health problems. One study found that two-thirds of all air traffic controllers in the United States have peptic ulcers, probably as a result of the demands of a job in which a mistake may mean death for hundreds of people.[13] Stress is also associated with heart disease. A study of lawyers, dentists, and physicians found a strong correlation between the amount of stress associated with their specialty and their rates of heart disease; thus, general-practice lawyers had less heart trouble than trial lawyers, who had less heart trouble than patent lawyers. But a study conducted by Columbia University found that such jobs as waitress and telephone operator, which place heavy demands on workers but give them little decision-making control, were the most highly correlated with heart and circulatory problems.[14]

One estimate puts the annual cost of stress related insurance claims and lost productivity at $150 billion a year. According to *Business Week* magazine, over 90 percent of America's 500 largest corporations now have some kind of program to deal with employee stress.[15] But the unexpected stress from sudden changes in living patterns may be even more hazardous than routine occupational stress. Parkes, Benjamin, and Fitzgerald's study of 4486 widowers found that their death rate was 40 percent higher than normal for the first year after the death of their wife.[16] And Taylor found a higher-than-normal death rate and more illness among widows after the death of their husband.[17]

Environmental Hazards The pollutants that industries dump into the environment are more than just an ugly nuisance; they are killers. Air pollution has been found to be related to deaths from bronchitis, heart disease, and emphysema as well as several types of cancer. The contamination of water with poisonous wastes, such as lead and mercury, has already taken hundreds of lives, and the list of new dangers grows daily. American industry alone creates 3,000 new chemicals every year, and most of the hundreds of thousands of chemical compounds used by modern industry have never been thoroughly tested to find out how dangerous they are.

19th-Century Social Problems

Dr. H. B. Cole, health officer, reported to the council, as board of health, that the present year, according to the opinions of celebrated authorities, is to be a year of great danger as regards to epidemics, etc., and recommended that our citizens be required to use unusual care in the disposition of garbage and slops, and that all pig stys in the thickly settled portion of the city be declared nuisances, and that none be allowed except they maintain a floor and it be cleaned twice a week during the summer, that privies be thoroughly disinfected, and that slaughter houses be not permitted to run the blood on the ground and let the hogs create as much filth as before.

May 7, 1886

These selections, which appear throughout the text, are from the *Badger State Banner*, a newspaper published in Black River Falls, Wisconsin.

Not surprisingly, the most serious problems may be found among laborers who work directly with dangerous substances. Steelworkers are 7.5 times more likely to die of cancer of the kidney and 10 times more likely to die of lung cancer than people in other occupations. But steelworkers are lucky compared with asbestos workers. Almost half of the 500,000 workers who were exposed to high doses of asbestos will die as a result: 100,000 are expected to die of lung cancer, 35,000 of asbestosis (another lung disease), and 35,000 of mesothelioma (an otherwise rare cancer of the linings of the lungs and stomach).[18] It is estimated that one in every four American workers is exposed to a serious health hazard at work. About 5.5 million workers are injured or made ill, and about 75,000 workers die from "job induced" causes every year.[19]

Contagious Disease Cancer and diseases of the heart and circulatory system are the most common causes of death in wealthy industrial societies. But such killers are seldom the causes of our daily health problems. Most of our most common difficulties result from the relatively minor contagious diseases that are a seemingly inevitable part of daily life. A ten-year study of families in Cleveland, Ohio, found that common respiratory and intestinal diseases (colds, bronchitis, flu, and the like) accounted for 76 percent of all illnesses. The average person in this study had 5.6 respiratory and 1.5 intestinal diseases a year.[20]

Although these relatively minor ailments remain a continuing problem, great progress has been made against the death-dealing epidemics that once threatened all humanity. Improvements in sanitation and water treatment have all but eliminated such waterborne diseases as cholera and typhoid from the industrialized nations and sharply reduced their incidence in the poor nations of the Third World. Vaccinations have had even greater success against other dread diseases such as polio and smallpox. For a while it seemed that we were on the way to eliminating the killers that had threatened the human race for countless centuries. But recently the tide has shifted in the other direction, and it is obvious that the battle against contagious disease is far from over.

Some of our current problems stem from overconfidence and neglect. Measles—a well-known disease most common in children—provides a good example. A vigorous program of vaccination slashed the number of cases in the United States from over 400,000 in 1960 to fewer than 2000 in the early 1980s. But declining federal support and general overconfidence has led to a reduction in the percentage of children who have been vaccinated, and the total incidence of measles is once again on the increase.[21] There have also been "miniepidemics" of some diseases among such vulnerable groups as the homeless and intravenous drug users. Although conditions in the Third World have improved, the struggle against contagious disease has never been as successful there as it has been in the industrialized nations. Half the world's people lack safe drinking water, and three-fourths have no sanitary facilities. Fewer than 40 percent of the children of the Third World have been vaccinated against measles, tetanus, whooping cough, diphtheria or the other major childhood diseases which take about 4 million young lives every year.[22]

Although the effects of this kind of neglect were predictable, the other blow to our efforts to control contagious disease came from an entirely unexpected source: the emergence of a deadly new virus. That virus, of course,

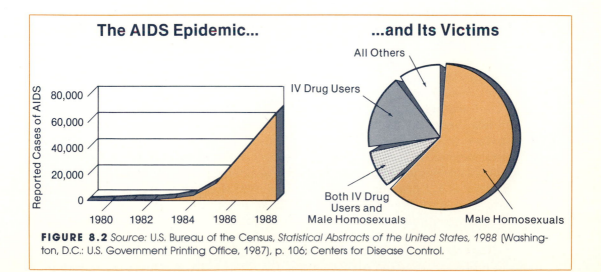

FIGURE 8.2 *Source:* U.S. Bureau of the Census, *Statistical Abstracts of the United States, 1988* (Washington, D.C.: U.S. Government Printing Office, 1987), p. 106; Centers for Disease Control.

The victims of the growing AIDS epidemic must not only deal with the knowledge that the disease is almost always fatal but also face fear and rejection from the general public.

causes acquired immune deficiency syndrome (AIDS). Virtually unknown in 1980, there were over 64,000 known cases in the United States in 1988, and the number is doubling every year. The disease attacks the body's immune system, leaving it vulnerable to a host of other diseases. AIDS is almost always fatal and there is no known cure. Although it develops quite slowly, over 36,000 people have died in the United States alone.[23]

Fortunately, AIDS is not very easily transmitted from person to person. Some direct exchange of body fluids is usually necessary, and the most common forms of transmission are anal intercourse and needle sharing among intravenous drug users. About 72 percent of the victims of AIDS in the United States are homosexual men, and about 24 percent are intravenous drug users. (There is a 7 percent overlap of these two categories, that is, gay men who are also intravenous drug users.)[24] Like most other health problems, AIDS is most common among the poor and minorities. Blacks make up about 12 percent of the population of the United States, but they are 25 percent of the AIDS victims and, similarly, Hispanics are about 7 percent of the population but 14 percent of the AIDS victims. Even more disturbing is the fact that 78 percent of the AIDS victims under the age of 13 are black or Hispanic.[25] (See Figure 8.2.)

The most frightening thing about the AIDS epidemic is the projections of how many people it may strike down in the near future. Federal health officials believe that as many as 1.5 million Americans have already been exposed to the disease, and they predict that there will be about 450,000 active cases of AIDS by 1993.[26] A 1987 poll by the *Los Angeles Times* found that one out of five Americans said that they had changed their life-style because of the AIDS epidemic, and a frightening 42 percent said that some civil liberties must be suspended to fight the epidemic.[27] But as serious as the AIDS epidemic is, it is important to keep it in perspective. Although AIDS is by far the most serious contagious disease in the industralized nations, on a global scale it ranks far down the list. Worldwide, about 5 to 10 million people are believed to be infected with the AIDS virus, but about 200 million people have schistosomiasis, another 200 million are infected with hepatitis, and about 220 million more with malaria.[28] In Africa alone, about 1 million children die of malaria ever year.[29]

Poverty There is overwhelming evidence that poor people have more health problems than those who are better off. The effects of poverty are obvious in the over-populated agricultural nations. Lack of clothing, housing, and food takes a frightening toll. The infant mortality rate in such countries as India, Zaire, and Iran is about ten times higher than in the United States, epidemic disease is commonplace, and 10 to 20 million people simply starve to death every year (see Chapter 17).[30] The problems of the poor in the industrialized nations are less visible, but they are no less real. They include lower life expectancies, higher rates of infant death, and more contagious disease, heart ailments, arthritis, and high blood pressure. Black children are twice as likely as white children to die in their first year of life, and a number of studies show that the poor and members of the ethnic minorities are sick more days a year than are the wealthy.[31] When asked about their health, poor people are about three times more likely to say that their health is only fair or poor, or that they have some serious chronic illness.[32]

Poverty is the indirect cause of most of these problems. About 25 million Americans cannot afford to keep themselves adequately fed and are therefore particularly susceptible to illness and disease. Because their diet contains more cheap, fatty foods, poor people are more likely to be overweight. Lack of proper sanitation and protection from rain, snow, cold, and heat also take their toll. Reports of rat bites in slum areas number in the thousands each year, and contaminated water is a problem for many native Americans. Moreover, the daily lives of the poor are filled with stress because they are often worried about getting the money to pay their bills and buy groceries. As Syme and Berkman put it, the poor have "higher rates of schizophrenia, are more depressed, more unhappy, more worried, more anxious, and are less hopeful about the future."[33] Finally, as we will see, the poor receive inferior care when they get sick.

HEALTH CARE

Medical science has made enormous progress in the past century. Unfortunately, improvements in the delivery of health care services have lagged behind advances in medical knowledge. People in poor countries seldom receive adequate health care, and millions die from easily preventable diseases like cholera and typhoid. Even the richest nations find the ballooning cost of today's sophisticated medical technology a heavy burden.

In the past, those who could not afford health care simply did without. As late as 1967 the American Medical Association held medical care to be a privilege, not a right. But most people now believe the sick deserve health care even if they cannot afford to pay for it. Virtually all the industrialized nations except the United States have adopted a system of government-supported health care available to all citizens. The United States took a different course, creating a medical-welfare system for the poor and the elderly, but leaving the rest of the health care system in private hands. But rising costs and inadequate government funding mean that a growing number of Americans still lack basic health care.

Health Care in the United States The 4 million Americans who are employed in the health care industry have much to be proud of. A large portion of America's 7000 hospitals are among the most modern and best equipped in the world. America's 450,000 physicians are rigorously trained to the highest standards. American health care is certainly among the best that money can buy. The problem is that many people cannot afford to pay the price.

In 1986 Americans spent $458 billion on health care, which amounts to almost 11 percent of the national income.[34] Despite this massive expenditure, many indicators show that the health of U.S. citizens lags far behind that of comparable industrialized nations. Infant mortality rates, for example, are shockingly high in the United States, compared with those for such nations as France, Italy, and Japan.[35] Of course, the U.S. health care system is not entirely responsible for these differences. Variations in life-style, culture, and diet are important too. Nevertheless, it appears that Americans are not getting their money's worth for their health care dollars.

In the United States, health care services are purchased very much like other goods and services. Those who have the money or the insurance can buy the best care, while others cannot. As a result, the wealthy receive excellent health care, while the poor receive indifferent and decidedly inferior care.

Until recently, poor people in the United States saw physicians much less often than did wealthier people. With the coming of medicare for the aged and medicaid for the poor—two government-paid health care programs—the poor began seeing doctors more often. This does not mean, however, that equality has been achieved. As we have seen, the poor are generally less healthy than other people and therefore they are still less likely to see a physician than a wealthy person with a similar health problem. Moreover, recent changes in the medicare and medicaid programs have excluded a

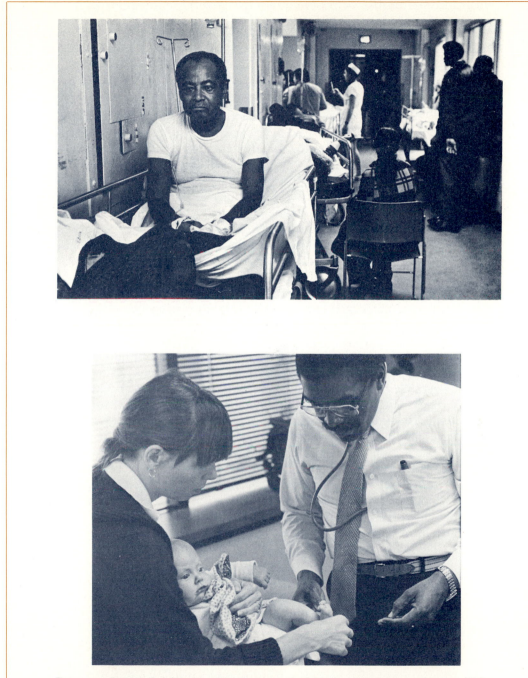

The poor often must wait in long lines to see a physician in overcrowded public hospitals, while people from the middle and upper classes receive better and more convenient care from private sources.

significant number of people from the government-supported health care system.[36]

Regardless of how often poor people visit doctors, it is clear that they receive lower-quality care. For one thing, they are less likely than others to be cared for by specialists.[38] For another, many of the best physicians refuse to accept medicare and medicaid patients because of the paperwork involved and because the government will not pay the high fees these physicians normally charge. As a result, the poor are more likely to go to hospital emergency rooms and clinics, while more wealthy people go to the private practitioner of their choice. Geographic distribution is a factor too: the best specialists practice only in wealthy residential areas.

Widespread disorganization poses another serious problem in the U.S. health care system. Independent physicians, small medical groups, and huge hospitals all compete for the same patients. Despite a great shortage of general practitioners, new doctors flock to the overcrowded specialties such as surgery, where the money is. Isolated rural areas go begging for physicians, while urban centers have many more than they need. Some patients pay their own bills, while others rely on charitable organizations and a bewildering variety of insurance plans and agencies of local, state, and federal governments. The result of this disorganization is waste and inefficiency on a grand scale.

Doctors and Nurses Physicians command more respect and admiration than people in virtually any other profession. Books, movies, and television programs picture the physician as unselfish and dedicated, a "saint in white." As far back as the 1940s, a study of occupational prestige found that physicians were second only to members of the Supreme Court. More recent studies have shown that medical doctors have maintained their high status.[37] And as is so often the case, high income accompanies high prestige.

Despite the great prestige of American doctors, there is growing discontent with their performance. An increasing number of health care consumers seem to be complaining that physicians are more concerned with their incomes than with the well-being of their patients. As medical technology has become more and more complex and the health care system more bureaucratic, the doctor-patient relationship has become increasingly depersonalized. The old general practitioner who was a family advisor and friend has been replaced by an army of narrow specialists. As late as 1931, general practitioners outnumbered specialists by five to one. Today that ratio is reversed: only about 12 percent of American physicians are general practitioners.[38]

Two decades ago there was serious concern about a shortage of physicians in the United States. But increases in medical school enrollments and the immigration of physicians from other countries has led to substantial growth in the supply of physicians. In 1960 there were 151 physicians for every 100,000 persons in the United States; today there are about 240.[39] The effects of this increase are, however, open to debate. Some fear that physicians, like monopolistic corporations, will raise their fees to maintain their current incomes while treating fewer patients. Others believe that increased competition will result in better service at a lower price. Evidence from U.S. cities that already have a surplus of physicians, such as San Francisco, indicates that medical costs have remained high. But health care has improved as highly trained specialists become willing to take on more minor cases, physicians show more willingness to make house calls, and so forth.[40] There are, however, some other studies that indicate that physicians charge higher fees in areas with more competition in order to keep their salaries up.[41] And despite the recent increases there are several countries that have more physicians per person than the United States,[42] and no one can really say what the ideal doctor-to-patient ratio really is.

Whatever number of new doctors is really needed, it is clear that the physicians we have are poorly distributed. Some fields of medicine are overcrowded, while there is a serious shortage of doctors to provide basic medical care, especially general practitioners, internists, and pediatricians. Currently, there is only about one pediatrician for every 1350 children in the United States.[43] At the same time, prestigious specialties, such as surgery, have a surplus of physicians.[44] The surplus of surgeons has in turn led to much unnecessary and potentially dangerous surgery. In the middle 1970s, a subcommittee of the House of Representatives estimated that 2.4 million unnecessary surgical operations, costing $4 billion and 11,900 lives, were performed each year. The American Medical Association (AMA) responded that these estimates were based on false and misleading data.[45] But the committee did not change its conclusions, and in a later report it held that widespread publicity and efforts by government and the medical community had not significantly improved the situation.[46] A 1987 RAND Corporation study of three common operations once again found extremely high rates of unnecessary surgery. The worst of the three procedures was the "corotid endarterectomy," intended to reduce the risk of stroke. The RAND study concluded that only about a third of the 100,000 of these operations performed every year were clearly appropriate to the needs of the patient.[47]

The geographic distribution of physicians is also uneven. As was already noted, physicians are heavily concentrated in the affluent districts of cities and in suburbs, leaving many rural and poor areas with a critical shortage. Wealthy states such as Massachusetts and Connecticut have twice as many physicians per person than do poor states such as Alabama and Arkansas.[48]

At least four conditions contribute directly to this maldistribution of physicians. First, it is not surprising to find that doctors, like other educated Americans, prefer to live in cities, with their superior cultural and recreational facilities. Second, physicians have become dependent on the support of laboratory technologists and their sophisticated equipment, and rural areas do not have the number of patients needed to maintain such facilities. Third, physicians are overwhelmingly white and from middle-class and upper-class backgrounds, and they are often most comfortable with patients from a similar social background. In 1986 only 3.3 percent of U.S. physicians were black, and only 4.1 percent were Hispanic.[49] Fourth, and probably most important, affluent areas guarantee larger incomes than can be expected in poor areas. As Howard Schwartz puts it, "two-thirds of American physicians treat the one-third of the population that is most able to pay."[50]

Once a patient gets in to see a doctor, his or her problems may be just beginning, for many times patients are hurt rather than helped by their physician. A 1981 study of a major university hospital found that more than one out of every three of its patients suffered from some sort of physician-caused disease—most commonly, an adverse reaction to the medications they were given.[51] A study by Dr. Sidney Wolfe concluded that the antibiotics prescribed in U.S. hospitals are unnecessary in a full 22 percent of cases, and that these unnecessary drugs can be expected to cause about ten thousand potentially fatal adverse reactions a year.[52] And, of course, that is in addition to the more than 10,000 deaths a year caused by the unnecessary surgeries already discussed.

If American physicians are so well trained, why do such problems occur? Of course, doctors are only human, and no matter how well trained they are, some will make mistakes that cost patients their health or their lives. But some physicians have had inferior training in questionable foreign medical schools, and others have failed to keep up with current medical techniques. Further, the medical profession refuses to weed out incompetent physicians. Neither patients nor government officials are as well qualified as physicians to judge professional competence. For this reason the burden of protecting the public from incompetent physicians falls on the medical profession itself. Unfortunately, it has failed to shoulder this responsibility. The ethics of the profession discourage physicians from criticizing their colleagues, and only the most grossly incompetent physicians are forbidden to practice medicine.

Whereas physicians are the elite of the medical profession, nurses are its "working class." The doctors make the diagnosis and prescribe the treatment, but it is generally the nurses who carry out those instructions and do the other work necessary to the day-to-day operation of the hospital. Many nursing jobs require long hours and entail an enormous burden of responsibilities that may mean life or death to patients. Yet nurses seldom receive the recognition or the pay that their work warrants.[53] In 1987 the average physician made about $120,000 but the average nurse made less than $28,000.[54] It is not surprising, then, that there is a critical shortage of nurses. Moreover, the situation is likely to get worse before it gets better. In 1984 there were 80,312 graduates from U.S. nursing schools, but by 1990 that number is expected to be only about 67,000.[55]

The Hospitals Hospitals were originally *hospices*, places of refuge where the poor could go to die. Not until modern times did the hospital become a place where sick and injured people were given medical treatment. Today hospitals are the nerve centers of the medical profession. A hospital determines which physicians will be allowed to use the hospital and, thus, which patients will be admitted. Hospitals control much medical teaching and research and provide a wide range of outpatient services through clinics and emergency rooms.

The soaring cost of hospital care has been a major cause of the rapid increase in health care costs in the last three decades. Between 1960 and 1982 hospital costs increased 900 percent—three times faster than the cost of physicians and twelve times faster than the cost of drugs and medications.[56] In 1983 stiff new cost-control measures were instituted by the federal government (see the next section), yet total hospital costs continued to increase far faster than the general rate of inflation. In 1987 alone, hospital costs increased 16 percent. There were also great differences in hospital costs from one part of the country to another. The average daily charges in Rhode Island were $474 in 1987, while in Nevada they were $1,204.[57]

One would think that institutions charging such large fees would be highly profitable ventures, but many hospitals are now experiencing a financial crisis that is having a major impact on the quality of health care. One major problem is that overbuilding and shorter stays by patients have produced a large number of surplus beds. From 1960 to 1985 the average occupancy rate of hospital beds dropped from 85 to 70 percent.[58] Another problem is that the costs of new medical technology have continued to escalate, while cost containment efforts by government health care plans and private insurers have made it more difficult for less efficient hospitals to pass along all their expenses. There has also been a rapid increase in the number of profit-making hospitals, which have skimmed some of the most lucrative business away from traditional nonprofit and government-owned hospitals.[59] Not only are these profit-making hospitals more likely to charge the highest possible rates; they seem to have less commitment to meet the needs of the general public. Profit-making hospitals tend to serve well-insured middle- and upper-class patients and to turn their backs on the poor who cannot afford their services.

New government restrictions on payments by medicare and medicaid have meant that nearly half of U.S. hospitals lose money treating such patients.[60] And an increasing number of the poor and working-class people have no private health insurance but are not eligible for federal health care programs. As a result, a growing list of public and nonprofit hospitals that have attempted to meet the needs of less advantaged citizens have simply closed their doors and gone out of business. The ones that remain are getting more and more crowded, leading to an inevitable decline in the quality of health care for the needy.

The Rising Costs Like the cost of hospitalization, the cost of all health care in America has been rising at an alarming rate (see Figure 8.3). In 1950 Americans spent 4.4 percent of their gross national product on health care; today that figure has more than doubled to about 11 percent.[61] There are at least three common explanations for this trend. The first focuses on the way the health care industry is financed. Because most physicians are paid on a **fee-for-service basis,** there is a strong financial incentive to subject patients

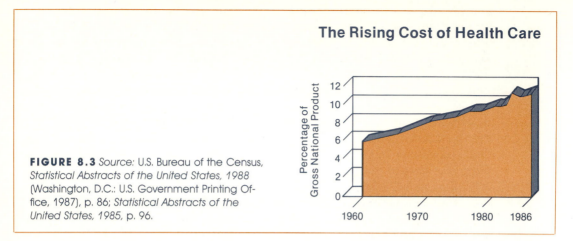

The Rising Cost of Health Care

FIGURE 8.3 *Source:* U.S. Bureau of the Census, *Statistical Abstracts of the United States, 1988* (Washington, D.C.: U.S. Government Printing Office, 1987), p. 86; *Statistical Abstracts of the United States, 1985*, p. 96.

to as many medical procedures as possible. A study of the amount of surgery performed on government employees covered by different health insurance plans revealed some startling facts. Employees covered by Blue Shield insurance, which pays doctors on a fee-for-service basis, had more than twice

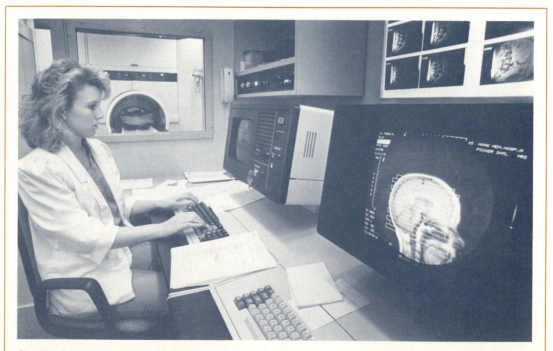

The development of complex and expensive new techniques has been a major factor in the rapid increase in the cost of medical care.

as much surgery as employees with group medical plans offering doctors no financial incentives for unnecessary operations.[62] Obviously, some physicians' decisions to operate are based on the profit to be gained rather than on the needs of their patients. Moreover, the fact that less than 30 percent of health care costs are paid directly by patients means that they have fewer incentives to look for the least expensive care or take other steps to hold costs down.[63]

A second important cause of increasing health care costs has been the development of expensive new drugs and medical techniques. Such procedures as organ transplants and renal dialysis (the use of artificial kidney machines) are extremely costly and tend to drive up the overall cost of health care. A third factor is that patients have discovered that they can sue doctors for malpractice and win. As a result, the number of those suits has quadrupled in the last decade.[64] All doctors—competent or not—now must pay large fees for malpractice insurance. The increasing number of malpractice suits has increased health care costs in an indirect way as well. The fear being charged with malpractice has forced many doctors to practice *defensive medicine;* that is, they order a large number of costly tests that are not really necessary because they do not want to be accused in court of having forgotten something important.[65]

Finally, although the AIDS epidemic has not yet had a major impact on our health care costs, it is expected to become a critical problem in the years ahead as new treatments allow patients to survive longer and the total number of cases reaches into the millions.

Paying the Costs Traditionally, Americans have bought medical care the way they buy beans, pork chops, and cars: purchasing the services they desire and can afford. But direct payments by patients have been supplemented by government programs and private insurance, which now pick up most of the tab. But these changes were carried out in a poorly planned and haphazard way, and as a result there are huge gaps and inequalities in the system.

Private insurance companies paid about 31 percent of Americans' health care costs in 1986.[64] Although most Americans have some kind of health insurance, in 1988 about 17.6 percent of those below age 65 had no coverage at all (most persons 65 or older are covered by medicare), and the problem is getting worse every year. A recent study by the UCLA School of Public Health found that the number of uninsured Californians has jumped by 50 percent in the last seven years.[67] And even those who have health insurance may still face serious problems paying for the care they need, for few policies cover all health care expenses. Some have little or no coverage for office visits or preventive care, while others have deductible payments, requiring the insured person to pay a minimum amount before the policy goes into effect. Most policies also limit the total amount the insurer will pay. Thus, those with serious health problems may find that the cost of their care has exceeded the limits of their policy, or that their insurance company has canceled their policy and refuses to pay for any future illnesses.

The government's contribution to the payment of medical expenses comes primarily from the two programs mentioned earlier: medicare and medicaid. **Medicare** buys medical services for people over 65 years old, while **medicaid** is designed to help the poor, the blind, and the disabled. The medicare program is relatively uniform throughout the nation. Medicaid, however, is administered by the states, and each state has its own standards of eligibility and levels of benefits. The benefits are extremely low in some states. Neither medicare nor medicaid pays all the costs of a patient's medical care. Both programs require patients to pay for part of the initial treatment and a percentage of all additional costs.

There are also significant gaps in the coverage these programs provide. The worst hit are the poor and near poor who are not eligible for medicaid and cannot afford private insurance. Medicare coverage for the elderly is far less restrictive—almost everyone over 65 qualifies. But medicare still has some glaring omissions, especially its failure to cover the costs of nursing homes. A recent report from the House Subcommittee on Aging concluded that half of all elderly couples with one member in a nursing home are driven into poverty within six months, and that 90 percent of single people in nursing homes are impoverished within a year.[68]

The medicare and medicaid programs have not overcome the fraud, waste, and inefficiency associated with some private health insurance plans. In fact, they seem to have provided a strong inducement for fraud and corruption among health care workers. Dishonest physicians and medical laboratories charge huge fees for unnecessary tests and treatments, and even submit bills for services that were not performed. The government—the taxpayer—pays. Some laboratories have been caught giving kickbacks to physicians who order laboratory tests for their patients. A 1982 report prepared for the House of Representatives concluded that the government is defrauded of $2.5 to $6.2 billion a year in medicaid swindles by hospitals, nursing homes, and pharmacies.[69]

The general increase in medical costs and the increasing number of elderly people eligible for benefits pose an even more serious problem for government health care programs. In 1983 the fear that the medicare trust fund would soon be exhausted spurred the federal government to make a major change in the way it makes hospital payments. Instead of allowing hospitals to set their own charges for the care of the elderly and simply bill the government, the new system established 468 categories of illness, known as diagnostic related groups, and provided a fixed payment for each one. It also established peer review organizations with the power to refuse medicare payment for unjustified medical treatments.

This new system seems to have had some success in reducing the huge yearly increases in the cost of federal health care programs, but it has created new problems as well.[70] In many cases, the new payment plan has led hospitals to release their patients too quickly because they receive the same amount of money regardless of the length of stay. Moreover, since the most profitable patients in each diagnostic category are those who are the least sick, severely ill persons may have trouble getting any treatment at all in some institutions.

Other Health Care Systems   The percentage of people served by government health care programs is smaller in the United States than in any other Western nation. Citizens of those nations pay few doctor or hospital bills; however, their taxes are higher in order to cover the costs of medical care. A look at the health care systems of other English-speaking nations provides some interesting contrasts. The British health care system is often held up both as a model of effectiveness and as an illustration of the dangers of socialism. The Canadian system combines elements of the British and American systems.

Great Britain In England, Northern Ireland, Scotland, and Wales, most medical care is provided at very little direct cost to the patient. The government owns the hospitals and pays most of the physicians. It also pays most of the costs of dental care and drugs. The National Health Service operates a two-tiered system of health care. Everyone signs up with a general practitioner, who is the one they go to first with any ailment. Most general practitioners have about 2,000 patients. They are paid on the basis of how many patients they have on their list, not on how many procedures are performed, and as a result there is no financial incentive for "overdoctoring." When patients need special services, they are referred to a consultant in a hospital. The consultants are paid a fixed salary that doesn't depend on the number of patients or the procedures performed. Many consultants work only part-time for the National Health Service and also have a private practice in which they charge fees directly to their patients.[71]

In many ways the British system is more efficient than the American one. Britain spends only about 6 percent of its national income on health care, while the United States spends around 11 percent; yet the death rates for most age groups in the two countries are very similar.[72] The British system is clearly superior in providing health care for the poor, since everyone has equal access to the National Health Service. On the other hand, financial restraints mean that expensive procedures are informally rationed, so that there may be delays in receiving some kinds of treatment that can be safely postponed.[73] Moreover, Britain, like all other industrialized nations, is having trouble meeting the needs of an aging population and coping with the exploding costs of medical technology. British Prime Minister Thatcher's Conservative government has failed to provide sufficient funding to meet these new expenses. And as a result, there are often long delays before a patient can receive a needed operation, and about 10 percent of the British people have now taken out private insurance to supplement the public system.[74] Thus, the gap between the quality of health care for the rich and the poor has grown wider in recent years.

Canada Although the Canadian and American cultures are similar, Canadians have always been more enthusiastic than Americans about government social programs. As a result, Canada became involved in government-sup-ported health care much earlier and to a much greater extent than the United States. As far back as 1914 the province of Saskatchewan established a hos-pital insurance program and followed it with comprehensive health insur-ance in 1948. By the end of the 1950s, hospital insurance had gone nation-wide, and by the end of the next decade it included doctor visits as well.[75]

The Canadian system is quite different from the British one. For one thing, it is decentralized. Each Canadian province secures health care for its citizens and pays three-fourths of the bill; the rest is paid by the federal government. As a result, health care programs differ from one province to another, even though all programs are managed according to federal guide-lines. Canadian governments, whether federal or provincial, do not own hos-pitals or employ staffs to run them. Canadian doctors are paid on a fee-for-service basis rather than on a capitation basis as in Britain.

But the amount they are paid is set in a contract with the provincial government that is periodically renegotiated. Physicians are allowed to "ex-tra bill" on top of the government payment, but it is discouraged and most do not do it. The Canadian provinces exercise much tighter cost controls than does the U.S. government, and as a result the system is far more effi-cient. In 1972, a few years after the start of national health insurance in Canada, health care costs in the United States and Canada were both about 7.5 percent of their gross national products. But today, Canada spends only a little more (7.8 percent in 1985) than it did then, while costs in the United States have shot up to 11 percent.[76]

The death rate for infants in Canada is a little lower than in Great Brit-ain, and both rates are lower than that in the United States.[77] Again it is clear that low-income Canadians, like low-income Britishers, have better access to health care than low-income Americans.

Ethical Dilemmas   To most outsiders, the moral responsibility of the medical profes-sion seems clear: to save lives and help patients be as healthy as possible. But the increasing power of medical technology and the breakdown of so-ciety's old moral consensus has created perplexing ethical dilemmas for which we have yet to find satisfactory answers. The views of those on op-posing sides of the abortion issue are presented in the debate in this chapter: "Should Abortion Be Legal?" But abortion is only one of many controversial issues of medical ethics.

An equally difficult problem concerns the so-called heroic efforts phy-sicians use to extend the lives of dying patients. Medical costs mount rapidly in the final weeks of a patient's life as greater and greater efforts are needed to prolong life. One-third of medicare's entire budget is spent on people in the last year of their life.[78] Most of us would say that money should not be the standard to decide who lives and dies. But in a world in which millions of people starve to death every year, the money used to keep one dying American patient alive for another month could save a thousand hungry babies in the Third World. Is this fair? An ethical problem arises even if the financial cost of keeping a patient alive is minimal. Does the medical profes-

DEBATE

Should Abortion Be Legal?

YES To deny a woman the right to have an abortion is to deny her the right to control her own body. As the Supreme Court has said, the government has no justification for interfering in the private lives of its citizens to force a mother to have a child she does not wish to bear. Those who demand that the government stop all abortions are urging us down the road to a totalitarian society in which the police and the courts would control our most personal decisions.

Those who oppose abortion claim that a fetus is a fully formed human being and to abort it would be murder. Such claims lack any scientific support. A fetus is not an independent living creature and can survive only as long as it is attached to its mother's body. If it is murder to abort a fetus that cannot live on its own, then it is murder to practice birth control and cut off the unfertilized egg's chance of survival.

In addition to the obvious immorality of giving the state authority over the private workings of our bodies, there is another important reason to keep abortion legal. The plain fact is that the laws prohibiting abortion have never stopped such operations. What they do is force hundreds of thousands of women and girls to go to incompetent, untrained abortionists, and many of them pay with their lives. If the antiabortion crusaders are successful, we will once again start up the vicious business of black-market abortions, and thousands of women will be its victims.

NO Abortion is murder, plain and simple. When a fetus is aborted, a human life is ended. An aborted fetus dies just as surely as a baby shot with a gun. A society that claims to respect human life cannot allow the continuation of this slaughter.

The supporters of abortion claim that the old antiabortion laws created a flourishing business in illegal abortions that injured or killed many of its customers. They are certainly right in pointing out the harm the illegal abortionists did to many of these mothers. But they ignore the harm that abortions—legal or illegal—do to innocent fetuses. The way to stop the black-market abortion business is not to legalize it but to demand tougher law enforcement to stamp it out.

There is also another important reason to make abortion illegal again: to preserve the sanctity of the family and to reinforce our society's support of the fundamental value of human life. When society permits a mother to take the life of her unborn child, it tells us all that human life is a cheap commodity to be thrown away for the sake of mere convenience. Mothers should be required to carry their babies the full term necessary for their survival. Unborn babies have a right to life.

sion have an obligation to keep patients alive for a few more weeks of agonizing pain and slow physical deterioration? Even if they don't wish to live? How long should patients be maintained on artificial life support?

No one has a simple answer to these troubling questions, yet society must somehow formulate social policies to guide the medical profession. Some people have made out "living wills" that spell out how far they wish their physicians to go in using heroic means to extend their lives. Yet even the principle of self-determination implied in such "wills" is not widely accepted in our society. Under current law, for example, a physican can be charged with murder for helping a terminally ill patient end his or her own life.

RESPONDING TO PROBLEMS OF THE SICK AND THE HEALTH CARE SYSTEM

There are two approaches to the problems of the sick. The first is to try to prevent health problems by changing life-styles and eating habits, reducing pollution, and increasing the use of preventive medicine. The second aims at improving care for people after they become sick. The latter approach includes proposals designed to create equal access to health care regardless of income and to improve the overall quality of these services at less cost.

Healthier Living There is much that we can do as individuals to improve our health. A balanced diet is the first essential. In North America, dietary problems usually stem from eating too much of the wrong kinds of food. Most of us

Regular exercise is an important component of healthy living, and growing numbers of people are making an effort to incorporate more physical activity into their lives.

would be better off if we ate less and avoided foods that are high in sugar, fats, and artificial additives. Regular exercise is another essential component of healthy living. The growing recognition of this fact has encouraged many people to run, swim, play tennis, and engage in other physical activities. Recent reductions in death rates from heart and circulatory disease may well be a result of such activities. Finally, it is important to avoid health hazards such as smoking and excessive stress.

There are, however, many health hazards that can be reduced only through collective action. It is easy to tell a business executive or a factory worker to avoid stressful situations, but how can one avoid stress when trying to earn a living in one of the world's most competitive economic systems? Overall levels of stress will be reduced only when changes have been made in our economic and political institutions. But there are proposals for more limited change that might bring some immediate improvements. Much stronger government action is needed to reduce occupational health hazards and make sure that companies that have killed or crippled their employees at least pay for the damage they have done. Stronger antipollution laws combined with more vigorous enforcement efforts could make another major contribution to public health (see Chapter 18). One of the most effective things we could do is to take action to encourage a more equal distribution of wealth, for it is clear that poverty takes a devastating toll on the health of our poorest citizens (see Chapter 6).

Preventive Medicine   The old saying that "an ounce of prevention is worth a pound of cure" is as true today as it was 100 years ago. As we have noted, the remarkable drop in death rates in the past century was due mainly to improvements in preventive medicine. Improvements in sanitation and nutrition have saved more lives than all hospitals combined. Yet health care systems continue to emphasize treatment rather than prevention of disease. A delicate heart operation is much more dramatic than the dull business of educating people to avoid heart trouble through proper diet and regular exercise. Yet the second approach is both cheaper and more effective.

In its broadest sense, **preventive medicine** includes a wide range of programs to encourage healthier living, including school courses in nutrition, personal hygiene, and driver training, as well as campaigns against excessive use of tobacco, alcohol, and other drugs. Even efforts designed to attack poverty, racism, and discrimination can be considered part of an effective program of preventive medicine.

Medical Pesonnel   The United States needs to train more general practitioners, pediatricians, and nurses. By restricting the number of students in overcrowded specialties such as surgery, medical schools could help move physicians into fields where they are badly needed, particularly general practice. Medical schools could also train more paramedics: medical personnel who, although less broadly trained than M.D.'s, are qualified to perform many services that are now restricted to physicians.

But the most pressing need is for higher pay and more professional authority for nurses. Not only would this attract more people into the nursing profession, but it could even save money if nurses were allowed to do more of the services now carried out exclusively by physicians. During the last two decades the nursing profession has been moving in this direction with the development of a new category of nurse, known as a nurse practitioner, whose duties and responsibilities are halfway between the traditional nurse and the physician. Although the first nurse practitioners did not graduate until the early 1970s, they have been providing effective low-cost care, and their numbers have been increasing rapidly in recent years. However, regulations concerning nurse practitioners vary greatly from state to state, and they have had to fight numerous battles with physicians who see them as a threat to their professional status.[79]

National Health Insurance   The United States is the only developed nation in the world that does not have some form of government-financed medical care available to its entire population. It seems to be only a matter of time before some form of comprehensive health care coverage is adopted. A 1987 Gallup poll found that 63 percent of all Americans believe that the nation should have such a health insurance program.[80]

Despite such widespread support, important questions about how a national health insurance program should be organized remain. If hospitals stay in private hands, with doctors paid on a fee-for-service basis, the dangers of creating an unresponsive government bureaucracy will be minimized. But individual corruption and profiteering are a serious problem in this type of system. Without proper quality and cost controls, such a system could accelerate the already astronomical rise in the costs of health care. A national health insurance program with physicians paid varying salaries, as in England, would be cheaper in the long run. But American doctors oppose such a system, and the tremendous power of the AMA and other physicians' organizations will make it very difficult to win approval of such a system.

The state of Massachusetts recently approved a mixed plan that contains incentives for businesses to provide health-insurance coverage for all their employees and provides state insurance for those who still remain uncovered. But this law remains a halfway measure, since the insurance provided still does not cover all health care costs, and it takes no effective action to fight runaway medical inflation.

Health Maintenance Organizations   Some physicians have banded together to form clinics that provide health care on a prepaid basis. Such **health maintenance organizations** (HMOs) are essentially group practices. A group of medical personnel, including specialists, offer a complete range of medical services. Subscribers pay a fixed monthly fee that does not, in individual cases, increase when a subscriber needs care and treatment in the clinic. Physicians either are paid a fixed salary or receive a flat fee for each patient.

Health maintenance organizations remove the financial incentives for "overdoctoring." They are also more efficient than individual private practice on a fee-for-service basis. Although doctors working in health maintenance organizations have more office visits than private physicians, they hospitalize their patients less frequently and perform fewer operations. As a result, a patient's total expenses for health care are greatly reduced. The quality of care varies greatly from one HMO to another, as it does from one private physician to another. But well-run HMOs can provide excellent care to their patients.

Health maintenance organizations were roundly condemned by the AMA when they were first established. Although many doctors still oppose HMOs, they do provide some benefits for physicians as well as for patients. Among the advantages that a health maintenance organization offers physicians are retirement and sick pay, regular working hours, reduction of bookkeeping and insurance costs, and easy availability of peers for consultation and support.

It is possible that health maintenance organizations will become more wasteful and ineffective as they become more popular. There are now over 17 million Americans in health maintenance organizations,[81] and some HMOs are already being accused of being bureaucratic and impersonal, with physicians who are unresponsive to their patients' needs. Nonetheless, the problems of health maintenance organizations seem to be less severe than those of current fee-for-service systems.

SOCIOLOGICAL PERSPECTIVES ON PROBLEMS OF THE SICK

Concern about the increasing gap between the high-quality health care that modern medicine can provide and the care that most people receive has made health care an important social problem. Social scientists of every persuasion have tried to explain why the social organization of health care is not better, given the fact that it is now a multibillion-dollar business with the knowledge and technology necessary to provide excellent services for everyone.

The causes of ill health have also been a subject of great concern to social scientists. Conflict and functional theorists are concerned primarily with large-scale health problems such as environmental pollution, which is discussed in Chapter 18. But the basic differences between the two perspectives are simple. Functionalists see the unhealthy conditions created by pollution as unintended (latent) dysfunctions of industrialization. Conflict theorists place the blame on industrialists who put profits ahead of the health and well-being of the people.

The Functionalist Perspective   Viewed functionally, the jumbled health care system is a result of the rapid development of medical technology and the changes in public attitudes about medical care. In the nineteenth century, medical knowledge was so limited that private doctors could handle almost all demands for health care. Rapid growth of medical knowledge and techniques greatly increased the kinds of services doctors had to offer. Because these services were effective, the demand for them boomed. People came to see good health care as a fundamental right, but the system of health care was unable to adapt efficiently. The idea that health care is a commodity, to be bought the way a homemaker buys a sack of potatoes or one hires a carpenter, is still with us, as is the conviction that medical care should be provided by a private practitioner and not by a corporation, a group practice, or a government bureau.

Because of this lag, functionalists say, the U.S. health care system is failing to do its job efficiently. Health care services are still sold privately. But this individualistic "free-enterprise" system has been supplemented, in patchwork fashion, by a great variety of cooperative organizations: clinics, hospitals, group practices, and health maintenance organizations. It has also been supplemented by many new sources of funding: employers, unions, insurance companies, and a host of government agencies.

In short, the U.S health care system is disorganized because it has grown rapidly and haphazardly, without proper planning. Obviously, the solution to this problem is reorganization. But functionalists do not agree on the form this reorganization should take. Some would have us return to complete free enterprise in the health care business. Such a system would allow physicians to sell their services at whatever price the market will bear, and let those too poor to pay that price turn to private charity or go without. Others believe that we should merely streamline the present system. They call for reallocating medical personnel, reducing fraud and malpractice, lowering costs, and training more nurses and other medical personnel.

The Conflict Perspective   Conflict theorists see the U.S. health care system in a different light. They argue that its problems and deficiencies stem from the fact that it is designed to serve the needs of the rich and powerful (including doctors themselves), thus neglecting the needs of low-income groups. Health care is a business dominated by businesspeople with medical degrees who try to sell their services at the highest price. Because physicians have a legally enforced monopoly on medical services, they are in a position to rig prices. Their services are sold at inflated prices that only the rich or well insured can pay, and programs that would reduce profits or require physicians to provide cheap health care for the poor are opposed. Further, conflict theorists claim, physicians have created an aura of mystery about their profession in order to boost their occupational prestige and cover up their shortcomings. In this atmosphere, patients are not expected or allowed to judge the quality of the medical care they are receiving—"the doctor knows best." Incompetents and profiteers are not weeded out because patients are kept in the dark about the true nature of the medical care they are receiving.

Sociologist Paul Starr's research has shown that the U.S. health care system's reliance on unrestricted fee-for-service payments by insurance companies and government agencies was created by powerful interests in the medical industry itself.[82] According to Starr, the largest, most important health insurance company, Blue Cross/Blue Shield, was intended to protect the interests of hospitals and physicians. Blue Cross, which originally covered only hospital expenses, was started in response to the financial crisis of U.S. hospitals during the Great Depression, and was directly controlled by the hospital industry. Blue Shield, which originally covered doctors' expenses, was created and controlled by physicians. Starr also argues that the generous system of medical payments in the original medicare legislation was put there as a result of pressure from the medical lobby.

Conflict theorists would resolve the health care problem by reducing the medical profession's control over the financing and organization of the health care system. This power would then be transferred to the government to ensure good medical care for all citizens regardless of their ability to pay. Most conflict theorists call for government-financed health care that is available without charge to individual patients. They also argue that such changes will come about only if those who receive inadequate health care organize themselves to counter the tremendous power of the health-care establishment.

Social Psychological Perspectives   Health and health care are obviously of tremendous psychological importance to every individual. Although social psychologists rarely deal directly with the organization of health care services, they have made significant contributions to the health care field. They have shown, for example, that the socialization process in medical schools often has unanticipated consequences, making doctors into something less than the humanitarians many medical students aspire to be. They have shown, further, that people learn to be "sick" (to play the role of sick people) just as they learn to be parents, factory workers, or lawyers. It follows that health care services sometimes make people sick rather than well.

Social psychological research is the foundation for the popular notion that effective medical care should meet patients' emotional needs as well as their physical needs. The oft-heard calls for more "family medicine" and general practitioners are a response to current medical practice which relies on specialists and large clinics and treats patients more like objects than people ("the ulcer in room 12," "the pregnancy in the waiting room"). Impersonal bureaucracies, whether financed publicly or privately, are poorly suited to meet an individual's emotional needs.

Social psychologists are also concerned about the causes of health problems. Personality theorists focus on the relationship between character traits and health problems. For instance, Rosenman and his colleagues found that people with "type A" personalities—hasty, impatient, restless, aggressive, and achievement oriented—are more likely to have heart disease than the easygoing "type B" personality.[83] Behaviorists and interactionists are concerned with the ways we develop unhealthy habits and life-styles. Attitudes toward exercise, diet, smoking, and drinking are learned from our primary groups and reflect the attitudes of our culture as well. Social psychologists point out that unhealthful behavior is often encouraged by the mass media,

KEY TERMS

fee-for-service compensation	medicaid
health	medicare
health maintenance organization	preventive medicine

FURTHER READINGS

Howard D. Schwartz, *Dominant Issues in Medical Sociology*, New York: Random House, 1981.

Rashi Fein, *Medical Care, Medical Costs*, Cambridge, Mass.: Harvard University Press, 1985.

Howard Hiatt, *America's Health in the Balance: Choice or Chance?* New York: Harper & Row, 1987.

David Mechanic (ed.), *Handbook of Health, Health Care and the Health Professions*, New York: The Free Press, 1983.

Peter MacGarr Rabinowitz, *Talking Medicine: American Doctors Tell Their Stories*, New York: New American Library, 1983.

Paul Starr, *The Social Transformation of American Medicine*, New York: Basic Books, 1982.

- How does society respond to the process of aging?

- Is there an "erosion of childhood"?

- Why do adolescents face an identity crisis?

- What problems do the elderly face in today's society?

- How can we improve the financial security of the young and the old?

Chapter 9
THE OLD AND THE YOUNG

From the time we are born until the time we die, we are constantly aging. Most people see this strictly as a biological process, but aging is a social process as well. Although the problems of aging are rooted in the physiological changes we experience, society tells us what these changes mean and what is expected of people of any particular age group. Thus, the problems of aging are social problems. For example, many of the tragic difficulties the elderly face in our society stem from the fact that they receive little of the respect and consideration that elderly people enjoyed in the past. In Colonial times, Americans dressed to make themselves look as old and dignified as possible; today there is a multibillion-dollar industry devoted to making us look younger than we really are. Yet at the same time that we idolize youthful beauty, we seem to be indifferent to the real needs of the young. Compared with older people, the young are far more likely to be poor, to be unemployed, and to suffer from a deep confusion about who they are and where they are going. Society cannot eliminate the need to adjust to the changes brought on by such things as sexual maturity or the physical deterioration of old age. But we can do a far better job of dealing with the social and biological realities of aging.

AGING AND THE LIFE CYCLE

Everyone is familiar with the biological changes that we experience as we age. They occur most rapidly in our earlier years, as we grow from a baby, to a child, to a sexually mature adult. The changes occur more slowly after physical maturity, but they never stop. As we grow older most of our physical abilities eventually decline. The most obvious signs are the external ones—the graying of the hair and the wrinkling of the skin—but the changes are much more far-reaching than that. Such things as hearing, eyesight, muscular strength, reaction time, and heart and lung capacity all decline. But although such changes are inevitable, the rate at which they occur is profoundly affected by such social factors as diet, exercise, medical care, and life-style. Not only have the improvements in diet and public health made us taller and healthier than our ancestors, but children today reach their full height and mature sexually at an earlier age than they did in past generations.[1] The physical deterioration associated with advancing age is subject to the same kind of social influences. Exercise and a good diet can help slow down the process of deterioration. Research even shows that new opportunities and new stimulation increase the IQ scores and mental abilities of elderly people.[2] But our social environment can have the opposite effect as well. Skid-row alcoholics and homeless transients, for example, often seem 10 or 15 years older than they actually are.

In addition to its influence on the physical process of aging, society also tells us what we have to do to "act our age." Every known society is divided into what anthropologists call **age grades:** groups of people of similar age. The **life cycle,** then, consists of a series of passages between the social roles expected of people in different age grades. As we progress from one age grade to another, we are presented with a predictable set of new social expectations and a new set of problems that go with them.

The transition itself may also present a difficult challenge of its own. On the one hand, people experiencing such transitions must cope with the feeling of loss at seeing an end to a major period of their lives. On the other, they must face the difficult task of learning new roles. Young adults must conquer their fears and learn how to shoulder the new responsibilities expected of them. The elderly must learn how to reorganize their lives after the stability of child rearing and employment is torn away.

Most cultures have what are known as **rites of passage** to mark transitions from one stage of life to another. These ceremonies and rituals provide individuals who are in transition with group support and symbolic confirmation of their new status. Although our culture still maintains a few rites of passage, such as marriage, confirmation, and bar mitzvah ceremonies, most people do not receive much social support when making critical transitions from one age grade to another.

Age grades and the behaviors associated with them vary tremendously from one society to another, and even within a single society over the course of history. Our current ideas about age and what it means are very complex, and different experts see the stages of aging in different ways. In this chapter we will consider four broad age grades typical of contemporary industrialized society—**childhood, adolescence, adulthood,** and **old age**—but each one of these can also be subdivided into two or more smaller categories.

Historian Philippe Aries argues that childhood was an invention of the eighteenth century and did not exist before that time.[3] Pointing out that the children in sixteenth-century paintings do not have the proportions of real children but of miniature adults, Aries argues that once out of infancy, children were simply seen as small adults. While he may overstate his case, it is clear that the world of childhood was far less distinct and less sheltered than it is today. In the past, people were expected to work on the farm and carry many important responsibilities at an early age.

The next stage in the life cycle—adolescence—was clearly a product of the industrial revolution. Of course, young people have always experienced the physiological changes accompanying puberty, but until the industrial revolution there was no extended period during which a physically mature person was considered too young to assume adult responsibilities. Childhood ended abruptly when people became adults. Adolescence developed as a response to industrialization and the need for a prolonged period of education before entering adult life. The word itself was not in common usage until 1904, when psychologist Stanley Hall used it to refer to those young people who had reached puberty but were denied adult responsibilities and privileges.[4]

The remainder of this chapter will focus on the problems of those at the two ends of the life cycle: the young and the old. By most sociological standards, those in their middle years are an advantaged group and do not require special attention here. But despite the fact that those in mid-life have higher incomes, more prestige, and more power than others, there is growing recognition that these advantages do not necessarily translate into personal happiness or satisfaction. For one thing, those in mid-life are often responsible for the care and support of both the young and the old, and they often feel those responsibilities as a heavy burden. In addition, there are the acute problems associated with what has come to be known as the **mid-life crisis.** This crisis typically occurs in the late 30s or 40s when persons in mid-life come to question their dreams and illusions, and grapple with the reality that their youth is gone and that death is the inevitable end of their journey. Those devoted to a career must often come to terms with the fact that their dreams of success may never come true, or the even more difficult conclusion that success itself was an empty goal that has left them dissatisfied and unfulfilled.[5] Thus, the adjustment to mid-life can be as difficult as any other role transition, even if it is not aggravated by as many economic and social restrictions.

PROBLEMS OF THE YOUNG

Childhood To most of us, childhood conjures up memories of a happy, carefree time that we would love to relive. But although adolescence is usually the most difficult period of a young person's life, children do face some very real problems as well. The important issues of child abuse and molestation (see Chapters 11 and 15) have been the subject of increasing national concern. But the economic problems faced by our children have unfortunately received far less attention. In 1986 the poverty rate for children under 16 was more than 50 percent higher than the national average and double the rate for those in their middle years.[6] At the same time that the poverty rate was soaring among the young, the government seemed to have turned its back on their needs. School lunch programs were slashed, eligibility requirements for Aid to Families with Dependent Children were raised (see Chapter 6), and federal support for education was cut (see Chapter 4). The plain fact is that unlike the elderly, the young cannot vote and have virtually no political power.

There is also growing concern about the "erosion of childhood": the deterioration of the special status accorded childhood and a return to something more like the sixteenth-century idea of children as small adults. There are still strong restrictions on child labor (as much to protect the jobs of older people as the welfare of children), but the ever-increasing importance of education and the relentless materialism of the consumer revolution have made many children's lives highly competitive ones. The sharp increase in family instability and single-parent homes have forced many children to take on adult roles and responsibilities at an earlier age than they did in the recent past. But no factor has been as important in breaking down the barrier around the world of childhood than television. In the past, parents controlled their children's access to information about such things as sex, crime, and the injustices of life. But the media now bring the harshest adult realities

DEBATE

Are We Turning Our Backs on the Problems of the Young?

YES We were far more concerned about the problems of our children a few generations ago than we are today. Television was tightly regulated to make sure that its programs were suitable for even the youngest viewers. The movies contained only the tamest sex and far less graphic violence than they do today, and pornography was banned from all respectable newsstands. Even parents seemed more willing to sacrifice their own happiness and stay together for the sake of their children.

Perhaps some of these changes were the inevitable result of the process of industrialization and the aging of the population, but even the government seems to have forgotten about the needs of our children. The funding for education is grossly inadequate. Federal programs to provide such things as free school lunches and welfare benefits to poverty-stricken families have been slashed, parks and playgrounds in hundreds of cities have been shut down, and nothing is being done to stop the advertisers' shameless exploitation of the young. Commercials tell our children that processed breakfast cereals laden with sugar are part of a nutritious breakfast and urge them to buy everything from ice cream and candy bars to war toys, and the government just looks the other way.

The babies that used to be considered a "bundle of joy" are now more often seen as a noisy, messy, nuisance. Parents are glared at when they bring their infants into a movie or a restaurant, "adults only" apartment buildings have sprung up across the country, and the birthrate itself has plummeted as more and more young

NO Today's society is a far better place for children than it ever was before. Improvements in public health, sanitation, and medicine have slashed the infant mortality rate and allow more children to grow into healthy adults. The number of years an average child attends school has gone up and illiteracy has gone down. Children are now more likely to have braces on their teeth and vaccinations against serious diseases, and their parents generally keep a much closer watch on their diet and their physical safety than they ever did in the past.

The increase in sexually oriented material in the media has nothing to do with our attitudes about children. It is a result of changing attitudes about sex. Similarly, the increase in divorce is not the result of a declining concern for children, but a decline in the belief that keeping an unhappy marriage together is really good for the children.

Far from turning its back on children, the government is much more involved in protecting their welfare than it ever was before. The safety of toys, for example, is much more tightly regulated, and many popular toys from the fifties and sixties can no longer be sold at all. We used to all but ignore the problems of child abuse and molestation, but today they are major social concerns. The public is more vigilant, the police more willing to investigate, and the courts more likely to send the offenders to prison than at any time in the past. A hundred years ago, children commonly worked long hours in dirty sweat shops and dangerous factories, and severe beatings were accepted as normal discipline; but today all that is against the law. There simply is no doubt couples decide that extra spending money is more important than children. Today's children are the forgotten Americans. Their needs clearly come last on our list of national priorities.

that we are more, not less, concerned with the welfare of our children than we were in the past.

---

onto the television screen and thereby into the world of childhood. In the early days of television, programs were carefully screened to make sure that they were appropriate for family viewing. The results may often have been bland and boring, but they did protect the sheltered world of childhood. Today, however, the media is straining to win the lucrative "baby boom" market, and even early-evening programs are often filled with sex and violence.[7]

Adolescence   Of all the stages in the life cycle, society's expectations of the adolescent are the most contradictory and confusing. No longer children, but not yet adults, adolescents live in a kind of limbo between two worlds. On the one hand, they are told that they must act their age and behave in a responsible and mature manner; but at same time, they are told that they are not old enough to get married, have sex, drink, vote, or hold down a well-paying job. It is therefore hardly surprising that psychologist Erik Erikson concluded that the **identity crisis**—the pressing need to figure out who we are and how we fit into the scheme of things around us—is the central problem of adolescence.[8]

Adolescents must also face a host of difficult decisions that will shape the rest of their life. Children have most of their decisions made for them, and those later in life are more likely to just follow along in a long-established course. But the adolescent must decide critical questions about such things as relationships with the opposite sex, marriage, school, and career, with little previous experience to fall back on. Another problem that springs from adolescents' position in contemporary society is their sense of powerlessness. Although they feel themselves to be physically mature and capable of running their own lives, they are constantly under the authority of their elders, whether they be parents, teachers, or the local police.

In response to their unique problems and experiences, adolescents in most industrial societies have created their own subculture. Many of the characteristics of this so-called **youth culture** can be seen as a response to teenagers' pressing need to create a viable identity.[9] The constantly changing fashions in speech, clothing, and music provide a sense of belonging and a way for the followers of such fashions to gain status and feel a part of an in-group. These symbols also allow teens to see themselves as separate and somehow "cooler" than the adults that exercise such power over their lives.

This symbolic rejection of the adult world becomes a much more direct and violent challenge in the delinquent subculture that has long made up an important current within the overall youth culture. This subculture, along with the drug culture popular among some young people, certainly contributes to the fact that the arrest rate for 16-to-21-year-olds is higher than for any other age group.[10] But all delinquency is certainly not caused by such deviant subcultures. Adolescents face many difficult choices, and it is hardly surprising that they might experiment with various kinds of deviant activities. If nothing else, adolescents are less likely to have the responsibilities of a well-paying job or a family to support and therefore have far less to lose if caught breaking society's rules.[11]

There has been a disturbing increase in a problem that used to be quite rare among the young: suicide. Between 1970 and 1985 the suicide rate among those aged 10 to 14 more than doubled, and the rate for 15-to-19-year-olds increased by about 70 percent.[12] Although the exact causes of this trend remain unclear, it appears to be related to the increase in family instability and a growing awareness of suicide as a possible response to the difficulties of the adolescent years (see Chapter 19).

One of the most difficult problems adolescents must face is coming to terms with their sexuality. If anything, society's norms and expectations for adolescent sexual behavior are even more confused than they are for other aspects of their lives. Teenagers are bombarded with books, movies, and advertising emphasizing the importance of being sexy and attractive. Everything from soft drinks to jeans is given the sexual sell. Yet at the same time, parents, teachers, and religious leaders tell young people that they are not ready for sex and all the complications it involves. Unlike young people in most European countries, American teenagers are also strongly discouraged from using birth control. And as a result of all this, unmarried teenagers in the United States have the highest birthrate of any country in the industrialized world (see Chapter 11).[13]

Finally, something must be said about the serious economic problems

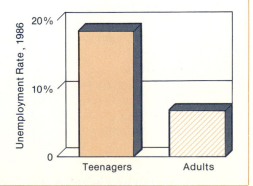

FIGURE 9.1 *Source:* U.S. Bureau of the Census, *Statistical Abstracts of the United States, 1988* (Washington, D.C.: U.S. Government Printing Office, 1987), p. 268.

faced by many adolescents. Most teenagers still derive their economic status from their family, and because poor people have larger families, a disproportionate number of teenagers are trapped in poverty. The poverty rate for teenagers is higher than for any other age group in the United States except those under 13.[14] In 1986, teenaged males who worked in full-time jobs still made less than a third as much as those in their peak earning years.[15] But despite their low wages, those working teenagers were the lucky ones. The unemployment rate for teenagers was two and a half times higher than the national average in 1986.[16] (See Figure 9.1 p. 257.) The problem is so bad that black teenagers looking for work in many ghetto neighborhoods are more likely to end up unemployed than working.

PROBLEMS OF THE ELDERLY

In traditional societies with extended family systems, increasing age is usually accompanied by increasing prestige. But with the breakup of the extended family, the status of the elderly has suffered a severe decline. No longer are old men and women the respected heads of an ongoing social unit. Rather, they are increasingly isolated and alone. Youth and vigor are cultural ideals in North America, and there is widespread belief that older people have little or nothing left to contribute. In a common phrase, the elderly are said to be "over the hill."

The problems of the elderly have been drawing increasing attention in recent years, probably because there are more old people than ever before. Since 1900 the average life expectancy in the United States has increased by 24 years, and the percentage of the population over age 65 has more than doubled. There are now almost 30 million people aged 65 or older, about 12 percent of the U.S. population,[17] and projections indicate that the elderly population will continue to grow rapidly in the years ahead.

Health   Of all the problems that trouble older people, health seems to concern them the most. There is good reason for this concern: the elderly have more severe health problems than other age groups. But although most Americans over age 65 have at least one chronic illness such as arthritis or heart disease, elderly people actually have fewer acute illnesses (such as colds and infectious diseases) than others. However, their recovery time from such illnesses is much longer than that of younger adults.[18]

Despite the prevalence of chronic illness among the elderly, only 15 percent are too sick to care for themselves, and only about 1 out of every 20 people over 65 lives in an institution. Most elderly people say that they are in reasonably good health, perhaps because they have learned to put up with illness and physical impairment as an inevitable part of the aging process (see Figure 9.1).[19]

The elderly have trouble getting care and treatment for their ailments. Most hospitals are designed to handle injuries and acute illnesses that are common in the young but are inadequate to treat the chronic degenerative diseases of the elderly. Many doctors are also ill prepared to deal with such problems. As Fred Cottrell points out, "There is a widespread feeling among the aged that most doctors are not interested in them and are reluctant to treat people who are as little likely to contribute to the future as the aged are reputed to."[20] And even with the help of medicare, the elderly in the United States have a difficult time paying for the health care they need (see Chapter 8).

Money   For most of this century, the elderly were much more likely than other people to be poor. Recent statistics reveal a remarkable turnaround in the general financial condition of older people. In 1986, 12.4 percent of persons over 65 were below the poverty line, while that figure was 13.6 percent for the entire population and 21 percent for children under 18.[21] The main reason for the improving economic status of the elderly is that since 1970 social security benefits have automatically been adjusted for inflation. Since then, the real buying power of the average social security check has increased 25 percent, while the buying power of the assistance provided to families with dependent children (AFDC) declined by 33 percent.[22]

The financial condition of the elderly is not as rosy as these figures might suggest, however. Poverty among the elderly is still significantly higher than it is for those in their middle years, and there are some very serious pockets of poverty among older people, especially among widows and members of minority groups.[23] Also, government statistics underestimate the amount of poverty among the elderly because they do not acknowledge the fact that older persons need more money than younger persons to enjoy the same standard of living. Medical bills increase, and as the elderly grow more feeble, they must hire people to do many of the heavier jobs that they once did themselves.

One source of these financial problems is that as people grow older, they are less likely to be employed. While over 90 percent of American men in their middle years are in the labor force, the figure is about 16 percent for men over 65.[24] Most older people look forward to retirement and the escape it offers from the pressures of the working world, but some find that they can no longer muster the strength and stamina that their jobs require.

Another employment problem for older people arises from technological changes that may suddenly make the skills that older workers have acquired over a lifetime obsolete. Older people who know only how to bake bread or build fine cabinets or repair shoes are bound to have a tough time as bakeries become bread factories, cabinets are made of plastic, and cheap shoes are imported in huge quantities. They cannot even get unskilled jobs because employers want the energy of youth. Employee training programs that might lead to new skills are closed because training directors believe that older men and women will not work long enough to repay the cost of the training.

Discrimination in hiring and promotion is a fact of life for the elderly. Employers give a variety of reasons for their reluctance to hire senior citizens. They fear that older workers will take longer to learn a new job, will not be as productive, and will be sick more often than their younger counterparts. Although such fears are not groundless, they do not apply to the majority of older workers. A more realistic objection to hiring older workers stems from the fact that on the average they will not stay on the job as long as younger workers. This means that expensive training procedures must be repeated more often and that the costs of pensions and retirement benefits are likely to be higher for the company employing older workers.

Retired men and women receive income from a variety of sources, including pensions, social security, and personal savings. Most workers dream of retiring on a "fat pension," but only a minority of the retired receive any pension at all, and such pensions are seldom "fat."[25] The single most important source of income for elderly people in the United States is payments from Old Age and Survivors' Insurance, commonly called **social security** benefits. More than 90 percent of all elderly people in the United States collect social security or public assistance, and over half the elderly have no other source of income.[26] About 60 percent of the elderly in the United States would be living in poverty if they did not receive social security. Still, social security benefits are hardly extravagant, despite the automatic cost of living adjustments. In 1986 the average retired worker received only $488 a month, and an average couple received $831.[27]

Overall, the social security program has been a resounding success. Polls show that the current system is seen favorably by over 80 percent of the American public.[28] Still, an increasing number of younger people are becoming concerned about the future of their retirement benefits. The source of their concern is obvious. Today, people over 65 make up about 12 percent of the total population of the United States, but that figure is expected to skyrocket in the years ahead. There obviously will be a smaller number of workers supporting each retired person. Although today's young workers probably will have to pay far more for the benefits they receive, there is little danger that the social security system will collapse. The popularity of the program and the political power of the elderly virtually assure that social security will continue as a viable social program.

Housing   Decent housing is especially important to the elderly because they spend so much time at home. In central cities elderly people living in run-down rooms must accept the risks and discomforts of life in a slum. Inexpensive housing that is within walking distance of stores and a doctor's office is likely to be substandard and in a neighborhood plagued with pollution, vice, and crime. For personal comfort the elderly need higher room temperatures than the young require, but housing for the elderly often lacks proper heating. Those who are physically handicapped or disabled also need wheelchair ramps, elevators, and other special facilities. Even owning a home is not easy for many elderly people. There are mortgage payments to meet, and the costs of rising taxes and insurance must also be paid. Because many of the homes in which the elderly live were built before World War II, they are old by U.S. standards. New roofs and other needed repairs may be left undone because most elderly people are unable to do the work themselves and cannot afford to hire outside help.

So-called retirement communities are one of the most successful responses to the need of the elderly for decent housing. But unfortunately, most of these are private, and thus, the better ones are available only to people with substantial means. Often built in sunny climates, these complexes of houses or apartments are designed especially for the elderly and usually include special recreational facilities. Some are run like hotels or make hotel-like arrangements for residents who can afford them. Retirement communities have often been criticized because they weaken the ties between generations and create a kind of "old people's ghetto." Nevertheless, many older people move to retirement communities precisely because they seek the companionship of others who share their interests and experiences.

Only about 5 percent of people over 65 live in an institution, but that percentage increases sharply with advancing years. Almost a quarter of all Americans over the age of 84 live in a nursing home.[29] Most of these institutions, privately owned and managed, are profit-making businesses. Many that charge high fees give excellent service, but some of these, and most of the less expensive ones, do not do much "nursing" and are in no sense

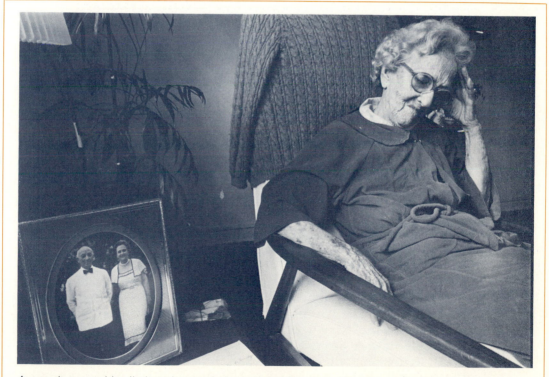

As people grow older, their environment changes and friends and loved ones die. One result may be loneliness and isolation.

"homes." The worst of these facilities are old, overcrowded, unsanitary firetraps. There are not enough toilets, the sewers back up, and the light switches don't work. Residents complain that they are served only the cheapest foods and do not get a balanced diet. And even those who live in good nursing homes may face serious psychological problems, for many people feel that entering a nursing home is a disgrace—a sign of final rejection by friends and family and proof that no one really cares.

Problems of Transition   Elderly people somehow learn to adjust to the profound role changes that are thrust upon them. But the transition to old age is a difficult one because it usually involves the loss of status, while role changes for younger people are likely to involve more prestige and responsibility. The three most significant personal transitions that the elderly must face are retirement, increasing isolation, and death.

Retirement The idea of retiring from work on a pension after a certain age is relatively new. It developed only after the industrial system had matured enough to make retirement economically possible. Although the first retirement program was begun in 1810 for British civil servants, such programs did not become common until well into the twentieth century.

After a person has been employed for decades, the transition to retirement can be painful. The daily routine that has given direction to the worker's life is suddenly yanked away. This change is difficult enough when it is voluntary, but it presents special problems to people who are required to stop working when they reach a mandatory retirement age. The transition is not just a matter of finding new things to do but requires adjustment to the idea that people who do not work are not "pulling their weight." It demands a new answer to the first question strangers are likely to ask each other: "What do you do?" Although retirees are no longer viewed as loafers, some stigma remains. An old saying held that "it is better to wear away than to rust away." People who are rusting away on park benches and shuffleboard courts are seen as a little immoral as well as useless. To make matters worse, retirees usually suffer a sharp drop in income and can no longer afford many of the things that they were used to buying—another sign of "failure."

Despite these problems, studies show that most retired people are satisfied with their lives. When a Harris poll asked a sample of retired people "Has retirement fulfilled your expectations for a good life or have you found it less than satisfactory?" 61 percent of the respondents said that retirement had fulfilled their expectations, while only 33 percent felt that it was less than satisfactory. The two most common complaints involved health and income. Lack of satisfying work was third on the list.[30] Other research shows that retirement does not usually affect health adversely and may even improve it. Retirement also appears to have little effect on morale, satisfaction with life, or self-esteem; so while the transition to retirement may be difficult, most people seem to be able to handle it satisfactorily.[31]

Normlessness and Isolation More difficult than retirement is the transition to old age itself. Because elderly people do not have clear-cut roles in our society, many find themselves in an ambiguous position. Such normlessness can produce a sense of alienation and even despair. Because no one seems to need their talents, many elderly people develop a growing sense of uselessness. But this normlessness can be a kind of liberating experience to some, who find that they are finally free to "be themselves" without having to worry about what others think of them.

Aimless or free, the social world of the elderly shrinks as the years accumulate. There are fewer social contacts as friends and relatives die, and moving from place to place becomes increasingly difficult. Old social roles are dropped, and even sex differences blur as a single role, that of "old person," is accepted.

Old people look and behave differently, and so are increasingly shunned by the young. If they have children or sisters and brothers, they are fortunate, for ties with surviving family members normally remain strong. Those without close living relatives find their world growing smaller and smaller.

Sooner or later old people die. If one member of a married couple dies, the survivor must cope without a partner. Most survivors are women, both because most wives are younger than their husbands and because women tend to live longer than men. Normlessness, isolation, and loneliness can be particularly severe in widowhood. The older the widow, the greater the problems. There is no sex, no love, no help with daily tasks, and less income. Problems of transition begin immediately after the husband's death. The woman who depended on her husband to make the decisions and handle family affairs must, in the midst of her grief, work her way through a maze of medical bills, insurance claims, funeral expenses, and tax payments. She is likely to discover that she is eligible for little or none of her husband's pension benefits, and may have to choose among looking for a job, trying to live on social security, or remarrying. Remarriage is not likely to be easy, however, for there are not enough eligible older men. Moreover, after living with one man for most of a lifetime, the idea of taking up with another may not be attractive.

Becoming a widower has its problems too. Should the elderly widower desire to remarry, his chances of finding a mate seem brighter because there are more elderly women than men. But if he does not remarry, his life may become more difficult. In most families it is the wife who keeps up contacts with friends and relatives, arranges parties, and runs the household. Consequently, a man who loses his wife is likely to lose touch with many of his friends as well. Further, although some widows can fall back on their maternal roles, widowers generally have weaker ties to their children and therefore are likely to be lonely and isolated.[32]

Death Death is the final personal transition. In many societies where death is a common occurrence, it is accepted for what it is: a natural part of daily

who are available and give more teenagers a chance at their first job. If the government supported job retraining programs for all workers, there would be no need to choose between the young and the old.

The United States, like other nations, has tried to deal with the problem of age discrimination by passing laws against it. The Federal Age Discrimination in Employment Act of 1967 prohibits most types of age discrimination against workers between the ages of 40 and 65. As a result, the most blatant signs of age discrimination have decreased significantly. But more subtle forms of discrimination continue. Laws of this type are difficult to enforce because it is hard to prove why an employer hired one person rather than another. In actual practice, the law is enforced on a hit-or-miss basis because there isn't enough money to enforce it across the board. Moreover, the current laws are far too narrow, and do nothing to fight discrimination against young workers. Although legislation of this kind can never be a complete answer to the problem, a revision of the law to include all kinds of age discrimination and a significant increase in the funding to enforce the law would certainly be a step in the right direction.

Social Welfare   The very old and the very young are often unable to fend for themselves. Traditionally, the family has been responsible for providing food, shelter, and clothing for these dependent individuals. But the profound changes that have shaken the contemporary family have left it far less able to meet these needs. The government has tried to step in and fill this gap, but its effort has left much undone.

The Young As we have seen, the government substantially reduced its commitment to young people during the 1980s. Although such short-sighted policies may achieve some immediate saving, in the long run their social and financial costs are likely to be staggering. The problems of neglected youth do not simply go away but grow progressively worse as the years go by.

The obvious place to start to reaffirm our commitment to the young is by increasing the funding for the AFDC program. Whatever the shortcomings of the parents, this aid is primarily intended to help the children, and steps should be taken to ensure that none of them fall below the minimum standard of living expected in our society. Of course, few critics of social programs openly reject the notion that the government has the responsibility to help feed, clothe, and shelter poor children, but instead claim that welfare benefits are siphoned off by undeserving parents ("welfare chiselers"). But there are many types of programs, such as those that provide a free lunch for schoolchildren, that are immune to such problems, and they have fared no better in the political climate of the 1980s. Other programs to help the young could include such things as funding to provide one nutritious meal to every child every school day, and a national program to provide high-quality day care to all children who need it. A program that has met with success in European nations is a family allowance—that is, a direct payment made to all parents regardless of income.

But a real commitment to the young must go beyond merely providing the basic necessities for survival. Our young people desperately need a better system of education, and that will require the kinds of costly reforms discussed in Chapter 4. And along with better education, our society needs to take more interest in the social needs of the young. The financial problems of local government have resulted in the closing of many parks, swimming pools, and basketball courts, and the elimination of sports programs. A new commitment to the young would mean a reversal of this trend and a greater effort to see that young people are provided positive, healthy outlets for their energy.

The Elderly Although the government programs designed to help the elderly are different than those for the young, their goals are much the same: to assist a group of deserving people who cannot always provide for themselves. Social security is the major source of income for most elderly Americans. Although it is one of the most popular and widely accepted social programs in the United States, it is experiencing some serious difficulties. As we have seen, benefits are too low to support some elderly people, yet the system is having trouble meeting the financial commitments it already has.

The original idea behind the social security system was that all workers would contribute part of their income to a pension fund, and those contributions would be matched by the employer. When workers retired, they would be entitled to regular payments from these savings. In practice, however, the contributions of workers have not been saved up; they have been paid out as needed. Social security's current financial problems arise from the fact that the number of retirees is increasing much more rapidly than the number of workers (see Figure 9.2). Thus, today's workers must pay higher social security taxes than in past decades. This burden is particularly heavy on low- and middle-income people because the social security tax rate does not increase with increasing income (as income tax rates do). Those with high incomes do not pay taxes on their entire earnings but only on the portion below a fixed level.

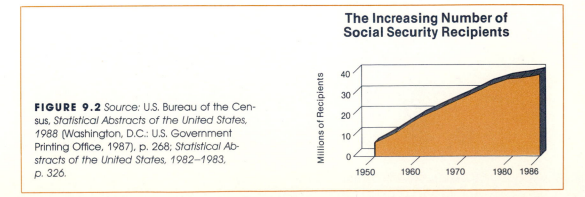

FIGURE 9.2 *Source:* U.S. Bureau of the Census, *Statistical Abstracts of the United States, 1988* (Washington, D.C.: U.S. Government Printing Office, 1987), p. 268; *Statistical Abstracts of the United States, 1982–1983,* p. 326.

The Increasing Number of Social Security Recipients

Because of these problems, it is unlikely that social security revenues can be increased significantly without a change in the tax base. The possibilities include making all income subject to social security tax, instituting a progressive social security tax that increases as income increases, and supplementing social security funds with other tax monies. Such changes would increase social security revenue without placing the burden on struggling low- and middle-income wage earners.

In addition to improving the social security system, the elderly could benefit from a variety of other programs as well. One of the most pressing needs is for more government-subsidized housing for those who are too poor to own their own home or live in a retirement community. To help middle-income retirees squeezed by inflation and health care costs, several states allow the elderly to defer their property taxes until after their death, when the equity in their house is used to pay the taxes due. Finally, a universal program of national health insurance that contained effective cost-control measures would help the elderly, the young, and many of those in their middle years as well (see Chapter 8).

Cultural Change   The problems of the elderly and the young are rooted in the cultural traditions of our society. There is, for example, a strong negative stereotype of elderly people. This attitude probably arises from observing the miserable conditions in which some elderly people must live, but eliminating poverty

Retirement communities with many specialized facilities are becoming increasingly popular, but they are expensive and most old people cannot afford to live in them.

among the aged will not necessarily change the stereotype. A public-opinion survey sponsored by the National Council on Aging found that older people consistently described themselves in more positive terms than those used by the general public. For instance, people over 65 were almost three times as likely as those under 65 to say that the elderly are "very open-minded and adaptable." The general public also saw the elderly as much less active and more bored than the elderly saw themselves. Those under 65 were more than twice as likely to believe that the elderly spend a lot of time sleeping or doing nothing, and they were four times as likely to say that "not having enough to do" is a serious problem for the elderly.[36] Such stereotypes become self-fulfilling prophecies that lead to the exclusion of the elderly from employment opportunities and other forms of social involvement. Further, because many elderly people accept these stereotypes, they may feel that they are obliged to give up their more active pursuits.

The most effective way to change this situation is to encourage the elderly to participate in community life, putting their wealth of wisdom and experience to work for the good of others. A number of government programs are aimed toward these ends. For example, the Foster Grandparent Program helps both the young and the old at the same time by paying older people to work part-time at child care centers and institutions. The elderly get meaningful work and additional income, and the children receive the benefits of personal attention and concern. Senior citizens' centers, which are funded by public and private sources, also employ older people in community projects. Perhaps more important, these centers provide a place where the elderly can congregate, make new friends, and get a hot meal.

The problems of adolescents stem less from negative stereotypes about them—although these certainly abound—than from the contradictory demands and expectations of the adult world. If we are to significantly reduce juvenile delinquency, drug and alcohol use, suicide, and the general sense of boredom and aimlessness among the young, we must provide a more clear-cut set of expectations for their age grade, and more rewarding and worthwhile things for them to do. Reducing teenage unemployment would obviously be a big help. But in addition to making money, history has shown us that young people are idealistic and want to make a useful contribution to the world. It is up to the rest of society to tap this youthful idealism and channel it into worthwhile projects. Not only can such endeavors help give purpose and meaning to those involved, but they can produce real benefits for the recipients of their aid.

SOCIOLOGICAL PERSPECTIVES ON PROBLEMS OF THE LIFE CYCLE

Each of us must come to terms with the realities of growth, aging, and death as we pass through the stages of the life cycle. This may appear to be a lonely, individual struggle, but it is not. Although the major sociological perspectives focus on different issues, they all show us how such seemingly individual problems are inextricably bound up with the social order in which we live.

The Functionalist Perspective   Functionalists see much confusion in the institutions and agencies that are supposed to meet the needs of our youngest and oldest citizens. At the root of the problem are the changes that continue to transform Western culture. In the past, death came at an early age, and there were relatively few elderly people. Most of those who did grow old were cared for by their families. But with the improvements in sanitation and food supplies brought about by industrialization, the percentage of elderly people in the population has increased enormously. At the same time, economic changes caused a breakdown in the traditional extended family, leaving many older people isolated, alone, and without the financial means to support themselves.

These changes are, moreover, having just as profound an effect on children and young adults as on the elderly. Increasing family instability has created intense social and psychological problems for many young people. And as the demand for untrained and uneducated labor has declined, the young are finding themselves increasingly excluded from the job market. Society created the new age grade of adolescents, but the expectations and social roles for this group have yet to be clearly defined.

From the functionalist perspective, it is necessary to reorganize the social institutions that traditionally cared for the young and the elderly or to develop new agencies that can do so more effectively. The fact that the government has been taking increased financial responsibility for the elderly

Our culture views old people as useless and incompetent, but few of them actually meet this stereotype. The store of information and wisdom accumulated by the elderly is especially useful to the young as they are growing up.

can be seen as an attempt to get the machinery of society running smoothly again. But there is a great deal of disorganization in the administration of government programs for the elderly, just as there is disorganization in the far smaller programs for the young. These programs are often cumbersome and inefficient, and they spend far too much of their budget on administrative costs. But the most serious problem is that these agencies do not have enough money to meet the needs of these people.

There are signs that society is at least beginning to come to terms with the problems of the elderly. Stereotypes about the elderly are beginning to change, and senior citizens' centers, retirement communities, and other organizations designed to meet the needs of the elderly are becoming increasingly common. But at the same time, we seem to have forgotten about the problems of the young, and far more needs to be done for them.

The Conflict Perspective   Many social scientists are convinced that the government's seeming indifference to the problems of the old and the young is no accident, but a product of class conflict. They argue that the wealthy and powerful have blocked efforts to help these groups because it is not in their best interests to do so. The wealthy do not need government assistance for their children or their old age and do not care to pay for such assistance for others.

Value conflicts also play an important part in these problems. Ideas about the value of competition, self-reliance, and personal responsibility clash with the effort to care for people who are not productive. Thus, the ideology of individualism (see Chapter 6) blames the elderly for their poverty, assuming that they deserve to suffer because they have failed to provide for their future. Similarly, single parents are blamed for their failure to follow traditional family patterns. On the other side, many people see such prob-

Conflict theorists are convinced that increased political activism is the most effective way to solve the problems of the elderly in our society.

lems as the product of social forces beyond the control of any single individual; and if these problems are created by society, it follows that society should do something to help resolve them.

From the conflict perspective, the most effective response to these problems is political action. And in fact, senior citizens have already organized themselves into an effective lobby. Acting through such organizations as the American Association of Retired Persons, senior citizens have been able to protect social security from the kind of cutbacks that hit most other social programs in the 1980s. Children and adolescents are, however, in a much weaker position. They lack political experience, have little money, and cannot even vote. Their only hope for political representation lies with concerned adults who are willing to fight for their interests.

Social Psychological Perspectives   Social psychologists who take the biosocial perspective emphasize the importance of the physical changes we undergo as we age. Some argue that the high rates of crime and violence among young people are the direct result of the high sex drive and physical vigor characteristic of this age group (see Chapters 14 and 15). Similarly, the emotional problems of the elderly are linked to the physiological deterioration brought on by advancing age. Although few have proposed biological treatments for the problems of the young, some scientists feel that new medical breakthroughs may make it possible to slow the process of degeneration that accompanies aging. But whatever the future may hold, it is clear that some of the physical degeneration of the elderly is due to improper diet, inadequate heating and shelter, and lack of exercise—conditions that are social rather than biological. Thus, major scientific breakthroughs are not necessary to markedly improve the health of older people.

Most social psychologists are more concerned with the social than the biological process of aging. Both behaviorists and interactionists point out that social behavior is learned from other people. As people reach different age levels, their group memberships change and they assume new roles. The key to successfully negotiating these role transitions lies in the nature of the new groups. If one is accepted by his or her new peers and given some positive ideal to emulate, the transition is likely to be an easy one. But those entering adolescence are often confronted with a confusing barrage of competing groups with conflicting ideals and expectations, and as a result they find it difficult to discover their own direction. On the other hand, people entering old age find that their previous roles disappear, along with friends and loved ones, but that their new role is poorly defined. There are far fewer expectations of any kind placed upon them and fewer goals to pursue. Although this can be a liberating experience, feelings of aimlessness and apathy are the more common result.

Despite the great differences in their perspectives, most social psychologists recommend the same kind of solution to the problems of young and old alike: help integrate them into supportive social groups that offer a constructive role to play in society. But although this conclusion is almost universally accepted for adolescents, there are some who feel that it is less appropriate for the elderly. The majority of social psychologists adhere to what is known as **activity theory,** which urges older people to remain active and involved in community life. However, **disengagement theory** rejects this recommendation and holds that old age is best negotiated by accepting the inevitable contraction of one's social world and gradually disengaging from social involvements and responsibilities as death comes nearer. While the idea of disengagement clashes with the activist bent of Western culture, it is the accepted ideal of Hindu life that the elderly should withdraw from everyday activities and focus their attention on spiritual pursuits.

SUMMARY

Aging is a social as well as a biological process. All societies divide their members into age grades—groups of people of similar age—and the members of the various age grades have different rights and duties. Sociologically, the life cycle is a series of transitions from one set of social roles to another, and such role transitions are difficult. The individual making such changes must adapt to a new set of expectations and leave behind the rewards and security of earlier roles. The four principal age grades in industrial societies are childhood, adolescence, adulthood, and old age.

Although childhood is seen as a carefree time, children still face significant problems in today's society. There is a great deal of concern about child abuse and molestation, and the poverty rate is higher for children than for any other age group. Moreover, the special sheltered status children have enjoyed in most of the twentieth century seems to be eroding. Changes in family structure have forced many children to assume adult responsibilities at an earlier age, and television and the other mass media are bringing adult attitudes and problems into the world of childhood.

Adolescents are seen neither as children nor as adults, and society's expectations for them are probably more contradictory and confusing than for any other age grade. Adolescents face many difficult problems, including constructing a viable personal identity, dealing with their awakening sexuality, and making critical decisions about education and jobs. To make matters worse, adolescents have a higher poverty rate than any other age group except young children. One response to this situation is the youth culture, which helps tie adolescents together and supplies some common answers to these perplexing questions.

Because Western culture puts high value on beauty and vigor, it fails to give the elderly the prestige and respect that they receive in many other cultures. Elderly people have more chronic diseases and poorer overall health than the general population, but most elderly people say that they are in reasonably good health. Money worries are common among the aged. Most elderly people are not eligible for a private pension, and the private pensions that the elderly do receive are usually inadequate. Over half of all the elderly people in the United States live almost entirely on social security payments or public assistance. Retirement as such is not bad for a person's health and does not, by itself, have devastating effects on morale. But because the elderly lose old friends and relatives as well as most of the social roles they once performed, they are more likely to be lonely and isolated. The death of a spouse makes matters worse. After a brief period of support and sympathy, the new widow or widower must take up a new life. Widows have some special problems of adjustment because their incomes are greatly reduced and their chances for remarriage are slim. And all elderly people are faced with the reality that their own death is drawing near.

Many different responses to the problems of our youngest and oldest citizens have been suggested. A program to create more jobs would help all workers regardless of their age. A broader prohibition against age discrimination and stronger enforcement of existing laws are other common suggestions. A reform of social security financing that allowed higher payments to retirees could do much to help the economic problems of the elderly. Young people would benefit from an increase in Aid to Families with Dependent Children, free school lunches, and more recreational facilities and programs. Both groups would be helped by a comprehensive national health insurance program, and, perhaps most of all, by cultural changes that gave them both a more positive role to play in our society.

Functionalists see the problems of the old and the young as one more product of the social disorganization that follows rapid economic and social change. From this perspective, it is necessary either to restore the extended family or to develop new organizations to take its place. Conflict theorists are convinced that groups suffer because the wealthy and powerful profit from their misery. They advocate more and better organization for political action by these groups and their supporters. Social psychologists study how age-graded roles are learned and emphasize the need of all people to be integrated into supportive social groups.

KEY TERMS

adolescence	life cycle
adulthood	mid-life crisis
age grade	old age
childhood	rite of passage
identity crisis	youth culture

FURTHER READINGS

The Life Cycle

David Allen Karp and William C. Yoels, *Experiencing the Life Cycle: A Social Psychology of Aging,* Springfield, Ill.: Charles C. Thomas, 1982.

Daniel J. Levinson, *The Seasons of a Man's Life,* New York: Alfred A. Knopf, 1979.

The Elderly

Beth B. Hess and Elizabeth Markson (eds.), *Growing Old in America*, 3d ed., New Brunswick, N.J.: Transaction Books, 1985.

Lyn Lofland, *The Craft of Dying: The Modern Experience of Death*, Beverly Hills, Calif.: Sage, 1979.

Alan Pifer and Lydia Bronte (eds.), *Our Aging Society: Paradox and Promise*, New York: W. W. Norton, 1986.

The Young

Erik H. Erikson, *Childhood and Society*, rev. ed., New York: W. W. Norton, 1964.

Joseph M. Hawes and N. Ray Hiner (eds.), *American Childhood: A Research Guide and Historical Handbook*, Westport, Conn.: Greenwood Press, 1985.

Hans Sebald, *Adolescence: A Social Psychological Analysis*, Englewood Cliffs, N.J.: Prentice-Hall, 1984.

Chapter 10
WOMEN AND MEN

We have all watched a movie hero fight his way through fire, flood, or corruption to save the defenseless heroine from disaster. But we would be amazed if the woman were shown rescuing the man while he clung helplessly to her skirts. The first plot fits our ideas about the proper behavior of men and women. The second does not.

Our ideas about differences between the sexes have deep historical roots. For generations, these ideas were accepted uncritically, but new economic and social conditions are forcing us to rethink out traditional attitudes. Women are moving into the "man's world" of employment and competition, while men are beginning to explore the "woman's world" of family and children. Indeed, this redefinition of what it means to be a woman or a man may be one of the most significant developments of modern times.

At first glance these changes hardly qualify as a social problem; but our identity as a male or female is a critical part of the way we see ourselves, and even minor changes have far-reaching implications. For many people, perhaps most, the new roles are a welcome release from unreasonable social restrictions. Some people, however, are experiencing confusion and anxiety. Even more important, people are becoming aware that the inequality between men and women is as unjust as racial, ethnic, and class inequality. Women are now recognized as victims of exploitation and oppression similar in many ways to ethnic minorities.

GENDER ROLES

Like veteran actors, each of us plays many roles. The list is almost endless—parent, child, student, worker, pedestrian, automobile driver, shopper, consumer. **Gender roles** are assigned to us on the basis of our biological sex. These roles contain sets of expectations both for what we are supposed to do and what we are not supposed to do. A woman who spends hours dyeing her hair and applying just the right makeup before going out meets our gender role expectations; a man who does the same thing violates those expectations.

Gender roles are assigned early in life. Children quickly learn that they are girls or boys and act accordingly. Most keep their gender identity for life. Nevertheless, adult gender roles are complex, involving both personality and behavioral characteristics. Women are expected to be passive, warm, and supportive. In contrast to men, who are expected to suppress their feelings, women are encouraged to express emotions openly. Women are also expected to be dependent and to need emotional support. Men, on the other hand, are expected to be active, independent, and self-controlled. An essential part of the male role is aggressiveness and dominance. The henpecked husband is the butt of jokes because he deviates from cultural expectations. No one jokes about a woman who does her husband's bidding.

The focus of the traditional male role is the world of work. The husband is the breadwinner and the provider of financial security for the family. He is supposed to protect and defend his family from outside dangers, make important decisions, and provide family leadership. He must also show courage and strive for achievement.

The traditional female role centers on home and family. Most women are under strong pressure to marry and have children, and their responsibility is to run the home and rear the children. Whereas men's prestige is derived from their own efforts in the world, women's prestige is usually derived from that of their husbands.[1]

Obviously, the roles of women and men in our society are not only distinctly different, they are highly unequal. Men are assigned the positions of power and importance and are expected to have the personality traits that go with them. Women, on the other hand, are given the subordinate role. Their ideal personality is therefore giving, compliant, and supportive.

The movement of women out of the home and into the workplace has led to a vigorous challenge to those old notions about the natural differences between the sexes.[2] In the past, people who did not fit the expectations for their gender were shunned and laughed at. Today, some argue that the healthiest individuals display both strong masculine and strong feminine characteristics, and that the new ideal should therefore be a single **androgynous** one combining traits traditionally assigned to different genders.[3] Others hold that the whole distinction between masculine and feminine characteristics is harmful, and should be abandoned altogether.[4] Nonetheless, these traditional roles and stereotypes are still a powerful force in our society, and their consequences will be with us for a long time to come.

Nature or Nurture?   What, then, are the origins of the differences that we see in the behavior of women and men? As with many other issues in the social sciences there is a vigorous debate about the relative importance of nature (biology) and nurture (learning).

The two most significant biological differences are the greater size and strength of the male and the female's ability to bear and nurse children. In physical contests most males have a clear advantage. Not only is the average male taller than the average female, but testosterone, a male sex hormone, promotes muscular development and strength. The female has a much closer biological tie with the process of reproduction. Childbearing is, of course, the exclusive domain of the female. And before the development of baby bottles, only the female could feed the child for the first months of its life. Because a sexually active woman who lives in a farming society will become pregnant about once every two years without the use of contraceptives, the average woman in most agricultural societies was either pregnant or nursing a small child during most of her adult life.[5]

Despite the male's advantage in physical strength, females are clearly the healthier sex. Males are subject to a variety of sex-linked genetic defects, including hemophilia and color blindness. They are also more susceptible to some diseases, and they grow and mature more slowly than females.[6] Although more male infants are born, their rate of death is significantly greater. Females have longer life spans in all modern societies.

Changes in life style have significant effects on physique. Muscular strength used to be considered "un-feminine," but such attitudes are changing. Florence Griffith Joyner, shown here winning one of her Olympic medals, has become as famous for her beauty as for her athletic ability.

The relationship between sex hormones and behavior is a highly controversial issue. Numerous researchers have attempted to show that male hormones are linked to such things as aggression and dominance, and female hormones to mothering and nurturant behavior. Studies have been made of children exposed to high levels of male hormones in the womb because of a hereditary defect in the function of the adrenal gland (adrenogenital syndrome), and of children exposed to high levels of a female hormone (progesterone) given to mothers because of difficulties in pregnancy. In general, these studies have found girls exposed to male hormones to be more "masculine," and males exposed to female hormones to be more "feminine." However, the interpretation of these results is far from clear. The cause of the lower levels of aggression and physical activity in the "feminized" boys may have been their mother's problems during pregnancy and not the drug prescribed to deal with those problems. Similarly, the active "masculinized" behavior of girls with adrenogenital syndrome may be due to the regular doses of cortisone (a drug which can cause hyperactive behavior in adults) prescribed by their physicians, or the expectation of parents and friends that they will be more masculine than other girls (at birth their external genital organs may appear to be those of a male).[7]

Other researchers have attempted to show a correlation between high levels of the male hormone, testosterone, and aggressive behavior in adult men. But such studies have produced mixed results. Some have shown a significant correlation between high levels of testosterone and aggression and hostility, but most have not. But even if a correlation between the two were clearly established, that would still not prove that the hormone causes aggression. Numerous studies have shown that testosterone levels are strongly affected by an individual's environment and emotional state. For example, researchers have found that men's testosterone levels go up after winning a tennis match and down after losing one.[8] Moreover, the practice of castrating prisoners or giving them drugs that neutralize male hormones have proven to have little effect in preventing violence.[9]

If gender roles are determined by biology, it is logical to assume that they should be the same in all cultures. Most researchers agree that some degree of male dominance is a common characteristic of all known societies.[10] But anthropological studies have shown that there are still enormous differences in the gender roles of different cultures, and historians have found that gender roles change within the same culture over time. For example, in many hunting and gathering societies both males and females are peaceful and cooperative, and in other societies, such as the Mundugumor of New Guinea, both males and females are highly aggressive and competitive.[11] Some societies even have more than two genders. Among the Crow Indians, for example, there was a third gender that was seen as neither male nor female, for men who did not fit into the roles expected of their sex.[12] Thus, different social and economic conditions produce different gender roles.

Further evidence against the biological determination of gender comes from the study of people who have been raised as members of the opposite sex. This usually occurs because of a physical abnormality of the genitals, but it occasionally occurs for other reasons as well. The general conclusion from this research is that a woman raised as a man will act like a man, and that a man raised as a woman will act like a woman.[13] In other words, people act the way they are taught to act; their behavior is not predetermined by a biological program.

Two conclusions seem justified from the evidence. First, although there may be some biological tendencies for men and women to behave in different ways, cultural learning is far more important and can easily override any biological predispositions that may exist. As individuals, our gender roles are determined by society, not biology. Second, the gender roles that society creates are nonetheless strongly influenced by biological considerations. Because men tend to be stronger and larger than women and are not destined to bear and nurse children, it is not surprising that they engage in more activities that involve strength and travel, or that women are more concerned with childbearing and the responsibilities of the home. The typical pattern of male dominance can be seen as a result of the greater physical strength of the male. The typical "family-oriented" female pattern can be seen as a consequence of childbearing and breast feeding. But as we will see in the next section, the influence of the biological constraints that helped shape traditional gender roles has been greatly weakened in modern industrial societies.

The Historical Development of Gender Roles   The roles given to women and men have changed over the centuries as the economic system has changed. The earliest human societies obtained food by hunting animals and gathering edible plants. Because these societies left no written records, there is little hard evidence about their culture. However, by examining contemporary hunting and gathering societies, some educated guesses can be made about the earliest human societies.

Hunting and gathering societies were small, often consisting of fewer than 50 people. There was little surplus wealth, so the differences between rich and poor were small. Politically, these societies also tended to be egalitarian, with little or no formal leadership. Leaders would emerge in response to specific problems and then dissolve back into the group when the problems were solved. Under these conditions of relative political and economic equality, the most important and lasting social division was between men and women. Ernestine Friedl has described the relationship between the sexes in present-day hunting and gathering societies as follows:

> Economic and sexual cooperation between [the sexes] is necessary, but their interdependence is full of difficulties. . . . The cleavage between men and women can be great, and relationships are sometimes hostile. Nevertheless, both men and women have considerable autonomy, and those of each sex have, in most foraging societies, the basis for acquiring self-esteem.[14]

Friedl concluded that the most important difference in these societies stems from the male monopoly on hunting large animals. The meat from hunts, which is usually distributed to the entire group, gives the successful hunter a source of prestige and power that women do not share. However, other anthropologists reject this conclusion, holding that women provide other services of equal social value to the meat from the hunt.[15] Despite such disputes, anthropologists generally agree that the relationships between the sexes, like other relationships in hunting and gathering societies, tend to be egalitarian.

A major change in human society occurred with the discovery that plants could be grown specifically for human use. Horticultural societies used the hoe and the digging stick but did not have the plow or irrigation. The style of life was quite different from that of the hunters and gatherers. The development of a more dependable food supply made it unnecessary to wander from place to place in search of food. The sedentary life promoted the growth of clans and the extended family. Trade grew, and with it developed inequalities in wealth and power. Because these societies produced surplus food, they were able to support specialized economic, religious, and political roles.

In contemporary horticultural societies men almost always have a monopoly on warfare and do the initial clearing of land. Typically, both men and women share in cultivation, although this task is sometimes assigned exclusively to women. Child rearing is typically a female task, but both sexes may share in the responsibilities. The distribution of power between the sexes varies with economic conditions. In societies with little trade and commerce and few class distinctions, males tend to be strongly dominant. In

There are wide variations in sex roles among the various cultures of the world. Hunting-and-gathering societies, such as the one pictured here, generally have egalitarian relationships between the sexes.

horticultural societies in which trade is an important activity, women usually have a much better position. In many such societies women can gain prestige by displaying trading ability in the marketplace.[16]

The next major change in human societies came with the development of agriculture. Agricultural societies make use of such technological advances as the plow, irrigation, and the harnessing of domestic animals. Inventions that originated in horticultural societies were refined in agricultural societies. Economic surpluses grew, and with this growth came greater sex-role specialization, a more elaborate division of labor, and more social and economic inequality. Agricultural societies created written language and the first bureaucracies. The surplus food produced by agriculture permitted the growth of the first real cities. Large centralized empires developed in many agricultural regions.

Although there were many cultural variations, the development of agriculture usually meant a decline in the status of women. Because of the strength required for plowing and irrigation, men did more of the agricultural labor, and women lost the influence that came from their important role in horticulture.[17] Men also came to monopolize the powerful political and religious bureaucracies.

The industrial revolution once again created profound changes in human society. As noted in Chapter 5, the extended family deteriorated, and the nuclear family became the norm. Economic changes that made children a financial burden instead of an asset led to fewer births and a smaller number of children. Industrialization reduced the importance of physical labor, the family was displaced as the primary unit of economic production, and women joined the work force in increasing numbers.

This transformation of the family and the economic system had a particularly significant impact on gender roles. Because technological and social development sharply reduces the importance of the biological differences between the sexes, their roles change as societies industrialize. The male's greater size and strength means much less in an age of machines and automation. The qualities necessary for economic success are now related more closely to personality and intelligence than to physique and are possessed equally by women and men. At the same time, birth control, smaller families, bottle feeding for babies, and the great increases in life span mean that child rearing no longer takes up most of a woman's adult life.

But although there have been significant improvements in the status of women in industrial societies, cultural change still lags behind technological change. Women are no longer seen as the property of their husbands, they have equal inheritance rights, and they are generally considered equal in theory if not in practice. But despite the fact that democratic countries now given men and women an equal vote, men still dominate the political system. The traditional pattern in which the husband works and the wife stays home to raise the children also remains the ideal among many people. A new pattern in which both the wife and husband work and share family duties in developing, but the working wife is usually burdened with a disproportionate share of the domestic and child rearing duties. Moreover, working women still receive substantially lower pay than their male counterparts.[18]

GENDER SOCIALIZATION

Socialization is the process by which we learn the essentials of life in our culture. Customs, behavior, mores, values, how to speak, even how to think—all these are learned in the course of socialization. **Gender socialization** is part of this process. It is the way we learn the behavior and attitudes that are expected of the members of our sex. It should not be concluded, however, that gender socialization creates identical males and females. There is always room for interpretation and creativity. In response to their unique experiences, each individual creates her or his own definition of what it means to be a woman or a man.

Sexual stereotyping starts almost from the moment of birth, when boys are wrapped in blue blankets and girls in pink ones. Girls' and boys' bedrooms are often decorated differently and contain different kinds of toys. Researchers have found that boys are given a wider variety of toys than girls, and that the boys' toys are more likely to encourage activities outside the home.[19] But the most important differences are learned as children begin to master a language. For one thing, most languages require the speaker to make frequent distinctions between the sexes. The use of the words *he* and *his* or *she* and *hers* continually draws the child's attention to the importance of gender differences. In addition, the structure of every language conveys social assumptions about the nature of the differences between the sexes. The child quickly learns that the male is given first-class status, while the female takes second place. In English, for example, male pronouns and adjectives are used to describe people whose gender is unknown ("No person shall be compelled in any criminal case to be a witness against himself"). When one is referring to the entire human race, the term *man* or *mankind* is often used. The male is primary in our language, the female a vaguely defined "other."[21]

The older and more aware children become, the greater the differences in the family's expectations for boys and girls. Because the male role is narrowly defined, young boys come under some particularly intense pressures. They are continually told not to be "sissies" and not to "act like a girl." A boy who playfully puts on a dress and lipstick is likely to receive a hostile and even panicky reprimand from his parents. The root of many of these attitudes is the deep-seated homophobia (fear of homosexuality) in Western culture. Some argue that the training boys receive to repress their feelings of love for other males eventually leads to a repression of all sorts of emotional expression, and there is little doubt that most boys learn to reject and even fear the feminine at an early age.[22]

A major problem faced by most young boys is that they spend much more time with their mother than with their father and must repress the natural tendency to imitate this central figure in their life. Because most girls are raised by members of their own sex, they have a much clearer idea of what is expected of them as adults than do boys. Perhaps for this reason, there is less fear among girls of "acting like a boy." It is far worse to be a sissy than a tomboy. But with the coming of adolescence, it is the girls who find their lives increasingly restricted by the demands of their gender role. While the the boys are allowed and even encouraged to "sow some wild oats," girls are denied such freedom. Not only are they far more closely watched, but they quickly learn that appearing too strong and assertive will make it more difficult to form the marital relationship that will be so critical to the rest of their lives.

From their earliest years, girls are taught the vital importance of personal relationships, and they are encouraged to develop the traits that promote them: empathy, expressiveness, and sensitivity to others. Boys, on the other hand, are urged to be self-reliant, assertive, and achievement oriented. The results of this differential socialization are reflected in the relationships that girls and boys create. Girls tend to have fewer, more intense friendships, whereas boys form larger and therefore less intimate groups.[23]

Boys generally have more trouble adjusting to school than do girls. Because boys develop more slowly, they are often less able to live up to the expectations of the school than girls of the same age. Since boys are given much more encouragement to be independent and assertive, they also tend

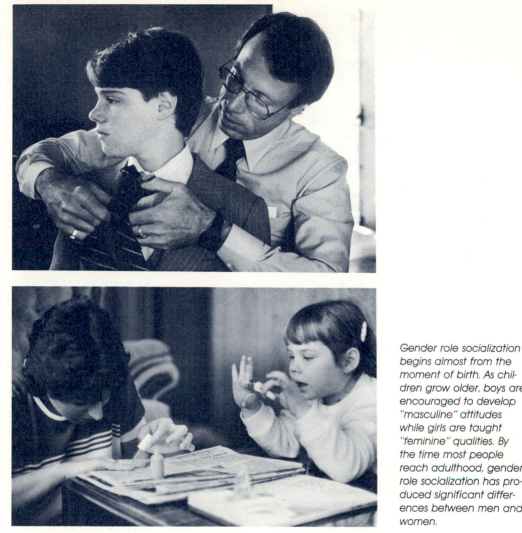

Gender role socialization begins almost from the moment of birth. As children grow older, boys are encouraged to develop "masculine" attitudes while girls are taught "feminine" qualities. By the time most people reach adulthood, gender role socialization has produced significant differences between men and women.

to find the docile, cooperative behavior expected of schoolchildren far more frustrating than girls. Boys are therefore more likely to act up and get into trouble.[24] Perhaps for this reason, studies of teacher-student interaction have found that boys get more attention, both positive and negative, than girls. As Myra Sadker and her associates put it: "Boys are the central figures . . . and girls are relegated to second-class participation."[25]

Research shows that teachers' expectations have a powerful influence on the way students perform in the classroom (see Chapter 4). This creates a serious problem for girls because most teachers accept the sexual stereotypes so common in our society. Teachers expect a good male student to be active, adventurous, and inventive, whereas good female students are expected to be calm, conscientious, and sensitive.[26] These expectations also involve more specific abilities. For example, John Ernest found that 41 percent of the teachers he interviewed believed that boys were better than girls at math, and none felt it was the other way around.[27] Moreover, Kelly found that most teachers actually believed that those differences were genetic.[28] Teachers who believe that girls are genetically inferior at math are bound to have lower expectations for them and convey that message to their students. Thus, such expectations become a self-fulfilling prophecy.

Despite some recent improvements, males and females are still directed into different kinds of classes in junior and senior high school. Girls are encouraged to take courses that help them fulfill their traditional gender roles, such as sewing, cooking, and typing. Boys are more likely to take classes in carpentry, sheet-metal work, and automobile repair. Counselors encourage college-bound girls to enter such "feminine" careers as nursing, social work, and teaching, whereas boys are urged to consider professions like business, engineering, medicine, and science. Most of the careers that girls are encouraged to pursue have two things in common—low pay and limited opportunity for advancement.

The mass media also have a profound effect on the definition of personal gender roles. A variety of research studies show that television, motion pictures, radio, books, and magazines all tend to reinforce traditional gender role stereotypes. Children's television programs are particularly important in the early socialization process, consistently depicting men and women in traditionally stereotyped ways.

Male characters are shown in such active and prestigious occupations as physician, lawyer, and police officer, while women are relegated to such secondary roles as mother, secretary, and helper. Commercials also reflect the same biases. Feldstein and Feldstein found that boys are overrepresented in advertisements for every type of toy except dolls, while the girls who are shown are far more likely to be given only a passive role.[29] Even children's cartoons are stereotyped. One study found that male cartoon characters outnumbered female characters by three to one.[30] But beyond simply showing more males, the cartoons depict males as being more powerful and having a greater impact on their environment than females do.[31]

How does the media's message of male dominance and female passivity affect children? Numerous studies of children from preschool to adolescence show that those who watch more television are more likely to accept traditional gender stereotypes.[32] Of course, it is possible that children with traditional attitudes are simply more likely to watch television. However, Michael Morgan's two-year study of the impact of television viewing on a group of teenagers indicates otherwise. The subjects who were the least sexist to begin with—girls with high IQs—were the most affected by television. The high-IQ girls who watched a lot of television showed a significant increase in sexist attitudes over the two-year period, while the attitudes of those who were light television viewers were unchanged.[33]

Of course, sexist stereotypes are not limited to children's television. The advertising aimed at adult audiences reveals the same bias. Women are used to attract attention to a man's sales pitch—perhaps wearing a bikini while sipping a new drink, wearing a silk gown while slithering into a sports car, or staring seductively at a man who uses the right brand of shaving cream. The prime concern of the "good housewife" is the whiteness of her wash and whether she can see her face reflected in her dinner plates. Research on the contents of popular books, movies, and magazines points to much the same conclusion: women are consistently portrayed as sex objects, passive by-standers, and willing assistants, whereas men are more often active, aggressive, and dominant.[34]

GENDER INEQUALITY

In Western society the roles of females and males are not only substantially *different* but also *unequal*. As we have seen, the male is given the dominant position. In a sense he is the star actor, whereas the female plays only a supporting role. The male is expected to have superior strength, greater stamina, higher intelligence, and better organizing ability. Psychologically, the male is trained to play the dominant, superior role of decision maker, whereas the female is programmed to be submissive and obedient. Inequality in sex roles is reflected in our basic institutions. In education, employment, and political power, women clearly are treated as inferiors. They are victims of **sexism** (sexual stereotyping, prejudice, and discrimination) in much the same way that blacks are victims of racism.

Education We have already discussed some of the subtle ways in which schools encourage achievement among males and discourage it among females. But not all sexism in education is so subtle. Most older colleges and universities were originally open only to men, and until recently graduate and professional schools commonly excluded women. Such discrimination has been strongest at the most desirable and prestigious schools. Harvard University excluded women from its law school until 1950 and from its graduate business program until 1963.[35] Because recent laws have forbidden sexual discrimination, women's educational opportunities have improved, but sexism remains a fact of life for most women in schools, colleges, and universities.

In the past, many more boys than girls graduated from high school, but in recent years female graduates have slightly outnumbered the males. There are still many more men with bachelor's degrees than women, but that too seems to be changing. In 1980 the number of women enrolled in college exceeded the number of men for the first time and today about 52 percent of first-year college students are female.[36] It is in graduate school that the difference between the sexes is the largest: men receive half the master's degrees, but more than two out of three Ph.D.'s. This is nonetheless a significant improvement from the 1950s, when women received less than one in every ten Ph.D.'s.[37]

Equally important are the differences in the majors taken by men and women. Most female students are concentrated in the liberal arts and teaching areas, while more men study science, engineering, business administration, and other majors that lead directly to high-paying occupations. Once again the trend is toward greater participation of women in formerly all-male fields, but there is still a long way to go before equality is achieved.

Why are women less likely to go to graduate school or to major in the fields that lead to the highest-paying jobs? One factor is economic. If a family cannot afford education for all its children, sons are likely to be given preference over daughters. Gender role stereotypes both inside and outside the school also serve to discourage women from competing in traditionally male fields. A young woman is expected to find an appropriate mate and then to shape her life—including her educational plans—to fit his needs. Further, many rewarding careers in such fields as engineering and business are seen as "unfeminine" work for which men are better suited.

Employment   The role of women in the work force is undergoing a remarkable change. Fifty years ago, fewer than 25 percent of all adult women in the United States worked outside the home. Today, over 50 percent are employed, and the percentage is growing steadily. In 1890 women accounted for only 17 percent of the total work force. By 1960 this figure had risen to 33 percent, and by 1986 over 44 percent of all workers were women.[38] A similar trend is evident in Canada, but women account for a smaller percentage of the total work force than in the United States. And both countries are still slightly behind such northern European nations as Denmark, Finland, and Sweden.[39]

Although the gap between men's and women's pay has narrowed in recent years, it continues to be a large one. In 1975 a woman working full-time for the entire year earned about 59.5 percent as much as a man working full-time. A decade later that figure had increased to 68.2 percent.[40] Unfortunately, this change was caused more by a decline in men's earnings than by an increase in women's earnings. Moreover, women's wages are still far below those of their male counterparts (see Figure 10.1). A woman with a college degree earns only a little more than a male high-school dropout, whereas a male college graduate earns half again as much.[41]

Many women receive lower paychecks than men because they enter lower-paying jobs and hold lower-ranking jobs within their occupation. Yet there are substantial differences in pay even between men and women who do the same type of work.

Saleswomen earn only half of a salesmen's pay; female executives earn about 60 percent as much as male executives; and professional women earn about 65 percent as much as their male counterparts.[42] Employers traditionally justified this inequality by claiming that men need higher pay because they must support their families and that women just work for "extra" money. The sharp increase in female-headed families and new legislation making such discriminatory practices illegal means that few employers openly use such rationalizations anymore, but they nonetheless persist in

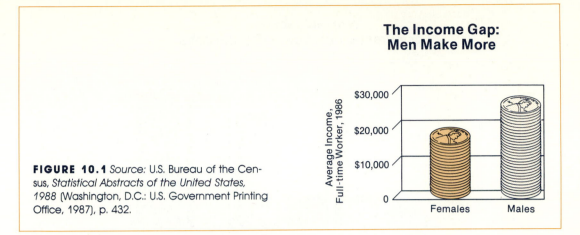

The Income Gap: Men Make More

Average Income, Full-time Worker, 1986

$30,000

$20,000

$10,000

0

Females   Males

FIGURE 10.1 *Source:* U.S. Bureau of the Census, *Statistical Abstracts of the United States, 1988* (Washington, D.C.: U.S. Government Printing Office, 1987), p. 432.

paying men more. Some economists explain such differences by pointing out that the average male worker has more years of experience than his female counterpart, and others argue that women are more likely to put the demands of their family ahead of their job. Although such factors do explain part of the pay differentials, the fundamental cause is simple discrimination. Employers pay women less for the same work because they can get away with it: they know that the prevailing wages are lower for women, and that their female workers probably cannot get another job at "men's wages."[43]

Most occupations are clearly "sex typed": that is, they are considered either men's jobs or women's jobs. Two-thirds of all university professors are men, as are 90 percent of all police officers and 93 percent of all engineers. In contrast, 73 percent of all primary and secondary teachers, 87 percent of all librarians, and 98 percent of all secretaries are women.[44] "Women's jobs" almost always have lower pay and lower status than comparable "male" positions (see Figure 10.2). The nurse (usually female) is subordinate to the doctor (usually male), just as the secretary (usually female) is subordinate to the executive (usually male). Jobs that are relatively autonomous are usually typed as male, as in the case of truck drivers or traveling sales personnel.

"Women's jobs" also offer less chance for advancement. The secretary does not become a top executive, nor the nurse a doctor. Even when a woman enters a company in a high-level job, she and the male executives are likely to be on different "tracks." Women employed in high-level corporate jobs are usually in dead-end positions (such as administering affirmative-action programs or supervising the hiring process) rather than in the production, sales, and financial posts that lead to the top corporate jobs. About 97 percent of top executive jobs are held by men.[45] Successful female executives often complain about a "glass ceiling" that keeps them out of the highest corporate jobs. One study based on interviews with 100 male and female executives from three major U.S. corporations concluded that there was a clear double

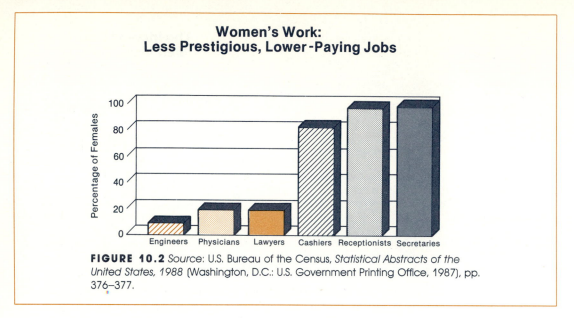

FIGURE 10.2 *Source*: U.S. Bureau of the Census, *Statistical Abstracts of the United States, 1988* (Washington, D.C.: U.S. Government Printing Office, 1987), pp. 376–377.

standard in promotions, and that women had to perform significantly better than their male counterparts in order to get ahead.[46]

There are, nonetheless, some hopeful signs. As Blau and Ferber point out, there has been a slow but steady decrease in occupational segregation since the 1960s, and many women have managed to breach the walls that kept them out of better-paying "men's jobs."[47] In 1960 only about 6.5 percent of U.S. physicians were women; today that number is over 17 percent. Women have made even greater strides in the legal profession: fewer than one out of twenty lawyers and judges were women in 1960, but today it is almost one in five.[48]

Political Power   Politics has been considered a man's business in almost all societies throughout the world. Women were not even allowed to vote in most democracies until this century. The few women who have gained power have usually had the benefit of family connections to overcome objections to their sex. Benazir Bhutto in Pakistan and the hereditary European monarchs such as Queen Elizabeth II in England are good examples. Neither the United States nor Canada has ever had a female head of state.

In 1988, only 4 percent of the members of the U.S. Senate and 5.3 percent of the House were women. Moreover, no woman has ever held a key position of power in Congress, such as majority leader or speaker of the house. As of the late 1980s, women still appear to be locked out of the inner circles of power in Congress and the White House.[49] And they have fared little better with the judicial branch where only one woman has ever been a Supreme Court justice in the history of the United States.

Women, nonetheless, have enormous political potential. Most of the volunteer workers essential to modern political campaigns are women. Even more significant is the fact that women outnumber men and could easily outvote them. But until recently, women have voted much as their husbands have, showing little awareness of their own special political interests. But things began to change with the 1980 elections, when a significant "gender gap" between the voting patterns of men and women first developed. Polls show that women look more favorably on welfare programs and environmental protection, but are more likely to oppose military spending and an aggressive foreign policy. In the last three presidential elections, substantially more women than men voted for the Democratic candidate.[50] So far the gender gap has not been a decisive factor in U.S. politics, but the potential is certainly there.

Social Life   Sexism in education, employment, and politics is obvious to anyone who cares to look. But women and girls are also victims of more subtle forms of discrimination. They are told in many subtle ways that they are second-class citizens. They are seen as emotional, unstable, and unable to direct their own lives. All too often the heroine in popular stories proves unable to solve her own problems and must be rescued by a man. Women are taught from childhood that beauty and sex appeal are the keys to happiness. Success comes not from their own efforts but from the ability to appeal to the right man. They may be seen as wives and mothers of important people, but seldom as important individuals in their own right.

Women are routinely expected to repress their desires and ambitions in ways that are seldom demanded of men. Studies of dual-career families (in which both husband and wife work) reveal that it is the wife who must sacrifice her career if it interferes with that of her spouse. The working woman is also expected to carry most of the homemaking and child-rearing responsibilities in addition to her job (see Chapter 5).

Women are expected to repress their sexuality in the same way that they are expected to repress their career ambitions. During the Victorian era women's sexuality was almost entirely denied. The "good" woman did not enjoy sex; she put up with it for her husband's sake. Recent research shows that although the **double standard** for sexual behavior has weakened in recent years, it is still very much with us. Young men are expected to "sow their wild oats," but the "slut" is still condemned. And those who berate an unfaithful wife often condone a husband's infidelities with a wink.

But paradoxically, at the same time that women are told to repress their sexuality, they are often subject to **sexual harassment** at work and on the streets.[51] Although definitions of sexual harassment vary, they usually include everything from unwanted sexual comments and gestures to direct physical assaults. A recent survey of 13,000 federal employees found that 42 percent of the females reported experiencing some kind of sexual harassment on the job.[52] In many cases it may be nothing more than a minor annoyance, but sexual harassment can be much more serious. Countless women have

DEBATE

Should Federal Legislation Be Enacted to Require That Women Be Given Comparable Pay for Comparable Work?

YES Virtually everyone agrees that women deserve pay equal with that of men. Existing legislation forbids occupational discrimination and requires that men and woman who do the same work receive the same pay. Despite inadequate enforcement, these laws have promoted the ideals of social justice. Now, the struggle for equal employment for women is confronting a new barrier: sex typing in employment. Study after study has shown that job categories dominated by women receive substantially lower pay than less demanding, lower-skilled jobs performed primarily by men. For example, skilled nurses are commonly paid less than the grounds keepers who trim the hospital trees, and executive secretaries upon whose skills an entire firm's future may rest are payed less than the plumbers who unclog the drains. This double pay scale demeans women and violates the most fundamental principles upon which our society claims to be based. Justice demands that it be ended once and for all.

The only real issue is how to eliminate such discrimination. Some people say that women should simply change to traditional male jobs that offer higher pay and better chances for advancement. But such claims are so unrealistic they can hardly be taken seriously. How are the millions of secretaries, nurses, and saleswomen suddenly going to develop new skills, and where could they all possibly find jobs if they did? Other critics say that legislation requiring comparable pay would only create another cumbersome bureaucracy, one that would raise the costs of business and government and make us less competitive in world markets.

The same argument could also have been used against the abolition of slavery. Legislation requiring equal pay for equal work did not harm our international competitiveness, and neither will legislation requiring comparable pay for comparable work. The enforcement of such legislation would certainly require some bureaucracy, but it need not be cumbersome or inefficient unless its opponents try to make it that way. When all is said and done, there is no other way to give women an equal chance in our society. We must enact comparable pay legislation, now!

NO There is now strong social support for women's demands for equal pay. Both private employers and government employers are making vigorous efforts to implement this new policy. We even have laws requiring that employers pay the same wages to men and women for the same work. But the demand that the government somehow analyze every job in the country, decide which ones are comparable, and then require that their pay be equalized is, in the words of former President Reagan, "a cockamamie idea."

The most obvious drawback of the proposal for comparable worth legislation is this: Such a law would be impossible to enforce. How can anyone determine if a welder's job and a respiratory therapist's job have comparable worth? The only efficient way to make such decisions is through the operation of the free market. If one job is overpaid, more people will be attracted to it and wages will decline. If another job is underpaid, employers will not be able to hire the people they need and wages will improve. The intrusion of government into this system would create a bureaucratic nightmare. You can be sure that politically sensitive government employees would never order anyone's salary cut, so the final result of such legislation would be a huge jump in inflation that would seriously hurt our already precarious position in world markets. Such legislation would require that the government set salaries without regard to market conditions. How would we make adjustments between the kinds of work people desire and the needs of the economy? Hundreds of thousands of people would scramble to get the overpaid jobs, while the underpaid ones would go begging. The net result would be economic chaos that would benefit neither men nor women. Comparable pay for comparable worth is another of those ideas that sounds good in theory but would be a disaster in practice.

been fired from their jobs because they rejected their boss's sexual advances, while others have been forced into physical relationships that they did not want. In many traditionally all-male jobs, repeated sexual harassment is used as a tactic to drive away female workers.

RESPONDING TO THE PROBLEM OF GENDER INEQUALITY

The inequality between women and men has been the subject of intense debate in the last two decades. But to understand the current controversy over how to respond to this problem, it is necessary to understand the history of the women's movement. In North America, its origins are usually traced to the nineteenth century and the struggle to free the slaves. Many idealistic women who became involved in the abolitionist movement came to realize that they too were part of an oppressed group. These early feminists made wide-ranging demands for sexual equality, but the movement they created eventually came to focus on a single issue: women's right to vote. After years of struggle these "suffragettes" built themselves into a powerful political force and won their battle for universal suffrage. But after that success, the movement began to fade. It was not until the 1960s, when the civil rights movement was once again calling attention to the racial injustices of North American society, that the feminist movement was reborn.

The modern feminist movement has scored some remarkable successes. Women's liberation and sexual equality are now widely discussed, and more and more women are entering occupations that were formerly closed to them. Through effective court and legislative action, feminists have successfully attacked employment and promotion practices that discriminate against women. Government-sponsored affirmative-action programs now require employers to hire and promote more women and members of minority groups. Feminists have even made some inroads on the sexual biases built into the English language. Women are increasingly identifying themselves as *Ms.* rather than *Miss* or *Mrs.*, and new sexually neutral words such as *chairperson* and *humankind* are replacing the traditional masculine terms. But as we have seen in this chapter, we are still a very long way from full sexual equality.

As in other social movements, all feminists do not agree on the best ways to win their objectives. The liberal feminists are the largest group in the

The feminist movement has a long history in North America, dating back to the struggle for women's suffrage. Today's feminists are seeking complete equality between the sexes.

movement, and their approach is the predominant one in the National Organization for Women (NOW). Drawing on the values of freedom and individual liberty central to the liberal tradition, these feminists call for a vigorous government attack on all forms of prejudice and discrimination. They urge a strengthening of affirmative-action programs (see Chapter 7), and new laws requiring not only that women be given the same pay for the same work but that those working in "women's jobs" be paid in the same range as those working in comparable "men's jobs." Liberal feminists advocate a concerted effort to send rapists to prison and crack down on sexual harassment in the workplace. They support women's reproductive rights, which include access to contraception and abortion. Liberal feminists are also strong advocates of a system of government-funded and -supervised day care centers, so that all parents can be assured that their children have safe, high-quality care while they are away at work.

The liberal feminists have, however, been under attack on two fronts. Other feminists have criticized the liberals for failing to make the connections between the problems of individual women and the structural conditions that create them. Socialist feminists argue that the exploitation of women arises from the capitalist system and that only fundamental changes in our economic institutions can liberate women. Radical feminists focus more on the social arena, calling for a new "woman-centered" culture to replace the current pattern of patriarchal (male-dominated) society. At the same time, all feminists are being attacked by those who feel that they are undermining the family and traditional social values.[53]

What, then, are the prospects for the future? There is little doubt that the feminist movement has suffered some significant setbacks in the last decade. The most painful was certainly the failure to win ratification of the Equal Rights Amendment, which would have explicitly guaranteed equal protection under the law regardless of sex. Recent surveys also show that young women are often reluctant to identify themselves as feminists because feminists are seen as being too radical or "antiman."[54] Yet most young women, and many young men as well, already accept the basic ideas that feminists have fought for: the equality of the sexes and the right to fair and equal treatment for everyone. Despite the inevitable shifts in the political winds, the overall trend in all industrial societies has been toward greater sexual equality, and that trend seems likely to continue in the years ahead.

SOCIOLOGICAL PERSPECTIVES ON PROBLEMS OF GENDER

Distinct roles for males and females are found in every society. These gender roles become a social problem only when a significant number of people object to them. And such objections are certainly being voiced today. Functionalists, conflict theorists, and social psychologists have all noted the gap between the growing ideal of equality and the reality of male domination over females. They differ on the question of why this gap exists and what should be done about it.

The Functionalist Perspective   Functionalists say that the problems of gender roles stem directly from the historical changes discussed earlier in this chapter. Traditionally, gender roles were based on biological differences between the sexes: women were concerned primarily with child rearing and men with providing economic support. But changes brought on by the industrial revolution threw this arrangement out of balance. The decline in infant mortality and the spread of effective methods of birth control made it possible to depart from traditional roles. It was no longer necessary for women to devote most of their adult lives to the raising of small children, and automation wiped out the importance of the male's greater strength in most types of work. However, attitudes and expectations about the proper role of women have changed much more slowly than social and economic conditions. This cultural lag is therefore the principal source of today's problems.

To resolve these problems, most functionalists suggest that expectations be made to conform more closely with actual conditions. Some advocate a return to the stable past, believing that too great a shift toward sexual equality is dysfunctional. They note that the traditional division of labor between men and women was highly efficient, enabling society to train people for specialized roles that meshed together in stable families. Other functionalists, however, advocate a redefinition of sex roles to bring them into line with changed economic, political, and social conditions. Although these functionalists do not agree on the exact form the proposed changes should take, they do agree on the need for a shift toward full sexual equality and a reconstruction of women's roles to encourage economic competition and achievement. Along with this change, basic institutions would also have to be modified to eliminate sexual discrimination. The current family system, for example, would have to undergo extensive changes to accommodate new roles for both men and women.

The Conflict Perspective   Prejudice and discrimination against women come as no surprise to conflict theorists, since they see exploitation and oppression as universal human problems. Conflict theorists say that men first used their greater size and strength to force women into a subordinate position. Then, like any other dominant group, they created institutions that serve to perpetuate their power and authority. Men gain economic advantages by paying women low wages and excluding them from positions of economic control and political power. Men also benefit from women's subordinate role in the family. The "good" woman, we are told, blindly serves her husband and obeys his will like a domestic servant. The traditional wedding vows reflect the strong social support for the subordination of women. Only the bride must pledge to love, honor, and *obey* her spouse. Even the structure of our language serves to reinforce the belief in male dominance. Conflict theorists hold that the position of women in most societies today is similar to that of a subordinate ethnic minority, such as blacks in the United States.

There are many indications, however, that the traditional male advantages are declining in importance. The superior strength of the male means little in a highly mechanized society. The real barriers to women's liberation are now the institutions and attitudes that were established in the days of unquestioned male dominance. An increasing number of women are coming to realize this fact, and they are organizing themselves to break these barriers. According to the conflict perspective, the feminist movement is thus both a reflection and a cause of the growing strength of women in industrial societies. Conflict theorists advise women to continue publicizing their grievances, bring all women and sympathetic men together in a unified movement, and solicit the support of other dissatisfied social groups. For the conflict theorist, social action is the road to social change and a just society.

Social Psychological Pespectives   Social psychologists see gender roles, and the sense of identity we derive from them, as critical components of human personality. Most social psychologists are convinced that sexual identity develops in the early years of childhood in interaction with parents, peers, teachers, and the mass media. Once formed, these ideas and concepts are quite durable. Social psychologists note that prejudice and discrimination against women arise from differences in socialization. Females are conditioned to be passive and dependent and are therefore less dominant than males, who are trained to be more aggressive and independent. Thus, both sexes are often taught to see females as inferiors.

Biosocial theorists, however, are yet to be convinced that gender-role differences are simply a product of socialization. They argue that the personality and social differences between men and women are biological in origin. Clearly, there are differences in physical and biochemical makeup between men and women that cannot be ignored, but it is not clear how important they are in contemporary society. If gender roles are determined entirely by biology, little can be done to change them or to reduce sexual inequality.

Behaviorists, personality theorists, and symbolic interactionists are more optimistic. They are convinced that gender roles and the inequality they promote can be changed if the content of the socialization process is altered. These theorists argue that girls should be encouraged to be more aggressive and that boys be urged to accept the passive, dependent side of their natures. Because parents have been socialized into traditional gender roles, persuading them to teach their children to behave differently is extremely difficult. Schools, which are an increasingly important influence in socialization, can be changed more easily. Feminists are already pressing to remove sexual stereotypes from schoolbooks and lectures and to promote higher educational and occupational aspirations for talented girls. The media, particularly radio, television, and film, could also promote these changes. Showing women as powerful, assertive figures and allowing men who do not live up to the code of male dominance to be heroes equal to "he-men" would do much to foster equality between men and women.

Most social psychologists also hold that greater tolerance of human differences is also needed. No matter what characteristics a culture attributes to the ideal woman or the ideal man, there are many who do not conform. The nonconformist is made to pay an enormous personal cost for merely being a little different. There is no reason, aside from prejudice and bigotry, why traditional sex roles cannot exist side by side with a variety of other arrangements.

SUMMARY

Gender roles (sets of expectations about the proper behavior for each sex) are basic components of individual personalities as well as of the larger social system. In Western culture the male role has centered on work and providing for the family. The male is expected to be more aggressive than the female and to have tighter control over his emotions. The female role has centered on child rearing and the family. Females are expected to be emotionally expressive, dependent, and passive. Gender roles show a wide range of variation among cultures, and in our culture, as in others, the behavior of many men and women does not fit the expected patterns.

Two important conditions seem to have influenced the development of gender roles: biology and culture. The fact that females bear and nurse children has had an obvious influence on the definition of sex roles, as has the fact that males tend to be larger and stronger than females. Despite the importance of biology in the origin of gender roles, the individual's role is determined primarily by culture. Studies show that a man who is raised as a woman will think and act like a woman, and vice versa. Many cultures assign what we consider "feminine" traits to both sexes, while others assign "masculine" traits to both.

In early hunting and gathering societies the relationships between men and women were generally egalitarian. Horticultural societies had a wide range of gender relationships, from rough egalitarianism to strong male dominance, depending chiefly on the economy. With the coming of agriculture—that is, the use of the plow, irrigation, and domesticated animals—the power of women declined because their contribution to agricultural production was reduced. But the economic and social conditions accompanying industrial society neutralized many male advantages. Mechanization made physical size and strength less important, and the sharp drop in infant mortality and the spread of birth control reduced women's child-rearing burdens.

Gender socialization is the process by which children learn the behaviors and attitudes expected of their sex. The family plays a critical role in this process. Parents begin treating boys as boys and girls as girls almost from the moment of birth. Schools reinforce the traditional gender roles learned at home. Teachers, counselors, and textbooks encourage high aspirations in boys and discourage them in girls. Radio, television, and motion pictures also convey sexual stereotypes.

The roles we assign to each sex clearly promote gender inequality. Men are given the dominant position, and a variety of evidence reveals a clear pattern of discrimination against women in education, employment, politics, and everyday social life.

The feminist movement emerged when women organized to protest against discrimination and to work actively for their economic, political, and social rights. Liberal feminists advocate a vigorous attack on all forms of discrimination against women, and laws that guarantee comparable pay for comparable work, reproductive rights, and government-supported child care. Other feminists criticize the liberals for failing to recognize the connection between the discrimination against women and the social institutions that create it. Traditionalists accuse all feminists of undermining essential social values.

Functionalists see the problems of present-day gender roles as stemming from economic changes that upset the traditional cultural pattern. They advocate a reduction in the gap between expectations and actual conditions. Conflict theorists are convinced that these problems arise from domination and exploitation of the weak by the strong. They advise women to organize and to use political power to gain equality. Most social psychologists are convinced that gender roles and sexual identity are learned in the process of socialization, but biosocial theorists cling to the idea that sex differences have biological origins. The consensus among most social psychologists is that sexual inequality can be eliminated by changing gender roles, and that gender roles will change if the content of the socialization process is changed.

KEY TERMS

androgynous
double standard
gender role

gender socialization
sexism
sexual harassment

FURTHER READINGS

Gender Roles

Laurel Walum Richardson, *The Dynamics of Sex and Gender*, 3d ed., Boston: Houghton Mifflin, 1988.

Hilary M. Lips, *Sex and Gender: An Introduction*, Mountain View, Calif.: Mayfield, 1988.

Suzanne M. Bianchi and Daphne Spain, *American Women in Transition*, New York: Russell Sage Foundation, 1986.

Barbara Ehrenreich, *The Hearts of Men: American Dreams and the Flight from Commitment*, New York: Anchor, 1983.

Problems and Solutions

Beverly A. Stitt et al., *Building Gender Fairness in Schools*, Carbondale, Ill.: Southern Illinois University Press, 1988

Laurel Richardson and Verta Taylor, *Feminist Frontiers: Rethinking Sex, Gender, and Society*, New York: Random House, 1983.

PART THREE
Conformity and Deviance

Chapter 11
SEXUAL BEHAVIOR

Western culture has traditionally held some of the most negative attitudes toward sex found anywhere in the world. The Puritans, who played such an important role in the colonization of North America, condemned all sexual activity outside of marriage and even disapproved of sexual relations between husbands and wives except for the purpose of reproduction. In a culture with such repressive attitudes it is not surprising that sexual behavior was considered a serious social problem.

Despite the enormous changes in values and attitudes that have taken place since Puritan times, sexual behavior remains a troubling problem for many people. The old attitudes have been challenged by a number of more liberal standards, but none of them has won universal acceptance. What is normal and natural to some people is still sinful to others. The consensus that such things as homosexuality and prostitution are harmful to society and deserve strong punishment has broken down. But many of the old laws have remained on the books, and people continue to be harassed, even jailed, for private sexual activities that are perfectly acceptable to large segments of society. Ironically, these same laws have not proven effective in stopping child molestation, rape, and other sexual activities that almost everyone agrees are wrong.

The sexually charged atmosphere of modern-day America creates still other problems. Images of bathing beauties and muscular young men are used to sell everything from automobiles to deodorants. Books and movies routinely depict explicit sexual activities. Personal attractiveness and "sex appeal" have taken on enormous importance. In such an environment many young people become involved in sexual activities before they are emotionally prepared for them, and end up with an unwanted pregnancy; and people of all ages may feel restless and inadequate when they are unable to match the impossible sexual ideals promoted by the mass media.

HUMAN SEXUALITY

Few areas of social life are kept more secret than our sexual behavior. As a result, many myths, half-truths, and falsehoods have come to be accepted as fact. Among the most common errors is the belief that the sexual acts that are acceptable in our society are the only natural ones and that other acts are violations of "human nature." Anthropological studies have revealed a wide range of sexual customs and behavior in cultures around the world. Indeed, almost every form of sexual behavior is considered normal somewhere under some circumstances.

Historically, Western culture has been sexually conservative. Ford and Beach found that only 10 of the 190 societies they studied share our traditional disapproval of both premarital and extramarital sex.[1] The Polynesian peoples of the central Pacific, for example, have long been noted for their free sexual attitudes. Before the growth of Christian influence, Tahitians worshipped physical beauty. Young people of both sexes were encouraged to engage in masturbation and premarital intercourse, and both activities were openly discussed and practiced.[2]

Although North Americans are shocked by the thought of sexual activity among children, it is encouraged in many places. In some cultures intercourse is believed to be necessary if preadolescents are to mature sexually. The Trukese of the Caroline Islands build small huts especially for this purpose. Among the Alorese of Indonesia, mothers routinely masturbate their children in order to pacify them.[3]

Yet such liberalism is far from universal. The men of Yap Island believe that intercourse causes physical weakness and reduces resistance to disease. At one time Yap attitudes toward sex were so negative that the Yap people almost became extinct. The Manus of New Guinea consider intercourse degrading—a disgusting act that a woman must endure in order to produce children. The neighboring Dani tribe do not have sexual relations until two years after marriage, and refrain from sex for five years following the birth of each child. Closer to home, the Shakers, a Protestant sect founded in New England, banned all sexual activities, acquiring children only by adoption. Rural Ireland is also notable for its repression of sexuality. Marriages are delayed until later in life—about age 35 for men and 26 for women. Men and women are segregated in public places, and there is a strong taboo against the discussion of sexual matters. Women's capacity to experience orgasm is denied by some and considered deviant by others.[4]

Western culture has traditionally held that sexual activities are unclean and that children have no interest in sex. Today, social psychologists agree that sexual interests and exploration are a normal part of growing up.

The kinds of sexual behavior that are considered deviant also vary widely from culture to culture. The use of force to obtain sexual favors is strictly forbidden in our culture and in most of the rest of the world. But among a tribe living in southwestern Kenya normal intercourse is a kind of ritualized rape.[5] Women are encouraged to frustrate men with sexual taunts, and the men overcome this resistance with force, often inflicting pain and humiliation in the process. Attitudes toward homosexuality also show enormous variation. Most of the societies studied by Ford and Beach disapproved of homosexuality in general, but 64 percent of them tolerated, approved, or even required homosexual acts in some circumstances for some people.

A number of societies consider homosexuality normal among adolescent males but look less favorably on it in other groups. Among many Melanesian societies homosexuality is considered a more mature form of sexual behavior than masturbation and is common among young men. However, heterosexual relations are valued more highly, and homosexuality is rare after marriage. Heterosexuality is preferred over homosexuality in virtually all societies, at least in part because of its essential role in reproduction. Yet there are at least two known societies in New Guinea in which homosexuality is more highly valued. The Marind-anim people are so strongly homosexual that they must kidnap children from other tribes to maintain their population.[6] At the opposite extreme are such peoples as the Rwala Bedouin, who consider homosexuality so base that it is punishable by death. Even the **incest taboo** (the prohibition of sexual relations between parents and their children or between the children themselves), which is certainly the most common restriction on sexual behavior, is not universal.

There is clearly nothing innate in human beings that makes certain types of sexual behavior normal and other types abnormal. The distinction between "normal" and "deviant" sex comes from society, not biology. We are all born with a sex drive, but it is amazingly flexible and can be satisfied in a great variety of ways. We learn to satisfy our sex drive with one type of object and not another in the same way that we learn to satisfy our hunger drive with socially acceptable foods and not with dog meat or human flesh.

CONTEMPORARY SEXUAL BEHAVIOR

The study of sexual behavior is a difficult and confusing task. Social scientists have repeatedly found that people do not care to describe their sexual behavior to even the most objective investigators. As a result, it is impossible to say how common various forms of sexual behavior actually are. North American researchers find it hard even to describe public attitudes toward sex because there are such deep conflicts over sexual morality. At the heart of the matter is the conflict between restrictive traditional standards and the growing belief in the value of individual choice and personal freedom. Many religious groups continue to advocate the traditional values, while the media pour out an increasing stream of sexually arousing advertising and entertainment. Because of this confusion and uncertainty, sex researchers have found themselves in the uncomfortable position of influencing as well as describing contemporary sexual standards. Some people evaluate their own sexual behavior by comparing it with the findings of the sex surveys, apparently assuming that unusual sexual behavior may be wrong, but that "if everyone else is doing it, it must be all right."

A Historical Sketch   After the fall of the Roman Empire, Western society adopted a very restrictive sexual morality. In general , sexual relations have been approved only between a husband and wife, often only for the purpose of reproduction. The origins of this attitude are to be found in the Judeo-Christian religious tradition, particularly the New Testament teachings of Saint Paul and the lectures of early Christian leaders such as Saint Augustine. These leaders held sexual abstinence to be the ideal but allowed that "it is better to marry than to burn." Sex was seen as something evil and degrading, to be avoided as much as possible. Although such standards continued to be supported by religious and secular leaders for centuries, it is doubtful that more than a small percentage of the population adhered to them.

The Puritans of the seventeenth century reemphasized the strict moral code of the early Christians and demanded almost complete repression of sexuality. Puritan immigrants in North America helped establish this rigid code as a dominant force on the new continent. The Victorian era, during the ninteenth century, was also noted for its repression of sexuality. Victorians avoided discussion of anything that could be considered even remotely sexual . Legs became limbs, sweat became perspiration, and underwear became "unmentionables." Masturbation was believed to cause defects ranging from mental disorders to blindness. The double standard was so strong that female sexuality was almost entirely denied. The Surgeon General of the United States reflected prevailing opinions of the time when he said that "nine-tenths of the time decent women feel not the slightest pleasure in intercourse."[7] But the Victorian era is noted for its hypocrisy as well as its sexual repression. Prostitution and pornography flourished, and there appears to have been a wide gap between what people said and what they did.

In general, the history of sexual behavior in Western culture is marked by alternating periods of stern repression and quiet permissiveness. It is impossible to determine how closely the public's behavior conforms to its principles during periods of repression. But it seems likely that the original Puritans were the most effective in enforcing their standards and that later moral crusades became increasingly less effective.

A Sexual Revolution?   There is no doubt that sexual attitudes and practices have become much more liberal since the time of the Victorians. In reporting these changes, the media often picture them as a revolutionary break with the past. Indeed, some commentators have predicted that our "moral decay" will have dire consequences for Western society. But not everyone agrees that a "sexual revolution" has taken place. Some argue that today's young people are sim-

19th-Century Social Problems

Young men who have become the victims of solitary vice, that dreadful habit that sweeps annually to an untimely grave thousands of young men of exalted talent and brilliant intellect, can call with confidence. [front-page ad about masturbation]

August 5, 1897

These selections, which appear throughout the text, are from the *Badger State Banner*, a newspaper published in Black River Falls, Wisconsin.

ply more open in discussing their sexual activities than their grandparents were and that actual behavior has not changed very much.

One point about which there is no disagreement is that there have been remarkable changes in the media's use of sexual material. Magazines with pictures of scantily clad women were condemned by our grandparents but are now a fixture of supermarket magazine racks. Over the years illustrations revealed more and more of the body until nudity became the accepted style. Next, mass circulation magazines such as *Playgirl* broke the strong taboo against male nudity, and even relatively conservative women's magazines now carry erotically oriented advertising and frank discussions of sexual matters. Similar changes have occurred in movies and plays. Many writers and producers now feel that one or two sex scenes are necessary to the financial success of a new production. Even television programs openly deal with subjects that would have been shocking just a few decades ago.

Methodological problems make it difficult to measure the extent of the actual changes in sexual behavior. Sex surveys such as the pioneering studies conducted by Alfred Kinsey and his associates in the 1940s and 1950s are the best sources of data available, but they have serious methodological weaknesses.[8] Kinsey interviewed volunteers, including people in social clubs and prisons, and it is doubtful that his subjects were representative of the overall population.

More recent research has avoided some of the problems of Kinsey's work but has serious shortcomings of its own. Few scientific studies of sexual behavior have had strong financial backing, and they therefore tend to use small local samples of high school or college students and neglect the rest of the population. Magazines often rely on responses from whoever happens to send in published questionnaires, and even broad surveys that use normal sampling techniques are flawed, in that an unusually high number of people refuse to respond to their questions. As a result, there are probably important differences between those who respond to sex surveys and those who do not.

And given the sensitive nature of the subject, many respondents are undoubt-edly less than honest in their replies. Despite all these methodological weak-nesses, conclusions based on these studies are still vastly superior to the unsupported opinions and generalizations voiced by so many people. But it should be kept in mind that the percentages given in this chapter are just rough estimates and may be very wide of their mark.

When Kinsey's report on male sexual behavior was published in 1948, it shocked the nation. Kinsey concluded that 85 percent of all American men had experienced premarital intercourse, 70 percent had visited a prostitute, and over one-third had participated in at least one homosexual act. Kinsey's data suggest that the first wave of sexual liberation in the United States occurred much earlier than is usually believed, probably in the generation that came of age after World War I. His study found that only 8 percent of white women born before 1900 had premarital intercourse by age 20, but that among those born between 1910 and 1929 the figure was 22 percent. Later surveys indicate that a second wave of liberation occurred in the sec-ond half of the 1960s and the early 1970s.[9]

An important part of these changes was the decay of the double standard, discussed in Chapter 10. Traditionally, both sexes were supposed to refrain from "sinful" sexual activities, but violating this taboo was considered a greater sin for women than for men. To be a "loose woman" or an unfaithful wife was a social disgrace, but young men were expected to gain sexual experience before marriage, and a husband's carousing was often passed over with a wink. A century ago the "good" woman was not supposed to enjoy sex; she was to merely tolerate it for her husband's sake.

Although the double standard has not disappeared, it has certainly weak-ened. There has been some increase in the amount of premarital sexual ex-perience reported by males since the 1940s, but the change was much more dramatic for females. Whereas one-third of all the women in Kinsey's sample reported having engaged in **premarital intercourse** by age 25, well over two-thirds of the women in Hunt's survey were sexually experienced by that age;[10] and Shah and Zelnick found that the trend toward more premarital intercourse among females has continued since then.[11] Kinsey's data indicate that about a quarter of all married women had experienced an **extramarital affair,** and McCary and McCary conclude that "it is generally accepted that the incidence of extramarital coitus among married women has increased significantly since Kinsey's time—perhaps doubling his figure."[12] One should not conclude, however, that because women are enjoying more of the free-doms formerly reserved for men, the double standard no longer exists. It is still with us. Rates of female participation in both premarital and extra-marital sex, for instance, are still substantially lower than the rates for men.

The surveys indicate that there is more sexual activity within marriage as well as outside it. Particularly striking is the sharp increase in oral-genital sex. Kinsey found that only 40 percent of the married males he surveyed had ever engaged in oral sex with their wives, whereas 63 percent of Hunt's male subjects said that they had done so in the past year.[13] There is also evidence

Kinsey's research indicated that, contrary to popular belief, the first wave of sexual libera-tion occurred in the generation that came of age in the "roaring twenties."

that married couples have intercourse more often than they did in the past, and that masturbation is more common among both married and single people.[14] However, all forms of sexual behavior have not become more common. There is no evidence that male or female homosexuality has in-creased,[15] and several studies indicate that prostitution has actually de-clined.[16] As women have become more sexually active, men apparently have felt less need to use the services of prostitutes.

The increase in sexual freedom described in these surveys is one result of the sweeping cultural changes of the twentieth century. The weakening of the influence of traditional religious morality has lowered the barriers that once prevented many kinds of sexual activity. There has been, as was men-tioned earlier, an erosion of the double standard, and as women have gained economic and political power, they have gained greater equality in sexual matters as well. The development of more effective birth control techniques has reduced the fear that sexual relations will lead to an unwanted pregnancy. Growing emphasis on individual freedom and self-determination has made many people more willing to challenge traditional ideas and customs. The increasing use of erotic materials to entertain and to sell products has exerted an influence in many subtle ways. Finally, sexuality itself seems to be undergoing a basic redefinition. Although sinful and degrading to Victorians, sexual activity is now a routine part of a normal life.

PROBLEMS AND ISSUES

Considering the conflict about sexual morality in the twentieth century, it is hardly surprising that many people do not agree about which sexual behaviors are a social problem and which are not. The issues discussed in this section fall into three general groups. The first are unintended problems that arise as a consequence of sexual activities, such as unwanted pregnancy and sexually transmitted disease. The second group involve the sexual victimization of one person by another, as in child molestation and rape (which will be discussed in Chapter 15). Finally, there are homosexuality, prostitution, and pornography, in which the persons involved are usually participating voluntarily. Problems in the first group (unwanted pregnancy and sexually transmitted disease) are generally not considered criminal matters; activities in the second category (child molestation and rape) are almost universally condemned as serious crimes; but there is great variation in the legal response to such things as homosexuality, prostitution, and pornography.

Adolescent Sex and Unwanted Pregnancy   Many surveys have been done about adolescent sexual behavior, but their results have not been consistent. In the eight studies reported by Adams and Gullotta, the percentage of females from age 16 to 19 who report having had intercourse ranged from 18 to 57 percent, and for males the range was 21 to 72 percent.[17] There is, however, general agreement about one point: young people are having sex at a somewhat earlier age than they did in the past. This is just one part of an overall trend toward more liberal sexual attitudes and behaviors, but it also poses some special problems. In the erotically charged atmosphere of today's society, young people are often confused about how to deal with their own sexuality. They see the overwhelming importance given sexual attractiveness in the media, yet they also hear their parents and religious advisers telling them sex is wrong. As a result, many young people begin having sex without really intending to and without taking proper precautions against pregnancy.

In 1960 only about 15 of every 1000 unmarried teenage girls (age 15 to 19) gave birth to a child, but by 1985 that number had increased to almost 32 births per 1000 (see Figure 11.1; also see Chapter 5 for a discussion of the difficulties these young women are likely to face).[18] Teenagers in other industrialized nations, however, have far lower pregnancy rates. Some of this difference can be attributed to the high pregnancy rates of black teenagers in the United States. But white American teenagers are still twice as likely to become pregnant as British or French teenagers, and six times more likely

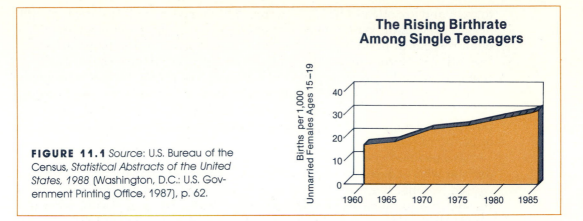

The Rising Birthrate Among Single Teenagers

FIGURE 11.1 *Source*: U.S. Bureau of the Census, *Statistical Abstracts of the United States, 1988* (Washington, D.C.: U.S. Government Printing Office, 1987), p. 62.

than Dutch teenagers. The cause of this difference is clear. Although studies show that American teenagers are no more sexually active than their European counterparts, they are far less likely to use contraceptives.[19]

Why don't more sexually active teenagers use contraceptives? In some cases they actually want to have a child, but most of the time a teenage pregnancy is an accident.[20] Many teenagers are simply ignorant about sexual matters and believe such myths as "you can't get pregnant the first time" or "you won't get pregnant if you only have sex once in a while." Teenagers are also influenced by parents and religious leaders who tell them not only to abstain from sex but from using birth control as well. Of the two, it is certainly far easier to abstain from the second than from the first. Many teenage girls feel that planning out a sexual encounter is immoral, but that if you are swept off your feet and are unable to stop you can't be blamed for your actions. Finally, teenagers often do not know how to get birth control devices or are afraid that their parents will get angry if they do.

Sexually Transmitted Disease   **Sexually transmitted disease** (diseases passed from one person to another during intercourse) is an old problem. Descriptions of such diseases have been found in records dating back thousands of years. Traditionally, the two major sexually transmitted diseases were syphilis and gonorrhea, which are both bacterial infections. In addition, chlamydia, another bacterial disease which was often ignored in the past, is increasingly recognized as a major problem as well. If left untreated, these diseases can have serious complications. Syphilis is the most dangerous. There was, for example, a major epidemic in sixteenth-century Europe that took a very heavy toll in lives. Fortunately, the bacteria that cause these diseases are susceptible to treatment with modern antibiotics. Although there are some newer strains of penicillin-resistant gonorrhea, a cure is usually a relatively simple matter if the problem is discovered and treated in the early stages.[21]

The sexually transmitted diseases caused by viruses are more difficult to treat and are often impossible to cure. The most common of these is genital herpes. The main symptom is blisters or sores in the genital region. They often reoccur at periodic intervals, and the disease is communicable only at these times. Herpes is not life threatening, and the most serious complications are usually psychological rather than physical. However, a pregnant woman can pass the disease along to her child during delivery, and doctors recommend a cesarean section if the disease is active at that time. There are now drugs available that repress the symptoms, but a complete cure has yet to be found.

The problems caused by other sexually transmitted diseases pale in comparison with **acquired immune deficiency syndrome** (AIDS)—a killer disease caused by what is apparently an entirely new virus. The AIDS virus destroys the victims' immune system, leaving them vulnerable to a host of other diseases. Although it often stays dormant for years after first exposure, once it reaches its active phase, the disease is almost always fatal. Virtually unknown in 1980, by 1988 there were 64,000 known cases. And some estimates place the number of people now carrying the virus as high as 1.5 million. Over 36,000 persons have already died in the United States alone, and the death toll is expected to go much higher (see Chapter 8).[22]

This new epidemic has touched off a near panic among some people. Unfounded fears that one can get AIDS by shaking hands with a victim or that children can get it by playing with an infected classmate are common. In reality, AIDS is not a particularly easy disease to transmit. It is possible for AIDS to be passed on by heterosexual vaginal intercourse, but it is far more likely to be transmitted through anal intercourse, which is why most AIDS sufferers in the United States are male homosexuals. For the other main group of AIDS victims, intravenous drug users, the disease is not sexually transmitted, but passed on by sharing unclean hypodermic needles.

Child Molestation   There are few kinds of deviant behavior more repugnant to the general public or more frightening to parents than the sexual molestation of a child. But the image most people have of the child molester as a demented stranger who seizes a child and forces her to have intercourse with him is highly inaccurate. It is generally estimated that 50 to 80 percent of **child molestations** are committed by family friends, relatives, or acquaintances.[23] Most cases of child molestation do not involve actual intercourse, but such things as exposure, fondling, and masturbation. Jaffe found that only 11 percent of victims were physically penetrated by the offender,[24] and McCaghy concluded that physical violence is used in no more than about 3 percent of molestation cases.[25] The only accurate part of the popular stereotype is that most offenders are male and most victims are female, but even that is not always the case.

Determining the amount of child molestation and incest (a molestation involving immediate family members, usually a father and daughter) is even more difficult than for other types of sexual behavior. In a recent survey, one in ten Boston parents reported that their child had been the victim of sexual abuse or attempted sexual abuse, and 15 percent of the mothers and 6 percent of the fathers said that they themselves had been abused as children.[26] Other estimates have put the female victimization rate as high as 54 percent.[27] Although some claim that there has been a big increase in child molestation in recent times, there is no convincing evidence to support this assertion. The estimates produced by the Kinsey studies, for example, were within the same range as the more recent research. One thing that has increased is the willingness to acknowledge the problem and talk about it, and as a result the number of cases of child molestation reported to the police has gone up in the last few years.

Child molestation stems from complex social and psychological causes, and no single theory explains them all. The most common psychological profile of child molesters depicts them as men who are insecure and sexually inadequate. As a result, they turn away from adult sexual relationships to seek out children, who are less threatening and more easily controlled.[28] However, some child molesters are married men with normal sexual relationships, and many inadequate men never become involved in child molestation. There is also mounting evidence that child molesters often learned that behavior in their own childhood, when they themselves were the victims of sexual abuse. Father-daughter incest, on the other hand, most often occurs in disturbed families. Oftentimes there is no sexual relationship between the husband and wife, and the daughter is forced to assume that part of the mother's normal role.[29]

Homosexuality As with many other forms of sexual behavior, there are many common myths and half-truths about homosexuality. For instance, it is widely believed that all male homosexuals put on a flashy display of femininity, and that female homosexuals all lift weights and dress like men. In fact, most homosexuals look and act like everyone else. The few who fit the popular stereotype are just more noticeable. Another common myth is that homosexuals and heterosexuals have different personality characteristics. An experiment by Evelyn Hooker, however, showed that even experienced clinical psychologists were unable to identify the sexual orientation of a mixed group of subjects by examining their responses to a battery of psychological tests. Nor were any differences found in personal adjustment.[30] Many people believe that homosexuals endanger children, but there is no evidence to indicate that homosexuals are more likely than others to be child molesters. Finally, many people are not aware that many homosexuals form stable long-term relationships just as heterosexuals do.

A major source of confusion about homosexuals is the tendency of many people to see sexual preference in absolute terms. Most people assume that individuals are either sexually attracted to members of the opposite sex (and thus are heterosexual) or to members of the same sex (and thus are homosexual). In reality, most people have both homosexual and heterosexual urges at one time or another. The differences among **homosexuals, bisexuals,** and **heterosexuals** are a matter of degree. Kinsey found that many otherwise heterosexual males had briefly engaged in homosexual activities during their adolescent years. The choice of sexual partners may also be determined by the environment, regardless of an individual's personal preference. Many prisoners engage in homosexual activities while they are locked up but are strictly heterosexual outside prison walls.

Causes There are many theories about the causes of homosexuality, but little conclusive evidence. One popular explanation is that homosexuals are "born that way." The strongest evidence to support the contention that homosexuality is hereditary comes from studies of twins. Several studies have found that identical (one-egg) twins are more likely to show the same sexual preference than fraternal (two-egg) twins.[31] However, the problem with such studies is that identical twins are more likely to be treated alike by family and friends; thus, their similarities may be due to environment, not heredity.

Some biological theorists argue that homosexuality is determined by sex hormones. Although no significant differences in the levels of sex hormones have been found in homosexual and heterosexual adults, some claim that there may be differences in receptivity to those hormones or in exposure to them before birth.[32] But all biological theories of homosexuality have difficulty explaining the significant differences in the amount of homosexuality in various cultures and the reasons that some people are homosexual during one period of their life and heterosexual during others.

Classical psychoanalytic theory views homosexuality in males as the result of an excessively close relationship with the mother and a distant and rejecting father. Numerous studies based on interviews with heterosexuals and homosexuals have generally supported this conclusion, although a recent study by the Kinsey Institute for Sex Research did not. Studies also show that lesbians report much more fear and hostility toward their fathers than heterosexual women.[33] It may be, however, that some of this parental rejection is the result of the deviant behavior of the children, not its cause. In one of the few long-term studies of the same group of subjects, psychiatrist Richard Green found that a homosexual orientation begins long before adolescence. Three-fourths of the "feminine" boys he studied went on to homosexual lives as adults, while only one of the "masculine" boys became involved in homosexual activity.[34]

Sociologically, homosexuality is explained by examining the conditions in which it is learned. Given the enormous range of sexual behavior in the cultures of the world, it would actually be much harder to explain the absence of homosexuality in large and diverse societies like the United States and Canada than its presence. Although a strong social condemnation of homosexuality discourages homosexual tendencies, homosexuality is encouraged in many other ways. For instance, when adolescents first begin to feel strong sexual urges, society forbids them to engage in heterosexual intercourse. Young males and females are not permitted to sleep or shower together, but these activities are acceptable for members of the same sex. The encouragement of specific sex role differences, combined with the pres-

Although a small percentage of homosexuals make a showy display of the characteristics usually associated with the opposite sex, most homosexuals look and act like everyone else. Demonstrations such as the one shown here are part of the efforts of homosexuals to win greater social acceptance.

sures of mate selection, makes association with the same sex less painful and embarrassing than association with the opposite sex. Some adolescents can carry on homosexual activities without arousing the suspicion of their parents, whereas heterosexual activities would be out of the question. Further, the widespread belief that one is either homosexual or heterosexual often causes individuals who engage in exploratory homosexual behavior to define themselves as homosexuals. And once such a self-concept takes hold, it is likely to persist, perhaps for a lifetime.[35]

The Homosexual Community There is considerable disagreement about how common homosexuality actually is. The various surveys of sexual behavior that have been done over the years have reached widely different conclusions.[36] The most commonly accepted estimate puts the number of men who have had extensive homosexual experience at about 10 percent of the total population, with somewhere around 2 to 3 percent of all men being primarily or exclusively homosexual. Almost all the surveys show less homosexuality among women. Most estimates indicate that women are only about half as likely as men to engage in homosexual activities.[37]

Unlike many other minorities, homosexuals can conceal their differences from the public if they choose to do so. "Closet queens" disguise their sexual preference and pass as heterosexuals. But such deception places them under great emotional stress. Discovery and possible blackmail are constant dangers. In the last two decades there has been a growing trend among homosexuals to "come out of the closet" and openly participate in the homosexual community. But "coming out" means more than just publicly admitting one's homosexuality; it also means admitting it to oneself.

The homosexual community provides many services for its members including a supportive environment that rejects the people who reject them. In some cities homosexuals have developed a system of mutual assistance in business and employment, much in the manner of religious and ethnic groups. Thus, a homosexual who needs the services of a carpenter will find a homosexual carpenter; a homosexual who wants to buy a house will find a homosexual real estate agent; and so on. Bars that cater to homosexuals are also important to the homosexual community. They are places for socializing and relaxing, and serve as centers for making new sexual contacts. Such bars are frequented by both men and women, but **lesbians** (female homosexuals) are less likely to "cruise" bars looking for pickups or to have a large number of sex partners. Lesbians, like other women, tend to place great importance on the bonds of family and friendship.[38]

Since the 1960s homosexuals have been making steady progress against the prejudice directed at them for so many years. However, the epidemic of AIDS among male homosexuals in the 1980s has been a severe blow to the liberation of the homosexual community. Irrational fears that one might catch that fatal disease from casual contact with a homosexual have led to a new wave of hostility toward gays. And at the same time, homosexuals themselves now have to live with the fear that any new sexual contact might be a fatal experience, or the even more frightening thought that they may already have an undetected case of the disease. The AIDS epidemic has produced major changes in sexual behavior among male homosexuals. Many "bath houses," which served as sex clubs, have been closed, and there has been a sharp decline in all sorts of casual sexual contact.

Homosexuality and the Law The Judeo-Christian religious tradition has long condemned homosexuality as a vile sin, and Western nations have acted accordingly. During the Middle Ages homosexuals were commonly tortured to death. They were burned at the stake in Paris as late as 1750. In Britain homosexual activities were punishable by life imprisonment until 1956.[39]

The recent trend has been toward repeal of legal penalties for homosexuality. Britain canceled its most repressive laws in 1965, thus legalizing homosexual behavior in private between consenting adults. Other European nations followed suit, and such behavior is now legal in France, Spain, Italy, Denmark, and Finland. Canada passed a law similar to Britain's in 1969, but some official harassment of homosexuals has persisted.

The trend toward legalization has developed more slowly in the United States. Seventeen states have legalized homosexual acts between consenting adults, but others continue to threaten homosexuals with penalties as severe as life imprisonment. However, in states where homosexuality remains a crime, the laws are not vigorously enforced. Only a few unlucky or unwise individuals are arrested, prosecuted, or punished. Moreover, enforcement efforts are directed almost exclusively against male homosexuals. Lesbian activities are usually ignored. And even in jurisdictions where criminal penalties have been reduced or abolished, homosexuals still suffer from open legal discrimination. In some places the professions of law, medicine, and teaching are closed to homosexuals, and the U.S. military still refuses to accept homosexuals as recruits.

Like many ethnic minorities, homosexuals have been organizing and demanding an end to the discrimination against them. The American Psychiatric Association was persuaded to drop homosexuality from its list of mental disorders; television stations have been pressured to stop programs that cast homosexuals in an unfavorable light; and a number of cities—including Los Angeles, Minneapolis, and Seattle—have passed legislation protecting homosexuals from various forms of discrimination. However, the movement has had its failures as well. The United States Supreme Court refused to ban prosecution and imprisonment of people for homosexual activities, even if those activities were conducted in private between consenting adults. Also, the gains of homosexual activists have often stirred vigorous counterattacks. In several cities gay rights laws already on the books have been repealed as a result of such opposition.

Prostitution **Prostitution** has declined dramatically in the past half-century. Kinsey's data suggested that prostitution had begun to decline in the 1940s, Hunt found that prostitution had decreased by over 50 percent since the time of the Kinsey report, and other studies show the same trend.[40] It appears that the demand for prostitution has decreased as sexual freedom has increased. Nevertheless, it is unlikely that prostitution will disappear by itself, and repeated efforts to stamp it out have been remarkably unsuccessful.

Prostitution continues because it satisfies important needs for both prostitutes and customers. The primary reward for most prostitutes is, of course, money. Even a moderately successful prostitute earns much more money than a waitress, store clerk, or professor. As for the customers, a prostitute offers sex without emotional ties and obligations. Customers do not have to "woo and win" the prostitute, and they have no obligation to be nice afterward. Prostitutes will also perform sexual activities that may be difficult for the customer to obtain elsewhere. Prostitutes are easily available to those who lack the time or social skills necessary for normal dating, to servicemen and others who are isolated from women, and to men with severe physical handicaps.

The Social World of the Prostitute Prostitutes are condemned and rejected by "respectable" people, but within their own world they have a status hierarchy like those of other professions. Call girls are the best paid and the most respected. They are highly selective about their customers, charge high fees, and see the same clients again and again. Because they seldom accept unknown customers, their chances of arrest are low. The woman who works in a house of prostitution is a step below the call girl in status. The "house girl" does not have to walk the streets in search of customers, but neither can she screen her customers. She must service a large number of clients each night and must split her fees with the operator of the house, who is usually known as a madam.

Streetwalkers are on the bottom rung of the status ladder. They must prowl the streets in search of clients, often rob their customers, and are themselves highly vulnerable to assault, robbery, and arrest. Most streetwalkers work for a pimp who takes most or all the income. In return the pimp pays for the prostitute's apartment, buys her clothes, arranges legal services, provides protection, and gives her emotional support and affection.

Many people think that all prostitutes are women, but male prostitution is also common. Male prostitutes sometimes have female clients, but most of their business comes from other men. In his interviews with male prostitutes in Chicago, Luckenbill found another clear-cut occupational hierarchy. At the bottom are the "street hustlers," similar to female streetwalkers

Streetwalkers, both female and male, are the lowest status prostitutes. Those who work in a house of prostitution are somewhat better off, while the call girl (or call boy) has the highest status and the best working conditions.

except that they did not work for a pimp.[41] Next are the "bar hustlers," who find their customers in bars, and at the top of the hierarchy are the prostitutes who work for an "escort service."

Although prostitutes come from all walks of life, most are young unmarried women from low socioeconomic backgrounds. They typically have done poorly in school and in "straight" jobs.[42] Studies have shown that they usually drift into the occupation one step at a time. They begin by giving sex in exchange for presents from boyfriends, progress to occasional "tricking," and then become full-time professionals.[43] Weisburg's study of adolescent prostitutes found that many of the females were encouraged to become professionals by a pimp, but that was not true of the males.[44]

Prostitutes use several strategies to maintain a positive self-image in the face of social condemnation. Most commonly, they reject those who reject them. Prostitutes say that everyone has a "hustle," and that they are at least more honest about it than the middle-class women who exchange sex with their husbands or boyfriends for their financial support.[45] Not all prostitutes reject middle-class values, however. Some carry on quite ordinary private lives, concealing their occupation as much as possible. Others fail to maintain their self-respect and sink into alcoholism or drug addiction.

Prostitution and the Law During the Middle Ages prostitution was seen as a kind of necessary evil and was rarely illegal. With the coming of the Protestant Reformation and a growing concern about the spread of syphilis, prostitution was outlawed. It has been widely prohibited in the Western world ever since, though antiprostitution legislation has not always been strictly enforced.

A hundred years ago prostitution was widespread in North America. It was illegal, but it was carefully ignored by most police departments. At that time most prostitutes worked in brothels (houses of prostitution) concentrated in the "red-light" districts of larger cities. Madams paid police officers to leave their girls alone, and they were not disturbed as long as they did not venture out of their district. In the early part of the twentieth century, this cozy arrangement was upset by a wave of vice crusades. The American Society of Sanitary and Moral Prophylaxis, the American Purity Alliance, the YMCA, and other organizations mounted a powerful offensive against prostitution. One by one the red-light districts were closed down and increasing numbers of prostitutes became streetwalkers instead.

Today prostitution is illegal everywhere in North America except a few counties in Nevada. Nevertheless, prostitution seems to be practiced more openly today than it was in the 1940s and 1950s. Enforcement is sporadic and is aimed at prostitutes, while largely ignoring their clients.

The laws that were intended to solve the problems of prostitution have on the whole made them worse. Closing houses of prostitution increased the number of streetwalkers, who pose a more serious problem than "house girls" because they solicit men who are not interested in their services, invade areas in which they are not welcome, and are often involved in criminal activities such as robbery and narcotics dealing. The prohibition of prostitution also encourages organized crime to enter the business in order to realize its enormous potential for tax-free profits.

Pornography   Strictly speaking, **pornography** is not a form of sexual behavior. It consists of obscene books, pictures, sights, and sounds. But the attempts to clearly define what is obscene have ended in failure and confusion. One popular definition holds that any material that is intended to be sexually arousing is obscene and, thus, pornographic. But by this definition a large percentage of all advertising, books, and movies would be pornographic. According to the Supreme Court, sexually explicit materials are not obscene unless they (1) appeal to "prurient" (lewd, lustful, indecent) interests, (2) are contrary to community standards, and (3) lack all "redeeming social value."[46] But although these criteria appear to be clear and precise, they are impossible to apply objectively. Any book, magazine, or film can be said to have some social value. In fact, in 1970 the President's Commission on Obscenity and Pornography found that 60 percent of all Americans believe that exposure to erotic materials provides information about sex and entertainment, both of which appear to be of "redeeming social value." A 1985 survey by *Newsweek* found that only one out of five Americans favored a ban on magazines that show nudity, and less than one out of three favored a ban on rentals of X-rated films.[47]

Critics of sexually explicit materials, such as the Moral Majority, charge that they lead to immorality and social decay. However, standards of sexual morality differ so widely that it is difficult for sociologists to even determine what is or is not considered immoral, much less to decide whether or not pornography encourages it. There is, moreover, considerable evidence to support the argument that looking at "dirty" books and pictures does not lead the viewer to rape, child molestation, or other sex crimes. Wilson found that his sample of sex offenders had less exposure to pornographic materials than the average citizen, and this finding has been confirmed by other researchers.[48] Even more telling evidence comes from Denmark, the first European nation to repeal its pornography laws. Studies revealed a substantial reduction in exhibitionism (58 percent), peeping (80 percent), and child molesting (69 percent) as erotic materials became more easily available.[49] Studies of criminal statistics show no relationship between the amount of pornography available in a state and its rate of forcible rape.[50]

Critics of such studies, however, point out that they often fail to consider the important differences between the different types of materials that are labeled as pornography. A nude photograph or an explicit love scene are very different from a graphic video tape showing a woman being raped and murdered. There is good reason to believe that violent pornography contributes to violent sex crime. For one thing, laboratory studies have found a correlation between exposure to violent pornography and favorable attitudes toward rape[51] and a greater willingness to inflict suffering (electric shocks) on other experimental subjects.[52] Moreover, the much more extensive research on television violence indicates that it does encourage violence in real life (see Chapter 15). After a thorough review of the available literature, Donnerstein, Linz, and Penrod concluded that the scientific evidence generally supports the idea that violent pornography promotes real sexual violence. On the other hand, they found only weak and inconclusive evidence that materials showing "degrading" sex (for example, a film showing a woman having sex with numerous men in a short period of time) promote violence or other criminal behavior, and they concluded that depictions of "nondegrading" sex and simple nudity do not promote illegal activities.[53]

These findings are quite consistent with the attitudes of the general public. Polls show that most Americans believe that violent pornography and so called "kiddie porn" (sexually oriented materials involving children) should be banned, but that other kinds of erotic material should not be prohibited. Seventy-four percent of the subjects in the *Newsweek* poll mentioned earlier favored a total ban on magazines that show sexual violence, and 68 percent favored a ban on movies that depict sexual violence.[54] Research shows, however, that most hard-core X-rated movies actually show very little violence. It is the R-rated "slasher" movies that are the worst offenders.[55]

It is also important to keep in mind that any type of restriction on freedom of the press creates its own problems. Censorship has a chilling effect on personal freedom as well as on artistic expression. Works ranging from Shakespeare's plays to *Alice in Wonderland* have been banned at one time or another. If censors are given broad powers to prohibit "pornography," many works of art will be affected as well. Because pornography is so difficult to define, there is also a real danger that the decision to ban a particular book or picture would be based on political considerations and that authors who threaten powerful special interests would be more likely to have their works censored.

RESPONDING TO PROBLEMS OF SEXUAL BEHAVIOR

The diverse problems and issues surrounding sexual behavior obviously require different kinds of responses. But most proposals for dealing with them can be put into one of two categories: those that rely on education and prevention, and those that advocate changes in the laws and the criminal-justice system. One set of proposals in the first category aim to correct the irresponsibility of the broadcast media. According to a study sponsored by Planned Parenthood, the average viewer saw about 14,000 references to sex in the 1987–88 television season. Yet that viewer would see only 165 references to such things as birth control, abortion, sexually transmitted diseases, or sex education.[56] The three major networks not only refuse to run public service announcements to inform sexually active teenagers about the importance of birth control but will not even accept paid advertising from the manufacturers of birth control products. Given this attitude, that sexual titillation is fine but that birth control is dirty, it is hardly surprising that unmarried teenage girls exposed to this programming have such a high birth-rate. A law requiring television stations to run public service birth control announcements would help change the message that we are giving young people. Such announcements could also be a major force in the fight against AIDS and other sexually transmitted diseases if they forcefully promoted the use of condoms—the only technique of birth control that is also effective in the prevention of disease. Unfortunately, such proposals are opposed by powerful groups that confuse the advocacy of birth control and safe sex with the advocacy of promiscuity.

Another common proposal to reduce teenage pregnancy is to create a more comprehensive program of sex education in the schools. A 1982 study by the Urban Institute concluded that the average high school student receives less than five hours of sex education a year. However, a study by Douglas Kirby found that it was much more effective to create clinics on school campuses to distribute contraceptives to students than it was to increase educational programs. Several of the 31 such clinics now operating in the United States have reduced the number of pregnancies in their school by over 50 percent—a record unmatched by any other type of program. Moreover, recent studies indicate that the fear that such programs will encourage teenagers to engage in sexual activity is unfounded. The evidence shows that girls in schools with birth control programs actually begin sexual intercourse at a somewhat later age than girls in schools without such programs.[55]

The control of child molestation and rape falls primarily to the criminal-justice system, and general proposals for improving its operations will be discussed in Chapter 14. Here it is sufficient to point out how difficult a task it is to convict offenders in child molestation cases or even to know if a crime actually took place. Often the only witnesses to such crimes are too young even to give reliable testimony to investigators, much less to give it under the intense pressures of a public trial. There is, however, one factor that has greatly helped enforcement: the new public awareness of the problem of child molestation.

The use of the power of the law to punish sexual activities in which there is no victim poses some very different issues. Aside from the legislation against homosexuality and prostitution already discussed, the government forbids its citizens to engage in numerous other sexual practices. An unmarried couple who have sex are guilty of a criminal act in 19 states and may receive penalties as severe as a fine of $10,000 and four years in prison. If one or both of them are married to another person, they would also be committing the crime of adultery in 26 states and might be penalized with a prison sentence of as much as five years. But even if the couple were married to each other, they could still be sent to prison if they engaged in sexual activities of which the government does not approve. In 18 states a married couple could be jailed if they had anal sex, and in 20 states they could go to prison—in some places for as long as 20 years—for having oral sex.[56] The fact that most of the laws prohibiting such acts are seldom enforced points out our confusion about the proper relationship between government and

DEBATE

Should the Schools Provide Free Birth Control to Teenagers?

YES The time has come to face facts. We may not want our teenagers to have sex, but they are having it. We continue to pretend that "good girls" don't use birth control, and the result is that our unmarried teenagers have a higher birthrate than in any other industrialized nation. These young mothers often drop out of school and into years of welfare dependence. Many of their children are raised in poverty by a single parent unready for the burdens of motherhood. Too often the ultimate result is a negligent and abusive parent, and a disturbed child who grows into a troubled adulthood.

Fortunately, there is an effective and inexpensive way to deal with this problem: realistic sex education and free birth control provided directly in the schools. This kind of program has already been tried and proven effective in numerous schools, and if applied nationwide, it could slash the birthrate among single teenagers. Critics say that such programs encourage teenagers to have sex, but there isn't a shred of evidence to support such a claim. Surveys show that teenagers in European countries that have easier access to birth control are no more sexually active than in the United States. And studies of the U.S schools that already have these programs show no increase in sexual activity among the students. The real reason that there is such vehement opposition to effective birth control programs is that self-righteous moralists want to make these girls suffer for their "sins." What these young mothers really suffer from is our short-sighted birth control policies, and it is time for a change.

NO The proposal that the schools should give out condoms and birth control pills like popcorn in the movies is offensive and wrong. The way to deal with the shocking increase in illegitimate births among our teenagers is to return to the traditional values that have made our society strong. You stop illegitimate births by convincing teenagers to wait until they are married to have sex, not by helping them violate one of the most sacred commandments in the Judeo-Christian tradition.

A program to allow the schools to give out birth control information and devices would be a highly unwelcome intrusion of government power into the private lives of millions of families. If parents do not want their children to use birth control, what right does the government have to go ahead and give it to them anyway? One of the most important of all parental duties is to teach our children how to tell right from wrong. But what chance do parents have to instill a strong sense of sexual morality when the government steps in and helps our teenagers behave in an immoral way?

The problem of unmarried mothers is indeed a serious one, but pursuing a policy that will encourage sexual promiscuity is certainly not the way to deal with it. All this classroom discussion of sex and the easy availability of contraceptives would certainly encourage many students to become sexually active and might well result in more, not less, illegitimacy. But even if it prevents a few illegitimate births, the moral damage such a program would cause is far too high a price to pay.

citizens. The heart of the conflict can be stated in a single question: Is the government justified in attempting to force people to conform to its standards of sexual morality?

Some officials are convinced that these laws are necessary to preserve traditional standards and to prevent moral decay that may lead to social corruption. However, most social scientists who have studied the effects of these laws advocate their repeal. They point to the injustice of permitting one segment of society to force its morality on everyone else. It has also been shown that this type of legislation tends to create a wide variety of other problems. Herbert Packer, a Stanford University law professor, made a long list of such problems, including the following:

1. Because forbidden sexual acts are hard to detect, police must rely on questionable techniques, including the use of undercover agents, decoys, spies, and paid informers.
2. Laws prohibiting these acts encourage the development of a deviant subculture as violators form links and bonds to protect themselves from the police.
3. No real harm is caused by the forbidden activities.
4. Wide-scale violation of these laws creates a climate which encourages disrespect for the law as well as police corruption.[57]

SOCIOLOGICAL PERSPECTIVES ON SEXUAL BEHAVIOR

Because sexual behavior is deeply rooted in human biology, many people lose sight of the fact that it is socially controlled and directed. Instead, they believe that the sexual standards of their social group are a part of human nature and that those who do not follow those standards are abnormal or unnatural. Such ethnocentric attitudes help to make sexual behavior a social problem by fostering concern about "abnormal" sexual activities and by promoting campaigns to stamp out sexual deviance. These problems are particularly severe in North America because there are so many different cultures and subcultures with contradictory standards of sexual behavior. The conflicts between moral standards and the rapid changes that have occurred in sexual attitudes have made sexual behavior a controversial social issue.

The Functionalist Perspective Kingsley Davis's early analysis of prostitution set the pattern for most of the functionalist work on this subject.[58] Following Davis's lead, most functionalists hold that prostitution is inevitable. As long as there are sexual restrictions in a society, the argument goes, sex will be for sale. Functionalists also note that prostitution benefits society by creating jobs for people with few skills, by providing a sexual outlet for people who would otherwise be without one, and by reducing the risk that frustrated, hostile men might use violence to satisfy their sexual desires. Consequently, many functionalists, including Davis, advocate the legalization of prostitution.

At the same time, however, other restrictions on sexual expression are considered functional. Thus, the prohibition of premarital and extramarital sex is seen as a device to keep society's kinship system intact, ensuring a clear knowledge of a child's paternity and thus facilitating the transmission of money and power from parents to children. Sexual restrictions in general are considered to be functional because they direct individuals' energy away from personal pleasure seeking and into more socially beneficial activities. Pornography is held to be dysfunctional because it encourages extramarital affairs and therefore threatens an essential social institution: the family. Similarly, many functionalists believe that homosexuality should be banned because this sexual outlet does not contribute to society's need for new members. In other words, homosexuality is dysfunctional because it does not contribute to reproduction. But considering the current overpopulation of the world, it can now be argued that some amount of homosexuality is actually functional.

The Conflict Perspective It is obvious that many of the problems of sexual behavior stem from conflicting ideas about sexual morality. There are many different standards of sexual behavior, but supporters of traditional standards have the lion's share of the power and have been able to write their convictions into law. Those whose sexual morality differs from the values of dominant groups are made into criminals and threatened with imprisonment. Conflict theorists see such actions as part of a larger effort by traditional groups to maintain their cultural dominance by controlling the criminal law. The same power struggle leads to the imprisonment of marijuana smokers, bigamists, political radicals, and others who challenge the beliefs and customs of dominant groups.

Conflict theorists see attempts to stamp out prostitution and homosexuality as the oppression of "sexual minorities," similar to the oppression of ethnic minorities by segregation laws. Aside from noting the obvious injustice of such policies, conflict theorists point out that such oppression causes secondary problems, such as the creation of a black market for the forbidden goods and services and a burning hostility among these groups to the current social order.

Conflict theorists recommend that homosexuals, prostitutes, and other so-called sexual deviants organize and agitate for social change, as they have already begun to do. In addition, conflict theorists encourage them to form alliances with other oppressed groups such as drug users and religious and ethnic minorities. The "problem" of sexual behavior would be far less severe, according to conflict theorists, if we repealed laws prohibiting sexual acts between consenting adults and passed laws banning discrimination against homosexuals and others who engage in unpopular sexual activities.

Social Psychological Perspectives Biosocial theorists point out that humans are the most sexually active animals on earth. The human female is unique because she is sexually receptive at all times, whereas the females of other species are receptive only around their periods of fertility. Thus, whereas other species mate only on a periodic basis, humans can do so continually, a situation that creates many problems of sexual adjustment.

Biosocial theorists often attribute the differences in male and female sexual behavior to evolutionary forces. According to one theory, men are naturally promiscuous because it increases the chances of their genes being passed on to the next generation. The more women a man has sex with, the more children he is likely to father, and the more descendants he is likely to leave. However, a woman's reproductive success is not enhanced by having sex with numerous men but by attaching herself to a single man who will protect the children she bears, and women therefore tend to be more monogamous.[59] Critics of this theory point out that even monkeys must learn how to have sex or they will be unable to reproduce, and humans have a far greater capacity for learning than monkeys. Moreover, the critics charge that the rigid programming of sexual behavior hypothesized by some evolutionary theorists would actually be maladaptive for a species whose survival is dependent on effective cultural adaptation to a changing environment.

Personality theory holds sexual conduct to be a product of psychological traits and characteristics that are established early in life. Homosexuality, for instance, is usually seen as the result of experiences in early childhood, particularly those that promote identification with the opposite sex. Behaviorists and interactionists also hold that sexual behavior and preferences are learned, but claim that one learns to engage in homosexuality or prostitution in the same way that one learns to engage in heterosexual activities. That is, the homosexual or prostitute simply receives more rewards and fewer punishments for such behavior than for socially acceptable alternatives.

Many social psychologists have become concerned about the effects of the constant use of sex to sell consumer goods and to boost television ratings, motion picture receipts, and magazine sales. This erotic bombardment creates serious psychological problems for many people who cannot live up to the demands for sexual attractiveness and instant fulfillment created by the media. Although such problems are common among people of all ages, they are particularly prevalent among the young, who have little sexual experience and are more likely to accept uncritically the expectations created by the media. The mystique of sexuality used to sell products and attract audiences has also made an important contribution to the extremely high rate of pregnancy among teenage girls. In response to this problem, social psychologists recommend more effective sex education in the schools, therapy and counseling for those with sexual problems, easier availability of contraception, and greater social responsibility on the part of advertisers and the media. The resolution of these problems seems unlikely in the short run, but many social psychologists are optimistic that as the novelty of the new liberal sexual attitudes wears off, a healthier, more matter-of-fact attitude toward sex will replace the current state of confusion.

SUMMARY

In view of the enormous range of sexual customs and beliefs found in different cultures, it is clear that all sexual behavior is not biologically determined. It derives from a biological drive, but a drive that is channeled, directed, and controlled by social forces.

Traditionally, Western culture has been sexually conservative. Intercourse was permissible only between a husband and wife, and then only for reproduction. But these attitudes and values have changed. Comparison of surveys taken over the past four decades shows that there has been a substantial increase in many types of sexual activity. The double standard has weakened but has not disappeared; premarital and extramarital sex have increased significantly, as has sexual activity between married couples. The same surveys show no change in the incidence of homosexuality, and a decrease in prostitution. A number of forces have contributed to the increase in sexual activity, including changing attitudes about sex, a weakening of the power of families to control the sexual behavior of their children, and improvement in birth control techniques.

Single teenage girls in the United States have sex about as often as do single teenage girls in other industrialized nations, but because they are less likely to use birth control, they are more likely to get pregnant. In addition to the possibility of unwanted pregnancy, another unintended complication of sexual activity may be the exposure to a sexually transmitted disease. The worst of these is acquired immune deficiency syndrome (AIDS), but there are a host of other sexually transmitted diseases including syphilis, gonorrhea, genital herpes and chlamydia.

Child molestation is a very different kind of problem: the intentional sexual victimization of one person by another. Contrary to popular opinion, most cases of child molestation involve sexual behaviors that stop short of intercourse, and the offenders are not usually strangers but family friends or relatives. Psychologists argue that child molesters are usually sexually inadequate people who turn to children because they cannot handle adult sexual relations. Sociologists point out that many child molesters learned that behavior when they themselves were victimized as children.

Homosexuality is another often misunderstood form of sexual behavior. Contrary to popular belief, the differences between homosexuals, bisexuals, and heterosexuals are not absolute but are a matter of degree. Psychologists often argue that homosexuality is learned in the early years of childhood, but strong prohibitions against adolescent heterosexuality also encourage homosexual experimentation. In the past most homosexuals concealed their sexual preference, but now many are "coming out," publicly acknowledging their sexual preference. Most European countries, Canada, and 17 of the United States have repealed their antihomosexual legislation, but homosexuals are still subject to both occupational and social discrimination.

Prostitution has declined in this century, but it is unlikely that it will ever disappear. Prostitution offers its customers several advantages, including sex without ties or obligations, hard-to-obtain services, and sex for social isolates. Prostitutes have an occupational prestige system. The call girl has the highest rank; next is the woman who works in a house of prostitution; and at the bottom is the streetwalker, who must search out her customers in public. Although most prostitutes are females, there are a substantial number of men in the profession as well. Legal efforts to restrict prostitution have often aggravated the situation. Closing houses of prostitution created more streetwalkers, who are a far greater social problem than the "house girls" they replaced.

Legally, pornographic material must be lewd, contrary to community standards, and without redeeming social value. But applying these standards is quite difficult, especially because almost any book or picture can be shown to have some redeeming value. Many believe that all sexually explicit materials promote sex crimes, but scientific evidence suggests that most is harmless. Sexually explicit materials that contain violence or use children as sexual objects do, however, have damaging social consequences. Opponents of censorship argue that legislation restricting pornography is more harmful than the pornography itself, since censorship threatens civil liberties and stifles artistic expression.

Several different responses to the problems of sexual behavior are commonly suggested, including (1) an effort to balance the unrealistic image of sexuality presented in the media with public service announcements promoting birth control and the use of condoms to prevent sexually transmitted disease; (2) more sex education in the schools and easier access to contraceptives for teenagers; (3) legalization of all sexual behavior between consenting adults in private; and (4) better enforcement of laws protecting children and other victims of sexual aggression.

Functionalists analyze the effects of homosexuality, prostitution, and pornography on society. Prostitution, for example, is said to serve society by providing sexual outlets for people who would otherwise lack them. But some other restrictions on sexual expression—including homosexuality—are generally considered to be functional, since they help fulfill society's need for more children. Conflict theorists say that problems of sexual behavior stem from value conflicts and from efforts by powerful groups to force their morality on others. Biosocial theorists stress the fact that humans are the most sexually active of all animals and argue that a great deal of our sexual behavior has been biologically predetermined by the process of evolution. Personality theorists are primarily concerned with identifying psychological traits that are acquired early in life and determine later sexual behavior. Interactionists and behaviorists argue that sexual behavior is primarily learned, not hereditary.

KEY TERMS

bisexual	pornography
child molestation	premarital intercourse
heterosexual	prostitution
homosexual	sexually transmitted disease

FURTHER READINGS

Sexual Behavior

James Leslie McCary and Stephen D. McCary, *McCary's Human Sexuality,* 4th ed., Belmont, Calif.: Wadsworth, 1982.

Barbara Ehrenreich, Elizabeth Hess, and Gloria Jacobs, *Remaking Love: The Feminization of Sex,* New York: Anchor/Doubleday, 1988.

Problems and Issues

Arlene Carmen and Howard Moody, *Working Women: The Subterranean World of Street Prostitution,* New York: Harper & Row, 1985.

Kenneth Plummer (ed.), *The Making of the Modern Homosexual,* New York: Barnes & Noble, 1981.

David Finkelhor, *Child Sexual Abuse: New Theory and Research,* New York: Free Press, 1984.

Chapter 12
MENTAL DISORDERS

Few things are more frightening than the thought of "going crazy." Literature since the time of the ancient Greeks has portrayed pathetic lunatics and madmen and madwomen raging against imaginary demons. Although mental disorders are sometimes shown in a comic light, they are more commonly associated with tragic personal failure. Perhaps it is for this reason that most people react uncomfortably to any discussion of mental illness. Dark fears that mental illness may run in the family make the relatives of mental patients reluctant to discuss the issue openly. Some people act as though mental disorders were contagious, fearfully avoiding any contact with the mentally disturbed.

Psychologists estimate that over five million Americans suffer from schizophrenia or acute emotional disturbances and that over 20 percent of the population have some kind of mental disorder that seriously interferes with their life.[1] Millions of people receive treatment for mental problems every year. American men between the ages of 14 and 45 spend more time in the hospital for mental disorders than for any other cause, and only the delivery of a child accounts for more days in the hospital for women of this age.[2] Yet most people who have mental problems never get to a hospital or receive professional help of any other kind. Some turn to friends or to one of the dozens of new "pop psychology" books published every year. But many others simply ignore their problems and hope that somehow they will go away.

WHAT ARE MENTAL DISORDERS?

The terms *mental illness* and *insanity* bring to mind the most dramatic types of mental problems. A common image of the mentally disordered is that of a madman in a straitjacket, foaming at the mouth and struggling to free himself in order to attack anyone who happens to be nearby. Another is that of a dirty, disheveled woman, babbling incoherently and engaging in random sexual relations with anyone who is interested. But these images are misleading, for most mental disorders are neither bizarre nor dramatic; instead, they are the common experiences of anxiety or depression with which we are all familiar.

Despite years of research and study, there is no widespread agreement on the meaning of terms such as *mentally ill, insane, mentally disturbed,* and *crazy.* One person's craziness is another person's individuality. If a man says that he has talked to God and received instructions to save humanity, he may be considered crazy by most of us; but some may see him as a prophet or a saint. The difference turns not so much on what he says as on whether his audience believes him. An old woman who gives away her fortune may be considered mentally ill by her family, but those who receive the money will see her as a generous philanthropist.

Speaking generally, a person may be said to have a **mental disorder** if he or she is so disturbed that coping with routine, everyday life is difficult or impossible. But this definition—and most others as well—is vague. Exactly how does one determine whether individuals can or cannot cope with their everyday affairs? There is no clear-cut answer. This does not mean that it is impossible to tell whether an individual has a psychological problem, for the behavior of some mental patients is so bizarre that few people would question their inability to cope. The catatonic schizophrenic may stand motionless for hours, even days, and must be fed through a tube. But most cases are not so obvious. People with serious physical illnesses are usually aware of their need for help. In contrast, the greater a person's mental disturbance, the more difficult it is for the person to be conscious of the trouble.

Although many psychiatrists, psychologists, and sociologists have attempted to define *mental disorder* precisely, none of these efforts has received universal acceptance. Some experts see mental disorder as an illness; others consider it to be personal maladjustment; and still others feel that it is simply a label applied to people whose behavior we wish to condemn.

Mental Illness   The most widely accepted approach to mental disorders uses a medical model that assumes that mental illnesses are very much like physical illnesses. Thus, the concepts and methods of modern medicine are used to diagnose and treat mental illness in the same fashion as a broken arm or measles. Mental illness is believed to be the result of a disruption in the normal functioning of the personality, just as physical illnesses are caused by some disturbance in the normal functioning of the body.

Psychiatrists who use this approach try to identify specific types of mental illnesses that, like the measles and smallpox, are assumed to have specific causes. After identifying the patient's specific illness, the psychiatrist tries to cure the illness by eliminating the cause. This model is most appropriate when the mental problem can be shown to be a result of an organic condition such as an overdose of drugs, syphilis, or a biochemical condition. But because most mental disorders do not have easily defined physical causes, they are attributed to such abstractions as repressed hostility, frustration, and personal conflict.

In medieval times, mental disorders were believed to be caused by demons and spirits. "Treatments" such as flogging, starving, and dunking the sufferer in hot water were used to drive the devils out. The idea that mental disorders are a form of illness developed as a part of a humanitarian reaction against these practices. The denial of supernatural influences on the mind opened the door to scientific experimentation and study. The belief that mental disorders are similar to other common illnesses also helped reduce the shame of disturbed people.[3]

The perception of mental disorder as an illness was a great advance over demonic beliefs, but critics charge that the medical model has outlived its usefulness. They point out that although there is general agreement on the symptoms and causes of physical disorders such as appendicitis and pneumonia, there is little agreement about the symptoms and causes of mental illnesses. Most physicians agree that surgery is the best treatment for appendicitis and that antibiotics are most effective for pneumonia, but there is no agreement about the most effective means of treating mental illness. The treatment a patient receives is as likely to be determined by the theoretical perspective of the therapist as by his or her actual symptoms.

Pneumonia is pneumonia, regardless of the culture in which it occurs; but mental illness is different in different cultures. Thomas Szasz, a psychiatrist and a strong critic of the medical model, argues that the whole idea of mental illness is a myth used to make the values and opinions of the psychiatric establishment resemble scientific fact.[4] He notes, first, that although everyone knows what it means to be physically healthy and agrees that being healthy is a good thing, there is no similar agreement about the nature of mental health. Second, he sees the proponents of "mental health" as mere moralists who are trying to tell others how they ought to live. Third, he argues that diagnosing people with mental problems as "mentally ill" robs them of personal responsibility for their condition and therefore undermines the moral fabric of society.

Personal Maladjustment   According to another perspective, mental disorders arise when someone is unable to deal effectively with his or her personal problems. It is assumed that disturbed behavior is caused by the same forces that govern normal behavior and that such behavior is one end of an unbroken continuum. Therapists who use this approach do not look for symptoms of a specific disease. Instead, the person's overall adjustment to his or her environment is examined.[5] James C. Coleman has described this approach as follows:

> Life is a continuous process of adjusting, in which we strive to meet our own needs and maintain harmonious relations with our environment. When an individual deals with his problems effectively, he is said to be *well* adjusted—to be adapting successfully to both the inner and outer demands being made upon him. Conversely, when his problems prove too much for him—as shown by anxiety, inefficiency, unhappiness, or more serious symptoms—he is referred to as *maladjusted.*[6]

Szasz uses this approach in a modified form. Although he prefers to talk of problems in living rather than personal maladjustment, the two phrases have similar implications. The basic difference is this: Szasz sees problems in living as universal and inescapable, whereas the personal-maladjustment approach implies that all normal men and women have a well-adjusted relationship to their environment.[7]

The personal-maladjustment model has three advantages over the medical model. First, it does not consider individuals in isolation from their environment, as a physician would when treating a broken leg or a "mental illness." Second, because abnormal behavior is seen to be produced by the same processes as normal behavior, it discourages the assumption that mentally disturbed people are freaks or lunatics. Third, it accepts the fact that any diagnosis of mental problems is a very uncertain affair and, therefore, that there are no specific cures for these problems.

19th-Century Social Problems

*A woman was recently found wandering about the streets of
Eau Claire with a dead baby in her arms. She was from Chippewa
County and had lost her husband and was destitute.*

July 5, 1885

These selections, which appear throughout the text, are from the *Badger State
Banner*, a newspaper published in Black River Falls, Wisconsin.

The personal-maladjustment approach has some serious shortcomings,
however. Although it does not ignore the individual's environment, as the
medical model is prone to do, the basic assumption is that mental problems
are personal problems. Thus, the individual—not the social order—is assumed to be responsible for the problems. But personal problems sometimes
stem from an unlivable environment rather than from the individual. The
healthiest individuals are not always those who are best adjusted to their
environment; and refusal to accept an unjust social order is certainly not
abnormal or harmful.

Social Deviance   The newest approach to mental disorders emphasizes their social
aspects. The proponents of this approach hold that there are no objective
standards by which a person's mental health may be judged. The determination that someone is or is not mentally disordered is strictly a cultural
matter. What is considered mental illness or maladjustment in one society
is considered healthy adjustment in another. From this perspective, what
people call "mental illness" is merely social deviance. In other words, people
are labeled "mentally ill" because they have violated society's rules about
how they are supposed to behave, not because they have a specific disease.

Most deviants violate clearly understood rules and therefore are labeled
in ways that emphasize their moral failure.[8] If a man kills another person,
he is labeled "murderer"; if a woman accepts money for sexual relations,
she is labeled "prostitute." According to Thomas Scheff, however, the rules
that are violated by those who are labeled "mentally ill" are *residual*, meaning that they are commonly accepted and observed in a way that makes
them appear to be part of human nature. There is no law against staring
intently at a person's ear or foot when carrying on a conversation, but those
who do so violate such residual rules and are considered rather strange. The
same is true of a man who claims to be Jesus Christ or who smears feces on
his clothing before leaving for work in the morning. Because most people
cannot understand why anyone would violate unstated rules of everyday life,
they perceive deviants as sick or mentally ill and label them accordingly.

The difference between being labeled a prophet and being labeled mentally disturbed depends on the reaction of the audience. This photograph shows the victims of the mass suicide in Jonestown, Guyana. The followers of Jim Jones considered him a great religious leader, but others said his role in encouraging this carnage was the act of a deranged mind.

Because the social-deviance approach places responsibility for mental disorders on the social environment rather than on the individual, the stigma of mental illness is removed. Therapists are encouraged to deal with the patient's family and personal environment rather than assuming that the patient is suffering from a personal defect or disorder. However, this approach has been severely criticized by experts who hold more traditional ideas about mental health and mental illness. These experts point out that the labeling approach neglects the disturbed individuals themselves. Even if no one were labeled "mentally ill," they argue, disturbed people would still have problems. Further, labeling people "mentally ill" is the only way we can identify those who are in need of help.

Each of these theories of mental disorder has its weaknesses, but each also has something to contribute. There is no good reason for insisting that mental disorder is entirely a medical problem, entirely a problem of maladjustment, or entirely a problem of labeling. Mental problems are far too complex for such simple answers. After centuries of study and thought, we still remain uncertain about their ultimate cause. We must therefore admit the limitations of our knowledge and draw insight from any available source.

CLASSIFICATION OF MENTAL DISORDERS

Mental problems are as diverse as the people who suffer from them. In one way or another every individual problem is unique. But those who work with the mentally disabled have long sought a standardized system to help make sense out of these diverse problems. One of the most widely accepted classifications of mental disorders appears in the American Psychiatric Association's *Diagnostic and Statistical Manual of Mental Disorders* (DSM), and its major categories are summarized in Table 12.1.[9] But the value of this classification is still a very controversial issue. The World Health Organization's *International Classification of Disease* uses a somewhat different system, and the American Psychological Association is working on a classification of its own.[10] Labeling theorists, moreover, question the value of any such scheme, and the psychiatric association itself has repeatedly changed its classification.

In 1973 the American Psychiatric Association undertook a major revision of the DSM, which was not published until 1980 (DSM-III), and another less-sweeping revision was made in 1987 (DSM-III-R). The new classification threw out many familiar terms found in previous editions which are still in common use among the general public. Most notably absent were the **neuroses**—a very widely used term referring to a personal problem that is accompanied by anxiety and chronically inappropriate responses, but that falls short of a full-fledged **psychosis** in which the victim loses contact with reality. Critics charge that the changes in the classification have been as much a response to political pressure and public opinion as to new scientific discoveries. Gay advocates demanded and won the removal of homosexuality from the list of mental disorders, but less well-organized groups such as sadomasochists remain on the list. Similarly, as the antismoking movement gained power, tobacco dependence appeared as a mental disorder for the first time.

If we look at the diagnoses given hospitalized mental patients in North America, we find that **schizophrenia** is by far the most common. Typical symptoms of schizophrenia include extreme disorganization in personality, thought patterns, and speech. Schizophrenics tend to withdraw from social life and live in a private fantasy world. They also tend to have delusions (false beliefs that are maintained in spite of contradictory evidence) and hallucinations (apparent sensory experiences of something without an objective source, such as hearing voices that no one else can hear).

The second most common cause of hospitalization is the **substance abuse disorders**, most of which are alcohol related. Next are the **mood disorders**, which involve disturbances in mood and emotion rather than in thought

---

TABLE 12.1 Major Mental Disorders According to the American Psychiatric Association

1. **Disorders First Evident in Infancy, Childhood, or Adolescence**
   Includes such things as mental retardation, stuttering, and anorexia
2. **Organic Mental Disorders**
   Disorders with organic causes (for example, senility and brain damage)
3. **Substance Use Disorders**
   The abuse of alcohol and/or other drugs
4. **Schizophrenic Disorders**
   Symptoms include such things as withdrawal from ordinary social contacts, bizarre thought processes, and hallucinations.
5. **Paranoid Disorders**
   Involves persistent irrational delusions, often a fear of persecution
6. **Mood Disorders**
   Emotional disorders such as depression or exaggerated mood swings
7. **Anxiety Disorders**
   Phobias, panic, extreme anxiety, and stress from traumatic experiences, (for example, battle shock)
8. **Somatoform Disorders**
   Psychological problems that manifest themselves as symptoms of physical disease (for example, hypochondria)
9. **Dissociative Disorders**
   Problems in which part of the personality is dissociated from the rest (for example, multiple personalities and amnesia)
10. **Sexual Disorders**
    Sexually related problems such as transsexualism, exhibitionism, and inhibited sexual desire
11. **Sleep Disorders**
    Insomnia and other problems with sleep
12. **Disorders of Impulse Control**
    The inability to control certain undesirable impulses (for example, kleptomania, pyromania, and pathological gambling)
13. **Adjustment Disorders**
    Difficulty in adjusting to the stress created by such common events as unemployment or divorce

Source: American Psychiatric Association, DSM III-R.

---

patterns as in schizophrenia. The most common affective disorder involves deep depression, although some people experience wide swings of emotion that include a manic or hyperactive phase. **Organic disorders** are caused by a physical problem in the brain. In some cases it is hereditary; in others it is caused by an injury or by substance abuse. **Paranoid disorders**, which involve overpowering irrational fears, are a less common reason for hospitalization in North America, but this is a more frequently used diagnosis in some European countries.

THE DISTRIBUTION OF MENTAL DISORDERS

It is difficult to measure the incidence of mental disorders in different social classes, in urban areas compared with rural areas, or even among men as compared with women. Rates of admission to mental hospitals are not accurate measures because people from one category may be more likely to seek treatment than people from another. Further, hospitals have different criteria for admission, and even outpatient treatment by a psychiatrist may be determined as much by income and attitudes toward "going to a shrink" as by the need for treatment. At the same time, surveys of communities to determine how many people are mentally ill also have serious weaknesses. Mental disturbances are so poorly defined that the results of such surveys may reflect the biases of the researchers as much as the distribution of mental disorders. Consistently, the following discussion relies on approximations and estimates because most of the evidence is far from conclusive.

Social Class   One of the earliest investigations of the relationship between social class and mental disorder was carried out by Robert Faris and Warren Dunham in the 1930s.[11] These researchers obtained information about the original place of residence of patients who had been admitted to Chicago's four state mental hospitals and eight private mental hospitals between 1922 and 1934. They found the highest rates of mental disorder in the central areas of the city, where the population was poor and had little living space. The lowest rates were found in the more stable, wealthy residential areas on the outskirts of Chicago. Faris and Dunham concluded that the social disorganization of the central city, with its mobility, extreme poverty, demoralization, and cultural heterogeneity, was responsible for the higher incidence of mental disorder there.

A second major study was conducted by Hollingshead and Redlich in the 1950s.[12] They obtained data on the class background of mental patients seeing private psychiatrists and those in public and private hospitals in New Haven, Connecticut. Like Faris and Dunham, they found that the psychoses, particularly schizophrenia, were much more common among lower-class people. However, the neuroses were more common among people with higher status and income. They also found that social class had a very strong influence on the type of treatment a patient received. The poor people were most likely to be treated in hospitals, whereas the wealthy were more likely to be treated by private psychiatrists. Lower-class men and women who were hospitalized for mental disorders remained in the hospital much longer than other patients. Hollingshead and Redlich concluded that it was impossible to tell whether higher rates of psychosis for lower-class people were caused by the conditions in which they lived or by the inferior treatment they received.

A third study was conducted in Manhattan by Leo Srole and his associates.[13] Rather than using hospital admissions or other statistics pertaining to treatment, these researchers conducted a door-to-door survey of 1700 men and women, asking a variety of questions designed to determine whether the respondents had any psychological problems and what sort of treatment, if any, they had received. The startling conclusion was that over 23 percent of the respondents were significantly impaired by a mental disorder and that less than 20 percent were completely healthy. Srole and his co-workers found significant differences between social classes. In the lowest class almost half were impaired, whereas in the highest class only one in eight (12.5 percent) had a significant problem. The Manhattan study also found a close relationship between social class and psychiatric treatment. Only 1 percent of the impaired people in the lowest class were receiving treatment at the time of the interview, compared with 20 percent of the people in the upper status level.

The finding that lower-class people have more psychological problems has been confirmed by many other researchers. After reviewing 44 studies, Bruce and Barbara Dohrenwend concluded that "analysis of these studies shows that their most consistent result is an inverse relation between social class and reported rate of psychological disorder."[14] In other words, the lowest social classes have the highest rates of mental disorder.

Communities The relentless growth of cities and the change in traditional life-styles that has accompanied this growth have led many people to wonder about the impact of urban life on mental health. It is generally assumed that the congestion, anonymity, and stress associated with urban living cause mental problems, but the evidence for this belief is far from conclusive. It is easy to show that rates of hospitalization for mental problems are higher in urban areas, but the meaning of this fact is not clear. Because there are more hospital facilities in urban areas, it is much easier for city dwellers to get to a hospital for treatment.

The Manhattan study just discussed seems to indicate that mental problems are extremely common in the most densely populated borough of New York City. But it is quite possible that the high rates of mental disorder revealed by this study resulted from the kinds of questions the researchers asked, and therefore do not reflect the actual rates of mental disorder in Manhattan. A similar survey by the National Center for Health Statistics found slightly fewer reported psychiatric symptoms among residents of big cities than among people who live in small towns.[15]

A study of rural Hutterite communities in Montana, the Dakotas, and Canada did not yield the results that most students of mental disorders expected. Hutterite communities are close-knit, homogeneous, and highly integrated, and have steadfastly resisted the inroads of modern civilization. Yet Joseph Eaton and Robert Weil found that the rate of severe mental disorder among Hutterites was roughly equal to the rate of hospitalization for mental disorders in New York State.[16] The most important difference was that the Hutterites usually cared for their disturbed people in their homes rather than in hospitals. A comparable study by Eleanor Leacock found a high rate of psychosis in some decaying rural areas and a low rate in some relatively well-off urban areas.[17] It therefore appears that the nature of an individual's immediate community has more to do with mental health than does the number of people who live in it.

Gender, Age, and Marital Status Men and women are equally likely to receive treatment for a mental disorder, but there are some important differences. Men are more often hospitalized while women more often receive outpatient care. The two sexes are very similar in their rates of diagnosed schizophrenia, but women are twice as likely to be treated for depression. Men are commonly thought to be four or five times more likely to suffer from alcoholism.[18]

These figures are influenced by our gender-role expectations in several important ways. The willingness of women to admit that they are having psychological problems and to seek early care contributes to their higher rates of outpatient treatment. Men, on the other hand, seem to be more inclined to ignore their problems unless they become so severe that hospitalization is necessary. Similarly, the higher rates of alcoholism among men reflect, in part, the greater acceptability of heavy drinking among men than among women. This difference in attitudes also makes women more likely to conceal their alcoholism, thus exaggerating the statistical differences between the sexes. Feminist critics of the mental-health-care system charge that it serves to perpetuate women's second-class status by encouraging them to "adjust" to the domination and exploitation of their husbands. Feminists also charge that because most therapists share in the sexist attitudes of our culture, they are more likely to label independent women who violate traditional gender-role expectations as mentally ill.[19]

Marital status also has a considerable bearing on the odds of being treated for a mental disorder. Married people have the lowest rates of treatment, while rates for those who have never married are considerably higher for men but only slightly higher for women. However, among divorced, widowed, or separated people the rates are high for both sexes. Age is significant too: although the highest rate of treatment appears in the 18 to 44 age group, the elderly are much more likely to be treated for organic psychoses due to senility. But it is important to remember that these statistics are for the rates of *treatment* and do not necessarily reflect the true rates of mental disorder in these groups.

CAUSES OF MENTAL DISORDERS

Considering the amount of disagreement over the definition and classification of mental disorders, it is not surprising that there are arguments about their causes as well. Although this issue has received much scientific scrutiny, many difficult questions remain. What are the family conditions that promote emotional problems? How important is heredity? What role do the reactions of others play in the behavior of mentally disturbed people? Do different kinds of mental disorders have different causes? Conclusive answers to these questions cannot be given; in fact, the principal theories about the causes of mental disorders disagree on most of the important issues.

Biosocial Theories   Because some drugs produce mental states that are very similar to psychoses, it seems reasonable to believe that psychotics are suffering from a biochemical problem. Prolonged use of amphetamines, for instance, produces a state that is similar to paranoia. However, there are also significant differences between amphetamine abusers and psychotics. And although tranquilizers seem to improve the behavior of some psychotics, that alone hardly proves that the causes of their behavior are biological.

Most psychologists and psychiatrists believe that there is an inherited predisposition to contract schizophrenia, but they often disagree about the relative importance of inheritance versus environment. The bulk of the evidence for the importance of heredity comes from the study of twins. Kallmann and Roth studied 17 pairs of identical twins (from one egg) and found that if one twin had schizophrenia, the other had the same problem 88.2 percent of the time.[20] However, the rate of concordance (if one has it, both have it) was only 22.9 percent for the 35 pairs of fraternal twins (from two eggs) that they studied. More recent studies have also concluded that close genetic relationships between twins are reflected in higher concordance rates. However, the differences found were not nearly as large as those reported by Kallmann and Roth. For instance, Hoffer and Polin found a concordance rate of 15.5 percent for identical twins and 4.4 percent for fraternal twins in a sample of almost 16,000 twins in the American armed forces.[21] Critics of these studies argue that their findings may be due to the fact that the physical similarity of identical twins leads their family and friends to treat them alike, but other research shows a higher concordance rate among identical twins even when they have been raised apart.[22] Researchers also believe that they have located a specific gene defect common among the members of one large Amish family that greatly increases the likelihood of manic-depressive psychosis (a serious type of mood disorder).[23]

Developmental Theories   One of the most popular explanations among professional psychotherapists is that mental disorders are caused by disturbances in the individual's early psychological development. Details vary from one theory to another, but many of them borrow extensively from Sigmund Freud and his psychoanalytic school. Freud held that the unusual behavior of the mentally disturbed is merely a symptom of deeper unresolved conflicts locked in the unconscious mind of the patient. He treated mental disorders with psychoanalysis: a slow and detailed examination of the patient's mental life. This method attempts to bring subconscious conflicts into the open, thereby permitting patients to understand and resolve them. Although critics of psychoanalysis say it is slow, costly, and ineffective, Freud's theories and methods remain part of the framework used by most clinical psychologists and psychiatrists.

Most of the early conflicts analyzed by developmental theorists occur in the family. For example, it is generally believed that parental love and affection are vital to the normal development of a child. Children who are rejected by their parents may develop a variety of psychological problems, including anxiety, insecurity, low self-esteem, and hostility. Parental standards of discipline are also important for proper development. Harsh, rigid standards may produce either a hostile and rebellious child or a passive, guilt-ridden one. Lack of discipline is thought to encourage antisocial aggressive tendencies. Much has been made of the harm done by overprotective parents, whose children sometimes develop "passive-dependent personalities."[24] Such behavior is tolerated, even expected, of females. But the "mama's boy" finds it difficult to adjust to society's expectations, and psychological problems may develop as a result.[24]

Gregory Bateson and his associates have advanced a theory of schizophrenia based on what they call the **double bind.**[25] This occurs when a parent gives a child two conflicting messages at the same time. For example, a boy may hear his mother say "I love you" but observe that she flinches or pulls away whenever he touches her. Children who receive such conflicting messages are in a double bind: they desperately want to believe what their parents are saying, but are constantly exposed to evidence that what is said is false. Thus, they come to mistrust and misinterpret normal communications, eventually becoming so disoriented that serious psychological problems emerge.

Critics note that the development approach does not specify the exact conditions that produce mental disorders. Almost every family has some conditions that developmental theorists consider conducive to mental disorder, but most children do not develop mental problems. David Mechanic, among others, has criticized psychologists for their tendency to seize on a minor problem in an individual's life history as an explanation for mental disorder:

> . . . the usual variances in childrearing patterns appear to play a relatively small part in producing such profound difficulties. . . . The contexts which appear to breed pathology are those which are emotionally bizarre or deprived and in which the child experiences profound rejection, hostility, and other forms of social abuse. . . .[26]

Learning Theories   Psychologists have been studying the process of learning for many years, and this knowledge is now being applied in the explanation and treatment of mental disorders. Learning theorists do not believe that biochemical processes or hidden inner conflicts cause mental disorders. Instead, they see such disorders merely as inappropriate behavior that has been learned, as other behaviors are learned.

According to learning theorists, there are two basic mechanisms by which people learn behavior, whether normal or abnormal: classical conditioning and operant conditioning. **Classical conditioning** is quite passive, whereas **operant conditioning** requires the active participation of the subject.

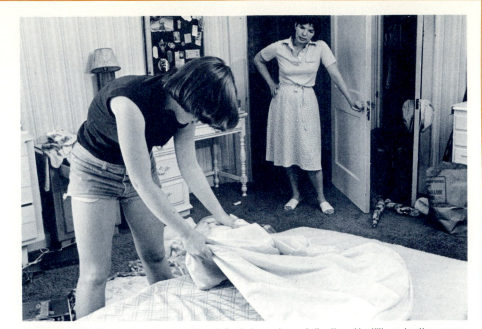

Some mental disorders are caused by defects in early socialization. Hostility, rejection, over-protection, lack of love, and the conflicting messages of a double-bind situation all promote mental problems.

For instance, in classical conditioning it is first observed that a dog's mouth will water if the animal is shown a juicy steak. Then a neutral stimulus, such as the ringing of a bell, is presented along with the mouth-watering meat. After a few trials the dog learns to associate the two stimuli and will salivate at the ringing of the bell alone. Operant conditioning, on the other hand, involves learning by the rewards and punishments that certain behaviors produce. For instance, if a pigeon is rewarded with a kernel of corn whenever it pecks a lever, the bird will peck until it is full. However, if the pecking bird is not rewarded, the pecking will eventually stop.

According to learning theorists, psychological disorders are little more than a series of maladaptive behaviors learned by humans the same way a dog learns to salivate or a pigeon learns to peck a lever. Critics point out that this perspective ignores everything that cannot easily be seen or measured, and they maintain that abnormal behavior reflects deep psychological problems rather than merely learned patterns of behavior.

Social-Stress Theory   Stress theory is based largely on commonsense ideas about psychological problems that are widely accepted in our society. Simply put, the

Social-stress theories hold that some mental disorders are the result of excessive environmental stress. Such stress among soldiers in combat produces a disturbance known as "battle fatigue."

theory holds that each individual has a breaking point and that if stress builds up beyond this level, the individual will experience serious psychological problems. This theory is used by military psychiatrists to explain the symptoms of "battle fatigue." But it can also be used to account for the behavior of harried parents, pressured executives, or overworked students. Since sociologists have found that social stress is much greater among the poor than among the affluent, it is not surprising to find a higher rate of serious mental disorder in the lower classes.

The relationship between stress and mental disorder is, however, more complex than our simple illustrations suggest. A certain amount of stress is actually beneficial because it provides a challenge that motivates an individual to respond in new and creative ways. But too much stress over too long a period of time seems to exhaust individual resources. The problem is to determine how much stress is appropriate and how much is harmful. Individuals have different tolerance levels, so that something that constitutes a healthy challenge for one person may bring serious psychological consequences to another.

19th-Century Social Problems

The spectacle of a middle aged man rushing along the avenues, pursued by a mob of howling, jeering school boys who hurled tin cans, sticks, and other missiles at him, was witnessed by scores of indignant citizens at East Superior. The boisterous mob was reinforced at every corner by urchins of all sizes and descriptions . . . there were perhaps 100 in the crowd . . . the fleeing man was pelted unmercifully from all directions. Finally he rushed into a private residence and the crowd dispersed. The man was a resident of West Superior, sometimes called "Simple Joe." He had been to church at the East End, and when leaving . . . was attacked.

April 2, 1896

Labeling Theory For more than two decades a school of sociologists, psychiatrists, and social psychologists has been challenging accepted ideas about mental disorders and the way they should be treated. The members of this school argue that there is nothing inherently normal or abnormal in human behavior. Whether behavior is abnormal or normal depends on the label that is attached to it. Thus, "mental illness" is just a label that is given to individuals who behave in ways that others do not like or accept. Few labeling theorists try to explain why people do things that cause them to be labeled "mentally ill." They merely note that once someone has been declared mentally ill, he or she experiences increasing pressure to behave like others who have been similarly labeled. Opportunities for labeled individuals to act out "normal" roles are steadily reduced. Others may laugh at them and shun them. Prospective employers may think of them as too unreliable and unstable to hold a responsible job. Even their efforts to shed the label are taken as evidence of their instability. Because everyone behaves as though the labeled person is sick, he or she eventually comes to believe it and to act that way. Indeed, the sick role becomes attractive to some victims of labeling. It allows them to escape from responsibilities, behave as they wish, and relax their battle against the label.[27]

Critics of labeling theory vigorously object to the idea that mental illness is just a social label. They argue that labeling theorists ignore the fact that mental disorders have clearly defined characteristics that can be seen in all cultures. An increasing number of developmental and social-stress theorists are nonetheless coming to accept the idea that labeling has harmful effects on mental patients. A study by Bruce Link, for example, showed that labeled mental patients end up with lower income and lower occupational status than people with the same background and the same psychological symp-toms who have not been labeled.[28] However, these theorists generally reject the idea that mental disorders are produced by the labeling process itself. Although there are some interesting case studies showing the impact of la-beling on particular individuals, critics of labeling theory point out that it has little to say about the reasons someone does the "crazy" things that get them labeled in the first place.[29]

An extreme form of labeling theory is used by R. D. Laing, a British psychiatrist, who claims that "disturbed" individuals are in fact well and that it is society that is sick.[30] Schizophrenia, from Laing's perspective, is a normal response to a deranged society, and the "normal people" are the ones who are really sick: "What we call 'normal' is a product of repression, denial, splitting, projection, introjection and other forms of destructive action on experience. It is radically estranged from the structure of being."[31] Laing sees schizophrenics as courageous explorers of "inner space and time," not as twisted and tortured individuals. In fact, he says, schizophrenia is an attempt to deal with one's "normal" consciousness as well as with the sick-ness of everyday life: "Can we not see that this voyage [schizophrenia] is not what we need to be cured of, but that it is itself a natural way of healing our own appalling state of alienation called normality?"[32] Needless to say, most traditional therapists and mental-health experts scoff at Laing's approach. They argue that if everyone had Laing's "healthy" mental disorders, society would collapse and millions of people would starve to death.

RESPONDING TO PROBLEMS OF MENTAL DISORDERS

The way we deal with mental disorders is always linked to some notion about their cause. Ancient peoples believed that mental disorders were caused by demons that had taken possession of the afflicted individual. Treatment, log-ically enough, consisted of driving the demons out. One of the earliest known treatments was trephining: chipping away an area of the skull to permit evil spirits to escape. Later, a common treatment was exorcism: attempting to drive out evil spirits by performing rituals, including incantations, noise making, prayer, and drinks made from sheep dung and urine. Medieval Christians believed that the devil could be driven off by verbal assaults, so they bombarded mentally disturbed people with a barrage of insults. But not all the techniques of exorcism were so innocent. "Madmen" were also starved, beaten, whipped, burned, and tortured in order to make their bodies such unpleasant places that the demons and devils would leave.

The Greeks were the first people to ascribe mental disorders to natural cause. Hippocrates, for example, believed that mental disorders were caused by hereditary brain pathologies. Greek and Roman physicians prescribed rest, pleasant surroundings, entertainment, and exercise for individuals with mental problems. After the fall of Rome this scientific approach was carried on by the Arabs. The first mental hospital was established in Baghdad in A.D. 792 as a humane refuge for the mentally disordered.

The insane asylums that appeared later in western Europe hardly deserved to be called hospitals. By present-day standards, conditions in the early asylums were horrible. Residents were chained like dogs, some fastened in a standing position so that they could not lie down to sleep. Whippings, beatings, and sexual abuse were routine.[33]

The advent of democracy brought the first humanitarian reform of insane asylums. Philippe Pinel, who was placed in charge of a Paris mental hospital during the French Revolution, removed the chains from mental patients and began treating them like sick people rather than wild beasts. The patients responded remarkably well to this humane handling, and Pinel's experiment was considered a great success. In North America, Dorothea Dix was an effective crusader for reform of insane asylums. In the mid-nineteenth century, Dix, a former New England schoolteacher, carried on a relentless campaign to alert the public and the government to the horrors of insane asylums. She also raised millions of dollars to establish more humane hospitals in the United States and Canada.[34]

Types of Treatment   As suggested earlier, the causes of most mental disorders have not been clearly identified. For this reason there are wide variations in the treatments recommended for these disorders. Indeed, the type of treatment a disturbed person receives depends more on the therapist than on the symptoms. Each psychological school has its own treatment methods, and new therapies come and go like the latest fashions in clothing. The three general types of treatment discussed here, however, have been widely used and accepted over the years.

Biological Therapies The use of **chemotherapy** (drugs) has grown at an amazing pace in the past three decades. Three major types of drugs are routinely used in private practice as well as in mental hospitals. The *antipsychotics* are tranquilizers that have a very powerful calming effect on the patient. *Antianxiety drugs,* such as Valium and Miltown, are minor tranquilizers that have a milder calming effect. *Antidepressants* are stimulants used to elevate mood and counteract depression.

The use of these chemicals has revolutionized the treatment of the mentally disordered, especially in mental institutions. Since the advent of the tranquilizing drugs, hospitals have been able to abandon straitjackets and similar restraining devices. The patients seem to have benefited remarkably. Many psychotics have been able to return to a reasonably normal life when they would otherwise have been required to remain in an institution.

But chemotherapy has vigorous opponents. Among them are ex-patients who have formed organizations such as NAPA (Network Against Psychiatric Assault) to oppose what they consider excessive chemotherapy. They charge that tranquilizers are used to keep patients quiet and manageable rather than to help them. Some former hospital patients have charged that drugs are used in a punitive way to maintain the authority and power of some staff members. Equally serious is the charge that chemotherapy treats symptoms, not causes. Few people deny the improvements brought about by modern drugs, but in many cases those drugs are used too often and for the wrong reasons. Drugs should be used only for the patient's benefit, not the staff's, and in combination with other therapy.

The use of **electroconvulsive therapy** (also known as ECT or shock treatment) has declined with the growing use of antidepressant drugs. However, shock therapy is still widely used. Many psychiatrists consider it an effective technique for dealing with severe depression, even though the reasons for its therapeutic effects are not known. But ECT, like chemotherapy, has come under attack in recent years. There is considerable evidence that it can cause hemorrhages, brain damage, and loss of memory.

Behavior Modification Based on the principles of learning theory discussed earlier, **behavioral therapy** aims to do exactly what the name implies: modify the behavior, not the personalities, of mentally disordered people. Behavioral therapists use a variety of specific techniques, depending on the type of problem under treatment. In all cases, however, the objective is to manipulate patients' environments in order to modify their behavior. Some behaviors are modified by removing the reinforcement (reward) for them. This is called **extinction.** For instance, if a young girl is disruptive in class, the therapist might suggest that her parents and teachers ignore her behavior, thereby cutting off the reward (attention) she receives from the behavior. **Systematic desensitization** is used to treat phobias and irrational anxieties. In this form of treatment the patient is gradually exposed to the feared stimulus so that the fear is slowly overcome. **Aversion therapy** is old-fashioned punishment with a few modern refinements. For example, behavioral therapists have treated alcoholics by administering a mild electric shock whenever the patient takes a drink. Therapy that employs rewards rather than punishment is also widely used to change inappropriate behaviors.

Behavior modification therapies are relatively recent arrivals on the therapeutic scene. They have had some remarkable successes, but they—like other therapies—have not been very successful with the most severe mental disorders, such as schizophrenia and extreme depression. Therapists who focus on personality problems say that behavioral therapy, like chemotherapy, deals only with symptoms, not with causes.

Psychotherapy There are so many different kinds of **psychotherapy** that it is impossible to discuss all of them here; however, most share certain common assumptions. Particularly important is the belief that mental disorders are symptoms of defective personalities. Therapy therefore consists of helping individuals first to understand and then to overcome the causes of their personality problems.

Psychoanalysis, one of the first and most influential psychotherapies, was founded by Sigmund Freud, an Austrian neurologist (1856–1939). It is a long-term procedure designed to uncover the repressed memories, motives, and conflicts that are assumed to be at the root of the client's psychological

problems. Techniques used in this procedure include free association (encouraging the patient to talk at length and without restriction), dream interpretation (analyzing the client's dreams for hidden, symbolic meanings), and
analysis of resistance (close examination of thoughts or ideas that the patient
is reluctant to discuss). Psychoanalytic therapy is often criticized for being
too slow and too expensive, for putting too much stress on sexual conflicts,
and for the failure to produce experimental evidence of its effectiveness.

Carl Rogers developed another popular technique called **client-centered
therapy,** or nondirective therapy.[35] Rogers saw men and women as basically
rational and good. He therefore believed that given the opportunity and a
little assistance, patients could work out their own problems. Unlike Freudians, Rogerian therapists do not try to guide or direct therapy sessions. The
client chooses the topic and sets the pace and direction of the session. It is
not assumed that therapists know more than clients. Therapists listen as
clients discuss their problems; they provide encouragement and support; and
they try to help clients clarify their own feelings and attitudes.

Another recent innovation in psychotherapeutic techniques is **group
therapy.** Some group therapy is merely individual therapy administered to
more than one client at a time. More commonly, the group itself is the therapist. Each individual is encouraged to reveal his or her problems and experiences to the group, which then discusses and examines them. Some
groups employ psychodrama in which the members are asked to take roles
and act out their problems; others conduct marathon sessions continuing
around the clock for several days.

The Mental Hospital   A mental hospital is much more than just a place where patients
are treated for mental problems. People who live in mental hospitals lead a
very different life from those who stay at home and make periodic visits to
a psychiatrist. Hospitalized patients are cut off from the outside world and
are closely supervised and controlled by staff members. Their personal needs
either are met by the institution or are not met at all. They live in what
Erving Goffman called a **total institution,** defined as "a place where a large
number of like-situated individuals, cut off from the wider society for an
appreciable period of time, together lead an enclosed, formally administered
round of life."[36]

The mental hospital is similar to other total institutions, such as boarding schools, monasteries, and army posts. But it resembles a prison most
closely. Indeed, some mentally disturbed persons are committed to prisons
and some criminals are committed to mental hospitals. The mental hospital
must try to meet two distinct goals: custody and treatment. No matter what
treatment methods are used, they must be administered within a custodial
framework. Patients, like prisoners, are policed to ensure that they do not
escape or injure one another. Only after these essentials have been provided
for can the remaining time and money be devoted to treatment.

But the budgets of most state mental hospitals are so meager that there
is not enough money for adequate custody, let alone treatment. This means

that there are hundreds of patients for each nurse, psychiatrist, psychologist, and social worker. Attendants are untrained and poorly educated, and the buildings are often old, dark, and gloomy. Patients must live in wards where they have little personal privacy. Clearly, the environment of most mental hospitals is hardly designed to brighten the spirits of those who are depressed and confused.

Goffman's study of a mental hospital revealed some of the perplexing problems faced by new patients.[37] They often come into the institution with a sense of betrayal, believing that they have been tricked and manipulated by their friends and family. Upon admission, they are stripped of their clothing and personal possessions. They are poked, prodded, examined, and classified by the hospital personnel with normal medical objectivity and detachment. These "degradation rituals" strip the patients of their identity and their dignity, and leave them confused and demoralized. It is little wonder that mental hospitals often do more harm than good, regardless of the treatment programs used.

D. L. Rosenhan conducted a series of experiments that dramatically demonstrated the labeling effect of commitment to a mental institution.[38] He had eight normal persons present themselves to several different mental hospitals, complaining of hearing voices. After admission, each of these bogus patients was told to act normally, making no further pretense at mental illness. Not one of the phonies was recognized or diagnosed as being sane. After an average stay of 19 days, they were released as schizophrenics "in remission." Rosenhan concluded that it is impossible to distinguish the "sane" from the "insane" in our mental hospitals because the environment in those institutions is so abnormal.[39] Critics of Rosenhan's research claim that the fact that the "patients" were only kept in the institution for a couple of weeks shows that the staff really did recognize that they were not severely disturbed.

Deinstitutionalization and Community Treatment   In recent years there has been a reaction against mental hospitals, and a growing movement to **deinstitutionalize** mental patients and return them to the community. By 1984 there were only about 20 percent as many people in mental hospitals in the United States as there were in 1955.[40] There were two main reasons for this major shift in the way we treat the severely mentally disturbed. The first was humanitarian. The recognition that bureaucratic total institutions are not very good places to help troubled people made many doubt the wisdom of sending so many people into mental hospitals. Civil libertarians also made strong protests against forcing people into an institution very much like a prison without the legal safeguards that we grant even the most dangerous criminals.[41] (See the debate in this chapter for a discussion of the pros and cons of involuntary commitment.) The second reason was financial. State and county governments across the nation discovered that mental patients could be treated more cheaply in community-based facilities than in mental hospitals.

DEBATE

Should the Government Be Allowed to Commit People to Mental Hospitals Against Their Will?

Yes Contrary to the claims of some radical psychiatrists and psychologists, mental illness is no myth. The unfortunate fact is that there are hundreds of thousands of people who are so mentally disturbed that they have lost all contact with reality. They forget to eat or wear proper clothing. They cannot keep a job or perform the other tasks necessary to live in our society. They are often homeless wanderers helplessly drifting from place to place with no direction or control of their lives. These people need the protection and care of a mental hospital. But the very problem that makes them need hospitalization also makes some resist all efforts to help them. Such unfortunate people must be committed to an institution even if they object. Otherwise, they will eventually do serious harm to themselves or someone else.

Opponents of involuntary commitment claim that it is a threat to our civil liberties, but there is no good evidence to support this contention. The Soviet Union and some other totalitarian societies have used mental hospitals as a weapon to imprison political dissidents, but there is little danger of similar abuses in a democratic society. If government officials tried to have their political opponents committed to mental institutions, there would be a deafening public outcry of the sort that is never heard in the Soviet Union. No system is perfect, and one can find cases of people who were wrongfully committed. But such things are rare, and current legal safeguards make it far more likely that we will be unable to commit someone

No It is a violation of fundamental human rights to lock innocent people up because someone thinks they have a "mental illness." Mental hospitals are nothing more than prisons by another name. The mentally disturbed should be given the same right to a fair trial that we give everyone else. If it can be proven that they have committed a crime, they should be sent to a prison or a "hospital." But if they have broken no law, they deserve no punishment.

Supporters of involuntary commitment make a host of false claims to justify this barbaric practice. First, they say that the government must protect society from the mentally disturbed. But very few of these people are dangerous, and those who are can be sent to prisons if they violate the law. Second, they claim that mental hospitals do not punish the mentally disturbed but help them. But taking away someone's freedom is extremely punitive, and that is why so many disturbed people would rather take their chances on the streets than live in a mental hospital. Third, they hold that these people are being committed in order to protect them. But since when is it the government's job to protect people from themselves? Those few persons who are so disturbed that they cannot even feed and clothe themselves do not usually object to a stay in a mental hospital, and those who do can be given food and shelter on the outside. The real reason we force these people into institutions is simply that we don't like to see them or talk to them on the streets.

who desperately needs it, than the other way around. The involuntary commitment of those who need psychiatric help provides a real service to them and to the community as a whole, and it must be continued.

The history of the Soviet Union's use of mental hospitals as jails to house its political opponents shows the dangers inherent in any system of involuntary commitment. We should abolish ours before any more harm is done.

Critics of deinstitutionalization argue that it is merely a convenient justification for ignoring the problems of the mentally disturbed. It is estimated that about a third of the nation's growing body of homeless men and women suffer from serious mental disorders. Former mental patients are commonly seen wandering aimlessly in city streets, eating food from garbage cans, and sleeping in alleys and parks. Although there seems little doubt that these people need more help than they are receiving, defenders of deinstitutionalization point out that the original intent of the reforms was never carried out. The idea behind deinstitutionalization was to treat fewer mental patients in hospitals and more in the community. But most of the mental patients who were released from the hospital never received adequate treatment on the outside. It is estimated that about two thousand community centers were needed to support deinstitutionalized mental patients, but only about seven hundred were ever built. Although about 63 percent of the persons with serious mental disorders are now at large in the community, two thirds of state and local funding still goes to mental institutions.[42]

It is therefore clear that a considerable increase in the funding for community-based mental health services is urgently needed. Despite all the failures of deinstitutionalization, well-organized community-based care still has many advantages for all but the most seriously disturbed patients. Patients who remain in the community during treatment avoid the shock of being taken out of their normal environment. They also escape the labeling, humiliation, and feeling of powerlessness that accompany institutionalization, and the painful readjustment period that follows it.

Most government-supported community health care centers offer five basic services: short-term hospitalization, partial hospitalization (allowing patients to return home at night or in the evenings), therapy for patients who live in the community, emergency care for special problems, and consultation and educational services for the community at large. These centers thus provide many more services than were previously available, ranging from one-time counseling to complete hospitalization.

In addition, other kinds of community programs can also help deal with the problems of the mentally disturbed. For example, physicians, teachers, police officers, and others who are likely to come into contact with people who need mental health care should be taught the best ways of handling those individuals and should be familiarized with agencies that can provide help. Many private organizations can also help meet community mental health needs. Citizens working without pay for agencies such as Hotline answer phone calls from people in need of help, refer them to appropriate agencies, try to head off suicides, or merely lend a sympathetic ear to lonely voices. "Free clinics" that attempt to meet a broad spectrum of poor people's health needs also offer counseling and therapy for mental problems.

Directions for the Future   Scientists and researchers have given more attention to mental disorders than to virtually any other social problem discussed in this book. A tremendous number of innovative approaches to prevention and treatment have been developed since World War II. One of the most promising new trends is toward the treatment of entire families in their home environment. This approach sees mental disorder as a process of interaction between two or more people, and thus, more than one person must be included in the treatment process. For instance, the parents of a disturbed child or the husband of a woman with severe depression can be taught more effective, less debilitating ways of interacting with the troubled person. More significant, the entire family can be taught to develop new patterns of interaction that will benefit each member of the family.

Investigation of the biochemical basis of mental disorders is another exciting frontier. Some researchers believe that they will soon be able to identify the exact biochemical process that generates schizophrenia and related disorders. Once such a discovery is made, it might then be possible to develop an effective treatment.

It seems unlikely, however, than any treatment—chemical, psychological, or social—will eliminate all mental disorders. We must therefore continue to learn how to interact with disturbed people and how to deal with them humanely when ordinary interaction is impossible. One giant step in this direction would be to stop using such stigmatizing labels as *insane*, *crazy*, and *nuts*. Most people scoff at Laing's suggestion that schizophrenics are really the sanest people among us. Yet if this attitude prevailed, it would bring us much closer to removing the shame and humiliation that now go hand in hand with mental disorders.

SOCIOLOGICAL PERSPECTIVES ON MENTAL DISORDERS

Although human beings experience an extraordinary array of thought patterns and behaviors, all cultures limit the amount of variation that it is permissible to display. These expectations about how people should think and act give a measure of stability and permanence to people's lives. Neverthless, in every culture there are individuals who seem unable to share in the reality experienced by others. They think and behave in ways that are incomprehensible to most members of their society. In contemporary societies these people are considered mentally disturbed, and the tools of science are used to explain and to change their behavior.

The Functionalist Perspective   Functionalism is a broadly based social theory that is primarily concerned with large groups and institutions. It does not attempt to account for the causes of mental disorders on the individual level. Rather, it examines the social conditions that affect the rates of mental disorder. Around the turn of the century, the famous French sociologist Émile Durkheim showed that suicide rates were higher among people who were not integrated into supportive social groups. Following Durkheim's lead, present-day functionalists argue that social disorganization, which tears people loose from their social supports, is a major cause of both suicide and mental disorders. According to the functionalists, people who live in disorganized societies have higher rates of mental disturbances than others. Moreover, people who live in disorganized neighborhoods have more psychological problems than those who live in more integrated communities. Functionalists often cite the high rates of schizophrenia in urban slums and ghettos as proof of this proposition.

Considerable disorganization can also be seen in the way treatment services are delivered, or not delivered. No one wants mental hospitals to be understaffed, and no one wants them to give greater priority to custody than to treatment. But inadequate financing and lack of strong community support makes it impossible for the staff or the administrators to be more effective. Thus, many aspects of mental hospitals and other treatment programs are dysfunctional. Crowding, depersonalization, and rejection of mental patients makes some of them worse rather than better.

Functionalists argue for a twofold attack on the problems of mental disorder. First, a concerted effort must be made to reduce social disorganization and bring lonely, isolated individuals back into a supportive social network. Second, mental hospitals and other treatment facilities must be improved. More money and more effort must be invested in a serious effort to help the mentally disordered. Community treatment programs should be expanded so that they can treat anyone who can benefit from their services. Mental hospitals should be reduced in size and reserved only for the most seriously disturbed patients. Hospital staffs must be better trained and large enough to give the kind of personal treatment that is often impossible today.

The Conflict Perspective   Like functionalists, conflict theorists do not pretend to explain the origins of all mental disorders. Instead, they are concerned with the forces that create the high rates of mental disorder in North America. To most conflict theorists, the origins of our psychological problems are to be found in the economic system. The North American economy is the most competitive in the world. Every individual is expected to engage in a constant struggle to succeed. The insecurity that results from this system produces intense feelings of anxiety and tension. And those pressures, in turn, produce high rates of mental disorder. Many conflict theorists agree with Laing's contention that mental disorders are a normal reaction to the insanity of modern society.

Conflict theorists are also interested in the way the incidence of mental disorder is distributed within a society. They are particularly concerned about the high rates of psychological disorders among the poor and under-privileged—which they believe to be the result of social, political, and economic exploitation that places great stress on poor people. Moreover, the alienation and powerlessness of most workers is itself a kind of mental disorder. Frustrations build up among people who can do little to change the conditions of their lives, and serious mental disturbances are often the result.

The system for delivering treatment services to the mentally disturbed also favors the rich and powerful, who receive private treatment from highly skilled professionals. The poor cannot afford such help, and their troubles are ignored until they create a disturbance. Then they are locked up in underfunded mental hospitals, where they receive little real help. In stark contrast to the individualized psychotherapy private therapists provide for those who can afford it, the poor can expect little more than massive doses of tranquilizers and perhaps group therapy led by a poorly trained and inexperienced therapist.

Conflict theorists recommend changes in our treatment programs. They generally believe that all funding for facilities should come from the government, so that everyone will receive the same high-quality care that only the rich can now afford. But in order to achieve a long-term solution to the problem of mental disorder, drastic social changes will be necessary. Conflict theorists advocate a restructuring of our economic system to reduce excessive competition and to eliminate exploitation of the workers and the poor.

Social Psychological Perspectives Because the problem of mental disorder is necessarily a social psychological matter, we have already discussed the social psychological perspectives in some detail. Each of the explanations of the causes of mental disorder described in this chapter are based on one of the major social psychological theories. Most of the therapeutic techniques we discussed were also developed from the ideas and perspectives contained in these theories. For example, behavior modification developed from the behaviorist perspective, while most psychotherapies have their roots in the personality or interactionist theories.

SUMMARY

The economic and personal costs of mental disorders are staggering. Nevertheless, there is no widespread agreement on the meaning of terms such as *mentally ill*, *insane*, *mentally disturbed*, and *crazy*. Those who support the mental-illness approach view mental problems the way they view measles and chicken pox; that is, each disordered person has a specific illness and may be helped by a specific treatment. Others advocate the personal-maladjustment approach, in which mental disorders are seen as products of the individual's inability to cope effectively with social life. Still others prefer the social-deviance approach, noting that people are labeled "mentally ill," "crazy," and so on, when they violate commonsense rules about how people are supposed to behave.

There is a lot of debate about the best way to classify mental disorders. The American Psychiatric Association's *Diagnostic and Statistical Manual of Mental Disorders* is the most widely used classification, but it still has many critics. Schizophrenia, which entails extreme disorganization in personality and thought pattern, is the most common diagnosis among hospitalized mental patients. Next most common are the substance abuse disorders, and then the mood disorders. Organic disorders caused by physical problems in the brain and paranoid disorders based on overpowering irrational fears are less common diagnoses.

A number of studies have investigated the relationship between social class and mental disorders. The general conclusion is that people in the lower classes are more likely than middle-class and upper-class people to have psychoses. However, it has not been established that this difference is due to emotional stress caused by poverty.

No single explanation of mental disorder is satisfactory. Biosocial theories contend that some mental disorders, such as schizophrenia, are caused by biochemical imbalances. Developmental theory holds that the source of each mental disorder is to be found in an individual's early psychological history. Although there are many versions of this theory, the basic idea is that mentally disordered patients are individuals who did not develop properly as children. Learning theorists see mental disorders as inappropriate behavior that is learned the way other behavior is learned. Stress theory holds that mental disorders result from strains imposed on individuals by the environment. Labeling theory contends that "mental illness" and "abnormality" are labels attached to individuals who behave in ways that others do not like.

The type of treatment a patient receives depends a great deal on the therapist. Biological therapies use tranquilizing and mood-elevating drugs, and electric shock. Behavior modification employs the principles of learning theory to reward appropriate behavior and extinguish inappropriate behavior. Psychotherapy applies a variety of techniques designed to give patients insight into the psychological bases of their problems, including psychoanalysis, client-centered therapy, and group therapy.

Many studies show that state mental hospitals are not good places to help mentally disordered people recover. The budgets of some hospitals are so low that little money is left for treatment once the expenses of custodial care have been met. Hospital patients experience the humiliation and degradation associated with life in "total institutions." Hospital populations are being reduced as more disturbed people are being deinstitutionalized and sent to community treatment centers. Unfortunately, far too few centers have been created, and the existing ones cannot deal with the flood of deinstitutionalized patients.

The three principal sociological perspectives on mental disorders attempt to describe the causes of such disorders and how they should be treated. To functionalists, mental disorders are caused or aggravated by the condition of the society and the immediate social environment. Even some aspects of treatment services are dysfunctional, making patients worse instead of better. Conflict theorists attribute the high incidence of mental disorder among the poor to alienation resulting from exploitation, which leads to frustration and serious breakdowns. The social psychological perspective consists of the biosocial theories, behavioral theories, personality theories, and interactionist theories.

KEY TERMS

affective disorder
chemotherapy
deinstitutionalization
mental disorder
neurosis

organic disorder
paranoid disorder
psychosis
psychotherapy
schizophrenia

FURTHER READINGS

Understanding Mental Disorder

Robert C. Carson, James N. Butcher, and James C. Coleman, *Abnormal Psychology and Modern Life*, 8th ed., Chicago, Ill., Scott, Foresman, 1988.

William Cockerham, *Sociology of Mental Disorder*, Englewood Cliffs, N.J.: Prentice-Hall, 1981.

Gerald N. Grob, *Mental Illness and American Society: 1875–1960*, Princeton, N.J.: Princeton University Press, 1983.

Labeling Theory

Thomas Scheff (ed.), *Labeling Madness*, Englewood Cliffs, N.J.: Prentice-Hall, 1975.

Thomas Szasz, *The Myth of Mental Illness*, rev. ed., New York: Harper & Row, 1974.

Responses to Mental Problems

David Mechanic, *Mental Health and Social Policy*, Englewood Cliffs, N.J.: Prentice-Hall, 1978.

Erving Goffman, *Asylums*, New York: Doubleday, 1961.

- Is drug use increasing or decreasing?
- Which drugs create the most serious problems?
- Why do people use drugs?
- How has legal repression affected drug use?
- How can we deal with the drug problem?

Chapter 13
DRUG USE

Few other social problems are surrounded by more myths and misinformation than drug use. The confusion starts with the very meaning of the term, for many people mistakenly believe that only illegal substances like heroin, cocaine, or marijuana are drugs. But alcohol and tobacco alter the minds and moods of those who use them and can be just as dangerous as the illicit drugs. Nor is drug use confined to a few ragged deviants on the margins of society. Drugs are a big business. Americans spend billions of dollars a year for coffee, tea, cocoa (which contains the stimulants caffeine and theobromine), tobacco, and alcohol, and the manufacturers of these products have a respected place among the corporate giants of today's economy.

One of the most widespread myths is that we are in the midst of a rising "drug epidemic." It is true that the use of most drugs increased rapidly in the 1960s and 1970s, but drug use has been declining in the last decade. The sales of whiskey, vodka, and most other distilled liquors have dropped every year since 1981. And although the population of the United States has grown significantly during the 1980s, there has been no increase in the amount of beer produced, and wine production has decreased by almost a third.[1] The percentage of tobacco smokers in the population decreased from 37 percent in 1970 to 30 percent in 1985.[2] Surveys show that the use of marijuana, the most popular illicit drug, peaked in about 1979 and has been decreasing steadily since then, as has the use of most other illicit drugs. The one major exception is cocaine, which gained in popularity in the early 1980s. But there is evidence that cocaine use peaked around 1986 and has also begun to decrease.[3]

One commonly held belief about the drug problem that is certainly not a myth is that it is widespread and extremely costly. According to the National Safety Council, about 60 percent of all drivers killed in automobile accidents have drunk enough alcohol to impair their driving skills. Alcohol abuse is estimated to cost over $25 billion each year in lost work days, medical expenses, and accidents. But some of the most tragic problems occur among adolescents who turn to drugs to escape the intense emotional problems that they face (see Chapter 9). According to government surveys, about 31 percent of Americans from age 12 to 17 use alcohol at least once a month, 12 percent use marijuana, and 2 percent cocaine.[4]

DRUGS AND DRUG ADDICTION

While everyone uses the terms *drug addiction* and *drug addict* at one time or another, *addiction* is a technical term that is difficult to define. In the broadest sense addiction refers to an intense craving for a particular substance. But this definition can be applied to almost any desire or craving, whether it is for ice cream, potato chips, or heroin. To avoid this problem, drug addiction is sometimes erroneously defined as the physiological dependence that a person develops after heavy use of a particular drug. Most addicts, however, experience periods when they "kick" their physical dependency, yet their psychological craving continues undiminished and they return to drug use as soon as possible. The most accurate definition therefore is that **addiction** is the intense craving for a drug that develops after a period of physical dependence stemming from heavy use.

Two essential characteristics of an addictive drug are tolerance and withdrawal discomfort. **Tolerance** is another name for the immunity to the effects of a drug that builds up after heavy use. For instance, if someone takes the same amount of heroin every day for a month, the last dose will have much less effect than the first. If the user wants the same psychological effect at the end of the month, the dosage must be increased. **Withdrawal** discomfort is the sickness that habitual users experience when they stop taking drugs. Addictive drugs produce both tolerance and withdrawal distress. Drugs that produce tolerance but no withdrawal discomfort, such as LSD, are not addictive.

Drug addiction is not solely a physiological matter, however. Psychological craving supplements biological dependence. Moreover, the behavior of those who use specific drugs is influenced by cultural expectations that are quite independent of the drug's physiological effects. For example, anyone who drinks a large quantity of alcohol will pass out—a physiological reaction. But behavior while drunk but not dead drunk varies greatly from culture to culture and even from group to group within a culture.[5] Many people erroneously believe that alcohol reduces inhibitions and generates violent behavior through its effects on body chemistry. It is true that some people do indeed become less inhibited when drinking alcohol, but this is because they have learned to behave in that way when drinking, not because of changes in body chemistry. Thus, it is just as important to understand individual and group attitudes toward a drug as it is to understand its physiological effects (see Figure 13.1).

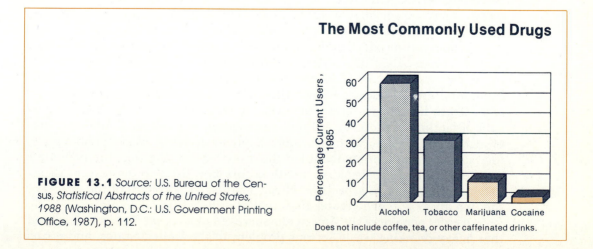

FIGURE 13.1 *Source:* U.S. Bureau of the Census, *Statistical Abstracts of the United States, 1988* (Washington, D.C.: U.S. Government Printing Office, 1987), p. 112.

The Most Commonly Used Drugs

Percentage Current Users, 1985

Alcohol Tobacco Marijuana Cocaine

Does not include coffee, tea, or other caffeinated drinks.

Alcohol The use of alcohol is an accepted part of our culture. Business people make deals over three-martini lunches, college students escape the pressures of final exams with a keg of beer, restaurants offer champagne brunches and expensive wine lists, and of course there are the neighborhood bars that serve as social centers for many local residents. The fact that alcohol is so widely accepted and so widely used means that it creates more problems than other drugs. As the National Commission on Marijuana and Drug Abuse put it: "Alcohol dependence is without question the most serious drug problem in this country today."[6]

Alcohol, like most other drugs, is rather harmless when used in moderation (except in the case of pregnant women), but is extremely dangerous when used to excess. Alcohol is called a **depressant** because it depresses the activity of the central nervous system and thereby interferes with coordination, reaction time, and reasoning ability. Large doses of alcohol produce disorientation, loss of consciousness, and even death. As has already been noted, the psychological reaction to alcohol varies from person to person, from group to group, and from culture to culture. However, the physiological effects of alcohol clearly increase as the level of alcohol in the blood increases. The effects of alcohol first become apparent when the concentration of alcohol in the blood reaches 0.05 percent, and extreme intoxication occurs at 0.25 percent. A user with over 0.4 percent blood alcohol is likely to pass out, and concentrations over 0.6 percent are usually fatal.[7]

Prolonged heavy drinking may generate a number of health problems. Alcoholic beverages are high in calories but have little other food value. For this reason, heavy drinkers often lose their appetite and suffer from malnutrition. The harmful effects of excessive drinking on the liver are well known; the end result may be cirrhosis, a condition in which liver cells are destroyed by alcohol and replaced by scar tissue. Heavy drinkers are more likely than others to have many types of heart problems, and there is evidence that they suffer from a higher rate of cancer as well. The drinkers' problems may also be passed on to their children. Studies show that the children of alcoholic mothers have lower birth weights, slower language development, lower IQs, and more birth defects than other children.[8]

Alcohol will produce addiction if used in sufficient amounts over a long period. The so-called DTs (short for *delirium tremens*) are actually symptoms of alcohol withdrawal. These symptoms commonly include nausea, vomiting, and convulsions; sometimes they involve hallucinations and coma as well. Death from heart failure or severe convulsions occurs in about 10 percent of victims of the DTs. A much more common cause of death is the use of alcohol in combination with other depressant drugs. Many people have, for example, unintentionally killed themselves by taking sleeping pills after an evening of heavy drinking. Death occurs because two depressant drugs taken together have a *synergistic* effect. That is, the strength of the effects of the two drugs is much greater than that of either drug taken alone.

Over 90 percent of the Americans surveyed in a recent Harris poll agreed that heavy drinking was a serious problem in the United States, and a surprising 32 percent reported that someone in their household has a drinking problem.[9] It is doubtful that all these persons should be considered alcoholics, but the term is often used so loosely that anyone who takes more than an occasional drink might be included. For the purposes of this book, we will define an **alcoholic** as a person whose drinking problem disrupts his or her life, interfering with the ability to hold a job, accomplish household tasks, or participate in family and social affairs. Although many people use alcohol as a means of improving their self-esteem, in the long run it usually has the opposite effect. Statistics suggest that alcoholics can expect to die 10 to 12 years sooner than other people. Estimates of the number of alcoholics in the United States range from 8 to 17 million, more than the total number of users of most illicit drugs.[10]

Alcohol causes thousands of deaths on the highway every year. In 1986 about 24,000 people died in accidents in which the driver had been drinking.[11] As a result of this huge death toll, the victims of drunken drivers and other concerned citizens have banded together in organizations such as MADD (Mothers Against Drunk Drivers) to publicize the problem and push for stiffer punishments for drunk drivers. The new concern about this problem seems to be having some positive effects. That 1986 death toll actually represents a significant decline from the 28,000 to 30,000 who were dying a few years before.[12] A survey of college students by Hanson and Engs found that the percentage reporting having driven after having had too much to drink dropped from 41 percent in 1982 to 35 percent in 1988.[13] In addition to the problem of drunk driving, alcohol is also involved in about a third of all suicides, half of all murders and sexual assaults, and the majority of all violent incidents in the home.[14]

19th-Century Social Problems

The beer garden recently started on this side of the river, by permission of our town board, continues to grow offensive. The rabble from the city and the country meet there and sometimes form nothing less than drunken mobs. It is not safe for women to pass along the road near this place. Bloody fights are of a daily occurrence and drunken men may be found lying around in the bushes on all sides. Wife whipping has come into vogue since the new institution was forced upon us. . . . What it may end in need hardly be conjectured.

July 10, 1890

These selections, which appear throughout the text, are from the *Badger State Banner*, a newspaper published in Black River Falls, Wisconsin.

Studies show that around 70 percent of all adults in the United States drink alcoholic beverages.[15] After years of steady increases, the use of alcohol by both juveniles and adults has now begun to decrease. However, the prevalence of drinking varies widely among different social and ethnic groups. Most studies indicate that more men drink (about 75 percent) than women (about 65 percent), but that drinking has been increasing among women as they have gained more freedoms and taken on more financial burdens. The prevalence of drinking is greatest among the college educated and those with higher incomes.[16] It is estimated that about 80 percent of all college students drink, and student alcoholism is a serious problem on campuses throughout North America.[17] Despite their visibility, skid-row alcoholics who live on the streets or in cheap hotels known as flophouses make up fewer than one of every twenty alcoholics.[18]

Tobacco   About 30 percent of Americans over the age of 17 smoke cigarettes, and the percentage of adolescent smokers between 12 and 17 is about half that number.[19] Men smoke more than women, but the use of tobacco has been declining more rapidly among men (see Figure 13.2.), and teenage girls are now actually more likely to smoke than teenage boys.[20] About 70 percent of all smokers use more than 15 cigarettes a day, making tobacco one of the few drugs that addicts use practically every waking hour of every day.[21] The sales of tobacco, like those of alcohol, have been declining in recent years. Since 1981 the number of cigarettes sold in the United States has decreased more than 2.5 percent a year.[22]

The principal drug in tobacco is nicotine, which is clearly addictive. Withdrawal symptoms include drowsiness, nervousness, anxiety, headaches, and loss of energy. Nicotine is a **stimulant** that raises blood pressure, speeds up the heartbeat, and gives the user a sense of alertness. However, nicotine

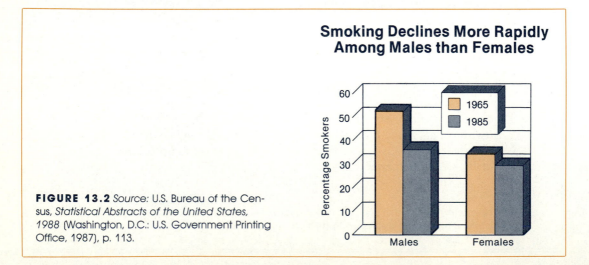

FIGURE 13.2 *Source:* U.S. Bureau of the Census, *Statistical Abstracts of the United States, 1988* (Washington, D.C.: U.S. Government Printing Office, 1987), p. 113.

also seems to have the contradictory effect of producing a feeling of relaxation and calm in the user. Some claim that this relaxation is due to the ritual of smoking and not the drug itself, but the issue remains unclear.[23]

In 1964 the Surgeon General's Advisory Committee on Smoking and Health issued its famous report concluding that smoking is hazardous to health, and since then the annual report issued by the federal government has painted an ever bleaker picture of the effects of smoking on health. Commenting on the particularly detailed 1979 report, the Secretary of Health, Education and Welfare said that it: "reveals with dramatic clarity that cigarette smoking is even more dangerous—indeed, far more dangerous—than was supposed in 1964."[24] In issuing the 1988 report, the Surgeon General took another major step by forcefully acknowledging the addictive properties of nicotine and its similarity to heroin and other illegal drugs.[25]

Cigarette smoking has been linked to cancer of the larynx, mouth, and esophagus, as well as to lung cancer. Other diseases linked to smoking include bronchitis, emphysema, ulcers, and heart and circulatory disorders. It is estimated that smoking more than two packs a day reduces normal life

As cigarette sales have weakened, tobacco companies have developed cigarette brands aimed at specific groups such as women and blacks.

expectancy by eight years and that light smoking (half a pack a day or less) reduces it by four years. The babies of women who smoke weigh less than other babies and have slower rates of physical and mental growth.[26] Recent statistics from the U.S. Public Health Service indicate that tobacco kills far more people than all other drugs combined.[27]

Why, then, do so many people smoke? One reason is that cigarette smoking is addictive and most smokers find it difficult to stop. But what about the substantial number of young people who begin smoking for the first time every year, despite medical warnings? Most young people surely have heard warnings about the health hazards of smoking, but many pay little heed. The answer seems to be that the tobacco industry has succeeded in establishing an association in the public mind between smoking and maturity, sophistication, and sexual attractiveness. Cigarette manufacturers spend billions of dollars a year advertising their products, and the smokers in those ads are invariably young, good looking models and actors with strong sex appeal. As the sales of cigarettes have decreased in recent years, the tobacco industry has responded with ever more sophisticated marketing campaigns targeted at very specific groups. The popularity of smoking among women is certainly related to the special efforts the tobacco companies have made to encourage them to smoke, and similar campaigns have been directed at blacks and Hispanics.[28] Not surprisingly, the rates of lung cancer and other respiratory diseases have shown an alarming increase among these groups in recent years.[29]

Caffeine Caffeine is the most widely used stimulant in the world. It is found in coffee, tea, cola drinks, and even chocolate candy. Caffeine is a weak stimulant, but it produces many of the effects of stronger ones: increased alertness, restlessness, and the alleviation of fatigue. Mild doses taken in coffee, tea, or other beverages produce little tolerance or withdrawal symptoms. Higher doses of caffeine (five or more cups of coffee) produce mild withdrawal discomfort including depression and a jittery, nervous feeling. These higher doses may produce agitation and insomnia; and extremely large amounts can be fatal, although there are only six known cases in which this has occurred.[30]

The debate about the effects of more normal doses of caffeine has raged on for years. At various times caffeine has been accused of causing heart disease, cancer, low blood sugar, and birth defects, among other ailments. But current research has failed to substantiate any of these claims. Voltaire, the famous French philosopher and avid coffee drinker, seems to have summed things up quite accurately when he said that, "It is poison, certainly—but a slow poison—for I have been drinking it these 84 years."[31]

Marijuana Marijuana is the most widely used illegal drug. About one in four Americans say that they have tried marijuana, and a little less than one in ten are classified as current users (that is, they report using the drug at least once within the previous month). Marijuana use is most frequent among those between 18 to 25 years of age and drops off sharply after age 35. Marijuana is more popular among males than females and among those who live in the Northeast and on the Pacific coast.[32] The evidence indicates that the use of marijuana increased sharply during the 1960s and 1970s, but like most other drugs, marijuana use has been decreasing in the 1980s.

Marijuana has been subject to an unusually long-running and intense scrutiny. Starting with the 3000-page Indian Hemp Drugs Commision Report published in 1894, there have been dozens of lengthy reports on marijuana and its effects on the user. In the 1980s alone, there were major reports by the National Academy of Sciences, the World Health Organization, the Institute of Medicine, and the National Institute on Drug Abuse.[33] It is generally agreed that the measurable effects of marijuana use are not very dramatic: an increase in heart rate, a reddening of the eyes, a dryness in the mouth, and a disruption in short-term memory. There is a continuing debate about whether or not users develop a tolerance to marijuana, since first-time users often report feeling no effects at all. If there is a buildup of tolerance it is a rather weak one. Similarly, it is possible to induce a withdrawal syndrome among experimental subjects given extremely large doses of THC (tetrahydrocannabinol, the active ingredient in marijuana), but there is only one recorded case of marijuana withdrawal occurring outside the laboratory.[34]

The health hazards of marijuana are still the subject of an emotional debate that has often had more to do with politics than with objective scientific research. Like caffeine, numerous claims have been made about the damage caused by marijuana smoking that have later proven to be false. The current evidence indicates that the main health hazard in marijuana use is the risk of cancer and other lung problems caused by inhaling the smoke. Some studies indicate that the way marijuana is usually smoked (deep inhalations which are held for a long time) makes it more damaging than tobacco, puff for puff.[35] However, this is more than offset by the greater number of cigarettes smoked by tobacco users. Two or three "joints" a day is considered heavy marijuana use (the fact that marijuana is usually shared among a group of people means that each user smokes less), whereas many heavy tobacco users smoke more than 50 cigarettes a day. There is also enough evidence that marijuana may harm a user's unborn baby to strongly recommend that pregnant women do not use the drug. Thus, those who claim that marijuana is harmless are wrong: there are clearly significant health hazards involved in the excessive use of marijuana. However, it is also clear that marijuana is less dangerous than alcohol, tobacco, cocaine, and most of the other widely used recreational drugs.[36]

The psychological effects of smoking marijuana are strongly influenced by the social environment and the expectations of the users. Howard S. Becker has shown that users must learn from their peers how to identify the effects of the drug before they actually get "high."[37] Descriptions of the drug's psychological effects vary considerably from one person to another. Typical effects include euphoria, relaxation, increased sensitivity, and hunger. Although those who use marijuana occasionally tend to report more negative reactions than those who use it frequently, reactions, whether positive or negative, probably reflect the expectations of the users more than the effects of the drug itself. Orcutt has shown that the more contact a marijuana user has with the drug subculture, the less likely he or she is to have a negative experience.[38]

Opiates The **opiates** are a group of natural (opium, codeine, morphine, and heroin) and synthetic (meperidine, methadone) drugs with similar chemical compositions. The pain-relieving properties of the opiates are extremely important to modern medicine. Although people who are under the influence of an opiate can still feel pain, it no longer seems to bother them. Just as opiates relieve physical pain, they deaden psychological distress. Other physiological effects of opiates include reduced rates of metabolism and respiration. Psychologically, the opiates tend to induce a state of tranquility, peace, or euphoria.[39]

All opiates are highly addictive. Users rapidly develop a tolerance and must continually increase their dosage to get the same effects. Although the intensity of opiate withdrawal distress varies with the amount being taken and with the individual involved, withdrawal seldom causes the screaming agony depicted in so many books and movies. Withdrawal distress usually resembles a bad case of the flu accompanied by a feeling of severe depression. In some cases, however, it can be much more severe.

Opiate addiction has severe consequences for the health of the addict. Ironically, most of these problems come not from the drug itself but from the way in which it is used. When addicts receive a continuous supply of pure drugs in a reasonably sanitary environment, drug use does not make

19th-Century Social Problems

We are about to have a gold cure institute in this city. Dr. A. E. White and E. Krohn have purchased the right for this section to use the celebrated improved "Tri Chloride of Gold Cure" and are about to establish here an institution for the cure of the liquor, opium, morphine, and tobacco habits. . . . They guarantee a cure for a stipulated fee. The time required for treatment is 3 weeks. The patient is required to deposit the full fee in the bank, payable to the doctors when a cure is perfected, the patient agreeing to follow directions strictly. Medicine is taken internally every 2 hours, and 4 hypodermic injections are given each day. . . . We presume they will have few patients for the cure of other than the liquor habit.

June 2, 1892

them ill.[40] However, the opiate addict's life-style, as well as impure drugs and infected needles, produce severe health problems. Addicts often share the same needles without proper sterilization, and this spreads disease. Until recently, hepatitis, a serious liver infection, was the most serious problem. But intravenous drug users are now stalked by a much more deadly disease: AIDS. Almost a quarter of all AIDS sufferers are intravenous drug users, and a majority of the addicts in some cities are believed to be infected with the virus.[41] Death from overdose is another threat to the addict's survival, and is a major cause of death among young males in many big American cities. In many cases, however, death can more properly be attributed to the combination of opiates with other depressant drugs such as alcohol. A new problem comes from the synthetic opiates derived from an anesthetic known as fentanyl. Some of these new drugs are as much as 10,000 times stronger than heroin, and if cut incorrectly, they can be killers.

Despite all the publicity, opiate use is actually quite rare. The latest survey by the National Institute on Drug Abuse did not find a single group in which the percentage of current heroin users exceeded 0.5 percent.[42] Well over half of all heroin addicts in the United States live in its three largest cities, with the heaviest concentration in New York City. Addiction is an urban phenomenon in Canada as well, with its major center in Vancouver. Despite some increase in heroin use among middle-class people, most addicts are young males from the poorest segments of society.

If opiate use is so uncommon, why is there so much concern about it? For one thing, heroin addicts project a very dramatic image that fits well into the plots of books, television shows, and movies. Almost everyone has seen or read about the skinny, haggard "junkie" prowling the streets in a desperate search for the money to buy his next "fix" (injection of heroin). Although most fictional descriptions of junkies are greatly distorted, the stories do contain a grain of truth. Most heroin addicts depend on crime to support their habits, and some will do almost anything to get a "fix." However, not all heroin users fit this stereotype. There are more addicts in the medical profession than in any other occupation, yet they are seldom involved in crime or violence. There are also many addicts who must buy their drugs at high black-market prices but do not commit crimes to support their habits.[43]

Psychedelics   Although the physiological effects of the **psychedelics** are rather slight, they produce greater psychological changes in the user than any other drugs. There are many different psychedelic drugs. LSD (lysergic acid diethylamide) and mescaline are among the most popular in North America. The use of peyote cactus (from which mescaline is derived) has a long history among native Americans. It seems to have been an important element in their religions long before Europeans came to the continent. The use of peyote continues today as a central part of the ritual of the Native American Church of North America, which claims 250,000 members from various tribes. The members of this church have been successful in defeating government efforts to ban their use of peyote.[44] MDMA (methylenedioxymeth-amphetamine), one of the newest arrivals on the drug scene, has some psychedelic effects and is chemically related to both mescaline and the amphetamines. Sometimes known as "ecstasy" when sold on the streets, the drug is the center of a controversy between some psychiatrists, who believe that it is a useful therapeutic tool, and drug enforcement officials, who have succeeded in banning its use.

Unlike mescaline, LSD is completely synthetic. Colorless and tasteless, a tiny dose of LSD produces a tremendous psychological effect that is highly unpredictable. Some users report an intensely beautiful experience, whereas others find it the most frightening experience of their lives, and still others swing from one extreme to the other on the same "acid trip." Aside from such profound emotional changes, the psychedelics also produce hallucinations and perceptual distortions. Colors and smells often appear more intense or uniquely beautiful under the influence of these drugs.

Users of psychedelic drugs rapidly develop a tolerance, but most of these drugs produce no withdrawal symptoms. Few people become heavy (once a week or more) psychedelic users, and those who do usually give up the drug after a few years. Although some have charged that LSD produces brain damage and birth defects, there is little evidence to support this claim.[45]

The greatest dangers of psychedelic drugs are psychological rather than physical. The "bad trip"—a terrifying experience that often throws the user into a panicky state—is always a possibility, especially among inexperienced users. Such bad trips have apparently brought on serious mental disorders in some susceptible persons. Because the environment is so important in determining whether a psychedelic experience is wonderful or terrifying, many users take the drug with a "guide" who understands the effects of the drug and can help point them in the right direction. Another psychological problem associated with these drugs is the "flashback": a reoccurrence of the psychedelic state that can occur unexpectedly weeks or even months after the last use of the drug.

Sedative-Hypnotics   **Sedative-hypnotics,** such as barbiturates and tranquilizers, depress the central nervous system. In moderate doses, these drugs slow down breathing and normal reflexes, interfere with coordination, and relieve anxiety and tension. Speech becomes slurred, the mind clouded. In larger doses, they produce drowsiness and sleep. Medically, these drugs are used to produce two effects: relaxation (sedation) and sleep (hypnosis).

The sedative-hypnotics are popular both with recreational users and as a treatment for such problems as insomnia and persistent anxiety. Taken as a whole, the sedative-hypnotics rank as the third most frequently used illegal drugs behind marijuana and cocaine.[46] However, there are many different drugs in this category, and by themselves none of them approaches the popularity of either marijuana or cocaine.

Among recreational users, the barbiturates are the most popular of the sedative-hypnotics. The psychological effects of barbiturates are similar to those of alcohol. Indeed, the state of intoxication that barbiturates produce is often indistinguishable from alcoholic drunkenness. And, like alcohol, the barbiturates are addictive. Repeated doses produce a growing tolerance, and heavy use can produce severe withdrawal distress when terminated. Addiction to barbiturates differs from addiction to opiates in two significant respects. First, physical dependence develops much more slowly; thus, the doses required to induce sleep will not usually be addictive. Second, withdrawal symptoms are more severe and may cause hallucinations, restlessness, and disorientation. Barbiturate withdrawal is fatal for about one in every twenty persons who abruptly terminate their habit. Alcohol and barbiturates are similar enough that the use of one will prevent the withdrawal symptoms caused by the other. When taken at the same time, these drugs have a synergistic effect that makes their combination much more dangerous than either taken alone.[47]

Methaqualone, known under the brand names of Quaalude and Sopor, is not chemically a barbiturate. However, its effects are very similar to those of barbiturates. Originally synthesized in the 1950s, a heavy advertising campaign a decade later promoted methaqualone to physicians as a safe nonbarbiturate sleeping pill. The result was a massive increase in prescriptions for what physicians believed to be a nonaddictive aid to sleep. The drug soon caught on among recreational users in the black market as well. In reality, however, methaqualone is as highly addictive as the barbiturates, and the loss of coordination it produces is even greater.[48] In the 1980s methaqualone declined in popularity as its dangers became more widely known and law enforcement cracked down on its use.

A large number of tranquilizers are now on the market that are prescribed for various psychological problems. Some are so strong that they are seldom used except in the treatment of severely disturbed mental patients, but "minor" tranquilizers are widely used by the public to reduce tension and to relieve anxiety. Librium and Miltown are well-known brand names of minor tranquilizers, and they are sometimes used for recreational as well as medical purposes. Valium has become particularly popular among drug users. Although many people believe this drug to be harmless, it actually has many of the same effects and dangers as the barbiturates. Valium is addictive and will produce a withdrawal syndrome when heavy use is discontinued.

Another popular illicit drug first synthesized by pharmaceutical companies in the 1950s is phencyclidine, often known as PCP or angel dust. In low doses it usually produces a sleepy, dreamlike state similar to that produced by other sedatives, although the effects may vary considerably from one person to another. In larger doses it produces hallucinations, and therefore PCP is sometimes classified as a psychedelic drug. Still larger doses of PCP produce unconsciousness, and for this reason it has been used as a surgical anesthetic. PCP is reputed to cause fits of uncontrollable violence in some users and has been a subject of growing national concern in recent years. Unfortunately, little reliable research on the illicit use of PCP has been conducted to date.[49]

Amphetamines   The amphetamines are a group of synthetic stimulants that includes benzedrine, dexedrine, and methedrine. These drugs used to be widely used as "diet pills," although more and more physicians are turning to other methods to help patients lose weight. They reduce the appetite, increase blood pressure, and increase the rate of breathing. In moderate doses they produce increased alertness, even excitement. Continuous heavy doses of an amphetamine produce a psychosislike state that is often indistinguishable from schizophrenia. Fear and suspicion are common symptoms, and fits of violent aggression may occur. Hallucinations, delusions, and general personal confusion are also common. Amphetamines produce tolerance with repeated use, and withdrawal symptoms, mainly severe depression, also occur.

Most amphetamine users take the drug orally in pill form, but some inject it directly into the bloodstream, producing a brief but extremely intense high or "rush." Such heavy use takes a tremendous toll on the health of the user, and so-called speed freaks often go on "runs" lasting several days, during which they get no sleep or proper nutrition. Long-term users lose their hair, teeth, and a large portion of their normal body weight. And, of course, the amphetamine-induced psychosis becomes increasingly severe.[50]

Cocaine   Cocaine is a natural stimulant derived from the leaves of the coca plant, which Peruvians have chewed for at least fifteen hundred years. Until 1906 it was a major ingredient of Coca-Cola and a number of patent medicines. The effects of cocaine are similar to the effects of amphetamines except for two differences. First, cocaine is a powerful local anesthetic; second, the effects of cocaine are not as intense and do not last as long as those of amphetamines. This means that cocaine users often repeat their doses every hour or so as the effects wear off. Because of this difference, and because cocaine is more expensive than amphetamines, psychotic reactions from cocaine use are less common, but they still occur. Heavy cocaine use also produces other adjustment problems, not the least of which is the financial burden of paying for the drug. Many wealthy cocaine users report having spent hundreds of thousands of dollars on their drug habit. Recent evidence indicates that a few individuals are biologically unable to metabolize cocaine, which may explain the cocaine-related deaths of several well-known athletes.[51]

Most users sniff cocaine powder into their nose through a tube or straw. Heavy users who "snort" cocaine in this way often suffer damage to the nasal passages and a constantly runny nose. Smoking cocaine has grown increasingly popular in recent years because it produces a very intense and immediate high, but it also has the potential to produce serious lung damage as well.[52] Street cocaine cannot, however, be smoked until it is chemically treated in a process known as freebasing. In response to the increasing popularity of freebasing, dealers introduced "crack": a special form of cocaine that comes in a small "rock" that can be smoked immediately without fur-

Cocaine is one of the few drugs whose use has sharply increased during the 1980s.

ther chemical treatment. The enormous popularity of this new drug among hard-core drug users has created serious problems both for law enforcement and for the communities in which such drug users live. In addition to the damage to the users' health, many cities have experienced a series of gang wars between different groups trying to control this lucrative new trade.

In the early part of this century cocaine use was concentrated mainly among poor blacks, but the demographics of cocaine use have changed dramatically since then. In the 1970s and early 1980s, cocaine became known as a "rich man's drug" because of its high cost and popularity among the middle class. However, the increasing use of crack among members of the underclass, as well as more negative attitudes in the middle class, seems to be reshaping the demographics of cocaine use once again.

A number of famous athletes and entertainers have voluntarily admitted having a cocaine problem, and other users have been uncovered in a series of scandals that have rocked all the major professional sports in the United States. There is, however, no reason to believe that cocaine use is more common among athletes than among the members of other highly paid professions. Athletes are simply more visible to the public. Almost 3 percent of the people in the United States over the age of 12 use cocaine; so it is not surprising that they are represented in all occupational groups.[53]

WHY USE DRUGS?

Researchers seem to be fascinated with the question of why we use drugs. A tremendous amount of effort has gone into the investigation of this topic, much of it on the assumption that if we can find out why people take drugs, we can find ways of preventing them from doing so. Most explanations are based on one or more of the social psychological perspectives.

Biological Theories Many believe that drug problems are caused by the nature of the drugs themselves: once someone takes too much of a drug he or she become addicted and is simply unable to stop. Although such theories are probably most popular with the general public, biological explanations of drug problems have also won increasing attention from scientists in the last decade. One of the earlier theories was advanced by Vincent Dole and Marie Nyswander, founders of the famous methadone treatment for heroin addiction.[54] They argued that people have different "neurological susceptibilities" to opiates. If susceptible individuals use an opiate, they quickly develop a "drug hunger" that continues even when they are no longer physically dependent. Because people become addicts for physiological reasons, Dole and Nyswander argue, addicts should be given methadone to keep their drug hunger under control until a chemical cure is found. But Dole and Nyswander's theory remains a weak one because they never specified what makes someone susceptible to this drug hunger, nor did they present convincing evidence that this susceptibility has biological origins.

More recent research has tended to focus on alcohol rather than opiates. A Danish study found that 65 percent of people whose identical twin was an alcoholic became alcoholics themselves, compared with only 25 percent for nonidentical twins. Although much of this difference may be due to the fact that identical twins are treated more similarly than fraternal twins are, some studies indicate that alcoholism in adopted children correlates more closely with the alcoholism of biological parents than with the alcoholism of adoptive parents.[55] In one of the best-known biological theories of alcoholism, E. M. Jellinek argued that it is a disease with a consistent pattern of symptoms and not voluntary behavior.[56] More recent research has attempted to find the exact biochemical reason that one person is more susceptible to alcoholism than another. The evidence shows that alcoholics have higher levels of a chemical (acetaldehyde) that is produced by the metabolic breakdown of alcohol in the body. Some hold that these high levels of acetaldehyde are the result, not the cause, of alcoholism. But others argue that persons who are better able to metabolize alcohol are more likely to become alcoholics. Because they show a higher tolerance to the effects of alcohol, such persons drink more heavily, which in turn produces more of the chemicals that create the physical addiction to alcohol.[57]

We must, however, be careful not to let the impressive findings of the new biological research lead us to unwarranted conclusions. Although there apparently is a genetic predisposition toward particular drug problems in some individuals, drug use is still learned behavior that is created and controlled by society. There are no alcoholics or heroin addicts in cultures where the use of those drugs is unknown or is practiced only in tightly controlled ritual situations. Today's drug problems are so much more severe than they were two hundred years ago because of the wrenching changes brought on by industrialization, not because there has been a genetic change in our population. But although biological theories cannot explain the historical changes in drug consumption or the reasons that drug problems are so much worse in big cities than in traditional small towns, they do help us understand why one person develops a drug problem while another person with similar experiences and background does not.

Behavioral Theory   Psychologists have done extensive studies of the effects of drug use on animals. They have found that animals can be trained to use drugs and that some become habituated. Behaviorists argue that such experiments show that drug use is learned through a process of conditioning. The use of a drug often provides a reward (positive reinforcement), and when experimental animals or humans use a drug and find it rewarding, they are likely to use it again.

Alfred Lindesmith turns this behavioral theory on its head.[58] Rather than being attracted to a pleasant experience, he says, the addict is trying to escape the unpleasant experience of withdrawal distress (negative reinforcement). According to Lindesmith, addicts use drugs so frequently to relieve withdrawal discomfort that they begin to associate the drug with the relief it brings. They continue to use drugs even when there is no physiological dependence because they associate drug use with the elimination of discomfort and pain.

The basic idea behind behavioral theory—that people use drugs because they find them pleasurable and continue to use them because doing so prevents withdrawal distress—is not new. The behaviorist contribution lies in careful examination of the learning processes that promote or discourage drug use.

Personality Theories   Many psychologists have tried to explain drug problems by investigating users' personalities. However, there is no general agreement among psychologists about the personality characteristics of addicts and drug abusers. Drug addicts have thus been classified as narcissists, psychopaths, sociopaths, dependent personalities, immature, schizophrenic, neurotic, and character disordered, to list only a few of the labels used.

The most common theory is that alcoholics and drug addicts have weak personalities and low self-esteem and therefore turn to drugs to try to escape their problems. G. E. Barnes, for example, argued that there is an "alcoholic personality" that displays such characteristics as "neuroticism, weak ego, stimulus augmenting [a hypersensitivity to the environment that results in fear and anxiety], and field dependency [a passive-dependent orientation to life]."[59] Because these characteristics may be a response to alcoholism rather than its cause, psychologists also talk about a "prealcoholic personality." The characteristics that are believed to lead to alcoholism include impulsivity, gregariousness, and nonconformity.[60]

Isador Chein and his associates reached similar conclusions about their sample of heroin addicts.[61] They found that heroin addicts have major personality disorders originating in the addicts' early family histories. The mother was usually the most important parent figure to the child, with the father cold or even hostile. Children from these homes were found to be overindulged or frustrated, and were uncertain of the standards they were expected to observe. These conditions were said to produce such personality traits as passivity, defensiveness, and low self-esteem.

Critics of these studies charge that they are little more than a reflection of the popular stereotypes that condemn those who suffer from drug problems. They argue that heavy drug users have as many diverse personality characteristics as any other group of people, and that the findings of these psychologists are based on their own prejudices and the fact that those with inadequate personalities are more likely to come to them for treatment. Support for this position comes from an unusually comprehensive 40-year longitudinal study of 660 young men drawn both from Harvard University and from an inner-city slum. Although the study found a strong correlation between alcoholism in the parents and the children, no personality differences were found between those who became alcoholics and those who did not.[62]

Despite weaknesses in these theories, there is no question that personality plays a critical role in a person's decision to use a drug. The problem is that there is no single type of personality that is most likely to lead to addiction. A great number of learned behavior patterns and personality traits interact in a given environment either to promote or to discourage drug use.

Interactionist Theory   Most social psychologists see drug use merely as one more behavior pattern that is learned from interaction with others in our culture. They observe, for example, that most people in our society drink alcohol, not because they have some personality defect or a biological urge to drink, but because drinking is a widely accepted cultural pattern. Most children see adults use alcohol, and they learn attitudes, beliefs, and definitions that are favorable to alcohol use. When such children reach adulthood, they are likely to use alcohol just as their parents did.

Interactionists hold that the use of illegal drugs is also culturally learned, although in a slightly different way. Because the dominant culture encourages negative attitudes toward illegal drugs, some contact with a drug sub-

Drugs are used in many social settings. According to interactionist theory, people use drugs because of the attitudes and values they learn in their daily contacts with other people.

culture is necessary before most people start using such drugs. The longer and more intense a person's contact with a drug subculture, the greater the likelihood that that person will accept attitudes and definitions that are favorable to drug use. Once a person actually begins to use an illicit drug, he or she is likely to grow closer to other drug users and to become more deeply committed to the values of the drug subculture. In fact, some people use drugs for the companionship of other drug users as much as for the effects of the drugs themselves.

The key point in interactionist theory is that drug use is determined by individuals' attitudes toward drugs, the meaning drug use has for them, their overall world view, and their system of values—all of which are learned from interaction with people in a certain culture or subculture. Drug users, according to interactionist theory, quit only when their attitudes and values change and the drugs involved are redefined in more negative terms.[63] Labeling theorists point out that such changes are much more difficult when a drug user has been discovered and publicly labeled "addict," "alcoholic," "junkie," or "pill head." Those who have been branded in this way often find that they are excluded from contact with groups and individuals who might support their attempts to reform.

DRUG CONTROL IN NORTH AMERICA

European colonists who came to North America brought their drinking customs with them. Before 1700 most drinking was moderate and socially accepted. The most common beverages were beer and wine. Strong religious and family controls limited drunkenness and disorderly conduct. However, as expansion to the west continued, drinking patterns changed. The traditional restraints of family and religion were ineffective among rugged frontiersmen, and heavy consumption of distilled spirits became commonplace. This type of drinking, often accompanied by violent destructive behavior, was the first alcohol problem to gain widespread social attention. At the same time, total abstinence was becoming more popular among rural farmers.

By the nineteenth century there were two different drinking patterns among Americans. Rural middle-class people were largely abstainers, while the frontiersmen and the thousands of immigrants in the big cities tended to be alcohol users. Three waves of state prohibition laws swept the United States as small-town dwellers tried to stamp out the customs of urban drinkers. The last wave resulted in the passage in 1919 of the Eighteenth Amendment to the Constitution, which prohibited the manufacture, sale, and transportation of intoxicating liquors. This amendment was repealed in 1933 by the Twenty-first Amendment.

Just as the drive against alcohol intensified in the nineteenth century, so also did the drive against the use of other drugs, particularly the opiates. At that time, opium was sold legally in over-the-counter patent medicines as a cure for everything from diarrhea to whooping cough. Morphine was widely used as a painkiller during the Civil War, and veterans spread the word about its beneficial effects. After the war, extensive advertising campaigns for opiated medicines also contributed to the spread of opiate use. Products such as Mrs. Winslow's Soothing Syrup and McMumm's Elixir of Opium were widely used.[64]

The nineteenth-century opiate user was quite different from today's junkie. Most opiate users were middle-aged, middle-class women. They were no more involved in crime or deviant behavior than anyone else.[65] The critical difference between them and contemporary addicts may be seen in the way early addicts defined the drugs and themselves. Indeed, the nineteenth-century users did not define themselves as addicts at all. They perceived the drugs as medicine and therefore did not see themselves as deviant or abnormal. In contrast, twentieth-century junkies define opiates as dope and themselves as addicts.

Opium smoking among Chinese immigrants on the west coast was the first use of opiates to be associated with crime, and this negative image soon spread to other methods of opiate consumption. In 1896 the *New York Sun* coined the term *dope fiend*, and an anti-opiate drive was soon under way. Near the turn of the century some states began restricting the use of opium. All nonprescription use of opiates was prohibited in Canada in 1908 and in the United States in 1914.[66]

This prohibition produced a sharp drop in the number of opiate users. However, users who were unwilling or unable to quit were placed in a very difficult position. They found themselves labeled "dope fiends" and were virtually forced to associate with smugglers and other criminals if they were to obtain supplies of the drug. This small group of opiate users was the beginning of the subculture of opiate addiction that has become such a problem in recent years. The price of illicit opiates rose steadily, and so did users' need for money. The method of consumption changed from drinking opiated medicines to injecting morphine and heroin. Within a few decades after opium prohibition, the modern junkie emerged: predominantly young, predominantly male, and often deeply involved in crime.[67]

Alcohol prohibition had equally negative effects on American society. While the prohibition law was in effect Americans witnessed an unprecedented wave of crime and gangsterism. The drinking public was not willing to give up alcohol, no matter what the law said. They turned to illegal sources of supply, thus creating a huge illicit market for alcohol. Organized criminals and many independent operators jumped into the alcohol business, and speakeasies (illegal bars) sprang up in every city.[68]

Marijuana was the last major drug to be prohibited in this era of "temperance." As late as 1930 only 16 states had laws prohibiting marijuana use, and these laws were not vigorously enforced. Although the climate of the early 1930s was right for another antidrug campaign, a single government agency, the Federal Bureau of Narcotics, played a major role in promoting marijuana prohibition in the United States. This agency was set up to enforce opium prohibition in 1930, and its director became convinced that marijuana use was an area of wrongdoing that should be under his jurisdiction. Accordingly, the bureau began an intensive program of lobbying both state and federal governments for the prohibition of marijuana. It also circulated a number of phony horror studies like the following, written by the Federal Commissioner of Narcotics and published in a popular magazine of the time:

> An entire family was murdered by a youthful [marijuana] addict in Florida. When officers arrived at the home they found the youth staggering about in a human slaughterhouse. With an axe he had killed his father, mother, two brothers, and a sister. He seemed to be in a daze. . . . He had no recollection of having committed the multiple crime. The officers knew him ordinarily as a sane, rather quiet young man; now he was pitifully crazed. They sought the reason. The boy said he had been in the habit of smoking something which youthful friends called "muggies," a childish name for marijuana.[69]

Virtually no one challenged the distortions, half-truths, and outright lies circulated by the Federal Bureau of Narcotics. In 1937 Congress passed the Marijuana Tax Act, which was designed to stamp out use of the drug, and every individual state eventually passed an outright prohibition of its own.

Most of the new drugs that have become popular among recreational users in the twentieth century have been produced by the pharmaceutical corporations and have often been promoted with erroneous claims that they were less addictive than their predecessors. Heroin was synthesized in 1874 and first placed on the marked by Bayer Laboratories in 1898. It was widely promoted as a safe substitute for codeine and a cure for morphine addiction. The first barbiturate was clinically tested in 1903, and by the 1930s the barbiturates were in common use. Although references to barbiturate intoxication and withdrawal convulsions were made as early as 1905, it was not until 1950 that a controlled study was done to prove their addictive properties. Methaqualone was, as we have seen, falsely advertised as a safe substitute for the barbiturates that were coming to be recognized as a major drug problem. LSD was first created in 1938. Although it was never promoted as a prescription drug, the Sandoz laboratories did give LSD samples to a very wide variety of scientists from 1953 to 1966. It has now come to light that the Central Intelligence Agency and the U.S. Army conducted experiments with LSD during this period that included dosing unsuspecting citizens with the drug to observe its effectiveness as a combat weapon.[70]

THE DISTRIBUTION OF DRUGS

The history of drug use in North America points out the tremendous impact of the method of drug distribution on both the drug user and society as a whole. Drugs are distributed through three main channels: the legal over-the-counter market, the prescription market, and the illegal black market. Users of a black-market drug face an array of problems that are not experienced by others, and they, in turn, contribute to other social problems. The most critical task faced by policy makers in the drug field is that of determining the best method of distributing each psychoactive drug.

The Over-the-Counter Market   The legal over-the-counter market is by far the most popular means of distributing psychoactive drugs. Alcohol, nicotine, and caffeine are distributed in this way. A number of nonprescription medicines, such as Sominex and Sleep-Eze, are sold over the counter as well. Sales of some drugs, such as alcohol and tobacco, are limited by minimum age requirements or other restrictions such as regulations setting minimum distances liquor stores must be from schools and the hours during which they can do business. Nevertheless, the drugs sold in the over-the-counter market are the most readily available to the public and are generally the most commonly used.

The Prescription Market   A wide variety of drugs are legally available only with a doctor's prescription. The minor tranquilizers are prescribed most often, followed by the sedatives and hypnotics. About 75 percent of the psychoactive drugs prescribed by doctors are used to produce sedation, tranquility, and sleep, and about 25 percent are prescribed to increase energy or treat depression. About two-thirds of all users of prescription drugs are women, whereas men are far more likely to use black market drugs.

The prescription market is, in a sense, halfway between open legal sales and complete prohibition. The idea is to allow the public to use these drugs, but only with the advice and consent of a qualified physician. All drugs on the prescription market are not, however, treated alike. The federal government classifies drugs into five categories known as "schedules." Schedule I drugs are the most tightly controlled and may only be used in carefully regulated scientific experiments (heroin and marijuana are in this category). Schedule II drugs such as morphine, cocaine, and most barbiturates are available by prescription, but their production is still strictly limited by the government. The production of Schedule III, IV, and V drugs is not limited, and prescriptions are less tightly monitored than for Schedule II drugs.[71]

The Black Market   Many of the drugs prescribed by doctors are also available on the black market. Amphetamines and barbiturates are prime examples. Holders of legitimate prescriptions for such drugs sometimes give or sell them to other users. More significant are the large quantities of these drugs that are diverted from the prescription market into the black market for direct sale to users. A large percentage of the illegal amphetamines and barbiturates consumed in North America have at various times been manufactured by legitimate pharmaceutical companies and secretly purchased by underground drug dealers.

Among the drugs that are not available legally but are sold on the black market are marijuana, most psychedelics, and heroin. (Opiates other than heroin are available by prescription, but they are very tightly regulated.) Most marijuana used in the United States and Canada is grown on farms in Latin America and smuggled across the American border by individuals or small criminal organizations, but there are also many domestic cultivators who make their living growing marijuana indoors or in hidden fields in rural areas of North America.

The production and marketing of heroin and other opiates is more complex. For years opium poppies grown in Turkey and the Middle East were refined and sent to France for final processing, then smuggled into North America. Now, as a result of efforts by the U.S. government to discourage cultivation of the opium poppy in Turkey, more heroin comes from other countries, especially Latin America and Southeast Asia. Organized crime dominates the distribution system, principally because the importation and wholesale distribution of opiates requires huge amounts of cash. The risks of confiscation and long prison terms are high, but the profits are enormous, and fortunes can be made with one successful shipment. Once heroin reaches the United States, it moves through a chain similar to that of any legitimate importing-distributing-wholesaling-retailing business. Each participant in the chain buys and then sells. Each also dilutes the heroin with milk sugar or other additives. The street-level dealer is an independent businessperson who purchases at wholesale prices and sells at retail prices. The cost to the consumer is about five hundred times the cost at the point of importation.

The distribution pattern of cocaine is similar. First, almost all cocaine comes from coca leaves grown in South America. Second, juvenile gangs appear to be far more heavily involved in the distribution of cocaine and especially of crack. Several U.S. cities have experienced gang wars and violence that spring from the attempts of these young criminals to expand and protect their business.

RESPONDING TO THE DRUG PROBLEM

Drug use has long been considered an important social problem, at least partly because of the social costs already discussed. The Protestant ethic—which demands that individuals work hard and show self-discipline—also is a source of the concern about drug use. Although these values have changed over the years, their influence remains strong. Thus, some are opposed to drug use itself, regardless of any damage it may do, because it is associated with laziness and self-indulgence. But most people are primarily concerned with the physical and psychological problems excessive drug use may cause. Proposals for dealing with drugs can be grouped into four categories: prevention, treatment, legal repression, and increased tolerance.

Prevention   Most people agree that the best way to deal with drug problems is to discourage young people from using drugs before they start. But how is that to be done? One common approach is to try to frighten them by presenting horror stories in "drug education" classes. Such attempts seriously underestimate the awareness and intelligence of our youth. Sooner or later they discover that they have not been told the whole truth, and they may even come to doubt the accurate information they have been given about drug problems. A more reasonable approach is to present the best factual information available regardless of whether or not it is likely to discourage students from using drugs. Critics of educational programs argue that so much talk about drugs in the classroom will excite some students' interest in using them. Blum, Blum, and Garfield concluded that students exposed to drug education programs may actually be more likely than other students to use drugs, although they do so in a more moderate fashion.[72] In contrast, less informed students had a greater tendency to be either abstainers or heavy drug users. Education programs need not, however, be administered exclusively by the schools. Another approach is to run public-service advertising about alcoholism, lung cancer, and other problems caused by drugs, and to prohibit the advertising of drugs in any media.

Others believe that prevention programs are doomed to failure because they are pursuing an unrealistic goal. They think a certain amount of drug use is inevitable in our complex and insecure society, and that the goal therefore should be to encourage moderation, not total abstinence. Recent research, moreover, indicates that moderate drug use does not usually cause serious psychological or physical problems. A ground-breaking UCLA study published in 1988 tracked 739 young people from junior high until young adulthood and concluded that the harm caused by drugs depends largely on the level of use. No measurable harm was found from moderate drug use, but as use increased so did its damage.[73]

Many therefore advocate more balanced educational programs that allow students to make a rational choice based on all the available information. In this view, the best way to prevent drug problems is to openly accept a certain level of use but encourage the creation of clear social standards about how much is too much. Researchers have found, for example, that the rate of alcoholism is low among Italians (and Italian Americans) even though their per capita alcohol consumption is significantly higher than in most countries. Italian culture does not condemn drinking, but contains clearly defined norms that limit total alcohol consumption to meal times and other social occasions. On the other hand, alcohol use was not part of the traditional culture of American Indians, and their high rate of alcoholism today is often attributed to the weakness of such norms.[74]

Treatment   The treatment approach, like prevention programs, tries to discourage drug use. The difference is that treatment programs attempt to help people stop using drugs after they have already developed a drug problem. A variety of treatment programs have been tried, but no single program works for everyone. Many drug users go through several programs before kicking the habit.

Individual psychotherapy has proven to be one of the least successful approaches to drug problems.[75] No matter how much psychiatric care most drug users are given, strong social support is needed to motivate them to give up the drug habit. Aversive therapy is designed to associate the effects of the drug with some unpleasant sensation such as an electric shock or nausea. Aversive techniques are widely used to discourage smoking (for ex-

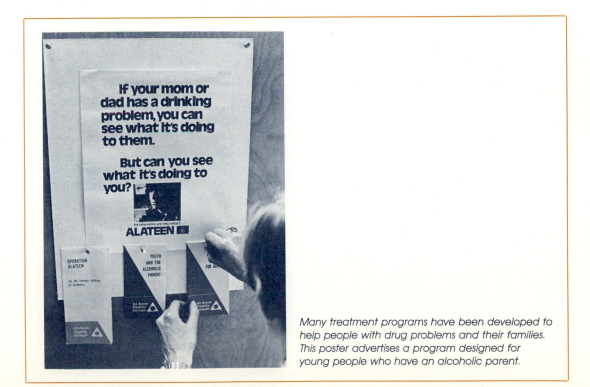

Many treatment programs have been developed to help people with drug problems and their families. This poster advertises a program designed for young people who have an alcoholic parent.

ample, by the Schick Centers), but they have had less success with problem drugs such as alcohol and heroin.

The most successful treatment programs involve some kind of group support. Alcoholics Anonymous (AA) is one of the oldest such groups and is now a worldwide organization. Treatment takes the form of meetings where members give accounts of their troubles with alcohol and the help they have found in Alcoholics Anonymous. Members are encouraged to call on one another for help when they feel a desire to start drinking again. The AA program is religiously oriented, but its success seems to derive primarily from its system of encouraging each member to try to reform others, thus reinforcing the reformer's own nondrinking behavior.

Some group-oriented programs for drug addicts are adaptations of AA techniques for use in therapeutic communities where drug users live together in a house or dormitory. The first of these was the famous Synanon, founded in Santa Monica, California, in 1958. Synanon members were ex-users who maintained strict discipline, prohibited all drug use, and helped each other avoid drugs. Frequent group sessions were held in which members discussed their problems and criticized individuals who failed to live up to the expectations of the group.[76] Although Synanon has changed drastically in recent years, other therapeutic communities still follow its original principles.

Most therapeutic communities claim high rates of success but have seldom conducted rigorous research to support their claims. One major problem is that these programs appeal only to drug users who can accept their ideology and discipline. It has been estimated that only 10 to 20 percent of those who join these communities finish the program, but at least a majority of these individuals do remain drug free.[77] Another problem with some therapeutic communities is that those who complete the program successfully often have great difficulty leaving. Many who do manage to leave become "professional ex-addicts" working in halfway houses or other drug programs.

19th-Century Social Problems

Thomas Galt died at his home in this city Friday night last . . . from the effects of the Ackerman anti-dipsomania gold cure which he was taking. He was 37 . . . he contracted the drink habit and it so obtained the mastery of him that he was much of the time incapacitated for labor. He was so anxious to break the fetters that enslaved him . . . that he risked and lost his life. . . . He was a great sufferer throughout the treatment.

November 16, 1893

Legal Repression   When the use of a particular drug comes to be seen as a problem, the most common response has been to make it a crime, usually by prohibiting the manufacture and sale of the drugs and punishing the users. This approach has been tried with almost all psychoactive drugs except caffeine and nicotine. The idea is that people will not use drugs if there are none available, but it is difficult to evaluate the success of this approach. For example, opiate use declined sharply after it was declared illegal, but marijuana use has increased enormously since its prohibition. Supporters of this approach argue that its failures are due to a lack of tough laws and enough money to enforce them. It does seem fair to conclude that the prohibition approach usually does reduce (but not eliminate) the use of the condemned drug. However, the matter is a good deal more complex than that. For one thing, the cost of effectively repressing a popular drug may be far more than society can afford. As the drug becomes more scarce, the price is driven up and drug dealers have more money to offer in bribes and corruption (a key reason for the frequent failure of this approach). Political factors also obstruct the enforcement effort. Evidence has emerged showing not only that the Central Intelligence Agency has been involved with drug-dealing schemes to help finance its secret operations but that several presidential administrations have intentionally ignored drug-running activities by their allies in volatile Third-World countries.

But even if the enforcement effort could somehow dry up the supply of illicit drugs, this approach would still have unintended side effects. A policy that completely removed all popular drugs from the black market, while allowing free over-the-counter sales of alcohol, seems likely to achieve little more than the substitution of one dangerous drug for another.

In the real world, of course, some black market almost certainly would remain and that fosters the growth of organized crime. When a drug is prohibited by law, legitimate businesses are forced out of the market. The demand for the drug is still there, however, and criminals organize to meet it. Because such criminals have no competition from legitimate enterprise, legal prohibition guarantees them huge profits. The classic example of this process is the prohibition of alcohol in the United States during the 1920s and early 1930s. As many Americans sought new sources of alcoholic beverages, gangs of criminals began to supply them. The result was widespread gangsterism and disrespect for the law. Gang bosses like Al Capone, who built his illegal empire by bootlegging alcohol, virtually controlled some American cities.

In addition to organized crime, drug prohibition also encourages the growth of deviant subcultures among users who band together to share their experiences and defeat the government's efforts to cut supplies of their drug. Many marijuana users report that they originally were more attracted to the comradery and friendship of other drug users than to the effects of the drug itself. And finally, the enforcement effort itself poses a serious threat to civil liberties. Drug offenses seldom have victims who call the police. Law enforcement agencies must therefore resort to such questionable techniques as the use of wiretaps, undercover agents, and spies to uncover violations.

Of course, these criticisms do not necessarily mean that the enforcement approach should be abandoned, for the results may be judged to be worth the price. But they do suggest that it is far preferable to reduce the demand for drugs through education and treatment if at all possible.

Increased Social Tolerance An alternative approach to the drug problem is to increase social tolerance for drug use. This approach includes a variety of solutions, ranging from reductions in penalties for some types of drug offenses to full legalization of all drugs. Advocates of such proposals claim that a less punitive reaction to drug use would reduce the negative side effects stemming from legal repression and, in the long run, reduce the need for treatment. If drugs could be obtained legally, it is argued, their attractiveness as "forbidden fruit" would decrease. Further, legalization would take the profit out of drug distribution, thus taking drugs off the street. But even if this approach failed to reduce drug use, its advocates assert, it might still reduce the drug problem by reducing organized crime, destigmatizing drug users, undermining drug subcultures, and promoting the growth of more effective informal controls for drugs that are currently illegal.

Legalization Proponents of **legalization** believe that attempts at legal repression of drug use have been so disastrous that the problem can be solved only by taking the government out of the drug-law enforcement business. In practice, regulation by government agencies would undoubtedly continue, as it does in the case of alcohol. Minors would be prohibited from purchasing drugs, and taxation and regulation of quality standards could be expected.

Most proponents of legalization do not advocate over-the-counter sales for all drugs. In fact, marijuana is the only drug for which full legalization has widespread support. Those who do advocate the legalization of all drugs often base their arguments on philosophical opposition to government interference in individuals' lives. The psychiatrist Thomas Szasz, for instance, feels that the decision to use a drug is entirely an individual matter in which the government has no legitimate concern.[78]

Decriminalization **Decriminalization** is a step halfway between prohibition and full legalization. Its advocates argue that the penalties for possession and use of a given drug, usually marijuana, should be dropped but that the sale of the drug should continue to be illegal. The aim is to stop punishing those who use illicit drugs but to discourage such use by forbidding sales. Critics of this policy point to the contradiction between allowing legal possession and penalizing sale or purchase. Its advocates, who fear that legalization would encourage a new wave of drug use yet want to reduce the repression of users, propose decriminalization as a compromise. Decriminalization of marijuana use, or reduction of penalties for possession and use of marijuana, has been endorsed by American and Canadian commissions on drug use, the American Medical Association, and the American Bar Association. Eleven states decriminalized possession of small amounts of marijuana during the 1970s. But the new wave of concern about drug abuse has stopped this trend, and no new states have joined them in the 1980s.[79] A 1986 poll found that 57 percent of those questioned opposed the decriminalization of marijuana and 36 percent supported it.[80]

DEBATE

Should We Prohibit Involuntary Drug Testing?

YES The phony "drug epidemic" whipped up by politicians and sensationalistic journalists has reached hysterical proportions and threatens to sweep away our most cherished civil rights. The fact of the matter is that drug use is going down, not up. But no matter what the latest trends may show, it is intolerable to allow the government and the corporations to dictate the standards by which we must lead our personal lives.

Employers have every right to fire employees whose drug use interferes with their work. But what right does an employer have to fire someone who is doing a good job, because he or she smoked marijuana at a party on Friday night? Another injustice inherent in drug testing comes from the tests themselves, which are highly inaccurate and often give false results. Moreover, they are not equally sensitive to all drugs. Marijuana, a relatively harmless drug, can be detected weeks after it has been used, whereas more dangerous drugs such as heroin cannot. Thus, marijuana smokers would be encouraged to change to cocaine, heroin, and other more hazardous drugs. And what about alcohol? If we are going to fire marijuana smokers, shouldn't we fire alcohol drinkers too? And for that matter, what about tobacco smokers, caffeine drinkers, unfaithful husbands, or political radicals? The new programs of involuntary drug testing are a step toward a totalitarian police state and must be stopped now!

NO Drugs are a menace to the very survival of our society. Drugs corrupt children, break up families, and lead hundreds of thousands of people to an early grave. Mandatory drug testing is a serious measure, but only serious measures can solve this frightening problem.

Because drug use has become so widespread in our society, mandatory testing is the only way to ensure that our aircraft pilots, railroad engineers, police officers, and other vital personnel are fit to do their jobs. Without drug testing we can expect to see thousands of innocent people lose their lives in drug-related accidents. But the economic consequences of drug abuse are just as serious as its toll of deaths and injuries. One of the major reasons that our products and our businesses are doing so poorly in world trade is that so many of our workers have drug problems. The workers in Japan and South Korea do not use drugs, and mandatory drug testing is the only way that we are going to remain competitive and ensure a drug-free workplace.

Of course, it would be preferable if workers simply refrained from using drugs without being tested. And if we crack down on drugs now, someday we may reach that goal. But until we do, mandatory drug testing is the most effective weapon we have in the battle against the drug menace, and we must use it.

Maintenance Maintenance programs supply addicts or habitual users with a drug while denying it to the public at large. This approach is usually advocated for the opiates, but it could also be applied to other addictive drugs. The only widely used maintenance program in the United States and Canada is the distribution of methadone (a synthetic opiate) to heroin addicts. Although methadone maintenance is often called treatment, it has little in common with real treatment programs. In essence, these programs simply provide a restricted legal supply of an opiate to people who otherwise would obtain opiates illegally.

Supporters of methadone maintenance programs believe that methadone has several advantages over heroin: its effects last longer, it can be given orally, and it does not generate the intense high that is produced by heroin. However, many heroin addicts refuse to participate in methadone programs because they prefer heroin. Critics, including some ex-addicts, argue that methadone is just another narcotic and that dispensing it to heroin users does nothing to solve the addiction problem.

Another issue concerns the method used to distribute methadone. In current programs the addict must go to a special clinic and is only given a small dose. This technique is designed to minimize the diversion of methadone into the black market. Critics say that these programs throw addicts into association with one another just when they are trying to escape the culture of addiction, that they unreasonably restrict addicts' freedom to travel, and that they are demeaning because they require addicts to wait in line for their daily handout. Some have proposed that a different kind of maintenance program be established, one that allows individual physicians, rather than government clinics, to distribute any opiate the patient needs, including heroin.[81]

SOCIOLOGICAL PERSPECTIVES ON DRUG USE

The drug problem should not be dismissed as the outcome of individual faults or weaknesses. Although some people seem to have more difficulty limiting their drug use than do others, social psychologists have shown that anyone can become a drug addict, regardless of moral character. Sociologists have repeatedly demonstrated the enormous influence social forces have on all types of human behavior. The severe problems North American society has with drug use are the result of its culture and social structure, not the weakness of its people. Repeated claims that drug users are sick, degenerate, or abnormal are simply misguided name-calling that obscures the real source of the problem.

The Functionalist Perspective Functionalist theory does not attempt to explain the specific reasons why individuals use or do not use drugs. It concerns itself with the social conditions that have caused the tremendous increase in drug use in recent decades. The general assumption is that drug use is a means of escaping from difficult and unpleasant social circumstances. Consequently, the current wave of drug addiction is seen as a response to other social problems such as the instability of the modern family, the breakdown of traditional moral standards, and the weakening of religious institutions. Functionalists are also likely to note that inefficiency characterizes the agencies that are charged with enforcing drug laws, thus contributing to the growing use of illegal drugs.

If drug use is indeed a secondary effect of other social problems, an effective solution will not be easy to find. What is needed is a wide-ranging attack on the primary problems. Hundreds of proposals for dealing with these and other pressing problems have been made, but reducing social ills to levels that would no longer motivate people to misuse drugs would be extremely difficult. A simpler response would be to devote more time and money to the enforcement of drug laws, thus attempting to cut off the supply. However, functionalists as well as other sociologists are often skeptical about such an approach, mainly because past enforcement efforts have been so unsuccessful.

The Conflict Perspective   Some conflict theorists also assume that drug users are escapists, and they agree that drug use is caused by other social problems. However, they hold that these social problems stem from exploitation and social injustice rather than from social disorganization. Like functionalists, these conflict theorists advocate a direct attack on the primary problem— exploitation—rather than on the symptoms of the problem—drug use. They argue that drug use will decrease only after a just society, free from racism, poverty, and oppression, is created.

Other conflict theorists strongly disagree, asserting that drug use itself is neither escapist nor a social problem. Rather, it is normal behavior that occurs in all societies around the world. According to these theorists, drug use becomes a problem only when groups who oppose drugs use the power of the state to force their morality on everyone else. The inevitable result of such actions is social conflict, violent repression of drug users, and a booming black market.

Most conflict theorists argue that people should not be jailed for using drugs if their behavior causes no harm or danger to others. Conflict theorists also say that the attempt to repress drug use creates secondary social problems such as organized crime and a seething discontent with the legal system. Those who hold this viewpoint advocate a simple solution to the drug problem: legalize the prohibited drugs and stop jailing people who have done nothing worse than refusing to accept the dominant society's idea of what is good for them.

Social Psychological Perspectives   Most research into the causes of and solutions to the drug problem has been at the social psychological level. As our previous discussion has suggested, each of the four major social psychological theories has its own explanations of drug use and its preferred treatments. Biosocial theorists say that drug addiction is a physiological problem and recommend more research to develop a biochemical cure. Personality theory holds that addiction is caused by defects in the addict's personality and recommends psychotherapy. Interactionists and behaviorists agree that drug addiction is learned behavior and recommend treatment programs designed to help addicts learn less destructive patterns of behavior.

SUMMARY

Many people have mistaken ideas about drug use. For example, it is widely believed that alcohol and tobacco are not drugs because they are legal, but there is actually little difference between these drugs and the illegal ones. Another misconception is that drug use is a new epidemic that is sweeping through our society. Surveys and sales figures indicate that total drug use has actually gone down in the 1980s.

Many drugs are habit-forming, meaning that continual use produces tolerance and that the user becomes sick when the drug is withdrawn. Addiction is the strong craving that often develops when one uses habit-forming drugs.

The most popular drug, for recreational purposes, is alcohol, and it also creates the most problems for society. It is a depressant and is addictive if used in excess. Tobacco is another widely used legal drug. Cigarette smoking has been shown to cause a variety of health problems, yet large numbers of people start smoking every year.

Marijuana is the most widely used illegal drug. Although most of the evidence indicates that it is less harmful than alcohol, there is considerable controversy concerning its legal status. The opiates are all highly addictive. Although the drugs themselves do not appear to cause great physical harm, the way they are used and the life-style of most addicts make these drugs extremely dangerous. Mescaline and LSD are two of the most popular psychedelic drugs, and both produce powerful psychological changes in the user, including hallucinations and alterations of mood and perception. The psychedelics produce few health problems but create serious emotional disturbances in some users. The sedative-hypnotics depress the central nervous system and are frequently prescribed by physicians, but there is also a flourishing black market for many of these drugs.

The most widely used stimulant is caffeine, which is not dangerous in moderate doses. The amphetamines are much stronger and more dangerous stimulants. Excessive amphetamine use produces a psychotic state as well as considerable physical damage. Cocaine is a natural stimulant with effects similar to those of the amphetamines. It is one of the few drugs that has increased in popularity in the 1980s.

Biological theories hold that addicts use drugs because of an overwhelming need created by the physiological effect of the drugs. Behavioral theory sees drug use and addiction as products of conditioning: people use drugs because they find the experience to be rewarding, and addicts continue to use drugs because they want to avoid painful withdrawal. Personality theorists argue that individuals who use drugs have inadequate or impulsive personalities. According to interactionist theory, drug use stems from attitudes, values, and definitions favorable to such behavior, often learned in drug subcultures.

The early North American colonists had few problems with drugs. Later, heavy drinking patterns developed among single men on the frontier, while more respectable farm families began to give up drinking. Several prohibitionist movements swept North America in the twentieth century and resulted in the banning of alcohol, opiates, and marijuana. Prohibition of these drugs fostered drug subcultures among the users, who were branded as criminals. The "junkie" or "dope fiend" subculture, which developed among heroin users, has become a particularly severe problem.

The method by which a drug is distributed has an important effect both on society and on the user. Some drugs are distributed legally in over-the-counter sales; others are available by prescription. Still others—including some prescription drugs—are distributed illegally in the black market.

Proposals for dealing with the drug problem fall into four main categories. The first consists of prevention programs designed to stop people from getting involved with drugs or using them to excess. The second approach is treatment of drug users to help them stop using drugs. The most successful treatment programs use some form of group support. A third set of proposals aim to increase legal repression of drug use. This approach discourages drug use but has damaging side effects, including the growth of organized crime and drug subcultures. Increased social tolerance of drug use is a fourth alternative. Included in this category are legalization, decriminalization, and maintenance clinics that supply addicts with substitutes for illegal drugs.

Functionalists generally assume that drug use is a means of escaping from unpleasant social conditions that have arisen as society has become disorganized. Some conflict theorists also assume that drug users are escapists, but they are convinced that these problems stem from exploitation rather than from social disorganization. Other conflict theorists consider drug use to be normal behavior and argue that the problem lies in the state's attempts to repress it. The social psychological perspective includes biosocial theory, personality theory, behavioral theory, and interactionist theory. Each of these social psychological theories tries to explain why persons become drug users, and each implies a specific approach to treatment.

KEY TERMS

addiction
alcoholic
decriminalization
depressant

stimulant
tolerance
withdrawal

FURTHER READINGS

The Drug Problem

Sidney Cohen, *Substance Abuse Problems, vol. 2,* New York: Haworth, 1985.

Oakley Ray, *Drugs, Society and Human Behavior,* 3d ed., St. Louis: C. V. Mosby, 1983.

Katheleen Whalen Fitzgerald, *Alcoholism: The Genetic Inheritance,* New York: Doubleday, 1988.

Herbert Hendin et al., *Living High: Daily Marijuana Use Among Adults,* New York: Human Sciences Press, 1987.

Jack H. Mendelson and Nancy K. Mello, *Alcohol Use and Abuse in America,* Boston: Little, Brown, 1985.

Jay Stevens, *Storming Heaven: LSD and the American Dream,* New York: Atlantic Monthly Press, 1987.

Legal Response to Drug Use

Ronald Hamowy (ed.), *Dealing with Drugs: Consequences of Government Control,* San Francisco Pacific Research Institute for Social Policy, 1987.

Thomas Szasz, *Ceremonial Chemistry: The Ritual Persecution of Drugs, Addicts, and Pushers,* rev. ed., Holmes Beach, Fla.: Learning Publications, 1985.

- Are official crime statistics accurate?
- What causes criminal behavior?
- What are the most important types of crime?
- How does society deal with crime?
- Does punishment reform criminals?
- What can be done to reduce crime?

Few of us would deny that crime is a major social problem. Almost one in every four American households is touched by crime each year, while less than 3 percent are touched by death from any cause, and only about 1 percent are touched by heart disease or cancer.[1] Although it is impossible to determine the exact economic costs of all the various types of criminal activity, the total certainly runs to many billions of dollars a year in the United Sates alone. But even more serious are the human costs of crime—the loss of life and liberty, the physical injuries, and the nagging fear that we may be next on the long list of victims.

Public concern about the danger of crime has increased tremendously in the last 30 years. However, crime has not increased nearly as much as the fear of it. In fact, crime was actually going down in many of the years that the public thought we were in the midst of a crime wave. During the 1980s those who believed that crime was increasing outnumbered those who felt that it was decreasing by from two to one to as many as thirteen to one.[2] But as we will see, the evidence shows that crime was actually decreasing. Why was the public so misguided? The answer is not entirely clear, but the media's exploitation of dramatic crime stories to keep up ratings and newspaper sales was certainly a major factor, as were the efforts of many politicians to use the crime issue for political advantage.

THE NATURE OF CRIME

A crime is a violation of the criminal law. No matter how indecent or immoral an act may be, it is not a crime unless the criminal law has listed it as a crime and provided a punishment for it.

In practice, of course, it is not always easy to tell whether a specific act is or is not a burglary, a robbery, a rape, or some other crime. It often takes a trial to determine what a particular law means. For example, the criminal law forbids the unlawful killing of human beings (murder), but is an aborted fetus a human being? The criminal law forbids stealing (larceny), but what is stealing? The definition has changed over time as ideas about property have changed. If students take library books with no intention of returning them, it is stealing; but is it stealing if they take books without properly checking them out and read and return them? Is it stealing if a student takes a library book, photocopies it, and then returns it?

Such questions must be decided by someone; and criminal justice is the process by which such decisions are reached. It is not a mechanical process in which a precise criminal law is uniformly applied to all cases. Any fair judgment as to guilt or punishment requires wisdom, sensitivity, and a sense of balance.

Roscoe Pound, a famous American legal scholar, once pointed out that there is a great difference between "law on the books" and "law in action." What the criminal law says and what police and the courts do are often quite different. For example, some old laws—such as those outlawing certain sex acts—remain legally valid but are almost never enforced. Even more recent laws, such as those making it a crime to go nude on a beach, are sometimes ignored. In addition, police officers and courts enforce most laws selectively. This means, for example, that an act might be called burglary if it is committed by a poor person—especially one with a criminal record—but might be called trespassing or some other minor offense if it is committed by someone who is more "respectable."

Certain types of acts, such as murder, are condemned in almost all societies. Other acts are illegal in some nations and legal in others. Some countries allow a man to have many wives, but in other countries the same man would be guilty of the crime of bigamy. There are places where alcohol use is legal and marijuana use is not and places where marijuana smoking is legal but drinking is not. In the United States and many other large nations, there are variations from state to state and even from city to city. The point is that the creation and modification of criminal laws is a political process. When values change or political power shifts, the "law in action" changes, even if the "law on the books" remains the same.

IS THERE A CRIME WAVE?

Many average citizens throughout the industrialized world are convinced that a massive crime wave is threatening their property and personal safety. But changes in the amount of crime are hard to measure, and few people take the time to examine the evidence about the real trends in crime. The most common source of statistics about the number of crimes committed is official police records. Because all crimes are not reported, these statistics underestimate the total amount of crime. But they do not necessarily distort the *trends* in crime. In the United States the FBI annually publishes statistics on arrests and on crimes known to the police. These statistics, like those published by other Western nations, showed a steady increase in crime for three decades after the end of World War II. However, reported crime peaked in 1980 and then decreased for several years, before turning up a bit in 1986. (see Figure 14.1).

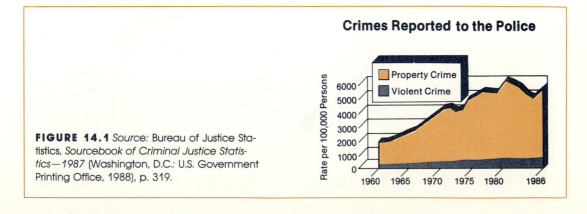

FIGURE 14.1 *Source:* Bureau of Justice Statistics, *Sourcebook of Criminal Justice Statistics—1987* (Washington, D.C.: U.S. Government Printing Office, 1988), p. 319.

Crimes Reported to the Police

There are, however, many doubts about the accuracy of these statistics. Many police departments try to show as large an increase as possible to justify their requests for more money and personnel. Conversely, when a city's police are criticized because the crime rate is too high, they may reverse themselves and try to show a decrease in crime. For instance, the FBI reported a 4 percent drop in total crime in 1972—the first reduction in 17 years—and it was charged that the figures were intentionally reduced to strengthen the Nixon administration's "law and order" image just before the presidential election.[3] In addition to such intentional manipulation of the figures, many criminologists believe that there are other reasons the FBI figures may exaggerate the increase in crime. Greater confidence in the police, quicker and easier ways of reporting crime, improved record keeping, and the growing popularity of theft insurance (which requires victims to report a crime in order to collect) have all tended to boost the number of crimes that are reported.

The most convincing evidence that the FBI statistics distort the trends in crime comes from **victimization surveys** (see Figure 14.2). In 1973, the U.S. Department of Justice began the National Crime Survey (NCS), which bypasses police reports by directly asking a sample of Americans which crimes, if any, they had been victims of in the last year. While the FBI figures showed an increase in crime throughout most of the 1970s, the National Crime Surveys show a downward trend in crime that has continued on into the 1980s.[4] Of course, the National Crime Survey has weaknesses too. Victims may be unwilling to tell interviewers about their problems (the crime surveys do, however, reveal the existence of much more crime than do the police reports used by the FBI), or they may mistakenly report a crime that actually occurred several years before the period they are being questioned about.

Despite this conflicting evidence, it seems clear that crime has decreased since 1980, for both the FBI's figures and the NCS show the same downward trend in most years. The period in the 1970s in which the two measures of

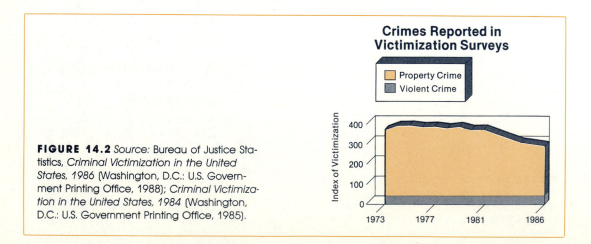

FIGURE 14.2 *Source:* Bureau of Justice Statistics, *Criminal Victimization in the United States, 1986* (Washington, D.C.: U.S. Government Printing Office, 1988); *Criminal Victimization in the United States, 1984* (Washington, D.C.: U.S. Government Printing Office, 1985).

Crimes Reported in Victimization Surveys

Property Crime
Violent Crime

Index of Victimization

400
300
200
100
0

1973   1977   1981   1986

crime do not agree is more difficult to interpret. But on the whole, the NCS has more credibility, and it therefore appears that crime was also undergoing a slight decline during this time as well. But what about the "crime wave" that has gained so much media attention? It is difficult to be sure but, if it did in fact occur, it was probably during the 1960s. The FBI's figures were going up at an unprecedented rate during that period, and because there were no national victimization surveys, there is nothing to refute the claim that crime was in fact increasing at a rapid pace.

THE DISTRIBUTION OF CRIME

Despite their limitations, crime statistics from different sources suggest that the crime rates for certain categories of people are either higher or lower than the average. These distributions tell us a great deal about crime causation. The five most important relationships of this kind are those between crime and gender, age, social class, ethnic group, and residential area.

Gender   Males dominate the world of crime. If you were asked to use a single trait to predict which children in your town would become criminals, you would make the fewest mistakes if you chose gender as the trait and predicted that the boys would be criminals and the girls would not. The prediction would be wrong in many cases. Most of the boys would not become criminals and a few of the girls would. But you would be wrong in more cases if you used some other trait, such as age, ethnic group, family background, or a personality characteristic. As Sutherland and Cressey put it:

> The crime rate for men is greatly in excess of the rate for women—in all nations, all communities within a nation, all age groups, all periods of history for which organized statistics are available, and for all types of crime except those peculiar to women, such as infanticide and abortion.[5]

In the United States, more than 4 times as many men as women are arrested, and about 20 times as many men are sent to prison. Similar ratios exist in other industrialized countries. In Canada the ratio of males to females convicted of serious offenses is about 15 to 1. This difference is even greater in traditional societies, where there is greater inequality between men and women. In such countries the male arrest rate may run as much as 20,000 times greater than the female arrest rate. The ratio of men to women also varies greatly with the type of crime. Only men are arrested for forcible rape, and in general the gender differences are much greater for violent crimes than for property crimes.

Differences between the crime rates of men and women have, however, been decreasing in recent years. The rates for women have been increasing more rapidly than those for men, bringing the two sexes closer together. Between 1976 and 1985 the arrest rate for women increased twice as fast as it did for men.[6] Contrary to some claims, the biggest increases among women were for property crimes. Men continue to greatly outnumber women in arrests for violent crimes. It seems that the more women become involved in the world outside the home and the more financial responsibilities they carry, the more they become involved in property crime. When full sexual equality is achieved, there will probably be a much smaller difference between the crime rates of men and women.

Age   Records of arrests and convictions from industrialized countries around the world show that teenagers and young adults commit the most crimes. Statistics from the United States indicate that very few people under the age of 13 or over the age of 60 are arrested. The likelihood of arrest increases sharply throughout the teenage years, peaks among 19-to-21-year-olds, and then slowly declines.[7]

But the age of the average criminal varies greatly from one crime to another. Contrary to the popular stereotype of the violent teenage hoodlum, minors are actually less likely to commit violent crimes than young adults. If we look at the crimes that have been solved by the police, we find that 20 percent of them were attributed to someone under 18. But those young people committed less than 10 percent of the violent crimes, and almost a quarter of the thefts.[8]

Social Class   Official statistics suggest that people from the lower classes are more likely than others to become involved in crime. Two-thirds to three-fourths of the men and nine-tenths of the women in prison are from the poverty class or the working class. Studies of arrests and convictions also show a disproportionate percentage of lower-class people. Criminologists who have compared the crime rate in poor neighborhoods with that in more affluent areas have found substantially more crime among the poor.

But there are serious problems with using official records in this kind of study. The reliability of statistics on the backgrounds of criminals has been questioned even more strongly than statistics on gender, age, and ethnic group. Because middle- and upper-class criminals have greater personal resources, they are better able to protect themselves from detection, arrest, conviction, and imprisonment.

Many attempts have been made to use other measures to offset the bias in official statistics. However, the studies of victimization mentioned earlier still support the belief that the poor commit more crimes. Findings from the National Crime Survey indicate that a poor family is significantly more likely to be victimized by a property crime than a wealthy one.[9] Since wealthy people are unlikely to go into a poor neighborhood to commit a burglary (the take would most likely seem too small to be attractive), the high burglary rate among the poor suggests that it is other poor people in the same neighborhood who are committing the crimes.

Another technique for determining the role of social class in crime is to ask people what kinds of crimes they have committed and a considerable number of such "self-report" studies have been done. In a well-known article published in 1978, Tittle, Villemez, and Smith reviewed 35 self-report studies and found little consistent evidence that lower-class people were more criminal. They therefore concluded that the official statistics were a product of class bias and did not reflect a real difference in crime rates among the different classes.[10] A new self-report study and a reanalysis of the older ones by Delbert Elliott and his colleagues has called this conclusion into question, however. They found that the research showing similar crime rates for the middle class and the lower class used measures that were slanted in favor of minor offenses. When the comparisons were based on serious offenses like burglary, assault, or vandalism, the lower class was once again found to be more heavily involved in crime.[11]

But there is a grave weakness in all this data, whether it is from official statistics, victimization surveys, or self-report studies, and that is the failure to include white-collar crimes such as embezzlement, false advertising, and consumer fraud. Few people are arrested for such crimes, and most of their victims do not even know that they have been victimized. But middle- and upper-class people are obviously much more heavily involved in white-collar crime than poor people. One sociologist has argued that if all crime could be counted, a U-shaped curve would emerge, indicating more crime in the lower and upper classes and less in the middle.[12] But the plain fact is that criminologists do not really know whether poor people commit more crimes than others. We can say that poor people probably commit more "street" crimes such as murder, burglary, and theft; but that is all.

Ethnic Group   American crime statistics show considerable variation in the rates for different ethnic groups. Blacks, Hispanics, and native Americans have higher than average rates, while Jews and Japanese have lower than average rates. Although blacks make up only 12 percent of the population of the United States, they account for about 27 percent of those arrested each year. This difference is particularly pronounced for violent crimes: 48 percent of those arrested for murder, 46 percent of those arrested for rape, and 62 percent of those arrested for robbery in 1985 were black.[13] However, such statistics cannot be taken as an accurate measure of the amount of crime committed by blacks or whites, since many criminologists believe that blacks are more likely to be arrested, indicted, and imprisoned than whites who have committed the same offense.[14]

Studies of the victims of crime are a much more reliable source of data than arrest statistics. And because the criminals and victims in the vast majority of crimes are of the same race, we can infer that the group with the highest rate of victimization is also the group with the highest crime rate. Of the murders known to the police in 1985, about 44 percent of the victims were black, but only about 12 percent of the entire population was black. This means that blacks were about six times more likely to end their life as the victim of a murder than other Americans. Another source of data is the National Crime Survey, which asks victims to identify the race of their offender. In cases in which victims saw their offender, he or she was identified as being black in about 20 percent of the assaults, 25 percent of the rapes, and 45 percent of the robberies.[15] On the basis of this and other evidence, most criminologists have concluded that there is a real, not just statistical, difference between the rates of violent crime for blacks and whites. It also appears that blacks are somewhat more likely to commit the kinds of property crimes that are usually reported in police statistics. However, whites are more likely to hold white-collar jobs and thus probably commit many more white-collar crimes. And as is the case with social class, the lack of reliable statistics on white-collar crime makes it impossible to assess black–white differences in property crime as a whole.

Residential Area   For at least a century, studies from all over the world have shown more crime in big cities than in small towns and rural areas. Skeptics have wondered whether the difference is merely statistical, because more rural and small-town crime is handled informally rather than reported to a police agency. But recent studies of victimization have confirmed earlier studies using official statistics. According to the National Crime Survey, a person living in the central city is 52 percent more likely to be a victim of a violent crime than other Americans, and about 20 percent more likely to be victimized in a property crime.[16] But there are crime rate differences *within* individual cities as well. The rates are highest in decaying inner-city slums, and they decrease regularly as one moves out from the central city to the better residential areas.

There are a number of reasons for the higher rates of crime in urban areas. For one thing, the urbanite lives in a world of strangers where a criminal is not likely to be recognized. Further, the anonymity of the big city breeds alienation, and many people are isolated from supportive social groups that might prevent crime informally. Finally, the city attracts young single people, who as a group have the highest crime rate no matter where they live.

THE CAUSES OF CRIME

Systematic study of crime rates and criminal behavior goes back only about two centuries. Until about the time of the American Revolution, crime was considered a product of innate depravity prompted by the devil. Because something outside the society and outside the individual was thought to be responsible for crime, the notion that crime could be reduced by modifying the conditions that produce it was entirely foreign.

The birth of modern criminology can be traced to 1764 and the publication of Cesare Beccaria's book *On Crimes and Punishments*. Beccaria was an Italian nobleman. The great English philosopher Jeremy Bentham applied Beccaria's ideas to legislation, and these two men became the leaders of what came to be called the classical school of criminology. They thought that all people were guided by a rational desire to seek pleasure and avoid pain. According to the classical school, persons who commit a crime choose to do so. They weigh all the options and find that a crime will give them the most pleasure for the least amount of pain. This was regarded as a complete explanation of crime, and its inventors saw no need for research on economic, personal, political, or social conditions associated with crime. Although the psychology on which the classical school was founded has long since been discarded by most social scientists, this approach continues to dominate Anglo-American criminal law and its administration.

The early members of the classical school were reformers who tried to soften the cruel methods used by kings and emperors to maintain social order and protect their privileged positions. Bentham, for example, helped make punishments less severe and arbitrary. He contended that all laws should be clearly stated and that all people who violate a specific law should receive identical punishments regardless of age, social class, or circumstances. In other words, the punishment was to fit the crime. The solution to the crime problem, according to Bentham, was to punish as many offenders as possible. Such punishment—which was to be severe enough to deter crime but no more severe than that—was expected to outweigh the pleasures anyone might gain from crime, thus teaching people that it was in their interest to obey the law.

The so-called positive school of criminology developed under the leadership of an Italian physician, Cesare Lombroso, in the last quarter of the nineteenth century. Lombroso and other positivists rejected the classical school's belief in free will and the criminal's ability to decide rationally whether or not to commit a crime. They saw crime and criminal behavior as products of natural causes. In the past hundred years criminological research has taken the positivist path, meaning that researchers have assumed that crime and criminality have external causes and are not merely willed by individual actors.

Biological Theories   Lombroso thought criminals were born with the savage instincts of wild animals.[17] In other words, they were throwbacks to humanity's pre-human ancestors. According to Lombroso, these "born criminals" could easily be distinguished from normal individuals by physical traits such as sloping foreheads, small brains, large ears, overdeveloped jaws, and other apelike characteristics. Lombrosian ideas about the physical characteristics of criminals have been totally discredited in the scientific community, but the idea that some tendency toward criminality is inherited has gained renewed attention in the last two decades.

One of the first objects of this new interest in biological theories of crime was an abnormality in sex chromosomes reported to be far more common among prisoners and patients in mental hospitals than among the general public. The idea is that an extra Y (male) chromosome in males causes the individual to be uncontrollably aggressive. But a thorough review of this research concluded that "XYY males in an institutional setting are *less* violent or aggressive when compared with matched chromosomally normal fellow inmates, and their criminal histories involve crimes against property rather than against persons."[18]

More recent biological research has tended to ignore the search for specific genes that produce crime. Instead, criminologists have looked to see if those who have a close biological relationship to known criminals are themselves more likely to be involved in crime. As in the research on mental disorder discussed in Chapter 12, some criminologists have compared crime rates among identical and fraternal twins. The assumption is that if crime is inherited, the criminal records of identical twins (whose genetic makeup is supposed to be the same) ought to be more similar than those of fraternal twins; most but not all of these studies have found that to be the case.[19] However, such studies are not very convincing because of the fact that parents and friends tend to treat identical twins more similarly than fraternal twins.

A better methodological approach is found in studies that compare the crime rates of adopted children with those of their biological parents. Once again, most but not all of these studies have found higher crime rates among adopted children whose biological parents were criminals than among those whose biological parents were not. Hutchings and Mednick's study of 1,145 boys adopted in Copenhagen, for example, found that having a biological parent as a criminal significantly increased a boy's chances of growing up to be a criminal and that the highest crime rates were among those boys whose adoptive and biological parents were both criminals.[20]

But the adoption studies still have serious weaknesses. Since both adoption and criminality are rare events, it is difficult get a good sample of people with both characteristics. In most cases, researchers have relied on official records as their only measure of criminality, and as we have seen, such records have serious deficiencies. But the most crucial problem is the tendency of adoption agencies to place babies in homes from the same ethnic and social groups as their biological parents. This means that some or all of the similarity in crime rates between biological parents and their children who were given up for adoption may be due to the similarity in their social experiences. Thus, although there is some evidence that a tendency toward criminality is hereditary, it is far from proven.

Another problem with biological theories is that they have yet to determine exactly what inherited characteristics contribute to criminal behavior. Wilson and Herrnstein speculate that it might be low intelligence or an impulsive personality, but there is little conclusive evidence on the matter.[21] Crime obviously cannot be directly inherited because crime is defined by legislators and politicians and the definition of what is criminal and what is not is continually changing. It seems likely that inherited traits are related to criminal behavior only by virtue of the fact that people have learned to react to them in a certain way. For example, a student with high intelligence will be more likely to do well in school and receive praise and support from teachers, whereas a student with lesser abilities is far more likely to feel rejected and rebel against school authorities.

Personality Theories   There is a widely held belief that many criminals, especially violent ones, are mentally disturbed. After a particularly gruesome murder has occurred, we often hear the comment, "A person would have to be crazy to commit a crime like that." Although such statements express understandable shock and disbelief, they are misguided. In the first place, psychiatric examinations of convicted criminals show that only a small percentage are psychotic. Moreover, psychiatric records show that most psychotics are not criminals and have not attacked or harmed other people.[22] In the second place, research on the relationship between psychoses and crime is complicated by the fact that a person who is "insane" at the time that a legally forbidden act is carried out does not commit a crime. For example, a man charged with murder may defend himself in court by showing that he was insane at the time that the act occurred, just as another man may plead that his act was performed in self-defense. *Insanity* is a legal term, not a psychiatric one, and it refers to the fact that a person did not know the nature or quality of the harmful act or did not know right from wrong. "Insane" people, like infants, are legally incapable of committing crimes.

The psychoses are not the only psychological conditions that have been studied as potential causes of crime. Criminal behavior is often said to be caused by emotional disturbances or certain personality traits. Dozens of personality tests and rating scales have been used to compare criminals and noncriminals, but despite the claims of some psychologists and psychiatrists, few significant differences have been found. For example, the most widely used personality test is the Minnesota Multiphasic Personality Inventory (MMPI), and numerous studies have been made of the differences between the scores of criminals and noncriminals over the years. Three comprehensive reviews of the studies using the MMPI or other personality scales—one by Schuessler and Cressey in the 1950s, a second by Waldo and Dinitz in the 1960s, and a third by Tennenbaum in the 1970s—have all concluded that there was little evidence to support the claim that criminals have distinctive personality characteristics.[23]

Many psychologists and psychiatrists who routinely examine convicted criminals have nonetheless concluded that they often have **sociopathic personalities.** This term is quite vague, but it refers to an inability to form close social relationships combined with a lack of moral feelings or concern for others. Some psychiatrists think that this personality type is hereditary, but the most common explanation is that it develops in early childhood. The method of diagnosing a sociopathic personality is not at all standardized. For this reason, the labels "sociopathic" and "sociopath" can be applied to almost anyone. It appears that this idea of causation is circular. People are labeled sociopathic because they have broken the law, and then it is claimed that people break the law because they are sociopaths. This approach has been called neo-Lombrosian because it continues Lombroso's search for a criminal type, with an emphasis on personality rather than anatomy.

Sociological Theories   There are dozens of sociological theories of crime and criminality. The central idea is that criminal behavior is produced by the same social processes that produce other behavior. Analyses of the social processes and conditions producing criminality have taken two principal forms. First, sociologists have shown that variations in crime rates are associated with variations in social structure, including mobility, social class, population composition, and cultural conflict. Second, sociologists have studied the processes by which a person becomes a criminal.

For generations, sociologists have been trying to explain why lower-class people commit more crimes than others. As we have seen, this kind of study has been handicapped by the apparent unreliability of crime statistics. But some sociologists, convinced that there really is an excess of crime among lower-class people, have gone on to try to explain it. Probably the most influencial of these sociologists is Robert K. Merton, who developed what is often called **strain theory**.[24] Crime, according to this theory, is produced by the strain in societies that (1) tell people that wealth is available to all but also (2) restrict people's access to the means for achieving wealth. In more traditional societies where citizens are taught to be content with their lot, they do not experience such frustration. And of course, if all people "made it" in societies stressing ambition and upward mobility, there would not be much frustration either. Societies with high crime rates, Merton said, are those that tell people they can get ahead but in fact block achievement for some of them. Because lower-class people in such societies cannot legally obtain the things they are taught to desire, they are more likely to try to reach their goals in some other way—by breaking the law. This produces a high crime rate among lower-class people.

Not all sociologists agree that lower-class people are unhappy and discontented with their lot in life. Walter B. Miller, for example, held that American lower-class culture is distinctively different from middle-class culture and that it is much more conducive to crime.[25] Miller argued that lower-class behavior patterns might have originated in a process similar to the one described by Merton, but that strain and frustration are not the causes of the high rates of crime among the lower classes. He argued that lower-class culture is organized around six central values—trouble, toughness, smartness, excitement, fate, and autonomy—and he held that it is allegiance to these values that produces delinquency.

Much social psychological research has supported Miller's conclusion that criminal behavior is learned in a process of association with values that lead to trouble with the law. Indeed, a major theory of crime causation, **differential association**, proposes that people become delinquents or criminals when they have experienced an excess of such associations.[26] Briefly put, this theory—developed by Edwin H. Sutherland—says that people become criminals because they are exposed to more attitudes and definitions that are favorable to a certain kind of crime than are opposed to it. Thus, a person may come into contact with an excess of behavior patterns favorable, say, to shoplifting, but an excess of behavior patterns unfavorable to burglary or robbery. However, all associations and personal contacts do not have the same influence. The longer, the more frequent, the more intense, and the more important an association is to a person, the stronger its influence. Most criminal behavior, like most noncriminal behavior, is therefore learned in intimate personal groups and not from impersonal sources such as movies and television.

Deviant subcultures are an important source of crime. Such groups have developed perspectives, attitudes, and values that support criminal activity. The more people are involved with members of such a deviant subculture, the more they are likely to be influenced by their opinions and to join in their criminal activity. Miller considered the entire lower-class subculture to be deviant because he saw that anyone growing up in it will be more likely to violate the law. The drug subculture and the subculture of juvenile-gang members also are distinctive perspectives on the world, and both reject at least parts of the conventional morality embodied in law. For a lower-class boy who is a drug addict and a member of a juvenile gang, crime of one kind or another is almost automatic. He does not have to "choose" whether or not to commit a crime. His associations make the selection for him.

The theory of differential association is one of the most widely accepted sociological theories about crime causation, but it is far from perfect. For one thing, it is stated in quite general terms and therefore is very hard to test. The theory implies that an observer can simply add up the number of a person's associations that favor crime, compare them to the associations that are opposed to crime, and decide whether or not that person will become a criminal. In practice, that is impossible. Another criticism focuses on opportunities to commit crime. For example, suppose there were two women with exactly the same ratio of associations favorable to shoplifting and unfavorable to shoplifting. One might live in a large city and have an opportunity to commit the crime easily and safely, while the other might live in a rural area, never have such an opportunity, and never become a criminal. The differential-association principle seems to be concerned only with people who have equal opportunities to commit a crime, but this point is not clear.

The differential-association theory is considered irrelevant by some sociologists who believe that crime is normal and natural. If all people are born with an "aggressive instinct," or automatically commit crimes for some other reason, it is not useful to ask why they commit crimes. It is more reasonable, according to this way of thought, to ask why people do not commit crimes. **Control theorists** ask this question, and they answer it by saying that noncriminals are controlled and constrained by society and thus are prevented from breaking the law.

Some control theorists emphasize the importance of the internal controls that society builds up in the individual through the process of socialization. They say a strong conscience and sense of personal morality stops most people from breaking the law. Others say attachment to small social groups is what keeps people in line. According to this idea, most of us refrain from committing crimes because we fear disapproval and rejection by the people who are important to us. Still other control theorists have abandoned positivism and returned to a basic assumption of the classical school, namely, that most of us do not commit crimes because we fear arrest and imprisonment. These different versions of control theory are not mutually exclusive.

In fact, the most convincing form of control theory sees all three types of control working simultaneously.[27]

Critics point out that control theory, like the theory of differential association, is extremely broad and virtually impossible to prove or disprove. The critics have passed particularly harsh judgment on control theory's assumption that people "naturally" commit crimes. Like the religious idea that human beings are evil by nature, it is an assumption that is almost impossible to study scientifically.

Labeling theorists, like differential-association theorists, believe that criminals learn to be criminals. As the name suggests, labeling theory is concerned with the process of branding people as criminals and the effects that such labeling has on individuals. Labeling theory holds that, contrary to popular opinion and control theory, branding someone as a deviant often encourages rather than discourages criminal behavior.

For example, take the case of an adolescent boy whose "play" includes breaking windows, climbing over roofs, and stealing hubcaps. He might look at such activities as akin to the fun of Halloween. To most adults, however, his behavior is delinquent and must be curtailed. Law enforcement personnel, school officials, and his parents demand that he stop his delinquent activities. As it continues, there is a shift away from the definition of the *acts* as delinquent to the definition of the *boy* as delinquent. The boy, realizing that he is being branded as "bad," draws closer to others who share his "play" activities and therefore are experiencing similar problems.

Once the community is convinced that the boy is a delinquent, he is singled out for special treatment. He is threatened, punished, counseled, tested, analyzed, supervised, perhaps committed to an institution. He acquires a record with the police and other agencies. As the community copes with him, it crystallizes its conception of him and his conception of himself. He defines himself as he is defined, as a "delinquent"—by this time an incorrigible one, committed to a long-term criminal career.

Labeling theory has not been as widely accepted as the differential-association or control theories. Its principal defect is its inability to explain why people commit the acts that get them labeled in the first place. It is not enough to say that "everyone breaks the law," even though that is probably true. The challenge is to explain why they do so. Another problem arises because labeling sometimes discourages delinquency and crime. Many people who are arrested and labeled as criminals are so shocked and ashamed that they never repeat the behavior that got them into trouble.

TYPES OF CRIMES

There are so many different criminal laws that it would take a massive book just to describe them all. Criminal laws vary tremendously from place to place, and hundreds of new criminal laws are passed, changed, or repealed every year. Crime, then, is a rather diffuse hodgepodge of different kinds of behavior. Much effort has gone into attempts to classify crimes in some orderly way. Crimes are legally classified as **felonies** or **misdemeanors.** The more serious offenses are called felonies and are usually punishable by death or by confinement in a central prison; the less serious ones are called misdemeanors and are usually punishable by confinement in a local jail or by fines. However, this distinction is not very useful as a sociological classification because both categories still contain a bewildering variety of different and largely unrelated crimes.

For statistical purposes crimes are usually classified as offenses against persons (violent crime), crimes against property (property crime), and offenses against public decency and order (victimless crime). The official statistics compiled by the FBI are classified this way. Eight offenses are called "index crimes" or "major crimes." This category includes four violent crimes—murder, forcible rape, robbery, and assault—all of which involve the use of force or the threat of force. It also includes four property crimes—burglary, larceny-theft, arson, and automobile theft—three of which involve stealing something belonging to another. Less serious versions of these crimes are also classified as crimes against persons or crimes against property. Examples are minor assaults, vandalism, and sex offenses other than rape or prostitution. But the great majority of all offenses fall into the third category: crimes against public decency and order. These include prostitution, gambling, drug offenses, drunkenness, and vagrancy.

Of all the arrests reported to the police (excluding arrests for traffic violations), only about 20 percent are for the "major" crimes. Homicide arrests account for about 0.15 percent, rape for 0.3 percent, robbery for 1 percent, and aggravated assault for 2.5 percent. Thus, the four most serious crimes account for less than 5 percent of all arrests. By way of contrast, about 35 percent of all arrests are for only four of the many "public order" crimes: drunkenness (8 percent), driving under the influence (15 percent), narcotics (7 percent), and disorderly conduct (6 percent).[28]

19th-Century Social Problems

Victoria Hanna, a middle aged woman of Kaukauna, Outagamie County, was bound over to Commissioner Bloodgood the other day in the sum of $500 on the charge of sending obscene matter through the mails. The woman had a spite against a neighbor and mailed her a letter of the filthiest description.

May 14, 1886

These selections, which appear throughout the text, are from the *Badger State Banner,* a newspaper published in Black River Falls, Wisconsin.

Classifications of crimes for theoretical or educational purposes do not necessarily follow the schemes used for statistical purposes. Various types of crimes are grouped together in ways designed to focus attention on some particular part of the total crime problem. Violent crime is one such grouping, and in the next chapter, we will show that this category includes offenses ranging from teenage fist fights to cold-blooded murder. Three other categories of crime—victimless crimes, youth crimes, and white-collar crimes— deserve some special attention in this section.

Crimes Without Victims   Crime usually involves a victim who suffers either financial or physical harm at the hands of one or more offenders. But there are a substantial number of crimes in which there is no clear-cut victim. The use of illegal drugs, gambling, prostitution, and homosexuality, for example, have been called **victimless crimes** because the harm, if any, is not suffered by anyone except the offender.

Enforcing the laws against such acts is a tremendous burden for police departments and other criminal-justice agencies. According to official statistics, almost half of all arrests in the United States are for victimless crimes. Many criminologists argue that these arrests are taking valuable resources away from the effort to control more serious offenses. Moreover, the very fact that a crime is victimless means that few people are likely to call the police to report it. For example, the customers of prostitutes and bookmakers (takers of illegal bets on horse races and athletic events) do not report the activities of these criminals. If police officers are to make arrests for such offenses, they must seek them out on their own. In doing so they often use the services of spies and informers. Such secret police operations pose a potential threat to the civil liberties of all citizens, not just those who have committed a crime. Further, a substantial number of people do not think that such activities as smoking marijuana and gambling are wrong; consequently, laws against them create hostility and disrespect for the legal system. Finally, prohibition of victimless crimes often fosters the growth of deviant subcultures that may in time encourage crimes other than victimless ones.

If these laws create so many problems, why aren't they abolished? The answer, of course, is that a majority or a powerful minority of the people feel that the outlawed behaviors are wrong. They use the law-enforcement machinery in an effort to reduce the incidence of what they see as sin. However, in large, complex societies, and even in some small ones, not everyone agrees on what is sinful and what is not.

Juvenile Delinquency   The difference between crime and **juvenile delinquency** is not simply a matter of age. It is true that adults who violate criminal laws are called criminals, while juveniles who do the same things are called delinquents. But this is only part of the story. A substantial portion of all juvenile delinquents have never even been accused of doing anything that would be against the law if they were adults. Runaways, truants, violators of curfew laws, and youngsters who get drunk, for example, are delinquents only because they have broken laws pertaining to the behavior of juveniles. Further, criminal laws must try to present clear definitions of the acts they outlaw, but juvenile codes define delinquency in vague terms. Indeed, some state codes define a delinquent child but do not define specific delinquent acts. For example, youngsters who are "incorrigible" and those who are in danger of leading an "immoral life" are often defined as delinquents. But such terms as *incorrigible* and *immoral* are not defined clearly. The vagueness of juvenile codes gives police officers and other state officials broad power to decide what kind of behavior is delinquent and what is not.

It is no accident that juvenile courts have jurisdiction over juveniles who are considered to be in need of supervision as well as those who are accused of theft, robbery, assault, and other crimes. Juvenile-court procedures were established to *help* juveniles, whether they have committed harmful acts or not. It followed logically that neglected children as well as young criminals should be called delinquents because that was a way of initiating a program to help them. Precise definitions were not needed, the argument went, because the court was to be a welfare agency. For example, deciding whether a youth had or had not stolen something—in imitation of the criminal courts—was not to be the business of juvenile courts. Instead, the judge was to decide what help should be given to juveniles whose thefts suggested that they needed help, just as the judge was to decide what help should be given to an orphan or a neglected child.

Anthony Platt has shown that the concept of delinquency was created in the latter part of the nineteenth century by middle-class reformers whom he calls "child savers."[29] Despite the good intentions of the child savers, Platt argues, their efforts resulted in increasing governmental control over youthful behavior that did not violate the criminal law but did violate middle-class standards. In the 1960s civil libertarians began voicing strong objections to the practices of juvenile courts. They noted that juveniles were in fact being stigmatized and punished by the juvenile-justice process, not helped or treated. The Supreme Court then held that broad definitions of delinquency and the absence of criminal-law procedures violate the constitutional rights of juveniles. As a result, juvenile courts have grown more similar to criminal courts. For instance, many states no longer define running away, incorrigibility, and other **status offenses** (juvenile offenses that do not violate the criminal law) as delinquency. At the same time, juveniles are increasingly being prosecuted for their delinquencies in the same ways as adults are prosecuted for their crimes.

Juvenile delinquency—at least the acts of juveniles that would be crimes if committed by adults—has probably been studied more carefully than any other category of crime. The principal explanations of crime were developed from the study of delinquency as well as adult criminality, and all of them are used to explain delinquency as well as crime. Nevertheless, juveniles have special problems and should not be considered merely young criminals.

Juvenile courts were created to help young people in trouble and were given very broad powers. They are now becoming more and more like criminal courts, however, because of both a concern about juveniles' civil rights and an increasingly punitive attitude on the part of the courts.

For one thing, the influence of the family is certainly greater in the lives of juvenile delinquents than in the lives of adult criminals. A number of studies show that children from homes in which one or other of the parents are criminals are much more likely to become delinquent. Discipline and training are also important. Many studies show that children from single-parent homes are more likely to become delinquents than children from two-parent homes. However, the low income level of most single-parent families is probably as important as the family disruption itself.[30]

Another unique problem of juvenile offenders is their youth. In traditional cultures people go directly from being a child to being an adult. But in industrialized nations there is an extended in-between period of adolescence in which difficult demands are placed on young people. Adolescents are not considered old enough for marriage and family responsibilities of their own, yet they are too old to remain totally dependent on their parents. In a sense they are between two worlds and part of neither.

Finally, the problem of juvenile gangs deserves mention. Adolescents all over the world form groups based on friendship and mutual interests. When these groups meet social approval we call them clubs; but when the community condemns them, they are called gangs. Juvenile gangs of streetwise young toughs roam the streets of most urban slums and ghettos. The primary motivation of the "fighting gang" is to control their "turf" (territory) and defend their honor, sometimes to the death. Some gangs have long histories, going back 30 or 40 years, and gang fights and killings have been a fact of life in some urban neighborhoods for generations.

White-Collar Crime   **White-collar crimes** cost more money and more lives than all other types of crime put together. Although accurate tallies of the financial costs of white-collar crime are hard to come by, a conservative estimate would place the yearly losses from 20 to 30 times higher than the losses from street crime.[31] In 1985, for example, the average robbery netted only about $628, while in that same year a single white-collar criminal, Ivan F. Boesky, agreed to pay $100 million in fines and penalties for his illegal stock market dealings.[32] Yet that huge sum was probably far less than he made from his crimes.

Most people do not think of white-collar offenses as violent crime, and it is true that the criminals seldom intend to injure or kill anyone. Nonetheless, the yearly death toll from unsafe products, worker safety violations, the illegal dumping of toxic wastes, and other corporate crimes is far higher than that from murder. The cover-up of the deadly hazards of asbestos by the Mansville Corporation and the other major asbestos producers will prob-

White-collar crime costs the public far more than the "street crimes" that get so much attention. Ivan Boesky, pictured here, made tens of millions of dollars, while the average robbery nets only a few hundred dollars.

ably cost as many lives as all the murders in the United States for an entire decade. And in addition to our lives and our money, white-collar criminals threaten something else as well: political freedom. The assassinations of foreign political leaders, the illegal surveillance and harassment of groups opposed to government policy, election fraud, and the kind of political dirty tricks involved in the Watergate scandal are all important white-collar crimes.[33]

Edwin Sutherland originally coined the term "white-collar crime" to call attention to the weaknesses in theories that say crime is due to personal pathologies or poverty (such theories obviously cannot account for most criminal activities among the upper classes). He defined white-collar crime as any "crime committed by a person of respectability and high social status in the course of his occupation."[34] There are two basic types of white-collar crime. **Organizational crimes** are committed by people who are acting on behalf of the organization for which they work. **Occupational crimes** are committed solely to advance the personal interests of the criminal. For example, when employees embezzle money from a bank, the crime is occupational because the employees are obviously not working for the interests of their employer. But when an executive fraudulently claims that an addictive new drug isn't habit-forming, it is an organizational crime because the offense was committed to benefit the company.

There are white-collar criminals in every type of occupation, from accounting to zoology, and in every type of organization, from the corner grocery store to huge government bureaucracies. Many of the victims of such criminals do not know that they have been victimized and therefore do not complain to the police or anyone else. For this reason the public is often unaware how serious the problem of white-collar crime really is.

Numerous studies have also shown that those charged with white-collar crimes are less likely to be prosecuted and convicted than those charged with comparable "street crimes." And when the defendants in white-collar cases are convicted, they receive a lighter sentence.[35] But the most leniency goes to the big corporations. The famous University of Wisconsin study of corporate crime headed by sociologist Marshall B. Clinard found that the major corporations were seldom given any real punishment for their illegal activities. Almost half of the "penalties" given to the 477 largest manufacturing corporations in the United States for their illegal activities were merely warnings. The corporations were fined for fewer than a quarter of their offenses, and those fines averaged only about $1000—hardly a significant punishment for a multibillion-dollar corporation.[36]

There are several reasons why white-collar criminals receive such lenient treatment. For one thing, they can afford the best legal defense available. More important, the laws themselves are generally written to favor high-status criminals, particularly those who commit crimes that benefit, rather than harm, their companies. Children are a favored group in our society, and special juvenile delinquency laws and procedures have been developed to deal with their offenses; similarly, special laws and procedures have been developed to deal with the crimes of businesspeople, another favored group.

Finally, the thousands of victims of such white-collar crimes as false advertising and price fixing lose only a few dollars each; so there is less public
resentment than there is when a criminal strikes more heavily at a few individual victims. Indeed, as has already been noted, many of the victims of
white-collar crimes never know they have been victimized.

DEALING WITH CRIMINALS

The criminal-justice process reflects a conflict between two very different
social goals. On the one hand, there is the need to stop crime and rid society
of troublemakers. On the other hand, there is the need to protect, preserve,
and nourish the rights and liberties of individuals. All societies pit these two
needs against each other. Some are police states, in which the methods of
crime control bulldoze citizens into submission. At the other extreme is
chaos, in which individuals run wild. Democratic societies take a middle
ground, tempering the need to repress crime with concern for the rights of
their citizens.

But even in democratic societies few people agree on what the proper
balance should be. Some North Americans favor what Herbert Packer called
the **crime-control model** of criminal justice, a program for the speedy arrest
and punishment of all who commit crimes. Others advocate a **due-process
model** that tempers the rush to punishment with concern for human rights
and dignity.[37] Speaking generally, those who fear official abuse of power
favor the due-process model, while those who fear crime more advocate the
crime-control model. But the matter is not so simple. The person who supports one model today may support the other tomorrow, depending on the
merits of specific cases For example, parents might cry for the crime-control
model when their daughter is raped but call for the due-process model when
their son is arrested for selling heroin to a police informer.

The matter is further complicated by the fact that criminal law itself
stresses crime control, while the legal rules for the administration of justice
emphasize the rights of the accused to due process of law. Every criminal
statute calls for strict control of criminal behavior. Each says, specifically,
that whoever behaves in a certain way must be punished in a certain way.
Each is thus a command issued by lawmakers to all who are paid to process
suspects, defendants, and criminals. These officials are ordered to punish
criminals on the assumption that punishment will hurt them so much that
they will be afraid to repeat their crimes.

But other laws soften this harsh crime-control procedure. They do so
mostly by (1) specifying rules about arrests, court processes, and the conditions of imprisonment and (2) authorizing criminal-justice workers to adjust
punishments to the circumstances of each offense and the background of
each offender. Thus, the crime-control model is softened by laws saying that
police looking for evidence of crime cannot break into houses, that courts
must give accused persons an opportunity to cross-examine their accusers,
and that punishments may not be cruel or unusual. The criminal-justice
process is also softened by laws authorizing judges to suspend punishments

and place offenders on probation and, more generally, by rules permitting officials to use their judgment in deciding which crimes may be overlooked in the name of justice.

The Police   Police officers are on the cutting edge of the criminal-justice process. They are much more visible than other criminal-justice personnel, and they have more contacts with the citizenry. They have become the symbols of the whole system of justice. The kind of job they do therefore has an enormous influence on public confidence in the institutions of government.

In addition to their symbolic importance, police officers are the gate-keepers for the other criminal-justice agencies. They cannot possibly arrest all suspected lawbreakers. First, considerations of cost and due process limit the number of officers; police chiefs cannot put an officer at every citizen's elbow. Second, if the existing police force arrested all criminal suspects, there would not be enough courts to process them or enough jails and prisons to house the guilty. Third, it is not always easy to tell whether a violation of law has in fact taken place. Criminal laws are written in general terms to

Police officers spend more of their time providing public services than enforcing the law.

cover a wide variety of behaviors, and police officers must decide whether they fit the individual case at hand. For example, statutes outlaw "assaults" but do not outlaw "scuffles," and officers are hard put to decide which is which. Fourth, police officers may not arrest a person on mere suspicion. An arrest is not legal unless the facts suggest that there is good reason to believe that the arrested person has committed a crime.

All in all, then, the work of police officers is highly discretionary. The judgment of individual officers, in turn, determines how much business there will be for the criminal-justice agencies down the line.

Of equal importance to understanding police activities is the fact that only a small part of all the work done by a police department is directly concerned with fighting crime. For example, only 10 to 20 percent of the calls to most police departments require officers to perform law-enforcement duties, and most of the incidents an officer handles on any given day are not criminal matters.[38] Outsiders who have observed police activities confirm the idea that the terms *peace officer* or even *social worker* describe the work of police personnel more adequately than *law-enforcement officer*.

Even when performing law-enforcement duties, police officers are in a difficult position. They are expected to behave according to the crime-control model, meaning that they are supposed to apprehend lawbreakers and maintain order. But they are also expected to perform according to the due-process model, strictly meeting all the legal requirements for proper police procedures. They are criticized for not catching enough criminals, but they are also criticized if they exceed their legal authority.

There is no clear-cut solution to this dilemma. No one wants to "handcuff the police," but most citizens recognize that personal freedoms perish when legal safeguards are ignored. In the long run, police officers and citizens alike will be better off if the population comes to realize that police officers operate more like diplomats than like soldiers engaged in a war on crime.

The Courts   After an arrest, police officers must take the suspect promptly before a lower-court magistrate (judge). If the magistrate decides that a suspect must come back to the lower court for further proceedings, the magistrate sets the conditions under which temporary release on bail can be granted.

The cases of those accused of minor offenses are decided when they return to the lower court. But those accused of serious crimes are first given a **preliminary hearing.** At this hearing, the magistrate decides whether the evidence against the accused is sufficient to justify further legal proceedings. The preliminary hearing is wholly for the benefit of the suspect. Its purpose is not to determine whether the accused is innocent or guilty. It is to determine whether the state has enough evidence to justify further court proceedings. If the evidence against the accused is insufficient, the suspect is discharged. Otherwise, the accused must await further proceedings by a higher court.

Under the American **bail** system, accused persons put up a sum of money to be forfeited if they do not show up for trial. In most courts, the accused can pay a relatively small fee to a bail bondsman, who then provides the financial security (called a bail bond) necessary for release. It is a well-known fact that the bail system discriminates against the poor. The amount of money required is usually determined by the charge against the suspect rather than by the person's character and responsibility. Poor people who cannot raise enough money stay in jail, while the more affluent go free on bail. At least half of all American defendants are unable to make bail. They remain in jail awaiting trial, sometimes for months.

Felony cases that are not dismissed at the preliminary-hearing stage move up to a trial court. Each defendant is informed of the charges and asked to plead guilty or not guilty. Defendants who plead guilty are sentenced; those who plead not guilty are scheduled for trial at a later date. However, statistics show that the trial plays a very small part in the criminal-justice process. A recent study of federal courts showed that about 89 percent of felony convictions came on a guilty plea, whereas only about one in ten came from a jury trial.[39]

The defendant does not, however, always plead guilty to the original charges. A single act usually involves more than one crime. For example, a person who commits burglary also commits the lesser crimes of unlawful entry and trespassing. Similarly, a grand-theft charge automatically accuses the defendant of petty theft as well: it is impossible to steal a lot (grand theft) without also stealing a little (petty theft). In a process that has come to be called **plea bargaining,** many defendants make a deal with prosecutors to plead guilty if the charge is reduced. The state is thus saved the expense of a trial, and the defendant receives a punishment lighter than the one that might have been imposed if he or she had gone ahead with a trial on the original charge and had been found guilty.

Settling cases out of court with the plea bargaining process is much faster and cheaper than taking each case to trial. Moreover, the process provides for much greater flexibility than the trial process. It permits prosecutors and defense attorneys to soften laws that call for a penalty that seems too harsh in light of what the defendant actually did. Nevertheless, plea bargaining has recently come under a torrent of criticism. Civil libertarians complain that it takes justice behind closed doors, where violations of defendants' rights are hidden from judicial and public view. They also claim that the very existence of the negotiation process coerces defendants into pleading guilty: those who exercise their right to a trial and are convicted receive longer sentences than they would have received if they had pleaded guilty to a lesser charge. Plea bargaining also has been attacked by those who claim that it allows criminals to escape the severe punishment they deserve.

After defendants have pleaded guilty or have been found guilty, they are called back to the courtroom for sentencing. When the influence of the classical school of criminology was at its height, sentencing was rather routine. In theory, the judge had no choice about the sentence. The law ordered specific punishments for specific offenses, and the judge merely asked that they be administered. But with the development of the positive school, the

DEBATE

Will Sending More Criminals to Prison Solve the Crime Problem?

YES The spread of crime and lawlessness threatens the very survival of our society. Yet the criminal-justice system is hamstrung by pointless rules and regulations and obsessed with safeguarding the rights of criminals. The result is that law-abiding citizens go unprotected. The maze of legal restrictions are so complex that it practically requires the service of a lawyer for the police to make a legal arrest. Criminals are commonly turned loose because of minor technical errors that are not related to their guilt or innocence. Even if they are brought to court, plea-bargaining arrangements allow many dangerous felons to plead guilty to minor crimes. Convicted criminals are freed by judges or parole boards after serving little or no time in prison. This leniency permits thousands of criminals to remain at large, threatening the lives and property of decent citizens.

Despite the claims of liberals, putting criminals in prison is an effective way of preventing crime. Criminals obviously cannot victimize the public when they are locked up. Therefore, more criminals in prison means more safety on the streets. Fear of imprisonment is a powerful deterrent to crime. If criminals were given the tough punishment they deserve, more people would be afraid to break the law. But even if strict punishment failed to reduce crime, simple justice demands that the leniency in our criminal-justice system be ended. Law-abiding citizens are cheated when criminals go free. A crackdown on crime and lawlessness would make society better for everyone.

NO A larger portion of the population of the United States is in prison than in any other democratic nation. The proposal to solve the crime problem by locking up even more people is foolish and misguided. Prison actually encourages more crime. To be locked up with hundreds of criminals is to enter a school for crime in which degrading and inhumane conditions generate bitterness and resentment. The inevitable result is more crime, as is shown by the high percentage of offenders who return to prison for a second, third, or fourth time. The answer to the crime problem will not be found in imposing even more severe punishment on criminals but in changing the economic and social conditions that cause crime.

Even if packing more people into our prisons would reduce crime, such a "get tough" policy poses an unacceptable threat to civil liberties. Many conservatives would dismantle the constitutional safeguards that regulate the criminal-justice process, in order to catch more criminals. Under such a system no one would be safe from the prying eyes of the government. Police could stop people and search them without reasonable cause; they could enter homes, tap telephones, or investigate our private lives. Can we trust the government with such unbridled power? Numerous government scandals prove that the answer is no. Sooner or later this enormous power would be turned to political ends. The rights of all citizens—including criminals—must be protected. We cannot surrender our freedom to an oppressive state even if it promises to solve the crime problem.

offender rather than the offense became the focus of attention and judges were given a wide range of alternatives for dealing with criminals. Generally speaking, the severity of the sentence was supposed to be matched to the background of the offender as well as to the seriousness of the crime. Judges were, and are, permitted to place one murderer on probation, commit another to prison, and order the execution of a third. However, concern about disparities in the sentences judges hand out, and a feeling that they have been too lenient, has led to a trend toward a narrowing of the range of sentencing alternatives.

Judges and other sentencing authorities are on the spot. They are supposed to give equal punishments, no matter what the social status of the defendants involved. Yet they are also supposed to give individual punishments because the circumstances of each crime and the motivations of each criminal are always different: a just punishment for one burglar or car thief may be completely inappropriate for another. Judges are in a difficult position, then, because they are supposed to order uniform punishments for all burglars or automobile thieves but are also supposed to order different punishments for the various individuals convicted of violating the burglary or car-theft statutes. As judges try to satisfy these conflicting demands, they are bound to be denounced as unfair. The judge's task, like the police officer's task, is to walk a thin line between the crime-control model and the due-process model, balancing demands for repressing crime against demands for human rights and freedom.

Corrections   Until about two hundred years ago, there were few alternatives to punishing criminals. Authorities assumed that criminals would change their ways if they were punished **(specific deterrence)**. They also assumed that punishment of criminals would frighten others so much that they would not break the law, thus keeping the crime rate low **(general deterrence)**. But in the past century a new idea developed that criminals ought to be helped to change their ways by nonpunitive programs run by probation departments, prisons, and parole agencies. This new approach grew increasingly popular until the early 1970s. But in more recent years it has lost favor to the old idea that the criminal-justice system's primary goal is to make criminals suffer for their crimes.

If there is one key to understanding modern criminal-justice practices, it is this conflict between the idea that criminals should be changed by punishment and the idea that they should be changed by positive actions. The latter approach is the foundation on which probation and parole systems were constructed. It also was the principle underlying the idea that prisoners should be "diagnosed" and then "cured" by prison rehabilitation programs.

Probation Probation workers do not try to make criminals suffer but instead offer an alternative to the suffering they would experience if they went to prison. Probation thus represents a distinct break with the punitive ideal. In theory, only offenders who stand a good chance of changing their criminal

behavior are selected for probation. In practice, neither the methods of selecting people for probation nor the methods of helping them change their
behavior have been very effective. For example, the presentence investigations made by probation officers are by no means scientific. They consist
largely of routine interviews with prospective probationers. And if the investigation is defective, it follows that any treatment or intervention program
cannot be based on a real understanding of why the probationer broke the
law. Most probation departments do not have enough money to hire enough
well-trained workers. This means that the efforts of probation workers are
mostly devoted to keeping watch over criminals. Little time is left to try to
change probationers. Petersilia estimates that about two-thirds of those convicted of a crime are given probation,[40] but the rate is lower for more serious
offenses. A study of prosecutions in 37 big cities found that only 39 percent
of those convicted of a felony receive probation,[41] and another study of 18
local jurisdictions found that just 28 percent of convicted felons received
probation instead of going to prison.[42]

A recent Rand Corporation study of 1600 probationers found that about
two-thirds of them were eventually rearrested, and about half that number
went back to prison.[43] Although that is certainly not a good record, other
research shows that people placed on probation are still less likely to commit
new crimes than are those sent to prison. But of course, the most hardened
and dangerous criminals are not placed on probation; therefore, such studies
are not really helpful in evaluating the effectiveness of probation in preventing crime. The supporters of probation point out that it keeps offenders
from associating with one another in prison, and it is considerably cheaper
and more humane than imprisonment. Critics counter that probation lets
criminals off too lightly and therefore fails to discourage crime.

Prisons Imprisonment as a punishment for crime is, by and large, an American invention. In nonliterate societies and in ancient and medieval civilizations, imprisonment was rarely used as a penalty. Until the time of the
American Revolution, it was used primarily as a means of detention before
trial and as a means of enforcing the payment of fines. The major changes
that have occurred in prisons in the past two hundred years have been guided
by the idea that restricting a criminal's liberty is, by itself, punishment. As
democracy developed, restriction of freedom came to be regarded as a proper
system for imposing pain on criminals. Consistently, prison officials now say
that criminals are committed to prison *as* punishment rather than *for* punishment.

The public has set four main goals for criminal law that imprisonment
is supposed to achieve. First, they want to get even **(retribution).** The prison
is expected to make life unpleasant for people who, through their crimes,
have made others' lives unpleasant. Second, they want to scare people so
much that they will be afraid to commit crimes **(deterrence).** Third, they
want protection. The prison is expected to isolate criminals so that they
cannot commit more crimes against the public **(incapacitation).** Fourth, they

want criminals changed so that they will commit no more crimes even when free **(rehabilitation)**.

During the 1940s and the 1950s, the idea that prisoners should be rehabilitated hit at the very roots of the idea that prisons should change criminals by punishing them. Although the methods of rehabilitation were never precisely defined, the emphasis was on psychotherapy. The mental hospital was often used as a model of what the prison should be. Despite a great deal of talk, however, the prison remained a place of punishment. Wardens were not asked to replace programs designed to produce reformation through punishment with programs designed to rehabilitate through treatment. They were asked to set the new programs alongside the old ones and thus to be punitive and nonpunitive at the same time.

Evaluations of prison rehabilitation programs have shown that they help very few offenders.[44] As a result, it is now fashionable to argue that prison rehabilitation efforts should be abandoned. Indeed, they *are* being abandoned. The misguided idea that a criminal can be treated for criminality in

During the 1950s and 1960s, the idea that prisoners should be changed so they would no longer engage in criminal activities gained increasing popularity. Now, a growing fear of crime has led to a return to the idea that prisons are places to punish criminals and nothing else.

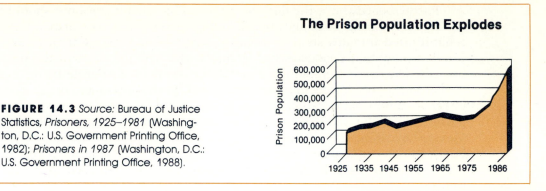

The Prison Population Explodes

FIGURE 14.3 *Source:* Bureau of Justice Statistics, *Prisoners, 1925–1981* (Washington, D.C.: U.S. Government Printing Office, 1982); *Prisoners in 1987* (Washington, D.C.: U.S. Government Printing Office, 1988).

the way that a mental patient can be treated for schizophrenia is no longer popular in criminal-justice circles. Appearing in its place is the idea that the prison is a place for punishing people and nothing else. At least in part as a result of such ideas, American prisons are once again becoming "jungles." Murder, assault, and homosexual rape are everyday events in many prisons, and it will not be long before mere survival is the primary goal of every inmate. The failure of our prisons to change criminals by using punishment and fear has been shown again and again. Although it is a matter of some dispute, the most commonly cited figure is that about two-thirds of those released from prison commit another serious crime.[45] A recent study by John Wallerstedt concluded that about half of all those released eventually return to prison.[46]

Despite such evidence of failure, America's prison population has reached an alarming size. At the end of 1987, over 580,000 persons were in state and federal prisons and another quarter of a million people were in local jails.[47] In the conservative climate of the 1980s, our prisons have literally undergone a population explosion: between 1980 and 1987 the prison population increased by 76 percent.[48] (See Figure 14.3.) As a result, prisons have become increasingly overcrowded and living conditions have gone from bad to worse. The federal prisons, for example, are now believed to be operating somewhere from 37 to 73 percent over their maximum capacity.[49]

Parole Like probation, parole represents a break with the classical theory of criminology. **Parole** is the act of releasing a criminal from prison after part of the sentence has been served. The prisoner who is granted parole must maintain good behavior. Like probation, parole ideally includes assistance to the offender. Parole is granted by a board that is part of the executive branch of government, and it is always preceded by imprisonment. The idea is to continue outside the prison the rehabilitation efforts that have begun inside the prison, while holding parolees under the threat of more severe punishment (return to the institution) if they do not maintain good behavior.

Parole boards have the duty of determining when a prisoner should be released on parole. Although boards give lip service to the principle that rehabilitated inmates shall be released, they seldom follow it in practice. Studies show that seriousness of offense is the best indicator of the parole board's decision.[50] Complaints about inconsistencies in parole board decisions, and a growing feeling among the public that prisoners ought not to be released until their full sentence is served has led to a movement to abolish parole altogether, and that is exactly what Illinois, Maine, Indiana, and New Mexico have done. Other states such as California, no longer allow the parole board to determine when most offenders are to be released, but parole officers still supervise prisoners for a time once they are returned to the community.

Despite this trend, there is good reason to think that both the ex-convict and the community can benefit from a well-run parole program. An ideal program ought to help parolees get and keep a job, and assist them to deal with the difficult psychological adjustment to the outside world, while keeping a close watch to make sure that they do not return to crime. Not only would this reduce the likelihood that they will still find a criminal career to be attractive, but the community is also given the extra assurance that parolees can quickly be returned to prison if they go back to their old ways. The problem with the current system is that with caseloads running as high as 200 or 300 parolees per agent, low pay, and inadequate training, the states simply cannot meet those goals.

RESPONDING TO PROBLEMS OF CRIME AND DELINQUENCY

Everyone seems to have an idea about how to stop crime. Politicians, police officers, criminologists, sociologists, and ordinary citizens propose one solution or another almost every day. Many of these proposals are contradictory, but it would seem to be possible to use the best features of each proposal in one comprehensive program.

Impose More Pain   The United States punishes its criminals more severely than any other democratic nation. American criminals receive longer prison terms than criminals in any similar country. Further, a higher percentage of America's population is in prison at any given time than in any other industrialized nation except South Africa and the Soviet Union.[51] Despite the severity of punishment in the United States, many Americans believe that the solution to our crime problem is to get even tougher. Their proposal has two parts. First, they demand that punishment be made more certain. Their ideal system would catch, convict, and punish a greater percentage of the people who violate the law. Second, they demand that punishments be more severe, that prison terms be lengthened, and that more criminals be executed. Both ideas are popular with the general public and with politicians who believe that they cannot afford to be "soft on crime."

Supporters of this approach argue that the decline in the crime rate in the 1980s was at least partially due to the "get tough" policies of the criminal-justice system. And indeed, there seems to be little doubt that locking more people up will produce a short-term drop in the crime rate. But critics charge that the long-term effects will be just the opposite. Sooner or later almost all prisoners are released, and their prison experience is likely to leave them more bitter and more hardened in their criminal ways than when they went in. A second problem is financial. It costs more to keep a criminal in prison than it does to keep a student in Harvard or Yale. In the next few years billions of dollars will have to be spent by hard-pressed state governments just to provide adequate facilities for those who are already in prison, much less to accommodate the steady increase in prison population. Finally, critics charge that this crime-control approach to criminal justice is a threat to the due process of law and thus to our most fundamental personal freedoms.

Divert and Ignore   The insights of labeling theory have led many sociologists to argue that we should avoid processing people as delinquents and criminals whenever possible because arrest, conviction, and imprisonment encourage some offenders to commit further crime. Influenced by this observation, criminal-justice workers have introduced programs to divert offenders out of criminal-justice agencies and into community programs of various sorts. Most of these **diversion programs** are aimed at keeping juveniles out of the criminal courts, and even out of juvenile courts. But many have had the opposite effect: they have become systems for getting more, not fewer, people processed by state agents.[52] For example, before diversion programs were introduced, a police officer might merely lecture a boy about a minor infraction and let him go. Now the existence of a diversion program run by the state encourages the officer to make an arrest and send the youngster into the program.

Edwin Schur has gone a step beyond the idea of diversion. He calls for "radical nonintervention" in dealing with juveniles, meaning that the criminal-justice system should stop arresting and labeling so many young people.[53] He observes, as many others have observed, that programs for changing juvenile delinquents have not been very successful and may well be harmful. He concludes that the best response is no response at all: leaving young people alone whenever possible creates fewer problems than trying to do something, be it punitive or rehabilitative. The critics of this position argue that the real reason there is so much juvenile crime is that we are already too lenient, and that violent thugs can literally get away with murder if they are young enough. In the eyes of most criminologists and politicians, ignoring juvenile crimes would simply make the problem worse.

Reform the Law   State and federal legislatures enact many laws for emotional or political reasons, giving little thought to their long-range effects. But just because a new law pleases the electorate does not mean that it will be beneficial. Some popular laws produce disastrous results. A classic example is the law that made it a crime to manufacture, distribute, or drink alcohol. Current laws prohibiting other victimless acts—such as prostitution, gambling, and taking drugs—have similar effects. Many criminologists are convinced that eliminating ineffective and harmful laws would be a major step toward cutting the crime problem down to manageable size.

Promote Equal Justice   Everyone is supposed to be equal before the law, but lawyers, judges, social scientists, and many others are convinced that the very legitimacy of government is threatened by existing inequalities in criminal-justice procedures. Eliminating these injustices is no easy task. The power and influence of individual white-collar criminals makes it far easier for them to conceal their illegal activities. And even in the few cases in which the rich and powerful are actually arrested, they are usually treated leniently by the criminal-justice system. But the problem of bringing corporate criminals to justice is even more difficult. Not only do the major corporations have far more money and better lawyers to defend themselves than the government has to prosecute them, but they have the political power to stop investigations and prosecutions before they even begin, as well as the power to shape the laws so that the penalties are weak and ineffective. To deal with these huge problems, the government must enact tougher laws and allocate far more money than it now does to enforce them. But that is unlikely to happen unless the public rises up and demands it.

Prevent Crime   Proposals for punishing criminals, increasing our defenses against criminal activities, and social intervention are all concerned with preventing crime. Crime is prevented when criminals are afraid to commit new crimes. Crime is also prevented when criminals are killed or kept behind bars, and when citizens lock up their valuables and themselves, thus frustrating people who would behave criminally. Crime is prevented when the personal and social situations of criminals are improved or when the economic, political, and social order that generates high crime rates is modified so that it no longer does so.

Of the three methods, intervention is, or could be, the most effective procedure. We have seen that crime is rooted in the economic, political, and social order. Most social scientists realize that it is foolish to leave this situation the way it is and then try to reduce crime by punishing criminals or defending against them. But punishment and defense are easier than carrying out some of the sweeping social changes that have been proposed—eliminating poverty, unemployment, and discrimination, for example. In the long run, however, genuine crime prevention—changing the conditions that cause crime—will be both cheaper and more effective.

Better knowledge about crime and criminals does not necessarily mean that crime will be eliminated. Nevertheless, valid knowledge must be the basis of all prevention policies and programs. In the short run, efforts can be made to reduce crime through punitive and defensive measures. In the long run, crime must be controlled the way diseases have been controlled:

by developing valid knowledge about its causes and then using that knowledge to eliminate those causes. To put it another way, the most practical program for preventing crime is one that uses criminological theory to uncover the roots of crime and then digs them out.

SOCIOLOGICAL PERSPECTIVES ON CRIME AND DELINQUENCY

As was noted earlier, the central thesis of the sociological school of criminology is that criminal behavior results from the same processes as other social behavior. Studies of the ways in which these processes create crime and delinquency have taken two principal forms. First, functionalists, conflict theorists, and others have tried to relate variations in crime rates to variations in social organization such as the distribution of wealth, income, and employment, and to variations in population density and composition. Second, social psychologists have studied the processes by which people become delinquents and criminals. These studies are related to general studies of social learning and have used such principles as frustration-aggression, differential association, and reinforcement.

The Functionalist Perspective   Functionalists study crime rates rather than criminal behavior. They hold, generally, that a certain amount of crime is inevitable in any society because crime makes a contribution to social order. For instance, crime is said to promote the solidarity of the group, just as war does, by providing "common enemies" (in this case criminals). It is also argued that crime is functional because it provides an "escape valve" for the pressures arising from unjust laws or excessive conformity. But although some crime is natural and even healthy, too much crime is highly dysfunctional. Today most functionalists, like the general public, feel that current levels of crime pose a major social problem.

Functionalists hold that increases in the crime rate have been caused by the hectic pace of social change in the twentieth century and the social disorganization it has caused. Old traditions have been shattered, but a new consensus has not yet developed to take their place. Nowhere is this problem more apparent than in the family. Functionalists believe that the increase in divorce, illegitimacy, and family instability has deprived a growing number of children of the discipline and guidance they need to grow into responsible adults. As a consequence, many of these children drift into delinquency, and from there into a life of crime. The schools, faced with increasingly unruly students and a chronic shortage of funds, have compounded the failures of the family. Discipline has broken down, and some schools have been allowed to drift into virtual chaos. Unable to respond quickly enough to the rapid increase in crime, the criminal-justice system has also become increasingly disorganized. Backlogs of cases have piled up, and criminals have escaped their just punishment in the rush to speed up the system. Indeed, the criminal-justice system has become so disorganized that many criminologists refuse to call it a system at all.

To deal with these problems, functionalists call for greater social integration and a return to the traditional values of the past. Their most straightforward recommendation is for a reorganization of the criminal-justice system so that criminals can be handled in a more efficient and a more just manner. Functionalists also recommend a thorough reorganization of the schools to reemphasize the fundamentals of education and to restore order to the classroom. Much more difficult to carry out is their call for a return to a more stable family system and to the traditional values on which it was based.

The Conflict Perspective Conflict theorists emphasize the fact that both crime and the laws defining it are products of a struggle for power. They argue that a few powerful groups control the legislative process and that these groups outlaw behavior that threatens their interests. For example, laws outlawing vagrancy, trespassing, and theft are said to be designed to protect the interests of the wealthy from attacks by the poor. Although laws prohibiting such things as murder and rape are not so clearly in the interests of a single social class, the poor and powerless are still much more likely to be arrested if they commit such crimes.

Conflict theorists also see class and ethnic exploitation as a basic cause of many different kinds of crime. Much of the high crime rate among the poor is attributable to a lack of legitimate opportunities for improving their economic condition. This exploitation of the poor and ethnic minorities creates a sense of hopelessness, frustration, and hostility. Such feelings often boil over into acts of rage that are aimed not only at the system that oppresses the underprivileged but also at their friends, relatives, and neighbors. More generally, many conflict theorists hold that the greed and competitiveness bred by our capitalist consumer culture encourage crime among all social groups. Every day we are given countless subtle and not-so-subtle messages that wealth is the measure of a successful woman or man. It is therefore hardly surprising that even our richest citizens are often willing to break the law to further enhance their fortunes and outdo their competition.

Conflict theorists believe that crime will disappear only if class inequality and the exploitation of the weak by the powerful are eliminated. But because that is obviously a very distant goal, they often advocate more limited responses to the crime problem as well. For example, they ask that the state's criminal-justice processes treat the different classes and ethnic groups more equally. Thus, they ask that more attention be given to white-collar crime, they support bail reform and programs for providing better defense lawyers for the poor, and they call for elimination of class and ethnic discrimination by police officers and correctional workers. They also call for the repeal of laws that attempt to enforce one group's cultural dominance over another. Included here are laws prohibiting the use of marijuana, laws prohibiting private sexual acts between consenting adults, and laws prohibiting such activities as bigamy and gambling.

Although functionalists believe that crime performs some social functions, they see our high level of crime as a serious social problem.

Social Psychological Perspectives   Most social psychologists regard criminal behavior as a product of primary-group interaction. As we have seen, however, they have developed different theories about the specific kinds of interactions that produce crime. Personality theorists focus on personal traits and characteristics that encourage criminality, as well as on family environments that promote the development of such characteristics. Behaviorists argue that people commit crimes because they are rewarded for doing so: a bank robber is rewarded with money, a rapist with sexual gratification, and so on. Interactionists believe that people commit crimes because they learn attitudes and motivations that are favorable to crime: a boy who associates with other boys who believe that stealing is exciting is likely to adopt that attitude and start to steal.

The social psychological perspective helps us understand why one 18-year-old ends up in prison while another ends up in college. But the conditions producing criminal behavior are very hard to change. The government in a free society cannot intervene significantly in child-rearing practices and can hardly change the character of a person's associations. The social psychological approach does have something practical to say about how to deal with criminals, however. For instance, it notes that punishment is not necessarily bad: if used sparingly and intelligently, it contributes to learning. Also, care should be taken to avoid the contagion of youngsters by confirmed criminals, as sometimes happens in juvenile halls and prisons. Finally, offenders should be integrated into primary groups that strongly discourage criminal behavior. Ideally, this is the aim of good probation and parole programs. Social psychologists argue that the many programs that aim merely to keep tabs on probationers and parolees must be reorganized to meet this goal.

SUMMARY

A crime is a violation of the criminal law. However, it is not easy to apply this definition to actual behavior. Because of vagueness and ambiguities in statutes, unequal enforcement, and the sheer complexity of human behavior, "law in action" differs from "law on the books."

There are two main sources of data about the trends in crime: the Uniform Crime Reports (UCR), based on crimes reported to the police, and the National Crime Survey (NCS), based on a nationwide survey of the victims of crime. The UCR showed a steady increase in crime from the end of World War II until the 1980s, when it finally started to decrease. The NCS has shown a declining crime rate since it was first taken in 1973.

Official arrest records and other crime statistics suggest that the crime rates for certain categories of people are higher than average. Males have higher rates than females, and teenagers have higher rates than children or mature adults. Similarly, blacks, Hispanics, and native Americans have higher than average rates, as do lower-class people and urban dwellers. There are serious problems with these data because the police tend to regard people with such characteristics as more likely to be criminals and therefore to watch them more closely.

There are many different explanations of crime. Members of the classical school of criminology argue that people choose to commit crime because they think that they have more to gain than to lose by breaking the law. Members of the positive school see crime and criminality as products of natural causes, not free will. Based on studies comparing the criminal histories of twins, and those of adopted children and their biological parents, biological theorists argue that a predisposition toward crime is hereditary.

Psychologists and psychiatrists argue that crime is caused by personality defects such as emotional disturbances and sociopathic traits. Two important sociological theories address the higher crime rates among the poor. According to strain theory, crime rates will be high if people are told that wealth and prestige are available to all when in fact opportunities for achieving these things are limited. The other theory holds that a distinctive lower-class culture is the cause of crime among the poor because it emphasizes values that encourage criminal behavior. Differential-association theory holds that criminal behavior is learned in primary groups just like any other kind of behavior. Control theory holds that people commit crimes because society has failed to stop them either by instilling an internal sense of morality or by threatening severe punishment. Labeling theory argues that people who are stigmatized as delinquents or criminals are unintentionally encouraged to commit further crimes.

Crimes have been classified in many ways. Legally, they are classified according to their seriousness, as felonies and misdemeanors. For statistical purposes, they are classified by the character of the victim, as crimes against persons, crimes against property, and crimes against public decency and order.

There are two general models of how the criminal-justice process should operate. The crime-control model stresses the need to isolate troublemakers from the rest of society and calls for speedy arrest and punishment of all who commit crimes. The due-process model, on the other hand, stresses the need to preserve civil liberties. It calls for softening the rush to punishment and for considering human rights and the rights of accused persons.

Police officers have come to symbolize "the law." Yet only a small percentage of the work done by a police department is directly concerned with crime. When performing as law enforcement officials, the police are expected to use the crime-control model (that is, they should catch criminals), but they are also expected to use the due-process model (that is, they should protect the rights of the accused).

After an arrest has been made, the suspect is taken before the magistrate of a lower court. The magistrate sets bail. Accused people who cannot raise the money for a bail bond are held in prison. Felony cases that are not dismissed in lower-court hearings move to a higher court. There, most defendants plead guilty as a part of a process called plea bargaining, in which the suspect agrees to plead guilty in exchange for a reduction in the charges.

For about a century there has been a distinct movement toward correctional programs for sentenced criminals. Probation and parole systems and prison rehabilitation programs grew out of the effort to understand and correct criminals rather than merely punish them. The most recent trend, however, is toward a return to programs designed to make criminals suffer for the crimes they have committed.

The most common proposal for solving the crime problem is increased punishment. Other proposals include general programs for diverting criminals out of criminal-justice agencies, eliminating unnecessary laws, promoting equal justice, and preventing crime by changing the economic, political, and social conditions that produce it.

The central theme in sociological studies of crime is that criminal behavior results from the same processes as other social behavior. Functionalists study crime rates rather than individual criminal conduct. Their main theme is that the growing crime rate is but one symptom of increasing social disorganization. Conflict theorists argue that many criminal laws are designed to protect the interests of the wealthy and that legal procedures discriminate against the poor and the powerless. Most social psychologists believe that criminal behavior is a product of the individual's interaction with primary groups; however, different theories stress different types of interaction.

KEY TERMS

control theory	plea bargaining
crime-control model	probation
differential association	sociopathic personality
due-process model	strain theory
juvenile delinquency	victimless crime
labeling theory	white-collar crime

FURTHER READINGS

General Criminology
Frank E. Hagan, *Introduction to Criminology: Theories, Methods and Criminal Behavior,* Chicago: Nelson-Hall, 1986.
Sue Titus Reid, *Crime and Criminology,* 5th ed., New York: Holt, Rinehart & Winston, 1988.

Criminal Justice
William Chambliss and Robert Seidman, *Law, Order and Power,* 2d ed., Reading, Mass.: Addison-Wesley, 1982.
John Irwin, *Prisons in Turmoil,* Boston: Little, Brown, 1980.

Special Crime Problems
Clemens Bartollas, *Juvenile Delinquency,* New York: John Wiley & Sons, 1985.
James William Coleman, *The Criminal Elite: The Sociology of White-Collar Crime,* 2d ed., New York: St. Martin's, 1989.
Harry King and William J. Chambliss, *Harry King: A Professional Thief's Journey,* New York: John Wiley & Sons, 1984.

- What are the most common types of violence?
- How much violence is there?
- What causes violence?
- Do television programs promote violence?
- Would gun control reduce violence?

Chapter 15
PERSONAL VIOLENCE

From teenage fist fights to cold-blooded murder, violence is a perennial problem. Every day television, radio, and newspaper reporters tell us new horror stories. We are informed that rape, child abuse, and wife beating are on the rise. Old people are afraid to unlock their doors, and the fear of violent criminals haunts our cities and suburbs. To make matters worse, fictional violence has become the mainstay of movies and television. We are, it seems, obsessed with violence.

Presidential commissions have studied and denounced violence. So have garden societies, PTAs, and scientists. But an effective program to deal with violence has yet to be launched. When state or federal restrictions on the instruments of violence are proposed—gun control, for example—the opposition is overwhelming. The crux of the matter is that we like violence. We denounce and condemn it, but we are still fascinated by it. Our heroes solve their problems with blazing pistols, and acts of violence are seen as proof of manhood. Violent men are cool, sexy, and desirable. With the passage of time, frontier hoodlums like Jesse James, Davy Crockett, and Daniel Boone have become gentle Robin Hoods, shining examples of honor and dignity. The young boy who won't fight is a sissy. The man who will not fight is a coward.

This is not to say that people admire acts of wanton aggression. Only violence that is "right" is approved. Yet these acts of "good" violence lead inevitably to acts of "bad" violence as well.

THE NATURE OF VIOLENCE

Violence is a common enough term, and we all think we know what we are talking about when we use it. Yet violence is much more complex than it appears at first glance. Although violence may properly be defined as behavior intended to cause bodily pain or injury to another person, this definition can be misleading. Most people who use it are thinking only about acts that they do not like. When a criminal knocks down an old lady, it is clearly an act of violence. When a police officer knocks down a criminal, it is necessary force. Because the two acts are equally violent, the real distinction is between *legitimate* and *illegitimate* violence. Illegitimate violence is what people have in mind when they speak of "the problem of violence." The catch is that there is no clear-cut distinction between legitimate and illegitimate mayhem. One person's self-defense is another person's aggression. One person's spanking is another person's child abuse.

When most people think about violence, they think about murders, stabbings, and beatings. There is nothing wrong with this view. Interpersonal violence is a serious problem. But an equally important kind of violence is collective. Terrorism and warfare—to be discussed in Chapter 19—are examples of collective violence. Individual violence and collective violence have different causes and therefore require different explanations and different social responses. Despite outward appearances, there is little similarity between a wife who murders her husband in a fit of anger and a terrorist who coolly assassinates a political leader.

Illegitimate violence is against the law, and may therefore properly be called violent crime. Only a small percentage of all crime is violent, but it is this kind of crime that most worries the public. A nationwide survey found that over half of all American women and one-fifth of the men said that they were afraid to walk outdoors at night even in their own neighborhood.[1] It seems that an atmosphere of fear hangs over many U.S. cities like a suffocating fog.

Reports from industrialized countries all over the world show an alarming rise in violent crime. However, criminologists believe that these figures are exaggerated by police and news media to promote their own interests. Strong support for this belief comes from the U.S. Bureau of Justice Statistics, which has conducted a nationwide survey of the victims of crime every year since 1973. Although substantial increases in the rates of violent crime have been reported by the police in the last decade,[2] the victimization surveys show the opposite trend. Between 1973 and 1987, the likelihood that an average American household would be touched by violent crime decreased by 21 percent.[3] Unlike police departments, the Bureau of Justice Statistics has little to gain or to lose from the statistics it collects and publishes. Its figures are therefore much more likely to be accurate. Thus, the popular belief that we are in the midst of a new wave of violent crime is not supported by the scientific evidence.

Differences in methods of assembling criminal statistics make international comparisons risky. It appears, however, that there are wide differences in the amount of violence from one culture to the next. The best indicators of these differences are murder rates, because murder is the most accurately reported crime. Although a few Third World countries such as Thailand and the Philippines report higher murder rates, the United States has the highest rates of any industrialized nation. According to data from the World Health Organization, the murder rate is five times higher in the United States than in Canada, and seven and a half times higher than in Europe. Data from the International Police Organization (Interpol) indicate that murder in the United States is three times more common than it is in Canada and five times more common than in Europe. Although the data are less reliable for other crimes, the United Nations, Interpol, and the World Health Organization all agree that the rate of rape in the United States is higher than in any other country in the world, and that the United States is among the highest in its robbery rates.[4]

Murder and Assault   **Murder** is not the same as **homicide,** which is any killing of a human being. Murder is a special kind of homicide: the unlawful killing of a human being with malice aforethought. Thus, the killing of enemies in wartime, killing in self-defense, and killing in lawful execution of a judicial sentence are all homicides, but not murders, because they are neither malicious nor unlawful. **Manslaughter** is the unlawful killing of another person without malice aforethought, as in a traffic accident caused by a reckless driver.

An **assault** occurs when one person attacks another with the intention of hurting or killing the victim. There is often little difference between murders and assaults. The fact that the victim of an armed attack got to a hospital in time to be saved may spell the difference between one crime and the other. Most assaults do not involve deadly force, however. A punch in the belly is an assault. So is a slap in the face. But the essence of assault is the intention to do harm. If your professor raises his fist at you in a menacing manner, you have been assaulted. You are also assaulted by anyone who takes a swing at you and misses. "Aggravated assault" is assault committed with the intention of committing some additional crime, or which is peculiarly outrageous or atrocious, as when a deadly weapon is used.

Newspaper and television reports focus on dramatic crimes such as mass murders, "gang wars," and particularly brutal and vicious attacks. This press coverage misleads the public. The fact is that few people are attacked or killed by a demented stranger. About half of all murders occur in the home of the victim or the offender[5] usually among relatives, friends, or acquaintances. Indeed, the closeness of the relationship may add to the violence of the attack when someone feels betrayed or insulted. As we pointed out in

Although mass murders receive a great deal of public attention, we are much more likely to be assaulted or killed by someone we know.

19th-Century Social Problems

Mr. Axel, a farmer living about 6 miles east of Kiel, Manitowoc County, cut his wife's throat a few days ago so that she might not recover and then killed himself. There were various rumors as to the cause of the tragedy such as domestic infelicity etc., but a few who had dealings with Axel of late attributed the act to an aberration of mind.

May 14, 1886

These selections, which appear throughout the text, are from the *Badger State Banner,* a newspaper published in Black River Falls, Wisconsin.

Chapter 5, beatings, slashings, stabbings, chokings, and shootings are common in many homes. The full extent of husband-wife violence is not known, but it is probably the most common form of violence in North America. Such violence is often the result of the husband's attempts to dominate and control his wife. Alcohol is another contributing factor in family violence, as it is for violent crime in general. Slightly over half of all prisoners in jail for murder or assault report that they were under the influence of alcohol or some other drug at the time of their offense.[6]

Marvin Wolfgang's classic study of murder in Philadelphia found that only 15 percent of the 550 murders he analyzed occurred between strangers; almost 60 percent occurred between relatives or close friends.[7] More recent data show much the same picture. Only about 18.5 percent of the murders for which we had information in 1986 were committed by strangers.[8] Studies of assault show that victims are less likely to know their attackers but are still acquainted in almost half of the cases.[9] One's chances of being assaulted or killed therefore depend more on one's relationship with relatives and friends than on the whim of some predatory stranger.

Rape Although the legal definition of rape varies from place to place, **forcible rape** is usually considered to be sexual intercourse forced upon a person without consent. So-called **statutory rape** is not really a violent crime. It is sexual intercourse with a female (in some places males are also included) below the legally defined age of consent, usually 16 to 18 years old. Many jurisdictions now use the more appropriate term, "illegal intercourse," for this offense.

Studies show that there are two distinct patterns of forcible rape. In the first type, the rape occurs between friends or acquaintances on an unplanned, spur-of-the-moment basis, and is sometimes known as "date rape." The other pattern of rape is a calculated act usually involving a stranger as the victim.

The rapist, often a repeat offender, actively seeks out a victim with the prior intention of raping her. The rapist may wait on a dark street for a lone woman to walk by, search for an unsuspecting hitchhiker, or break into a woman's home. Because the first type of rape is much less likely to be reported to the police, it is difficult to determine which pattern is more common. According to the 1986 National Crime Survey, the victims of attempted rape were about equally divided between those who knew their attacker and those who did not,[10] but the findings of other research has not provided consistent support for this or any other conclusion on this issue.[11]

It is extremely difficult to measure the amount of rape accurately. The National Crime Survey puts the rate of victimization at about 1.2 rapes for every 1000 women over the age of twelve,[12] but other research using different methodology and different definitions of rape has put the figure far higher. Studies of college women, for example, have found that somewhere between 11 and 25 percent report having been forced to have sexual intercourse by their date or boyfriend,[13] and other estimates hold that as many as 44 percent of all women have been the victims of a rape or an attempted rape some time in their life.[14] Whatever the exact number, the fear of rape has a profound effect on the way most women live their life, forcing them either to severely restrict their freedom of action or to run the constant risk of victimization. As one woman put it: "I know what I can't do and I've completely internalized what I can't do. I've built a viable life that basically involves never leaving my apartment at night unless I'm directly going someplace to meet somebody. It's unconsciously built into what it occurs to women to do.[15]

Unlike the victims of other violent crimes, most rape victims are female. For every male who reported being the victim of a rape to the 1986 National Crime Survey, there were 12 females.[16] The attackers, on the other hand, are overwhelmingly males. Only about one in fifty victims of a single attacker reported that she was a female, while about 18 percent of the victims of gang rape reported that the assailants were all females or a mixed group of males and females. Thus, even most male victims are raped by other men.[17] In other respects, however, the victims of rape are typical of the victims of other violent crimes. Women between 16 and 25 years of age are two to three times more likely to report being victimized; black women are more likely to report a rape or rape attempt than white women; and about half of all rape victims between 1978 and 1982 had a family income of less than $10,000. Data from the National Crime Survey also indicate that victims who physically resist their attackers are often successful in preventing the completion of the rape. The attacker completes the rape in only 32 percent of the cases in which the victim resists, but in 56 percent of the cases where she does not. However, resistance by the victim is also related to an increase in the probability of such injuries as black eyes and cuts.[18]

Robbery   **Robbery** is theft by force. Robbers take something from their victims by using force or threatening to use it. About 35 to 40 percent of all robberies in the United States are committed with a gun, and about the same percentage with a knife. But surprisingly, victims are more often injured by an unarmed robber, perhaps because they are more likely to resist.[19]

Because robbery is really a kind of theft, it seems to have more in common with the property crimes than with rape, murder, or assault. Unlike other violent crimes, few robbers know their victims. According to the National Crime Survey, over three-fourths of all robberies occur between strangers,[20] and other sources put that figure as high as 90 percent. Robberies are far more likely to occur in the street and in parking lots and outdoor areas than other violent crimes. Murder, assault, and rape usually involve persons with similar social characteristics. Young adult males with low incomes and a minority background are more likely than others to be the offenders and the victims in these crimes (except for rape in which the victims are usually female). The typical robber is also likely to have these same characteristics, but his victims tend to be older and nonminority (most victims are still males, however).[21] The main cause of these differences is that other violent crimes tend to be crimes of passion that erupt unexpectedly out of the social interactions between people. Robbery, on the other hand, is more calculated and more rational. The offenders want money and consequently seek out a victim who can provide it. The offenders do not want to be arrested and therefore avoid victims who might be able to recognize them.

Suicide   Although **suicide** is against the law in some states it is seldom actually treated as a crime[22]—perhaps because the successful "criminal" is beyond the reach of the law. Suicide is nonetheless a major social problem. Nearly fifty percent more Americans die from suicide than as a result of violent crime (see Figure 15.1),[23] and this ratio is even higher in most other industrialized countries. Although the United States has far more violent crime than any other industrialized nation, that is not true of suicide. The United States has a higher suicide rate than Italy or Great Britain, but its rate is slightly lower than Canada and only about half as large as Switzerland or Denmark.[24]

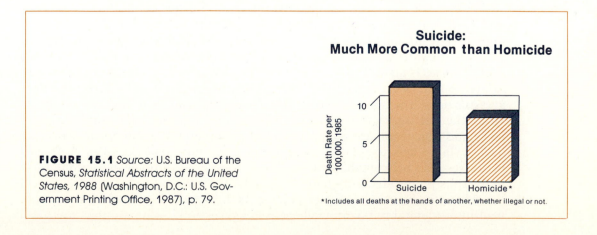

FIGURE 15.1 *Source:* U.S. Bureau of the Census, *Statistical Abstracts of the United States, 1988* (Washington, D.C.: U.S. Government Printing Office, 1987), p. 79.

**Suicide:
Much More Common than Homicide**

Death Rate per 100,000, 1985

Suicide   Homicide*

*Includes all deaths at the hands of another, whether illegal or not.

The suicide rate has shown a small increase in the last two decades, primarily because suicide has gone up among the young. For the population as a whole, however, it is the elderly who are most likely to kill themselves. This is true primarily because of the extremely high suicide rate among older white males. The suicide rate of white females peaks in their late forties and early fifties, and for blacks the peak comes even earlier. As a whole, suicide is only half as common among blacks as among whites. And regardless of ethnic group, males are more than three times more likely to kill themselves than females, even though females are more likely to attempt suicide.[25]

With the exception of some relatively rare acts of self-sacrifice, most people kill themselves because their lives seem so painful and unpleasant that they no longer want to continue living. But what makes people feel that way? Émile Durkheim, the famous French sociologist, argued that it was the lack of supportive social groups that leaves people aimless and unhappy. Durkheim mustered an impressive battery of statistics to show that suicide rates are higher among those who are not part of a cohesive group.[26] Psychologists, on the other hand, tend to focus on more individual characteristics, for example, a disturbed childhood or a mental disorder such as acute depression.[27] Although their acts may seem pointless to others, suicidal individuals may actually be trying to accomplish something by their attempts at self-destruction. A suicide attempt is often a way of calling for help, or an effort to punish relatives or loved ones who the victims believe have let them down.

EXPLAINING PERSONAL VIOLENCE

Violence has been blamed on everything from human instincts to television. The explanations of it are similar to those used to explain all crime, non-violent as well as violent. But theories of violence are not restricted to illegitimate violence. They are concerned with making sense of this widespread form of human behavior, whether it is socially accepted or condemned.

Biological Theories   For centuries people have blamed violence on human instincts, and such notions are still popular today. Robert Ardrey, for example, has argued that humans have an innate drive to conquer and control territory and that this drive is the root of our inhumanity to one another.[28] Behind such theories is an idea about evolution. It is said that the animals (including humans) that were most likely to survive through the years were the aggressive ones. The instinctively aggressive animals survived and reproduced, while the less aggressive ones died off. Konrad Lorenz maintains that violence and aggression are useful because they spread the members of a species over a large territory, thus helping to even out food supplies.[29] These processes also help establish a system of dominance among individual animals, thus giving structure and stability to groups.

There is, however, no particular reason to believe that the process of evolution inevitably favors violence and aggression. Some animals are violent and aggressive and others are not. It can just as easily be argued that violence-prone individuals will kill themselves off and that peaceful individuals will be the ones to survive and reproduce.

Daly and Wilson propose a much more sophisticated evolutionary theory of violence.[30] They argue that the basic motives and structure of the human psyche evolved to serve one evolutionary goal: the survival of our genes. Utilizing admittedly incomplete data, they argue that within the family we are most likely to kill those with whom we do not share common genes (for example, spouses and adopted children) and least likely to kill those who carry our genes (biological children). They see violence between strangers as rooted in the conflicts between males over access to the reproductive powers of females and the right to father as many children as possible. This "Darwinian psychology" raises some interesting new questions, but at least at present it seems to be unable to account for the known patterns of violent behavior. As we have seen, the one person we are most likely to kill is ourself, and that obviously is an act that will greatly diminish our chances of passing our genes on to the next generation.

Psychological Theories   Sigmund Freud, perhaps the most influential psychologist of modern times, painted a very bleak picture of human nature. Like many biological theorists, he felt that we are engaged in a continuing struggle with our natural impulse toward aggression and violence, and that we are barely held in check by the forces of civilization. For psychologists of the Freudian school, the question is not why some people are violent; it is why most people are not. Their answer is that society trains us while still children to develop a *superego* (conscience) that inhibits destructive impulses and violent acts. People who do not develop normal, healthy superegos cannot stop their destructive impulses. For example, it is said that the average man wants to have sexual relations with every woman he finds attractive, with or without the woman's consent. However, the superegos of most men block these impulses, often so thoroughly that they are not even aware of them. From this perspective, a rapist is simply a man with a weak superego who cannot block his natural impulses. Freudian theories have, however, been declining in popularity among psychologists for at least 30 years, and all the criticisms of biological-instinct theories apply equally well to the Freudian theories.

A more convincing psychological theory holds that aggression and violence are caused by individual frustration.[31] People become frustrated when they want something they can't have, and the stronger the blocked desire, the stronger the frustration. If a person's level of frustration is high enough, the idea goes, it overcomes inhibitions, with the result that the frustrated person responds with aggression and even violence. The frustrated person may lash out at the source of his or her frustration or displace that hostility to someone else. Thus, many contemporary criminologists see rape as more a product of anger and hostility than a simple desire for sex.

This **frustration-aggression theory** is one of the simplest and most popular explanations of violence, be it a family murder or a massive riot. However, like most psychological theories, it has its problems. In the first place, frustration does not always produce aggression. Frustration may find an outlet in peaceful activities such as a vigorous workout or a talk with a sympathetic friend, or it may remain bottled up. In the second place, much aggression and violence seems to be unrelated to frustration. A professional killer does not have to be frustrated to carry out a job, and the same can be said of the mugger, the robber, and the soldier.

Sociological Theories   There are two principal types of sociological explanations of violence. The *macro* theories look at the ways violence is created by large-scale social structures. On the other hand, *micro* theories focus on the ways violence is learned from other people.

Theories that blame violent behavior on the social structures are linked to the two psychological theories just discussed. The **control theory** used by some sociologists pictures violence as a universal human tendency that is expressed when society fails to keep tight enough restraints on its members. To control theorists, society's first line of defense is group norms that discourage violence. People who are not controlled by families and other primary groups are controlled by police officers and fear of the law. When both of these controls fail, violent behavior is expressed. In many ways this theory is like Freudian theory. The difference is that violence is said to be controlled by society rather than by a mechanism within the individual. And like Freudian theory, control theory provides a reasonable explanation of why some people are violent and others are not, but both are based on the unproven assumption that people are naturally violent.

Sociologists also use the **frustration-aggression theory** on a macro level. They say that much of the frustration that leads to violence stems from the inequalities and injustices of society. They point to the statistics that show higher rates of violence in inner-city slums and other ghettos, then argue that poverty and lack of opportunity in those areas are very frustrating to their residents. Slum dwellers want all the material goods that everyone else wants, but are unable to get them legitimately. As a result, they become frustrated and lash out in bursts of violence. This social form of the frustration-aggression theory has the same weaknesses as the original. It provides a reasonable explanation for some violence, but fails to explain the presence of violence among more affluent people and the lack of violence among many frustrated poor people.

The most widely accepted theory is that people learn to be violent the same way that they learn any other kind of behavior. The process of learning may take place in the family, in a subculture, or in an entire culture. Some individuals learn norms and values that define violence as a good thing in certain situations. Others learn a view of the world that makes violence appear to be the only way of getting what they want. Still others may learn from the experience of having been the victim of a violent attack.

Although few parents consider violence a good thing, many consider it a necessary part of life: a behavior pattern that a child, particularly a boy,

Children learn to be violent in the process of socialization.

must learn. The gender roles that teach us that a boy must be tough, strong, and aggressive are therefore a major part of the problem of violence (see Chapter 10). A survey conducted for the National Commission on the Causes and Prevention of Violence found that 70 percent of the respondents agreed with the statement "When a boy is growing up it is important for him to have a few fistfights."[32] Although they didn't ask about girls, it is highly doubtful that most parents would feel that those fistfights would be a good thing for their daughters.

Numerous studies have shown that people who come from violent families are much more likely to be violent themselves. Straus, Gelles, and Steinmetz found that men who grew up in families where violence was prevalent were ten times more likely to beat their wives than men from nonviolent families.[33] Children seem to learn more from the violent example set by their parents than from admonitions to be nonviolent, especially when the children themselves are the victims of violence. A number of studies also show that people who were abused as children are much more likely than others to become child abusers.[34] Straus, Gelles, and Steinmetz found that "over and over again, the statistics . . . suggest the same conclusion. Each generation learns to be violent by participating in a violent family."[35]

Sociologists have long known that attitudes toward violence differ greatly from one group to another within the same society. Marvin Wolfgang and Franco Ferracuti presented considerable evidence along this line in their book *The Subculture of Violence*.[36] They showed that in the United States there is a large subculture that has positive attitudes toward violence and that these attitudes encourage or even require violence in many circumstances. Members of this subculture admire the style of tough, aggressive

19th-Century Social Problems

Lydia Berger, a 15-year-old girl, is in jail having confessed to the crime of arson. Several days ago she left her home on a farm north of Milwaukee and went to town to go to . . . the carnival. . . . She was out late that night and the next day her father whipped her for staying away without permission. She sought revenge by setting fire to the little cottage in which they lived. It was burned to the ground. A neighbor gave the family shelter and the next day the girl set fire to the house of their benefactor. Her mother ordered her to harness a team of horses which was temporarily quartered in a barn belonging to the Wisconsin Lake Ice Company. The girl went to the loft and set fire to the barn, which, with 64 tons of hay, was burned to the ground. The girl says she set fire to the places simply to have revenge on her father for whipping her.

July 19, 1898

masculinity, sometimes known as **machismo**. Any personal slight—even the most trivial one—is seen as a direct insult, often requiring a violent reply. An accidental bump on the street or an unguarded glance that most people would hardly notice may trigger a physical attack.

The most controversial aspect of Wolfgang and Ferracuti's work is their theory that this violent subculture is more common among ethnic minorities and the lower classes and is a principal cause of the higher rates of violence for these groups. Critics argue that these groups place no higher value on violence than anyone else and that their violent behavior is the result of their social circumstances. Strength, courage, and a willingness to use violence are often the only assets that an uneducated lower-class male has in the struggle to win the things that are valued by our society.

America: Land of the Violent?   As we have seen, the United States is clearly the most violent of all the Western democracies (see Figure 15.2). American violence is often seen as a holdover from the rowdy days of frontier expansion. According to this view, violence became a way of life as an unending stream of settlers pushed westward in search of land and profit. The new Americans fought wars with Spain, England, and Mexico. They almost exterminated the native Americans, and they fought among themselves. In the expansive stretches of the Old West, points of law were settled with rifles, pistols, knives, and fists, and vigilante groups killed troublemakers.[37] Today's social conditions are very different, but movies and television dramas still celebrate this violence.

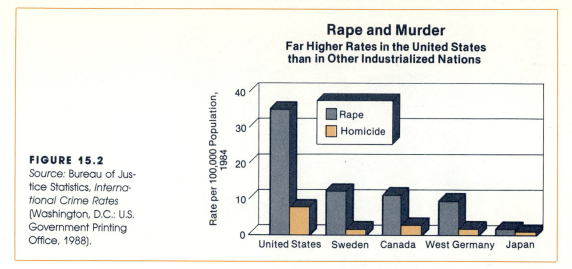

FIGURE 15.2
Source: Bureau of Justice Statistics, *International Crime Rates* (Washington, D.C.: U.S. Government Printing Office, 1988).

Canada and Australia were also settled by "roughnecks," but the citizens of those countries apparently have not passed down a violent frontier tradition. Although America's violent past does not alone explain its extreme contemporary violence, the American frontier did have some characteristics that were not found in other areas. For example, in Canada:

The inhospitable Laurentian Shield (a range of mountains which formed a barrier to migration) deflected pioneers southward into the United States; when railroads opened the Canadian prairie provinces to British settlement in the late nineteenth century, the frontiersman came directly from the more traditional east and the process of settlement was not nearly as prolonged as was the American experience.[38]

Aside from its unique frontier tradition, America has other characteristics that seem to contribute to the violence of its people. The United States is much larger than the other Western democracies, and it contains a much broader spectrum of ethnic groups. Tensions and conflicts are to be expected in a nation with such a low level of social integration. Further, America is a wealthy nation but, compared with other Western countries, has less economic equality and inferior welfare and social programs for the poor. Thus, we can expect class conflicts and the frustrations of being poor in a rich land to be greater in the United States.

Violence and the Mass Media   John Hinckley shot President Ronald Reagan after repeatedly watching a movie in which the hero coolly stalked a senator with a gun. A group of adolescents raped a fellow student with a broom handle after a similar incident was shown in a television drama. A gang in a different city copied a television program they had seen by burning an elderly woman to death.

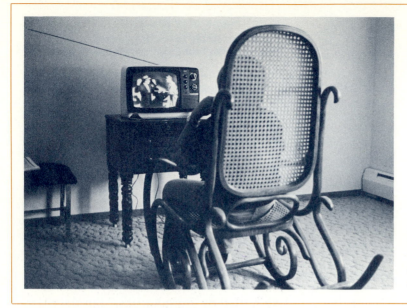

The evidence indicates that watching violent television programs encourages violent behavior in some people.

Such incidents have made violence in the media an issue of great public concern. Supporters of the media claim that everyone realizes media violence is just a fantasy, and that it does not encourage real-life violence. But two comprehensive examinations of all the available research—one by the U.S. Surgeon General in 1972 and another by the National Institute of Mental Health in 1982—concluded that media violence does indeed promote real violence.[39] Numerous studies have found that children in laboratory settings act more violently when they are shown violent television programs than when they are shown nonviolent programs. Such experiments have been criticized because they are carried on in artificial settings, but many other types of studies lead to similar conclusions. Particularly persuasive are two studies of Canadian Indians that found that violent behavior increased among children after television was introduced into their communities.[40] As Jeffrey Goldstein concluded, "After nearly three decades of research social scientists are now almost unanimous in their agreement that portrayed violence increases aggressive behavior."[41]

How does violence in entertainment cause real-life violence? For one thing, watching violence on television increases the chances that viewers will regard it as a justifiable means of settling disputes in everyday life. Television stories show people responding to frustration with aggression: they strike out, smash, and even kill in what looks like blind rage. They do not seek or even discuss more peaceful alternatives. The viewer learns that it is "natural" for people to go berserk, and this increases the chances that viewers will fly into a violent rage when they are frustrated or provoked.

DEBATE

Should Television Violence Be Censored?

YES We are experiencing a sweeping epidemic of violence that threatens the very foundations of our society. Our television stations have added to the toll of murders, rapes, and assaults by using violence as a tool to boost their ratings and improve their profits. Scientific studies have shown that violent television programs encourage real-life violence, and our television is certainly full of wanton violence.

Civil libertarians often claim that a government program to remove violence from our airwaves would soon be censoring broadcasts for their political content as well and would ultimately contribute to the growth of totalitarianism. Such charges are highly misleading. Although it is true that any censorship has a potential for abuse, a well-planned program could easily avoid this danger. For instance, if the law spelled out the specific kinds of violent acts that were to be prohibited and expressly forbade censorship on any other grounds, there would be little danger of abusing civil liberties.

The prohibition of violent dramas on television would not, of course, be the entire answer to the problem of violence, but it would be an important step in the right direction. It would show our children that violence is not an acceptable solution to personal conflicts. And compared with the other proposals for dealing with this difficult problem, a program to clean up television would be cheap, simple, and effective.

NO No matter how well intentioned, censorship of the press is always a threat to democracy. Once the censorship boards are set up to stop television violence, other pressing "problems" demanding censorship will soon come along. In the end, our freedom will be lost. All censorship boards claim to achieve important social goals, but that does not make them any the less totalitarian. The end does not justify the means.

No one doubts that violence is a major social problem. But how much good would television censorship really do? Scientific studies do show a relationship between watching violent programs and real-life violence, but it is a very weak relationship. Most violence is learned from parents, on the streets, or in the schools. Even if we took all the violence off television tomorrow, the effects would probably be so small that we couldn't even measure them.

Besides, violence can be removed from television by much less dangerous means. If citizens are concerned about this problem they should write to their local stations, to the networks, and to the sponsors and ask that violent programs be taken off the air. They should also turn off their television sets and encourage their friends and neighbors to do the same. If sponsors find that advertising on violent programs does not improve the sales of their products and if network executives find that violence no longer improves their ratings, the problem of television violence will soon disappear.

Television dramas also contribute to violent crime in a more general way. Television creates the impression that violence is a rather routine everyday event, so the viewing public may become indifferent to all but the most sensational crimes of violence. In this respect television dramas might have effects similar to the sensationalistic coverage of crime in the newspapers and on radio and television. Both news stories and television dramas help blunt our indignation about violence and encourage a kind of "tuning out" of real-life horrors. For instance, one study found that the physiological changes that go with emotional reactions to violence were diminished in a "high TV exposure" group of children as compared with a "low TV exposure" group.[42] A population for whom violent crime has become routine is less likely to do anything to try to stop it.

These research findings do not mean that exposure to dramatizations of violence, even repeated exposure, will change a peaceful man or woman into a violent one. The home, the community, and the schools certainly have a greater influence on children than television or movies. But the media can have a very significant effect on those who are already poised on the brink of violence.

Firearms and Violent Crime   Americans like guns. No one knows exactly how many privately owned firearms there are in the United States, but 46 percent of those questioned in a 1987 survey said that they had some kind of gun in their home.[43] About one-third of these are handguns—weapons that are good for little else except target practice and killing people at close range. Although reliable statistics are hard to come by, police agencies also believe that there has been a substantial increase in the private ownership of military-style rapid-firing weapons such as the Uzi submachine gun and the M16 assault rifle.[44] About 60 percent of all American murders are committed with firearms (usually handguns), as are 35 percent of the robberies and a quarter of the rapes.[45]

There is, however, considerable debate about the impact of firearms on violent crime. Years ago Wolfgang argued that widespread possession of firearms has little impact on the total number of murders.[46] His reasoning, which has been adopted by sportsmen and gun manufacturers, is that killers would simply use other weapons if guns were not available. There is a great deal of evidence on the other side, however. It appears that the difference between assault and murder often turns on the type of weapon involved. A recent study of criminal violence in St. Louis, for example, revealed that a person was almost twice as likely to die if he or she were attacked with a small-caliber gun than with a knife, and three times more likely to die if attacked with a larger-caliber weapon.[47] According to FBI figures, guns are used in only one-quarter of all aggravated (serious) assaults but in the majority of all murders.[48]

Many criminologists believe that a significant reduction in privately owned firearms would have little effect on the total number of personal attacks but would significantly reduce the number of deaths resulting from such attacks. However, there are those who believe that the number of attacks would decrease as well. For one thing, an assault with a gun requires no physical strength and therefore gives the attacker a much wider number of potential victims. Perhaps more important, it takes only a split second to shoot a gun, while other types of assaults take longer and may provide time for second thoughts.

RESPONDING TO PROBLEMS OF VIOLENCE

Many different proposals for reducing violence have been made. Some of them, such as gun control, are fairly specific and limited, and therefore would be relatively easy to put into effect. At the other extreme are more difficult, but no less important, proposals for sweeping changes in our social structure.

Gun Control   The United States has extremely loose and ineffective gun regulation. The laws vary enormously from one state to another, and the only consistent policy is that convicted felons are not supposed to own guns. Most, but not all, states also prohibit the carrying of a concealed weapon without a license.[49] But because guns are so easily available to everyone, few criminals

Firearms are more readily available in the United States than in almost any other democratic nation.

have any trouble getting a gun if they want one. In Canada all firearms must be registered, but control there is still rather loose compared with most European countries.

Despite the lack of effective legislation, Gallup polls starting as far back as 1959 have repeatedly shown that Americans favor registration and other gun-control measures. A 1985 poll, for example, found that 70 percent favor mandatory registration of all handguns, and a 1986 poll found that 60 percent of the people want stricter gun control and that fewer than one in ten want to loosen the current laws.[30] Why then aren't tougher laws passed? The major opposition consists of several organizations that are known collectively as the gun lobby. These organizations represent sportsmen, civil libertarians, and firearms manufacturers who see their interests threatened by gun control. The desires of the people cannot seem to compete with well-financed and highly organized special-interest groups like the National Rifle Association.

Many types of gun control programs have been proposed. Most center on the handgun or "Saturday night special," a weapon that is useless for anything except homicide. The National Commission on the Causes and Prevention of Violence recommended prohibiting the possession or ownership of handguns except for those who can prove that they have some special need for such a weapon. Owners of rifles and shotguns would merely be required to obtain identification cards, which would be granted to anyone over the age of 18 who was not a criminal or mentally incompetent.

Opponents of gun control often use catchy sayings to summarize their arguments. One of them is "When guns are outlawed, only outlaws will have guns." The slogan implies that honest citizens need firearms to protect themselves from criminals. And it is indeed true that many people, especially those who live in inner cities, believe that they need guns to defend themselves against robbers, burglars, and rapists. However, the statistics do not bear out their fears. As we have seen, the greatest number of homicides and assaults occur between friends and relatives, not strangers. Another slogan is "Guns don't kill; people do." The argument here is that criminals, not guns, should be controlled. If killers and other felons were all locked up, the idea goes, then there would be no need even for laws making it a crime to own a gun. The chances of jailing all potential killers are, however, virtually nil. Gun control is also opposed on the ground that our citizens might someday need guns to fight for freedom if a dictator were to seize power. Overlooked is the fact that even if such an unlikely event should take place, pistols and rifles would hardly be a match for hand grenades, tanks, jet fighters, and nuclear bombs. But few advocate that private possession of such weapons be legalized.

Helping the Victims   Traditionally, the criminal-justice system considered the victim of a violent crime—or any other crime, for that matter—to be just another witness. Once the accused person had been convicted, the state usually forgot about the victim. But the victim of a violent crime may have enormous medical expenses, miss weeks or months of work, and even be blinded or crippled. Until recently such victims, like the destitute children of murdered parents, had few legal remedies for their loss. They could sue the offender, but such attempts are rarely successful. For one thing, the attackers must be identified and the police must be able to find the suspect and make an arrest. For another, most violent criminals, like most victims, are penniless. Even if the victim wins a damage suit, the criminal usually has no money with which to pay. If they are convicted, violent criminals go off to prison for long terms and therefore have no way of earning money to pay their victims.

As the public became more aware of these problems in the 1980s, a host of new legislation was enacted to help the victims of violent crime. Thirty-one states now have some kind of "victims' bill of rights," which includes such things as the right to be notified about the outcome of the case in which they are involved, protection from intimidation, and the return of property held as evidence. Twenty-seven states have funded programs to assist victims (and often other witnesses) in dealing with the court system. And most important, 43 states and the federal government now have some kind of program that gives financial compensation to the victims of violent crime.[51] These programs are not all the same, but in general, the victim applies to a government board, which examines the case and sets compensation based on such things as medical costs, lost income, the severity of injuries, and the role the victim played in the crime. However, most of these plans have not been given enough money to do the job, so the compensation still doesn't cover all the victim's losses. Obviously, the best way to protect the victim's rights is to prevent the crime before it happens, but failing that, more and better-funded programs to assist victims can help reduce their suffering.

Cultural Change Unjustified, "bad" violence clearly is condemned in our society. At the same time, however, we lavish praise and admiration on war heroes, tough cops, and others who use "good" violence. High rates of violence arise in part from the fact that "good" as well as "bad" violence has a way of breeding more violence.[52] Further, there is no simple answer to the question of which violence is good and which is bad. The typical murder begins with a petty disagreement, escalates into a heated argument and a few slaps or blows, then ends with the use of a deadly weapon.[53] Both parties may be right in some ways and wrong in others.

Many people have proposed that the mystique of violence, so often reflected in television and the movies, be replaced with an ethic of nonviolence. This ideal is advocated by most of the world's great religions. Nonviolence was a cornerstone of the politics of the great American civil rights leader Martin Luther King, Jr., and of Mahatma Gandhi, the leader of the independence movement in India. Many other political leaders have also called for long-range changes in violent cultural traditions. It is clear that the stronger our collective denunciation of violence and the fewer situations in which we justify its use, the more peaceful our society will be.

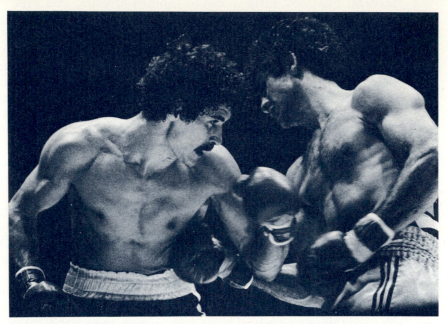

Many forms of violence are permitted in our society. Legitimate violence promotes attitudes and values favorable to criminal violence. To reduce the problem of violence, we must promote the positive ideals of nonviolence.

Criminal Justice   It is often suggested that a tougher and more efficient criminal-justice system would reduce violent crime. As was noted in Chapter 14, advocates of such policies argue that improved law enforcement will catch convicts and punish a higher percentage of those who commit violent crimes. There is considerable evidence that more severe punishment for murder does not prevent very many people from committing this crime, but the issue is by no means settled. Others argue for better defense rather than more severe punishment. For them, the idea is that murderers should simply be taken off the streets and isolated in prisons, where they can do no more damage. But the fact is that very few murderers repeat their crimes, whether they are imprisoned or not. Longer prison terms would affect them only slightly, if at all.

In contrast to murder, however, robbers and rapists often commit the same crimes again and again, and isolating more of them behind bars is more likely to bring about the desired results. For this reason, many states are now making it easier for courts to convict rapists. In the past, defense lawyers went out of their way to try to prove that the victim had consented to sexual intercourse or at least had "asked for it" with provocative behavior. As a result, many rape victims found that they, rather than the rapists, were being put on trial. Now police departments are relying more heavily on female officers to take rape complaints and are training them to minimize the victims' sense of shame and humiliation so that more victims will come forward. Also, some states now forbid defense attorneys to delve into the victim's past sexual behavior unless they have proved in advance that such inquiry is relevant to the case. These changes certainly will not stop all rapes. But they do make it easier for victims to cooperate with the police, and they ensure that fewer rapists go unpunished.

SOCIOLOGICAL PERSPECTIVES ON PERSONAL VIOLENCE

Violence has been a social issue ever since Cain killed Abel. For centuries, murder and other violent acts were believed to be prompted by evil spirits. Only two hundred years ago English courts not only accused defendants of violating the law but also accused them of "being prompted and instigated by the devil and not having the fear of God before [their] eyes." And as late as 1862 the Supreme Court of North Carolina declared that "to know the right and still the wrong pursue proceeds from a perverse will brought about by the seductions of the evil one."

During the period when such explanations of violence were most commonly voiced, the idea of natural causation had not developed. Few people could imagine that violence is a natural outcome of the way a society is organized, not of something outside the society. But sociologists have helped change all that. Functionalists and conflict theorists have shown that violence is linked to economic, political, and social organization. Social psychologists have shown that violent behavior is learned in interactions with others. None of these scientists believe that violence can be significantly reduced by heaping torture and suffering on violent people.

The Functionalist Perspective   In huge, poorly integrated societies many people have little association with the social groups and institutions that are supposed to regulate and direct behavior. As a result, many people are alienated, frustrated, and alone. In short, they suffer from anomie. Because so many people lack proper social direction and control, functionalists argue, some are bound to drift into violence, and others are violent because they know no other way of life.

Violence can be functional or dysfunctional, depending on the context in which it is used. The violence used by police to subdue a criminal is usually seen as functional, while the violence of the criminal is considered dysfunctional. But functionalists believe that, taken as a whole, the effects of violence in our society are overwhelmingly dysfunctional. The pervasive climate of violence fosters feelings of fear and insecurity, restricts individual freedom, and, perhaps most serious, has spawned a growing doubt about the ability of society to deal with the problem within a framework of constitutional civil liberties. Some functionalists warn that if the level of violence continues unchecked, it may undermine the foundations of our democratic system and the freedoms that rest on them.

The functionalist solution calls for an increase in social integration. Violence would decline if alienated people were linked to primary groups that met their psychological and social needs. Religious organizations provide this sense of belonging and personal direction, but of course in disorganized societies not everyone is attached to such groups. Social clubs, political organizations, and work groups also have that function. Speaking generally, functionalists are convinced that violent crime and suicide would decrease if communities were better organized for peace.

The Conflict Perspective   Conflict theorists see the violence in North American society as a legacy of historical injustice. Conquering the Spanish, the Mexicans, and the French and nearly exterminating the native Americans forged a powerful tradition of violence in American society and left a smoldering resentment among the descendants of history's victims. Moreover, ethnic minorities still do not get their fair share of the wealth and power, and many still live under the domination of alien institutions and agencies. As a result, they are likely to have little respect for the legal system that tells them that violence is wrong. Indeed, they often see that system as a part of the machinery of oppression that keeps their people down. Thus, the robbery of a liquor store or a bank can be justified as a blow against oppression. But even if it is not, it is hardly surprising to see the victims of oppression often using the same weapons that have been used against them; tragically, in their confusion and frustration they usually strike out at their friends and neighbors instead of their oppressors. This same frustration and hopelessness may even lead to self-destruction.

Violence is also a powerful weapon in the "war between the sexes." Conflict theorists point out that violence has always been one of the principal means of enforcing male dominance. Many feminists charge that as industrialization and modern technology eroded the underpinnings of male privilege, violence became an increasingly important tool in keeping women "in their place." Rape and physical brutality continue to be used as a means for men to degrade women who challenge their sense of superiority, and to express their rage against women in general. As a result, fear of violence forces women to change their ways of living, acting, and dressing, and thus deprives them of many basic freedoms.

The conflict theorists' solution to the problem of violence is to give oppressed people a fair share of the wealth and power. Women and other victims of violence would then be able to use the full power of society to stop the violence against them. Such changes would also increase respect for society and therefore would increase the willingness of all people to abide by its laws. Most conflict theorists advocate some form of collective political action directed at bringing about change of this kind. A few even advocate collective violence as a means of reducing interpersonal violence.

Social Psychological Perspectives   As we have already noted, biosocial theories consider violence to be a result of an aggressive instinct that was bred into the human race over the centuries as the timid were killed off and the violent survived. This kind of theory offers little hope for the elimination of violence. About all such theorists can recommend is to try to channel some of our aggression into violent sports and other "friendly" conflicts. However, few social psychologists use instinct theory of this kind. Interactionists, personality theorists, and behaviorists all see violence as a product of social learning.

Many young people clearly learn to be violent in their early socialization, either from the example of their parents and friends or indirectly as they view a world that makes violence appear to be a necessary tool for survival and success. Adults continue to learn violent behavior through years of association with it. Interactionists also note that the process of learning violence is strongly linked to male gender role socialization. Boys are encouraged to be tough, to "stand up for themselves," and not to be "sissies." Then, as they grow into men, most of them encounter situations that require either a violent response or the inescapable recognition that they have failed to live up to the ideals of manhood that have been instilled in them.

Most social psychologists argue that if violence is to be reduced, people must be taught to be nonviolent. Anything that is learned can be unlearned, but it is far from clear how such a change might be brought about. Programs of therapy and behavior modification may help individuals who are motivated to change, but these programs are unlikely to have a significant impact on the overall problem of violence. Large-scale cultural changes will be necessary to solve the problem. Nationwide educational programs implemented through the schools and the mass media are the most promising way to teach nonviolence. But winning the massive national commitment necessary to create an effective program will be a difficult task. Changes in the media's romanticization of violence also would be helpful, but it is not clear how such changes could be made without raising the specter of government censorship. One bright spot on the horizon is the changing definitions of gender roles. If current trends continue, we may someday see a new ideal of masculinity that emphasizes the strength of the peacemaker and not the warrior.

SUMMARY

Violence has been defined as behavior intended to cause bodily pain or injury to another person. However, the legitimate imposition of pain or injury is not ordinarily thought of as violence. The "violence problem" is therefore a problem of *illegitimate* violence. The catch is that there is no clear distinction between legitimate and illegitimate violence.

There are four main violent crimes: murder, assault, forcible rape, and robbery. Murder is the unlawful killing of a human being with malice aforethought. It is distinct from homicide, which is any killing of a human being, legally or illegally. An assault occurs when one person physically attacks another. There is little behavioral difference between some assaults and some murders, except that in one the victim survives and in the other the victim dies. Rape is sexual intercourse with a person without her or his consent. There are two patterns of rape: in so-called date rape the attack often occurs on an unplanned spur-of-the-moment basis, but in the second pattern, the rape is a planned and calculated act often committed by a stranger. Robbery is basically theft by force and therefore has many similarities with the property crimes. Although suicide is not usually treated as a crime, far more people die from suicide than at the hands of another.

It is unusual for someone to be murdered by a stranger. The victims and the attackers generally have similar economic, ethnic, and social backgrounds. The pattern of victimization in robbery is quite different, however. In over 75 percent of the cases, the victim and the attacker are strangers.

Violence has been blamed on everything from human instincts to television. Some biological explanations hold that violence is instinctive, whereas others hold that the evolutionary process favors certain kinds of violence and discourages others. Among the psychological explanations, the Freudian approach is the most popular. Freud accepted the biological theory that people have an instinctive tendency to be violent and aggressive. His followers believe that most people develop a superego that blocks these aggressive instincts, and when it fails to do the job violence results. Another important psychological theory holds that aggression and violence are responses to the frustration of an individual's goals. The more frustrated people become, the idea goes, the more likely they are to become aggressive.

Sociological explanations of violence picture it as a product of social structure and social learning. Some sociologists argue that violence occurs when society fails to provide strong enough controls on individuals' behavior. Others say that violence is a product of the frustrations that structural inequalities cause among the poor and minorities. Still others point out that people learn to be violent the same way that they learn any other kind of behavior. There is, for example, considerable evidence that violence is learned at home.

Compared with other Western democratic nations, the United States is very violent. A tradition of violence developed as rugged frontiersmen conquered the vast continent, and this tradition continues. Some violence also stems from the great size and ethnic diversity of the United States and from its relatively high level of economic inequality. Tensions and conflicts are to be expected in a society with such a low level of social integration.

The flood of fictional violence in the media is another factor in the problem of violence, and most researchers believe that it causes higher levels of real-life violence.

Heated debate centers on the effects of widespread ownership of firearms. On one side is the argument that firearms have little effect on violence: that if guns were not available killers would use some other weapon. On the other side is the observation that the difference between assault and murder often turns on the kind of weapon involved. Most murders and a significant number of rapes and robberies are committed with a gun.

Many proposals have been made to deal with the problem of violence. Among them are stricter gun control, more help for victims, cultural changes that would stop the romanticization of violence and place more emphasis on the values of nonviolence, and changes in the criminal-justice system.

Violence, like any other social problem, is an outcome of the way a society is organized, not of something outside the society. Functionalists and conflict theorists have shown that violence is linked to economic, political, and social organization. Social psychologists have demonstrated that violent behavior is learned in interactions with others.

KEY TERMS

assault	murder
forcible rape	robbery
frustration-aggression theory	suicide
homicide	violence
manslaughter	

FURTHER READINGS

Martin Daly and Margo Wilson, *Homicide,* New York: Aldine de Gruyter, 1988.

John Allen, *Assault with a Deadly Weapon: The Autobiography of a Street Criminal,* New York: McGraw-Hill, 1978.

A. Nicolas Groth and H. Jean Birnbaum, *Men Who Rape: The Psychology of the Offender,* Beverly Hills, Calif.: Sage, 1978.

Gordon W. Russell, *Violence in Intimate Relationships,* New York: PMA Publishing, 1988.

National Institute of Mental Health, *Television and Behavior,* Washington, D.C.: U.S. Government Printing Office, 1982.

Murray Straus, Richard J. Gelles, and Suzanne K. Steinmetz, *Behind Closed Doors: Violence in the American Family,* New York: Doubleday, 1980.

Ted Robert Gurr (ed.), *Violence in America,* 3rd ed., Beverly Hills, Calif.: Sage, 1989 (two volumes).

PART FOUR
Problems of a Changing World

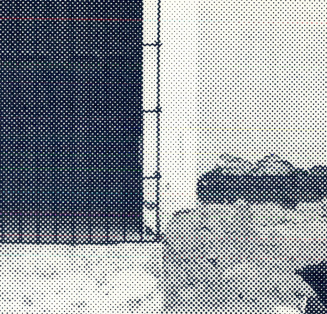

Chapter 16
URBANIZATION

The shift from rural to urban living is one of the most significant social changes of the past two centuries. **Urbanization** has profoundly altered the lives of millions of people in a relatively short period. In 1790, 95 percent of the population of the United States was rural (living on farms or in villages with fewer than 2500 inhabitants). Today, only one out of four Americans live in a rural area.[1] The same process has occurred in all other industrialized nations. Canada, for example, has about the same percentage of urban dwellers as the United States, Japan is slightly more urbanized, and over 90 percent of West Germans live in cities.[2] The **Third World** (the poor nations with little industrialization) has only begun its urban explosion, but its cities are now growing much faster than those in the industrialized nations. Today, about two-thirds of the people in the Third World live in rural areas, but in 35 years one-half will live in cities. In just 10 years, three of the four largest cities in the world will be in Third World countries.[3]

Although the shift to urban living is a recent development, the origins of the city are found at the very beginning of recorded history. The Sumerians, the first people to master the art of writing, are believed to have founded the first cities, with fabled names like Eridu and Ur. Other cities soon grew in Egypt, India, and China. However, these early cities were only tiny islands in a sea of rural farmers. Their populations seldom exceeded 5000 or 10,000.[4]

The industrial revolution set off a tremendous burst of urbanization. As agriculture became increasingly efficient, fewer people were needed on the farms, and the surplus labor drifted to the cities. Until well into the nineteenth century the only means of ground transportation was by foot or by horse, and only the rich could afford horses. Therefore, cities rarely had a radius of more than three miles. Advances in transportation have allowed cities to expand both in size and in population. Small satellite cities have sprung up on the outskirts of the major cities. The area between cities has steadily been filled, until vast stretches of land are entirely covered with buildings and roads. The term **megalopolis** is often used to refer to areas in which many cities fuse together to form one vast urban network. The largest megalopolis in North America is the unbroken stretch of cities and suburbs along the east coast of the United States from Boston to Virginia. Another sprawling urban area is growing in California from San Diego to San Francisco, and a third runs from Milwaukee through Chicago to northern Indiana. In Canada, 60 percent of the population live in a 600-mile strip from Quebec City to Windsor, Ontario. However, because these huge areas often have little overall political or economic integration, the U.S. Bureau of the Census uses a slightly more narrow concept, the **metropolitan statistical area** (MSA), which includes a central population center and the surrounding communities that are dependent on it.[5]

Although most nations of the Third World have yet to experience much of an industrial revolution, they are nonetheless undergoing a massive wave of urbanization. The principal motivation of urban migrants in the Third World is not so much the attractions of the city but the fact that rapid population growth and the spread of large export-oriented farming businesses have made it impossible for them to continue making a living on the land.

The cities of Third World nations are now growing almost twice as fast as those in the industrialized countries. By the year 2000 there will be twice as many people living in the cities of the Third World than in those of the industrialized nations, and by 2025 there will be four times as many.[6] Yet the poor nations have little money for new housing, roads, water, sanitation, or electricity.

THE CITIES

Civilizations have always been centered in cities. Despite the recent flight to the suburbs, modern cities are more dominant in our social life than ever before. In capitalist nations huge corporations spread their influence outward from a few major cities, just as the state bureaucracy does in the communist countries. The large newspapers and broadcasting companies, which set our tastes and define our world, are based in cities and reflect their realities. The cities spawn and attract actors, artists, writers, and other intellectual innovators who set the cultural style of our age. There is a particularly big gap between the sophisticated Western-influenced cultural life found in the major cities of the Third World and the life of the tradition-bound villagers. Foreign visitors and immigrants stop in the great cities, rarely in country villages. In North America, new immigrants first occupy the rundown sections of the cities, then move to more affluent areas as they become acculturated. This process has left the cities dotted with fragments of many different cultures—Irish, Italian, French, Chinese, Mexican, German, Russian, and more—thus adding to the diversity of city life.

Because big cities have these attractions, it is surprising that public opinion polls show that most people who live in them would rather live somewhere else.[7] Moreover, people in rural areas are almost two and a half times more likely to say that they are "completely satisfied" with their community than those in big cities.[8]

One of the most fascinating questions confronting urban sociologists concerns the nature of life in cities. Do urban people have a unique way of thinking, a special outlook on life? One of the first people to answer this question was the German sociologist Georg Simmel. In a classic essay published in 1903, Simmel noted that city dwellers are continually bombarded by a tremendous amount of "nervous stimulation."[9] Noise, traffic, crowds, the rapid pace of life, and dozens of other stimuli overload the urban resident. City dwellers simply cannot pay attention to everything that goes on around them, and as a result they become indifferent to their surroundings. Because urbanites deal with so many strangers, their relationships tend to be oriented toward external goals rather than direct personal satisfaction. On the whole, the city offers its people greater freedom, but it also increases the danger that they will be isolated and alone.

The most famous essay in urban sociology is Louis Wirth's "Urbanism as a Way of Life."[10] Published in 1938, this article summarized much of the thought of the "Chicago school" of urban sociology, which developed at the University of Chicago in the early twentieth century. Wirth painted with a broader brush than Simmel, but he reached similar conclusions about the psychological impact of urban life. To Wirth, the essential characteristics of a city are the size, density, and social diversity of its population: "The larger, the more densely populated, and the more heterogeneous a community, the more accentuated the characteristics associated with urbanism will be."

The diversity of social life is the most important of the city's characteristics. It springs from the size and density of the population, which create a "mosaic of social worlds." According to Wirth, urban dwellers are specialized in the work they do and in their relationships with other people. Being highly specialized, they know one another only in superficial and impersonal ways. One person will be recognized as a bank teller, another as a co-worker, and a third as a bus driver, but they are seldom known in an intimate way. Financial interests dominate this impersonal urban world. The city becomes a complex mass of people living close together but without deep emotional ties. The city dweller often feels lonely and isolated even in the midst of vast crowds. Urbanites learn to tolerate the attitudes and customs of other people, but they also learn to accept insecurity and instability as the normal state of the world. These characteristics work together to increase the incidence of what Wirth called "pathological conditions," including "personal disor-

The modern city has a rich diversity of people, life styles and architectures.

ganization, mental breakdown, suicide, delinquency, crime, corruption, and disorder."

Few contemporary sociologists agree that city life is as dismal as Wirth pictured it. Some argue that Wirth's ideas merely reflect small-town America's dislike of cities and their rapid growth. For example, Herbert J. Gans noted that Wirth overlooked the many city dwellers who have a strong sense of community.[11] Gans's studies have identified five distinct types of city dwellers, most of whom do not suffer from social isolation:

1. *Cosmopolites,* such as artists, writers, entertainers, intellectuals, and professionals, choose to live in the city because of its cultural activities.
2. *Childless people* live in the city to be near its job opportunities and social life.
3. *Ethnic villagers* live in self-contained ethnic communities and therefore are able to maintain their traditional ways of life and kinship patterns.
4. *Deprived people* include the poor, the handicapped, and minority groups.
5. *Trapped people* are sliding down the social scale or are retired and living on fixed incomes and thus are unable to leave their decaying neighborhoods.

Gans argued that only the last two types of people—the deprived and the trapped—experience the urban way of life described by Wirth. The others either belong to a supportive subculture or are in the city voluntarily because of the benefits it offers. More positively, Gans found that social class and age have a greater effect on urban life-styles than does city living itself. But whether it is the size, density, and diversity of cities or their population composition that causes them to have distinctive characteristics, there is no question that such characteristics exist. Surveys have shown that cities, in contrast to rural areas, have higher levels of education and income, greater social mobility, more foreign residents, smaller families, and less stable marriages. The reported rates of crime, alcoholism, drug addiction, and suicide are all higher in cities than elsewhere.

THE SUBURBS

More Americans now live in **suburbs**—the part of an urban area that lies outside the central city—than in cities or rural areas. The first suburbs can be traced back at least as far as the 1760s. By the end of the nineteenth century, most American cities had suburbs where the wealthy could live away from the congestion of the city. But the fastest growth took place in the two decades after the end of World War II, when millions of Americans poured into the suburbs.[12] In one sense the big city, with its congestion, crime, pollution, and decay, pushed them out. But in another sense the suburbs pulled families out of the cities. Some moved to the suburbs because they were attracted to the ideal of a "country home," but most had more specific reasons: space for growing families, good schools, personal safety, growing job opportunities, and a pleasant environment at a price that they could afford.[13]

But the modern suburbs did not simply spring into being because people wanted to live there. Enormous government subsidies fueled the suburbanization of the United States and diverted vitally needed funds away from the cities. The growth of these modern suburbs required three things: automobiles, highways, and private homes. The "highway lobby," composed of such diverse interests as the oil companies, automobile manufacturers, and truckers' unions, pushed through a massive program of freeway construction that laid the foundation for continued suburban growth. The government also spent billions of dollars subsidizing private homes for middle- and upper-class Americans. The biggest subsidy is the full tax deduction for interest paid on home mortgages. The government also worked to keep interest rates down on home mortgages, and even directly underwrote home loans through the Federal Housing Authority and the Veterans Administration.[14]

North Americans have a kind of love-hate relationship with the suburbs, seeing them as both the cause of and the solution of social blight. The proponents of suburban living picture it as a refuge from the troubles of the big city. In this view, neatly trimmed lawns and tidy, well-ordered, nuclear families greet suburban workers upon their return from their jobs in the city. Close to their new home is the symbol of modern suburbia: a shopping mall with dozens of stores filled with the latest consumer goods. The residents tend to be young and white. The men hold interesting white-collar jobs with promise for the future. The women are well-groomed, efficient, politically aware, and deeply concerned with the welfare of their young children. In general, suburbanites are outgoing and sociable, and because they resemble each other, they get along together and are active in local civic affairs.

The critics of suburbia picture it differently. They see the suburbs as an endless expanse of cracker-box houses that are so alike that it is difficult to tell one from the other. They say that because suburbanites are mostly from the white middle class, they lack individuality and diversity and are bland and dull. The suburbanite's life centers on nothing more important than washing the car, mowing the lawn, and shopping at the supermarket. The goal of each suburban dweller is to match or surpass his or her neighbors in the collection of cars, television sets, microwave ovens, barbeque pits, and other consumer goods.

Both these views are faulty, however, for they are based on an image of the suburb as a "bedroom community" for the affluent that is generations out of date. Although they started as residential areas for the wealthy, the suburbs are now heterogeneous and diversified. As people first moved to the suburbs, they were quickly followed by small shops and stores. Since then, suburban retailers have grown steadily more prosperous, while sales in the central city have stagnated.[15] Today's huge suburban shopping malls have every imaginable kind of product and service, and are important social centers as well. Along with the new jobs in retail has come a tremendous influx of manufacturing, wholesaling, and warehousing businesses that used to be found only in the central cities. Even the administrative offices of the major corporations have moved to the suburbs. There are now more corporate headquarters in the suburbs surrounding New York City than there are in the city itself. Overall, more than 70 percent of those who live in the suburbs of large metropolitan areas work in them too.[16]

As the suburbs have diversified economically, they have diversified socially as well. Because many older suburban neighborhoods have become less desirable, and builders have put up more apartment buildings, less affluent people have been able to move in. The poor and the minorities are now the fastest-growing segment of the suburban population.[17] However, this trend has not led to a new era of integration but rather to the reproduction of the same patterns of segregation found in the cities. About 86 percent of all suburban whites now live in segregated areas (areas in which less than 1 percent of the population is black).[18] And just as there are now black neighborhoods in the suburbs, there are other neighborhoods populated mainly by those with other particular ethnic or economic backgrounds.

Today's suburbs are therefore a checkerboard of widely divergent neighborhoods, and as Logan and Molotch point out, "In the suburban milieu, as in the larger world system (see Chapter 19), the advantages adhere to the places of the rich and the disadvantages to the places of the poor."[19] The rich neighborhoods have the best sanitation, fire, and police services, the best shopping, and the least pollution and crime. Because the process of suburbanization has fragmented the political control of metropolitan areas, the wealthy often live in their own towns and cities. One result is that their local taxes no longer go to help meet the pressing needs of the urban poor.

RURAL AREAS

Until the industrial revolution, most of the world's people lived in rural villages. Even today, most Third World people live in small rural settlements, which tend to be traditional in their cultural outlook and skeptical of new ideas and attitudes. Villagers are not only isolated from current world affairs and concerns, they generally have weak ties to their own nation. Illiteracy is still the rule, and because many Third World villages have no electricity, there is very little light after sunset, much less radio or television. The villagers' main concern is, therefore, with local events. Villages are very homogeneous places. Not only do the villagers share the same set of values, they have grown up together and know the intimate details of each others' lives.[20] Although most villagers are quite content to continue with their traditional life-style, population growth and changing economic conditions are making it harder and harder to do so (see Chapter 17).

In the industrialized nations, traditional village life is largely a thing of the past. Of course, there are still many people living on farms and in small towns, but their numbers have decreased sharply over the last two centuries. Only about one in four people in North America now live in rural areas.[21]

Moreover, the character of rural life has changed. People who live in open country and small towns are no longer as isolated as they were in the past. Universal education perpetuates a similar cultural outlook in people regardless of where they live and brings rural residents into the cultural mainstream by giving them the ability to read books and newspapers. The spread of telephones, radio, television, and modern transportation has also increased the integration of rural areas into a unified national fabric. Farm families no longer raise their own vegetables, butcher their own hogs, milk their own cows, or cut their own wood for lumber and fuel. They buy their beans, pork, and milk at the supermarket and order building materials and fuel oil from local distributors. Gone are the days when spare time meant sitting around the stove telling tales, mending clothes, or repairing tools. Today's rural families watch television or go to the movies, just as those in the cities and suburbs do.

Another major factor in the transformation of rural life is the decline of farming as an occupation. Traditionally, the vast majority of people who lived in the country were farmers. But as nations industrialize, farm technology improves and fewer and fewer people are needed on the farm. In North America, the decline of the farm population began in the nineteenth century and is still continuing. From 1960 to 1986 farmers decreased from 8.7 percent to 2.2 percent of the American population (see Figure 16.1).[22] Agriculture changed from a way of life into a business. Today's most successful farmers cultivate huge tracts of land and run their operations by modern corporate methods. In response to this challenge from "agribusiness," small farmers have taken on jobs that reduce their dependence on farm income. Middle-sized farmers have been the hardest hit by the realities of the new agricultural economy. Large numbers of them are being forced to sell their farms and find another way of life.

People born in rural areas continue to migrate to cities in search of opportunity, as they have for centuries. But in the last two decades, the number of people migrating from the cities to the rural areas and small towns has greatly increased. Between 1970 and 1986 the percentage of the population living in cities of over half a million people decreased, while the percentage of those living in communities of less than 50,000 went up.[23] The

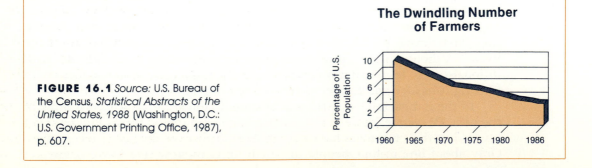

The Dwindling Number of Farmers

FIGURE 16.1 *Source:* U.S. Bureau of the Census, *Statistical Abstracts of the United States, 1988* (Washington, D.C.: U.S. Government Printing Office, 1987), p. 607.

reasons people are moving to small towns are probably much the same as the reasons they move to the suburbs: the lure of cheaper land, a slower-paced life-style, and the desire to escape from urban problems. Whatever their reasons for moving, these migrants bring their urban outlook with them, further diminishing the cultural distinctiveness of country people.

Despite all these changes, life on a farm or in a small town retains many special features. People know one another as people rather than as role players. The background of residents of rural communities tends to be more homogeneous than that of city dwellers, giving them a stronger feeling of group identity and a clearer sense of where they fit in as individuals. Deviant behavior is less common in rural areas than in urban ones; and though crime rates have been increasing faster in rural than in urban areas, they are still considerably lower.

Living in a small town has its drawbacks, however. There is less deviance because everyone watches everyone else. The absence of anonymity reduces opportunities for many types of crime, but it also affects personal freedom, innovation, and individuality. Because individuals cannot get lost in the crowd, their neighbors often know the details of their personal lives, and small-town gossip can be malicious and spiteful. Rural communities lack much of the spice of city life because they are so small and homogeneous. Still, people in rural areas report being far more satisfied with their community than do those in the cities.[24]

PROBLEMS OF URBANIZATION

As urbanization changed the way we live, it brought new problems as well. The urban population spilled over existing government boundaries, leaving local governments fragmented and disorganized. The price of housing rose so high that many poor people could not afford adequate shelter. Public transportation systems became overburdened, crime increased, and many rural areas were abandoned and left to decay.

Crisis on the Farm   No one has been harder hit by the process of urbanization than the farmers. The percentage of farmers in the U.S. population has been decreasing for generations. But on top of this long-term decline, the 1980s have seen an increase in farm foreclosures and bankruptcies of crisis proportions. In the last decade, as many as one in ten farms went out of business in some years, and experts predict that 30 percent of all U.S. farms may soon follow them.[25] Because the big farms are less likely to fail, farm employment has not decreased quite as rapidly, but it still dropped over 20 percent from 1980 to 1986.[26]

The reasons for the current farm crisis can be traced back to the 1970s, when a low dollar and a worldwide grain shortage led to fat profits. On advice from bankers and government experts, farmers borrowed heavily to buy new land and equipment to increase their production. But in the early 1980s, the dollar skyrocketed (making American grain more expensive overseas) and worldwide agricultural production increased substantially. As a result, the price of farm products fell and export markets dried up. The price of a bushel of grain decreased over 25 percent between 1978 and 1986, while inflation continued to push up the cost of growing it.[27] Deteriorating economic conditions led to a sharp drop in the value of farmland—28 percent from 1982 to 1986 alone. Without enough money to pay their mortgages or sufficient collateral in their farm to back their loans, thousands of farmers faced foreclosure.[28]

As a result, well-financed corporate farms have been able to buy up prime land at bargain prices. About 5 percent of the farms now hold half of all agricultural land. The agribusiness corporations also get most of the government farm subsidies, even though they were originally intended to help the family farmer.[29] Despite the fact that the dollar eventually went down again and export markets have shown some improvement, family farmers are still finding it difficult to survive.

Most rural people no longer work on the farm, but the plight of the family farmer has still sent economic shock waves through many parts of the country already facing hard times. The mass migration to the cities and suburbs and the narrow economic base of many rural communities have left their residents with lower average income, poorer health care, and less education than their urban counterparts. Some rural towns have been flooded with new immigrants, while others have seen their population dwindle away. Although an influx of new residents requires many difficult adjustments, the towns with declining populations suffer the worst problems. For one thing, a declining population means higher taxes because the cost of maintaining essential services must be carried by fewer people. Stores and businesses that depend on local trade go bankrupt, further reducing the tax base. As job opportunities dry up and education, health care, and other community services decline, even more people move out and the problem becomes more severe. To make matters worse, it is usually the young adults who migrate to the cities, leaving a disproportionately large dependent population of young children and elderly people who must be supported by the productive workers who remain.

Local Government The process of suburbanization has created a financial predicament for many local governments. As more and more affluent people move to the suburbs, cities are left with a high percentage of poor people who need many services but are unable to pay for them. The central cities are older and their **infrastructure**—roads, sewers, water systems, and other basic necessities—needs more repairs and upkeep; and they require additional fire protection as well. The crime rates are higher in the cities (see Chapter 14); so they need more money for police, courts, and jails. There is also more demand for social services such as welfare and public assistance. Taxes are higher than in the suburbs, but the cities still cannot raise them enough to meet their needs, for that would only accelerate the exodus of people and capital. But as the suburbs have grown larger and more diverse, these same problems have cropped up there. Taxes are low and the services generous in wealthy suburbs, but the poor ones are little better off than the central cities.[30]

Local governments are also beset by a variety of other problems, ranging from graft and corruption to wasteful duplication of services. Zoning changes, for example, have repeatedly been the focus of corruption scandals. Millions of dollars are often involved in an agency's decision to change the zoning of a piece of land. Developers and land speculators looking for a fast profit go to great lengths to convince officials to make the "right" decision. Officials are sometimes bribed with cash payments or given a percentage of the developer's profits. The result is likely to be a new suburban community that turns its developers into millionaires but fails to meet the needs of local residents.

Another product of urbanization is the creation of a confusing network of fragmented local governments and overlapping service districts. Metropolitan areas often have dozens of police chiefs, fire chiefs, and department heads when only a few would be sufficient. This overlap and duplication of services is expensive and inefficient. Many town and city governments have surprisingly little control over their own affairs because states place tight legal restrictions on their freedom to act, particularly with respect to the types and amounts of taxes that can be levied on their citizens. Further, local governments have come to rely on federal grants, which often come with orders that specify how the money is to be spent. Powerful corporations often influence federal and state governments to overpower local opposition to their plans.

Housing   The stunning increase in the cost of buying a private home has created a growing division between the haves and the have-nots in our society. Those who already own a home have received windfall profits, but first-time home buyers are increasingly shut out of the market. The cost of an average home more than doubled between 1977 and 1987 (see Figure 16.2). As a result, the average buyer was older and more likely to need two incomes to make the payments.[31]

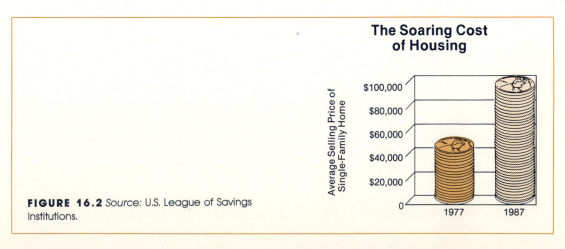

The Soaring Cost of Housing

Average Selling Price of Single-Family Home

$100,000

$80,000

$60,000

$40,000

$20,000

0

1977   1987

FIGURE 16.2 *Source:* U.S. League of Savings Institutions.

But these problems pale in comparison with the critical shortage of low-cost housing for those without comfortable middle-class incomes. Since 1978 more than two million units of low-cost housing have been abandoned or converted into more expensive housing.[32] One study of the 12 largest cities in the United States revealed that the number of low-income people increased by 36 percent between the late 1970s and early 1980s, while the supply of low-cost housing decreased by 30 percent.[33] As a result, an increasing number of people are being forced to move in with relatives and friends or are living in converted garages, old cars and vans, tents, or on the streets. Estimates of the number of homeless people in the United States vary widely from a low of 250,000 to a high of 4 million (see Chapter 6). But virtually everyone agrees that there has been a major increase in their numbers in the last decade.

What happened to the supply of low-cost housing? One problem is known as **gentrification**: the refurbishing of old, low-cost, neighborhoods to accommodate more wealthy people returning from the suburbs. One good example of this is the area known as Capitol Hill in Washington, D.C. In the 1960s it was occupied by poor and working-class blacks. But because of its close proximity to downtown employment centers, young artists, architects, and students began purchasing homes in the neighborhood and fixing them up. These first immigrants were soon followed by upper-income professionals and government workers. Over 90 percent of the newcomers were whites, and over 90 percent had college educations. The former residents had to move on to search for other accommodations from the city's shrinking supply of affordable housing.[34]

A second cause of this shortage can be laid directly at the government's doorstep. For one thing, the efforts of local community redevelopment agencies have tended to have much the same impact as private gentrification: old neighborhoods are renovated, and the poor are moved out to accommodate the affluent. Perhaps more important, the federal government has also turned its back on the housing needs of the poor. Between 1980 and 1987, the urban development budget was cut by almost 60 percent, and the Tax Reform Act of 1986 eliminated the tax breaks designed to encourage investment in rental properties.[35]

Transportation   It is often said that Americans have a love affair with the car. Even kings in their carriages did not know the speed, comfort, or convenience of the automobile that an average wage earner can now afford. But this romantic picture hardly fits the realities of American life where pollution fouls the air and over 45,000 people die in traffic accidents every year.[36] Traffic congestion is growing so bad in some urban areas that it is approaching **gridlock**, in which traffic simply stops moving and no one gets anywhere. Local, state, and national government spend billions of dollars a year in a losing battle to build roads faster than new cars clog them up. Still, four out of five commuters go to work by car, and most of those vehicles carry only a single passenger.[37] Our dependence on the automobile imposes a severe hardship on many of the one out of five households that do not own one,[38] making it difficult for the poor to get to work and the elderly to their doctor's office.

Why do we depend on such an inefficient system of transportation? Part of the answer is simply that we like cars. But there is another reason as well: the giant automobile, tire, and petroleum corporations decided that there was more money to be made from the automobile and they intentionally set out to impede the growth of public transportation. In Los Angeles, for example, General Motors and Standard Oil organized a corporation that acquired a controlling interest in the Pacific Electric Railway, which operated what was then the world's largest system of electric trolleys. The quiet and efficient trolleys were then replaced by polluting diesel-powered buses. The new owners gave up the special rights-of-way enjoyed by the trolleys and

The automobile provides one of the fastest and most convenient forms of transportation, but we have too much of a good thing. Traffic clogs city streets, exhaust pollutes the air, and engines consume huge amounts of petroleum.

pulled up the tracks. After these "improvements" passenger mileage plummeted, and Los Angeles is now one of the most automobile-dependent big cities in the world.[39]

Crowding There are many conflicting theories about the effects of crowding on human behavior. Laboratory studies suggest that overcrowding has alarming effects on experimental animals. The pioneering experiments of John Calhoun showed that the normal social patterns of rats are severely disrupted in overcrowded conditions.[40] Marauding males wander around the cage attacking both males and females and destroying the nests of weaker animals. Bands of "juvenile delinquents" engage in promiscuous sexual behavior and frequent fights. Some researchers concluded from these experiments that crowding is a major cause of urban problems. And because cities are becoming more and more crowded, they projected a very bleak picture of the future of urban life.

Researchers studying animals in the wild came to similar conclusions. They noted that some animals have a "territorial instinct" to claim a certain area as their own and to defend it against intruders. It was easy to conclude that humans have the same instincts and that the roots of human aggression are to be found in the violation of personal territory—which, of course, occurs more often in crowded conditions.[41] Again the implication appeared to be that urban problems will be solved only if population density is reduced.

However, there are many reasons for doubting these conclusions. For one thing, the animals studied lack complex cultural systems. Rats and other animals have fixed patterns of behavior that are very sensitive to any disturbance. If the pattern is disrupted, the animals cannot adjust. Human flexibility, in contrast, permits almost unlimited adaptation to the environment. Further, cross-cultural studies show no consistent relationship between crowding and crime or between crowding and aggression. Tokyo is one of the most densely populated cities in the world, but its crime rate is relatively low. Although this does not demonstrate that overcrowding has no bad effects on humans, it does suggest that high population density is manageable in human cultures.[42]

Ethnic Segregation Most large cities have a number of "ethnic villages": areas populated mostly by members of a particular ethnic group. Whether such a residential pattern is desirable or not is open to debate. As was noted in Chapter 7, pluralists hold that such communities provide support for new immigrants, and a place where their children and grandchildren can go to renew ties with their cultural roots. New immigrants often find jobs working for other members of their own group, and access to this supply of cheap labor provides an opportunity for other immigrants to move up the social ladder.[43] But the advocates of integration argue that the isolation of immigrants and minorities in ethnic communities actually cuts them off from many economic opportunities and makes them easy victims of exploitation, whether by members of their own group or of another. They point out that such segregated communities encourage the separate ethnic identities that divide Americans against each other and have created so much hatred and conflict through the years.

But whatever they think about the value of separate ethnic neighborhoods, both pluralists and integrationists agree that no one should be forced to live in them. Yet that is exactly the position in which many black and other nonwhite minorities find themselves. The laws explicitly requiring racial segregation have all been overturned, but racial minorities are still excluded from many neighborhoods by the hostility and prejudice of the residents, and by the realtors, landlords, and rental agents who cater to it. Although sociologists use different ways of measuring segregation, it appears that about three out of four blacks in American cities live in segregated neighborhoods.[44] Analysis of data collected by Karl and Alma Taeuber shows a slow decrease in the level of segregation in American cities over the years.[45] Logan and Molotch, on the other hand, found that segregation has been increasing in the suburbs,[46] while other recent research indicates that they are still less segregated than the central cities.[47] If this pattern of forced segregation is to be broken, the federal government will have to take much more vigorous action than it has in the last decade.

The Third World   The population explosion has prevented the problem of rural depopulation from developing in Third World nations, as it has in some industrialized ones. But with this one exception, the Third World has been experiencing all the problems of urbanization just discussed. Because Third World countries have more than double the population growth rate of the industrialized nations and only a fraction of their wealth, urban problems often take on staggering proportions. Moreover, the process of urbanization is occurring much faster in the Third World than it ever did in the West. In 1950 only 15 percent of the people in the Third World lived in cities, but 25 years later the percentage of urbanites had more than doubled, and it is expected to reach 43 percent by the end of this century (see Figure 16.3).[48]

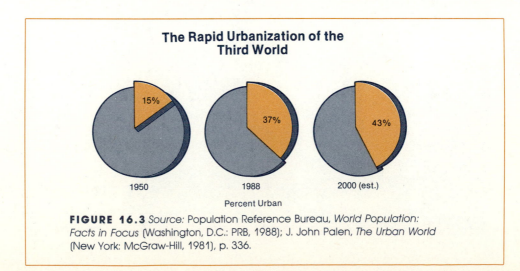

The Rapid Urbanization of the Third World

15%   37%   43%

1950   1988   2000 (est.)

Percent Urban

FIGURE 16.3 *Source:* Population Reference Bureau, *World Population: Facts in Focus* (Washington, D.C.: PRB, 1988); J. John Palen, *The Urban World* (New York: McGraw-Hill, 1981), p. 336.

The impact of this runaway urbanization can be more easily seen by comparing individual cities. In 1950 the population of Mexico City was less than one-fourth of the New York City area's 12 million people. In the next 25 years, Mexico City's growth rate was five times New York's, though in 1975 New York City was still larger, with 17 million people to Mexico City's 11 million. But by the year 2000, Mexico City will have over 26 million residents, making it the world's largest city, while New York will have about 15.5 million people. Mexico City's rapid growth is typical of most other large Third World cities as well. By the turn of the century, São Paulo, Brazil, will be almost as large, with a population of 24 million, and there will be *two* cities in India larger than New York, with a third quickly closing in.[49]

How are such impoverished cities to build enough new housing to accommodate all these people? Sadly, the answer is that they probably cannot. Most of the new people will either crowd into existing housing (most of it already crowded and dilapidated) or become urban squatters, building small shacks from whatever materials they can beg, borrow, or steal. Almost half the residents of Mexico City now live in slums and shantytowns, as do 55 percent of the residents of Manila in the Philippines, and 67 percent of the residents of Calcutta, India.[50] The slums are bad, but the shantytowns are worse. They are more than just overcrowded: they lack the basic services necessary for a decent life. The streets are unpaved, there is little fire or

Shanty towns, like the one in the background, are common in cities around the world.

police protection, clean water is scarce, and proper sewage facilities are nonexistent. As a result, health conditions are deplorable, death rates are high, and epidemic disease is common. Because urban squatters have no legal rights to the land they live on, they are in constant danger of losing their homes. If the government decides it needs the land for some new public-works project or that the squatters are an eyesore or a source of political unrest, they can simply be moved out. Ironically enough, however, the residents of these shantytowns are the lucky ones, for most large Third World cities have a substantial number of "pavement people" who sleep in the streets, without any permanent home. Calcutta, India, one of the world's most troubled cities, has between 330,000 and 1 million of these homeless people.[51]

Of course, all the residents of the Third World cities do not live in such deplorable conditions. The Westernized elite typically live in conditions of luxury that would make most middle-class Americans envious. And even the common people often find the city a far more rewarding place to live than rural villages. One survey of migrants who had been living in Mexico City for four years found that 80 percent of those interviewed were satisfied with their decision to move.[52] After all, millions of people wouldn't migrate to Third World cities every year if they didn't think that their life would be better there. The urban problems of Third World nations must therefore be seen in the context of the crowding, unemployment, and hunger of the rural areas.

RESPONDING TO PROBLEMS OF URBANIZATION

Despite the complexity of metropolitan problems, there is no shortage of proposals for solving them. Some are wildly utopian and others too narrow to be worthwhile. But all have one thing in common: their successful implementation will require two scarce commodities, money and the political will to get the job done.

Governmental Reorganization   Many proposals for solving metropolitan political and financial problems in the industrialized nations call for governmental reorganization. This means, generally, the creation of larger governmental units. For example, some planners suggest that cities be abolished and that county or even regional governments take their place. Others propose that only some functions of government be regionalized by creating larger school, water, sewage, airport and pollution control **districts.** Such regional governmental units could provide services more economically and would spread the tax burden more evenly over inner cities, suburbs, and rural areas. Some urban planners believe that these governmental units would eventually encourage a sense of regional cooperation and identity. A person would no longer be loyal to Boston or San Francisco; instead, he or she would identify with New England or the Bay area.

Annexation of suburbs or otherwise merging two or more governments appears to be the easiest form of reorganization. In the nineteenth century important mergers took place in New York City, Philadelphia, Boston, and New Orleans. But there seems to be increasing resistance to mergers and annexations. Voters in suburban areas are seldom willing to merge with nearby cities. They moved to their homes to avoid the problems of the big cities and see in proposed mergers only increased taxes and loss of autonomy.

A **federation** of metropolitan governments allows existing units to continue to operate independently on some issues but joins them to coordinate their activities on other issues. For example, each city may regulate and maintain its own streets, while several cities combine their efforts to handle schools or sewage. Such plans run into the same kind of opposition as proposals for annexations and mergers, and thus no large-scale federation has emerged in the United States. However, because local elections were not required, a Metropolitan Council was established in the area of Toronto, Ontario, over 30 years ago. Although this federation has its own critics, it has improved water supply and sewage disposal, established an advanced rapid-transit system, improved and unified law enforcement, and constructed new public housing and library facilities.[53]

However, some experts reject the whole idea of centralization. They argue that small governmental units are more responsive to the public will, promote a sense of community, and provide more opportunities for individual participation. For example, some plans for decentralization divide existing cities into smaller units with specific limited functions, while keeping overall control in the hands of the main city government. But whatever approach is used, the idea is to keep local government as close to the people it serves as possible.

Urban Renewal American **urban renewal** programs were begun during the Great Depression to improve housing and provide employment for construction workers. To this day urban renewal usually means housing renewal. From the beginning, urban renewal projects were plagued with problems. The original idea was simple: government agencies were to buy up decaying central-city areas, demolish the buildings, and sell the land to private developers, who would build apartments for people with low and moderate incomes. But the developers were not required to build inexpensive housing. Most built office buildings, factories, and luxury apartments, which bring in higher profits. The poor were forced to move from substandard homes in one area to substandard homes in another area. This caused many black leaders to say that urban renewal was just another term for "Negro removal."

The federal government also tried a smorgasbord of other programs, including building its own low-income housing and guaranteeing mortgages so that low-income people could afford to buy a home. One of the most popular programs provided subsidized loans for developers to build or substantially rehabilitate rental units for qualified low-income renters. The developer then rents the apartment to low-income families below the going rate, and the government makes up the difference with a cash payment. Many such agreements allowed the developer to pay off the loan after 20 years and then sell the building or divert it to some other use. According to a 1988 report from the National Housing Preservation Task Force, the United States may lose as many as 1.5 million units of such low-income housing by 1995.[54]

In the 1980s the federal government began moving away from such specific programs to deal with community problems and instead came to rely on general "block grants" and "revenue sharing," to be spent as the community sees fit. The idea that local leaders know more about the needs of their own community makes a great deal of sense, but such programs ignore the political reality that poor people have little influence over the decisions of their local government. According to research by Wong and Peterson, the block-grant program has resulted in a smaller proportion of federal money actually going to help the poor.[55] Moreover, the total amount of money available for low-income housing steadily declined in the 1980s.

The history of government programs to improve housing in the United States has been one of misplaced priorities. Most federal assistance has gone to the wealthy and the middle class in the form of low-interest home loans and tax exemptions for home mortgage payments. To deal with the growing need for low-income housing, these priorities must be reversed. For example, if some or all of the tax exemption for home mortgages were repealed, billions of dollars would be freed to provide housing for the poor.

Controlling Urban Growth   The need for more low-income housing has been recognized for generations, but the helter-skelter growth of our cities has created other serious problems that have only recently won public attention. The destruction of the natural environment, endless urban sprawl, traffic congestion, air pollution, and a feeling that our overall quality of life is declining have led us to question the old assumption that more growth means more prosperity and a better society. An increasing number of people are calling for tighter government controls to regulate growth and ensure that we protect the environment, expand public transportation, and conserve our natural resources. The logical approach is to redirect urban development away from the sprawling automobile-based suburbs and increase the population density of existing cities and towns. This high-density strategy has many advantages over the current policies that allow the endless proliferation of new suburban housing tracts. Not only does it protect virgin land from the developers' bulldozers, but higher-density housing is less expensive to build, more energy efficient, and much more compatible with effective public transportation. Another important way to save energy and alleviate transportation problems is to zone cities and suburbs so that residential areas are near the offices and factories where most people work.

The primary obstacle to the implementation of such proposals is economic. Developers stand to make far more money building whole new housing tracts on empty land, than they would remodeling existing buildings, tearing down and replacing dilapidated structures, and building on small

482 Part Four Problems of a Changing World

The struggle for power takes a different form in the Third World, but its effects are just as profound. Conflict theorists point out that the ruling class in most Third World nations (especially in those countries with large investments by foreigners) are much more Western in their outlook than the lower classes. As a result, they tend to support programs that will help generate the money they need to buy foreign luxury goods and maintain a Western standard of living. Peasants are often driven from their land to make room for large corporate farms, whose products are then sold on the world market. Government tax policies frequently place a heavy burden on rural villagers in order to pay for grandiose industrialization programs. The few well-paying jobs that are created by the new industries spur unrealistic dreams of urban affluence among poor villagers. The effect of all this has been a staggering wave of immigration to the cities that Third World nations have found impossible to handle.

Conflict theorists are convinced that the solution to urban problems lies in political organization and action. People in city slums and poor rural areas must band together and demand fairer treatment. Such a movement should not be directed at isolated problems such as poor housing or crime but rather should attack inequality in every social sphere. This kind of movement is particularly important in Third World nations, where conflict theorists often see the overthrow of the old ruling elites and the expulsion of the foreign multinationals that support them as the only hope for real improvement.

Social Psychological Perspectives   Most social psychological studies of community life have been concerned with the effects of urbanization on the psychological well-being of individuals. As noted earlier, Simmel and Wirth, among others, felt that city life has negative consequences for most people. But in a sense Simmel and Wirth were simply reflecting the traditional values that prize the qualities of rural living above those of urban living. Thomas Jefferson, for example, warned that city life would corrupt virtue and undermine political freedom. Such anti-urban values made the problems of urbanization seem like the fruits of evil living. Perhaps that is why, until quite recently, there were so few serious efforts to improve urban life-styles.

Even now, social psychologists seem to favor small-town life, with its sense of community and identity, over the cold impersonality of the city. Their recommendations for improving metropolitan life call for decentralization into smaller units so that people will have an opportunity to develop genuine neighborhoods. They note that many city dwellers have already rid themselves of the social indifference to which Simmel and Wirth objected. Many districts in today's cities are real communities in the sense that they have some of the social psychological characteristics of the village. The Chinese, Italian, and Polish neighborhoods in North American cities are often as tightly knit as any rural village. Similarly, some suburbs are characterized by a strong sense of neighborliness and mutual identity.

Serious psychological problems—mental illness, alcoholism, and drug addiction—are much more common among people who live in slums. Because there is little sense of community, old-fashioned social controls—gossip, ridicule, slander—are not effective. Police try to keep order, leading slum dwellers to complain that they are treated as though they were enemies whose territory is occupied by a foreign army. Such occupation, of course, produces new problems, which in turn require more occupation forces, and thus a vicious circle develops. The decentralization of government, social psychologists say, might break this chain of events by giving slum dwellers a stake in their own affairs and their own destiny. But such decentralization is not likely to occur unless there is a shift in power along the lines suggested by conflict theorists.

SUMMARY

The shift from rural to urban living in North America has profoundly altered the lives of millions of people. Traditionally, most families lived on farms in rural areas, but industrialization spurred the rapid growth of cities. In the past few decades there has been a new shift of population, this time toward the suburbs.

Pioneering sociologists such as Georg Simmel and Louis Wirth argued that city life creates certain characteristics in urban residents, including impersonal social relationships, a blasé attitude toward life, a materialistic outlook, and a feeling of indifference toward others. More recently, Herbert Gans has shown that this picture exaggerates the negative aspects of city life and is true only for some types of city dwellers.

The availability of government-backed loans, a growing system of highways, and the prosperity following World War II made it possible for many people to move to the suburbs. Although the stereotype of suburbia pictures miles of well-kept houses populated by young, middle-class, white professionals on the way up, there is actually a great deal of diversity in the suburbs. An increasing number of suburbs are business and industrial centers. As suburbs have aged, they have come to resemble the cities near them. They are no longer islands in a sea of urban problems, and the suburban way of life is coming to resemble the urban way of life.

Rural towns and villages have been deeply affected by urbanization and the decline in their population. With the growth of mass transportation and communication, rural life itself has become increasingly "urban." Yet life on a farm or in a small town retains its distinctive characteristics, including more personal relationships, a sense of identity and belonging, a homogeneous culture, and intolerance of deviant behavior.

The process of urbanization has contributed to a crisis on the farm that is making it increasingly difficult for middle-sized family farmers to survive. The growth of the suburbs has left us with an inefficient and environmentally destructive system of transportation, and has created a financial predicament for many local governments. Wealthy people and their tax dollars have moved out, leaving many communities with a large population of poor people and no way to pay for all the services that they need. The lack of enough low-cost housing is a growing national problem that is aggravated by segregation and housing discrimination against blacks and other minorities. But as bad as all these problems are, things are far worse in the poverty stricken and rapidly growing cities of the Third World.

There are many proposals for dealing with these problems. Some urban planners recommend that local governments be reorganized into larger and more efficient units, but others advocate the decentralization of local governments to bring them closer to the people they serve. So far, urban renewal programs have not been successful in producing adequate housing for the poor, and much greater efforts are needed to create low-cost housing and improve the living conditions in our urban slums. Environmentalists recommend tighter controls on suburban growth and policies that encourage greater urban density. Perhaps most important, programs of economic development and population control are needed to relieve Third World cities of their heavy burdens.

According to functionalists, rapid urbanization has disrupted the basic social institutions: economics, education, family, government, and religion. The rates of crime, suicide, and mental illness have grown as the disorganization brought about by this rapid urbanization has increased. Conflict theorists see the problems of urbanization as resulting from the competition between interest groups. Each group exercises power for its own benefit and not for the general welfare. Social psychologists are most concerned with the effects of urbanization on the psychological well-being of the millions of people who feel lost and lonely in large metropolitan areas. Their recommendations for improving city life include decentralization of metropolitan areas into small units so that people will have the opportunity to live in genuine communities and neighborhoods.

KEY TERMS

federation
gentrification
infrastructure
megalopolis
Metropolitan Statistical Area
   (MSA)

suburb
Third World
urbanization
urban renewal

FURTHER READINGS

Urbanization
Harvey M. Choldin, *Cities and Suburbs: An Introduction to Urban Sociology*, New York: McGraw-Hill, 1985.
Herbert J. Gans, *The Urban Villagers*, New York: Free Press, 1982.

Urban Problems

John R. Logan and Harvey L. Molotch, *Urban Fortunes,* Berkeley: University of California Press, 1987.

Thomas R. Shannon, *Urban Problems in Sociological Perspective,* New York: Random House, 1983.

Ida Susser and Norman Street: *Poverty and Politics in an Urban Neighborhood,* New York: Oxford University Press, 1982.

Katherine L. Bradbury, Anthony Downs, and Kenneth E. Small, *Urban Decline and the Future of American Cities,* Washington, D.C.: Brookings Institution, 1982.

- What is the cause of the population explosion?

- How does runaway population growth affect our way of life?

- Can food production keep up with population growth?

- How can population growth be controlled?

Chapter 17
POPULATION

The world's population is exploding. The number of men, women, and children is now over 5 billion—twice as many people as there were only 40 years ago. If the current rate of growth continues, the world's population will double again in the next 40 years.[1] Many scientists doubt that the earth can support such growth. They note that half of the world's people already have an inadequate diet and that 14 to 18 million people starve to death every year.[2] But these current problems seem minor compared with the disaster that many see on the horizon.

The dangers of runaway population growth can be seen in historical perspective by looking at the world population in units of 1 billion people. It took all of human history until 1800 for the world's population to reach 1 billion. But the next unit of 1 billion was added in only 130 years (1800–1930), the unit after that in 30 years (1930–1960), and the next in 15 years (1960–1975). The last billion people were added in only 12 years (1975–1987).[3] (See Figure 17.1.)

If this trend continues, the world will soon be adding a billion people a year, and eventually every month. Obviously, the earth will not be able to support such an enormous population. And indeed, United Nations demographers now expect the world's population to stabilize sometime in the next two centuries, but estimates vary widely as to when that will be and at what population. The earliest possible date would be around 2070, at which time

The sharp decline in death rates has created a population explosion in many parts of the world.

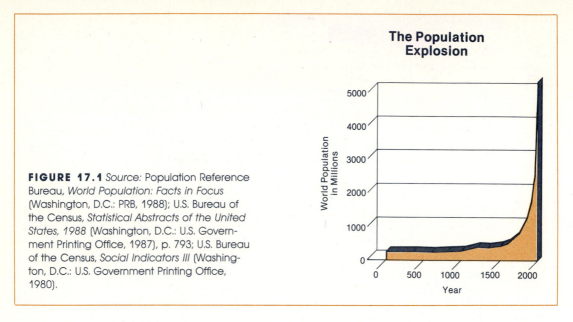

The Population Explosion

FIGURE 17.1 *Source:* Population Reference Bureau, *World Population: Facts in Focus* (Washington, D.C.: PRB, 1988); U.S. Bureau of the Census, *Statistical Abstracts of the United States, 1988* (Washington, D.C.: U.S. Government Printing Office, 1987), p. 793; U.S. Bureau of the Census, *Social Indicators III* (Washington, D.C.: U.S. Government Printing Office, 1980).

there would be about 8 billion people in the world. But the experts believe that zero population growth is more likely to be achieved some time in the twenty-second or twenty-third century at a population of between 10.5 and 14 billion people.[4] The crucial task facing the human race is to ensure that the population explosion is curbed by a rational program of population control and not by massive famines or devastating wars.

The long-range forecasts are ominous, but the population crisis is not a thing of the future. It is here now. Next year the world must house, clothe, and feed about 90 million more people. To make matters worse, the 239,000 who will be added in the next 24 hours will not be evenly distributed throughout the world.[5] Most will be born in the agricultural nations of Africa, Latin America, and Asia—Third World countries that are too poor to provide for the populations they already have (see Figure 17.2).

Although these poor nations may seem alike to Western eyes, there are important differences in their population problems. The most immediate crisis is in the overcrowded nations of Asia (including Bangladesh, India, Pakistan, Indonesia, and China), which already contain over half the world's people and have few resources to deal with population growth. The current growth rate in Asia (excluding migration) is 1.8 percent per year, much higher than the rates of the industrialized nations of Europe (0.3 percent) or North America (0.7 percent), but generally lower than those of poor nations in other parts of the world. Although current population densities are lower in Africa and Latin America than in Asia, the growth rate there is higher: 2.9 percent in Africa and 2.3 percent in Latin America.[6] But these continent-wide generalizations cover up many important differences between nations. Bangladesh, for example, has a growth rate of 2.7 percent a year, which is much

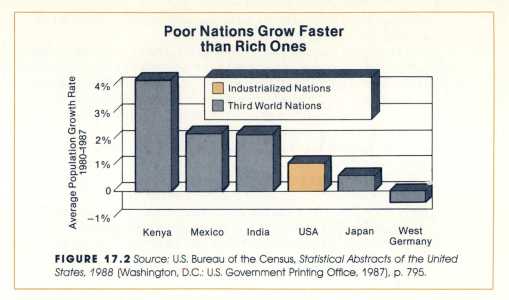

FIGURE 17.2 *Source:* U.S. Bureau of the Census, *Statistical Abstracts of the United States, 1988* (Washington, D.C.: U.S. Government Printing Office, 1987), p. 795.

higher than the average for Asia as a whole. At that rate, its population of 110 million will double in only 26 years. If its growth rate does not go down, Bangladesh will then have a population almost as large as the United States today, but with less than one-fiftieth the land area.[7]

WHY THE EXPLOSIVE GROWTH?

If the population explosion is to be brought under control, it must be understood. A scientific discipline, **demography**, has been established to study the causes and effects of the changes in human population. Demographers must be mathematicians as well, for they study such things as the rates of births and deaths, the flow of migration, and the age and sex distribution of a population.

Growth Rates   A nation's population obviously increases when the number of new arrivals exceeds the number of people leaving or dying. But the *world's* population is not affected by immigration and emigration: it is determined by birthrates and death rates alone. The **birthrate** is the number of babies born in a year divided by the total population. The **death rate** is the number of people who die divided by the total population. For convenience, the numbers refer to 1000 members of the population rather than to the total. For example, in 1986 the population of the United States totaled 240 million. In that year 3,687,000 births and 2,219,000 deaths occurred, for a birthrate of 15.3 per 1000 and a death rate of 8.7 per 1000. The **growth rate** is determined by subtracting the death rate from the birthrate and then adjusting the figures to account for migration. Thus, for every 1000 Americans in 1986, there were 6.5 more births than deaths, and immigration added another 2.5 people, making the total growth rate 0.9 percent.[8]

However, these are only crude rates. They are called "crude" by demographers because they do not take the sex and age composition of the population into account. National populations usually consist roughly of half men and half women, but age composition varies from time to time. Therefore, the age composition of a population must be examined to determine whether its growth rate is unusually high or low.

The percentage of the population below the age of 15 is much higher in poor countries (37 percent) than in industrialized ones (23 percent). Because the girls in this age group are normally too young to have children, the crude birthrate actually underestimates the differences in fertility between rich and poor countries. To measure this more accurately, demographers calculate the **total fertility rate**, which is an estimate of the number of children each woman is likely to have in her lifetime. The average woman in an industrialized country is now projected to have about 1.9 children, whereas a woman in a poor country can be expected to have 4.1 children. The replacement rate—the number of children each woman must have to keep the population from growing or shrinking—is between 2.1 and 2.5 children, depending on the death rate. Therefore, if the total fertility rate does not change, the population in the industrialized countries will eventually stop growing and begin a very slow decline, while the population of the poor countries will continue its rapid growth.[9]

Many people believe that increasing birthrates are the cause of the population explosion. But the real cause is the decrease in death rates resulting from the increase in the average life span. Throughout most of human history, the average life expectancy seldom exceeded 30 years. Under such conditions, a woman must have four children for two to survive to adulthood and have children of their own. As we have seen, this is just about how many children Third World women are having today,[10] but the life expectancy in these countries is now about 60 years, and the result is an exploding population.

The origins of the population crisis, thus, are to be found in the remarkable decline in death rates that began in Western Europe in the second half of the eighteenth century and later spread throughout most of the world. In the early years of the population explosion, the European nations and their colonies led the world in population growth. However, birthrates began decreasing in most of the industrialized nations in the latter part of the nineteenth century, thus reducing their rates of population growth. In agricultural nations birthrates did not begin to decrease until much more recently, and they have not kept pace with the rapid drop in death rates. As a result, the patterns of world population growth have been reversed, and the poor nations are now growing much faster. In 1988 the growth rate in Third World nations was more than three times higher than in the industrialized nations.[11]

The Demographic Transition   The need to understand these trends in world population has been one of the central tasks of modern demography. The most popular explanation is known as the theory of **demographic transition**. According to this theory, populations go through three stages. In the first stage, characteristic of all traditional societies, both birth and death rates are high and population growth is moderate. In the second stage, the process of industrialization begins and technological improvements bring a sharp decline in death rates. However, birthrates decline more slowly, and there is a "population explosion." Finally, in the last stage birthrates drop down far enough to balance death rates, and population stabilizes.

Why does industrialization bring down death rates? For one thing, industrial technology increases the food supply, thereby reducing the number of deaths from starvation. Industrialization also prolongs life by giving people pure water and better diets, clothing, housing, and sanitation. Insecticides prevent epidemics spread by insects and thus increase life spans even more. As was noted in Chapter 8, improvements in medical technology also contributed to declining death rates. Vaccinations have brought numerous contagious diseases under control, and the discovery of antibiotics produced a cure for such killers as syphilis and pneumonia.

Industrialization also brings down birthrates because it produces economic changes that affect family size. Children in agricultural societies make an important contribution to farm labor and usually support their parents when they grow old. In contrast, children in industrial societies are economic liabilities rather than assets. They make little economic contribution to the family, and they consume considerably more than their counterparts in agricultural societies. Changes in traditional gender roles also contribute to the lowering of birth rates. Bearing and rearing children is no longer a woman's only occupation. Some career women find it difficult to raise a large family, and they therefore consider a small family to be one of the costs of success. Other women find their careers more rewarding than rearing any children at all.

The invention of new methods of birth control, such as the contraceptive pill and the IUD (intrauterine device), and improvements in abortion and sterilization techniques have also been a factor in declining birthrates. Modern technology has made it easier for couples to have the number of children they want and no more, but we should not overestimate its impact. As Charles F. Westoff has pointed out, the lowest birthrates in many European countries occurred during the Great Depression of the 1930s, before the invention of the pill and the IUD, and before the legalization of abortion.[12] Thus, it appears that social change was a more important factor in bringing down birthrates than the mere availability of modern contraceptive technology.

The theory of demographic transition has clear implications for the future of world population. The Third World nations now undergoing the population explosion are in the second phase of the demographic transition.

Once these countries become industrialized, the theory holds that birthrates will come down and their population problems will be solved. But critics point out that the demographic transition is really a theory explaining the changes in population during the industrialization of the Western countries, and that things are quite different in the Third World than the theory implies.

DEBATE

Are Mandatory Limits on Family Size Needed to Control the Population Explosion?

YES The population explosion is the greatest problem facing humanity today. If forceful and effective action is not taken to reduce growth rates, it soon will be too late to head off international disaster. Near-starvation diets are already common in some countries, and unchecked population growth will certainly lead to a massive international famine, disrupting the political and economic balance of the entire planet. Battles between hungry nations for control of scarce food reserves would be likely, and it is doubtful that the industrialized world could avoid the spreading conflict. Because some of the poorest nations already have nuclear weapons and others are developing the capacity to build them, it is conceivable that the population explosion could lead to a nuclear holocaust.

In the face of such dreadful prospects, it is clear that population growth must be controlled. Mandatory limits on family size are repugnant, but there may be no other choice. Most voluntary programs have failed and unless a new approach is found, strict limits may be the only solution to this menacing problem. Legal restrictions on family size would violate some of our traditional rights, but it is far better to give up a little freedom than to face the international disaster that otherwise seems certain.

NO The world's population problem is not as serious as the alarmists claim. Many overpopulated nations are already reducing their growth rates. The claim that population growth will result in international disaster is wild speculation without scientific support. It would be foolish to invoke measures as drastic as mandatory population controls because of such fears. The world's food supply has always kept up with population growth, and it will continue to do so.

Limits on the number of children that parents could legally conceive violate basic human freedoms. How could we even send a person to prison for becoming a parent? Government has neither the right nor the wisdom to tell us how many children we may have. Trampling on individual rights may occasionally solve a problem, but democratic solutions are best in the long run.

If population problems became as serious as the doomsayers predict, parents would limit the size of their families voluntarily. Indeed, voluntary programs are already proving effective in a number of nations. Mandatory controls are therefore an unnecessary violation of our basic rights and should not be invoked.

There is little doubt that industrialization does indeed decrease death rates and birthrates. But it wasn't industrialization that brought down the death rates in the Third World, it was the importation of foreign technology and know-how. And because industrialization did not bring down death rates, it seems far too optimistic to assume that we can just sit back and wait for it to bring birthrates down.[13]

THE IMPACT OF POPULATION GROWTH

As we have seen, environmental limitations make it impossible for the human population to keep growing at its present pace. The question obviously is not *whether* the growth rate should decrease but, rather, *how* it will decrease. Only two remedies are possible: decreasing births or increasing deaths.

One of the first people to recognize the dangers of unrestricted population growth was an English minister, Thomas Malthus. His famous book, *Essay on the Principle of Population*, raised a storm of controversy when it was published in 1798.[14] Malthus argued that the human population naturally increases much more rapidly than its food supply. Food supplies increase arithmetically (1, 2, 3, 4, 5, etc.), but uncontrolled populations increase geometrically (1, 2, 4, 8, 16, etc.). The doubling effect occurs because two parents can produce four children; each of the four children can marry and produce four more children; and so on. Eventually, Malthus said, a population that keeps doubling in this way is doomed to outrun its food supply. He believed that only death-dealing disasters—famine, pestilence, and war—kept the human population within its environmental limits.

This gloomy theory was not popular in Malthus's time, when most Europeans believed in the inevitability of progress and the bright future of the human race. And it does seem that Malthus underestimated the world's capacity to produce food for its people. But most of the recent improvements in farming techniques require more energy. And contemporary demographers fear that as the world's supply of fossil fuel is used up, Malthus will be proven right after all.

Some scientists now conclude that unrestrained population growth will eventually produce the famine—if not the pestilence and war—predicted by Malthus. The poor nations with the highest growth rates are already exhausting their natural resources. The industrialized nations have food surpluses, but they have not eliminated hunger and poverty within their own boundaries, let alone in the rest of the world.

The Third World   Runaway population growth has meant hunger, poverty, and social instability for millions of people in the poor nations of the Third World.

Hunger   The histories of all the world's agricultural nations include periodic famines. Great Britain alone has suffered more than two hundred famines since the first century A.D. But the worst famines occur in the nations that have the greatest population problems. Cornelius Walford's description of the Chinese famine of 1877–1878 vividly conveys the tragic results of over-population:

> Appalling famine raging throughout four provinces (of) North China. Nine mil-lion people reported destitute, children daily sold in the markets for food. . . . The people's faces are black with hunger; they are dying by thousands upon thousands. Women and girls and boys are openly offered for sale to any chance wayfarer. When I left the country, a respectable married woman could be easily bought for six dollars, and a little girl for two. In cases, however, where it was found impossible to dispose of their children, parents have been known to kill them sooner than witness their prolonged suffering.[15]

Modern technology has enabled advanced industrialized nations to end the threat of famine for the first time in their history. But those who live in the poor agricultural nations are not so fortunate, and millions of people have already died in twentieth-century famines.

Since the end of World War II, food production has, nonetheless, more than kept pace with population growth. Between 1950 and 1986, world food production increased almost 30 percent per person, and as a result some significant improvements were possible in the diet of the world's people.[16] Although per capita food consumption went up in the Third World, most of the benefits went to the people of the industrialized nations, who were al-ready well fed. Moreover, the increases that did occur in the Third World have not been evenly distributed. In many countries the poor continue to starve, while the rich grow fat. And although several Asian nations have been very successful in improving their agricultural production, some other parts of the world have not. Since 1980 per capita food production has been de-creasing 0.8 percent a year in Latin America and 1.0 percent a year in Af-rica.[17] There have been nine major famines in the Third World since 1960, which have cost well over 12 million lives.[18]

Today's worst problems are in Africa, particularly the wide strip of semi-arid land just south of the Sahara desert known as the Sahel. A severe drought, which began in 1973 and carried on into the 1980s, brought a steady expansion of the desert, and starvation for hundreds of thousands of people who were no longer able to scratch a living from the land. But this was not simply a natural disaster, for much of the ecological problem in the area can be traced to destructive farming techniques and overgrazing caused by the need to feed more and more people from the same land. Although the prob-lems in the rest of Africa have not been as dramatic as those in the Sahel, they are still among the worst in the world. It is estimated that 60 percent of the African people from the tip of Cape Hope to the Sahara Desert go to bed hungry each night. The outside world has responded generously to pleas for help from the victims of the African famines.[19] But the countries with the worst starvation lack docks, roads, and transportation facilities to distribute the food, and corrupt governments often divert the donations to the black market.

Even though most people are able to get enough food to survive, from 10 to 20 percent of the world's people suffer from chronic hunger or malnutrition.[20] A poor diet during the childhood years delays physical maturity, produces dwarfism, impairs brain development, and reduces intelligence, even if the children affected receive an adequate diet later. The undernourished adult is apathetic, listless, and unable to work as long or as hard as the well-fed adult. Diseases caused directly by dietary deficiency, such as beriberi, rickets, and marasmus, are common in poor nations. Malnutrition also lowers resistance to disease; so the undernourished are likely to have a number of other health problems. The danger of epidemics is always high in overpopulated and underfed areas.[21] Moreover, research shows that the damage of malnutrition is passed on from one generation to the next. The babies born to malnourished mothers are weaker and in poorer health than the babies of well-fed mothers.[22]

Poverty By North American standards, the vast majority of the world's people live in grinding poverty. Differences in living costs, monetary exchange rates, and use of barter make comparisons of per capita income between different countries meaningless. But the modern industrialized nations clearly receive the largest share of all goods and services. The poorest 70 percent of the world's people account for only 12 percent of its economic production.[23]

The cities of these poor countries are largely slums. Millions of people live in tiny shacks made of whatever bits of cloth, metal, and wood they can find. The less fortunate have no shelter at all. They eat, sleep, and rear their children on public sidewalks, on open ground, and in the streets. In some Latin American cities, half the residents are *paracaidistas* (parachutists), people who live on the streets without permanent housing. In India, Pakistan, and Bangladesh, millions of babies born on the streets spend their entire lives there, seldom seeing the inside of a shack, let alone living in an apartment or house.

Because population is growing twice as fast in poor nations as in rich ones, an increasing percentage of the world's people are living in poverty. The portion of the world's population living in less developed areas increased from 64 percent in 1920 to 77 percent in 1988, even though several areas had undergone industrialization during this period.[24] The steady growth of the populations of Third World nations makes any improvement in living conditions impossible. At present rates of growth, the national incomes of most of these nations must expand more than 2 percent each year to keep the average citizen's income from falling. Egypt is a good example. Twenty-five years ago the Egyptian government, hoping to increase usable farm land and reduce poverty, began construction of the giant dam at Aswan. The completed dam increased Egypt's arable land area by over 12 percent. In the meantime, however, Egypt's population had grown by more than 71 percent.[25] The dam's economic benefits were swallowed up by the growth in population before the project had even been completed.

The people in this photograph live in the streets. Like millions of other people in the Third World, they have no permanent home, not even a crowded shack.

The age composition of the populations of Third World nations causes additional problems. In a rapidly expanding population there are so many children that working-age adults make up a bare majority of the total population. For example, Africa is growing much faster than North America, and as a result only 52 percent of all Africans are in their most productive years (15 to 64), compared with 66 percent of all North Americans.[26] And because a smaller percentage of working-age adults actually have jobs in Africa, every 100 workers must support about 92 dependents, whereas 100 workers in the industrialized countries support only 50 people. These heavily burdened workers are, nonetheless, the lucky ones, for about 45 percent of all workers in Third World countries are either unemployed or underemployed.[27] Yet these problems are only the beginning. As all the children in the poor countries grow up, they must find jobs, secure some other means of support, or die. According to projections from the U.S. Bureau of the Census, the world will have over 1.3 billion more people in their working years in two decades than it does today.[28]

Social Instability   The expanding population of the agricultural countries places new pressures on their traditional ways of life. Because tiny plots of family land cannot support all the family's members, young people migrate to the cities, where they join the masses of unemployed slum dwellers. The flood of immigrants from the countryside thus becomes an urban problem in an agricultural nation.

Few developing nations can industrialize fast enough to absorb this wave of new immigration to the cities. Some have followed China's lead and put official restrictions on such migration. The majority have not done so, perhaps reasoning that it is no worse to starve in the city than to starve in the country.

A substantial percentage of people in the major cities of the Third World already live in slums, and in shantytowns built by squatters on land they do not own. These homes often lack running water, sewers, and electricity, and the rapid urbanization projected for the next decade can only make matters worse. By the start of the next century, the majority of the world's people will live in cities for the first time in history.[29] As our discussion in Chapter 16 suggests, such headlong urbanization disrupts the traditions that hold agricultural societies together and greatly increases the likelihood of political upheavals and social unrest.

The Industrialized Nations   Population growth creates similar problems for agricultural and industrialized nations. The difference is in scale. The growth rates of industrialized countries are lower, but at the current pace their population will still double every 120 years.[30] If the growth rate of the United States remains unchanged (0.9 percent) for the next 200 years, its population will be almost 1.5 billion people. Most demographers expect these rapid growth rates to decrease, but until zero population growth is achieved, population changes will continue to have profound effects on the quality of life in industrialized countries.

For one thing, the cost of providing the necessities of life for a rapidly expanding population is enormous. For example, after World War II America's baby boom placed great economic strains on the nation. For a time elementary schools could not be constructed fast enough, and the quality of elementary education declined as schools were operated on half sessions. By the time the new elementary schools had been completed, the children had reached junior high school age, causing another shortage of buildings and equipment. Their next move, to high school, created similar shortages. Later, many high school graduates, some barely able to read, write, or do simple arithmetic, entered newly constructed or expanded colleges and universities. Today, unemployment has become a problem as those who were born during this period compete in a job market that has little room for them. In the years ahead, the social security system will be strained as the baby boom children move on to old age.

It should be noted, however, that the pattern of population growth causes severe economic problems even without booms and declines in the birthrate. The reason is simple: birthrates are higher among the poor than among the rich. Any nation that is determined to distribute its income more equally must face the fact that in periods of population expansion the poorer half of the population will increase more rapidly than the richer half.

Another important issue concerns the serious shortages of energy and essential raw materials expected in the near future. This problem will be discussed in Chapter 18. Here we merely note that the growing population of industrialized nations is a major contributor to the problem. One American baby will use more resources in its lifetime than 30 Asian babies. Thus, even the relatively slow population growth of the industrialized nations places great burdens on the environment and on available natural resources. If the population of the industrialized nations continues to grow, and demand for consumer goods is not curtailed, there may be no energy or raw materials left for the poor nations when they try to industrialize.

The effects of population growth on the overall quality of life in the industrialized nations are more difficult to measure. No dollar value can be placed on the loss of a beautiful lake or forest. Yet the cost of destroying nature so that more humans may live in comfort is certainly very high, and it is a cost that must be borne by all the generations to come. When the territories of birds, mammals, and reptiles are invaded and they become extinct, we are all poorer. Destruction of this kind is nothing new, but population growth has greatly accelerated the process. It is estimated that the world lost about 100 species of plants and animals in 1975, but by 1985 the figure had shot up to 1000, or about three a day. Scientists estimate that 500,000 to 1 million species will soon face extinction at the hands of the ever-growing numbers of humans on this planet.[31] As the population of the industrialized nations increases, there are other effects as well. The cities grow larger, the traffic gets worse, and the amount of noise, air pollution, and toxic waste inevitably increases.

RESPONDING TO POPULATION PROBLEMS

There are those who argue that there is no population crisis at all and that the dire warnings about the future are the cries of alarmists and doomsayers. But an increasing number of demographers, politicians, and informed citizens agree that the world faces a grave overpopulation problem. This awareness is itself a response to the population explosion. It is a first step toward implementing solutions to one or both of the two basic problems before us: increasing the amount of food available to poor people and restricting population growth.

Advocates for each approach have strong arguments to support their proposals. Those who focus on the need to expand food supplies point to the fact that food production has outpaced population growth since the end of World War II, and they predict that it will continue to do so if we keep working at it. Advocates of population control respond that it is unrealistic to believe that food supplies can expand indefinitely, and that unrestricted population growth will outstrip any conceivable increase in food production. Environmentalists also argue that even if we could feed the huge population that present growth rates will produce, the resulting overcrowding and pollution would have tragic effects on the quality of life of the world's people.

Feeding the Hungry   Scientists in laboratories around the world are working night and day to invent methods for growing more food. The greatest single advance in recent years was the creation of new strains of wheat and rice that yield much more food per acre. A "green revolution" occurred in places where these "miracle" seeds were planted. This new technique has been one of the main reasons that world food production has kept ahead of population growth in the last 30 years.[32] But the green revolution is not a cure-all for the problem of world hunger. The new strains of wheat and rice require more fertilizer, insecticides, and irrigation if they are to produce higher yields, and many poor farmers simply cannot afford such things. Moreover, all three depend upon petroleum, which was in short supply several times in the last two decades. Research also shows that increasing inputs of water, fertilizer, and pesticides produce diminishing returns: in the first few years of a green revolution crop yields increase dramatically, but as time goes on the increases level off. Finally, the green revolution has often been combined with a shift toward larger farms, and that has had a devastating effect on the peasants who are displaced from their traditional lands.[33]

The American way of improving agricultural production relies heavily on mechanization—another oil-dependent technology. Just as human power gave way to animal power, animal power gave way to petroleum-burning tractors pulling ingenious sowing, cultivating, and reaping machines. Thanks to such machines and to the intensive use of fertilizers and insecticides, farmers in the developed nations produce considerably more food per acre than farmers in poor countries.

Despite its success, however, the North American style of mechanization is not appropriate for most poor countries with severe population problems. Few of the world's farmers can afford even the least expensive tractors. When the price of such machines is subsidized by an outside agency, they still cannot be operated economically on the small plots of land owned by most peasant farmers. It is often suggested that small farms be consolidated and worked with modern labor-saving equipment. Even if such a program were politically feasible, it would create a staggering unemployment problem. It is hard to imagine anything that makes less sense for Third World countries with runaway population growth than spending their precious financial reserves on labor-saving machinery. Furthermore, a greater dependance on highly mechanized technology will only exhaust the planet's supply of petroleum that much faster.

The late English economist E. F. Schumacher advocated an ingenious compromise. He proposed that poor nations use **intermediate technology**: machines that are less sophisticated than the gas-guzzling marvels of the industrialized nations but more effective than the traditional reliance on human and animal power.[34] What the world needs, Schumacher said, is simple machines that can be manufactured in poor nations at low cost and are suitable for small-scale farming. Schumacher himself helped design a small gasoline-powered plowing machine that is more efficient than a horse or an ox but much less costly than a tractor.

Another way to get farmers to grow more food is to reorganize the agricultural economy. One of the most important steps is **land reform**: taking land away from rich landlords and redistributing it among the peasants who actually do the work. Land-reform programs in Mexico and Taiwan have clearly shown that people work harder and produce more when they own their own land and receive the benefits of their own labor. A different version of this approach has also proven effective in the communist nations. Officials in China and the Soviet Union have found that agricultural production is far higher from plots of land in which the farmers are allowed to sell their own crops and keep the profits, than from land in collective farms that provide fewer incentives for farmers to produce more food.[35] A serious problem in many poor nations is that their governments intentionally hold down the price of agricultural products to keep down the cost of food for urban workers. The result is that farmers often lose money on their crops, and production decreases. A better approach is to encourage farm prices to rise and subsidize the food budgets of the urban poor from taxes on the local elite.

A different proposal for feeding the world's population is to cultivate more land. But almost all the good land is already in use. The remainder would require large amounts of oil and other energy to produce even low yields. Some arid soil could be put into production with new irrigation projects, and perhaps new hydroelectric power would come as a bonus. However, the history of Egypt's Aswan Dam casts doubt on the notion that such projects can meet the growing demand for food. The proposal that tropical jungles be cleared for farming is even less realistic. Jungle land is not farmland. Brazil's attempts to farm the Amazon valley have shown that rainforest land has few plant nutrients and that tropical rains quickly wash away artificial fertilizers.[36]

As land runs out humanity must turn to the sea. Fish and other seafoods now contribute almost a quarter of all the animal protein consumed by humans.[37] During the 1950s and 1960s the world's catch of fish increased dramatically because of improved technology, but the increases have tapered off since then. The world's total catch of fish was only 8.5 percent higher in 1985 than it was in 1970, far less than the increase in the human population.[38] The lakes and oceans can support only a limited number of fish, and some species are nearing extinction. Nevertheless, experts believe that the total catch of fish could be expanded by concentrating on smaller and less appetizing species of fish, and through more careful management and control of the fishing industry. Several Asian countries, including China, South Korea, and Japan, raise fish specifically for human consumption, and "fish farming" is bound to increase as the human population grows. But future efforts to get more food from the sea will have to focus on plants as well as animals. Various forms of edible algae and seaweed are already being harvested in Asia, but if marine plants are to make a major contribution to the human food supply, they too will have to be farmed. Several experimental sea farms are now in operation, but it will be some time before this technology is economically feasible for large-scale use.

Finally, a different way to get more food for the hungry is to waste less. It has been estimated that people in the wealthy nations throw away one pound of food for every three that are finally eaten.[39] Poor nations also waste a great deal of food, but for different reasons: insects and rats eat up food in storage, and slow and inefficient methods of distribution allow more food to rot before it finds its way to the dinner tables of hungry people. Another way to increase food supplies without increasing food production is to get more people to eat a vegetarian diet. Eight to ten kilograms of grain must be fed to a cow to produce one kilogram of meat, and it is far more efficient, and often more healthy, to simply eat the grain and other vegetable products ourselves.[40]

Controlling Population Growth   Gaining control over the world's explosive population growth is the most urgent task before the human race today. If we fail, we will surely have to face our ancient enemies—famine, pestilence, and war—on a new and unprecedented scale. At present the industrialized nations are much closer than their Third World neighbors to achieving population control. The population of the industrialized nations is growing at about 0.6 percent a year, which is less than one-third the rate for poor nations. The following discussion will therefore focus on the nations with rapid growth rates. However, the proposals and programs designed for the poor nations can be modified to fit the industrialized nations as the need arises.

Some political leaders see a large population as a national asset and have used government programs to encourage population growth. As far back as the thirteenth century, a number of European nations established tax benefits for parents. Hitler's Germany enacted a variety of measures aimed at increasing its population, as have several communist countries. But the realities of explosive population growth are forcing one nation after another to adopt population control programs.

Many political leaders who are interested in controlling population focus their efforts on industrialization, believing that attitudes toward the family and reproduction will change as the economy develops. As we have already shown, industrialization does bring about a demographic transition—a change in basic birthrates and death rates that ultimately results in slower overall growth. Many leaders insist that the population problem will take care of itself if we wait for this "natural" process to occur in the agricultural nations. Such expectations are, however, ill-founded. The fact that industrialization has occurred in a few poor countries hardly means that it will occur in all of them. But even if all the poor nations of the world were somehow to industrialize, the demographic transition could not possibly occur fast enough to limit the world's population to a manageable size.

Industrialization is not, however, the only economic influence on population control. The key variable may be the maintenance of a minimum standard of living for the poor. As Jon Bennett put it: "High birth rates are primarily related to economic uncertainty. In nearly every country where

Because of the weaknesses in family-planning programs, some nations are now using programs that provide specific incentives for parents to limit the size of their families: bonuses for couples with few children and penalties for those with many children. The small country of Singapore, with over 2.5 million people crowded into only 226 square miles, has one of the most effective incentive programs in the world. The first two children in a family are given priority for admission to school; consequently, additional children may not receive an adequate education. Government hospital fees increase with each child. Women receive paid maternity leave for three children, but none for additional children. Small families are provided with low-rent housing, but large ones are not. Government employees with small families are viewed with favor at promotion time, as are some employees in private industry. As a result of this program, Singapore's birthrate has fallen year by year. The nation's population is now growing 1.0 percent a year, less than half the rate of neighboring Malaysia.[45] (See Figure 17.3.)

The most drastic proposals for population control call for mandatory limits on family size, often through compulsory sterilization of parents after the birth of their second or third child. India was one of the first countries to experiment with compulsory sterilization. The government of Prime Minister Indira Gandhi once refused to hire men with more than two children, and those who were already employed by the government were pressured to undergo vasectomy (a simple operation that makes men sterile but does not diminish their sexual interest or capacity). With encouragement from the central government, some Indian states began requiring mandatory sterilization of men after the birth of three children. The laws of the state of Maharashtra, in which Bombay is located, provided for a fine of at least $250 and up to one year in prison for those who refused to undergo sterilization.

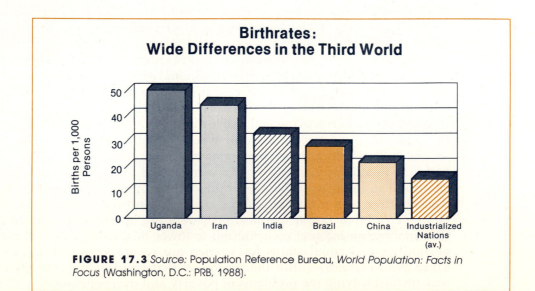

**Birthrates:
Wide Differences in the Third World**

FIGURE 17.3 *Source:* Population Reference Bureau, *World Population: Facts in Focus* (Washington, D.C.: PRB, 1988).

There were many reports of abuses, including charges that in some villages men were rounded up and sterilized regardless of the size of their families. This program immediately aroused intense opposition, including riots by Moslem villagers. International reaction was also negative. An American law passed in 1977 prohibited the use of foreign-aid money "for the performance of involuntary sterilization as a method of family planning" and directed foreign-aid recipients not to "coerce or provide any financial incentives to any person to practice sterilization."[46] The furor over compulsory population control contributed to Prime Minister Gandhi's defeat in the 1977 elections, and India returned to a poorly organized voluntary family-planning program.[47]

In contrast to the vacillation and confusion in India, the People's Republic of China has made great progress in reducing its birthrate. China's powerful and highly centralized government has urged its people to abstain from premarital sex, to delay marriage and childbearing, and to use birth control and abortion. China also has a strong incentive program designed to encourage each family to have no more than one child. Couples who agree to this limit are given a "single-child certificate," which entitles them to such things as priority in housing, better wages, a special pension, and preference in school admissions. Couples who have too many children are often fined and required to pay for all the maternity, medical, and educational costs

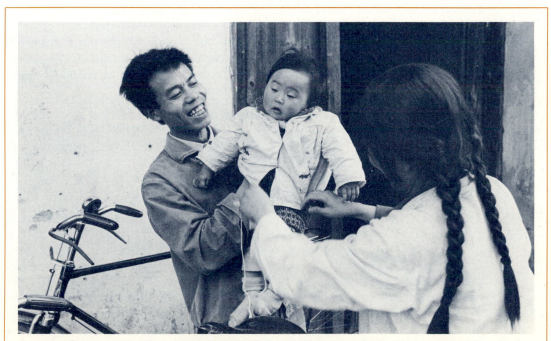

The population-control program in the People's Republic of China has been more successful than in any other large Third World nation.

their children may incur. As a result of this program, China's crude birthrate dropped 43 percent between 1972 and 1982.[48] Although an increase in the number of women in their prime childbearing years (due to a "baby boom" in the 1960s) has pushed the crude birthrate up a little since then, China's current growth rate is still only about 1.4 percent—an extremely low figure for a poor agricultural nation.[49] It is clear that China is now firmly committed to an all-out effort to stabilize the size of its population. Not only is that good news for the future of China, it is good news for the entire world, for one of every five people in the world lives in China.

These gains have not been made without considerable social cost. The government pressure for population control in China's highly centralized society has been so great that the one-child limitation has become virtually mandatory for most Chinese. This policy has placed a particularly great strain on rural villagers. Chinese peasants have traditionally placed a high value on having sons, who live with the extended family throughout their lives. Daughters, on the other hand, are expected to move in with their husband's family and are therefore considered more of a burden than an asset. The result has been a startling increase in female infanticide as the new population limitation measures have been put into effect. The Chinese government does, however, recognize the problem and has in some cases relaxed its rigid rules for rural families whose first child is a girl.[50]

Another hopeful sign is the continuing drop in the birthrates of the industrialized nations. Several European countries, including East and West Germany, Italy, and Hungary, have already reached zero population growth, and others will soon follow. Although the battle against the population explosion has just begun, there is considerable reason for optimism. The comments of the noted demographer Frank W. Notestein are as relevant today as they were when he made them more than 20 years ago:

> Optimism does not carry us to the point of forecasting that the problems will be solved without intervening tragedies. But we do have reason to believe that the problems can be solved by a world fully alert to the dangers and willing to devote serious resources and energy to attacking them.[51]

SOCIOLOGICAL PERSPECTIVES ON POPULATION

Population growth is an age-old social concern. In the past, however, the issue was how to keep population growing, not how to limit it. Plagues and famines repeatedly brought sharp reductions in population, and at times people must have felt the very survival of humanity to be in doubt. The combination of strong cultural values supporting fertility and improvements in food production and public health appeared for a time to have solved the population problem. Ironically, success in solving the old population problem created a new one: worldwide overpopulation. Only recently has this problem received serious scientific attention. It is now a major concern of sociologists, demographers, geographers, and other social scientists.

The Functionalist Perspective   Functionalists are interested in the social effects of rapid population growth. They have found that population expansion may perform several important functions. Because greater size often means greater strength, a large population provides more security during natural disasters and a stronger defense against foreign aggressors. Many economists believe that economic growth is essential to the prosperity of an industrial society and that an increasing population promotes growth by providing labor and creating new markets for consumer goods.

Population growth may also be dysfunctional, however. An expanding population requires the construction of more houses, the cultivation of more land, and the manufacture of more clothing. All these activities require an increase in the consumption of dwindling natural resources. The intense competition for jobs among the growing number of young adults and the resulting unemployment foster alienation and even despair. Overcrowding contributes to urban decay, the spread of disease, and a general decline in the standard of living.

When the world's population was low and there was no shortage of natural resources, the functions of population growth far outweighed its dysfunctions. Now the same social forces that promoted desirable population growth produce hunger, poverty, and social instability. For this reason, functionalists say, the population problem will be solved only when dysfunctional attitudes, values, and institutions that promote excessive birthrates are changed. Given time, the social system will reach a new balance. This balance should not come about as a result of famine, wars, or other disasters. It should come, instead, from well-organized programs to change traditional attitudes toward childbearing.

The Conflict Perspective   The conflict perspective sees the population problems of the Third World as a direct result of European colonialism and the growth of a world economy that is divided between rich industrialized nations and poor agricultural ones. In the nineteenth century, when technological advances were producing a sharp decline in death rates in Western Europe, the process of industrialization was creating economic incentives that were eventually to bring the birthrate down as well. Conflict theorists note that as these technological developments began lowering the death rate in the Third World, Europeans prevented their colonies from industrializing. As a result, the economic system continued to reward those with large families, and the population of the Third World exploded. Daniel Chirot cites the role of the British in India as a classic example of this process:

> Along with maintaining a colonial class structure, the British also prevented the imposition of protective tariffs which would have helped Indian industry compete against the more advanced British industries. . . . By the time India had escaped from British colonial rule, . . . the country's overpopulation problem was quite severe, and world technology still more advanced and capital intensive than in the early 1900s [thus making it still harder for India to industrialize].[52]

Conflict theory also provides important insights into the forces that oppose population control. Official opposition to birth control is viewed as a reflection of a conflict between the interests of the masses and those of ruling elites. Overpopulation is harmful to most people, but an expanding population is an economic and political asset to the ruling class. A large national population means greater international power. Population growth among a society's lower classes also helps the elite by keeping wages down and providing a large pool of laborers. Labor organization and strikes are less likely when jobs are scarce and there are many unemployed workers waiting to replace those who protest poor working conditions.

Perhaps the most significant contribution of the conflict perspective is its analysis of the problem of malnutrition and hunger. Conflict theorists point out that the current "food shortage" is really a problem of distribution, not production. The world currently produces more than enough food to provide an adequate diet for all people. Starvation and malnutrition result from the unequal distribution of the food that is produced. The rich industrialized countries have only a quarter of the world's people, but they consume more than half its food.[53] While millions of people starve to death every year in poor countries, many people in wealthy countries are suffering from obesity. Moreover, the same system of unequal distribution is also found within nations. The ruling elite in even the poorest countries eat well, while some of the poor people in rich countries such as the United States and Canada are malnourished.

The obvious solution to this problem is to redistribute the world's food so that everyone is adequately fed. But there are enormous political and economic barriers to any international program for redistributing the world's food supplies. Most of the surplus food is in the wealthy industrialized nations, and most of the hungry are too poor to pay for it. Even if the wealthy nations could be persuaded to give away a substantial proportion of their surplus food, which is doubtful, that might drive many marginal Third World farmers out of business and create even more poverty and deprivation. On a national level, however, the outlook for an effective program of redistribution is much brighter. In fact, such countries as Sweden and Norway already guarantee a good diet to the poor by means of welfare programs, and the Chinese government carefully controls, and when necessary rations, its limited food supplies to ensure that they are distributed fairly.

Social Psychological Perspectives   Biosocial theorists see human evolution as the root of the population problem. Because the most fertile individuals pass more genes on to the next generation, humans developed a high level of fertility. Throughout most of human history this process promoted the survival of the species. But although overpopulation is now a serious threat to human survival, the evolutionary process continues to promote high fertility. Many biosocial theorists see the development of more effective artificial means of birth control as the best solution to the population problem because such an approach directly attacks the biological tendencies that they consider the root of the problem.

Other social psychologists point out, however, that learned attitudes and beliefs must change before birth control measures can be effective. Peasant farmers in traditional societies have a fatalistic attitude toward life. The idea of planning a family, let alone a world population, is alien to them. Fertility continues to be seen as a sign of virility and competence. The "real man" is one who has fathered many sons, and the "real woman" is one who has borne and reared them. Even in industrialized nations childless couples are sometimes pitied, and the inability to bear children may be reason enough for a husband to divorce his wife.

Effective population control requires that these attitudes be changed. But social psychologists have demonstrated that attitudinal changes do not occur in a vacuum; rather, they interact with changing economic, social, and political conditions. Mere propaganda and personal appeals are not enough; they must be accompanied by concrete economic and social changes. For example, a sound social security plan can do much to convince people that a large family is not necessary for support in their old age. Similarly, women who are provided with alternatives to the roles of wife and mother will soon learn that caring for a large family is not the only important activity in life.

SUMMARY

The world's population is growing at a rapid rate. Demographers agree that the reason for the population explosion is that high birthrates have been maintained while death rates have been cut dramatically. According to the theory of demographic transition, this is caused by the process of industrialization. Industrialization increases the average life span by increasing food production and improving public-health conditions. In the early stages of industrialization, birthrates remain high and there is a population explosion. But eventually, economic changes make children more of a financial liability than an asset, and birthrates come down. Thus, this theory implies that industrialization will soon bring down the birthrates in the Third World, where the population growth is now the highest. But critics point out that unlike the rich countries, the decline in death rates in the Third World was not caused by industrialization but by the importation of foreign technology and know-how. Industrialization therefore seems far less likely to solve their current population problems.

Thomas Malthus was among the first to point out the dangers of unrestricted population growth. He argued that the human population naturally multiplies much faster than its food supply. Until recently, most demographers were confident that Malthus was wrong and that food supplies would keep up with population growth. But many modern demographers have come to feel that there is a limit to the number of people the world can support, and that Malthus will be proven right after all.

The runaway population growth of recent years has caused problems throughout the world. Poor agricultural nations with high growth rates are exhausting their land and other natural resources. Millions of people starve to death every year, and many of the world's people are underfed. At present rates of growth, the national incomes of most poor nations must expand by over 2 percent a year just to keep the average citizen's income from falling.

In Third World nations, increasing numbers of people are migrating to cities, where unemployment is high and social integration is low, thus increasing the chances of political upheaval. And industrialized nations must spend enormous sums to provide for their increasing populations. Providing for a booming population also has aggravated the world's shortage of essential raw materials and has severely damaged the environment.

There are two approaches to dealing with the population explosion: increasing the amount of food and lowering birthrates. Proposals for increasing the world's food supply include increasing the productivity of agriculture, increasing the sea's food production, and wasting less of the food that we do produce. Family-planning programs have been introduced by the governments of many countries. Such programs encourage the use of birth control devices, usually on the assumption that the birthrate will decline if couples have only the number of children that they desire. Because these programs have failed to reduce birthrates enough, some nations have introduced incentive programs that give bonuses to families with few children and penalize those with many. Another approach is to provide more economic and social opportunities for women, so that they will have a real alternative to the role of mother and child rearer.

There are signs of hope. The birthrates of industrialized nations continue to fall. The world's overall population growth rate has decreased, and food production is increasing. The solution is not in sight, but growing public awareness has resulted in the population explosion's being considered a social problem, and that is the first step toward a solution.

Many contemporary sociologists of all theoretical persuasions agree that the traditional attitudes toward reproduction and family life may threaten human survival. Functionalists note that as death rates have dropped, attitudes encouraging fertility have become dysfunctional. Conflict theorists point out that the current food shortage is caused by a distribution system that gives too much food to the wealthy and too little to the poor. Social psychologists have shown that the attitudes promoting high birthrates are learned; they have presented numerous proposals for changing people's opinions about the desirability of large families.

KEY TERMS

birthrate

death rate

demographic transition

demography

family planning

growth rate

intermediate technology

land reform

total fertility rate

FURTHER READINGS

Population

Thomas Malthus, *An Essay on the Principle of Population*, London: Reeves & Turner, 1872.

John R. Weeks, *Population*, 3d ed., Belmont, Calif.: Wadsworth, 1986.

Food Supplies

Jon Bennett, *The Hunger Machine*, Cambridge, U.K.: Polity Press, 1987.

William W. Murdoch, *The Poverty of Nations: The Political Economy of Hunger and Population*, Baltimore: Johns Hopkins University Press, 1980.

Dealing with the Population Problem

Lester R. Brown, *Building a Sustainable Society*, New York: W. W. Norton, 1981.

E. F. Schumacher, *Small Is Beautiful: Economics as if People Mattered*, New York: Harper & Row, 1974.

- How have we altered the natural environment?

- What are the long-term effects of pollution?

- What are the causes of the environmental crisis?

- How can we deal with the growing shortages of natural resources?

- Is an ecological disaster avoidable?

Chapter 18
THE ENVIRONMENT

For centuries we have seen our environment as a boundless storehouse of wealth. Nature was to be conquered, tamed, and used in any way we saw fit. Until recently only a few people realized how fragile and limited our world really is. Now the damage done by exploitive technologies and the enormous growth of the human population are forcing this realization on an increasing number of people. One by one the natural resources on which we have come to depend are dwindling away. And as they are used up, their by-products are fouling our land, air, and water and disrupting the delicate web of life on which our very existence depends.

It is a mistake to view the current environmental crisis solely as a product of personal greed and extravagance. Most of us do seem to have an insatiable desire for ever higher standards of living. But as social psychologists point out, we have acquired these desires and expectations from the culture in which we live. Thus, the environmental crisis is more accurately seen as a by-product of the industrial revolution and the collective greed embodied in the demand for profits and economic growth. The more productive the world has become, the more resources it has consumed and the more pollution it has produced. The industrial economy is based on the assumption that any kind of economic growth is a good thing, and we have come to depend on that growth to provide easy solutions to our social problems. Now, faced with shortages of raw materials and the buildup of dangerous pollutants, we must adjust to a new era in which the desire for a higher standard of living must be balanced against the need to build a sustainable society that is in harmony with its natural environment.

ECOLOGY

Western culture views us as special creatures, separate and apart from our environment. Humans are seen not as animals but as superior beings destined to rule over the planet and its lesser creatures. There is, however, no scientific evidence to support such beliefs. The science of **ecology**—the study of the interrelations among plants, animals, and their environment—has clearly shown that humans are but one part of a complex network of living things. No human could live more than a few seconds if separated from the sheltered terrestrial environment, with just the right proportions of water, oxygen, heat, and other essential components that support human life. These components, like our food, are entirely dependent on plants and on the non-human animals of the earth. We could not even digest our food properly without microorganisms that live inside our bodies.

Life on this planet exists in only a thin surface layer of soil and water and the air immediately surrounding it. This life zone, known as the **biosphere,** is a mere 14 kilometers (9 miles) thick. Within the biosphere there are many **ecosystems:** self-sufficient communities of organisms living in an interdependent relationship with one another and with their environment. Each ecosystem has its own natural balance, both internally and with other self-sufficient ecosystems, and human interference may set off a chain reaction with deadly consequences.

All ecosystems require energy, and virtually all energy comes from the sun. Green plants convert solar energy into food through a process known as **photosynthesis.** In addition to carbohydrates (food), photosynthesis produces the oxygen required for respiration in both plants and animals. Respiration, in turn, produces carbon dioxide, which is used in photosynthesis. Thus, like other aspects of an ecosystem, photosynthesis is part of a cycle that continually reuses the same basic elements. All that is needed from outside is the energy that comes from the sun.

Because animals cannot make direct use of the sun's energy for food production, all of our food ultimately comes from plants. The food produced by green plants usually goes through many transformations in what is known as a **food chain** before it decomposes enough for natural recycling. For example, a simple food chain may start with the grass and other green foliage eaten by a deer. The deer is then eaten by a wolf, and when the wolf dies, its decomposed body provides nutrients so that more grass can grow. Of course, most food chains are much more complex than this, involving many intricate relationships between plants and animals.

A variety of inorganic materials are, like sunlight, essential to life. Nitrogen, for example, passes through ecosystems in several cycles. The air we breathe is 80 percent nitrogen, but it can be used by plants only with the help of bacteria that convert it into more complex compounds. When food crops are planted over and over again in the same soil, the plants use up the nitrogen, thus disrupting this delicate cycle. Farmers must then use fertilizer to replace the nitrogen and other nutrients taken from the soil by crops.

THE HUMAN IMPACT

Early hunting and gathering people interfered very little with the ecosystems in which they lived. Their tools were limited, and muscle power was the main source of energy. As technology became more sophisticated and new sources of energy were tapped, the human impact on the environment grew ever larger. With the invention of agriculture, we attempted to replace the delicate complexity of the natural environment with the plants and animals that are best suited to supporting human life. The surplus food produced by agriculture made the development of cities possible. And with the cities came a host of new threats to the earth's ecological balance. Forests were cut down, rivers rechanneled, and tons of human waste dumped into the water and plowed into the soil. Some organisms were exterminated; others multiplied more rapidly than ever before. Humans soon became the single greatest force in changing the ecological balance of the planet. But this process did not stop there. Industrialization, with its countless new machines and technologies, once again increased our role in shaping the course of environmental change.

Time and again the human impact on the environment has produced unexpected, unpleasant, and even dangerous consequences. Logging and overgrazing changed hundreds of thousands of acres of fertile land into barren deserts. Improper plowing and tilling techniques caused fertile soil to wash away in heavy rains. Industrial wastes dumped into rivers and lakes killed or contaminated the fish that fed some of the humans who created the waste. The human species no longer faces danger from other predatory animals: we are our own worst enemy.

The damage created by some types of pollution, such as the release of poisons into our water supply, is obvious to any observer. But when a new substance, or an overabundance of an old one, disrupts a finely balanced ecosystem, the effects are not always obvious. Fishermen may not be aware that their dwindling catch is caused by a buildup of human-made chemicals in the waters they fish. Farmers may not realize that the extermination of wolves allows rabbits to multiply, thus threatening their crops. Or they may not know that wolves are eating their sheep because humans have killed the rabbits on which the wolves formerly fed. Only recently have we begun to understand that even pollution that does no economic damage makes the world a poorer place in which to live. As we scar our majestic forests with highways, hamburger stands, and litter, and drive species after species of animals and plants to extinction, we destroy our irreplaceable natural heritage.

Air Pollution Few of us give a second thought to the invisible and seemingly inexhaustible ocean of air in which we live. But consider the fact that a person can live for weeks without food and for days without water, but can survive for only a few minutes without air. We have been able to take our atmosphere for granted because rain and other processes naturally cleanse and renew it. But we are now dumping more pollutants into the air than can be removed by these natural processes. We are also creating new pollutants that nature cannot remove. Air pollution is worst in the big cities, but because the ocean of air connects all parts of our planet together, it is rapidly becoming a global problem. Smog has already been detected at the North Pole and the lead content of the northern ice caps has increased substantially.[1]

The single greatest source of air pollution in North America is transportation. Coal, oil, and natural gas used for heating and for generating electricity are also major contributors. Additional tons of pollutants are spewed into the air by paper mills, steel mills, oil refineries, smelters, and chemical plants. Even trash burning makes a substantial contribution to air pollution.[2]

The amount and kinds of pollutants in the air vary greatly from one area to another. The most common pollutants are carbon monoxide, hydrocarbons, oxides of sulfur, oxides of nitrogen, ozone, and tiny particles of soot, ashes, and other industrial by-products. The amounts of these pollutants vary in different industrial regions. Thus, areas that depend on oil for power have different pollution problems from those that use coal.

No matter which chemicals are involved, valleys and closed air basins are more likely to have air pollution problems than plains and mountains, where the air can circulate freely. Air quality can become especially bad when a layer of warmer air moves over a layer of cooler air and seals in

Although the exact composition of air pollution varies from one area to the next, it has become a common problem in cities around the world.

pollutants that would ordinarily rise into the upper atmosphere. This condition, known as **temperature inversion,** is temporary, but it may cause a pollution emergency. Local winds also affect the distribution of pollutants, carrying them from one area to another. Finally, climate has an important affect on the kinds of pollutants that are present in different areas. For instance, sunlight acts on oxygen, hydrocarbons, and nitrogen oxides to produce new compounds collectively known as **photochemical smog.**

Air pollution is not merely a minor irritant that burns our eyes and clouds the skies. It is a major health problem, contributing to many chronic diseases and killing a substantial number of people each year. Back in the 1930s, a spell of acute air pollution took dozens of lives in Belgium. One of the worst attacks of air pollution in the history of North America began on October 26, 1948, when a temperature inversion developed over the small industrial town of Donora, Pennsylvania. As the pollutants in the air built up, 6000 of Donora's 12,300 people became ill and 20 died. Similar conditions created London's famous "black fog" of 1952. Coal smoke from thousands of household and industrial chimneys combined with fog to reduce visibility to only a yard in some parts of the city. In some movie theaters audiences could not even see the screen. The intense pollution paralyzed London for two weeks and killed 4000 people. In December 1962 another attack of deadly air pollution killed 300 more Londoners. When a temperature inversion occurred over New York City during Thanksgiving weekend in 1966, air pollution caused 168 deaths.[3]

Acute attack of air pollution are frightening and dramatic. But literally thousands of scientific studies have shown that health problems also grow out of prolonged exposure to lower levels of pollution. The evidence suggest that air pollution contributes to the deaths of at least 53,000 Americans every year.[4] Air pollution has been linked to such serious respiratory diseases as bronchitis, emphysema, and lung cancer, as well as to heart disease and some other cancers.

The effects of individual pollutants on health are, however, difficult to determine because the various chemicals we release into the air combine to produce new pollutants. Further, all people living in a particular area are not necessarily exposed to the same amount of pollution. An executive who drives an air-conditioned car from her home to an air-conditioned office is exposed to less pollution than a traffic officer who breathes smog all day long. Some people even expose themselves to pollution intentionally, for instance, by smoking cigarettes.

The damaging effects of air pollution are not limited to humans. Although there has been little research in this area, it appears that domesticated animals living in polluted areas suffer much the same problems as humans. It has been shown that air pollution has harmful effects on trees, shrubs, and flowers. The orange groves of California and the truck farms of New Jersey both suffer from smog damage.

Chemicals from coal-burning power plants and other industrial sources combine with water in the atmosphere to produce acid rain. Not only do these rains harm plant life and eat away exposed metal surfaces and buildings made of limestone or marble, they decrease the fertility of some soils and destroy the life in streams and rivers. Acid rain has killed all the fish in hundreds of lakes in the United States, Canada, and northern Europe. Many scientists also believe that acid rain is a major contributor to the decline in forest lands in industrialized nations, but there are several other possible causes as well.[5] The control of acid rain poses a difficult international problem, because the pollution created in one country often rains down on another. For example, more than half the acid deposited in Canada by air pollution comes from the United States.[6]

Air pollution is also creating some very disturbing changes in the upper atmosphere and the thin ozone layer that protects us from the ultraviolet rays of the sun. Scientists have known for years that a group of chemicals known as the chlorofluorocarbons, used in air conditioners, refrigerators, and Styrofoam containers, decompose ozone. But many refused to take the threat to the upper atmosphere seriously until a giant hole in the ozone layer was discovered over Antarctica. Although the hole develops only during the spring months, it has been getting larger every year. Scientists' estimates of the amount of ozone that will be lost vary widely. But it seems almost certain to produce a range of damaging effects, such as a sharp increase in the rate of skin cancer (which has already begun), crop damage, and the destruction of plankton which is the foundation of the food chain for most marine animals.[7]

But of all the hazards of air pollution, perhaps the greatest potential problem is known as the **greenhouse effect.** The buildup of gases from the burning of various fuels and other human activities is changing the composition of the atmosphere. These gases are holding in more of the energy that comes to earth from the sun and are thereby increasing the temperature of the air, just like the greenhouse of an orchid grower. The biggest problem is with carbon dioxide, but methane and other gases also play a role. Worldwide, the air we breathe now contains about 25 percent more carbon dioxide than it did just a century ago.[8]

The greenhouse effect is expected to increase the average temperature of the earth from 3 to 8 degrees Fahrenheit over the next 50 years. Although that may not seem like much of a difference, the effects could be devastating. For one thing, the increases will not be spread evenly over the planet. Some areas will have much greater increases, while a few places may actually experience cooler weather. But more important, the changing temperatures will also change the pattern of rainfall, which could turn the American Midwest and other major agricultural areas into dust bowls. Moreover, as the temperature rises, the water in the oceans will expand and some of the polar icecaps will melt. The result will be an increase in sea level and the flooding of many low-lying coastal areas.[9]

Water Pollution   Over two-thirds of the world's surface is covered by water. This water is continually evaporating, forming clouds, and raining back to the earth in a cycle that provides a seemingly endless supply of clean water. Perhaps it is blind faith in the enormous reserves of water and the natural purification system that has led people to dump so much garbage into lakes, rivers, and oceans. For a time the earth's water resources could tolerate this onslaught. But with the population explosion and the increased dumping of industrial wastes, marine animals and plants began to die in large numbers.

Organic wastes are important water pollutants. In small quantities, they are quickly broken down by waterborne bacteria, but if too much organic material is dumped into the water, the bacteria use up available oxygen as they decompose the waste. Fish and other complex organisms suffocate, and a barren body of water is left. Human waste is a major contributor to the problem. The sewage from New York City alone produces 5 million cubic yards of sludge a year, which is dumped into the ocean and now covers over 15 square miles of ocean bottom.[10] However, the wastes from animal feedlots, oil refining, food processing, textile and paper manufacturing and other industries are actually a bigger source of pollution.

Chemical fertilizers have much the same effect as organic wastes and cause similar problems. When rains wash nitrogen fertilizers into rivers and lakes, they stimulate the growth of huge "blooms" of algae. When these blooms die, they decay, using up oxygen in the same way that other organic pollution does.[11]

Our rivers, lakes, and oceans are also polluted by a host of poisons and dangerous chemicals that include everything from industrial solvents to pesticides. Not only do these substances kill wildlife and threaten our drinking water, but many of them become more concentrated as they move up the food chain. When fish eat plants exposed to such things as arsenic, mercury,

19th-Century Social Problems

State Chemist Daniels has furnished an analysis of Ashland's drinking water and says that it is contaminated with sewage. . . . The typhoid fever epidemic from which Ashland is suffering is now directly attributed to the water supply. Efforts will be made by the Attorney General to have the water company's franchise annulled.

April 9, 1894

These selections, which appear throughout the text, are from the *Badger State Banner,* a newspaper published in Black River Falls, Wisconsin.

and pesticides like DDT, the pollutants build up in their tissues. When these fish are eaten by larger fish the toxins become still more concentrated, and so on. Because most of the seafood we eat comes from the top of the food chain, it is likely to have the highest levels of contamination.[12]

Heat is another dangerous pollutant. Power-generating plants, especially those using nuclear energy, greatly increase the temperature of the water they use for cooling. When this warm water is poured into a river, some species of fish and other cold-blooded animals cannot survive. Ducks, geese, and other migrating waterfowl stay on through the winter, causing additional ecological imbalances. If organic wastes are also dumped in the water, thermal pollution will speed up its decomposition, thus aggravating the oxygen-depletion problem.

To many people, the most important water is that coming out of the tap in their home. Water once commonly carried such dread diseases as cholera and typhoid, but modern water treatment has solved that problem. Now our drinking water is being threatened in another way: by contamination of the underground reserves. Dangerous industrial chemicals are seeping into the water supplies of many towns and cities, and the underground water in many agricultural areas now contains a host of different pesticides. Water from wells in Battle Creek, Michigan, was found to contain vinyl chloride and benzene, among other dangerous chemicals. The unusually high rate of certain types of cancers among residents of New Orleans is believed to be linked to carcinogens in its water supply.[13] A four-year study of women who live around California's famous "Silicon Valley" (a national center for the computer industry) showed that those who drank tap water had significantly more miscarriages than those who drank bottled water.[14]

The Environmental Protection Agency estimates that only about 1 to 2 percent of usable groundwater reserves in the United States are polluted, but that figure greatly underestimates the problem. For one thing, the water near heavily populated urban areas is most likely to be contaminated, and that, of course, is also the water we are most likely to drink. Furthermore, the federal government commonly tests for only 38 of the more than 700 chemicals that are found in drinking water and has failed to establish a comprehensive program to test the nation's underground water supplies.[15]

The Deteriorating Land   The wealthy industrialized countries have long been aware of the dangers of air and water pollution, but the poor nations, faced with overpopulation and shortages of food and housing, have often looked at the environment as a problem that only the rich can afford to worry about. But many of these poor nations are now beginning to realize that they are caught in the grip of an even greater environmental crisis then the one faced by their industrialized neighbors. The world's forests are shrinking at an alarming rate, while the desert wastelands grow, and most of these changes are occurring in the Third World nations (see Figure 18.1). Every year, the world loses 12 million hectares of tropical forest—an area about the size of England.[16] At this rate there will be virtually no tropical forest left in 30 to 40 years, and if the rain forests are destroyed, over a million unique species of plants and animals will die with them. **Desertification**—the transformation of productive land into desert—is a slower process. But it is estimated that 20 million square kilometers, an area twice the size of Canada, is at risk of turning into desert or is already in the process of transformation.[17]

There are many causes of this crisis on the land, but it is clearly not the result of natural forces such as the periodic droughts that have recurred through history. It is human activity that is causing this crisis. Desertification results from overgrazing by livestock, poor irrigation techniques that poison the soil with salts and alkalis, and desperate attempts to farm land that is not suited for it. Forests are being cut down for the fuel and lumber they provide, and to make room for the farms and cities demanded by an exploding human population. And of course, the destruction of forests promotes the growth of deserts.

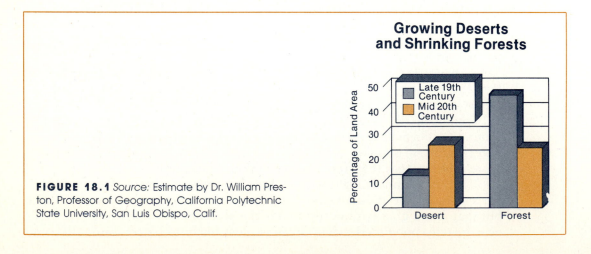

FIGURE 18.1 *Source:* Estimate by Dr. William Preston, Professor of Geography, California Polytechnic State University, San Luis Obispo, Calif.

Although things are worse in the Third World, the industrialized nations have serious problems of their own. Reforestation has allowed the industrialized nations to keep some of their temperate forests from shrinking,[18] but air pollution is still a serious threat. West Germany, for example, now reports that over half its forests are damaged or dying.[19] The heavily mechanized techniques used by agribusiness do serious long-term damage to the soil, and North America is now facing a serious erosion problem. The impact of years of environmentally damaging plowing techniques is adding up; and wind breaks, terraces, and antierosion ditches built during the 1930s are being torn out to make it easier to operate today's huge farming machines. The loss of topsoil from Iowa farms now averages almost 10 tons per acre per year.[20]

Another heavy burden on our beleaguered land is the huge quantities of solid waste produced by industry. Each year the United States generates about a ton of trash and garbage for every man, woman, and child in the country.[21] Some of this refuse is burned, thus adding to air pollution, but most of it is buried in landfills and dumps. This creates two problems. One is the increasing numbers of ravines, gullies, valleys, and sloughs that are being covered as the trash mounts up. Another is the increasing disposal of

Logged-out forests, such as the one shown in this photo, have become an increasingly common sight as a growing human population places more demands on limited environmental resources.

plastic and other synthetic materials, which, unlike organic material, never decompose. Americans dump about 100 million tires and 38 billion bottles and jars each year. Humans are the only form of life that generates wastes that are not consumed by some other plant or animal.

As if these problems were not enough, new threats to the land are looming on the horizon. Just when the population explosion demands that more and more land be used for agriculture, the shortage of energy and minerals is forcing us to use environmentally destructive methods to gather vital raw materials. For instance, there are enormous reserves of coal in North America, and much of it lies close to the surface. This makes it cheaper to extract, but the strip-mining technique that is normally used creates enormous environmental damage. Strip mines are long, shallow valleys gouged out of the earth. After the coal has been removed, the dislocated earth is dumped back into the hole. But unless the topsoil is carefully replaced (an expensive and time-consuming process), the land will not be fertile again for centuries, if ever.[22]

The growth of cities poses yet another threat to the ecological balance of our land. Great portions of North America, Europe, and Asia are covered by expanding cities and suburbs. These vast metropolitan areas are beginning to threaten the existence of the wilderness that harbors so many different species of plants and animals. Many ecosystems have already been destroyed by urban sprawl, and the outlook for the future is not bright. If population growth continues at its present rate, only the most remote mountains and deserts will remain unspoiled.

Chemicals and Radiation   The human race is dosing itself with thousands of chemicals. The air we breathe and practically everything we eat or drink contains synthetic substances. Although many of these chemicals seem harmless enough, the plain fact is that we know almost nothing about their long-term effects. Recent history is full of examples of supposedly harmless food additives, drugs, and industrial wastes that were found to be serious health hazards. A recent study by the National Academy of Sciences concluded that only 20 percent of the almost 710,000 chemicals in commercial use had been thoroughly tested, and a third had never been tested at all.[23]

Still, the toxic wastes that have been identified are a daunting problem. Each year the United States alone produces about 292 million tons of toxic wastes. A single day's waste is enough to fill the New Orleans Superdome four times.[24] The Environmental Protection Agency estimates that 90 percent of this waste is disposed of improperly. The EPA has already identified 25,000 toxic-waste sites in need of a clean up, and the General Accounting Office estimates that a thorough inventory would uncover at least another 350,000 sites.[25] Many people have already been burned or poisoned by these toxic wastes, and the contamination of drinking water with dangerous chemicals threatens to become one of the most serious public health problems of the next decade.

The Environmental Protection Agency has, however, done little to meet the toxic-waste crisis. In 1980 Congress created a $1.6 billion "superfund" to help clean up dangerous waste dumps. But seven years later, after the fund had been increased to $8.5 billion, only 13 of the 951 priority sites had been cleaned up, and the EPA itself admits that the list of priority sites could soon grow to over 2000.[26] Moreover, critics charge that the little work that was done was not done well. The EPA's approach to cleaning up most unsafe dumps is simply to move the dangerous chemicals to a different dump, which in many cases is no safer than the original site. The government has repeatedly been accused of dragging its feet on toxic-waste cleanups and, more generally, of supporting the interests of industrial polluters instead of the interests of the American public.

Radiation pollution frightens people even more than toxic chemicals, probably because we know so little about it. Small doses of radiation have no immediate effects. Moderate doses cause vomiting, fatigue, loss of appetite, and diarrhea. Death is practically certain for people exposed to high doses. However, no one knows much about the long-term effects of low and moderate doses of radiation. Studies of the survivors of the nuclear bombings of Hiroshima and Nagasaki show a high incidence of leukemia and other cancers, but it is not known exactly how much exposure is needed to produce cancer. There is ample proof that radiation causes genetic mutations, but again there is little information about how dangerous specific doses of radiation actually are. Although most of the radiation to which humans are exposed is natural, some scientists fear that the radiation we have already released into the biosphere has done genetic damage that will not become apparent for generations.

The ultimate environmental disaster—nuclear war—will be discussed in the next chapter. But there is also growing alarm about the spread of radiation from the use of nuclear reactors as a source of power and to produce nuclear weapons. Such reactors now contribute little to the overall levels of radiation in the world. But environmentalists fear that nuclear pollution will increase if the nuclear industry expands. One major concern is the danger of a nuclear accident. There is little chance of a reactor erupting in a nuclear explosion, but if the cooling system of such a plant should fail, the tremendous heat of the nuclear reaction would melt the concrete and steel surrounding it, thus releasing enough radiation to wipe out an entire city. Nuclear power plants have elaborate safeguards against such **meltdowns,** and advocates of nuclear power argue that the probability of such an accident occurring is very low. But the 1979 accident at the Three Mile Island reactor and the 1986 accident at Chernobyl in the Soviet Union have convinced many doubters that serious accidents are far more likely than the public has been led to believe.

Even if no more major accidents ever occur, the radioactive wastes generated by nuclear plants are deadly pollutants, and we still have no effective way to handle them. The main problem is that these wastes remain danger-

There is growing concern about the dangers of radiation pollution from both military and civilian sources.

ous for so long that scientists cannot agree on a safe disposal technique. For example, the EPA requires that spent fuel rods from nuclear plants be stored safely for 10,000 years. There are currently almost 50,000 of these old fuel rods stored temporarily at U.S. nuclear plants, but the federal government has yet to open a permanent disposal site. And even the temporary storage of nuclear wastes has proven to be inadequate. About 530,000 gallons of highly radioactive liquids have already leaked out of U.S. nuclear weapons plants. Although the public was never informed, there have apparently been over 14,000 leaks of radioactive waste from the Savannah River weapons plant alone.[27] It is becoming clear that the cloak of national security has been used to cover up horrible safety conditions that would never have been allowed at civilian facilities. Moreover, old nuclear power plants, whether civilian or military, are also a radiation hazard. Whatever technique is ultimately developed to decommission such plants, it is bound to be a slow and costly process.[28]

Another serious hazard in the use of nuclear energy is crime. Security is tight in nuclear power plants, but the more this energy source is used, the more shipments of radioactive materials there will be and the easier it will be for a terrorist group to steal them. Although it is difficult to turn low-grade nuclear fuels into bombs, there is still great danger. The explosion of a conventional bomb placed next to some radioactive materials could spread a deadly radioactive cloud big enough to poison a large area. A further problem might also spring from the development of breeder reactors that turn uranium 235, which is not usable as nuclear fuel, into plutonium, which is. Unlike other nuclear fuels, the plutonium produced by breeder reactors can easily be made into nuclear weapons. Thus, large-scale use of these reactors would create a distinct possibility that terrorists might seize some plutonium and hold entire cities for ransom or even destroy them with atomic explosions.

DWINDLING RESOURCES

Photographs of the earth taken from space have done much to further the cause of conservation. One look at a picture of that tiny blue-green globe hanging in the vast emptiness of space shows us how limited our world and its resources really are. Through most of human history we have been acting as though the world were a rich mine to be exploited. We are just beginning to realize that there are only limited amounts of oil, coal, and uranium. When the supply is used up, there will be no more.

The United States, with less than 5 percent of the world's people, uses a quarter of all the energy consumed each year.[29] All the industrialized nations combined hold only 25 percent of the world's people, but they use 85 to 90 percent of its resources. There is a growing feeling in Third World nations that the United States and the other industrialized countries are using up the world's resources so rapidly that there will soon be nothing left for them. There is much talk about industrializing the poor nations so that they can stabilize their population growth and bring their level of living up to Western standards. But with current technology, the world's supply of oil and minerals cannot possibly support all the world's people in the style to which the wealthy nations have become accustomed.

Energy   Modern industrial society would be impossible without massive supplies of energy. If enough energy is available, most raw materials—iron, copper, aluminum—can be recycled. But most of our current sources of energy are not renewable: once the supply is used up it is gone forever. The fossil fuels (oil, coal, and natural gas) are **nonrenewable**: they took millions of years to form from organic materials deposited in the earth and cannot be replaced.

We are just beginning to realize that our planet's resources are limited and that the web of life it supports is a fragile one.

Fortunately, other sources of energy are **renewable**. We can grow more wood and organic materials to burn in our fireplaces, and the supply of solar energy constantly renews itself whether we use it or not.

Worldwide consumption of nonrenewable energy resources has grown at a staggering pace. As recently as the nineteenth century, the vast majority of the world's energy came from renewable sources. Particularly important were human and animal labor and the burning of wood and dung. But the industrialized world's appetite for energy grew so rapidly that it could not be satisfied by these traditional sources. By the beginning of the twentieth century, coal was the world's principal source of energy and oil was just coming into use. Now the world gets over half its energy from oil and natural gas, and a quarter from coal. Only 18 percent of the world's energy comes from renewable sources, and in the United States it is less than 10 percent.[30]

The increasing use of nonrenewable energy resources made possible an enormous growth in consumption. Between 1960 and 1985, the world's energy consumption more than doubled. But although population growth has kept the total increasing, since 1980 energy use per person has actually decreased.[31] The reason, of course, was the energy crisis of the 1970s and the wild swings in the price of petroleum.

Until 1973 oil was plentiful and cheap. The price had been steadily decreasing for years,[32] and few people gave any thought to the possibility that we would ever run out of petroleum. But in 1973 the modern world was shaken by its first great energy crisis. War broke out in the Middle East, and the Arab oil producers tried to stop all shipments to nations that they believed to be supporters of their enemy, Israel. At the same time, the oil-producing countries quadrupled the price of oil. Although the oil boycott was soon ended, oil prices continued to rise. Energy consumption in the industrialized world fell the following year, but soon started to rise again. A second major petroleum shortage occurred in 1979, after the Iranian revolution disrupted that country's oil production. A "panic" soon followed, causing long lines and frustrated customers at gas pumps around the world. This second gas crisis seems to have been more effective than the first one in driving home the point that the energy supplies so essential to the industrialized nations are dependent on a fragile international web of political and economic relations. But as the prices of petroleum products have decreased from their record highs, that important lesson seems to be fading from memory.

No one knows how much longer the world's supply of oil will last. Experts disagree widely about how much oil remains to be discovered and the rate at which we are likely to consume it. If we continue to use petroleum at the present rate, and no new reserves are discovered, the world's supply will last only about 30 years.[33] But experts agree that neither assumption is likely to come true. The world's population is now growing at about 1.7 percent a year,[34] and a considerable effort will therefore be needed just to keep consumption from increasing. But as we approach the end of our supplies and one oil field after another goes dry, the price is bound to skyrocket, sharply reducing the consumption and making it profitable to explore more remote areas and develop more marginal reserves. But even if we eventually uncover three times today's proven reserves—and many experts believe this to be possible—most of the world's supply of oil will still be used up in another one hundred years.[35] Heavy oils from tar sands and oil shale could provide some additional reserves, but they will be costly and environmentally damaging to develop. And no matter what steps we take, it is clear that we are quickly approaching the day when there will be no more oil at affordable prices.

A worldwide disaster would be certain if there were no oil or natural gas tomorrow morning. North Americans, who use more energy per person than the citizens of other nations, would be hit particularly hard (see Figure 18.2). Millions of people would freeze. Factories would close. Transportation would stop. Even if crops could be planted, cultivated, and reaped by hand,

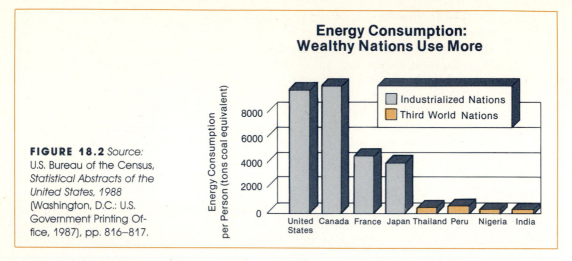

FIGURE 18.2 *Source:* U.S. Bureau of the Census, *Statistical Abstracts of the United States, 1988* (Washington, D.C.: U.S. Government Printing Office, 1987), pp. 816–817.

the land would become less productive without oil-based fertilizers, and millions would starve. Fortunately, it is highly unlikely that our oil supply could collapse so suddenly. But it is clear that we must take steps now to reduce our dependence on petroleum.

The world's reserves of coal are much greater than its reserves of oil and natural gas. Most experts believe that there is enough coal in the ground to meet the world's energy needs for several hundred years.[36] As with petroleum, however, the actual amount of coal available for human consumption is a matter of economics. The size of the world's usable coal reserves depends on the cost of mining them. Energy trade-offs must be considered too. Thus, the size of our usable coal reserves also depends on how much energy we must use to dig them up. Finally, we must remember that coal, like oil, is fossilized organic matter. No matter how much we pay for it, no matter how much energy we use to mine it, and no matter how much land we destroy in the process, someday the supply will be exhausted.

Some people believe that nuclear power plants will be able to supply more of the world's energy as oil and coal are burned up. Nevertheless, it is highly unlikely that nuclear reactors, at least in their present form, can replace the energy now obtained from fossil fuels. For one thing, it takes enormous amounts of energy and labor to build a nuclear power plant, so a substantial portion of the energy produced by the plant merely replaces the energy consumed by its construction. With staggering increases in the cost of building new nuclear plants and doubts about their safety in the wake of the accidents at Three Mile Island and Chernobyl, nuclear power seems to have reached a dead end in the United States. Plans for over one hundred plants have been canceled, and no new plants have been ordered since 1978.[37]

Even with over $44 billion in federal subsidies, the nuclear power industry is still not competitive with other sources of power.[38] Nuclear power costs up to three times as much as power generated by conventional means.[39]

One problem is that nuclear plants have generally been five to ten times more expensive to build than the original estimates. One typical example is the Callaway nuclear plant in Missouri, which was supposed to cost about $750 million but actually cost over $3 billion.[40] And once completed these plants have proved to be unreliable. In 1986 the 100 nuclear power plants in the United States operated at less than 57 percent of their full capacity.[41] But high costs are only one of the serious problems that plague the nuclear power industry. As we have already seen, nuclear power plants produce deadly radioactive wastes that are hard to dispose of. Furthermore, nuclear reactors depend on uranium, a nonrenewable element that is not abundant. Breeder reactors can stretch existing uranium supplies, but the use of such reactors would increase the danger of nuclear terrorism as well.

For the poorest third of the human population the real energy crisis is the shortage of wood to burn. Over two billion people in the world still rely on wood as their primary source of energy. More than half of them are unable to gather and too poor to buy enough to meet their needs, and the supply of wood is dwindling every year. For many poor families, it now costs as much to heat their supper bowl as to fill it. About half of all the wood cut every year is used for fuel, and that has been a major contributor to the acute problem of global deforestation.[42]

There are, fortunately, other sources of renewable energy that can yield greater energy. **Hydroelectric power,** generated by turbines turned by flowing water, is clean and efficient. New hydroelectric power stations appear every year, but the cost of transporting electricity limits the use of hydroelectric power. Currently, about 30 percent of America's electricity bill pays for the production of power; the other 70 percent is for transporting the power from the generators to the consumers. However, recent breakthroughs in superconductivity may someday allow us to slash these costs by sharply reducing the amount of electricity lost from the wires during transmission. Geothermal energy—the heat of the earth's inner core—can be used to generate electricity and steam and is thus a possible substitute for fossil fuels. At present, however, this energy can be harnessed only in places with very special geological conditions. **Solar energy** is just beginning to make a contribution to our energy supplies. The sun bathes the earth with an enormous amount of energy every day, and if that energy can be efficiently used, a clean substitute for coal, oil, and wood will be at hand.

Minerals   Although humans were using the earth's mineral wealth long before they used petroleum, it does not appear that there will be a mineral crisis any time in the near future. Modern industry depends on about 80 basic minerals. About three-fourths of them are either abundant enough to meet all needs or can be easily replaced. There are about 18 minerals that present more of a problem. The known reserves of zinc will last only about 40 years at the current rate of consumption, lead about 48 years, and copper 65 years.[43] Although both the known reserves and the rates of consumption are likely to increase, no one can say by how much. It is clear, however, that as high-grade deposits of these materials are used up, we will be forced to turn to deposits of ever lower quality, which are increasingly difficult to collect and refine.

The seas and oceans contain many minerals both in the water and on the bottom. If it were economically feasible to mine these resources, they would greatly increase the world's supplies of raw materials. Currently, it costs more to mine many of these minerals than they are worth, but technological advances are rapidly reducing the cost. As a result, bitter political battles have been fought over the control of undersea mineral resources. After nine years of negotiations, a United Nations conference finally agreed on a Law of the Sea Treaty in 1982. But several major powers including the United States, Great Britain, and West Germany refused to sign it because of provisions that they believed were too generous to Third World nations unlikely to develop their own undersea technology to exploit the mineral resources on the ocean floor.[44]

Unlike energy, most minerals can be recycled. A significant portion of the copper, lead, gold, silver, and aluminum being used today has been recycled at least once. Recycling of most other raw materials is not profitable at present prices. As world stores are emptied, prices will rise and recycling will look better and better, because it both conserves mineral resources and saves energy. One problem, however, is that some industrial metals stay in use so long that only small amounts are available for recycling.

ORIGINS OF THE ENVIRONMENTAL CRISIS

Many ecologists and demographers predict that an ecological disaster is on the way, most likely in the form of a devastating famine in the Third World. Although everyone is not so pessimistic, there is no disagreement about the fact that we have been destroying the very ecosystems that sustain us. Such irrational behavior is not easy to explain. Its complex causes have roots stretching far back into history. Ironically, the same characteristics that have made humans such a successful species—high intelligence and an enormous ability to manipulate the environment—have also contributed to the development of the technology and cultural orientation that are now threatening life on earth.

Technology More and more people are coming to realize that the magnificent technological advances that have made life so much more comfortable have a dark side as well. As we have seen, agricultural technology has brought havoc to the biosphere; industrial technology is polluting the environment; and military technology has for the first time in history given humanity the means to destroy itself. And even if we do not destroy ourselves directly with nuclear bombs, we may do it indirectly by disrupting ecosystems, food chains, and the whole life-supporting system.

But condemning technology as though it were separate from the humans who use it is both pointless and misleading. Every group of humans from prehistoric times to the present has used some form of technology to meet its needs for food, clothing, and shelter. Only a few of those technologies, however, have caused serious damage to the environment. The real culprit is **exploitive technology** designed to produce the greatest immediate rewards without regard to the long-term consequences to the environment or the quality of human life.

This problem is nothing new. Although the earliest hunting and gathering peoples did little damage to their environment, the human race has been using exploitive technologies for thousands of years. Historians now believe that many of the great agricultural societies of the past collapsed because unsound farming techniques led to an environmental crisis and a sharp reduction in food supplies. But the overall environmental damage done by industrial societies is far worse. For one thing, their technology is much more powerful and sophisticated, and for another they support many more people. Moreover, each of these people also demands a much higher standard of living than people had in the past, and that requires more intensive exploitation of the environment. Industrialization also brings about a qualitative change in the kind of technology we use. From nuclear radiation to the destruction of the ozone layer in the upper atmosphere, the cornucopia of modern science has produced problems undreamed of by our ancestors.

Growth   Each year the world is adding more new people than at any other time in human history. The average person in the industrialized nations has a higher standard of living and is using more nonrenewable resources than ever before. At the same time, the people of the Third World nations are struggling to feed millions of new mouths every year. The environmental effects of such growth are obvious. The more people there are and the more resources each of them uses, the faster they will pollute the environment and deplete the world's reserves of raw materials.

The damage caused by reckless growth is easily seen, but our traditional belief in economic expansion and progress has blinded many people to the problem. The governments of both capitalist and communist countries pursue policies concerned more with the quantity of possessions than with the quality of life. It seems that the process of industrialization depends on creating an almost insatiable appetite for more consumer goods in order to motivate people to work so hard and accept such wrenching changes in their lives. There is scarcely a nation in the world today that officially opposes economic growth. Fifty years ago the same thing could have been said about population growth. In the past quarter-century, however, the harsh realities of the population explosion have forced political leaders to change their minds and introduce population control measures. The same realities are now starting to eat away at the cherished belief in the value of economic growth.

One of the first widely publicized attacks on the values of growth came from a report published by a group known as the Club of Rome in 1972.[45] Working under the Club's direction, a team of scientists from the Massachusetts Institute of Technology constructed a computerized "world model." By programming the computer with different sets of figures, a variety of predictions about the future of the world were derived. All the projections led to the same conclusion, namely, that if humanity is to survive, it must abandon the age-old idea that growth is necessarily a good thing.

Numerous scientists have come to accept the idea that unless we change our attitudes and behavior the world is headed for an ecological disaster. As a group they are known as **neo-Malthusians,** after the famous demographer Thomas Robert Malthus (see Chapter 17). But businesspeople and industrialists, as well as average workers, are usually skeptical about such gloomy predictions and reluctant to abandon the ideal of growth that has been profitable for so long. The scientists who hold this perspective are known as **cornucopians,** and they argue that by the time our resources are gone, we will have found new resources and new technologies to keep the economy growing.[46] It is impossible to prove or disprove either set of claims. But it appears extremely unwise to continue using up our resources at the present rate, thus gambling our future on possible technological advances that may never occur.

Culture   Rapid population growth and increasing use of exploitive technologies are direct causes of the environmental crisis. But underlying such growth are culturally based attitudes toward nature and humanity's place in it. As was already noted, one characteristic of Western culture is the idea that humans are superior to the natural world they inhabit. According to the Book of Genesis, humans were made in the image of God, who told them, "Be fruitful, and multiply, and replenish the earth and subdue it; and have dominion over the fish of the sea, and over the birds of the sky, and over every living thing that moves upon the earth." Western culture tends to see nature as a wilderness to be conquered and subdued by human effort. The art, literature, and folktales of the West repeatedly show people in heroic struggles against the forces of nature.[47]

The attitudes of most "primitive" peoples are quite different. In these cultures human beings are seen as part of nature. They are expected to live in harmony with their environment, not to subdue or conquer it. American Indians, Australian aborigines, and many other "primitive" peoples see all of nature as sacred: the rocks, the trees, the mountains, the animals. To them, the Europeans' assault on the environment is not merely unwise, it is sacrilege: the desecration of holy places.

This attitude that nature is something to be subdued and exploited has been overlaid with newer beliefs in progress and materialism. The people of many ancient civilizations believed that the past contained some lost utopia, and they looked to the past for guidance in making important decisions. But a radically different idea took hold in seventeenth-century Europe. In this new perspective the golden era lies in the future, when scientific progress will banish poverty, ignorance, disease, and perhaps even death itself. Thus, the faster technological development and economic growth take place, the sooner the new utopia will appear. But such optimism about the future has been hard to sustain in a century that has seen the two most devastating

DEBATE

Is Rapid Industrial Growth in the Best Interests of the World's People?

YES The growth of industrial technology has brought wealth and prosperity to the world, and it is in everyone's best interests to encourage further growth. Before the industrial revolution, the majority of the world's people lived in horrible conditions. Even though most people were farmers, famines and starvation were common. Devastating epidemics often swept the land, and the average life span was less than half as long as it is today. Politically, the common people lived under the yoke of a few kings and princes, and democracy was virtually nonexistent. Industrialization brought about an enormous improvement in the quality of life, and there is every reason to believe that further industrial development will bring more improvements.

If we continue our industrial progress, we will see new technological inventions that rival, and even surpass, those of the past. As a result, we will enjoy even greater prosperity than we know today. Moreover, rapid industrialization is the only way the people in underdeveloped countries can hope to improve their standard of living and bring their runaway population growth under control.

The opponents of industrial growth believe that slower economic development would produce a more stable society. It would actually have the opposite effect. The modern industrial economy is a dynamic system; it cannot be frozen in place. Our economy depends on growth. If we restrict it, the result will be an economic collapse just like the one that caused the Great Depression of the 1930s. Economic growth is essential to our way of life, and we must encourage it in every way possible.

NO Uncontrolled industrial growth has brought the world to the brink of disaster and must be restrained. The modern consumer economy encourages insatiable greed. Advertising tells us that we must have the latest cut to our jeans, drive an expensive new car, and eat in the finest restaurants. Most people are left frustrated and unhappy because they cannot satisfy all these endless desires. And even the privileged few find that these things do not make their lives any happier.

Improvements in health and public sanitation, the increased productivity of agriculture, and the useful electronic devices spawned by industrial technology have made our lives healthier and more pleasant. Now it is time we learned to separate the real improvements from the useless baubles of consumer culture. We must use our energies to create more humane and ecologically sound technologies, and we must reject the foolish notion that producing ever more consumer goods necessarily means a better life.

We have cut down our forests, bulldozed our mountains, and poisoned our air and water to create products that we do not really need. This kind of environmental exploitation cannot continue forever. The industrialized nations have enough nuclear weapons to destroy the world several times over. If we continue to squander our resources, we may see those weapons used in a vicious war to win control of the resources that still remain. It is time to plan for a more rational future, and the first step is for the citizens of the rich industrialized nations to control their appetite for consumer goods and learn to live within their means.

wars in human history, the development and use of nuclear weapons, and the extermination of countless species of plants and animals. Many people, however, still see little choice but to continue down the perilous path of "progress."

Although our faith in progress may be shaken, our materialism seems stronger than ever. Day after day we are bombarded with advertising that tells us that we are what we own. A woman is judged by her clothes and jewelry, and a man by the car he drives. A society that sees the road to happiness in wealth and the accumulation of material things is hardly likely to value the environment over the economic rewards its destruction may bring.

It is easy to see how these attitudes have led to our current crisis. We have mastered some living things but destroyed others. We have transformed the natural world in our quest for wealth and progress, but we have not conquered it. Sooner or later we will inevitably pay the price for abusing the web of life on which we all depend.

RESPONDING TO ENVIRONMENTAL PROBLEMS

It was not until the 1970s that the public began to realize the seriousness of the environmental problems we face. Dozens of organizations, many of them with international memberships, are now working on everything from saving wildlife to developing new sources of energy. But pollution, energy consumption, and economic growth are interdependent problems. Effective programs for dealing with one of them often aggravate the others. For example, devices that clean automobile exhaust and reduce air pollution also decrease fuel economy, thereby using up our limited oil reserves more rapidly. Similarly, banning the burning of household trash reduces air pollution but increases oil consumption as trucks haul the trash to dumps. Exploiting new reserves of fossil fuel increases environmental pollution, as land, animals, and scenery are sacrificed for strip mines and oil wells, and the wastes produced by the fuel are dumped into the environment. On the other hand, ignoring the need for more energy retards the economy, thereby increasing unemployment and possibly reducing food production.

There is a way out of this trap. In a word, it is sacrifice. The fact is that there is no way both to clean up the environment and conserve natural resources without changing the life-style of people in the industrialized nations. The challenge is that of motivating people to make the necessary changes now, before a worldwide disaster forces much more difficult adjustments upon us.

Political Action Despite growing social awareness during the 1960s, environmentalism can hardly be said to have been a political issue in that decade. But starting with the nationwide observance of Earth Day on April 22, 1970, environmentalists began a political and educational campaign that not only raised public awareness of environmental issues but also won the passage of significant legislation to protect the nation's air, land, and water. Like most new laws, those bills were full of compromises and loopholes, but environmentalists believed that they would soon be followed by tougher regulations. In the 1980s, however, political opposition intensified, and environmentalists are still waging an intense struggle with the advocates of unlimited growth.

The problem is not that the public has turned away from environmental concerns. Although many people are still ignorant or misinformed about environmental problems, polls show that the public wants cleaner land, air, and water, and is willing to pay the price. As pollster Louis Harris put it: "During the 1980s, poll after poll has come up with similar results. Whenever the public is asked about environmental issues, the returns point almost always nearly unanimously in one direction: deep worry and concern about the ecological state of the country."[47] When asked if factories should be required to install the best possible antipollution systems even if it costs jobs, two-thirds of the Americans polled said yes. And more than 80 percent felt that a factory that has been shown to produce dangerous pollution should be required to install antipollution equipment, even if it means that the owners will lose money, that the workers will lose jobs, or that the whole factory will have to be shut down.[48]

The real problem comes from the wealth and power of the opponents of environmental protection. On the local level, environmentalists face rich land developers who can make large campaign contributions to the politicians who decide what land may or may not be developed. At higher levels of government, environmentalists face even more powerful foes: multinational corporations that stand to make big profits from despoiling the environment. Included here are some of the most powerful corporations in the world, such as the petroleum and mineral companies that want to sink oil wells and mines in fragile wilderness areas, the manufacturers that spew pollutants into the air and water, and the firms that sell products such as polluting automobiles and unsafe pesticides. Such corporations have spent hundreds of millions of dollars to persuade the government not to outlaw their destructive activities. The environmentalists and the concerned public simply do not have that kind of money.

If we are to preserve the natural environment for ourselves and the generations to come, two things must be done. First, a stronger educational campaign must be launched to make more people aware of environmental problems. Second, more ordinary citizens must join together and become involved in the political action necessary to strengthen antipollution laws, increase the enforcement effort, and protect our natural resources.

Conserving Resources   There is no doubt that our existing resources can be used far more efficiently. It is possible for a large-scale, multiple-stage recycling program to be introduced in imitation of natural ecosystems. Just as the necessities of life are used by one organism after another in various ecological cycles, so human society could reuse many of its essential raw materials over and over. To take a simple example, garbage could be used as fuel to run mills to make recycled paper, the wastes from which could be burned as fuel. Similarly, it is possible that community water districts will someday become closed systems, meaning that the water would be used again and again, never being discharged into an ocean or river. Some factories already have such closed systems. It is possible to envision larger closed systems designed so that no industrial material would ever be discarded as either waste or pollution.

Energy conservation can also stretch our natural resources. North Americans waste so much energy that significant amounts of oil, gas, and coal could be saved without lowering our standard of living. Sweden has a higher standard of living than Canada but uses 50 percent less energy per person.[49] Insulating homes, driving smaller cars at slower speeds, riding trains and buses instead of driving cars, recycling the heat used in factories, and restricting the manufacture of energy-wasting gadgets are obvious ways of eliminating waste. The immediate task is not to develop technologies that are more energy efficient; the challenge is to find ways of persuading people to use the conservation measures that are already available.

Better Technology   Conservation will stretch our energy supplies, but new sources of energy will be needed eventually. We have already mentioned proposals for more nuclear, hydroelectric, and geothermal power stations. Some scientists are now proposing the development of power plants equipped with nuclear reactors using fusion (the merging of atoms) rather than fission (the splitting of atoms). However, nuclear fusion generates temperatures comparable to those of the sun, and no one knows whether it is possible to control such a powerful force or how safe such a source of power would be.

A growing number of scientists and concerned citizens are coming to see solar power as the best answer to the world's energy problems. Solar power units use the endless supply of energy from the sun, are nonpolluting, and pose no threat of radiation or explosion. Solar energy is already being used on a small scale to heat water, homes, and offices. Most experts are confident that an efficient technology for storing and using the sun's energy can be developed. Considerable effort is being made to find cheap methods of turning sunlight directly into electricity. Other promising approaches use specially prepared ponds of water to trap solar energy or mirrors to concentrate it on a single location, where it can be used to generate electrical power. There are also many indirect forms of solar energy that can be tapped for human purposes. Power generated by wind, ocean tides, rivers, and dams all depend on the sun, and they all offer environmentally sound alternatives to our current dependence on burning fossil fuels. Such technology is an imitation of nature, since nearly all the energy in natural ecosystems ultimately comes from the sun.[50]

Limiting Growth   Technological solutions are attractive, but it is doubtful that they alone can resolve the environmental crisis. Any effective solution to the environmental crisis must include some form of population control. If the world's population keeps on doubling every 40 or 45 years, there is bound to be more pollution and an ever-increasing drain on natural resources. Re-

This house is one of many new homes designed to make efficient use of solar energy. Because solar energy is clean, abundant, and will never run out, it is one of the brightest prospects for our energy future.

strictions on unplanned economic growth will be needed as well. It seems inescapable that the wrong kind of economic growth means faster depletion of resources and more pollution.

It is often argued that industrial growth is necessary to create new jobs for a growing population. The advocates of growth who make this argument tend to ignore solutions to the problem of unemployment that do not require industrial growth. These include creating service jobs or working fewer hours a week in order to distribute the existing jobs among more people. Advocates of a decentralized solar technology point out that installing and maintaining solar collectors in millions of homes and offices would create far more jobs than the highly centralized technology based on burning fossil fuels that we now use. The argument that economic growth is necessary to eliminate poverty and create a more egalitarian society is also misleading. Despite decades of rapid economic growth, the industrialized nations continue to show enormous inequalities of wealth and power. The most egalitarian societies are those that depend on simple hunting and gathering technologies. This does not mean that the answer to the environmental crisis is for everyone to return to hunting and gathering; the world's current population is far too large to even consider such an idea. But it does seem likely that the world would be more peaceful and more secure if the people of the industrialized nations learned to accept a more leisurely life-style and a lower standard of living, while encouraging economic growth in the Third World.

SOCIOLOGICAL PERSPECTIVES ON THE ENVIRONMENT

Pollution of the air and water, degradation of the land, and wasteful use of oil and other natural resources seem to be topics for engineers, biologists, and geologists to ponder. Indeed, representatives of these disciplines, and economists and geographers as well, are making important studies of environmental problems, and it is they who have proposed most of the possible solutions. But environmental issues are also sociological issues. Sociologists take the broad view, repeatedly pointing out that social institutions are organized systems similar to the ecosystems of nature; that one must understand interacting physical, biological, economic, political, and psychological conditions if one is to understand collective human behavior; and that purposive human actions have unanticipated consequences. In short, sociologists try to teach people to understand that few human problems are as simple as they seem. The origins of the environmental crisis are not to be found in a few polluting industries but in the basic social organization and cultural outlook of the modern world.

The Functionalist Perspective Functionalists see today's environmental problems as latent dysfunctions of industrialization. Most of the technological advances that help society perform its basic functions easily and efficiently have had negative side effects as well. The manufacturing, distributing, and consuming processes that make increases in our standard of living possible also produce undesirable by-products: pollution and resource depletion. Thus, the economic changes that helped create modern industrial society also threw the environment out of balance and created our current problems.

To many functionalists, the answer to our environmental problems is simple: The dysfunctions of the industrial economy must be reduced through the use of more efficient pollution control devices and through new technological improvements that will produce more energy and utilize new raw materials. Thus, the environmental crisis is best solved by refining and improving our present way of doing things, not by making basic changes in our social and economic system. Thus, most functionalists are cornucopians: they believe that the solution to the problems of modern technology is more and better technology.

However, other functionalists disagree, arguing that the present industrial economy is inherently unstable because it depends on steady growth to maintain economic prosperity, yet is using up the resources that are necessary for that growth. To this way of thinking, minor reforms cannot solve our environmental problems. Basic changes must be made because many of the cental values of our social system have become dysfunctional. At one time, ideas about conquering nature and the importance of constantly increasing our personal wealth inspired the effort necessary for survival. Now, such attitudes threaten human existence because they ignore the long-term effects of the relentless pursuit of wealth by billions of people. The economic system is thus dysfunctional because it wastes resources and pollutes the environment in order to produce more than is necessary for the health and well-being of the people. To these functionalists, a solution to the environmental crisis will require major changes in our system of values and a reorganization of society.

The Conflict Perspective   Conflict theorists see exploitation of the environment as just one more result of social exploitation. More specifically, conflict theorists hold that the economic structure of capitalist nations not only depends upon the exploitation of the poor by the rich but also on an ever increasing exploitation of the natural environment. Private businesses must win the competitive struggle for profits if they are to survive, and that places enormous pressure on them to use exploitive technologies to gain quick profits regardless of the environmental costs. Conflict theorists argue that if a firm carried out more responsible policies, it would be driven out of business by less ethical competitors. One solution is obviously for the government to make firms pay for the environmental damage they cause. But conflict theorists point out that the giant corporate polluters are so powerful that they have been able to block the kind of effective environmental programs that are clearly in the interests of the vast majority of the people.

This same pattern of exploitation occurs internationally. According to conflict theorists, the wealthy industrialized nations are using their power to loot the poor nations of their irreplaceable natural resources, thus making the rich nations richer and the poor nations poorer. Now that the less developed nations are finally trying to industrialize, they find that the cheap energy and raw materials that helped develop the wealthy nations are gone (see Figure 18.3).

Conflict theorists insist that to solve the environmental crisis we must create a new world order based on equality and respect for the dignity of all humans. To stop the exploitation and destruction of our natural environment, we must reverse our priorities and put the welfare of humanity first and profits second. The competitive materialistic orientation that has produced such stunning economic achievements has also degraded us by making material possessions the measure of a person's worth. As long as this orientation, and the economic system that fostered it, continues, conflict theorists argue that we will continue to brutalize both the environment and ourselves.

Social Psychological Perspectives   Clearly, learned attitudes and values are at the root of the environmental crisis. The belief in progress, in materialism, and in our superiority to the natural world are all an important part of the problem. But social psychologists point out that more fundamental patterns of thought are also involved. Most of us evaluate the world in individualistic terms, doing what seems most likely to bring us what we want. Such an approach works fine for one or two isolated individuals, but when a large group all follow the individualistic road to happiness at the same time, the result is likely to be chaos and confusion. Environmental resources are often held in common for use by many people, and it is in the individualistic interest of each to use as much of these resources as possible before someone else does. In a phenomenon often known as the "tragedy of the commons," this individualistic pursuit of self-interest leads to the complete destruction of the resource and long-term harm to everyone.[51]

Such attitudes are learned. According to social psychologists, if we are to deal effectively with our environmental problems, these attitudes must be unlearned by an entire generation. As they are unlearned, new attitudes will take their place. Citizens of the twentieth century can learn what "primitive" people always knew: that our survival as individuals depends on our concern for the interests of the community; that nature is to be regarded with respect and reverence; and that a life-style that attempts to achieve harmony with nature is more satisfying than one that attempts to conquer it.

SUMMARY

As exploitive technologies have grown, the by-products of industrialization have fouled the land, air, and water, thus disrupting the delicate web of life on which human existence depends. The science of ecology—the study of the interrelationships between plants, animals, and their environment—has shown that humans are but one part of a complex network of living things.

Ecologists call the thin surface layer of air, water, and soil that supports all life on earth the biosphere. Within the biosphere are many ecosystems: interdependent communities of living organisms. The ultimate source of the food in any ecosystem is the sun, whose energy is transformed into plant life by a process called photosynthesis.

Humans have had a tremendous impact on natural ecosystems and are now the principal source of change in the biosphere. This interference has produced unintended effects that are harmful to humanity. Air pollution, for example, is a severe health hazard and is causing harmful changes in the world's weather and atmospheric conditions. Despite the world's enormous reserves of water, water pollution both above and below ground is becoming a serious problem. Organic wastes from human sewage and industry are water pollutants, as are the chemical fertilizers and pesticides used extensively in modern farming. Poisonous chemicals such as mercury and arsenic build up in the tissues of one marine animal after another, eventually reaching the humans at the top of the food chain.

Overgrazing, logging, urban sprawl, faulty irrigation, strip mining, and poor farming techniques have combined to deface the land. Over the years, forests have steadily shrunk as deserts, wastelands, and cities have grown. Further, new chemicals are used in business and industry every year, and many of them are being dumped on the land, in the water, and in the air. Although radiation pollution is not a major problem now, there is growing concern that nuclear reactors will foul the environment with cancer-causing waste.

The modern industrial economy is rapidly using up the world's irreplaceable natural resources. Many scientists estimate that the world's supply of oil and natural gas will be depleted in less than a century. Coal is more abundant, but even our coal reserves can supply the world's energy needs for only a limited period of time. Increasing emphasis is being placed on nuclear power, but the uranium that fuels nuclear reactors is another scarce natural substance that is not renewable, and there are growing doubts about the safety and high costs of nuclear power.

The complex causes of the environmental crisis have roots stretching far back in human history. Technology has become highly exploitive, using large amounts of energy and natural resources and producing a large volume of pollution in the process. The growth of the total human population and economic growth in the industrialized nations severely aggravate the problem. Underlying these conditions are three basic cultural attitudes: the belief in progress, the belief in materialism, and the idea that nature is something for humans to subdue and exploit.

The current concern about environmental problems first developed in the 1970s. The environmental movement met with some success, but government programs have often been stymied by powerful corporate polluters. Many programs for using existing resources more efficiently have also been proposed. Among them are recycling and education about how to avoid waste. Although conservation will stretch energy supplies, new sources of energy will eventually be needed. Many scientists believe that solar energy offers the brightest hope for the future. Other proposals for solving this social problem ask for population controls, and still others call for restrictions on economic growth. It seems inevitable that more economic growth will mean faster depletion of resources and more pollution, but no government in the world has officially sponsored a program for restricting its economic "progress."

Because social institutions resemble the ecosystems of nature, it is logical that sociologists should show concern for the interaction between human systems and environmental systems. Functionalists see environmental problems as latent dysfunctions of the industrial revolution: the attitudes that inspired the explosion of economic growth are no longer functional. Conflict theorists see exploitation of the environment as part of a continuing struggle between the rich and the poor. They note that profits have been given a higher priority than human welfare, and they call for a reversal of these priorities. Social psychologists have identified the attitudes and patterns of thought that underlie the environmental crisis. Such attitudes are learned, and if we are to deal effectively with our environmental problems they must be unlearned by an entire generation of citizens.

KEY TERMS

biosphere
cornucopian
ecology
ecosystem
exploitive technology

food chain
greenhouse effect
neo-Malthusian
photochemical smog

FURTHER READINGS

The Environment

Lester R. Brown, *The State of the World, 1989*, New York: W. W. Norton, 1989.

Durrell Lee, *State of the Ark: An Atlas of Conservation*, New York: Anchor Books, 1986.

G. Tyler Miller, *Living in the Environment: An Introduction to Environmental Science*, 5th ed., Belmont, Calif.: Wadsworth, 1988.

Norman Myers (ed.), *GAIA: An Atlas of Planet Management*, New York: Anchor Books, 1984.

Responding to Environmental Problems

John Berger, *Restoring the Earth: How Americans Are Working to Renew our Damaged Environment*, New York: Alfred A. Knopf, 1986.

Lester R. Brown, *Building a Sustainable Society*, New York: W. W. Norton, 1981.

Dave Foreman (ed.), *Ecodefense: A Field Guide to Monkeywrenching*, Tucson, Ariz.: Earth First!, 1985.

- What is the world system?
- Are there differences between international wars and revolutions?
- What would happen in a nuclear war?
- What are the causes of war?
- How does terrorism differ from conventional warfare?
- How can international conflict be prevented?

Chapter 19
WARFARE AND INTERNATIONAL CONFLICT

The mushroom cloud that loomed over Hiroshima on August 6, 1945, irrevocably changed the course of human history. Until that day, warfare was commonly considered an unavoidable evil like droughts, famines, and plagues. The dawning of the nuclear age forced the world to take a different attitude. The means for our own destruction were at hand, and people began to realize that future international conflicts must be controlled if the human race was to survive.

THE WORLD SYSTEM

Most of us picture the world as a confusing jumble of large and small nations, each pursuing its own interests, often in the most unpredictable ways. The order behind this chaos is hard to see, but it is nonetheless there. There is a **world system** of economic and political relationships that link the nations of our planet together. Although all nations participate in the world system, they play different roles. In fact, there is a kind of international class system made up of nations rather than of individuals. Australia, Japan, the rich nations of Western Europe and North America, and the industrialized nations of the communist block, such as East Germany and the Soviet Union, are members of the world's upper class. They form the industrial core of the world system and hold most of the political and economic power. The poorer agricultural nations, such as India and China, collectively known as the Third World, make up the world's lower class. In those societies, 70 to 80

The world system links nations together in a network of economic and political relationships. The crops that many Third World farmers grow are destined for sale on the world market, and they are therefore highly dependent on economic developments in the rich industrialized nations.

percent of the people live by farming, usually with inefficient traditional methods. The world's middle class is composed of such nations as Mexico and South Korea. Although they are part of the Third World, they are its wealthiest members. These nations have a large population of peasant farmers, but they also have a growing industrial sector. One group of nations that does not fit into this classification very well are the small oil-rich countries of the Middle East. Although clearly members of the Third World in most respects, vast oil reserves and small populations have made some of these nations richer than any of the advanced industrial powers.

The world system is relatively new. For most of human history, transportation was too slow and technology too primitive for societies in different parts of the world to have much contact with one another. But about five hundred years ago, revolutionary social, economic, and technological changes led European society on a course of worldwide expansion that was eventually to create today's world system. First Spain and Portugal and then Britain, Holland, and France set up huge colonial empires around the world. By the end of the nineteenth century, virtually the entire world was under the control of the Western powers. Most of North and South America, Africa, southern Asia, and the Pacific were colonies or former colonies of the Western nations, and the few remaining independent countries were still subject to the economic and political domination of the West. Under this system of **colonialism,** the "mother countries" in the West bought cheap raw materials from their overseas colonies and sold finished products back to them at much higher prices. The colonial rulers made sure that the countries they governed did not launch industrialization programs of their own, for that would create competition for the mother country. At least partially as a result of these policies, most of the former colonies now find themselves part of the international "lower class."

In the twentieth century, two devastating world wars and wrenching economic changes have transformed the world system. One by one, the colonies have gained their independence. Sometimes it was won through peaceful political pressure. In most cases, however, bloody revolutionary wars were required. The Western nations have only a few small colonies left today. Still, most of the former colonies are heavily dependent on their old masters. The poor nations continue to supply raw materials and cheap labor to the rich ones, and the rich nations still have the political and economic power to control key decisions in many parts of the Third World. Thus, the economic relationship between the Third World and the industrialized nations is sometimes described as "neo-colonialism" because the old colonial powers are still in the dominant position.

It is nevertheless true that the power of the industrialized nations of the West has declined from its peak in the earlier part of this century. Although these nations (with the addition of Japan) remain the world's most powerful political and economic block, they are being challenged on two fronts. First, the Russian Revolution and the subsequent industrialization of the Soviet Union created a new industrial power that is determined to substitute its leadership for that of the Western capitalist nations. Second, the euphoria that followed the first years of independence has worn off in most Third World nations, and their people have grown increasingly aware that they are still in a subordinate position in the world system. A growing number of voices are now demanding fundamental changes in the economic and political relations between the rich and the poor nations of the world.[1]

East Versus West   Most people in the industrialized nations see the split between the communist bloc of the East and the capitalist nations of the West as today's most important source of international conflict. The two sides have frightening arsenals of nuclear weapons, ready to destroy each other at a moment's notice. Both sides also wage a constant war of words and propaganda. The Eastern bloc charges that the West is exploiting the Third World, while the West hammers away at the economic failures and the brutal repression of human rights in the East.

Part of the reason for this conflict is ideological. Following the theories of Marx and Lenin, the communist nations see capitalism as an economic system based upon the exploitation of the poor and underprivileged, and they call for revolutionary change to create a new economic order. The capitalist nations, on the other hand, are believers in the principles of individual freedom and democracy. They see the communist nations as totalitarian states that demand conformity and obedience and ruthlessly crush anyone who dares to dissent from the official party line.

Behind these clashing beliefs is a nationalistic competition for international political power and the control of essential natural resources. Ideology clearly cannot explain why the United States is forming closer ties with communist China, while the Soviet Union sometimes backs right-wing military dictatorships. Most students of international affairs believe that if there is to be a devastating military conflict between the two sides, it will not be over ideology, but over control of the vast supplies of Middle Eastern oil or some other object of economic importance.

North Versus South   Although the immediate danger of a nuclear holocaust comes from East-West competition, the industrialized nations on both sides of the "iron curtain" have much more in common than they are usually willing to admit. In the long run, the most fundamental international conflicts are likely to be between the industrialized nations, located mainly in the northern part of the globe, and the poorer agricultural nations, located mainly in the south. Although the southern nations have broken the bonds of colonialism, they continue to be the poor relations of their powerful northern neighbors. Three-fourths of the world's people live in the south, but they earn less than one-fifth of its income. The average northerner can expect to live about 75 years, receive a free public education, and eat three meals a day. But in the south, one out of every five babies dies before the age of 5, the average life span is only about 59 years, and illiteracy is the rule not the exception. The diet of most southerners is inadequate, and 14 to 18 million of them starve to death every year.[2] (See Figure 19.1.)

FIGURE 19.1 *Source:* U.S. Bureau of the Census, *Statistical Abstracts of the United States, 1988* (Washington, D.C.: U.S. Government Printing Office, 1987), p. 804; Population Reference Bureau, *World Population: Facts in Focus* (Washington, D.C.: PRB, 1988).

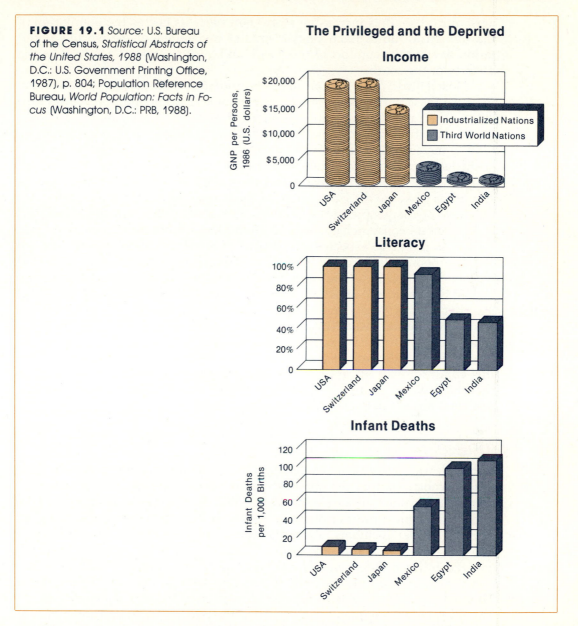

To make matters worse, the current trends are all running in the wrong direction. The 1980s have seen a steady decline in the living conditions in most parts of the Third World. Although Asia has made some progress, the average Latin American's income has decreased about 20 percent since 1980, and the situation is even worse in Africa, where per capita food production has been decreasing for over two decades.[3] Moreover, the population of the agricultural south is increasing more than twice as fast as the population of the industrial north. Each year, a smaller percentage of the world's population lives in the comfort of the north, and a larger percentage lives in the poverty of the south.

Most Third World nations are also riddled with deep internal conflicts. Because these nations have weak systems of education and mass communication, their people show much greater cultural differences than do the people of industrialized nations. Members of the ruling elite in poor countries tend to have strong cultural ties to the wealthy nations. For instance, many of the rich are educated in the West, and they are avid consumers of foreign luxury items. To buy such goods, they must sell their country's raw materials and labor power to the rich nations of the world. On the other hand, the vast majority of the people in the poor nations have little to do with Western culture or its consumer goods, and often have little in common with their rulers. As might be expected, the degree of inequality between the wealthy and the poor is far greater in the Third World than in the industrialized nations.[4] For example, the most affluent one-fifth of the households in the United States receive about 12 times the income of the poorest fifth. In Mexico, that ratio is 20 to 1, and in Brazil it is 33 to 1.[5] Such extreme inequality has led to internal instability and numerous revolutionary movements in the Third World. Disunity has prevented the south from taking strong action against the north, but the wealthy nations of the world cannot assume that this condition will always prevail. The growing desperation of so much of the Third World greatly increases the risk of a major North-South conflict, and thus poses a danger to the entire human race.

THE NATURE OF WAR

Although warfare is an ancient custom, it is difficult to define precisely. Part of the problem is that the difference between war and peace is a matter of degree. Everyone will agree that World War II deserves to be called a war and that a typical murder does not. Between these two extremes are a host of riots, border incidents, armed conflicts, civil upheavals, invasions, and "policings" of one nation by another. Such conflicts are called wars if organized military forces are in conflict, and if the conflict is lengthy. **War,** then, is protracted military conflict between two or more organized groups. This definition helps clarify the meaning of war, but it is obviously vague. The Arab-Israeli conflict of 1967 is called the Six-Day War, and some people still call America's lengthy participation in Vietnam a conflict rather than a war.

Throughout human history, war has been the rule and peace the exception. Small and Singer's study of warfare from 1816 to 1980 found only 20 years in which there were no international wars in progress.[6] This century alone has seen two "total" wars and dozens of lesser conflicts. Even in the most peaceful times, the next war is seldom far away. There are so many international and national tensions, and the traditions of warfare are so deeply entrenched, that the world is likely to show this pattern of almost constant warfare for years to come.

Wars are classified in many different ways, but for sociological understanding a simple division between **international wars** and **revolutionary wars** is most useful. The former are armed conflicts between governments of two or more sovereign nations. The latter are armed conflicts between an official government and one or more groups of national rebels. The American Civil War was thus actually a revolutionary war. The causes of international wars and revolutionary wars are quite different and will be discussed separately.

Armed conflicts are also classified according to the kinds of tactics used. A **conventional war** is one in which two or more armies meet in direct conflict. **Guerrilla war** is usually conducted by small bands of rebels who use hit-and-run tactics against their more powerful and better-supplied opponents. **Terrorism** involves attacks upon civilians in order to create chaos, win publicity, and use fear as a political weapon. Because terrorism is often used in situations that stop just short of full-scale war, it will be examined in a separate section. The development of nuclear weapons brought about such a massive leap in destructive power that conflicts in which they are employed deserve a special category. Thus, a **nuclear war** (of which there has been only one so far) is defined as any conflict in which nuclear weapons are used. But because a single war may involve many different tactics, this system of classification does not always produce satisfactory results.

THE ESCALATION OF MILITARY VIOLENCE

Traditionally, wars were limited. Their aim was a specific set of goals, not total destruction of an enemy nation. A small group of military men did the fighting, and the vast majority of the population watched from the sidelines. The behavior of these professional soldiers was governed by rules of gallantry and codes of honor. The opposing armies were directed by kings and nobles who would see the modern style of total war as barbaric and uncivilized.

Modern warfare, starting with Napoleon (emperor of France, 1805–1815), has been marked by a steady escalation of violence. The new style is total war—an all-out national effort to kill or subdue enemy civilians and soldiers alike. Today's armies are not composed solely of professional soldiers and privileged elites; they are mainly average citizens, often drafted against their will. Behind each army are many civilians, each making a contribution to the military effort: manufacturing ball bearings, producing oil, growing food. In modern warfare, victorious nations are those with the greatest productive capacity. It follows that civilians contributing to such production are prime military targets. The tremendous range and destructiveness of modern weapons have moved most civilians into the combat zone.

Over the years we have invented more and more efficient ways of killing our enemies at longer distances. The spear was replaced by the bow and arrow, which became the crossbow. The musket developed into the cannon, the rifle, and the machine gun. In World War I (1914–1918) the cannon and rifle were fused into the long rifle, a huge gun that enabled the Germans to shell Paris from a distance of 75 miles. The hand grenade of World War I became the bomb of World War II dropped from high-flying airplanes a thousand miles from their base. The TNT bomb gave way to the atom bomb, and the bomber was replaced with the guided missile.[7] Now a modern military force can wreak destruction virtually anywhere in the world at any time.

Some people consider this tremendous destructive power an instrument of peace. At a minimum, it makes total war less appealing than it was as recently as World War II, since even the victors in a nuclear war are likely to suffer terrible devastation. Although modern nations are organized for total war, the wars that have occurred since the development of nuclear weapons have been confined to limited areas, as in Korea, Southeast Asia, and Afghanistan. It appears that fear of a nuclear war has headed off global conflict. Nevertheless, the possibility remains that such limitations will be broken. All-out nuclear war remains a constant threat to human survival.

The frightening power of modern military technology has made it possible to wreak destruction in any part of the world at a moment's notice.

One of the main reasons that this threat remains so strong is **nuclear proliferation**: the spread of nuclear weapons to more and more nations around the world. At the dawn of the nuclear age, only the United States had these frightening weapons. But the Soviet Union, Britain, and France soon developed their own atomic bombs. Then, for a few years, nuclear weapons were exclusively in the hands of the major industrial powers. But in the 1960s China developed its own atomic bomb, and it was soon followed by its neighbor to the south, India, which admits having tested a nuclear bomb but denies having produced any more. However, Western experts believe that India now has between 12 and 20 nuclear weapons. It also seems certain that Israel has a large stockpile of nuclear weapons (probably over 100), since an Israeli nuclear technician, Mordechai Vanunu, published photographs of the inside of the Israeli nuclear weapons plant. Although the Israeli government still denies that it possesses nuclear weapons, Vanunu was subsequently kidnapped by Israeli agents and sentenced to 18 years in prison.[8] Although the evidence is less conclusive, it appears that one of Israel's Moslem enemies, Pakistan, has about four nuclear weapons, and that the racist regime in South Africa may have as many as 20.[9]

It is becoming increasingly clear that the "peaceful" nuclear power plants and technical know-how that the United States, Canada, and other Western powers have sold to nations around the world have made it much easier for these nations to make nuclear bombs. And as more nations develop their own nuclear weapons, it seems almost inevitable that someone, somewhere, will use them.

THE CONSEQUENCES OF WAR

Human history is filled with the records of warfare and the human carnage it brings. Small and Singer concluded that there have been an average of 7.9 international and 6.4 revolutionary wars every decade for the last 165 years.[10] And these wars have reaped a staggering toll in human lives. In the last two centuries, wars have killed over 150 million people.[11] The battles of World War II alone are believed to have cost about 15 million lives, and when civilian casualties are added in the total comes to almost 48 million deaths.[12] But the dead are not the only victims. Every war leaves a human legacy of the maimed and crippled, widows, grieving parents, and orphans.

Economically, the price tag for even a small war is astronomical. Property worth hundreds of millions of dollars has often been destroyed in a single day. Modern military technology has made it possible to transform a thriving community into a pile of rubble in a matter of seconds. But even without counting the destruction of civilian or military property, the costs of war are still enormous. Businesses fail; production of consumer goods slows down or stops; fields go unplanted and crops unharvested for want of labor. Many nations have plunged from affluence to starvation during a single war.

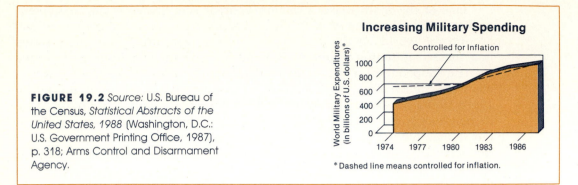

FIGURE 19.2 *Source:* U.S. Bureau of the Census, *Statistical Abstracts of the United States, 1988* (Washington, D.C.: U.S. Government Printing Office, 1987), p. 318; Arms Control and Disarmament Agency.

Increasing Military Spending

Controlled for Inflation

World Military Expenditures (in billions of U.S. dollars)*

1974 1977 1980 1983 1986

* Dashed line means controlled for inflation.

Even in times of peace, we pay a price for war. World expenditures for arms were $900 billion in 1987 (see Figure 19.2). Of this amount, about 20 percent was spent by underdeveloped nations that often have trouble just feeding their people.[13] These figures are so large that they are difficult to grasp. There are a number of ways to put them in perspective. We could, for example, build 12,000 high school buildings for the cost of a single aircraft carrier. The cost of developing one new bomber would pay the yearly salaries of one-quarter of a million teachers to staff those schools, and the cost of building just 14 jet bombers would provide free lunches for 14 million students. Yet as huge as these military costs seem to us, they are an even heavier burden to the poor countries, where money spent on human needs goes much further. The cost of one tank, a relatively low-priced piece of military hardware in the industrialized world, could buy 1000 classrooms in a Third World nation. And some experts believe that we could eradicate malaria with the money the world spends on the military in just 12 hours.[14]

Even in these relatively peaceful times, huge numbers of people devote their lives to fighting small wars and preparing for the next big one. Almost 11 million people are in the military forces of just three nations: the United States, the Soviet Union, and China.[15] And this figure does not include the reserves and the millions of civilians who work to produce the supplies and equipment used by the military.

Some economists argue that the enormous outlays for military spending are beneficial because they create jobs and stimulate the economy. This might be true. But if it is true, it also follows that much greater benefits would be reaped if the money were spent on goods and services that are economically useful. A nation is no better off economically with a thousand nuclear missiles than it is with one, but a nation is much better off with a thousand hydroelectric power plants than with only one. The two developed countries with the healthiest and fastest-growing economies, West Germany and Japan, both have small armed forces and low military budgets.

As heavy as all these military costs are, they are minuscule compared with those of a full-scale nuclear war. Because such a war has never occurred, it is impossible to be sure what would actually happen. But scientists have been able to make some educated guesses. The best source of data is an analysis of the only two explosions of atomic weapons in populated areas: the U.S. attacks on Nagasaki and Hiroshima killed 110,000 people in the first few seconds; another 100,000 people died within a year. Tens of thousands more were severely injured, and people are still dying from the long-term effects of radiation poisoning. Despite this horrible toll, the bombs dropped on those two cities were small and primitive by today's standards. There are about *53,000* nuclear warheads in the hands of the world's governments today, and some of them are over *4000 times* more powerful than the bombs dropped on Japan.[16] Scientists estimate that a nuclear exchange involving only about one-third of those weapons would kill over one billion people in the first few hours. As clouds of radiation spread throughout the globe, entire species of plants and animals would die, along with 50 to 75 percent of the world's human population.

Grim as this scenario is, scientists are coming to believe that it still may be too optimistic. Studies first published in 1983 and since subjected to intense scientific scrutiny indicate that a nuclear exchange would create a huge cloud of dust and smoke that would cover the globe. Estimates based on studies of much smaller clouds released by volcanic eruptions suggest that some 96 percent of the sunlight normally reaching the Northern Hemisphere would be blocked out. The result would be a **nuclear winter** in which the average temperature, even in warm areas, would drop below freezing for several months. The lack of sunlight and plummeting temperatures would have a devastating effect on the plants and animals that produce our food, perhaps changing the ecological system of the earth in an irreversible way.[17]

In some cases, however, it may be argued that wars have beneficial effects. The most obvious is the overthrow of oppressive and unjust governments. Both Germany and Japan developed stable democratic governments from the ashes of World War II. Some argue that even the most ruthless dictatorship can be changed by nonviolent resistance. But most people doubt that peaceful tactics would have been successful against history's many ruthless and bloodthirsty tyrants. It seems highly unlikely that the totalitarian leaders of prewar Germany or Japan would have relinquished their power peacefully. But no one lives forever, and a totalitarian society is no more immune to the forces of social change than any other.

War sometimes promotes the solidarity of groups, communities, and nations. Warfare also stimulates the development of science and technology. The most obvious examples are the improvement of the airplane, the invention of new medical techniques, and the development of nuclear energy. As Quincy Wright put it: "War has been like a fire which, if not too severe, may facilitate the growth of new vegetation by removing accumulations of dead grasses, brush, and logs."[18] There are, however, many other ways of acquiring the benefits of war without paying its staggering costs.

Modern technology has, as we have seen, brought great increases in the costs of war and reduced its benefits. Since it is quite possible that no human beings would survive an all-out nuclear conflict, the ancient practice of warfare can only be seen as a menacing social problem of the greatest magnitude for the modern world.

THE CAUSES OF WARFARE

Many people believe that warfare is part of human nature. The same "aggressive instinct" that is said to make us violent is also said to lead inevitably to war. However, there is a great deal of evidence that this is not the case. Most important is the fact that the people of some cultures have never gone to war. As Marvin Harris, a noted anthropologist, put it:

> Although humans may have aggressive tendencies, there is no reason that such tendencies cannot be suppressed, controlled or expressed in ways other than by armed combat. . . . There is no instinct for war. War is found only to the extent that it is advantageous for some of the combatants.[19]

Another common approach seeks to find the causes of a particular war in the specific acts that set it off and the leaders who make the key decisions.

It may be argued, for example, that if Hitler had not been born, World War II would never have happened. Since it is impossible to rerun history, there is no way of proving or disproving such claims. But it does appear that individual decisions have made the difference between war and peace in some cases. During the Cuban missile crisis of 1962, for example, the world seemed to be teetering on the brink of a nuclear war. The leaders of the United States and the Soviet Union made decisions that averted war, but one leader could well have plunged the world into an international holocaust. Even so, this theory can explain only the superficial causes of warfare. Certain social conditions must be present before war is possible. If the United States and the Soviet Union had not had enormous military machines and the willingness to fight, no conflict could have taken place, no matter what the decisions of their leaders.

Most sociologists therefore search for the underlying social forces that lead a society to war. But there are great differences between different wars and the forces that cause them. To simplify this complex task, we will examine the two main types of wars—revolutions and international conflicts—separately.

Revolutionary Warfare Revolutions are romantic. They have given us some of the most dramatic episodes in human history. Modern China, Cuba, Egypt, England, France, the Soviet Union, and the United States are all products of revolutionary struggles. The revolutionary theme—a small group of freedom-loving patriots fighting against overwhelming odds—has captured the imagination of writers and artists. Even American cowboy stories show plain and simple folk in heroic struggles against land barons and railroad tycoons. Several theories help make sense of revolutions—but these theories are far from perfect. All the conditions that are said to cause revolutions are sometimes present in societies in which no revolutionary conflict takes place, and revolutions sometimes take place in societies that lack the important characteristics mentioned by the theorists. The cultural traditions of individual societies play an important part in revolutionary struggles, as does the influence of individual leaders.

Exploitation and Oppression One of the earliest and most influential theories of revolution was formulated by Karl Marx and Friedrich Engels.[20] They believed that the injustices of capitalism would produce a worldwide revolution. As the workers in capitalist nations sank deeper and deeper into poverty and personal alienation, they would eventually come to realize that they were being exploited by the owners of the factories in which they worked. The workers would then band together, overthrow their oppressors in a violent revolution, and create a classless utopia with liberty and justice for all.

The Marxist theory of revolution is almost a century and a half old, and the revolutionary movement it predicted has not yet occurred. The revolutions fought in the name of Marxism in China, Russia, Cuba, and elsewhere did not happen the way Marx's theory predicted and did not produce anything like the communist utopia he described. Nevertheless, many Marxists and non-Marxists alike still believe that exploitation and oppression of the lower classes eventually does produce revolutionary action. Less accepted is Marx's idea that such a revolution will necessarily destroy capitalism and create a new, utopian economic system.

Relative Deprivation Considerable research since Marx's time suggests that it is relative poverty, not absolute poverty, that sparks revolutions. According to **relative-deprivation theory,** revolutions are caused by differences between what people have and what they think they should have.

James C. Davies, one of the leading exponents of this theory, presented some interesting data on several major revolutions.[21] He concluded that "revolutions are most likely to occur when a prolonged period of objective economic and social development is followed by a short period of sharp reversal."[22] In other words, the people were actually better off at the start of the revolutions he studied than they had been in previous decades. Apparently, improvement in social conditions creates an expectation of even greater improvement. If a sharp downturn occurs and the people are unwilling to reduce either their standard of living or their expectations, they rise up against the government.

Institutions and Resources Psychologically oriented approaches such as relative-deprivation theory hold, in effect, that misery breeds revolt. More recent theorists have argued that to understand why people rise up against their government, we also need to look at the imbalances in the social institutions of their society. Huntington, for example, holds that the changes created as a country modernizes its economy throw its institutions out of equilibrium. As people become more educated, their desire to become involved in politics increases faster than traditional political institutions can accommodate, and the result may be a revolution.[23]

Charles Tilly responded to Huntington's theory by pointing out that the discontent caused by such institutional imbalances is unlikely to lead to a revolt as long as the discontented remain disorganized and lacking in resources. Arguing that conflict is a normal part of politics, Tilly stressed that political violence is likely to occur only when dissatisfied groups are able to mobilize enough resources to mount a significant challenge to the existing government.[24]

Failure of the Government Studies of the world's great revolutions show that the people who ran the governments that were overthrown had been doing a very poor job of it. Crane Brinton's study of the American, British, French, and Russian revolutions concluded, for example, that the old ruling class in all these societies was "divided and inept."[23] The authorities seemed to make the wrong decisions and then overreact or underreact to the beginnings of revolutionary ferment. Further, Brinton showed, these prerevolutionary governments were teetering on the verge of bankruptcy, although the economies of their societies were reasonably sound.[26]

Theda Skocpol and other recent theorists emphasize the fact that governments do not always reflect the interests of the social elite of their society.[27] Often, the government and its top officials have special interests of their own that conflict with those of elite groups. For example, governments often become enmeshed in the game of international power politics, and the cost of the wars it sometimes creates may threaten the welfare of substantial segments of the elite. When this occurs, the likelihood of an armed revolt is greatly increased, especially when the elite have sufficient resources to mount a credible challenge to government forces.

Partitions and Divisions Virtually all sociologists who have studied the subject agree that class conflict precedes many revolutions. Before a revolution, the various social classes come to view one another as hostile economic competitors. The English and French revolutions, for example, were fueled by the revolt of the merchants and traders against the feudal aristocracy.

Other major sources of revolutionary conflict are geographic partitioning and ethnic differences. Regional differences were, for example, a major factor in the American Civil War. History is full of examples of revolts by an ethnic group in one part of a nation against the central government. When a rebellious group controls a regional government, these conflicts are similar to international war. Generally, if the rebels are successful, the nation is divided into two or more new countries. Sometimes, however, the rebellious group takes over the entire nation and reverses its relationship with the old dominant group.

International Warfare The causes of revolutionary and international wars are usually quite different, but in some cases the internal conditions conducive to a revolutionary uprising may also contribute to an international war. For example, political leaders who are having trouble at home sometimes stir up an international conflict in an attempt to divert the people's attention from domestic problems. It is said that "nothing makes friends like a common enemy," and such a strategy therefore sometimes reunites a nation. But in the long run the internal problems reemerge, often aggravated by the strains of the international conflict.

Militarism There are two faces of **militarism,** both of which contribute to international wars. The first is glorification of war. International warfare is obviously more likely when a society sees it as a heroic show of strength or when young people see it as a path to personal fame and fortune. Such attitudes are still common in the nuclear age, but they seem to be on the decline. The growth of complex military technology has taken the glory out of "man-to-man" combat, and the fear of nuclear annihilation has quieted the cheers of civilians.

The second face of militarism is the strong belief in "defense." With an apparent decline in justifications of war for its own sake, there seems to have been an increase in national desires to deter and ward off aggressors. These desires are reflected in enormous military budgets and constant preparation for war. Nations that devote major parts of their economies to military purposes now claim that they are doing so merely for defensive purposes. But the line between aggression and defense is fuzzy, as is indicated by the United States' "defense" of itself by moving into Vietnam or by the Soviet Union's "defense" of itself by moving into Afghanistan. The idea that the strength and integrity of a nation depend upon military superiority over its competitors often leads a country to a frantic effort to build up its military forces faster than its enemies. Such an "arms race" usually increases rather than decreases a nation's sense of insecurity and has often led to major international conflicts.[28]

Nationalism and Conflicting Ideologies Like patriotism, **nationalism** is a sense of identification with and devotion to one's nation. In the past, growing nationalism discouraged local wars by unifying petty feudal kingdoms into larger and more stable social units. In the modern world, however, unthinking nationalism all too often produces the opposite result.[29] Many wars have been fought over some petty incident that was interpreted as an affront to "national honor." Rational settlements based on fair compromise are difficult when nationalistic feelings are involved. After all, what wise politician

19th-Century Social Problems

The crushing of Admiral Cevera's fleet (at Santiago) has had a beneficial effect on the lumber market. . . . A large number of Eastern buyers are negotiating some large purchases at Marinette. Hayes and Company bought 2,000,000 feet of good lumber from Marinette growers.

July 21, 1898

These selections, which appear throughout the text, are from the *Badger State Banner,* a newspaper published in Black River Falls, Wisconsin.

Nationalism was an important part of the motivation for Nazi Germany's attempt to conquer Europe in World War II.

would dare compromise his or her nation's honor? Nationalism is also a critical part of the motivation for **imperialism** (the creation or expansion of an empire). As Quincy Wright pointed out in his classic study of war, some wars arise "because of the tendency of a people affected by nationalism . . . to acquire an attitude of superiority to some or all other peoples, to seek to extend its cultural characteristics throughout the world, and to ignore the claims of other states and of the world community."[30]

Nationalism is not, however, the only kind of ideology that can stimulate violent confrontations. Sometimes the conflict between secular political ideologies such as Marxism and capitalism has led to full scale war, but religion has more often played this role. From the European Crusades to the revolution in Iran, the belief that one must protect and expand one's faith by force of arms has sent millions of people off to war.

Economic Gain Most wars are fought for profit. One nation may attack another in an attempt to capture valuable natural resources, desirable land, or cheap labor. Sometimes an entire nation reaps economic benefits from its conquests, but more often only a small segment of a society benefits from a war. Some people stand to gain from an outbreak of almost any sort of war—for example, high-ranking military officers and those who supply the arms and materials necessary to keep a war going. Other interest groups may also profit from a war if it helps secure beneficial resources; exporters profit from the conquest of a new seaport, while farmers gain by winning access to valuable land or water.

It appears, however, that modern warfare has made it difficult for any nation as a whole to profit from an international war. As Finsterbusch and Greisman put it:

> Not only have the costs of wars increased greatly because of the vastly improved technology of devastation and the practice of total warfare, the benefits have also declined decidedly. Wars no longer gain booty, spoils, or tribute; and they infrequently gain economic concessions.[31]

The Vietnam War is an example of the economic burdens of modern warfare. It devastated most of Indochina and cost the United States alone over $150 billion and 50,000 lives. But despite this enormous cost, the Vietnam War produced virtually no economic benefits for the United States and left 2 million Vietnamese dead.[32]

International Political Organization The world's political organization is in many ways the most basic cause of international war. Our planet is divided into hundreds of sovereign states, most of which have their own military forces and a belief in their right to use them to protect or advance their national interests. With so many different governments and so many different armies, it is no surprise that international wars are frequent. Indeed, the threat of war is often just one more chip in the pokerlike political bargaining between nations. In the famous phrase of the nineteenth-century military strategist Karl von Clausewitz, "War is nothing but a continuation of political intercourse, with a mixture of other means."[33]

But despite appearances to the contrary, the nations of the world do not act like a pack of gunslingers in the Old West. There is a delicate and long-standing balance of power among the nations in the world system. Although it is often claimed that peace is most likely when there is rough equality between the groups of nations competing for power, Organski and Kugler found just the opposite to be true.[34] According to their research, peace is most likely when one power is clearly dominant and the others are afraid to challenge it, as was the case when Britain dominated the world system in the nineteenth century. Major wars break out when a new nation grows stronger than the old leader and upsets the balance.

TERRORISM

Plane hijackings, random bombings, political kidnappings, and assassinations—the nightly news is full of reports of terrorist attacks. Although the number of people involved in such incidents is very small compared with the number of those injured or killed in conventional warfare, the public is growing increasingly fearful of such seemingly random violence. Perhaps this is because the amount of terrorist activity has been increasing by about 10 to 12 percent a year since the beginning of the 1970s.[35]

The best known of the two principal types of terrorism is **revolutionary terrorism.** It is used by groups trying to bring about major political changes in a particular country. Some such groups believe that random terrorist attacks will create such chaos that the government they oppose will fall, or at least will meet their demands. Terrorists often try to goad a government into taking such extreme measures to combat them that it will lose popular support. Underground groups also hope that their acts of violence will make the public more aware of their cause, enabling them to recruit more members and build stronger popular support. Some of today's more sophisticated terrorists openly cultivate reporters and other representatives of the media by granting special interviews, releasing prepared statements for the press, and holding open press conferences. Some terrorists even time their attacks to avoid other newsworthy events that might compete for media attention.

Although acts of revolutionary terrorism, like this hijacking of a TWA plane to Beirut, receive the most publicity, repressive terrorism that governments direct against their own people actually cause far more deaths and injuries.

Revolutionary terrorists often secretly receive the help of established governments that support their goals and objectives.

Repressive terrorism is the opposite of revolutionary terrorism, in that its goal is to protect an existing political order. Although revolutionary terrorists receive most of the publicity, repressive terrorism is probably a far greater problem. Governments all over the world—from Chile and South Africa to the Soviet Union—use violence to terrorize their political opponents and maintain their grip on power. Government-backed death squads have been a fixture in the politics of Latin American countries for years. Again and again, the opponents of Third World leaders disappear and are never seen again. Torture and imprisonment without just cause are also common tools of repressive terrorists. The most extreme example since the end of World War II occurred in the small country of Cambodia (now known as Kampuchea), where about 2 million of its citizens were killed in less than four years.[36] Although the scale of the violence in Cambodia was unusual for such a small country, the danger of repressive terrorism is a fact of political life in most of the nations of the world today.

Many experts fear that terrorists might someday build or steal nuclear weapons. No one has ever used such nuclear terrorism, but it remains a disturbing possibility. Given a supply of the right fuel, a nuclear bomb is relatively simple to build. With such a weapon, a group of revolutionary terrorists would gain enormous power. Nuclear weapons are less suited to repressive terrorism. Still, a government controlled by a small and unpopular minority, such as South Africa's, might conceivably use such weapons against its own population. In the modern world, nuclear weapons are the ultimate source of terror.

PREVENTING WAR AND INTERNATIONAL CONFLICT

People have long dreamed of creating a world without war. Like other idealistic visions, this one may never come true. It may be that war cannot be altogether eliminated. But it is not too idealistic to believe that international conflict can be reduced in both frequency and scope. Ironically, this optimism is partially justified by the destructive power of modern military technology. Pacifists who would have been dismissed as head-in-the-clouds dreamers in the past are now given serious attention. Practically every educated person in the world recognizes the incredible destruction that a nuclear war would produce, and political leaders all over the world are trying to ensure that it will never happen.

Deterrence   Most military and political leaders assert that the best way to prevent another devastating world war is through **deterrence.** The idea is that our side (whichever one that is) must be so strong that its adversaries will be afraid to attack it. Thus, it is argued that building up a vast military machine actually promotes peace because it improves a nation's capacity to deter potential enemies. In the nuclear age this strategy has become known by a very appropriate abbreviation: MAD, short for mutual assured destruction. To guarantee mutual assured destruction both sides must not only be able to deliver enough nuclear weapons to devastate their opponent but be able to do it even after their opponent has launched a surprise attack and destroyed a good portion of their military forces.

As a strategy to prevent war, deterrence has serious weaknesses. It assumes that important political decisions are made in a cool, rational way. But in fact, nationalistic or religious fervor have often whipped nations into an emotional frenzy and led to an unrealistic belief in their invulnerability to the attacks of foreign enemies. Modern technology is also a destabilizing factor in the system of deterrence. New innovations in defensive techniques threaten to weaken one side's deterrent threat and touch off a new conflict. Moreover, the massive military forces both sides must keep in constant readiness greatly increase the chances of an accidental war no one really wants. And even if an armed conflict never breaks out, the constant preparations for war required by the deterrence strategy are extremely expensive.

All things considered, it seems obvious that a system of mutual deterrence cannot be counted on to maintain international peace. It is a desperate arrangement among enemies based on fear, not cooperation. Now that we are all the targets of nuclear weapons, it seems that our governments could do more than merely promise to kill our enemies if they kill us. Yet maintaining a strong deterrent threat seems to be one of the few things that the world's governments are doing to keep the peace, at least for the present.

Arms Control and Disarmament   The advocates of arms control argue that attempting to achieve peace by building up the means to make war is ridiculous. They recommend a balanced reduction in weapons or, ideally, total disarmament and the elimination of all means for making war. But even the call for a freeze on the manufacture of new nuclear weapons has met strong opposition. The major obstacle to arms control is distrust. Each nation is convinced that the others will cheat, perhaps by keeping weapons hidden for a surprise attack. It is for this reason that disarmament proposals must include inspection systems as well as agreements for the reduction of military forces.

Arms control also has an economic side. So much money is now being spent on weaponry that real disarmament would be a major shock to the world economy. In the Soviet Union and the United States (whose military budgets are almost equal but about ten times that of any other nation)[37], millions of people are involved in manufacturing weapons and other military supplies. The arms manufacturers and the military together form what President Dwight D. Eisenhower called the "military industrial complex," which is often a powerful political force against effective arms control. For this reason, most advocates of arms control call for a gradual reduction in arms accompanied by a slow adjustment to a peaceful economy. In the long run, the human race would certainly grow richer and more prosperous from such a commitment to world peace, even if some short-term economic problems occurred.

Many people reject the idea that the threat of mutual destruction is the best way to prevent a nuclear war, and they call instead for nuclear disarmament.

Some progress toward arms control has been made since the end of World War II, but it has come slowly—seemingly with one step back for every two steps forward. The Americans and the Soviets now say that they are committed to arms reduction, and there have been moves that could lead to real progress. In 1963 a partial ban on nuclear testing was signed. A 1972 treaty limited the use of antiballistic missiles. A treaty to stop the spread of nuclear weapons has been signed by many countries, but some of the nations that do not have such weapons are not enthusiastic about signing. Finally, the latest U.S.-Soviet agreement, the INF treaty, calls for the elimination of an entire class of weapons: intermediate range ballistic missiles. Even after these mid-range missiles are all dismantled, each side will still have enough weapons to destroy the other many times over. But such agreements can nonetheless have an enormous psychological value in promoting mutual trust and respect.

Social Justice   As was pointed out earlier, feelings of resentment among exploited groups are a major factor in uprisings, rebellions, and revolutions. Although it is possible to reduce such resentment without reducing inequality, the best way to prevent revolutionary violence is to change the conditions of inequality that cause the resentment. This seems to be a rather obvious principle, but it is seldom followed, largely because most elites—whether national or international—are either unable or unwilling to use it. Some are unaware that their special status is unjust; others simply don't care. They are indifferent to the need for compromise until it is too late. A stable government depends on **legitimation:** the consent of the governed based on their belief that the governors are just and fair. The sooner and more quickly a government moves to rectify just grievances, the more peaceful and secure it will be.

As the world develops into a more tightly knit economic and political community, the causes of international war will increasingly come to resemble the cause of revolutionary wars. The vast inequalities in wealth between the north and south are creating a festering sense of resentment and hostility in the Third World. Citizens of the industrialized countries are beginning to realize that something must be done to improve the standard of living of the world's impoverished masses. Handouts of food and other essential supplies can help stave off immediate disasters, but they are obviously not a long-term solution. Most poor nations are faced with two alternative strategies for developing their economies. One approach is to encourage investment by foreign multinational corporations in the hope that they will create more jobs and a higher standard of living. The other approach champions self-reliance. It encourages the government and domestic firms to begin their own investment programs.

A great deal of research has been addressed to the question of which of these two strategies is more effective. The consensus is that investment by foreign multinationals provides a short-term boost to local economies but that, in the long run, self-reliance is the much more effective approach.[38] Once the multinationals make their initial investment, the balance soon shifts, and they begin taking home more in profits than they invest in the local economy. A second problem is that expensive labor-saving Western technology is not well suited to the needs of poor countries with massive unemployment problems. Finally, the multinationals are run by foreigners whose goal is to maximize their own profits. These executives often make decisions that are contrary to the best interests of the host countries. Time and again, the vast financial resources and political power of the multinationals have enabled them to corrupt local officials and win major economic concessions.

The fact that self-reliance appears to be the best strategy of economic development does not mean that the Western nations should sit on their hands and do nothing. At least three important steps could be taken. First, tariffs, quotas, and import barriers could be dropped so that Third World products can compete freely in the rich markets of the industrialized nations. Second, more low-interest loans and grants could be made to Third World countries, helping them to buy the equipment and raw materials they need. Third, Western scientists, scholars, and businesspeople could provide guidance and assistance when it is needed. For example, many poor countries begin their development programs by launching grandiose industrialization projects aimed at catching up with the north in one giant leap; but most developmental experts now agree that because most of the people in Third World nations are farmers, economic development should begin with increases in agricultural production and improvement of the average citizen's diet.

Encouraging Global Cooperation   In addition to improving the poverty-stricken economies of the Third World, there are many other steps that must be taken to build the foundations for a more peaceful world. Cultural exchanges and direct networks of international communication help promote global understanding, and many more of them will be needed in the years ahead. Programs designed to encourage economic cooperation between different nations could also build stronger bonds of mutual support and understanding. Another necessary ingredient in the formula for world peace is international guidance and control. Just as national governments use their power and authority to settle disputes among their citizens, so a world organization could limit conflicts among nations.

Two components are needed in any serious effort to create international controls to prevent war. First is the formulation and acceptance of a body of international law. Like criminal law, international statutes must state what kinds of actions constitute international aggression and then specify punishments for each. The second requirement is an international organization to enforce the law. There must be an arrangement whereby an international body (a "court") decides whether or not an accused nation has broken the law and provides a legal arrangement to punish the violator.

A framework for international law already exists. The United Nations—and the League of Nations before it—have already created a considerable body of international law. The Universal Declaration of Human Rights, for example, is an international equivalent of the Bill of Rights in the Constitution of the United States, and it clearly prohibits the repressive terrorism practiced by so many countries around the world. International law also explicitly forbids aggression by one nation against another, which the United Nations defines as

> the threat or use of armed force across an internationally recognized frontier, for which a government, *de facto* or *de jure*, is responsible because of act or negligence, unless justified by necessity for individual or collective self-defense, by the authority of the United Nations to maintain international peace and security, or by consent of the state within whose territory armed force is being used.[39]

Although this definition is vague and general, it is no less specific than the statutes outlawing murder and manslaughter. In both cases there are bound to be heated trials to determine whether a specific action was justified because it was performed in self-defense. As in criminal law, international legal principles and traditions will develop only with experience.[40]

DEBATE

Is World Government the Way to Eliminate International Warfare?

YES As long as sovereign nations control their own military forces, there will be wars. World government is the only solution to this ancient problem. Such a government could curb international wars by limiting each nation's military strength and forcing nations to settle their differences in accordance with international law.

Although it would certainly be difficult to create a world government, critics who say that it cannot be done are wrong. The United Nations has already laid the foundation for world unification. World government would be weak and ineffective at first, but if it were well managed, its strength and unity would grow. There is no basis for the fear that such a government would violate national sovereignty and subject small countries to the domination of large ones. The new government would be a federation of independent states very much like the United States, Canada, or the Soviet Union. Each nation would be permitted to keep some armed forces and to control its domestic affairs. The international government would concern itself only with the economic and political relations between nations in order to promote the common good of all people. Just as the unification of the small feudal states of Europe provided great economic and social benefits for their people, world government would provide similar benefits for the entire human race.

NO Dreamers and idealists have talked about the need for a world government for centuries, but such an idea is as unrealistic today as it was a hundred years ago. History shows that governments rarely surrender their sovereignty voluntarily. In Europe, no international boundary has ever been changed except by war. Only the gun and the sword can meld small states into larger ones. The idea that this quarreling planet could be unified peacefully without an international holocaust is hopelessly naive. Can you imagine a government that even Russians, Chinese, and Americans could agree on? Getting the whole world to go along would clearly be impossible.

But even if world government were possible, it would be a mistake. No matter how decentralized and limited such a government might be in the beginning, it would inevitably grow larger and more powerful. Because the people of the democratic nations are vastly outnumbered by those who have been raised under totalitarian regimes, a world government would eventually reflect the political traditions of the totalitarian majority. The dictatorial superstate that could be expected to emerge would be vastly more powerful than today's totalitarian regimes, for it would not be hampered by pressure from other, hostile states. Its overwhelming power would leave its opponents no place to hide. Clearly, world government is both an impractical and dangerous idea.

A more fundamental stumbling block to international control over warfare is the difficulty of establishing an organization to enforce international law. Again, the basics are already in place. The problem is obtaining the consent of the governed. Most nations refuse to give up any of their authority to an international organization because they do not believe in international law. The United Nations has been effective only when its most powerful members, particularly the United States and the Soviet Union, were able to agree on a course of action. When the powerful nations disagree, it becomes obvious that the United Nations has no power of its own. And, unfortunately, there are many good reasons for such disagreements. The resolution of international grievances is such a delicate process that there are bound to be injustices. For example, suppose a nation's existing boundary was established years ago by clear military aggression on the part of its neighbor. Is the nation to be penalized if it tries to right this past wrong? As was pointed out in Chapter 15, it is extremely difficult to distinguish illegitimate violence from legitimate violence.

Despite these problems, there are signs of hope. The development of advanced technology and changes in the world economy have made nations more dependent on one another than ever before. No modern society can survive entirely on its own resources, and international trade and commerce can help build bonds between nations. For example, William Domke found that the more deeply involved a country is in foreign trade, the less likely it is to go to war.[41] As the nations of the world become more and more interdependent, the demand for greater international law and order is likely to grow.

SOCIOLOGICAL PERSPECTIVES ON WARFARE AND INTERNATIONAL CONFLICT

In political science more time and attention are given to warfare than to almost any other single subject. This is not true of sociology or of social science in general. Research on war and military matters is a minor specialty within the sociological discipline. For this reason, the three principal sociological perspectives are not as sharply defined with reference to warfare as they are with reference to, say, crime or poverty. In recent years, however, a great deal of attention has been paid to the economic development of the Third World and to other problems of the world system, and warfare itself is gaining increasing sociological attention.

The Functionalist Perspective   Functionalist theory sees international conflict and warfare as an inevitable result of the world's political disorganization. From time immemorial, humanity has been creating political structures that are conducive to warfare. When there is a multitude of large and small countries with conflicting interests, disagreements about physical and psychological boundaries are bound to occur. The international organizations set up to handle these disputes simply cannot do the job.

Given this high degree of international disorganization, war is actually functional because it is the only effective method for settling major international disputes. Warfare also provides short-term psychological and political benefits to individual nations and may function to keep a weak, divided society together for a time. For these reasons, we denounce warfare but nevertheless organize ourselves to retain it. It follows that the best solutions to the problem of international war are those that try to reorganize the world's political system. The primary need is for a program to replace our patchwork of international relations with a genuine world order.

To functionalists revolutionary warfare arises from a different kind of disorganization. When national systems do not work smoothly and become increasingly dysfunctional, revolution is one possible result. For example, a society might exclude capable people from positions of power and distribute its wealth so unequally that citizens become bitter, resentful, and revolutionary. Political organization also becomes dysfunctional when it champions established ways of doing things while the citizens' attitudes, values, and opinions are changing. Such rigidity is sometimes softened by revolution. Functionalists therefore believe that the best way to head off revolutionary conflict is to implement the kinds of gradual reforms already described in the chapters on economics, government, poverty, and ethnic minorities.

Although most functionalists recognize that the desperate poverty of the Third World is an unsettling factor in world politics, they find the causes of that poverty in the culture and social organization of the poor countries themselves. Functionalists are convinced that traditional values held in most poor countries do not provide strong enough encouragement for hard work, savings, and investment, or a scientific approach to the world. Furthermore, the political system in those societies is often dominated by an old landholding aristocracy, which blocks modernization efforts that might improve the conditions of the common people. In sum, functionalists feel that the less developed nations are still clinging to traditional culture and social structures that have become dysfunctional in the modern world. The solution to the problem of development thus lies in an all-out effort to change those dysfunctional values and institutions.

The Conflict Perspective   Conflict theorists ordinarily do not separate economics and politics. Instead, they speak of "political economy." To them, the world system is not disorganized; it is organized for economic and political exploitation. In this view, the people of the Third World are not poor because of their social or cultural characteristics. They are poor because they have been and are being exploited by the people of the industrialized nations. The colonial powers intentionally prevented industrialization in their colonies. They also systematically looted the colonies' wealth and natural resources, and shattered their traditional economic systems. Conflict theorists believe that international wars stem from the efforts of nations to establish or expand such exploitative empires. In contrast, revolutionary wars are generally seen as attempts by the people to free themselves from exploitation, whether by foreign or domestic elites.

According to the conflict perspective, the best way to eliminate warfare and international conflict is to eliminate oppression, both international and national. Some conflict theorists advocate a balance-of-power system, but one in which economic goods and the military power to protect them are distributed equally. Others call for radical economic changes that would make all government unnecessary; in this utopian state, both governments and the wars that they fight would vanish. But conflict theorists are not necessarily against war, at least in the short run. Their position is that conflict is basic to all human societies, and some recommend that collective violence be used to undo economic injustices that are maintained by military power. The ultimate aim of conflict theorists is, nonetheless, a peaceful world with full equality among all peoples.

Social Psychological Perspectives   Social psychologists have identified both individual and cultural characteristics that are conducive to warfare. The individual traits, as we have seen, are associated with an assumed instinctual aggressiveness. The cultural traits are clearly learned. Each culture champions a certain "ideal personality," and people are then encouraged in both subtle and open ways to develop personality traits consistent with this ideal. For example, people growing up in cultures that place great importance on honor and pride are likely to encourage warlike national policies, as are people growing up in cultures that emphasize competition and individual aggressiveness. Cultures in which people learn to put a high value on humility and cooperation are much more likely to be peaceful in both national and international affairs.

One's sense of nationalism or internationalism is also learned, as is the ethnocentric belief that one's own culture and social institutions are superior to others. Some people learn to identify so strongly with their country that any international setback is seen as a personal threat. Such people are not likely to encourage a peaceful foreign policy. Even Western religions put emphasis on conquering evil in an aggressive way. War allows people to identify enemies as evil and then win honor, glory, and a sense of righteousness by conquering them.[42]

In the long run, social psychologists say, the only sure way to reduce the frequency of warfare is to emphasize cultural characteristics that favor the peaceful resolution of differences. Rather than glorifying victory over evil, it would be more useful to applaud the rational compromise that heads off deadly conflict. The ideals of nonviolence must be substituted for the glorification of violence that is so common in the mass media and in our everyday lives.

SUMMARY

The pattern of economic and political relations that links the nations of our planet together is known as the world system. The two greatest sources of conflict in the world system are the divisions between the capitalist nations of the west and the communist nations of the east, and between the rich industrialized nations of the north and the poor agricultural nations of the south.

War can be defined as protracted military conflict between two or more organized groups. Wars can be classified on the basis of the groups involved as international (between independent nations) or revolutionary (between groups within a nation). They can also be classified on the basis of the tactics and weapons used as conventional wars, guerrilla wars, and nuclear wars.

Through the years, warfare has been more the rule than the exception. The cost of this warfare has been enormous. Hundreds of millions of people have been killed or injured in wars. Economically, the cost of war is staggering. But the greatest potential cost is the devastation of nuclear war.

Since the early nineteenth century there has been a steady escalation of violence in international armed conflicts. Wars once had specific, limited goals, but now they are "total." Civilians no longer sit on the sidelines watching fights between professional soldiers. They are participants and, thus, are military targets. Further, improved military technology has increased the scale and destructiveness of modern warfare.

The causes of revolutionary and international wars overlap but are nevertheless different. There are many theories about the causes of revolutionary wars. One says that they stem from exploitation and oppression of subordinate groups by a society's ruling elite. Another says relative deprivation stimulates the discontent essential to a revolution. Other theories hold that revolutions occur when the institutions of a society become imbalanced, when dissatisfied groups are able to mobilize sufficient resources to challenge the existing government, or when the government weakens and loses its political support. A final theory notes that class conflict, geographic divisions, and ethnic segregation all contribute to revolutionary conflict.

Militarism and the buildup of armaments are a major cause of international war. Ethnocentrism, when expressed in nationalism or dogmatic religious ideologies, may also encourage the conquest of other people. Plain greed cannot be ignored either: some wars are fought more for profit than for anything else. But underlying all international wars is the nature of the world's political organization. The large number of heavily armed independent states, each determined to advance its own interests, makes warfare almost inevitable.

Terrorism involves attacks on civilians to gain political ends and is often used in situations that stop just short of full-scale war. The two main types are revolutionary terrorism, aimed at changing an existing government, and repressive terrorism, aimed to protect it.

The most common proposal for preventing war urges nations to become strong enough to deter aggression by their neighbors. Because such an arrangement is inherently unstable, other proposals ask for some form of arms control or total disarmament. A third set of proposals calls for social justice and the economic development of the poor nations. If inequality were eliminated, the chief motivation for revolution would disappear and international tensions would relax. Finally, many religious, political, and intellectual leaders propose that military aggression be eliminated by the development of world government, including world law, world courts, and world law enforcement.

Functionalists see warfare and international conflicts as inevitable results of the way the world is organized politically. The world's political structures are dysfunctional, having been established to serve a bygone age. National systems do not function smoothly either, and revolution is evidence of this fact. Conflict theorists hold that the world system is far from disorganized. It is organized for economic exploitation of the weak by the strong. Conflict theorists favor a system in which economic goods and the military power to protect them are distributed equally. Social psychologists have identified personal and cultural traits that are conducive to warfare. In the long run, they say, the only sure way to prevent wars is to emphasize nonviolent cultural traits that favor the peaceful resolution of differences.

KEY TERMS

colonialism
deterrence
international war
militarism
nationalism

nuclear proliferation
revolutionary war
terrorism
world system

FURTHER READINGS

The World Order

Daniel Chirot, *Social Change in the Modern Era*, San Diego: Harcourt Brace Jovanovich, 1986.

Independent Commission on International Development Issues, *North-South: A Program for Survival*, Cambridge, Mass.: MIT Press, 1980.

Volker Bornschier and Christopher Chase-Dunn, *Transnational Corporations and Underdevelopment*, New York: Praeger, 1985.

Warfare

James F. Dunnigan and William Martel, *How to Stop A War: The Lessons of Two Hundred Years of War and Peace*, New York: Doubleday, 1987.

Ronald J. Glossop, *Confronting War*, 2d ed., Jefferson, N.C.: McFarland, 1987.

Jack A. Goldstone (ed.), *Revolutions: Theoretical, Comparative and Historical Studies*, San Diego: Harcourt Brace Jovanovich, 1986.

Gwynne Dryer, *War*, New York: Crown Books, 1985.

GLOSSARY

absolute approach   Defining poverty by dividing the poor from the nonpoor on the basis of an objective standard (e.g., income).

absolute deprivation   Lack of one or more of the necessities of life.

acquired immune deficiency syndrome (AIDS)   A fatal disease that attacks the body's defenses against illness.

activity theory   A theory of aging that holds that older people are happiest when they continue to be actively involved in social life.

addiction   The intense craving for a drug that develops after a period of physical dependence stemming from heavy use.

adolescence   The age grade of persons who have reached puberty but have not been given full status as adults.

adulthood   The age grade of persons who are considered to have reached full social and physical maturity.

affirmative action   A program designed to make up for past discrimination by giving special assistance to members of the groups that were discriminated against.

age composition   The percentage of a population in each age category.

age grade   People of similar age, such as children, adolescents, and adults.

aging   A set of biological and social changes that occur in all people throughout life, but at different rates.

alcoholic   A person whose work or social life is disrupted by drinking.

androgynous   Having both the characteristics traditionally ascribed to males and to females.

assault   An attack on a person with the intention of hurting or killing the victim.

authoritarian personality   A personality that is rigid and inflexible, has a very low tolerance for uncertainty, and readily accepts orders from above.

aversion therapy   A form of behavioral therapy that uses punishment to discourage a particular behavior.

bail   A sum of money put up as security to be forfeited if a person accused of committing a crime does not show up for trial.

balance of power   The condition in which the military strength of the world's strongest nations or groups of nations is roughly equal.

behavioral therapy   Modification of the specific behavior that is causing a patient's problems.

behavioral theory   A theory that explains human action in terms of observable behavior.

bilingualism   The policy of giving two languages equal legal status in a nation.

biosocial theory   A theory that explains social behavior by reference to biological traits.

biosphere   The life-containing region of the earth extending from about 200 feet below sea level to about 10,000 feet above it.

birthrate   The number of babies born in a year divided by the total population.

bisexual   Willing to have sexual relations with individuals of either sex.

blockbusting   A practice of realtors in which residents of a neighborhood into which a minority family has moved are convinced that property values in the neighborhood will fall; the residents sell cheaply to the realtors, who resell the property to minority families at a higher price.

blue-collar worker   Someone employed in a job requiring manual labor.

bourgeoisie   The class of people who, according to Marx, own capital and capital-producing property.

bureaucracy   A form of social organization characterized by division of labor, a hierarchy of authority, a set of formal rules, impersonal enforcement of rules, and job security.

business cycle   The ups and downs that characterize the economies of all capitalist nations.

capitalism   An economic system characterized by private property, the exchange of commodities and capital, and a free market for goods and labor.

case study   A detailed examination of specific individuals, groups, or situations.

chemotherapy   The use of drugs to treat mental disorders.

childhood   The earliest age grade, lasting from birth to the onset of puberty.

child molestation   A sexual act between an adult and a child.

class conflict   The disagreements and strife that develop between different social classes because of their different social, economic, and political interests.

classical conditioning   Learning that occurs without the active participation of the subject.

client-centered therapy   Psychotherapy in which the patient chooses the topic and sets the pace and direction of the therapy session, while the therapist provides encouragement and support. (Also called nondirective therapy.)

colonialism   A system in which one nation extends its political and economic control over other nations or other peoples and treats them as dependent colonies.

commune   A small self-supporting community voluntarily joined by individuals committed to living together in a familylike environment.

compensatory education program   A special program whose goal is to help disadvantaged students reach educational levels comparable to those achieved by more privileged students.

conflict perspective   A sociological perspective that sees conflicts between different groups as a basic social process and holds that the principal source of social problems is exploitation and oppression of one group by another.

conglomerate   A large firm that owns businesses in many areas of production and distribution.

control theory   A criminological theory holding that people commit crimes when social norms and other social forces no longer control them.

conventional war   A war in which two or more armies meet directly without guerrilla tactics or nuclear weapons.

cornucopian   Someone who believes that scientific progress will allow continued economic growth and prosperity despite population growth and the depletion of natural resources.

corporate interest groups   Groups of corporations that are controlled by the same financial interests.

corporate technostructure   The group of technically skilled corporation managers who, according to Galbraith, make the important decisions.

crime   Violation of a criminal law.

crime-control model   A model of criminal justice that favors speedy arrest and punishment of anyone who commits a crime.

cultural imperialism   The attempt by one social group to impose its values, beliefs, and standards of behavior on another group or groups.

cultural lag   The delay between technological change and a culture's adaptation to it.

culture   The way of life of the people in a certain geographic area, particularly their ideas, beliefs, values, patterns of thought, and symbols.

cyclical unemployment   Unemployment resulting from changes in the business cycle, which in turn cause changes in the demand for labor.

death rate   The number of people who die in a year divided by the total population.

decriminalization   The proposal that penalties for possession and use of a drug be abolished even if sales of the drug remain illegal.

de facto segregation   Segregation of minority groups that results from existing social conditions (such as housing patterns) but is not legally required.

deinstitutionalization   The movement to reduce the number of patients treated in mental hospitals.

de jure segregation   Segregation of minority groups that is required by law.

demographic transition   Changes in basic birthrates and death rates occurring during the process of industrialization.

demography   A scientific discipline dealing with the distribution, density, and vital statistics of populations.

depressant   A drug that slows the responses of the central nervous system, reduces coordination, and decreases mental alertness.

desertification   The transformation of productive land into desert.

deterrence   The strategy of preventing war by maintaining so strong a military force that other nations will be afraid to attack.

deviant   An individual who violates a social norm.

deviant subculture   A set of perspectives, attitudes, and values that support criminal or other norm-violating activity.

differential association   A theory holding that people become criminals because they are exposed to more behavior patterns that are favorable to a certain kind of crime than are opposed to it.

disarmament   Elimination of armed forces and armaments, usually by means of a treaty.

discrimination   The practice of treating some people as second-class citizens because of their minority status.

disengagement theory A theory of aging that holds that older people are best off when they slowly disengage from social activities as they age.

displacement of goals The shifting of organizational goals away from the organization's original purpose, as when an employee does something that interferes with the achievement of the organization's goals in order to protect his or her job.

diversion program A program whose goal is to keep juveniles out of the courts.

domination A national system in which one (ethnic) group holds power and other groups are subordinate to it.

double bind A situation in which a parent gives a child two conflicting messages at the same time.

double standard A code of behavior that gives men greater sexual freedom than women.

dual-earner family A family in which both wife and husband are employed.

due-process model A model of criminal justice that places more emphasis on protecting human rights and dignity than on punishing criminals.

dysfunction An action of an institution that interferes with the carrying out of essential social tasks.

ecology The study of the interrelationships among plants, animals, and their environments.

ecosystem A self-sufficient community of organisms living in an interdependent relationship with each other and their environment.

ego According to Freud, the individual's conscious, reality-oriented experience.

electroconvulsive therapy The use of electric shocks to treat mental disorders.

elitist One who believes that nations are ruled by a small elite class.

ethnic group A group whose members share a sense of togetherness and the conviction that they form a distinct group or "people."

ethnocentrism The tendency to view the norms and values of one's own culture as absolute and to use them as a standard against which to measure those of other cultures.

exclusion Income received from certain sources (e.g., municipal bonds) that is not counted for tax purposes.

executive branch The branch of government responsible for carrying out the laws.

experiment A research method in which the behavior of individuals or groups is studied under controlled conditions, usually in a laboratory setting.

exploitive technology Technology designed to produce immediate profits without regard to long-term consequences.

extended family Members of two or more related nuclear families living together in the same place.

extinction Modification of a behavior by removing the reinforcement (reward) for that behavior.

extramarital affair A sexual relationship of a married person with someone other than his or her spouse.

family A group of people related by marriage, ancestry, or adoption who live together in a common household.

family planning   A population control program whose objective is voluntary reduction of the birthrate.

federal system   A system of government in which national affairs are handled by a central government and local affairs are left to semiindependent local governments.

federation   A system of government in which each city, county, or state operates independently on some issues but fuses other activities with those of allied governments.

fee-for-service compensation   A form of compensation in which a physician is paid a fixed fee for each service rendered.

felony   A serious offense, usually punishable by death or by confinement in a central prison.

folkway   A custom whose violators are not strongly condemned.

food chain   The set of transformations beginning with production of food by green plants and ending with decomposition of the bodies of animals.

forcible rape   Sexual intercourse forced on someone against his or her will.

fraud   The acquisition of money or property through the use of deception or false pretenses.

free school   A school in which teachers encourage pupils to set their own educational goals and tempo.

frustration-aggression theory   A theory holding that frustration produces aggression.

function   The contribution of each part of society to the maintenance of a balanced order.

functionalist perspective   A sociological theory that sees society as a delicate balance of parts and holds that social problems arise when societies become disorganized.

fundamental education   Education that concentrates on the teaching of reading, writing, and arithmetic.

gender role   A social role assigned on the basis of biological sex.

gender socialization   The process by which a person learns the behaviors and attitudes that are expected of the female or male gender.

general deterrence   Punishment of criminals in order to frighten others so much that they will not violate the law.

generalized other   A person's system of values and standards that, according to Mead, reflect the expectations of people in general.

gentrification   The renovation of older low-cost neighborhoods in the central cities to accommodate more wealthy residents.

geothermal energy   The heat of the earth's inner core.

grade inflation   The assignment of higher student grades than were formerly given for the same quality of work.

great-man theory of history   The theory holding that individual decision makers determine the course of history.

greenhouse effect   The trapping of heat in the atmosphere.

gridlock   Extreme traffic congestion that virtually stops all traffic in an area.

group   A set of individuals with organized and recurrent relationships with one another.

group marriage   A family that includes three or more adults as the marriage partners.

group therapy   A procedure in which each member of a group is encouraged to reveal his or her problems and experiences to the group, which discusses and examines them.

growth rate   The birthrate minus the death rate.

guerrilla war   A war conducted by small bands of rebels using hit-and-run tactics.

health   A state of physical and mental well-being.

health maintenance organization   An organization in which a group of medical personnel offers a range of medical services to subscribers who pay a fixed monthly fee.

heterosexual   One whose preference is for sexual relations with persons of the opposite sex.

hidden curriculum   The things that students must learn in order to succeed in school that are not part of the formal curriculum, such as obedience to authority.

high-tech industry   An industry, such as computers, that is based upon rapidly changing and sophisticated technology.

homicide   The killing of a human being.

homosexual   One whose preference is for sexual relations with persons of the same sex.

id   The instinctual drives, particularly sex, that, according to Freud, motivate all human behavior.

imperialism   The creation or expansion of an empire.

incapacitation   The prevention of crime by imprisoning criminals so that they cannot commit more crimes against the public.

incest taboo   The prohibition of sexual relations between close relatives, e.g., parents and their children.

income   The amount of money a person makes in a given year.

identity crisis   The personal crisis, typical of adolescence, in which a person tries to define who he or she is and how he or she fits into society.

industrial espionage   The hiring of investigators to gain information about one's business competitors, for instance by "bugging" their offices and telephones.

inflation   An increase in the overall prices consumers must pay for the goods they buy.

infrastructure   The basic physical necessities of modern society, e.g., roads, power plants, and sewers.

institution   A relatively stable pattern of thought and behavior centered on the performance of an important social task.

institutional discrimination   Discrimination against minority groups that is practiced by economic, educational, and political organizations rather than by individuals.

institutional racism   Prejudice and discrimination against a particular race that are built into a society's economic, educational, and political institutions.

integration   A national system in which ethnic backgrounds are ignored and all individuals are treated alike.

interactionist theory A theory that explains behavior in terms of each individual's social relationships.

interlocking directorate The situation that exists when some of the same individuals sit on the boards of directors of competing firms, or when directors of competing firms sit together on the board of directors of a firm in a different industry.

intermediate technology Machines that are less complicated than expensive energy-intensive machines but more efficient than human and animal power.

international war Prolonged armed conflict between the governments of two or more nations.

iron law of oligarchy The tendency for any large organization to be ruled, according to Michels, by a few powerful people.

judicial branch The branch of government responsible for interpreting the laws and deciding on their constitutionality.

juvenile delinquency Behavior by minors (usually defined as individuals below the age of 18) that is in violation of the criminal law or the special standards set for juveniles.

labeling theory A theory holding that branding a person as a criminal often encourages rather than discourages criminal behavior.

land reform The redistribution of land from rich landlords to peasant farmers.

latent dysfunction A hidden dysfunction performed by a social institution or agency.

latent function A hidden function performed by a social institution or agency.

legalization The proposal that the use and sale of a drug be made legal, with government regulation.

legislative branch The branch of government responsible for enacting laws.

legitimation Consent of the governed based on a belief that those who govern have the right to do so.

lesbian A female homosexual.

life cycle The regular progression of persons through the age grades of their society as they grow older.

limited war A war whose goals are restricted to a set of specific objectives and in which a rather small group of military personnel do the fighting.

lobbying The activities of special-interest groups aimed at convincing lawmakers to pass the kind of legislation that they desire.

lower class The social class at the bottom of the social hierarchy, composed of people whose incomes are below the poverty line.

machismo Tough, aggressive masculinity.

macro theory A sociological theory that is concerned with the behavior of large groups and entire societies.

magnet schools Schools with special enriched programs designed to attract students from all ethnic groups, thus encouraging integration.

maintenance program A program that supplies addicts or habitual users with a drug, while denying it to the public at large.

manic depression   A mental disorder characterized by extreme swings in mood.

manslaughter   The unlawful killing of another person without malice.

market control   Domination of a market by a few giant firms.

medicaid   A U.S. program designed to help the poor, the blind, and the disabled pay for medical care.

medicare   A U.S. program that pays for medical care of people over 65 years old.

megalopolis   An area in which several large cities are fused together.

meltdown   An accident in which the cooling system of a nuclear power plant fails, allowing the heat of the nuclear reaction to melt the core, thus releasing huge amounts of radiation.

melting-pot theory   The belief that U.S. society acts as a sort of crucible in which people from around the world are blended together to form a new and distinctive culture.

membership group   A group of which an individual is a member, whether willingly or not.

mental disorder   A mental condition that makes it difficult or impossible for a person to cope with everyday life.

metropolitan statistical area (MSA)   The U.S. Department of Census term for a central city and the surrounding suburbs that depend on it.

micro theory   A sociological theory that is concerned with the behavior of individuals and small groups.

mid-life crisis   The crisis faced by middle-aged persons in which they must accept the passing of their youth and the limitations on their earlier aspirations.

middle class   The social class composed of professionals, managers, and most bureaucrats and white-collar workers.

militarism   (a) Glorification of war and combat. (b) Strong belief in "defense" combined with huge military expenditures.

misdemeanor   A minor offense, usually punishable by confinement in a local jail or by payment of a fine.

monogamy   The practice of being married to only one person at a time.

monopoly   The situation existing when a single corporation has gained complete control of a market.

mood disorder   A mental disorder involving severe disturbances in affect and emotion.

mores   Customs whose violators are punished or otherwise strongly condemned.

murder   The unlawful killing of a human being with malice aforethought.

nationalism   A form of ethnocentrism based on a sense of identification with and devotion to one's nation.

neo-Malthusian   Someone who believes that we are quickly approaching a crisis because of overpopulation, resource depletion, and environmental destruction.

neurosis   A personal problem, not as severe as psychosis, accompanied by anxiety and chronically inappropriate responses to everyday situations.

nonrenewable resource   A resource for which there is a fixed supply that cannot be replenished.

norm   A social rule telling us what behavior is acceptable in a certain situation and what is not.

nuclear family A married couple and their children.

nuclear proliferation The spread of nuclear weapons to an ever larger number of countries.

nuclear war Any war employing nuclear weapons.

nuclear winter The sharp decline in average temperatures produced by the dense clouds that would cover the earth after a major nuclear war.

occupational crime A crime committed in the course of the offender's occupation but without the support or encouragement of his or her employer.

old age The last age grade, usually considered to start around age 65.

oligopoly The situation existing when an industry is dominated by a few large companies.

open marriage A marriage in which the partners are committed to their own and each other's growth and which allows the widest possible range of outside contacts.

operant conditioning Conditioned learning that requires the active participation of the subject.

opiate Any of a group of natural and synthetic drugs with pain-relieving properties, including opium, codeine, morphine, heroin, meperidine, and methadone.

organic disorder A mental disorder that has a clear-cut physical cause, such as brain damage.

organizational crime A crime committed by someone acting on behalf of a larger organization, often his or her employer.

overeducation Training more people for occupations than there are jobs available in those occupations.

paranoid disorder A mental disorder in which the person suffers from overpowering, irrational fears.

parliamentary system A system of government in which the executive branch is not distinctly separate from the legislative branch; the prime minister is elected by the legislature and must resign if the party in power loses its legislative majority.

parole Release of a criminal from prison after part of his or her sentence has been served.

participant observation A research method in which the researcher participates in the activities of the group under study.

personal interview A research method that asks people about their activities and attitudes.

personality The relatively stable characteristics and traits that distinguish one person from another.

personality theory A theory holding that social behavior is determined by differences in personality.

photochemical smog A group of noxious compounds produced by the action of sunlight on oxygen, hydrocarbons, and nitrogen oxides.

photosynthesis The process by which green plants convert solar energy to food.

plea bargaining A process by which a defense attorney and a prosecutor agree to let

the defendant plead guilty in return for a reduction in the charge or other considerations.

pluralism A national system in which several ethnic groups maintain a high level of
independence and equality.

pluralist One who believes that political decisions are made by changing coalitions
of political forces.

political party An organized group whose goals are to get its members elected to
political office and to influence the decisions of those who already hold office.

political socialization The process by which people learn their political values and
perspectives.

polygyny The practice of being married to more than one wife at a time.

pornography A form of entertainment judged to be obscene.

poverty (a) The state of having an income below some specified level. (b) The state of
having significantly less income and wealth than the average person in the society
of which one is a member.

power The ability to force other people to do something whether they want to or not.

power elite A group of wealthy and powerful persons who, according to Mills, pursue
their own interests at the expense of the average citizen.

prejudice Antipathy, either felt or expressed, based on a faulty and inflexible generalization and directed toward a group as a whole or toward an individual because
he or she is a member of that group.

preliminary hearing A hearing at which a judge decides whether the evidence against
an accused person is sufficient to justify further legal proceedings.

premarital intercourse Sexual intercourse before marriage.

preventive medicine The theory or practice of staying healthy by maintaining good
health habits.

price fixing Collusion by several companies to cut competition and set uniformly high
prices.

price leader A firm whose prices are used as a guide by other firms in its industry.

probation Suspension of the sentence of a person who has been convicted but not yet
imprisoned, on condition of continued good behavior and regular reporting to a
probation officer.

proletariat The working class in an industrial society.

proportional representation An electoral system in which offices are won on the basis
of the proportion of the vote each party receives, and not on a winner-take-all basis.

prostitution The practice of selling the services of oneself or another person for purposes of intercourse or other sexual activities.

psychedelic A drug that produces hallucinations and other significant alterations in
the user's consciousness.

psychoanalysis Long-term therapy designed to uncover the repressed memories,
motives, and conflicts assumed to be at the root of the patient's psychological
problems.

psychosis A mental disorder in which a person has lost contact with reality and may
suffer hallucinations, delusions, and the like.

psychotherapy Any program for helping a patient understand and then overcome the
causes of his or her personality problems.

pushouts   Children who leave their family home because they are no longer wanted there.

race   People who are thought to have a common set of physical characteristics but who may or may not share a sense of unity and identity.

racism   Stereotyping, prejudice, and discrimination based on race.

reference group   A group with whose values and standards an individual identifies and of which he or she would like to be a member.

rehabilitation   The process of changing a person's criminal behavior by nonpunitive methods.

reinforcement   The reward or punishment received by an individual for a particular behavior.

relative approach   Dividing the poor from the nonpoor on the basis of the wealth and income of the average person.

relative deprivation   The situation in which persons have considerably less income, wealth, or prestige than they believe they deserve.

relative-deprivation theory   A theory holding that revolutions are caused by differences between what people have and what they think they should have.

renewable resource   A resource that is renewed through natural processes.

repressive terrorism   Terrorism intended to protect the existing political order in a nation.

retribution   The idea that the goal of the criminal justice process should be to make criminals suffer for their crimes.

revolutionary terrorism   Terrorism intended to bring about major political changes in a nation.

revolutionary war   Armed conflict between an official government and one or more groups of rebels.

rite of passage   A ritual that marks the transition from one state of life to another, especially from childhood to adulthood.

robbery   The unlawful taking of another person's property by force or threat of force.

role   A set of expectations and behaviors associated with a social position.

role conflict   The feelings experienced by people when two or more of their social roles place conflicting demands on them.

runaways   Children who move away from their homes without parental consent.

sample   A cross section of subjects selected for study as representative of a larger population.

scapegoat   A person or group that is unjustly blamed for the problems of others.

schizophrenia   A mental disorder involving extreme disorganization in personality, thought patterns, and speech.

sedative-hypnotic   A drug that depresses the central nervous system.

self-concept   The image one has of who and what one is.

sexism   Stereotyping, prejudice, and discrimination based on gender.

value conflict   A clash in the attitudes and beliefs held by different social groups.

victimization survey   A survey in which people are asked in personal interviews to report whether they have been the victims of various kinds of criminal offenses.

victimless crime   A crime in which the harm, if any, is not suffered by anyone except the offender.

violence   Behavior intended to cause bodily pain or injury to another; may be legitimate or illegitimate.

wage-price spiral   A repetitive inflationary circle in which prices are raised to cover the costs of higher wages, and wages are then raised to cover the increased cost of living.

war   Protracted military conflict between two or more organized groups.

wealth   A person's total economic worth (e.g., real estate, stocks, cash).

white-collar crime   Crime committed by people of respectability and high social status in the course of their occupations.

white-collar workers   Persons employed in nonmanual labor, such as business managers or office workers.

withdrawal   The sickness that a habitual drug user experiences when the drug is discontinued after a period of steady use.

workfare   A government program for welfare mothers that provides job training and placement.

working class   The social class made up of blue-collar and lower-level service workers.

world economy   The international system of economic relationships in which all countries participate.

world system   The system of economic and political relationships that link the nations of the world together.

youth culture   The distinctive subculture created by adolescents in industrial society.

REFERENCES

CHAPTER 1   SOCIOLOGY AND SOCIAL PROBLEMS

1. See Robert K. Merton, "The Sociology of Social Problems," in Robert K. Merton and Robert Nisbet, eds., *Contemporary Social Problems*, 4th ed. (New York: Harcourt Brace Jovanovich, 1976).
2. Herbert Blumer, "Social Problems as Collective Behavior," *Social Problems* 18 (1971): 298–306; Malcolm Spector and John I. Kitsuse, "Social Problems: A Reformation," *Social Problems* 21 (1973): 145–159.
3. See Robert H. Lauer, "Defining Social Problems: Public Opinion and Textbook Practice," *Social Problems* 24 (1976): 122–130.
4. See Howard S. Becker, *Outsiders* (New York: Free Press, 1963).
5. Edward C. Wilson, *Sociobiology: The New Synthesis* (Cambridge, Mass.: Belknap Press, 1975).
6. See, for example, Herbert Blumer, *Symbolic Interactionism: Perspective and Method* (Englewood Cliffs, N.J.: Prentice-Hall, 1969), and Tamotsu Shibutani, *Society and Personality* (Englewood Cliffs, N.J.: Prentice-Hall, 1961).

CHAPTER 2   PROBLEMS OF THE ECONOMY

1. U.S. Bureau of the Census, *Statistical Abstracts of the United States, 1988* (Washington, D.C.: U.S. Government Printing Office, 1987), p. 794.
2. Adam Smith, *An Inquiry into the Nature and Causes of the Wealth of Nations*, 1776 reprint edition (New York: Random House, 1937).
3. Ibid. p. 128.
4. Daniel R. Fusfeld, *Economics*, 2d ed. (Lexington, Mass.: Heath, 1976), p. 530.
5. Senate Committee on Government Affairs, *Voting Rights in Major Corporations* (Washington, D.C.: Government Printing Office, 1978).
6. New York Stock Exchange, *Fact Book* (New York: New York Stock Exchange, 1986).
7. Ibid.
8. See Beth Mintz and Michael Schwartz, *The Power Structure of American Business* (Chicago: University of Chicago Press, 1985).
9. David R. James and Michael Soref, "Profit Constraints on Managerial Autonomy: Managerial Theory and the Unmaking of the Corporate President," *American Sociological Review* 46 (February 1981): 1–18.
10. See Thomas R. Dye, *The Irony of Democracy*, 7th ed. (Monterey, Calif.: Brooks/Cole, 1987).
11. C. Wright Mills, *The Power Elite* (New York: Oxford University Press, 1956).
12. Wayne D. Thompson, *Canada 1986* (Washington, D.C.: Stryker Post, 1986), p. 106.

13. Stanley Meiser, "Canada Cools Efforts to Nationalize in Face of Tension with U.S.," *Los Angeles Times*, November 29, 1982, Part 4, p. 1; Statistics Canada, *Canada's International Position* (Ottawa: Queen's Printer, 1982).

14. Jonathan Peterson, "Weak Dollar Deficits Put U.S. on Sale," *Los Angeles Times*, February 24, 1988, Part 1, p. 13.

15. See Anthony Sampson, *The Sovereign State of I.T.T.* (Briarcliff Manor, N.Y.: Stein & Day, 1980).

16. Volker Bornschier and Christopher Chase-Dunn, *Transnational Corporations and Development* (New York: Praeger, 1985).

17. James William Coleman, *The Criminal Elite: The Sociology of White Collar Crime*, 2d ed. (New York: St. Martin's Press, 1989).

18. For a review of this and other studies on the frequency of price fixing, see Coleman, *The Criminal Elite*, p. 28.

19. Richard Austin Smith, "The Incredible Electrical Conspiracy," *Fortune* 63 (1961): 132–180, 161–224.

20. James William Coleman, "Law and Power: The Sherman Antitrust Act and Its Enforcement in the Petroleum Industry," *Social Problems* 32 (1985): 264–274; John M. Blair, *The Control of Oil* (New York: Vintage, 1976), p. 71.

21. Coleman, *The Criminal Elite*, pp. 49–51.

22. These and other techniques are described in detail in Edwin H. Sutherland, *White Collar Crime* (Hinsdale, Ill.: Dryden, 1949), pp. 56–58.

23. John Kenneth Galbraith, *The New Industrial State* (New York Library/ Signet, 1967), pp. 304–305.

24. Morton Mintz and Jerry S. Cohen, *America, Inc.*, (New York: Dial, 1971), p. 70.

25. Frederick C. Klein, "Some Firms Fight Ills of Bigness by Keeping Employee Units Small," *Wall Street Journal*, February 5, 1982, p. 1.

26. *Forbes*, July 1987, p. 116.

27. Robert S. Weiss, Edwin Harwood, and David Reisman, "The World of Work," in Robert K. Merton and Robert Nisbet, eds., *Contemporary Social Problems*, 4th ed. (New York: Harcourt Brace Jovanovich, 1976), pp. 608–609.

28. Louis Harris, *Inside America* (New York: Vintage, 1987), p. 17.

29. U.S. Bureau of the Census, *Statistical Abstract, 1988*, p. 389.

30. Jonathan Peterson, "Service Jobs Dominate the Economy," *Los Angeles Times*, September 24, 1987, Part I, pp. 1, 22–23.

31. U.S. Department of the Census, *Statistical Abstracts 1987*, p. 378.

32. Lee May, "No Frills Jobs: More Work for Less," *Los Angeles Times*, June 19, 1988, Part 1, pp. 1, 13.

33. David J. Charrington, *The Work Ethic* (New York: AMACON, 1980).

34. Lawrence White, *Human Debris: The Injured Worker in America* (New York: Putnam, 1983), p. 15.

35. U.S. Department of Labor, *The President's Report on Occupational Safety* (Washington, D.C.: U.S. Government Printing Office, 1980).

36. White, *Human Debris*, p. 23.

37. Coleman, *The Criminal Elite*, pp. 31–41.
38. Robert J. Samuelson, "Labor's Twilight Could be Dark for Business Too," *Los Angeles Times*, July 5, 1985; Henry Weinstein, "Union Membership Falls to 17 Percent of the Work Force," *Los Angeles Times*, January 23, 1988, Part 4, p. 2.
39. Michael Goldfield, *The Decline of Organized Labor in the United States* (Chicago, University of Chicago Press, 1987), pp. 45–46.
40. Coleman, *The Criminal Elite*, pp. 86–87.
41. Robert J. Samuelson, "Economics Needs More than a Slogan," *Los Angeles Times*, February 25, 1988, part 2, p. 7.
42. David M. Gordon, "American Dream Growing Elusive," *Los Angeles Times*, September 1, 1987, Part 4, p. 3; Pat Weschler, "Working Hard, Going Nowhere," *San Francisco Chronicle/Examiner*, This Week, pp. 9, 14.
43. U.S. Bureau of the Census, *Statistical Abstracts, 1987*, p. 295.
44. Paul Blumberg, *Inequality in an Age of Decline* (New York: Oxford University Press, 1980), pp. 135–136; Janet C. Norwood, "The Recovery in Productivity," *New York Times*, August 30, 1985, p. 26; Associated Press, "U.S. Productivity Surges in First Quarter of the Year," San Luis Obispo (California) *Telegram-Tribune*, June 7, 1988.
45. Diane Werneke, *Productivity: Problems, Prospects and Policies* (Baltimore: Johns Hopkins University Press, 1984), p. 10.
46. Blumberg, *Inequality in an Age of Decline*, p. 143; Elliot Currie and Jerome H. Skolnick, *America's Problems* (Glenview, Ill.: Scott, Foresman, 1988), pp. 399–400.
47. Blumberg, *Inequality in an Age of Decline*, p. 143–144.
48. U.S. Bureau of the Census, *Statistical Abstracts, 1988*, p. 321.
49. Wechsler, "*Working Hard, Going Nowhere.*"
50. Harris, *Inside America*, p. 17.
51. Ibid. p. 8.
52. Michael Kinsley, "Yes, The Rich Got Richer Under Reagan's Regime: The Poor Fared As Usual," *Los Angeles Times*, April 11, 1988, Part 2, p. 2.
53. Wechsler, *Working Hard, Going Nowhere*.
54. M. Harvey Brenner, *Estimating the Cost of National Economic Policy*, U.S. Congress, Joint Economic Committee, 1976.

CHAPTER 3   PROBLEMS OF GOVERNMENT

1. U.S. Bureau of the Census, *Statistical Abstracts of the United States, 1988* (Washington, D.C.: U.S. Government Printing Office, 1987), pp. 294–407.
2. Ibid. pp. 126, 280, 376, 828.
3. Max Weber, from *Max Weber: Essays in Sociology*, trans. Hans H. Gerth and C. Wright Mills (New York: Oxford University Press, 1946), pp. 196–244.
4. Max Weber, *The Theory of Social and Economic Organization*, trans

A. M. Henderson and Talcott Parsons (New York: Free Press, 1947), p. 337.

5. See Francis Rourke, *Bureaucracy, Politics and Public Policy*, 3d ed. (Boston: Little, Brown, 1984).

6. See Kenneth Janda, Jeffrey M. Berry, and Jerry Goldman, *The Challenge of Democracy* (Boston: Houghton Mifflin, 1987), pp. 427–457.

7. Thomas R. Dye and Harmon Zeigler, *The Irony of Democracy*, 6th ed. (Monterey, Calif.: Brooks/Cole, 1987), p. 319.

8. Ibid. pp. 172–203; Janda, Berry and Goldman, *The Challenge of Democracy*, pp. 221–267.

9. Paul N. McCloskey, "Congressional Politics: Secrecy, Senility and Seniority," in Alan Wells, ed., *American Society: Problems and Dilemmas* (Pacific Palisades, Calif.: Goodyear, 1976), p. 20.

10. See Dye and Zeigler, *The Irony of Democracy*, pp. 358–354.

11. U.S. Bureau of the Census, *Statistical Abstracts, 1988*, p. 248.

12. Ibid. p. 249.

13. Associated Press, "Young Blacks Outraced Whites in '86," San Luis Obispo *Telegram-Tribune*, October 7, 1987, p. 10.

14. Mary Deibel, "Congress's Dilemma on Campaigns," San Luis Obispo *Telegram-Tribune*, February 14, 1987, p. B11.

15. Robert W. Stewart and Tracy Wood, "Political Giving: Corporate Contributions Buy Access," *Los Angeles Times*, October 26, 1986, Part 1, pp. 1, 3, 36.

16. Maura Dolar, "Friendly Lawmakers Get Chemical Industry Help," *Los Angeles Times*, October 26, 1987, Part 1, pp. 1, 26, 27.

17. Thomas Byrne Edsall, "The Return of Inequality," *Atlantic Montly*, June 1988, pp. 86–94.

18. C. Wright Mills, "The Structure of Power in American Society," in *Power, Politics and People: The Collected Papers of C. Wright Mills* (New York: Ballantine Books, 1963), p. 288.

19. See for example, Thomas R. Dye, *Who's Running America: The Conservative Years* (Englewood Cliffs: Prentice-Hall, 1986); Leonard Silk and Mark Silk, *The American Establishment* (New York: Basic Books, 1980).

20. David Riesman, *The Lonely Crowd* (New York: Doubleday, 1953).

21. Arnold M. Rose, *The Power Structure: Political Process in American Society* (New York: Oxford University Press, 1967), p. 6.

22. G. William Dumhoff, *The Higher Circles: The Governing Class in America* (New York: Random House, 1970), p. 309.

23. Robert Michels, *Political Parties: A Sociological Study of the Oligarchical Tendencies of Modern Democracy* (New York: Free Press, 1962).

24. Ibid. p. 354.

25. U.S. Bureau of the Census, *Statistical Abstracts, 1988*, p. 321.

26. Ibid. p. 530.

27. Ibid. p. 314.

28. David R. Simon and D. Stanley Eitzen, *Elite Deviance*, 2d ed. (Boston: Allyn & Bacon, 1986), p. 138.

29. See Ron Haggart and Aubrey E. Golden, *Rumors of War* (Toronto: New York Press, 1971).
30. James William Coleman, *The Criminal Elite: The Sociology of White Collar Crime*, 2d ed. (New York: St. Martin's Press, 1989), pp. 55–72.
31. Ibid.
32. Associated Press, "Most Polygraph Use by Employers Banned," San Luis Obispo *Telegram-Tribune*, October 22, 1988, p. D1.
33. Francis J. Flaherty, "Truth Technology," *The Progressive* 46 (June 1982): 30–35; Constance Holden, "Days May be Numbered for Polygraphs in the Private Sector," *Science*, May 9, 1986, p. 9; Dan Collins, "Free Enterprise Rushes to Fill a Delicate Need," *U.S. News and World Report*, February 23, 1987.
34. Ted Gest, "Who is Watching You?" *U.S. News and World Report*, July 12, 1982, pp. 34–37.
35. Michael Harrington, "Inequality Haunts America as Taxes Favor the Rich, Penalize the Middle Class," *Los Angeles Times*, January 24, 1988, Part 5, p. 3.
36. Michael Kinsley, "Yes, the Rich Got Richer Under Reagan's Regime; The Poor Fared as Usual," *Los Angeles Times*, April 11, 1988, Part 2, p. 7.
37. Edsall, "The Return of Inequality," p. 89.
38. Tamar Jacoby, "Going After Dissidents," *Newsweek*, February 8, 1988, p. 29.

CHAPTER 4 PROBLEMS OF EDUCATION

1. Quoted in Mavis Hiltunen Biesanz and John Biesanz, *Introduction to Sociology*, 2d ed. (Englewood Cliffs, N.J.: Prentice-Hall, 1973), p. 616.
2. Gerald Gutek, ed., Standard Educational Almanac (Chicago: Who's Who, 1983), pp. 125–126.
3. U.S. Bureau of the Census, *Statistical Abstract of the United States, 1987* (Washington, D.C.: U.S. Government Printing Office, 1986), pp. 122, 149.
4. Beverly A. Stitt, *Building Gender Fairness in Schools* (Carbondale, Ill.: Southern Illinois University Press, 1988), pp. 19–57.
5. Robert James Parelius and Ann Parker Parelius, *The Sociology of Education*, 2d ed. (Englewood Cliffs, N.J.: Prentice-Hall, 1987), p. 265.
6. See S. Leonard Syme and Lisa F. Berkman, "Social Class, Susceptibility and Sickness," in Howard D. Schwartz, ed., *Dominant Issues in Medical Sociology*, 2d ed. (New York: Random House, 1987), pp. 643–649.
7. Parelius and Parelius, *The Sociology of Education*, pp. 280–282.
8. U.S. Bureau of the Census, *Statistical Abstracts, 1988*, p. 133.
9. James S. Coleman et al., *Equality of Educational Opportunity* (Washington, D.C.: U.S. Government Printing Office, 1966); Christopher Jencks et al., *Inequality: A Reassessment of the Effects of Family and Schooling in America* (New York: Harper & Row, 1972); Harvey A. Averch et al., *How Effective Is Schooling: A Critical Synthesis and Review of Research Find-

ings (Englewood Cliffs, N.J.: Prentice-Hall, 1974); Samuel Bowles and Herber Gintis, *Schooling in Capitalist America* (New York: Basic Books, 1976).

10. Michael W. LaMorte and Jeffrey D. Williams, "Court Decisions and School Finance Reform," *Educational Administration Quarterly* 21 (Spring 1985): 59–89.

11. Gutek, *Standard Educational Almanac*, p. 269.

12. U.S. Bureau of the Census, *Statistical Abstracts, 1987*, p. 117.

13. See Parelius and Parelius, *The Sociology of Education*, pp. 293–296.

14. Robert Rosenthal and Lenore Jacobson, *Pygmalion in the Classroom* (New York: Harper & Row, 1969).

15. See Roy Nash, *Teacher Expectations and Pupil Learning* (London: Routledge and Kegan Paul, 1976); Parelius and Parelius, *The Sociology of Education*, pp. 293–296.

16. D. G. Harvey and G. T. Slatin, "The Relationship Between a Child's SES and Teacher Expectations," *Social Forces* 54 (1975): 140–159.

17. See Parelius and Parelius, *The Sociology of Education*, pp. 297–301.

18. Karl Alexander, Martha Cook, and Edward L. Dill, "Curriculum Tracking and Educational Stratification," *American Sociological Review* 43 (1978): 47–66.

19. Meyer Weinberg, *The Search for Quality Integrated Education* (Westport, Conn.: Greenwood Press, 1983), pp. 231–234.

20. Christine H. Rossell, "Desegregation Plans, Racial Isolation, White Flight, and Community Response," in Christine H. Rossell and Willis D. Hawley, eds., *The Consequences of School Desegregation* (Philadelphia: Temple University Press, 1983), pp. 13–57.

21. David G. Savage, "Mandatory Busing: Era Whose Time Has Passed," *Los Angeles Times*, July 1, 1982, Part 1, p. 1.

22. Elaine Woo, "Judge Tells L.A. Schools, NAACP to Settle Lawsuit," *Los Angeles Times*, June 21, 1988, Part 1, pp. 1, 16.

23. Coleman et al., *Equality of Educational Opportunity*.

24. Rita E. Mahard and Robert L. Crain, "Research on Minority Achievement in Desegregated Schools," in Rossell and Hawley, *The Consequences of School Desegregation*, pp. 103–125.

25. Janet Ward Scholfield and H. Andrew Sagar, "Desegregation, School Practices, and Student Race Relations," in Rossell and Hawley, *The Consequences of School Desegregation*, pp. 58–102; Nancy H. St. John, *School Desegregation: Outcomes for Children* (New York: John Wiley & Sons, 1975), pp. 64–86.

26. Janet Eyler, Valerie J. Cook, and Leslie E. Ward, "Resegregation: Segregation Within Desegregated Schools," in Rossell and Hawley, *The Consequences of School Desegregation*, pp. 126–162.

27. Robert J. Rubel, "Extent, Perspectives, and Consequences of Violence in the Schools," in Keith Baker and Robert J. Rubel, eds., *Violence and Crime in the Schools* (Lexington, Mass.: Lexington Books, 1980), p. 17.

28. Joan Newman and Graeme Newman "Crime and Punishment in the

Schooling Process: A Historical Analysis,'' in Baker and Rubel, *Violence and Crime in the Schools*, p. 14.

29. Edwin H. Sutherland and Donald R. Cressey, *Criminology*, 10th ed. (New York: Harper & Row, 1978), pp. 239–240.

30. Delbert S. Elliot and Harwin L. Voss, *Delinquency and Dropout* (Lexington, Mass.: Lexington Books, 1974).

31. U.S. Bureau of the Census, *Statistical Abstracts, 1988*, p. 137.

32. National Commission on Excellence in Education, *A Nation at Risk: The Imperative for Educational Reform* (Washington, D.C.: U.S. Government Printing Office, 1983).

33. Ibid.

34. Ibid. pp. 19–20.

35. U.S. Bureau of the Census, *Statistical Abstracts, 1988*, pp. 119, 407.

36. U.S. Bureau of the Census, *Statistical Abstracts, 1987*, p. 116.

37. Anne C. Roark, ''Teaching: Poor Marks as a Career,'' *Los Angeles Times*, March 13, 1988, Part 1, pp. 1, 3, 34.

38. Tom Hayden, ''Running Short of Good Teachers,'' *Los Angeles Times*, June 24, 1983, Part 2, p. 5.

39. Parelius and Parelius, *The Sociology of Education*, pp. 334–335.

40. John R. Berrueta-Clement et al., *Changed Lives: The Effects of the Perry Preschool Program on Youths Through Age 19*, (Ypsilanti, Mich.: High/Scope, 1984).

41. David G. Savage, ''U.S. School Aid: Looking for Results,'' *Los Angeles Times*, April 11, 1985, Part 1, p. 1.

42. Michael Rutter, *15,000 Hours: Secondary Schools and Their Effect on Children* (Cambridge, Mass.: Harvard University Press, 1979).

43. James S. Coleman, Thomas Hoffer, and Sally Kilgore, *High School Achievement: Public, Catholic and Private Schools* (New York: Basic Books, 1982), p. 178.

44. A. S. Neill, *Summerhill: A Radical Approach to Child Rearing* (New York: Hart, 1960).

45. David G. Savage, ''Is the Basics Approach Deceiving?'' *Los Angeles Times*, November 30, 1981, p. 1.

46. Jonathan H. Mark and Barry Anderson, ''Teacher Survival Rates: A Current Look,'' *American Journal of Educational Research* 15 (1978): 379–383.

47. Tom Hayden, ''Running Short of Teachers,'' *Los Angeles Times*, June 24, 1983, Part 2, p. 5.

CHAPTER 5   PROBLEMS OF THE FAMILY

1. George P. Murdock, ''World Ethnographic Sample,'' *American Anthropologist* 59 (1957): 664–687.

2. Mark Hunter, *The Changing Family: Comparative Perspectives*, 2d ed., (New York: Macmillan, 1988), pp. 532–535.

3. For an analysis of the preindustrial family see Randall Collins, *Sociology*

of Marriage and the Family, 2d ed. (Chicago, Nelson-Hall, 1988), pp. 87–149.

4. See Hunter, *The Changing Family*, pp. 28–80.

5. "Size of Average American Household Continues to Decline," San Luis Obispo *Telegram-Tribune*, May 15, 1985, p. A8; U.S. Bureau of the Census, *Statistical Abstracts of the United States, 1987* (Washington, D.C.: U.S. Government Printing Office, 1986), p. 42.

6. U.S. Bureau of the Census, *Statistical Abstracts of the United States, 1988*, (Washington, D.C.: U.S. Government Printing Office, 1987), p. 42.

7. Ibid. p. 48.

8. Louis Harris, *Inside America* (New York: Vintage Books, 1987), p. 87.

9. James C. Coleman, *Intimate Relationships, Marriage, and Family* (Indianapolis: Bobbs-Merrill, 1984), p. 335.

10. U.S. Bureau of the Census, *Statistical Abstracts, 1988*, pp. 382–383.

11. Harris, *Inside America*, p. 87.

12. Joseph Veroff, Elizabeth Douvan, and Richard A. Kulka, *The Inner American: A Self-Portrait from 1957 to 1976* (New York: Basic books, 1981).

13. Harris, *Inside America*, p. 87.

14. See Ralph Linton, "The Natural History of the Family," in Ruth N. Ashen, ed., *The Family: Its Function and Destiny* (New York: Harper & Row, 1959); Louis Wirth, "Urbanism as a Way of Life," *American Journal of Sociology* 44 (1938): 1–24; Talcott Parsons, "The Kinship System of the Contemporary United States," *American Anthropologist* 45 (1943): 22–38.

15. For a good analysis of this debate see Arlene S. Skolnick, *The Intimate Environment: Exploring Marriage and the Family* (Boston: Little, Brown, 1987), pp. 135–142.

16. Claude S. Fischer, "The Dispersion of Kinship Ties in Modern Society: Contemporary Data and Historical Speculation," *Journal of Family History* 7 (Winter): 353–375.

17. U.S. Bureau of the Census, *Statistical Abstracts, 1988*, p. 59.

18. Ibid. p. 42.

19. Collins, *Sociology of Marriage and the Family*, pp. 360–361.

20. U.S. Bureau of the Census, *Statistical Abstracts, 1988*, p. 47.

21. Collins, *Sociology of Marriage and the Family*, pp. 357–358.

22. Judith S. Wallerstein and Joan Kelley, *Surviving the Breakup: How Children and Parents Cope with Divorce* (New York: Basic Books, 1980).

23. J. Ross Eshleman, *The Family: An Introduction*, 5th ed., (Boston: Allyn & Bacon, 1988), pp. 611–615.

24. James L. Peterson and Nicholas Zill, "Marital Disruption, Parent-Child Relationships and Behavior Problems in Children," *Journal of Marriage and the Family* 48 (May 1986): 295–301.

25. U.S. Bureau of the Census, *Statistical Abstracts, 1988*, p. 61.

26. Ibid. p. 85.

27. William J. Goode, "Family Disorganization," in Robert K. Merton and Robert Nisbet, eds., *Contemporary Social Problems*, 4th ed. (New York: Harcourt Brace Jovanovich, 1987), p. 519.

28. U.S. Bureau of the Census, *Statistical Abstracts, 1988*, p. 86.
29. Zack Nauth, "Poverty Up 53 Percent Among Children New Study Finds," *Los Angeles Times*, May 23, 1985, p. 5.
30. Mildred Daley Pagelow, Family Violence (New York: Praeger, 1984), pp. 67–68.
31. Murray A. Straus, Richard J. Gelles, and Suzanne K. Steinmetz, *Behind Closed Doors: Violence in the American Family* (New York: Doubleday, 1980), pp. 37–60, 148.
32. Ibid. pp. 190–197.
33. See Eshleman, *The Family*, pp. 573–577; for a dissenting view, see Pagelow, *Family Violence*, pp. 223–257.
34. Letty Pogrebin, *Family Politics* (New York: McGraw-Hill, 1985), p. 101.
35. Straus, Gelles, and Steinmetz, *Behind Closed Doors*, pp. 190–197.
36. Samuel X. Radbill, "A History of Child Abuse and Infanticide," in Ray E. Helfer and C. Henry Kempe, eds., *The Battered Child*, 2d ed. (Chicago: University of Chicago Press, 1974).
37. Murray A. Straus and Richard J. Gelles, "Societal Change and Change in Family Violence from 1975 to 1985 as Revealed by Two National Surveys," *Journal of Marriage and the Family* 48 (August 1986): 465–479.
38. David G. Gil, *Violence Against Children: Physical Child Abuse in the United States* (Cambridge, Mass: Harvard University Press, 1970), pp. 98–99; "Violence Aginst Children," *Journal of Marriage and the Family* 33 (1971): 644–648.
39. Straus, Gelles, and Steinmetz, *Behind Closed Doors*.
40. Harris, *Inside America*, pp. 130–131.
41. U.S. Bureau of the Census, *Statistical Abstracts, 1988*, p. 48; "Size of Average Household," San Luis Obispo *Telegram-Tribune*.
42. Associated Press, "Child Support Payments Dropping" San Luis Obispo *Telegram-Tribune*, August 21, 1987, p. B7.
43. U.S. Bureau of the Census, *Statistical Abstracts, 1988*, p. 48.
44. Bob Drogin, "True Victims of Poverty: The Children," *Los Angeles Times*, July 30, 1985, p. 1.
45. Joseph Rankin, "The Family Context of Delinquency," *Social Problems* 30 (1983): 466–479.
46. See Larry J. Siegel and Joseph J. Senna, *Juvenile Delinquency: Theory, Practice, and Law*, 3d ed. (St. Paul, Minn.: West, 1988, pp. 243–246; Clemens Bartollas, *Juvenile Delinquency* (New York: John Wiley & Sons, 1985), p. 236.
47. Siegel and Senna, *Juvenile Delinquency*, p. 246.
48. Thomas C. Taveggia and Ellen M. Thomas, "Latchkey Children," *Pacific Sociological Review* 17 (1974): 27–34.
49. Sheila B. Kamerman, *Parenting in an Unresponsive Society* (New York: Free Press, 1981).
50. Harris, *Inside America*, p. 96.
51. Ibid. p. 95.
52. Coleman, *Intimate Relationships*, p. 441.

53. Myron Brenton, *The Runaways* (New York: Penguin, 1978), pp. 28–32.
54. Joan Smith, "Transforming Households: Working-Class Women and Economic Crisis," *Social Problems* 5 (December 1987): 416–436.
55. Harris, *Inside America*, p. 19.
56. Janice Peskin, "Measuring Household Production for the GNP," *Family Economics Review* (Summer 1982): 10.
57. Harris, *Inside America*, pp. 39–40.
58. U.S. Bureau of the Census, *Statistical Abstracts, 1988*, p. 83.
59. M. D. Newcomb and R. R. Bentler, "Cohabitation Before Marriage," *Journal of Marriage and the Family* 41 (February 1980); 597–602.
60. J. Jacques and K. J. Chason, "Cohabitation: Its Impact on Marital Success," *Family Coordinator* 28 (January 1979): 35–39.
61. William Masters and Virginia Johnson, *Human Sexual Inadequacy* (Boston: Little, Brown, 1970).
62. Harris, *Inside America*, p. 99.
63. Alison Clarke-Stewart, *Daycare* (Cambridge, Mass.: Harvard University Press, 1982).
64. See, for example, George P. Murdock, *Social Structure* (New York: Free Press, 1949); William J. Goode, *The Family* (Englewood Cliffs, N.J.: Prentice-Hall, 1946); Kingsley Davis, *Human Society* (New York: Macmillan, 1949).

CHAPTER 6 THE POOR

1. U.S. Bureau of the Census, *Statistical Abstracts of the United States, 1988* (Washington, D.C.: U.S. Government Printing Office, 1987), p. 433.
2. Ibid. p. 429.
3. U.S. Congress, Joint Economic Committee, *The Concentration of Wealth in the United States* (Washington, D.C.: U.S. Government Printing Office, 1986).
4. A. Kent MacDougall, "Rich-Poor Gap in U.S. Widens During Decade," *Los Angeles Times*, October 25, 1984, p. 1.
5. See for example, Malcolm Sawyer, *Income Distribution in OECD Countries* (Paris: Organization for Economic Cooperation and Development, 1976).
6. J. Larry Brown, "Hunger in the U.S." *Scientific American* 256 (February 1987): 37–41.
7. Michael Kinsley, "Yes the Rich Got Richer Under Reagan's Regime; the Poor Faired as Usual," *Los Angeles Times*, April 11, 1988, Part 2, p. 7.
8. Joint Economic Committee, *The Concentration of Wealth in the United States*.
9. John A. Byrne et al., "Who Made the Most and Why," *Business Week*, May 2, 1988, pp. 50–58.
10. Richard Mand and David C. Mowrey, *Technology and Employment: Innovation and Growth in the U.S. Economy* (Washington, D.C.: National Academy of Science, 1987), p. 24.

11. U.S. Bureau of the Census, *Statistical Abstracts of the United States, 1987*, p. 74; Michael Parenti, *Democracy for the Few*, 3d ed. (New York: St. Martin's Press, 1980), pp. 41–42.
12. U.S. Bureau of the Census, *Statistical Abstracts, 1988*, p. 406.
13. See Paul Blumberg, *Inequality in an Age of Decline* (New York: Oxford University Press, 1980), pp. 65–107.
14. McDougall, "Rich–Poor Gap."
15. U.S. Bureau of the Census, *Statistical Abstracts, 1976*, p. 443.
16. U.S. Bureau of the Census, *Statistical Abstracts, 1988*, p. 436.
17. Ibid. p. 50.
18. Ibid. p. 437.
19. Ibid. p. 437.
20. Joe Davidson, "Differing Social Programs for Young, Old Results in Different Poverty Rates for Two Groups," *Wall Street Journal*, August 12, 1985, pp. 1, 14–15.
21. U.S. Bureau of the Census, *Statistical Abstracts, 1988*, p. 435.
22. Ibid, p. 429.
23. U.S. Bureau of the Census, *Characteristics of the Population Below the Poverty Level, 1984* (Washington, D.C.: U.S. Government Printing Office, 1988).
24. Greg J. Duncan, *Years of Poverty, Years of Plenty: The Changing Economic Fortunes of American Workers and Families* (Ann Arbor: Institute for Social Research, 1984).
25. Ken Auletta, *The Underclass* (New York: Vintage Books, 1983), p. 27.
26. Mary J. Bane and David T. Ellwood, "Slipping Into and Out of Poverty: The Dynamics of Spells," Working Paper No. 1199, National Bureau of Economic Research, Cambridge, Mass., 1983.
27. William Julius Wilson, *The Truly Disadvantaged: The Inner City, The Underclass and Public Policy* (Chicago: University of Chicago Press, 1987), pp. 6–8.
28. See Harold R. Kerbo, *Social Stratification and Inequality* (New York: McGraw-Hill, 1983), pp. 329–402.
29. Ellen L. Bassuk, "The Homelessness Problem," *Scientific American*, July 1984, pp. 40–45.
30. *Sacramento Bee*, June 12, 1988.
31. James D. Wright, "The Mentally Ill Homeless: What is Myth and What is Fact?" *Social Problems* 35 (April 1988):182–191.
32. David A. Snow, Susan G. Baker, Leon Anderson, and Michael Martin, "The Myth of Mental Illness Among the Homeless," *Social Problems* 33 (June 1986): 407–423.
33. Wright, "The Mentally Ill Homeless."
34. U.S. Bureau of the Census, *Current Population Reports: Consumer Income* (Washington, D.C.: U.S. Government Printing Office, 1985).
35. David Whitman et al., "America's Hidden Poor," *U.S. News and World Report*, January 11, 1988, pp. 20–24.
36. U.S. Bureau of the Census, *Statistical Abstracts, 1988*, p. 406.

37. Joe R. Feagin, *Subordinating the Poor: Welfare and American Beliefs* (Englewood Cliffs, N.J.: Prentice-Hall, 1975), pp. 91–92.
38. Ibid. p. 97.
39. Francis Fox Piven and Richard A. Cloward, *Regulating the Poor: The Functions of Public Welfare* (New York: Vintage Books, 1971): Michael Betz, "Riots and Welfare: Are They Related?" *Social Problems* 21 (1974): 345–355; Larry Isaac and William Kelly, "Racial Insurgency, the State and Welfare Expansion," *American Sociological Review* 45 (1980): 1348–1386.
40. Feagin, *Subordinating the Poor*, pp. 17–24.
41. Ibid. pp. 24–28.
42. Piven and Cloward, *Regulating the Poor*, pp. 61–62.
43. Ibid. pp. 184–185.
44. Daniel Patrick Moynihan, *The Politics of a Guaranteed Income: The Nixon Administration and the Family Assistance Plan* (New York: Random House, 1973).
45. Bob Drogin, "True Victims of Poverty: The Children," *Los Angeles Times*, July 30, 1985, pp. 1, 10–11; Kevin Roderick, "Case History of a 20-Year War on Poverty," *Los Angeles Times*, July 31, 1985, pp. 1, 8–9.
46. Alfred Kahn and Sheila Kammer, "Income Maintenance, Wages and Family Income," *Public Welfare*, Fall 1983, p. 28.
47. Marian Edelman, *Families in Peril* (Cambridge: Harvard University Press, 1987).
48. Elliot Currie and Jerome Skolnick, *America's Problems*, 2d ed. (Glenview, Ill.: Scott-Foresman, 1988), p. 120.
49. U.S. Bureau of the Census, *Statistical Abstracts, 1988*, p. 333.
50. U.S. Department of Health and Human Services, *Aid to Families with Dependent Children: A Chartbook* (Washington, D.C.: U.S. Government Printing Office, 1979).
51. Robert J. Samuelson, "Economy Needs More Than a Slogan," *Los Angeles Times*, February 25, 1988, Part 2, p. 7.
52. Bureau of Labor Statistics, *BLS News*, March 1988, pp. 2–3.
53. Lee May, "Hard-Core Jobless Have Little Hope," *Los Angeles Times*, June 6, 1988, Part 1, pp. 1, 12.
54. See Paul Jacobs, "Keeping the Poor Poor," in Jerome Skolnick and Elliott Currie, eds., *Crisis in American Institutions*, 5th ed. (Boston: Little, Brown, 1988), pp. 134–140.
55. Oscar Lewis, *La Vida* (New York: Random House, 1965), pp. xlii–lii.
56. Ibid.
57. Charles A. Valentine, *Culture and Poverty: Critique and Counter-Proposals* (Chicago: University of Chicago Press, 1968).
58. Herbert J. Gans, "The Uses of Poverty: The Poor Pay All," *Social Policy* 2 (1971): 21–23.
59. Associated Press, "Report: Poor Pay More in Sales Tax," *Los Angeles Times*, March 25, 1988, Part 4, p. 5.
60. Michael Harrington, "Inequality Haunts America as Taxes Favor Rich,

Penalize the Middle Class," *Los Angeles Times*, January 24, 1988, Part 5, p. 3.

61. David Whitman, "The Key to Welfare Reform," *The Atlantic*, June 1987, p. 23.

62. May, "Hard-Core Jobless," pp. 1–2.

63. Whitman, "Key to Welfare Reform," p. 25.

64. Kinsgley Davis and Wilbert E. Moore, "Some Principles of Stratification," *American Sociological Review* 10 (1945): 242–249.

CHAPTER 7   THE ETHNIC MINORITIES

1. Richard T. Schaefer, *Racial and Ethnic Groups*, 3d ed. (Glenview, Ill.: Scott-Foresman, 1988), pp. 9–10.

2. Ibid. pp. 473–478.

3. Ibid. p. 56.

4. See Paula S. Rothenberg, *Racism and Sexism: An Integrated Study* (New York: St. Martin's Press, 1988), p. 20.

5. Gordon W. Allport, *The Nature of Prejudice* (New York: Doubleday, 1956), p. 10.

6. Robert K. Merton, "Discrimination and the American Creed," in Robert M. MacIver, ed., *Discrimination and National Welfare* (New York: Harper & Row, 1949).

7. T. W. Adorno, E. Frenkel-Brunswik, D. J. Devinson, and R. N. Sandord, *The Authoritarian Personality* (New York: Harper & Row, 1950).

8. John Dallard, L. Doob, N. E. Miller, O. H. Mowrer, and R. R. Sears, *Frustration and Aggression* (New Haven, Conn.: Yale University Press, 1939).

9. See Judith Andre, "Stereotypes: Conceptual and Normative Considerations," in Rothenburg, *Racism and Sexism*, pp. 257–262.

10. For a Marxist analysis of the problems of racism and sexism, see Angela Y. Davis, *Women, Race and Class* (New York: Vintage Books, 1983).

11. Schaefer, *Racial and Ethnic Groups*, pp. 176–177.

12. Nancy Oestreich Lurie, "The American Indian: Historical Background," in Norman Yetman and C. Hoy Steel, eds., *Minority and Majority: The Dynamics of Racial and Ethnic Relations*, 4th ed. (Boston: Allyn & Bacon, 1985).

13. Schaefer, *Racial and Ethnic Groups*, p. 177.

14. Lurie, "The American Indian," p. 179.

15. Calculated from U.S. Bureau of the Census, *Statistical Abstracts of the United States, 1988* (Washington, D.C.: U.S. Government Printing Office, 1987), p. 10.

16. U.S. Bureau of the Census, *Statistical Abstracts, 1988*, p. 167.

17. Kurt Andersen, "New York: Final Destination," *Time*, July 8, 1985, pp. 36–39; William R. Doerner, "Asians: To America with Skills," *Time*, July 8, 1985, pp. 32–34.

18. U.S. Bureau of the Census, *Statistical Abstracts, 1988*, p. 125.

19. Carol McGraw, "Untold Human Need Found in Asian Community," *Los Angeles Times,* July 28, 1988, Part 2, pp. 1, 4.

20. Joseph H. Cash, "Indian Education: A Bright Path or Another Dead End?" in editors of the Winston Press, *Viewpoints: Red and Yellow, Black and Brown* (Groveland Terrace, Minn.: Winston Press, 1972), p. 14.

21. U.S. Bureau of the Census, *Statistical Abstracts, 1988,* p. 376.

22. Ibid. p. 422.

23. Ibid. p. 430.

24. U.S. Bureau of the Census, *1980 Census of Population and Housing Supplemental Report. Provisional Estimates of Social Economic and Housing Characteristics* (Washington, D.C.: U.S. Government Printing Office, 1982).

25. Ronald Takaki, "Asian Successes are Misleading," *San Francisco Chronicle,* February 9, 1985.

26. U.S. Bureau of the Census, *Statistical Abstracts, 1988,* p. 365.

27. Ibid. p. 429.

28. Jim Schachter, "Unequal Opportunity: Minorities Find that Roadblocks to the Executive Suite Are Still in Place," *Los Angeles Times,* April 17, 1988, Part 4, p. 1.

29. Quoted by Charles E. Reasons and Jack E. Kuykendall, eds., *Race, Crime and Justice* (Pacific Palisades, Calif.: Goodyear, 1972).

30. See D. Stanley Eitzen and Doug A. Timmer, *Criminology* (New York: John Wiley & Sons, 1985), pp. 439–445.

31. U.S. Bureau of the Census, *America's Black Population: A Statistical View* (Washington, D.C.: U.S. Government Printing Office, 1983), p. 23.

32. U.S. Bureau of the Census, *Statistical Abstracts, 1988,* p. 690.

33. James W. Vander Zanden, *American Minority Relations,* 4th ed. (New York: Knopf, 1983), p. 206; National Center for Health Statistics, *Health: United States, 1984* (Washington, D.C.: U.S. Government Printing Office, 1984), p. 53.

34. William Julius Wilson, *The Declining Significance of Race: Blacks and Changing American Institutions* (Chicago: University of Chicago Press, 1978).

35. U.S. Bureau of the Census, *Statistical Abstracts, 1988,* p. 70.

36. Ibid. p. 76.

37. Isabel Wilkerson, "Twenty Years After the Kerner Report: Three Societies, All Separate," *New York Times,* February 29, 1988, p. B8.

38. For a review of this research see Schaefer, *Racial and Ethnic Groups,* pp. 84–88.

39. Schaefer, *Racial and Ethnic Groups,* pp. 108–110.

40. Louis Harris, *Inside America* (New York: Vintage, 1987), pp. 188–192.

41. U.S. Bureau of the Census, *Statistical Abstracts, 1988,* p. 430.

42. George Ramos, "Rights Groups Urge Liberal Rules for 2nd Phase of Amnesty Program," *Los Angeles Times,* June 21, 1988, Part 1, p. 15.

43. "American Indians: Beggars in Our Own Land," *U.S. News and World Report,* May 23, 1983, pp. 70–72.

44. Amy I. Stevens, "Reagan View of Indians Called 'Ignorant,' " *Los Angeles Times,* June 8, 1988, Part 2, p. 3.

CHAPTER 8   THE SICK AND THE HEALTH CARE SYSTEM

1. Quoted in Paul I. Ahmed and Aliza Kolker, "The Role of Indigenous Medicine in WHO's Definition of Health," in Paul I. Ahmed and George V. Coelhi, eds., *Toward A New Definition of Health* (New York: Plenum, 1979), p. 113.

2. John B. McKinlay and Sonja M. McKinlay, "Medical Measures and the Decline of Mortality," in Howard D. Schwartz, ed., *Dominant Issues in Medical Sociology*, 2d ed. (New York: Random House, 1987), pp. 691–702.

3. U.S. Bureau of the Census, *Statistical Abstracts of the United States, 1988* (Washington, D.C.: U.S. Government Printing Office, 1987), p. 77.

4. See William L. Haskell, "Overview: Health Benefits of Exercise," in Joseph D. Matarazzo et al., eds., *Behavioral Health: A Handbook of Health Enhancement and Disease Prevention* (New York: Wiley, 1984), pp. 409–423; James F. Fixx, *The Complete Book of Running* (New York: Random House, 1977), p. 51.

5. See D. M. Hegsted, "What is a Healthful Diet?" in Matarazzo et al., *Behavioral Health*, pp. 552–574.

6. Otto Schaefer, "Pre- and Post-Natal Growth Acceleration and Increase in Sugar Consumption in Canadian Eskimos," *Canadian Medical Association Journal* 103 (1970): 1059–1060.

7. A. Keys et al., "Lessons from Serum Cholesterol Studies in Japan, Hawaii, and Los Angeles," *Annals of Internal Medicine* 48 (1958): 83.

8. *Newsweek*, January 22, 1979.

9. U.S. Bureau of the Census, *Statistical Abstracts, 1988*, pp. 114–115.

10. *Surgeon General's Report on Nutrition and Health* (Washington, D.C.: U.S. Government Printing Office, 1988).

11. Hegsted, "What is a Healthful Diet?"

12. Associated Press, "Koop: Tobacco like Heroin, Cocaine," San Luis Obispo (Calif.) *Telegram Tribune*, May 16, 1988, p. A1; Oakley Ray, *Drugs, Society and Human Behavior*, 3d ed., (St. Louis: C.V. Mosby, 1983), pp. 183–205; U.S. Department of Health and Human Services, *Smoking and Health: A Report of the Surgeon General* (Washington, D.C.: U.S. Government Printing Office, 1979).

13. Sidney Cobb and Robert M. Rose, "Hypertension, Peptic Ulcer, and Diabetes in Air Traffic Controllers," *Journal of the American Medical Association* 224 (1973): 489–492.

14. *New York Times*, April 3, 1983.

15. Sana Siwolop, "Stress: The Test Americans Are Failing," *Business Week*, April 18, 1988, pp. 74–76.

16. C. M. Parkes, B. Benjamin, and R. G. Fitzgerald, "Broken Heart: A Statistical Study of Increased Mortality Among Widowers," *British Medical Journal* 50 (1969): 740–743.

17. R. L. Taylor, "The Widowed: Risks and Interventions," *Wellness Resource Bulletin* 2 (1981): 1, California Department of Mental Health, Mental Health Promotion Branch.

18. James William Coleman, *The Criminal Elite: The Sociology of White Collar Crime*, 2d ed. (New York: St. Martin's Press, 1989), pp. 1–2, 35–36.

19. U.S. Department of Labor, *Interim Report to Congress on Occupational Diseases* (Washington, D.C.: U.S. Government Printing Office, June 1980), pp. 1–2; Patrick Derr et al., "Worker Public Protection: The Double Standard," *Environment*, September 1981.

20. John H. Dingle, "Ills of Man," in *Life and Death and Medicine* (San Francisco: W. H. Freeman, 1973), p. 53.

21. U.S. Bureau of the Census, *Statistical Abstracts of the United States, 1988* (Washington, D.C.: U.S. Government Printing Office, 1987), p. 106; Jonas Morris, *Searching for a Cure: National Health Policy Reconsidered* (New York: Pica Press, 1984), p. 189.

22. Howard Hiatt, *America's Health in the Balance: Choice or Chance?* (New York: Harper & Row, 1987), p. 121.

23. Marlene Cimons, "AIDS Panel Endorses Stiffer Anti-Bias Laws," *Los Angeles Times*, June 18, 1988, Part 1, pp. 1, 23.

24. Ann Fairbanks, "AIDS Frustrates County Health Workers," San Luis Obispo (Calif.) *Telegram-Tribune*, February 20, 1988.

25. Josh Getlin, "AIDS and Minorities: Fear, Ignorance Cited," *Los Angeles Times*, August 10, 1987, Part 1, pp. 1, 12.

26. Cimons, "AIDS Panel."

27. Robert Steinbrook, "AIDS Threat Changes Life Style of 1 in 5," *Los Angeles Times*, July 30, 1987, Part 1, pp. 1, 28; Robert Steinbrook, "42% Would Limit Civil Right in AIDS Battle," *Los Angeles Times*, July 31, 1987, Part 1, pp. 1, 21.

28. "AIDS: A Gobal Assessment," special supplement to the *Los Angeles Times*, August 9, 1987, p. 2.

29. Hiatt, *America's Health*, p. 121.

30. U.S. Bureau of the Census, *Statistical Abstracts, 1988*, p. 800.

31. U.S. Bureau of the Census, *Statistical Abstracts, 1988*, p. 75; S. Leonard Syme and Lisa F. Berkman, "Social Class, Susceptibility, and Sickness," in Schwartz, *Dominant Issues in Medical Sociology*, pp. 643–699.

32. U.S. Department of Human Services, *Health: United States, 1986* (Washington, D.C.: U.S. Government Printing Office, 1986), p. 20.

33. Syme and Berkman, "Social Class, Susceptibility, and Sickness," p. 644.

34. U.S. Bureau of the Census, *Statistical Abstracts, 1988*, p. 86.

35. Ibid. p. 800.

36. Harry Nelson and Anne C. Ruark, "Health Care Crisis: Less for More," *Los Angeles Times*, April 7, 1985, p. 1.

37. See Harold R. Kerbo, *Social Stratification and Inequality: Class Conflict in the United States* (New York: McGraw-Hill, 1983), pp. 175–177.

38. U.S. Bureau of the Census, *Statistical Abstracts, 1988*, p. 95.

39. Ibid. p. 93.

40. Marilyn Chase, "Will the Surplus of M.D.'s Be Good for Patients? A Look at San Francisco," *Wall Street Journal*, March 3, 1980, p. 1.

41. Howard D. Schwartz, "Irrationality as a Feature of Health Care in the United States," in Schwartz, ed., *Dominant Issues in Medical Sociology*, p. 478.

42. U. S. Bureau of the Census, *Statistical Abstracts, 1987*, p. 822.
43. Calculated from data in U.S. Bureau of the Census, *Statistical Abstracts, 1988*, pp. 13, 95.
44. Schwartz, "Irrationality as a Feature of Health Care in the United States."
45. *Los Angeles Times*, May 12, 1976.
46. *Los Angeles Times*, December 27, 1978.
47. Robert Steinbrook, "Thousands of Surgeries Called Unnecessary," *Los Angeles Times*, November 13, 1987, Part 1, pp. 1, 30.
48. Schwartz, "Irrationality as a Feature of Health Care in the United States," p. 477.
49. U.S. Bureau of the Census, *Statistical Abstracts, 1988*, p. 376.
50. Schwartz, "Irrationality as a Feature of Health Care in the United States," p. 477.
51. K. Steel, P. M. Gertman, C. Crescsenzi, and J. Anderson, "Iatrogenic Illness on a General Medical Service at a University Hospital," *The New England Journal of Medicine* 304 (1981): 638–642.
52. Boyce Rensberger, "Thousands a Year Killed by Faulty Prescriptions," *The New York Times*, January 28, 1976, p. 1.
53. See Howard D. Schwartz, Peggy L. DeWolf, and James K. Skipper, "Gender, Professionalization and Occupational Anomie: The Case of Nursing," in Schwartz, *Dominant Issues in Medical Sociology*, pp. 559–569.
54. Daniel S. Greenberg, "Lawyers' Pay Would Cure Nursing Shortage," *Los Angeles Times*, June 12, 1988, Part 5, p. 5; Associated Press, "House Leader: Cut Docs' Pay to Control Medicare," San Luis Obispo (Calif.) *Telegram-Tribune*, September 16, 1987, p. A10.
55. Greenberg, "Lawyers' Pay."
56. Nelson and Roark, "Health Care Crisis."
57. Associated Press, "Hospital Costs Up 16 Percent Nationwide in 1987," San Luis Obispo (Calif.) *Telegram-Tribune*, January 6, 1988.
58. U.S. Bureau of the Census, *Statistical Abstracts, 1988*, p. 99.
59. See David Mechanic, *From Advocacy to Allocation: The Evolving American Health Care System* (New York: Free Press, 1986), pp. 1–23.
60. Robert A. Rosenblatt, "Medicare Cuts Place Hospitals on Critical List," *Los Angeles Times*, Part 4, pp. 1, 13.
61. U.S. Bureau of the Census, *Statistical Abstracts, 1988*, p. 86.
62. See Coleman, *The Criminal Elite*, pp. 112–118.
63. U.S. Bureau of the Census, *Statistical Abstracts, 1988*, p. 89.
64. Harry Nelson, "Malpractice Suits: A New Epidemic Faced by Doctors," *Los Angeles Times*, April 1, 1985, pp. 1, 19–20.
65. Also see Irwin Press, "Predisposition to File Claims: The Patients' Perspective," *Law, Medicine and Health Care* 12 (1984): pp. 33–62.
66. U.S. Bureau of the Census, *Statistical Abstracts, 1988*, p. 86.
67. Claire Spiegel, "Number of Californians Not Covered by Health Insurance Jumps 50%," *Los Angeles Times*, August 2, 1988, Part 1, pp. 1, 18.
68. Associated Press, "Nursing Homes Impoverish Elderly," San Luis Obispo (Calif.) *Telegram-Tribune*, November 9, 1987.

69. Ellen Hume, "Medicaid Fraud Efforts Termed Disaster," *Los Angeles Times*, March 27, 1982, p. 6.

70. Robert A. Rosenblatt and Jonathan Peterson, ,"Medicare Change Stirs Concern for the Elderly," *Los Angeles Times*, April 14, 1985, pp. 1, 20–21.

71. Alan Maynard, *Health Care in the European Community* (Pittsburgh: University of Pittsburgh Press, 1975), pp. 196–197.

72. Harry Nelson, "Crisis Grips Health Care in Britain," *Los Angeles Times*, March 7, 1988, Part 1, pp. 1, 8.

73. Caroline Kaufmann, "Rights and the Provision of Health Care: A Comparison of Canada, Great Britain, and the United States," in Schwartz, *Dominant Issues in Medical Sociology*, pp. 491–508.

74. Nelson, "Crisis Grips Health Care in Britain."

75. Kaufmann, "Rights and the Provision of Health Care."

76. Ibid. p. 493

77. U.S. National Center for Health Statistics, *Health: United States, 1986* (Washington, D.C.: U.S. Government Printing Office, 1987), p. 94.

78. Roxane Arnold, "Medicine's Best Only Delayed the Inevitable," *Los Angeles Times*, April 7, 1985, Part 1, pp. 24, 26.

79. Schwartz, DeWolf, and Skipper, "Gender, Professionalization, and Occupational Anomie."

80. Allan Parachini, "Health Care Debate: Who Will Pay the Way?" *Los Angeles Times*, August 30, 1987, Part 6, p. 1.

81. Mechanic, *From Advocacy to Allocation.*

82. Paul Starr, *The Social Transformation of American Medicine* (New York: Basic Books, 1982).

83. R. H. Rosenman et al., "Coronary Heart Disease in Western Collaborative Group Study—A Follow-Up Experience of 4½ Years," *Journal of Chronic Disease,* 23 (1970).

CHAPTER 9   THE OLD AND THE YOUNG

1. See Vern L. Bullough, "Age at Menarche; A Misunderstanding," *Science* 213 (1981): 365–366.

2. P. B. Baltes and S. L. Willis, "Enhancement of Intellectual Functioning in Old Age: Penn State's Adult Development and Enrichment Program," in F. I. M. Craik and S. E. Trehrib, eds., *Aging and Cognitive Process* (New York: Plenum, 1982).

3. Philippe Ariès, *Centuries of Childhood: A Social History of Family Life* (New York: Vintage, 1962).

4. Stanley Hall, *Adolescence: Its Psychology and Its Relations to Physiology, Anthropology, Sociology, Sex, Crime, Religion and Education* (New York: Appleton, 1904).

5. See Daniel J. Levinson, *The Seasons of a Man's Life* (New York: Alfred A. Knopf, 1978).

6. U.S. Bureau of the Census, *Statistical Abstracts of the United States, 1988* (Washington, D.C.: U.S. Government Printing Office, 1987), p. 435.

7. Elizabeth Douvan, "The Age of Narcissism, 1963–1982," in Joseph M. Hawes and N. Ray Hiner, eds., *American Childhood: A Research Guide and Historical Handbook* (Westport, Conn.: Greenwood Press, 1985), pp. 587–617.

8. Erik H. Erikson, *Childhood and Society,* rev. ed. (New York: W. W. Norton, 1964).

9. Hans Sebald, *Adolescence: A Social Psychological Analysis* (Englewood Cliffs, N.J.: Prentice-Hall, 1984).

10. U.S. Department of Justice, *Sourcebook of Criminal Justice Statistics— 1986* (Washington, D.C.: U.S. Government Printing Office, 1987), p. 195.

11. See Clemens Bartollas, *Juvenile Deliquency* (New York: John Wiley & Sons, 1985), pp. 185–192, 262–286.

12. U.S. Bureau of the Census, *Statistical Abstracts, 1988*, p. 82.

13. Claudia Wallis, "Children Having Children," *Time,* December 9, 1985, pp. 78–90.

14. U.S. Bureau of the Census, *Statistical Abstracts, 1988*, p. 435.

15. Ibid. p. 432.

16. Ibid. p. 381.

17. Ibid. p. 15.

18. Arthur N. Schwartz, Cherie L. Snyder, and James A. Peterson, *Aging and Life,* 2d ed. (New York: Holt, Rinehart & Winston, 1984), pp, 37–38.

19. National Center for Health Statistics, *Health: United States, 1982* (Washington, D.C.: U.S. Government Printing Office, 1982), p. 80.

20. Fred Cottrell, *Aging and the Aged* (Dubuque, Ia.: Brown, 1974), p. 19.

21. U.S. Bureau of the Census, *Statistical Abstracts, 1988*, p. 435.

22. Joe Davidson, "Differing Social Problems for Young, Old Result in Contrasting Poverty Level for Two Groups," *Wall Street Journal,* June 27, 1985, p. 60.

23. U.S. Bureau of the Census, *Statistical Abstracts, 1988*, p. 435.

24. Ibid. p. 366.

25. Ibid. p. 344.

26. Beth B. Hess and Elizabeth Markson, eds., *Growing Old in America,* 3rd. ed. (New Brunswick, N.J.: Transaction Books, 1985), p. 14.

27. U.S. Bureau of the Census, *Statistical Abstracts, 1988*, p. 342.

28. Robert A. Rosenblatt and Jonathan Peterson, "Healthy Future Seen for Social Security," *Los Angeles Times,* August 12, 1985, pp. 1, 14–15.

29. Hess and Markson, *Growing Old in America*, p. 8.

30. Herman J. Loether, *Problems of Aging: Sociological and Social Psychological Perspectives,* 2d ed. (Encino, Calif.: Dickenson, 1975), p. 86.

31. See Walter R. Cunningham and John W. Brookbank, *Gerontology* (New York: Harper & Row, 1988), pp. 228–245; Robert C. Atchley, *The Sociology of Retirement* (Cambridge, Mass.: Schenkman, 1976), pp. 87–108.

32. Cunningham and Brookbank, *Gerontology*, pp. 247–248.

33. Schwartz et al., *Aging and Life*, pp. 281–300.

34. Elisabeth Kübler-Ross, *Questions and Answers on Death and Dying* (New York: Macmillan, 1985).

35. See Schwartz et al., *Aging and Life,* pp. 286–287.
36. See Jon Hendricks and C. David Hendricks, *Aging in Mass Society: Myths and Realities,* 2d ed., (Cambridge, Mass.: Winthrop, 1981), pp. 14–18.

CHAPTER 10   WOMEN AND MEN

1. See, for example, Hilary M. Lips, *Sex and Gender* (Mountain View, Calif.: Mayfield, 1988), pp. 1–26; Laurel Richardson, *The Dynamics of Sex and Gender: A Sociological Perspective* (New York: Harper & Row, 1988), pp. 9–12.
2. Suzanne M. Bianchi and Daphne Spain, *American Women in Transition* (New York: Russell Sage Foundation, 1986).
3. See, for example, Ann Ferguson, "Androgyny As an Ideal for Human Development," in Paula S. Rothenberg, ed., *Racism and Sexism: An Integrated Study* (New York: St. Martin's Press, 1988), pp. 362–371.
4. Sandra L. Bem, "Androgyny and Gender Schema Theory," in T. B. Sonderegger, ed., *Nebraska Symposium on Motivation: Psychology of Gender* (Lincoln, Neb.: University of Nebraska Press, 1985).
5. Jane B. Lancaster and Chet S. Lancaster, "The Watershed: Changes in Parental Investment and Family Formation Strategies in the Course of Human Evolution," in Jane B. Lancaster et al., eds., *Parenting Across the Lifespan* (New York: Aldine de Gruyter, 1988), p. 191.
6. See Lips, *Sex and Gender,* pp. 199–207.
7. Ibid. pp. 105–109.
8. Bruce Svare and Craig H. Kinsley, "Hormones and Sex-Related Behavior," in Kathryn Kelley, ed., *Females, Males and Sexuality: Theories and Research* (Albany: State University of New York Press, 1987), pp. 13–58.
9. Lips, *Sex and Gender,* p. 117.
10. Richardson, *The Dynamics of Sex and Gender,* p. 145.
11. See, for example, Richard Borshay Lee, *The !Kung San: Men, Women and Work in a Foraging Society* (Cambridge: Cambridge University Press, 1979); Margaret Mead, *Sex and Temperament in Three Primitive Societies,* (New York: Mentor Books, 1935).
12. James A. Doyle, *The Male Experience* (Dubuque, Ia.: Wm. Brown, 1983), pp. 82–85.
13. Margaret L. Andersen, *Thinking About Women: Sociological Perspectives on Sex and Gender,* 2d ed. (New York: Macmillan, 1988), pp. 49–52; John Money and A. A. Ehrhardt, *Man, Woman, Boy and Girl: The Differentiation and Dimorphism of Gender Identity from Conception to Maturity* (Baltimore: Johns Hopkins University Press, 1972).
14. Ernestine Friedl, *Women and Men: An Anthropologist's View* (New York: Holt, Rinehart & Winston, 1975), p. 31.
15. See, for example, Eleanor Leacock, "Women's Status in Egalitarian Society: Implications for Social Evolution," *Current Anthropology* 19 (June 1978): 247–255.
16. Friedl, *Women and Men,* pp. 61–64.

17. Richardson, *Dynamics of Sex Gender*, pp. 155–156.
18. Bianchi and Spain, *American Women in Transition*.
19. Anderson, *Thinking About Women*, pp. 82–83.
20. See Richardson, *Dynamics of Sex and Gender*, pp. 16–34; Simone de Beauvoir, *The Second Sex* (New York: Alfred A. Knopf, 1957).
21. Ruth E. Hartley, "Sex-Role Pressures and the Socialization of the Male Child," in Deborah S. David and Robert Brannon, eds., *The Forty-nine Percent Majority: The Male Sex Role* (Reading, Mass.: Addison-Wesley, 1976), p. 236.
22. Leslie Brody, "Gender Difference in Emotional Development: A Review of Theory and Research," *Journal of Personality* 53 (1985): 102–149.
23. Lips, *Sex and Gender*, pp. 232–233.
24. Richardson, *Dynamics of Sex and Gender*, pp. 56–59.
25. Myra Sadker, David Sadker, and Susan S. Klein, "Abolishing Misconceptions About Sex Equity in Education," *Theory into Practice* 25 (Autumn 1986): 220.
26. Beverly A. Stitt, *Building Gender Fairness in Schools* (Carbondale, Ill.: Southern Illinois University Press, 1988), pp. 29–32.
27. John Ernest, "Mathematics and Sex," *American Mathematical Monthly* 83 (1976): 595–614.
28. Alison Kelly, *Changing Schools and Changing Society: Some Reflections on the Girls in Sciences and Technology Project* (New York: The Open University, 1984).
29. J. H. Feldstein and S. Feldstein, "Sex Differences on Televised Toy Commercials," *Sex Roles* 8 (1982): 581–587.
30. F. E. Barcus, *Commercial Children's Television on Weekends and Weekday Afternoons* (Newtonville, Mass.: Action for Children's Television, 1982).
31. N. S. Feldman and E. Brown, "Male Versus Female Differences in Control Strategies: What Children Learn from Saturday Morning Television" (paper presented at the Eastern Psychological Association, Baltimore, April 1984).
32. For a summary of these studies see Lips, *Sex and Gender*, p. 229.
33. Michael Morgan, "Television and Adolescents' Sex Role Stereotypes: A Longitudinal Study," *Journal of Personality and Social Psychology* 43 (1982): 947–955.
34. See Richardson, *Dynamics of Sex and Gender*, pp. 69–82.
35. Cynthia Fuchs Epstein, "Sex Roles," in Robert Merton and Robert Nisbet, eds., *Contemporary Social Problems*, 4th ed. (New York: Harcourt Brace Jovanovich, 1976), pp. 431, 437.
36. U.S. Bureau of the Census, *Statistical Abstracts of the United States, 1988* (Washington, D.C.: U.S. Government Printing Office, 1987), pp. 141, 142.
37. Ibid. p. 149.
38. Ibid. p. 366.
39. Francine D. Blau and Marianne A. Ferber, *The Economics of Women, Men, and Work* (Englewood Cliffs, N.J.: Prentice-Hall, 1986), pp.

310–311; Don Irwin, "Women's Status: Sweden Put First, Bangladesh Last," *Los Angeles Times*, June 27, 1988, Part 1, pp. 1, 8.

40. Sara E. Rix, ed., *The American Woman 1987–88: A Report in Depth* (New York: W. W. Norton, 1987).
41. Ibid.
42. U.S. Bureau of the Census, *Statistical Abstracts, 1988*, p. 395.
43. Barbara R. Bergmann, *The Economic Emergence of Women* (New York: Basic Books, 1986), pp. 119–145; Blau and Ferber, *Women, Men, and Work.*
44. U.S. Bureau of the Census, *Statistical Abstracts, 1988*, pp. 376–377.
45. Jim Schachter, "Unequal Opportunity," *Los Angeles Times*, April 17, 1988, Part 4, p. 1 passim.
46. Ann M. Morrison, "Up Against a Glass Ceiling," *Los Angeles Times*, August 23, 1987, Part 4, p. 3.
47. Blau and Ferber, *Women, Men, and Work*, pp. 152–181.
48. U.S. Bureau of the Census, *Statistical Abstracts, 1988*, p. 376
49. Richardson, *Dynamics of Sex and Gender*, p. 161.
50. Ibid. pp. 162–163.
51. See Lips, *Sex and Gender*, pp. 145–146.
52. Eileen Putman, "Sex Harassment on U.S. Payroll," *Sacramento Bee*, June 30, 1988, pp. A1, A30.
53. See Josephine Donovan, *Feminist Theory* (New York: Frederick Ungar, 1985); Andersen, *Thinking About Women*, pp. 287–361.
54. See Richardson, *Dynamics of Sex and Gender*, pp. 248–250.

CHAPTER 11   SEXUAL BEHAVIOR

1. Clellan S. Ford and Frank A. Beach, *Patterns of Sexual Behavior* (New York: Ace Books, 1951), p. 14.
2. William H. Davenport, "Sex in Cross-Cultural Perspective," in Frank A. Beach, ed., *Human Sexuality in Four Perspectives* (Baltimore: Johns Hopkins University Press, 1977), p. 124.
3. Ian Robertson, *Sociology*, 3d ed. (New York: Worth, 1987), pp. 227–229.
4. Davenport, "Sex in Cross-Cultural Perspective," pp. 122–124.
5. Ibid. p. 125.
6. Conrad Phillip Kottak, *Cultural Anthropology*, 4th ed. (New York: Random House, 1987), pp. 152–153. For a more detailed description of the homosexual tribes of New Guinea, see V. van Baal, *Dema: Description and Analysis of Marid Anim Culture* (The Hague: M. Nijhoff, 1966).
7. Quoted in Robertson, *Sociology*, p. 230.
8. Alfred C. Kinsey, Wardell B. Pomeroy, and Clyde E. Martin, *Sexual Behavior in the Human Male* (Philadelphia: Saunders, 1948); Alfred C. Kinsey, Wardell B. Pomeroy, Clyde E. Martin, and Paul H. Gebhard, *Sexual Behavior in the Human Female* (Philadelphia: Saunders, 1953).
9. Morton Hunt, *Sexual Behavior in the 1970s* (New York: Dell, 1974), pp. 147–149.

10. Kinsey et al., *Human Female*, p. 333; Hunt, *Sexual Behavior*, p. 150.
11. F. Shah and M. Zelnick, "Sexuality in Adolescence," in B. B. Wolman and J. Money, eds., *Handbook of Human Sexuality* (Englewood Cliffs, N.J.: Prentice-Hall, 1980).
12. James Leslie McCary and Stephen P. McCary, *McCary's Human Sexuality* (Belmont, Calif.: Wadsworth, 1982), p. 391.
13. Hunt, *Sexual Behavior*, p. 34; Kinsey et al., *Human Male*, p. 386.
14. See McCary and McCary, *Human Sexuality*, pp. 367–369, 382–389.
15. Ibid. pp. 446–450.
16. Ibid. p. 431.
17. Gerald R. Adams and Thomas Gullotta, *Adolescent Life Experiences* (Monterey, Calif.: Brooks/Cole, 1983), pp. 330–335.
18. U.S. Bureau of the Census, *Statistical Abstracts of the United States, 1988* (Washington, D.C.: U.S. Government Printing Office, 1987), p. 62.
19. Claudia Wallis, "Children Having Children," *Time*, December 9, 1985, pp. 78–90.
20. Frank F. Furstenberg, *Unplanned Parenthood: The Consequences of Teenage Childbearing* (New York: Free Press, 1976), pp. 57–58.
21. See McCary and McCary, *Human Sexuality*, pp. 543–551.
22. Marlene Cimons, "AIDS Panel Endorses Stiffer Anti-Bias Laws," *Los Angeles Times*, June 18, 1988, Part 1, pp. 1, 23.
23. McCary and McCary, *Human Sexuality*, p. 413.
24. A. C. Jaffe, "Child Molestation," *Medical Aspects of Human Sexuality*, April 1976, pp. 73, 93.
25. Charles H. McCaghy, "Child Molesting," *Sexual Behavior*, August 1971, pp. 16–24.
26. Sue Titus Reid, *Crime and Criminology, 4th ed.* (New York: Holt, Rinehart & Winston, 1985), p. 260.
27. David Finkelhor, "How Widespread Is Child Sexual Abuse?" *Children Today* 13 (July/August 1984): 20.
28. Alex Thio, *Deviant Behavior*, 3d ed. (New York: Harper & Row, 1988), pp. 157–160; McCary and McCary, *Human Sexuality*, pp. 412–414.
29. See Reid, *Crime and Criminology*, pp. 261–263.
30. Evelyn Hooker, "The Adjustment of the Male Overt Homosexual," *Journal of Projective Techniques* 21 (1957): 18–31; and "Male Homosexuality and the Rorschach," *Journal of Projective Techniques* 21 (1958): 33–54.
31. See Philip Feldman, "The Homosexual Preference," in Kevin Howells, ed., The Psychology of Sexual Diversity (Oxford, U.K.: Basil Blackwell, 1984), pp. 20–22.
32. Hilary M. Lips, *Sex and Gender* (Mountain View, Calif.: Mayfield, 1988), pp. 114–115; Feldman, "The Homosexual Preference," pp. 22–24.
33. Feldman, "The Homosexual Preference," pp. 24–28; A. P. Bell, M. S. Weinberg, and S. K. Hammersmith, *Sexual Preference* (Bloomington, Ind.: Indiana University Press, 1981).
34. Richard Green, *The "Sissy Boy Syndrome" and the Development of Homosexuality* (New Haven: Yale University Press, 1987).

35. See Ronald L. Akers, *Deviant Behavior: A Social Learning Approach*, 3rd. ed. (Belmont, Calif.: Wadsworth, 1985), pp. 192–203.

36. Hunt, *Sexual Behavior*, p. 310.

37. See McCary and McCary, *Human Sexuality*, pp. 446–450.

38. Laurel Richardson, *The Dynamics of Sex and Gender: A Sociological Perspective*, 3rd. ed. (New York: Harper & Row, 1988), pp. 219–223.

39. Marshall B. Clinard, *Sociology of Deviant Behavior*, 4th ed. (New York: Holt, Rinehart & Winston, 1974), pp. 545–546.

40. Hunt, *Sexual Behavior*, p. 145; McCary and McCary, *Human Sexualty*, p. 431.

41. David F. Luckenbill, "Deviant Career Mobility: The Case of Male Prostitutes," *Social Problems* 33 (April 1986): 283–296.

42. D. Kelly Weisberg, *Children of the Night: A Study of Adolescent Prostitution* (Lexington Mass.: Lexington Books, 1985), pp. 158–159.

43. Jennifer James, *Entrance into Juvenile Prostitution* (Washington, D.C.: National Institute of Mental Health, 1980); Nanette J. Davis, "The Prostitute: Developing a Deviant Identity," in James M. Henslin, ed., *Studies in the Sociology of Sex* (Englewood Cliffs, N.J.: Prentice-Hall, 1971), pp. 297–322.

44. Weisberg, *Children of the Night*, pp. 155–157.

45. See Akers, *Deviant Behavior*, pp. 208–10.

46. *Report of the President's Commission on Obscenity and Pornography* (New York: Bantam Books, 1970), p. 49.

47. Aric Press, "The War Against Pornography," *Newsweek*, March 18, 1985, pp. 58–66.

48. W. Cody Wilson, "Facts Versus Fears: Why Should We Worry About Pornography?" *Annals of the American Academy of Political Science* 397 (1971): 105–117.

49. Ibid. p. 113; Clinard, *Deviant Behavior*, p. 534.

50. David G. Savage, "Violence and Women," *Los Angeles Times*, June 1, 1985, Part 2, pp. 1, 6; Press, "War Against Pornography."

51. See Frank E. Hagan, *Introduction to Criminology* (Chicago: Nelson-Hall, 1986), p. 247.

52. Edward Donnerstein and L. Berkowitz, "Victim Reactions in Aggressive Erotic Films as a Factor in Violence Against Women," *Journal of Personality and Social Psychology* 41 (1981): 710–724.

53. Edward Donnerstein, Daniel Linz, and Steven Penrod, *The Question of Pornography: Research Findings and Policy Implications*, (New York: The Free Press, 1987), pp. 172–179.

54. Press, "War Against Pornography."

55. Savage, "Violence Against Women."

56. Elizabeth Mehren, "New Study Claims TV Fails to Balance Sex, Responsibility," *Los Angeles Times*, January 27, 1988, Part 4, pp. 1, 12.

57. Tom Gorman, "Sex Classes: A Changing Direction" *Los Angeles Times* July 19, 1985, pp. 1, 19.; Wallis, "Children Having Children."

58. Clark Norton, "Sex in America," *San Francisco Examiner*, December 3, 1981, p. E11.

59. Herbert L. Packer, *The Limits of Criminal Sanction* (Stanford, Calif.: Stanford University Press, 1968), p. 304.

60. Kingsley Davis, "The Sociology of Prostitution," *American Sociological Review* 2 (1937): 744–755.

61. Donald Symons, *The Evolution of Human Sexuality* (New York: Oxford University Press, 1979).

CHAPTER 12   MENTAL DISORDERS

1. Robert C. Carson, James N. Butcher, and James C. Coleman, *Abnormal Psychology and Modern Life*, 8th ed. (Glenview, Ill.: Scott-Foresman, 1988), p. 4.

2. U.S. Bureau of the Census, *Statistical Abstracts of the United States, 1988* (Washington, D.C.: U.S. Government Printing Office, 1987), p. 101.

3. Carson, Butcher, and Coleman, *Abnormal Psychology and Modern Life*, pp. 28–43.

4. Thomas Szasz, "The Myth of Mental Illness," *American Psychologist* 15 (1960): 113–118.

5. David Mechanic, *Mental Health and Social Policy* (Englewood Cliffs, N.J.: Prentice-Hall, 1969), pp. 20–21.

6. James C. Coleman, *Abnormal Psychology and Modern Life*, 3d ed. (Glenview, Ill.: Scott-Foresman, 1964), p. 14.

7. Szasz, "The Myth of Mental Illness."

8. See Thomas J. Scheff, ed., *Labeling Madness* (Englewood Cliffs, N.J.: Prentice-Hall, 1975).

9. American Psychiatric Association, *Diagnostic and Statistical Manual of Mental Disorders*, 3rd. ed., rev. (Washington, D.C.: American Psychiatric Association, 1987).

10. World Health Organization, International Classification of Disease, 9th ed. (Geneva: World Health Organization, 1979); Anne C. Roark, "Psychiatric Bible: Bringing Order to Disorder," *Los Angeles Times*, September, 19, 1988, Part 1, p. 1.

11. Robert E. L. Faris and H. Warren Dunham, *Mental Disorders in Urban Areas* (Chicago: University of Chicago Press, 1939).

12. August B. Hollingshead and Frederick C. Redlich, *Social Class and Mental Illness: A Community Study* (New York: John Wiley & Sons, 1958).

13. Leo Strole, T. S. Langer, S. T. Michael, M. K. Opler, and T. A. L. Rennie, *Mental Health in the Metropolis: The Midtown Manhattan Study* (New York: McGraw-Hill, 1962).

14. Bruce P. Dohrenwend and Barbara Snell Dohrenwend, *Social Status and Psychological Disorder: A Causal Inquiry* (New York: John Wiley & Sons, 1969), p. 165.

15. Leo Strole, "Urbanization and Mental Health: Some Reformulations," *American Scientist* 60 (1972): 576–583.

16. Joseph W. Eaton and Robert J. Weil, *Culture and Mental Disorder* (New York: Free Press, 1955).

17. Eleanor Leacock, "Three Variables in the Occurrence of Mental Illness,"

in Alexander Leighton, John Clausen, and Robert Wilson, eds., *Explorations in Social Psychiatry* (New York: Basic Books, 1957), pp. 308–340.

18. U.S. Bureau of the Census, *Statistical Abstracts, 1988*, p. 52; Carson, Butcher, and Coleman, *Abnormal Psychology and Modern Life*, pp. 292, 369.

19. See, for example, Phyllis Chesler, *Women and Madness* (New York: Avon, 1972).

20. Franz Kallmann and B. Roth, "Genetic Aspects of Preadolescent Schizophrenia," *American Journal of Psychiatry* 112 (1956): 599–606.

21. A. Hoffer and W. Polin, "Schizophrenia in the NAS-NRC Panel of 15,909 Twin Pairs," *Archives of General Psychiatry* 23 (1970): 469–477; see also E. Kringlen, "Hereditary and Social Factors in Schizophrenic Twins: An Epidemiological Clinical Study," in J. Romano, ed., *The Origins of Schizophrenia* (Amsterdam: Excerpta Medica, 1968), pp. 2–14.

22. Seymour S. Kety, "The Biological Roots of Schizophrenia," *Harvard Magazine* 78 (1976): 20–26.

23. Associated Press, February 26, 1987.

24. Carson, Butcher, and Coleman, *Abnormal Psychology and Modern Life*, pp. 115–124.

25. Gregory Bateson, Don D. Jackson, Jay Haley, and John Weakland, "Toward a Theory of Schizophrenia," *Behavioral Science* 1 (1956): 251–264.

26. Mechanic, *Mental Health and Social Policy*, p. 39.

27. See Thomas J. Scheff, *Being Mentally Ill: A Sociological Theory* (Chicago: Aldine-Atherton, 1966), pp. 55–101.

28. Bruce Link, "Mental Patient Status, Work and Income: An Examination of the Effects of Psychological Labeling," *American Sociological Review* 47 (April 1982): 202–215.

29. See, for example, Edwin M. Lemert, "Paranoia and the Dynamics of Exclusion," *Sociometry* 25 (1962): 162–174.

30. See R. D. Laing and A. Esterson, *Sanity, Madness, and the Family* (Middlesex, England: Pelican Books, 1964); R. D. Laing, *The Politics of Experience* (New York: Ballantine Books, 1967).

31. Laing, *The Politics of Experience*, p. 27.

32. Ibid. p. 167.

33. Carson, Butcher, and Coleman, *Abnormal Psychology and Modern Life*, pp. 28–43.

34. Ibid. pp. 43–51.

35. Carl Rogers, *Client-Centered Therapy* (Boston: Houghton Mifflin, 1951).

36. Erving Goffman, *Asylums: Essays on the Social Situation of Mental Patients and Other Inmates* (New York: Doubleday, 1961), p. xii.

37. Ibid. pp. 126–169.

38. D. L. Rosenhan, "On Being Sane in Insane Places," *Science* 179 (1973): 250–258.

39. Ibid. p. 257.

40. Tom Morganthau, "Abandoned," *Newsweek*, January 6, 1986, pp. 14–19.

41. Luis Kutner, "The Illusion of Due Process in Commitment Proceedings,"

Northwestern University Law Review 57 (1962): 383–399; Thomas J. Scheff, "Social Conditions for Rationality: How Urban and Rural Courts Deal with the Mentally Ill," *American Behavioral Scientist* 7 (1964): 21–27; Daniel Oran, "Judges and Psychiatrists Lock Up Too Many People," *Psychology Today* 7 (1973): 20–22, 27–28, 93.
42. Morganthau, "Abandoned."

CHAPTER 13   DRUG USE

1. U.S. Bureau of the Census, *Statistical Abstracts of the United States, 1988* (Washington, D.C.: U.S. Government Printing Office, 1987), p. 718.
2. U.S. Bureau of the Census, *Statistical Abstracts, 1988*, p. 113.
3. Amy Stevens, "Student Drug Use Falls, but Alcohol Abuse is Unchanged, Survey Finds" *Los Angeles Times*, June 15, 1988, Part 1, pp. 1, 22; Marlene Cimons, "Cocaine Use by Students Fell 20% in '87, U.S. Says," *Los Angeles Times*, January 14, 1988; Associated Press, "Cocaine Use Down Among Students: Study Also Shows Marijuana Use Still on Decline," San Luis Obispo (Calif.) *Telegram-Tribune*, January 14, 1988, p. A8; Louis Harris, *Inside America* (New York: Vintage Books, 1987), p. 77; "Drugs: Effort Against Abuse Gains Attention," *Los Angeles Times*, October 20, 1986, Part 1, p. 1; U.S. Bureau of the Census, *Statistical Abstracts, 1985*, p. 118; U.S. Bureau of the Census, *Statistical Abstracts, 1988*, p. 112.
4. U.S. Bureau of the Census, *Statistical Abstracts, 1988*, p. 112.
5. See Craig MacAndrew and Robert B. Edgerton, *Drunken Comportment: A Social Explanation* (Chicago: Aldine-Atherton, 1966).
6. National Commission on Marijuana and Drug Abuse, *Drug Abuse in America: Problem in Perspective* (Washington, D.C.: U.S. Government Printing Office, 1973), p. 143.
7. Oakley Ray, *Drugs, Society and Human Behavior*, 3d ed. (St. Louis,: C. V. Mosby, 1983), pp. 166–67.
8. Jack H. Mendelson and Nancy K. Mello, *Alcohol Use and Abuse in America* (Boston: Little, Brown, 1985), p. 225.
9. Harris, *Inside America*, pp. 60–61.
10. Kathleen Whalen Fitzgerald, *Alcoholism: The Genetic Inheritance* (New York: Doubleday, 1988), p. xii; Ray, *Drugs, Society and Human Behavior*, p. 174.
11. Associated Press, "Drunken Driving Deaths Drop," San Luis Obispo (Calif.) *Telegram-Tribune*, December 10, 1987, p. D1.
12. Joel Fort, *The Addicted Society: Pleasure-Seeking and Punishment Revisited* (New York: Grove Press, 1981), p. 51.
13. *Potsdam College NEWS*, "National Study Indicates Decrease in Drinking, Drunk Driving Among College Students," March 3, 1988.
14. Katherine M. Jamieson and Timothy J. Flanagan, eds., *Sourcebook of Criminal Justice Statistics, 1986*, U.S. Department of Justice (Washington, D.C.: U.S. Government Printing Office, 1987), p. 398; Fitzgerald, *Alcoholism*, p. xii; Fort, *Addicted Society*, p. 52.

15. U.S. Bureau of the Census, *Statistical Abstracts, 1988,* p. 112.
16. Ibid.
17. *Potsdam College NEWS,* "National Study."
18. Ray, *Drugs, Society and Human Behavior,* p. 174.
19. U.S. Bureau of the Census, *Statistical Abstracts, 1988,* pp. 112, 113.
20. U.S. Bureau of the Census, *Statistical Abstracts, 1988,* p. 113; "Smoking: A Partial Success Story," *New York Times,* December 6, 1985, p. 36.
21. U.S. Bureau of the Census, *Statistical Abstracts, 1988,* p. 113.
22. Ibid. p. 719.
23. Ray, *Drugs, Society and Human Behavior,* pp. 199–202.
24. U.S. Department of Health and Human Services, *Smoking and Health: A Report of the Surgeon General* (Washington, D.C.: U.S. Government Printing Office, 1979); Matt Clark, "Slow-Motion Suicide," *Newsweek,* January 22, 1979, pp. 83–84.
25. Associated Press, "Koop: Tobacco Like Heroin, Cocaine," San Luis Obispo (Calif.) *Telegram-Tribune,* May 16, 1988, p. A1.
26. Ray, *Drugs, Society and Human Behavior,* pp. 195–197; Fort, *Addicted Society,* pp. 52–55; U.S. Department of Health and Human Services, *Smoking and Health.*
27. Associated Press, "Koop Urges Legislation as Tobacco Firms React," San Luis Obispo (Calif.) *Telegram-Tribune,* May 16, 1988, p. A3.
28. Donna K. H. Walters, "Cigarettes: Makers Aim at Special Niches to Boost Sales," *Los Angeles Times,* September 15, 1985, Part 5, pp. 1, 2.
29. Janny Scott, "Minority Lung Ailments Up as Smokers Are Wooed," *Los Angeles Times,* June 16, 1988, Part 1, pp. 3, 23.
30. Ray, *Drugs, Society and Human Behavior,* pp. 214–218.
31. Judy Stephens, "The Controversy Over Caffeine and Health Continues," San Luis Obispo (Calif.) *Telegram-Tribune,* November 25, 1987, p. A9.
32. U.S. Bureau of the Census, *Statistical Abstracts, 1988,* p. 112.
33. National Research Council, *An Analysis of Marijuana Policy* (Washington, D.C.: National Academy Press, 1982); Institute of Medicine, *Marijuana and Health,* (Washington, D.C.: National Academy Press, 1982); World Health Organization, *Report of AFR/WHO: Scientific Meeting on Adverse Consequences of Cannabis Use* (Toronto: Addiction Research Foundation, 1981); National Institute on Drug Abuse, *Marijuana and Health, 9th Report* (Washington, D.C.: Government Printing Office, 1982).
34. Ray, *Drugs, Society and Human Behavior,* p. 432.
35. Janny Scott, "Pot Takes a Hit in New Study of Health Dangers," *Los Angeles Times,* February 11, 1988, Part 1, pp. 3, 36.
36. See Ray, *Drugs, Society and Human Behavior,* pp. 430–441; Sidney Cohen, *Substance Abuse Problems,* vol. 2 (New York: Haworth, 1985), pp. 61–71; Fort, *The Addicted Society,* pp. 55–63.
37. Howard S. Becker, *Outsiders* (New York: Free Press, 1963), pp. 41–58.
38. James D. Orcutt, "Normative Definitions of Intoxicated States: A Test of Several Sociological Theories," *Social Problems* 25 (1978): 385–396.

39. Ray, *Drugs, Society and Human Behavior,* pp. 336–337.
40. Ray, *Drugs, Society and Human Behavior,* pp. 351–352; John Ball and John Urbaitis, "Absence of Major Complications Among Chronic Opiate Users," in John Ball and Carl Chambers, eds., *The Epidemiology of Opiate Addiction in the United States* (Springfield, Ill.: Charles C. Thomas, 1970).
41. Ann Fairbanks, "AIDS Frustrates County Health Workers," San Luis Obispo (Calif.) *Telegram-Tribune,* February 20, 1988; Josh Getlin, "AIDS and Minorities: Fear, Ignorance Cited," *Los Angeles Times,* August 10, 1987, Part 1, pp. 1, 12; "AIDS: A Global Assessment," special supplement to the *Los Angeles Times,* August 9, 1987, p. 2.
42. U.S. Bureau of the Census, *Statistical Abstracts, 1988,* p. 112.
43. Ray, *Drugs, Society and Human Behavior,* pp. 342–359; James William Coleman, "The Myth of Addiction," *Journal of Drug Issues* 6 (1976): 135–141.
44. Ray, *Drugs, Society and Human Behavior,* pp. 404–408; Robert M. Julien, *A Primer of Drug Action* (San Francisco: W. H. Freeman, 1975), pp. 147–148.
45. Ray, *Drugs, Society and Human Behavior,* p. 394.
46. U.S. Bureau of the Census, *Statistical Abstracts, 1988,* p. 112.
47. Ray, *Drugs, Society and Human Behavior,* pp. 314–319.
48. Ibid. pp. 311–314.
49. Ibid. pp. 413–416.
50. Ibid. pp. 303–312.
51. See Cohen, *Substance Abuse Problems,* pp. 15–20; Ray, *Drugs, Society and Human Behavior,* pp. 296–303.
52. Cohen, *Substance Abuse Problems,* pp. 15–20.
53. U.S. Bureau of the Census, *Statistical Abstracts, 1988,* p. 112.
54. Vincent Dole and Marie Nyswander, "Heroin Addiction: A Metabolic Disease," *Archives of Internal Medicine* 120 (1967): 19–24.
55. Sidney Cohen, *The Alcoholism Problems: Selected Issues* (New York: Haworth Press, 1983), p. 86; D. W. Goodwin, "Genetics of Alcoholism," in R. W. Pickens and L. L. Heston, eds., *Psychiatric Factors in Drug Abuse* (New York: Grune & Stratton, 1979).
56. E. M. Jellinek, *The Disease of Alcoholism* (Highland Park, N.J.: Hillhouse Press, 1960).
57. Fitzgerald, *Alcoholism: The Genetic Inheritance,* pp. 1–21.
58. Alfred R. Lindesmith, *Addiction and Opiates* (Chicago: Aldine-Atherton, 1968), pp. 64–67.
59. G. E. Barnes, "The Alcoholic Personality: A Reanalysis of the Literature," *Journal of Studies on Alcohol* 40 (1979): 622.
60. Ray, *Drugs, Society and Human Behavior,* p. 160.
61. Isador Chein, Donald Gerard, Robert Lee, and Eva Rosenfeld, *The Road to H* (New York: Basic Books, 1964).
62. George Vaillant, *The Natural History of Alcoholism* (Cambridge, Mass.: Harvard University Press, 1983).
63. James William Coleman, "The Dynamics of Narcotic Abstinence: An In-

teractionist Theory," *Sociological Quarterly 19* (1978): 555–564; Coleman, "The Myth of Addiction."

64. See Charles Terry and Mildred Pellens, *The Opium Problem* (New York: Bureau of Social Hygiene, 1928).

65. Coleman, "The Myth of Addiction."

66. D. F. Musto, "The History of Legislative Control over Opium, Cocaine, and Their Derivatives," in Ronald Hamowy, ed., *Dealing with Drugs: Consequences of Government Control* (San Francisco: Pacific Research Institutes for Public Policy, 1987), pp. 37–71.

67. Coleman, "The Myth of Addiction."

68. See Randy E. Marnett, "Curing the Drug-Law Addiction: The Harmful Side Effects of Legal Prohibition," in Hamowy, *Dealing with Drugs,* pp. 73–102.

69. Reprinted in Becker, *Outsiders,* p. 142.

70. Ray, *Drugs, Society and Human Behavior,* pp. 314–319, 334–335, 377–380.

71. Ibid. pp. 39–43.

72. Richard H. Blum, Eva Blum, and E. Garfield, *Drug Education: Results and Recommendations* (Lexington, Mass.: D. C. Heath, 1976).

73. Janny Scott, "Debate Resurrected over Risks of Casual Drug Use," *Los Angeles Times,* August 10, 1988, Part 1, pp. 1, 20.

74. See Marshall B. Clinard, *The Sociology of Deviant Behavior* (New York: Holt, Rinehart & Winston, 1974), pp. 412–419; Erich Goode, *Drugs and American Society* (New York: Alfred A. Knopf, 1972), pp. 147–148.

75. Roger Meyer, *Guide to Drug Rehabilitation* (Boston: Beacon Press, 1972), pp. 61–63.

76. See Rita Vokman and Donald R. Cressey, "Differential Association and the Rehabilitation of Drug Addicts," *American Journal of Sociology 69* (1963): 129–142.

77. Meyer, *Drug Rehabilitation,* p. 72; Ray, *Drugs, Society and Human Behavior,* pp. 360–362.

78. Thomas Szasz, *Ceremonial Chemistry: The Ritual Persecution of Drugs, Addicts, and Pushers,* rev. ed. (Holmes Beach, Fla.: Learning Publications, 1985).

79. Jamieson and Flanagan, *Sourcebook of Criminal Justice Statistics, 1986,* p. 65.

80. Ibid. p. 134.

81. For a discussion of maintenance programs see Ray, *Drugs, Society and Human Behavior,* pp. 362–366.

CHAPTER 14   CRIME AND DELINQUENCY

1. Bureau of Justice Statistics, *Households Touched by Crime, 1987* (Washington, D.C.: U.S. Government Printing Office, May 1987), p. 1.

2. Katherine M. Jamieson and Timothy J. Flanagan, eds., *Sourcebook of Criminal Justice Statistics, 1986,* U.S. Department of Justice (Washington, D.C.: U.S. Government Printing Office, 1987), p. 75.

3. Ronald J. Ostrow, "Ending FBI's Control Over Crime Statistics Proposed," *Los Angeles Times*, April 19, 1976.

4. Bureau of Justice Statistics, *Households Touched by Crime, 1987;* Bureau of Justice Statistics, *Criminal Victimization in the United States, 1986* (Washington, D.C.: U.S. Government Printing Office, August 1988).

5. Edwin H. Sutherland and Donald R. Cressey, *Criminology,* 10th ed. (New York: Lippincott, 1978), p. 130.

6. Sue Titus Reid, *Crime and Criminology,* 5th ed., (New York: Holt, Rinehart & Winston, 1988), p. 67.

7. Jamieson and Flanagan, *Sourcebook of Criminal Justice Statistics, 1986,* p. 295.

8. Ibid. p. 319.

9. Bureau of Justice Statistics, *Criminal Victimization, 1986,* pp. 34–35.

10. Charels R. Tittle, Wayne J. Villemez, and Douglas A. Smith, "The Myth of Social Class and Criminality," *American Sociological Review* 43 (1978): 643–656.

11. Delbert Elliott and Suzanne Ageton, "Reconciling Race and Class Differences in Self-Reported and Official Estimates of Delinquency," *American Sociological Review* 45 (1980): 95–110; Delbert Elliott and David Huizinga, "Social Class and Delinquent Behavior in a National Youth Panel: 1976–1980," *Criminology* 21 (1983): 149–177.

12. Walter C. Reckless, *The Crime Problem,* 4th ed. (Englewood Cliffs, N.J.: Prentice-Hall, 1967), pp. 110–112.

13. Jamieson and Flanagan, *Sourcebook of Criminal Justice Statistics, 1986,* p. 300.

14. See, for example, Marvin E. Wolfgang, Terence P. Thornberry, and Robert M. Figlio, *From Boy to Man, From Delinquency to Crime* (Chicago: University of Chicago Press, 1987).

15. Jamieson and Flanagan, *Sourcebook of Criminal Justice Statistics, 1986,* p. 266; Bureau of Justice Statistics, *Criminal Victimization, 1986,* p. 44.

16. Bureau of Justice Statistics, *Criminal Victimization, 1986,* pp. 30–31.

17. See Cesare Lombroso, *Crime: Its Causes and Remedies* (Montclair, N.J.: Patterson Smith, 1968).

18. Richard S. Fox, "The XYY Offender: A Modern Myth," *Journal of Criminal Law Criminology and Police Science* 62 (1971): 59–73.

19. See Frank E. Hagan, *Introduction to Criminology* (Chicago: Nelson-Hall, 1987), pp. 413–415; Larry J. Siegel, *Criminology,* 2d ed. (St. Paul: West, 1986), pp. 158–159.

20. Barry Hutchings and Sarnoff A. Mednick, "Criminality in Adoptees and Their Adoptive and Biological Parents: A Pilot Study," in *Biosocial Bases of Criminal Behavior,* S. A. Mednick and K. O. Christiansen, eds. (New York: Gardner Press, 1977); for a follow-up study with a different population, see Sarnoff A. Mednick, William Gabrielli, and Barry Hutchings, "Genetic Influences in Criminal Behavior: Evidence from an Adoption Cohort," in Katherine S. Van Dusen and Sarnoff Mednick, eds., *Prospective Studies of Crime and Delinquency* (Boston: Kluver-Nijhoff, 1983), pp. 39–57.

21. James Q. Wilson and Richard Herrnstein, *Crime and Human Behavior* (New York: Simon & Schuster, 1985).

22. See Sutherland and Cressey, *Criminology*, pp. 158–191.

23. Karl Schuessler and Donald R. Cressey, "Personality Characteristics of Criminals," *American Journal of Sociology* 55 (1950): 476–484; Gordon Waldo and Simon Dinitz, "Personality Attributes of the Criminal: An Analysis of Research Studies 1950–1965," *Journal of Research in Crime and Delinquency* 4 (1967): 185–201; David Tennenbaum, "Research Studies of Personality and Criminality," *Journal of Criminal Justice* 5 (1977): 1–19.

24. Robert K. Merton, "Social Structure and Anomie," *American Sociological Review* 3 (1938): 672–682.

25. Walter B. Miller, "Lower Class Culture as a Generating Milieu of Gang Delinquency," *Journal of Social Issues* 14 (1958): 5–19.

26. Sutherland and Cressey, *Criminology*, pp. 77–98.

27. Travis Hirschi, Causes of Delinquency (Berkeley: University of California Press, 1969); James Q. Wilson, *Thinking About Crime* (New York: Random House, 1975).

28. Jamieson and Flanagan, eds., *Sourcebook of Criminal Justice Statistics, 1986*, p. 291.

29. Anthony M. Platt, The Child Savers: The Invention of Delinquency (Chicago: University of Chicago Press, 1969).

30. See Clemens Bartollas, *Juvenile Delinquency* (New York: John Wiley & Sons, 1985), pp. 232–257.

31. See James William Coleman, *The Criminal Elite: The Sociology of White Collar Crime*, 2d ed., (New York: St. Martin's, 1989), pp. 6–8.

32. Michael A. Hiltzik, "Inside Trader to Pay Penalty of $100 Million," *Los Angeles Times*, November 15, 1986.

33. Jamieson and Flanagan, *Sourcebook of Criminal Justice Statistics, 1986*, p. 243; Richard T. Cooper and Paul E. Steiger, "Occupational Health Hazards—A National Crisis," *Los Angeles Times*, June 27, 1976, Part 1, p. 1.

34. Coleman, *The Criminal Elite*, pp. 6, 55–72.

35. Edwin H. Sutherland, *White Collar Crime* (New York: Dryden, 1949), p. 9.

36. Marshall B. Clinard and Peter C. Yeager, *Corporate Crime* (New York: The Free Press, 1980), p. 122–125.

37. Herbert L. Packer, *The Limits of Criminal Sanction* (Stanford, Calif.: Stanford University Press, 1968).

38. Bureau of Justice Statistics, *Report to the Nation on Crime and Justice: The Data* (Washington, D.C.: U.S. Government Printing Office, 1983), p. 47; Eric J. Scott, *Calls for Service: Citizen Demand and Initial Police Response*, National Institute of Justice (Washington, D.C.: U.S. Government Printing Office, July 1981), p. 26.

39. Barbara Boland, Wayne Logan, Ronald Sones, and William Martin, *The Prosecution of Felony Arrests, 1982*, Bureau of Justice Statistics (Washington, D.C.: U.S. Government Printing Office, May 1988), p. 7.

40. Joan Petersilia, *Probation and Felon Offenders*, National Institute of Justice (Washington, D.C.: U.S. Government Printing Office, 1985).
41. Boland, Logan, Sones, and Martin, *The Prosecution of Felony Arrests, 1982*, p. 8.
42. Bureau of Justice Statistics, *Felony Sentencing in 18 Local Jurisdictions* (Washington, D.C.: U.S. Government Printing Office, 1985).
43. Petersilia, *Probation and Felon Offenders*.
44. See Douglas Lipton, Robert Martison, and Judith Wilks, *The Effectiveness of Correctional Treatment: A Survey of Evaluation Studies* (New York: Holt, Rinehart & Winston, 1975) for a comprehensive review of the research on correctional treatment.
45. See Reid, *Crime and Criminology*, pp. 546–547.
46. John Wallerstedt, *Returning to Prison*, Bureau of Justice Statistics (Washington, D.C.: U.S. Government Printing Office, 1984).
47. Bureau of Justice Statistics, *Prisoners in 1987* (Washington, D.C.: U.S. Government Printing Office, April 1988); Jamieson and Flanagan, *Sourcebook of Criminal Justice Statistics, 1986*, p. 393.
48. Bureau of Justice Statistics, *Prisoners in 1987*.
49. Ibid.
50. Joseph E. Scott, "The Use of Discretion in Determining the Severity of Punishment," *Journal of Criminal Law and Criminology* 65 (1974): 214–224.
51. D. Stanley Eitzen and Doug A. Timmer, *Criminology* (New York: John Wiley & Sons, 1985), p. 482.
52. Donald R. Cressey and Robert A. McDermott, *Diversion from the Juvenile Justice System* (Washington, D.C.: U.S. Government Printing Office, 1974).
53. Edwin M. Schur, *Radical Non-Intervention: Rethinking the Delinquency Problem* (Englewood Cliffs, N.J.: Prentice-Hall, 1973).

CHAPTER 15   PERSONAL VIOLENCE

1. Katherine M. Jamieson and Timothy J. Flanagan, eds., *Sourcebook of Criminal Justice Statistics, 1987*, U.S. Department of Justice (Washington, D.C.: U.S. Government Printing Office, 1988), p. 141.
2. Ibid. p. 319.
3. Bureau of Justice Statistics, *Households Touched by Crime, 1987* (Washington, D.C.: U.S. Government Printing Office, May 1988).
4. Bureau of Justice Statistics, *International Crime Rates* (Washington, D.C.: U.S. Government Printing Office, May 1988).
5. Hugh D. Barlow, *Introduction to Criminology*, 4th ed. (Boston: Little, Brown, 1987), p. 127.
6. Flanagan and Jamieson, *Sourcebook of Criminal Justice Statistics, 1987*, p. 497.
7. Marvin E. Wolfgang, *Patterns in Criminal Homicide* (Philadelphia: University of Pennsylvania Press, 1958).

8. Calculated from Flanagan and Jamieson, *Sourcebook of Criminal Justice Statistics, 1987*, p. 339.

9. Bureau of Justice Statistics, *Criminal Victimization in the United States, 1986*, (Washington, D.C.: U.S. Government Printing Office, August 1988), p. 41.

10. Ibid.

11. See Barlow, *Introduction to Criminology*, pp. 159–160.

12. Bureau of Justice Statistics, *Criminal Victimization in the United States, 1986*, p. 16.

13. See Sue Titus Reid, *Crime and Criminology*, 5th ed. (New York: Holt, Rinehart & Winston, 1988), pp. 234–235.

14. Timothy Beneke, "Male Rape: Four Men Talk About Rape," *Mother Jones*, July 1983, pp. 13–22.

15. Quoted in Beneke, "Male Rape."

16. Bureau of Justice Statistics, *Criminal Victimization in the United States, 1986*, p. 16.

17. Ibid. pp. 43, 46.

18. Bureau of Justice Statistics, *Bulletin: The Crime of Rape* (Washington, D.C.: U.S. Government Printing Office, March 1985).

19. Flanagan and Jamieson, *Sourcebook of Criminal Justice Statistics, 1987*, p. 236; Barlow, *Introduction to Criminology*, p. 160.

20. Bureau of Justice Statistics, *Criminal Victimization in the United States, 1986*, pp. 40–41.

21. Barlow, *Introduction to Criminology*, pp. 180–182.

22. Irwin N. Perr, "Legal Aspects of Suicide," in L. D. Hankoff and Bernice Einsideler, eds., *Suicide: Theory and Clinical Aspects* (Littleton, Mass.: PSG Publishing, 1979), pp. 91–101.

23. U.S. Bureau of the Census, *Statistical Abstracts of the United States, 1988*, (Washington, D.C.: U.S. Government Printing Office, 1987), p. 79.

24. Ibid. p. 82.

25. Ibid. pp. 78, 82.

26. Émile Durkheim, *Suicide* (New York: Free Press, 1951).

27. See Eli Robins, *The Final Months* (New York: Oxford University Press, 1981).

28. Robert Ardrey, *The Territorial Imperative* (New York: Atheneum, 1967).

29. Konrad Lorenz, *On Aggression* (New York: Harcourt Brace Jovanovich, 1966).

30. Martin Daly and Margo Wilson, *Homicide* (New York: Aldine de Gruyter, 1988).

31. For the classic statement of this theory, see John Dollard, L. Doob, N. E. Miller, O. H. Mowrer, and R. R. Sears, *Frustration and Aggression* (New Haven: Yale University Press, 1939).

32. National Commission on the Causes and Prevention of Violence, *The Challenge of Crime in a Free Society* (Washington, D.C.: U.S. Government Printing Office, 1976).

33. Murray A. Straus, Richard J. Gelles, and Suzanne K. Steinmetz, *Behind*

Closed Doors: Violence in the American Family (New York: Doubleday, 1981), p. 101.

34. See, for example, Reid, *Crime and Criminology,* pp. 240–246; David G. Gil, *Violence Against Children: Physical Child Abuse in the United States* (Cambridge, Mass.: Harvard University Press, 1970), pp. 113–114.

35. Straus, Gelles, and Steinmetz, *Behind Closed Doors,* p. 121.

36. Marvin E. Wolfgang and Franco Ferracuti, *The Subculture of Violence* (London: Tavistock, 1967).

37. See Richard Maxwell Brown, "The Historical Patterns of American Violence," in Hugh Davis Graham and Ted Robert Gurr, eds., *Violence in America: Historical and Comparative Perspectives,* rev. ed. (Beverly Hills: Sage, 1979), pp. 19–48.

38. Graham and Gurr, *Violence in America,* p. 146.

39. National Institute of Mental Health, *Television and Behavior, vol. 1 Summary Report,* (Washington, D.C.: U.S. Government Printing Office, 1982); Surgeon General's Scientific Advisory Committee on Television and Social Behavior, *Television and Growing Up: The Impact of Televised Violence* (Washington, D.C.: U.S. Government Printing Office, 1972); and George A. Comstock and Eli Rubenstein, eds., *Television and Social Behavior,* vols. 1–5 (Washington, D.C.: U.S. Government Printing Office, 1972).

40. T. M. Williams, "Differential Impact on TV and Children" (paper presented at the meeting of the International Society for the Study of Aggression, Washington, D.C., 1978); G. Granszberg and V. Steinberg, *Television and the Canadian Indians,* Technical Report, Department of Anthropology, University of Winnipeg, 1980; see also *Television and Behavior,* p. 38.

41. Jeffrey H. Goldstein, *Aggression and Crimes of Violence,* 2d ed. (New York: Oxford University Press, 1986), p. 39.

42. Victor B. Cline, Roger G. Croft, and Steven Courier, "The Desensitization of Children to Violence," in Victor B. Cline, ed., *Where Do You Draw the Line: An Exploration into Media Violence, Pornography, and Censorship* (Provo, Utah: Brigham Young University Press, 1974), pp. 147–155.

43. Flanagan and Jamieson, *Sourcebook of Criminal Justice Statistics, 1987,* p. 168.

44. Mark Stein, "Firepower of Civilians Escalating," *Los Angeles Times,* September 9, 1985, pp. 1, 3.

45. U.S. Bureau of the Census, *Statistical Abstracts, 1988,* p. 160; Flanagan and Jamieson, *Sourcebook of Criminal Justice Statistics, 1987,* p. 236.

46. Wolfgang, *Patterns in Criminal Homicide.*

47. Barlow, *Introduction to Criminology,* p. 129.

48. Flanagan and Jamieson, *Sourcebook of Criminal Justice Statistics, 1987,* p. 236.

49. Ibid. p. 103.

50. Ibid. p. 172.

51. Ibid. pp. 98–100.

52. For example, Dane Archer and Rosemary Gartner, "Violent Acts and Violent Times: A Comparative Approach to Postwar Homicide Rates," *American Sociological Review* 41 [1978]: 937–963, show that war generally contributes to higher overall homicide rates.

53. David F. Luckenbill, "Criminal Homicide as a Situated Transaction," *Social Problems* 25 (1977): 176–186; and Lonnie H. Athens, "The Self and the Violent Criminal Act," *Urban Life and Culture* 3 (1974): 98–112.

CHAPTER 16   URBANIZATION

1. U.S. Bureau of the Census, *Statistical Abstracts of the United States, 1988* (Washington, D.C.: U.S. Government Printing Office, 1987), p. 16.

2. Population Reference Bureau, *World Population: Facts in Focus* (Washington, D.C.: Population Reference Bureau, 1988), pp. 9, 10.

3. Rafael M. Salas, "Cities Without Limits," *Unesco Courier*, January 1987, pp. 10–13, 16–17.

4. Harvey M. Choldin, *Cities and Suburbs: An Introduction to Urban Sociology* (New York: McGraw-Hill, 1985), pp. 73–74.

5. Ibid. pp. 143–144.

6. Salas, "Cities Without Limits."

7. See Claude S. Fischer, *The Urban Experience*, 2d ed., (New York: Harcourt Brace Jovanovich, 1984).

8. Choldin, *Cities and Suburbs*, pp. 303–304.

9. Georg Simmel, "The Metropolis and Mental Life," in Kurt Wolf, ed. and trans., *The Sociology of Georg Simmel* (New York: Free Press, 1950). This article was originally published in 1903.

10. Louis Wirth, "Urbanism as a Way of Life," *American Journal of Sociology* 44 (1938): 1–14.

11. Herbert J. Gans, "Urbanism and Suburbanism: Ways of Life," in Arnold M. Rose, ed., *Human Behavior and Social Processes: An Interactionist Approach* (Boston: Houghton Mifflin, 1962), pp. 625–648.

12. William A. Schwab, *Urban Sociology: A Human Ecological Perspective* (Reading, Mass.: Addison-Wesley, 1982), pp. 308–310.

13. Ivan Light, *Cities in World Perspective* (New York: Macmillan, 1983), pp. 214–215; Fischer, *The Urban Experience*, p. 209.

14. Light, *Cities in World Perspective*, pp. 208–215.

15. Choldin, *Cities and Suburbs*, pp. 363–366.

16. Ibid. pp. 366–367.

17. Ibid. p. 264.

18. John R. Logan and Harvey L. Molotch, *Urban Fortunes* (Berkeley, Calif.: University of California Press, 1987), p. 194.

19. Ibid. p. 198.

20. Choldin, *Cities and Suburbs*, pp. 478–479.

21. Population Reference Bureau, *World Population*, p. 10.

22. U.S. Bureau of the Census, *Statistical Abstracts, 1988*, p. 607.

23. Ibid. p. 32.

24. Choldin, *Cities and Suburbs,* pp. 303–304.
25. Louis Harris, *Inside America* (New York: Vintage, 1987), pp. 227–228.
26. U.S. Bureau of the Census, *Statistical Abstracts, 1988,* p. 607.
27. Jon Bennett, *The Hunger Machine* (Cambridge, U.K.: Polity Press, 1987), p. 171.
28. Laurent Belsie and Howard LaFranchi, "Rural America at a Crossroads: Is It Really a Depression?" in LeRoy Barnes, ed., *Social Problems 87/88* (Guilford, Conn.: Dushkin, 1987), pp. 160–168.
29. David Ehrenfeld, "Beyond the Farming Crisis, *Technology Review* 90 (July 1987): 45–56; James Wessel, *Trading the Future: Farm Exports and the Concentration of Economic Power in the Food System* (San Francisco: Institute for Food and Development Policy, 1983), p. 34.
30. See Logan and Molotch, *Urban Fortunes,* pp. 195–199.
31. Associated Press, "Home Buyers Older, Houses More Expensive— Study," San Luis Obispo (Calif.) *Telegram-Tribune,* February 4, 1988, p. C7.
32. Michael Dear, "Our 'Third World' of Housing Have-Nots Needs Action," *Los Angeles Times,* February 8, 1988, Part 2, p. 7.
33. James D. Wright, "The Mentally Ill Homeless: What is Myth and What Is Fact?" *Social Problems* 35 (April 1988): 182–191.
34. Choldin, *Cities and Suburbs,* pp. 333–334.
35. W. John Moore, "Lost in America: Low-Rent Housing," *Los Angeles Times,* June 12, 1988, Part 5, p. 2.
36. U.S. Bureau of the Census, *Statistical Abstracts, 1988,* p. 579.
37. Light, *Cities in World Perspective,* p. 209.
38. U.S. Bureau of the Census, *Statistical Abstracts, 1988,* p. 582.
39. Bradford Curie Snell, "American Ground Transport," in Jerome H. Skolnick and Elliott Currie, eds., *Crisis in American Institutions,* 7th ed. (Glenview, Ill.: Scott, Foresman, 1988), pp. 321–344; Light, *Cities in World Perspective,* pp. 210–211.
40. John B. Calhoun, "Population Density and Social Pathology," *Scientific American* 206 (1962): 139–148.
41. See, for example, Pierre van den Berghe, *Man in Society: A Biosocial View* (New York: Elsevier, 1978), pp. 52–59.
42. See Claude S. Fischer, *The Urban Experience,* 2d ed., (New York: Harcourt Brace Jovanovich, 1984), pp. 173–200.
43. Logan and Molotch, *Urban Fortunes,* pp. 124–126.
44. Calculated by Richard A. Shaffer from data in Choldin, *Cities and Suburbs,* pp. 247–249.
45. Choldin, *Cities and Suburbs,* p. 246.
46. Logan and Molotch, *Urban Fortunes,* p. 194.
47. Douglas S. Massey and Nancy A. Denton, "Suburbanization and Segregation in U.S. Metropolitan Areas," *American Journal of Sociology* 94 (November 1988): 592–626.
48. J. John Palen, *The Urban World* (New York: McGraw-Hill, 1981), p. 336.
49. Salas, "Cities Without Limit."

50. Ibid.
51. Palen, *The Urban World*, p. 406.
52. Choldin, *Cities and Suburbs*, p. 485.
53. Thomas Murphy and John Rehfuss, *Urban Politics in the Suburban Era* (Homewood, Ill.: Dorsey, 1976), pp. 254–258.
54. Moore, "Lost in America: Low-Rent Housing."
55. Kenneth K. Wong and Paul E. Peterson, "Urban Response to Federal Program Flexibility: Politics of Community Development Block Grants," *Urban Affairs Quarterly* 21 (March 1986): 293–309.
56. Logan and Molotch, *Urban Fortunes*, pp. 159–162.

CHAPTER 17   POPULATION

1. Population Reference Bureau, *World Population: Facts in Focus* (Washington, D.C.: Population Reference Bureau, 1988), p. 8.
2. Jon Bennett, *The Hunger Machine: The Politics of Food* (Cambridge, U.K.: Polity Press, 1987), p. 12.
3. U.S. Bureau of the Census, *Statistical Abstracts of the United States, 1988* (Washington, D.C.: U.S. Government Printing Office, 1987), p. 794; "Global Population: A Glimpse into the Future," *U.S. News and World Report,* August 2, 1982, pp. 48–49.
4. Charles B. Nam and Susan Gustavus Philliber, *Population: A Basic Orientation*, 2d ed. (Englewood Cliffs, N.J.: Prentice-Hall, 1984), p. 27.
5. Calculated from Population Reference Bureau, *World Population*, p. 8.
6. Population Reference Bureau, *World Population*, pp. 8–11.
7. Calculated from Population Reference Bureau, *World Population*, pp. 10, 14.
8. U.S. Bureau of the Census, *Statistical Abstracts, 1988*, p. 9.
9. Population Reference Bureau, *World Population*, pp. 8, 12.
10. John R. Weeks, *Population: An Introduction to Concepts and Issues*, 3d ed. (Belmont, Calif.: Wadsworth, 1986), p. 55.
11. Population Reference Bureau, *World Population*, p. 8.
12. Charles F. Westoff, "Populations of the Developed Countries," *Scientific American* 231 (1974): 114.
13. For an analysis of the theory of demographic transition, see Weeks, *Population*, pp. 39–48; Nam and Philliber, *Population*, pp. 42–48.
14. Thomas Robert Malthus, *Essays on the Principle of Population*, first published in 1798 (Baltimore: Penguin, 1971).
15. Quoted in Paul R. Ehrlich and Anne H. Ehrlich, *Population, Resources, Environment: Problems and Solutions* (San Francisco: Freeman, 1973), p. 15.
16. Calculated from Bennett, *The Hunger Machine*, p. 32; U.S. Bureau of the Census, *Statistical Abstracts, 1988*, p. 817.
17. U.S. Bureau of the Census, *Statistical Abstracts, 1988*, p. 817.
18. Lester R. Brown, "Putting Food on the World's Table," in Robert M. Jackson, ed., *Global Issues 88/89* (Guilford, Conn. Dushkin, 1988), pp. 87–97.

19. Charles T. Powers, "Hunger—Africa Seeks New Answers," *Los Angeles Times,* December 17, 1984, pp. 1, 24–25.

20. Bennett, *The Hunger Machine,* p. 12; G. Tyler Miller, *Living in the Environment,* 5th ed. (Belmont, Calif.: Wadsworth, 1988), p. 245.

21. See Miller, *Living in the Environment,* pp. 242–245.

22. Robert N. Ross, "The Hidden Malice of Malnutrition," in Jackson, ed., *Global Issues 88/89,* pp. 98–101.

23. Bennett, *The Hunger Machine,* p. 14.

24. Population Reference Bureau, *World Population,* p. 8.

25. Kingsley Davis, "The World's Population Crisis," in Robert K. Merton and Robert K. Nisbet, eds., *Contemporary Social Problems,* 4th ed., (New York: Harcourt Brace Jovanovich, 1976), p. 274.

26. Population Reference Bureau, *World Population,* pp. 8, 9.

27. Norman Myers, ed., *GAIA: An Atlas of Planet Management* (Garden City, N.Y.: Anchor, 1984), pp. 182–183.

28. U.S. Bureau of the Census, *Statistical Abstracts, 1988,* p. 794.

29. Rafael M. Salas, "Cities Without Limits," *Unesco Courier,* January 1987, pp. 10–13, 16–17.

30. Population Reference Bureau, *World Population,* p. 8.

31. Miller, *Living in the Environment,* pp. 295–296.

32. Ibid. p. 247.

33. Ibid. pp. 247–249; Bennett, *The Hunger Machine,* pp. 23–27.

34. E. F. Schumacher, *Small Is Beautiful: Economics as if People Mattered* (New York: Harper & Row, 1974), pp. 171–190.

35. Weeks, *Population,* p. 385.

36. Ibid. pp. 381–383.

37. Miller, *Living in the Environment,* p. 252.

38. Calculated from Miller, *Living in the Environment,* pp. 253–254.

39. Weeks, *Population,* pp. 385–386.

40. Bennett, *The Hunger Machine,* p. 37.

41. Ibid. p. 22

42. See Weeks, *Population,* pp. 417–423.

43. See Nam and Philliber, *Population,* pp. 298–301.

44. Weeks, *Population,* p. 423.

45. Ibid. pp. 427–428; Population Reference Bureau, *World Population,* p. 10.

46. Jeannie L. Rosoff, "House OKs Overseas Family Planning Authorization After Sterilization Debate," *Planned Parenthood—World Population Memorandum,* May 27, 1977, p. 2.

47. Miller, *Living in the Environment,* p. 163.

48. Weeks, *Population,* pp. 425–427.

49. David Holley, "China Orders New Drive to Prevent Unapproved Births," *Los Angeles Times,* February 16, 1988, Part 1, pp. 1, 19; Population Reference Bureau, *World Population,* p. 10.

50. "China Relaxing One-Child Policy," *International Herald Tribune,* June 25, 1985.

51. Frank W. Notestein, "The Population Crisis: Reasons for Hope," *Foreign Affairs* 46 (1967): 167–180.

52. Daniel Chirot, *Social Change in the Modern Era* (New York: Harcourt Brace Jovanovich, 1986), p. 177.

53. Bennett, *The Hunger Machine*, p. 34.

CHAPTER 18   THE ENVIRONMENT

1. Andrew Goudie, *The Human Impact on the Natural Environment*, 2d ed., (Cambridge, Mass.: M.I.T. Press, 1986), pp. 276–277; Norman Myers, ed., *GAIA: An Atlas of Planet Management* (Garden City, N.Y.: Anchor, 1984), p. 118.

2. U.S. Bureau of the Census, *Statistical Abstracts of the United States, 1988* (Washington, D.C.: U.S. Government Printing Office, 1987), p. 192.

3. R. F. Damann, *Environmental Conservation*, 5th ed. (New York: John Wiley & Sons, 1984), p. 398.

4. G. Tyler Miller, *Living in the Environment: An Introduction to Environmental Science*, 5th ed. (Belmont, Calif.: Wadsworth, 1988), p. 432.

5. Jon R. Luoma, "Forests Are Dying: But is Acid Rain Really to Blame?" *Audubon*, March 1987.

6. Miller, *Living in the Environment*, p. 432.

7. Sharon Begley, "A Gaping Hole in the Sky," *Newsweek*, July 11, 1988, pp. 21–23; Miller, *Living in the Environment*, pp. 438–440.

8. Miller, *Living in the Environment*, p. 441.

9. Sharon Begley, "The Endless Summer?" *Newsweek*, July 11, 1988, pp. 18–20.

10. Damann, *Environmental Conservation*, p. 402.

11. Miller, *Living in the Environment*, pp. 458–459.

12. Goudie, *The Human Impact*, pp. 178–179.

13. John Carey, "Is It Safe to Drink?" *National Wildlife*, February/March 1984, pp. 19–21.

14. *Sacramento Bee*, May 25, 1988, p. A5.

15. Miller, *Living in the Environment*, p. 474.

16. Myers, *GAIA*, p. 42.

17. Damann, *Environmental Conservation*, p. 179.

18. Myers, *GAIA*, p. 42.

19. "The State of the World: An Interview with Lester Brown," *Technology Review*, July 1988, pp. 51–58.

20. Tom Morgenthau, "The Disappearing Land," *Newsweek*, August 23, 1982, pp. 24–26.

21. U.S. Bureau of the Census, *Statistical Abstracts, 1988*, p. 193.

22. See Branley Allan Branson, "Is There Life After Strip Mining?" *Natural History* 95 (August 1986): 30–36.

23. Miller, *Living in the Environment*, pp. 499–500.

24. Ibid. p. 499.

25. Jeffrey Heil and James Van Blarcom, "Superfund: The Search for Consistency," in John Allen, ed., *Environment 88/89* (Guilford, Conn.: Dushkin, 1988), pp. 107–111.

26. Tim Smart, "The New Debate on Superfund: How Clean Is Clean Enough?" *Business Week*, July 13, 1987; Miller, *Living in the Environment*, p. 499.
27. Miller, *Living in the Environment*, pp. 375–376.
28. Ibid. pp. 376–378.
29. Calculated from U.S. Bureau of the Census, *Statistical Abstracts, 1988*, pp. 543, 795.
30. Miller, *Living in the Environment*, pp. 338–339.
31. U.S. Bureau of the Census, *Statistical Abstracts, 1988*, p. 543.
32. Ibid. p. 542.
33. Myers, *GAIA*, pp. 112–113.
34. Population Reference Bureau, *World Population: Facts in Focus* (Washington, D.C.: Population Reference Bureau, 1988).
35. See Miller, *Living in the Environment*, pp. 343–345.
36. Ibid. p. 354; Myers, *GAIA*, p. 113.
37. Christopher Flavin, "Reforming the Electric Power Industry," in Lester R. Brown et al., *State of the World, 1986* (New York: W. W. Norton, 1986), p. 100.
38. Miller, *Living in the Environment*, p. 379.
39. Flavin, "Reforming the Electric Power Industry," p. 101.
40. John E. Farley, *American Social Problems* (Englewood Cliffs, N.J.: Prentice-Hall, 1987), pp. 313–314.
41. U.S. Bureau of the Census, *Statistical Abstracts, 1988*, p. 551.
42. Miller, *Living in the Environment*, pp. 409–411; Myers, *GAIA*, pp. 114–115.
43. Myers, *GAIA*, pp. 110–111.
44. Ibid. pp. 96–97.
45. Donella Meadows, Dennis L. Meadows, Jorgen Randers, and William W. Behrens, *The Limits of Growth* (New York: Universe Books, 1972); Donella Meadows et al., *Groping in the Dark: The First Decade of Global Modeling* (New York: Wiley, 1982).
46. For a discussion of the differences between the neo-Malthusians and the cornucopians see Miller, *Living in the Environment*, pp. 17–19.
47. Louis Harris, *Inside America* (New York: Vintage, 1987), p. 245.
48. Ibid. pp. 248–249.
49. U.S. Bureau of the Census, *Statistical Abstracts, 1988*, p. 816.
50. See Miller, *Living in the Environment*, pp. 387–408.
51. See Garrett Hardin, "The Tragedy of the Commons," *Science* 162 (1968): 1243–1248.

CHAPTER 19   WARFARE AND INTERNATIONAL CONFLICT

1. See Daniel Chirot, *Social Change in the Modern Era* (New York: Harcourt Brace Jovanovich, 1986), for a good short description of the development of the modern world system.
2. Jon Bennett, *The Hunger Machine: The Politics of Food* (Cambridge, U.K.: Polity Press, 1987), pp. 3, 12, 21.

3. Arthur Simon, "Greed Keeps the Third World Hungry," *Los Angeles Times*, March 2, 1988, Part 2, p. 7; Juan de Onis, "Debt Payments Dampen Latin Economies—Study," *Los Angeles Times*, December 21, 1984; Charles T. Powers, "Africa: The Harsh Realities Dim Hope," *Los Angeles Times*, December 16, 1984, pp. 1, 24.

4. See Chirot, *Social Change in the Modern Era*, pp. 96–130, 231–261.

5. A. Kent MacDougall, "In Third World All But Rich Are Poorer," *Los Angeles Times*, November 4, 1984, Part 1, p. 1 passim.

6. Melvin Small and J. David Singer, *Resort to Arms: International and Civil Wars, 1816–1980*, (Beverly Hills: Sage, 1982), p. 293.

7. See Rudi Volti, *Society and Technological Change* (New York: St. Martin's, 1988), pp. 171–201.

8. Frank Barnaby, "The Nuclear Arsenal in the Middle East," *Technology Review*, (May/June, 1987).

9. Rod Nordland, "The Bombs in the Basement," *Newsweek*, July 11, 1988, pp. 42–45.

10. Small and Singer, *Resort to Arms*, pp. 293–294.

11. James F. Dunnigan and William Martel, *How to Stop a War: The Lessons of Two Hundred Years of War and Peace* (New York: Doubleday, 1987), p. 81.

12. Dunnigan and Martel, *How To Stop A War*, p. 239; Small and Singer, *Resort to Arms*, p. 91.

13. U.S. Bureau of the Census, *Statistical Abstracts, 1988* (Washington, D.C.: U.S. Government Printing Office, 1987), p. 318.

14. Rex de Silva, "Developing the Third World," *World Press Review*, May 1980, p. 48.

15. U.S. Bureau of the Census, *Statistical Abstracts, 1988*, p. 827.

16. G. Tyler Miller, *Living in the Environment*, 5th ed., (Belmont, Calif.: Wadsworth, 1988), p. 128.

17. Ibid. 129.

18. Quincy Wright, *A Study of War*, abridged by L. L. Wright (Chicago: University of Chicago Press, 1964), p. 85.

19. Marvin Harris, *Culture, People, Nature*, 5th ed. (New York: Harper & Row, 1988), p. 364.

20. Karl Marx and Friedrich Engels, *The Communist Manifesto* (Englewood Cliffs, N.J.: Prentice-Hall, 1955). This pamphlet was originally published in 1848.

21. James C. Davies, "Toward a Theory of Revolution," *American Sociological Review* 27 (1962): 5–19; James C. Davies, "The J-Curve of Rising and Declining Satisfactions as a Cause of Some Great Revolutions and a Contained Rebellion," in Hugh Davis Graham and Ted Robert Gurr, eds., *Violence in America: Histories and Comparative Perspectives* (New York: Holt, Rinehart and Winston, 1958), pp. 547–576.

22. Ibid. p. 5.

23. Samuel P. Huntington, *Political Order in Changing Societies* (New Haven: Yale University Press, 1968).

24. Charles Tilly, *From Mobilization to Revolution* (Reading, Mass.: Addison-Wesley, 1978).

25. Crane Brinton, *The Anatomy of Revolution* (New York: Random House, 1965), p. 51.

26. Ibid. pp. 28–39.

27. Theda Skocpol, *States and Social Revolution* (Cambridge, U.K.: Cambridge University Press, 1978).

28. See Ronald J. Glossop, *Confronting War* (Jefferson, N.C.: MacFarland, 1987), pp. 66–68.

29. Ibid. pp. 58–65.

30. Wright, *A Study of War,* pp. 213–214.

31. Kurt Finsterbusch and H. C. Greisman, "The Unprofitability of Warfare in the Twentieth Century," *Social Problems* 22 (February 1975): 451.

32. Dunnigan and Martel, *How To Stop A War,* p. 244.

33. Karl von Clausewitz, *On War,* trans. O. J. Matthkijs Jolles (Washington, D.C.: Infantry Journal Press, 1950), p. 16.

34. A. F. K. Organski and Jacek Kugler, *The War Ledger,* (Chicago: University of Chicago Press, 1980).

35. Brian Michael Jenkins, "The Future Course of International Terrorism," in Robert M. Jackson, ed., *Global Issues 88/89* (Guilford, Conn.: Dushkin, 1988).

36. Dunnigan and Martel, *How To Stop a War,* p. 247.

37. U.S. Bureau of the Census, *Statistical Abstracts, 1988,* p. 826.

38. See Volker Bornschier and Jean-Pierre Hoby, "Economic Policy and Multinational Corporations in Development: The Measurable Impacts in Cross-National Perspective," *Social Problems* 28 (April 1981): 362–377; Volker Bornschier and Christopher Chase-Dunn, *Transnational Corporations and Underdevelopment* (New York: Praeger, 1985).

39. Quoted in Wright, *A Study of War,* p. 186.

40. Also see Raymond J. Michalowski and Ronald Kramer, "The Space Between the Laws: The Problem of Corporate Crime in a Transnational Context," *Social Problems* 34 (February 1987): 34–53.

41. William K. Domke, *War and the Changing Global System* (New Haven: Yale University Press, 1988).

42. Walter H. Capps, "The Vietnam War and American Values," *The Center Magazine,* July–August 1978, pp. 17–26.

ACKNOWLEDGMENTS

Title page: *iii*, © 1982 Hazel Hankin.

Chapter 1: 1, Tannenbaum/Sygma; *5*, © Dion Ogust, The Image Works; *8*, Fullman, The Picture Cube; *16*, © Mercado, The Picture Cube; *25*, © Hrynewych, Stock, Boston.

Part One: *31*, Antman, The Image Works.

Chapter 2: 33, © 1982, Roberts, Photo Researchers; *37*, Herwig, Stock, Boston; *41*, © 1978, Reno, Jeroboam; *48*, Lawfer, The Picture Cube; *50*, AP/Wide World.

Chapter 3: 67, Hayman, Stock, Boston; *69*, © Hrynewych, Stock, Boston; *83*, AP/Wide World; *85*, Daemmrich, Stock, Boston.

Chapter 4: 96, © Mezey, Taurus; *99*, © 1986, Menzel, Stock, Boston; *101*, © 1976, Hamlin, Stock, Boston; *118*, © 1982, Eckert jr., EKM-Nepenthe.

Chapter 5: 124, © 1981, Kroll, Taurus; *129*, © 1977, Berkowitz, Taurus; *131*, © Scherr, Jeroboam; *140*, Barnes, Southern Light; *147*, © 1981, Siteman, Taurus.

Part Two: *155*, © 1979, Kroll, Taurus.

Chapter 6: 157, © 1976, Kroll, Taurus; *161 (left)*, © Skytta, Jeroboam; *161 (right)*, © Herwig, The Picture Cube; *168*, Player, NYT Pictures; *176*, © 1973, Gardner, The Image Works; *181*, © 1983, Kroll, Taurus.

Chapter 7: 188, McGovern, The Picture Cube; *199*, EKM-Nepenthe; *206*, Charles Gatewood; *210*, UPI/Bettmann Newsphotos.

Chapter 8: 221, © Rutledge, Taurus; *228*, © Eckert jr., 1982, EKM-Nepenthe; *231 (top)*, Pfeffer, Peter Arnold; *231 (bottom)*, © 1981, Menzel, Stock, Boston; *236*, Grant, The Picture Cube; *243*, © Johnson, Southern Light.

Chapter 9: 251, Bellerose, Stock, Boston; *261*, © Mendoza, The Picture Cube; *264*, © Gans, The Image Works; *268*, © 1982, Eckert jr., EKM-Nepenthe; *270*, Campione, Taurus; *271*, Lejeune, EKM-Nepenthe.

Chapter 10: 276, © 1984, Wood, Taurus; *279*, AP/Wide World; *282*, Muller, Woodfin Camp; *285 (top)*, © 1983, Hedman, Jeroboam; *285 (bottom)*, © Siluk, EKM-Nepenthe; *294*, UPI/Bettmann Newsphotos.

Part Three: *301*, Gatewood, The Image Works.

Chapter 11: 302, Carey, The Image Works; *304*, © Sidney, Southern Light; *309*, UPI/Bettmann Newsphotos; *315*, Eckert, EKM-Nepenthe; *318 (left)*, © 1983, Wood, The Picture Cube; *318 (right)*, © 1979, Roth, The Picture Cube.

Chapter 12: 331, © Levy, Photo Researchers; *336*, © The Washington Post 1978/Johnston, Woodfin Camp; *344*, Rosenthal, Stock, Boston; *345*, © 1986, Gray, Jeroboam.

Chapter 13: 359, © Rizza, The Picture Cube; *365,* © Alper, Stock, Boston; *373,* © Thompson, The Picture Cube; *377,* Carey, The Image Works; *383,* Beckwith, Taurus.

Chapter 14: 393, © Zucker, Stock, Boston; *410,* Sidney, Leo de Wys, Inc.; *411,* AP/Wide World; *414,* Franken, Stock, Boston; *420,* © 1986, Menzel, Stock, Boston; *427,* © 1980, Siteman, Jeroboam.

Chapter 15: 431, © Grant, Taurus; *434,* © Brilliant, The Picture Cube; *441,* Seder, Taurus; *444,* Gatewood, The Image Works; *447,* Reininger, Leo de Wys, Inc.; *450,* © 1981, Abramson, Stock, Boston.

Part Four: *457,* Mazzaschi, Stock, Boston.

Chapter 16: 459, © 1984, Reininger, Woodfin Camp; *462,* © Holland, Stock, Boston; *471,* © Jewett, EKM-Nepenthe; *474,* Menzel, Stock, Boston.

Chapter 17: 486, Franken, Stock, Boston; *487,* © Thompson, The Picture Cube; *496,* Laffont, Sygma; *502,* Botts, Nancy Palmer; *505,* © 1979, Kroll, Taurus.

Chapter 18: 512, © Mendoza, The Picture Cube; *516,* Eckert, EKM-Nepenthe; *521,* © 1979, Gardner, Stock, Boston; *524,* Scherr, Jeroboam; *526,* NASA; *537,* Antman, The Image Works.

Chapter 19: 543, Contact, Woodfin Camp; *544,* Franken, Stock, Boston; *550,* © 1985, Menzel, Stock, Boston; *558,* UPI/Bettmann Newsphotos; *560,* Nogues, Sygma; *563,* Carey, The Image Works.

AUTHOR INDEX

SUBJECT INDEX

Note: Page numbers in *italics* indicate glossary words.